ENCYCLOPEDIA OF COMPUTER SCIENCE AND TECHNOLOGY

VOLUME 27

INTERNATIONAL EDITORIAL ADVISORY BOARD

ENCYCLOPEDIA OF COMPUTER SCIENCE AND TECHNOLOGY

EXECUTIVE EDITORS

Allen Kent   *James G. Williams*

UNIVERSITY OF PITTSBURGH
PITTSBURGH, PENNSYLVANIA

ADMINISTRATIVE EDITORS

Carolyn M. Hall   *Rosalind Kent*

PITTSBURGH, PENNSYLVANIA

VOLUME 27
SUPPLEMENT 12

MARCEL DEKKER, INC.   NEW YORK • BASEL • HONG KONG

MARCEL DEKKER, INC.
270 Madison Avenue, New York, New York 10016

LIBRARY OF CONGRESS CATALOG CARD NUMBER: 74-29436
ISBN: 0-8247-2280-9

Current Printing (last digit)
10 9 8 7 6 5 4 3 2 1

PRINTED IN UNITED STATES OF AMERICA

CONTENTS OF VOLUME 27

CONTRIBUTORS TO VOLUME 27

MUSTAFA A. G. ABUSHAGUR, Ph.D., Associate Professor, Department of Electrical and Computer Engineering, University of Alabama in Huntsville, Huntsville, Alabama: *Optical and Optoelectronic Applied Science and Engineering*

RAJ K. BHATNAGAR, Ph.D., Assistant Professor of Computer Science, University of Cincinnati, Cincinnati, Ohio: *Reasoning in Uncertain Domains: A Survey and Commentary*

JOHN E. BIEGEL, Ph.D., P.E., Professor Department of Industrial Engineering and Management Systems, University of Central Florida, Orlando, Florida: *Expert Systems for Computer-Integrated Manufacturing*

H. JOHN CAULFIELD, Ph.D., University Eminent Professor, Department of Physics, Alabama A&M University, Normal, Alabama: *Optical and Optoelectronic Applied Science and Engineering*

DAVID I. CLELAND, Ph.D., Ernest E. Roth Professor and Professor of Engineering Management, School of Engineering, University of Pittsburgh, Pittsburgh, Pennsylvania: *Project Planning and Control*

JORGE L. DÍAZ-HERRERA, Member of the Technical Staff, Software Engineering Institute, Carnegie Mellon University, Pittsburgh, Pennsylvania: *Artificial Intelligence and Ada*

HANS W. GOTTINGER, Nuffield College, University of Oxford, Oxford, United Kingdom: *Statistical Expert Systems*

LARISSA A. GRUNIG, Associate Professor, College of Journalism, University of Maryland, College Park, Maryland: *Professional Responsibilities in a Global Context*

ZYGMUNT HAAS, Ph.D., AT&T Bell Laboratories, Network Systems Research Department, Holmdel, New Jersey: *Packet Switching*

JOSEPH Y. HALPERN, IBM Almaden Research Center,San Jose, California: *Reasoning About Knowledge: A Survey Circa 1991*

KEITH A. HAMEL, Ph.D., School of Music, The University of British Columbia, Vancouver, Canada: *Music Printing*

WILLIAM M. JOHNSON, Retired, U.S. Department of Agriculture, Soil Conservation Service, Washington, D.C.: *Professional Responsibilities in a Global Context*

LAVEEN N. KANAL, Ph.D., Professor of Computer Science, University of Maryland, College Park, Maryland: *Reasoning in Uncertain Domains: A Survey and Commentary*

LAWRENCE A. KURTZ, Director, Doric Computer Systems, Doric House, Waterford, England: *Database Management Systems: An Introduction*

CHRISTIAN J. P. LAVAULT, Ph.D., Professor, Department of Computer Science, INSA-IRISA, University of Rennes, Rennes, France: *Distributed Algorithms*

T. ANTHONY MARSLAND, Professor and Associate Chair, Computing Science Department, University of Alberta, Edmonton, Alberta, Canada: *Single-Agent and Game-Tree Search*

MIR MUJTABA MIRSALEHI, Ph.D., Assistant Professor, College of Electrical Engineering, University of Mashhad, Mashhad, Iran: *Optical and Optoelectronic Applied Science and Engineering*

ALFONSO M. MIOLA, Professor, Dipartimento Informatica e Sistemistica, Universita' "La Sapienza", Rome, Italy: *Symbolic Computation Systems*

PETER A. NG, Professor and Chairman, Institute for Integrated Systems Research, Department of Computer and Information Science, New Jersey Institute of Technology, Newark, New Jersey: *Systems Integration: Concepts, Methods, and Tools*

ANDRÉ OOSTERLINCK, Ph.D., Professor and Director, ESAT-MI2, Katholieke Universiteit Leuven, Leuven, Belgium: *Object Recognition and Visual Robot Tracking*

WILHELM ROSSAK,   Assistant Professor and Co-Director, Systems Integration Laboratory, Institute for Integrated Systems Research, Department of Computer and Information Science, New Jersey Institute of Technology, Newark, New Jersey: *Systems Integration: Concepts, Methods, and Tools*

JUDY SPEEDY,   School of Library and Information Science, University of Pittsburgh, Pittsburgh, Pennsylvania: *Evaluation of Software*

WILLIAM J. STEWART, Ph.D.,   Professor, Department of Computer Science, North Carolina State University, Raleigh, North Carolina: *The Numerical Solution of Markov Chains*

LUC J. VAN GOOL, Ph.D.,   Associate Professor, ESAT-MI2, Katholieke Universiteit Leuven, Leuven, Belgium: *Object Recognition and Visual Robot Tracking*

DAVID M. WEIMER,   Member of Technical Staff, Machine Perception Research Department, AT&T Bell Laboratories, Holmdel, New Jersey: *Raster Graphics*

EMMANUEL J. YANNAKOUDAKIS, Ph.D.,   Professor of Computer Science, Chairman of Computer Centre, Department of Informatics, Athens University of Economics and Business Sciences, Athens, Greece: *Statistical Measures of Languages: Entropy and Redundancy of the English Dictionary*

DAO-BIN ZHANG, Ph.D.,   Research Assistant, ESAT-MI2, Katholieke Universiteit Leuven, Leuven, Belgium: *Object Recognition and Visual Robot Tracking*

ENCYCLOPEDIA OF COMPUTER SCIENCE AND TECHNOLOGY

VOLUME 27

ARTIFICIAL INTELLIGENCE AND ADA

INTRODUCTION

The discussion about Artificial Intelligence and the programming language Ada [1], the new language recently mandated as the single implementation language for all military software systems, is motivated by a number of factors. First, the state-of-the-art programming language, at least with respect to software engineering standards, is Ada. The language addresses specific problems in the construction of large embedded systems. The solution to these problems is of paramount importance to the industrial base in general, and to the military establishment in particular, both of which are inextricably tied to the software element of computer systems. Ada represents the cornerstone of the U.S. Department of Defense software initiative, and its latest attempt to focus all software development on a single standard language (COBOL was the result of the first such an effort). The language is enjoying increasing international support especially for nonmilitary application areas.

Second, the dynamic growth and increased popularity of AI and the tremendous progress in hardware technology have made it inevitable for AI components to play a major role in embedded military systems. Although these next generation embedded systems posses some unique special purpose requirements (e.g., they will exhibit intelligent behavior such as introspection in the form of self-monitoring and self-description), they must be integrated with existing conventional software performing conventional real-time tasks, such as sensor reading and data fusion, control functions, actuator feedback, etc. Designers of these AI embedded applications face the same sort of problems and challenges as traditional software engineers. Such systems are best engineered using a language like Ada.

Natural and logical questions thus arise: Is the Ada language suitable for AI applications? But, what are the specific computational requirements of the next generation embedded AI systems? How does Ada match up with these requirements? What has Ada to offer here? And, more generally, how can these AI real-time embedded systems be implemented (with/without Ada) to meet current software engineering and military standards?

Without further exploration into what is actually understood by AI, it is practically impossible to try to answer any of these questions and to decide on the appropriateness of Ada. It also is awkward to present the Ada approaches to the problem without a discussion of Ada itself. Once this demarcation between AI and traditional programming is made, we can study the characteristics of the AI programming realm and identify essential language features for encoding such software systems in Ada.

The rest of this introductory section identifies general computational requirements of AI problems, and in particular those for embedded AI systems. In the following section, we briefly present the main issues being discussed today with regard to large-scale software development in general, highlighting the requirements of traditional (i.e., procedural) software development problems which Ada was devised to tackle, including an overview of the Ada language. The third section, AI software, constitutes the heart of the article. There, we identify specific requirements for nontraditional programming typical of AI software development bringing together AI and the language Ada, presenting the relevant aspects concerning the use of the Ada in these settings. Finally, in the conclusion, we provide several sample experiences of using Ada for implementing a number of AI systems, laying out future trends.

What Is Artificial Intelligence?

Many writers have defined Artificial Intelligence in terms of characteristics of "typical" AI systems and the techniques used as rule-based, planning, neural networks, common sense reasoning, multivalued and approximate logic, and the like. More abstract definitions can be found in the literature (see Table 1). It could also be said that AI deals with providing machine solutions to very complex problems which would otherwise be intractable by more traditional means. From a more pragmatic point of view, these techniques are intrinsically symbolic rather than primarily numeric.

But, what makes certain problems amenable to an AI treatment?

Bonasso [3] groups interesting AI problems into two large categories, namely analysis problems and construction problems. The former require interpretation of their environment but not a response to it, whereas the latter have in addition an effect on, and perhaps cause an alteration of, their environment.

Analysis problems use problem domain knowledge (known facts) in the deduction of new knowledge (unknown facts); this deductive process should be constrained somehow in order to limit an otherwise large progression of inferences (runaway inferencing). Typical analysis problems are: theorem proving; imprecise interpretation of rules and/or data; multi-sensor integration dealing with continuous streams of data attempting to detect a phenomenon evolving over time; natural language understanding; diagnosis; pattern recognition and scene analysis (visual perception or machine vision); and decision support, which involves interpreting raw data to prove an understanding of a situation based on a model of a problem domain.

Construction problems need to keep a history of environmental changes, their causes, and the circumstances (when/where) under which these changes were applied; all this information must be maintained in a relational cause–effect framework. Especially those changes that trigger more changes. The most well-known construction problems, and one of the first areas of AI research, is game playing. The main difficulty here is the combinatorial explosion of possible cause–effect situations (e.g., chess). Other typical construction problems are planning systems, automatic programming/design, and autonomous systems (ro-

TABLE 1.   Some Definitions of AI

Artificial Intelligence is a field of study that encompasses computational techniques for performing tasks that apparently require intelligence when performed by humans [2]

AI is the study of implementable ideas that enable computers to do things that make people seem intelligent [3]

The ultimate goal is to build a person . . . AI is the study of mental faculties through the use of computational models [4]

TABLE 2. AI Technology Deficiencies

- Traditional AI languages do not have adequate constructs for parallel and distributed processing and are weak in handling numeric types

- Multiple inheritance is not good for real-time due to its exponential nature.

- AI technology lacks standardization acceptance in the community

- AI tools provide poor support for team-oriented, programming-in-the-large software engineering environments, and for DoD standards in particular

---

botics). Planning systems involve the aggregation, association, and time-ordering of a series of actions, and analysis of their consequences, in order to attain a preset goal. Automatic programming and robotics are both influenced by developments on planning systems.

Bonasso further suggests that there are a number of distinguishing characteristics which indicate that a problem is an AI problem. These characteristics are: (1) voluminous, incomplete, or misleading data, (2) only a few constraints in the problem definition (i.e., a large solution space exists), and (3) a few human experts are usually able to provide plausible solutions. All in all, Artificial Intelligence's main problem is to be able to integrate perception, analysis, construction (deduction), and choice of reaction, all intrinsic human abilities, into a hardware/software system that can operate on a changing environment without human intervention.

AI Software Development

The state-of-practice of Artificial Intelligence is characterized by a variety of concepts, techniques, and linguistic tools independently developed in research laboratories, some of which are slowly finding their way into industrial and government shops. On the software development side, it is safe to say that the technology is not in place for the development of well-engineered AI applications. Table 2 lists many such deficiencies. Currently ad hoc techniques are used, and more often than not, it is the responsibility of the programmer (by patching) to make the system "work." This approach is of course inadequate for a number of reasons, namely (1) ad hoc methods cannot be exported to other projects, (2) performance becomes brittle with changes in the specification or in the environment, and (3) hand-tuning is time consuming since the programmer is performing an unconstrained search through the space of possible modifications to identify a subset that meets all constraints. Only a handful of existing AI software systems show any of the acceptable engineering attributes.

Typically, AI languages are higher-level than more traditional languages such as Ada, but they are lacking in several areas. Software technology at use in AI programming shops is at odds with more conventional software engineering practice. The use of common languages and standard software development practices is of crucial importance in software engineering in order to at least maintain a consistent quality control. Lack of standardization can only be detrimental to large scale projects for which the significant use of AI techniques is expected (e.g., NASA Space Station). Indeed, commonality and portability are issues of minor significance in the AI community. In fact, the sheer number of programming paradigms may prevent the development of a standard.

There is also lack of suitable AI real-time implementation tools (e.g., linguistic features to handle timing and synchronization constraints), and a general need for specialized training in real-time software engineering. In short, very few applications have progressed beyond the prototype stage for every day use in a real-time embedded set up. A basic premise is that AI software technology is not well-suited for implementing AI applications. Even extended versions of LISP (e.g., CLOS) do not address the issues of real-time computing. Specific real-time requirements are discussed next. More consolidated environments combining features originally found on individual paradigms have also been proposed [5, 6].

Real-Time AI Computing

According to J. Stankovic, *real-time computing* is "that type of computing where the correctness of the system depends not only on the logical result of the computation, but also on the time at which the results are produced" [7]. Traditional real-time technology relies on precise timing and tight control over the sequence and length of the execution of individual parts of the system. This approach depends on algorithms that are "serialized" according to predefined timing considerations, in which control flow is synchronized with a real-time clock, and thus making them deterministic (due to the tightly coupled nature of the computations performed).

Controlling complex systems by responding to rapidly changing data is a critical bottleneck in applying knowledge-based techniques in embedded real-time computing. If AI in general deals with problem solving, here we deal with a number of additional constraints in terms of much more stringent performance requirements. As Michalski and Winston have put it "Give me a reasonable answer immediately, even if somewhat general; if there is enough time, give me a more specific answer . . . " [8]. But, although a solution must be reached quickly, it must nevertheless be a good solution. Again quoting Michalski and Winston, "Give me a reasonable answer immediately, if there is enough time, tell me you are more confident in the answer or change your mind and give me another better answer . . ." [8].

These kinds of real-time (AI) systems would require a tremendous amount of adaptability with a high degree of autonomy and introspection, constantly assessing the relative importance of tasks and balancing the work load accordingly, thus precluding the use of static scheduling strategies typical of today's real-time systems. This situation is worsened by the nature of AI algorithms (in the way of resource utilization). Current AI technology does not have a good model of behavior from a resource utilization point of view for a number of techniques such as searching, rule-base, semantic nets, etc. Many of the commonly available knowledge representation and inferencing techniques do not seem suitable for real-time computing. AI developers (both practitioners and researchers) have not paid enough attention to the handling of timing constraints in the design of AI algorithms. Considerations of the ramifications of using exponential time AI algorithms in real-time systems, and reliability and fault-tolerance concerns are generally lacking in AI approaches to the problem. Actually, many have the misconception that real-time means fast! These generally perceived deficiencies in AI real-time technology are subject to the solution of more specific *technical problems*: A partial list of these problems is found in Table 3.

In this article, we discuss only issues related to the technical problems of using procedural languages on engineering AI embedded systems (problem 4 above), since these systems would also require high standards of documentation, verification, accreditation, and maintainability, all typical quality requirements of military systems. We have found that more traditional languages such as Ada, especially designed for implementing large and complex embedded software, are indeed able to support AI techniques [9]. Furthermore, a large percentage of AI code (between 80 and 85%) is procedural in nature! and thus better

TABLE 3. Real-Time AI Technical Problems

---

(1) Guaranteed Response Times: The best solution that comes too late is worse than a weaker solution on time.

An intrinsic concern is the fact that AI algorithms' performance degrades exponentially and worse case analyses would probably result in response times totally unacceptable. Garbage collection increases the problem of guaranteeing a maximum system latency. In fact, it may be impossible to predict all possible combinations of events that may occur in a real-time (on-line) situation.

(2) Accuracy: Making a best guess given a deadline . . . a solution must be reached quickly, but it must also be good.

This problem is compounded by the fact that data is not durable and decays in validity due to new data coming in from sensors or changes in the state of the system.

(3) Reliability: the system must be capable of continuous operation.

This refers to the capability of the system to keep operating despite the presence of faults, which implies close control of garbage collection. It must also have the capability of processing uncertain or incomplete data (noise) from faulty sensors.

(4) Procedural Programming: experimental programming, typical of AI software development, is incompatible at best with current software engineering standards.

---

expressed in software engineering languages like Ada. Before presenting specific details of the approaches taken, we provide an overview of current software engineering technology and of the Ada language.

ENGINEERING LARGE SOFTWARE SYSTEMS

In this section, we describe the environment within which current software technology has evolved. Figure 1 summarizes the situation in terms of cost/effectiveness ratios and orders of magnitude advancements in both hardware and software technology.

Software development (the process of going from system conception to deployment) is the essential component that controls the successful deployment of an application, and in many instances it even defines the application. In general, the demand for software, currently increasing at a rate of approximately 12 percent annually, far outstrips software development capabilities. The marvelous progress in hardware technology moves the computer incessantly into many new areas of application, placing additional responsibilities onto software development. In this sense, software is simultaneously becoming both (a) larger, more difficult, and more risky as found in complex unique systems, and (b) smaller, easier, and more manageable as for example cruise control systems for cars. At any rate, the scale of the efforts undertaken and the complexity of applications grow every year, thus making the shortage of software developers much more acute (increases in the number of "new programmers" grows at about 4% annually). In short, the gap between what could reasonably be programmed and what is required is growing larger and larger every day.

The tremendous increase in "computer power" has not been paralleled by anything even remotely similar in the way of software productivity. There has not been a significant software development to match current hardware technology, which in fact remains largely

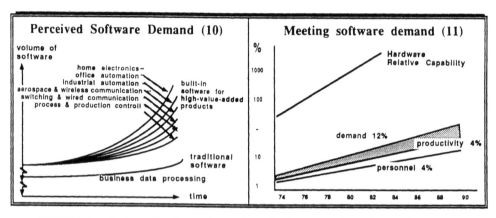

FIGURE 1.   Software/hardware demands and software productivity (Refs 10,11).

underused by an increasingly dissatisfied user community. The rate of growth in software productivity increases much more slowly at about 4 percent per year. This is because software systems are extremely difficult to write; programming has a very simple set of conceptual notions, but it allows the creation of extremely complex artifacts, perhaps one of the most complex things ever made by humans (the interrelation between the parts grows very quickly). This situation is compounded by a widespread belief that software development is not an engineering discipline: *software development is perceived as an almost artistic activity, subject to tremendous variations among individuals; in fact, the "right" programmer is seen as a virtual factor in the success or failure of a project!*

The prospects of continuing this practice represents a *serious deficiency in our capability to produce software!* This situation, commonly known as the "software crisis," is discussed in more detail next.

The Software Crisis

For several years now there has been considerable general discontent with the process of designing and producing software and the quality of the products delivered. This is one of the most important problems currently facing the software community. Despite the emergence of newer technology from large-scale software initiatives and the capabilities provided by abundant CASE tools, current software practice, even in the most advanced organizations, presents a host of difficulties that hinders the realization of the full advantage of computer systems. Many of the projects in serious trouble, especially those delivering defective software, are found to be ignoring modern software engineering technology and/ or not using proper software engineering languages.

Many computer programs released for routine use (as being checked out and operational) contain serious flaws (see Table 4). Software failures are not exclusive to the small newcomer, but common even in most technologically advanced organizations. A typical situation is that of a program that does not do exactly what the programmer has in mind, or that is an accurate implementation of the programmer's intent, but that intent turns out to be an inconsistent or incomplete reflection of the problem requirements.

Current efforts to address the problem include the use of modern software engineering methods, techniques, and tools, and the use of the higher-order languages that embody

TABLE 4. Traditional Software Development Deficiencies

• Unverified designs: Implementing the wrong thing. Software requirements are not understood completely. They generally are incomplete at the outset and do change during development; furthermore, many design decisions redefine the specification of the requirements.

• Unverified implementations: Inadequately tested programs, although programmers spend half of their time in debugging (Fig. 2).

• Low product's quality: Current software is highly unreliable, is not portable, is not maintainable, code is unreadable and incomprehensible. Poor coding practices due to a trade full of tricks.

• Time and cost overruns: Large software projects are difficult to manage (Fig. 2).

---

and enforce software engineering principles. The challenge is to put software process in place supported by methodologies and to develop tools that facilitate the creation and maintenance of software .

Software Engineering

A response to this crisis has been the emergence of the discipline called *software engineering*. Modern software engineering activities work in concert toward the achievement of preset *software engineering goals* that, if attained, will lessen the effects of the software crisis. These goals include, among others, maintainability, correctness, reusability, testability, reliability, and portability of software systems. A number of *software engineering principles* can be identified that contribute to the achievement of these goals. These principles involve the use of modular decomposition, encapsulation, step-wise refinement, information hiding, abstractions, stylistic conventions, etc., during software development. Due

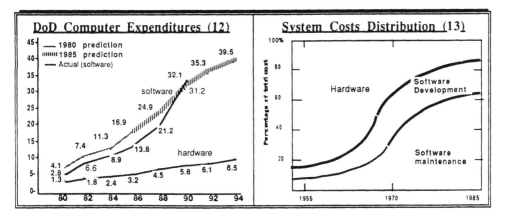

FIGURE 2. The rising cost of software (Refs 12, and 13).

to space constraints, we refer the reader to the general software engineering literature for a complete discussion of these goals and principles. We would, however, like to highlight maintainability, testability, and portability as being of paramount importance.

"*Maintenance*" of large systems, an activity covering both enhancements and corrective tasks which may be better termed *continued development*, usually involves many (incremental) changes to the operational system. Simple changes often trigger modifications in many other modules, sometimes at great expense, and additional design effort is needed to minimize this ripple effect. Software engineering principles directly supporting this goal are modular decomposition, information hiding, and abstractions. *Testability* refers to the ease with which each module, in a large collection of modules, can be independently tested as extensively as possible. A module's specification provides the basis for testing and it should include test criteria. The principles of abstraction and modularity play an important role here, for example, Abstract Data Types often make exhaustive testing possible. Testing strategies (e.g., bottom-up/top-down) are also related to respective incremental development strategies. *Portability* refers to the level of effort, and in fact to the possibility of being able to transport a system from one computing environment to another (with hardware/operating system differences). This is quite important since software large systems outlive the computing systems (specially hardware) for which they were initially developed. Portability is supported by modular decomposition and information hiding, as well as by standard coding practices. At the source level, it is achieved by using standard languages, whereas at the data interoperability level it depends on standard libraries and system software interfaces; machine-dependencies can be isolated.

Although software engineering principles are largely language independent, the right *notation* is important to both enforce the principles and to understandably express the underlying concepts. For example Ada, unlike earlier programming languages, embodies a collection of current knowledge of software engineering and a modern view of the process of developing large programs, thus incorporates specific constructs directly supporting these software engineering principles. In fact, the language cannot be effectively used without an understanding of the software engineering discipline in the first place.

In general, we can identify two approaches to software development, namely an *evolutionary* or *conventional* approach seeking to provide a more refined programming environment, and a *revolutionary* or *nonconventional* approach which tries to experiment with a new (more exploratory) paradigm "not based on the von Newmann bottleneck." It is useful to notice that AI software development is exploratory in nature and thus nonconventional. We will consider exploratory development in more detail shortly, but first we discuss the conventional approach.

Conventional Software Development

The conventional software development approach is characterized by a well-defined software process together with a variety of supporting methods and tools. The *software process* refers to the set of activities and intermediate products that are carried out in a more or less systematic manner for producing a deployable software system. In general, it is the process of translating problem requirements into software systems; in particular, it addresses both the decomposition of a problem into smaller more manageable subproblems, and the composition of solutions from more general subsolutions already stated.

A widespread software development process known as the *waterfall model* [14], illustrated in Figure 3a, prescribes a serial sequence of activities progressively leading to the production of software. Once the requirements analysis phase has produced a set of soft-

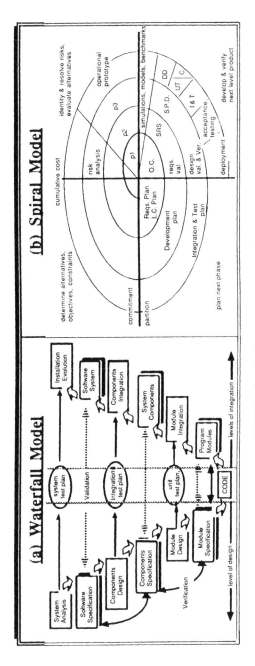

FIGURE 3.   Software process models.

ware specifications, the first step during the actual development process is software design, followed by module specification, coding, and testing. In addition, a set of review points (or managerial milestones), at which the results of the previous activity can be checked (and possibly, feedback given), is also defined. These correspond to the activities collectively known as verification and validation.

This traditional approach has evolved over the past three decades. This evolution is a response to the need for providing earlier feedback to system users, and has been made possible by the early production of prototypes. Rapid prototypes are generally of two kinds, throwaway and evolutionary prototypes. A throwaway prototype chiefly provides an early version of the user interface and it is populated with quick-and-dirty algorithms; whereas an evolutionary prototype is an early and scaled down version of the system which will progressively incorporate additional system functionality.

The software development process that incorporates the ideas of prototyping calls for an iterative development cycle. The approach known as the *spiral process model* [*15*], illustrated in Figure 3b, is the archetype of this evolutionary software development cycle. The spiral model suggests the use of throwaway prototypes for the early stages of development, followed by a series of evolutionary prototypes (p1, p2, . . ., pn) used in several incremental system builds converging into an operational prototype and finally into a deployable system. In this sense, it is a risk-driven process which cycles through four major phases (each represented as a quadrant in Fig. 3a). These phases are: (1) *Needs analysis*: determine objectives, alternatives, and constraints. (2) *Risk analysis*: evaluate alternatives, identify and resolve risks (includes prototyping). (3) *Development*: develop and verify next level product. (4) *Planning*: develop plans for for the next iteration. Each cycle is called a round, and the completion of a round constitutes a new evolution in the development of the deployable system. The spiral model provides a considerable flexibility in the choice of development approach. In fact, other models such as the waterfall, evolutionary development, exploratory development and transformational implementation [*16*] can be seen as special cases of the spiral model.

The Ada Language

The development of Ada was motivated by the software crisis. Ada is much more than another programming language; it is a robust and proven technology designed especially for use in well-engineered software systems. The language supports modern software engineering, risk reduction, and several development paradigms. Although software engineering principles and activities generally are language independent, Ada is becoming the first widely available language especially designed to directly support these diverse principles and activities. Initially the language was envisioned to be used for embedded real-time systems, but it has proven suitable in many dissimilar application areas, ranging from commercial data processing through Artificial Intelligence [*17*].

The Ada technology project is the focal point of much larger U.S. government and private efforts (e.g., FAA and NASA). The basic focus is on the enhancement of the environment in which software is developed and "maintained", the overall goal is to substantially reduce the cost of developing large software systems. This idea is to work closely with industry and academia to develop technology to increase productivity, to improve software quality (greater reliability and adaptability), to reduce the labor intensiveness of the process, etc. A great deal of activity has been generated, with many national and international interest groups formed and several annual conferences held in the United States, Europe, and Japan.

TABLE 5. Ada Design Goals

- Generality: The language meets a wide spectrum of needs, including support for real-time requirements.

- Reliability: Encourages software engineering principles, specially strong typing, and provides programmer-controlled exceptions handling.

- Modifiability: Good control and encapsulating (i.e., modular) structures together with powerful data abstraction facilities.

- Portability: Machine-dependent features are clearly marked, plus programmer defined physical representations of objects, and disciplined access to low-level hardware features.

- Productivity: Parallel development (top-down/bottom-up) directly supported, plus compiler enforced separate compilation and module obsolescence control, as well as facilities to interface with other languages.

Among the design goals of the language (see Table 5) the concern for programming as a human activity takes paramount importance. Program readability is much more prominent than program writing. Other weighty goals are those of portability and transportability of source Ada programs. To this end, the language provides a "software bus" based on a standard programming support environment (an area in which the language is unique) specified as a multilayered system with a clear distinction between host and target systems. A flexible tool interface—known as the CAIS [*18*, *19*], has been approved as an accompanying standard. Also in support of portability, I/O operations are not an intrinsic part of the language, but defined as standard library units whose implementation dependencies are clearly marked in an appendix of the referenced manual. The provision of capabilities for programmer defined object representations such as storage layout, addresses, and literal values, is another aspect supporting portability and transportability, since these allow the specification of machine dependencies in Ada itself.

An Ada compiler must comply with the ANSI-MIL-STD-1815A standard, which must be implemented in its entirety, and nothing can be implemented that is not in the Standard.

The language validation and certification process tests implementation conformance, not performance, to the Ada standard by testing that a compiler properly implements all legal language constructs and that it identifies and rejects illegal ones. Validation also identifies behavior which is implementation dependent. A compiler must correctly process the entire validation suite [*20*] and demonstrate conformity to the standard by either meeting the pass criteria given to each test or showing inapplicability to the implementation.

The Ada Validation Organization (AVO), on behalf of the Ada Joint Program Office (AJPO), is the controlling center for all validations also in charge of resolving implementers' disputes. A parallel organization, the Ada Maintenance Organization (AMO) is responsible for the control of the ACVC (Ada Compiler Validation Capability). The actual validations are performed by the AVF's (Ada Validation Facilities), distributed two in the United States and three in Europe (Fig. 4). At the time of writing, there were more than 300 compilers validated under ACVC 1.10 (containing about 4000 test programs.)

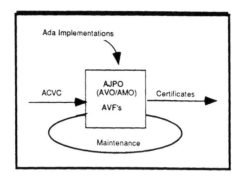

FIGURE 4.   Ada Validation.

Historical Perspective

Several important events have marked the steady development of the technology that the language brought about, a partial list of which is shown in Table 6. In January 1975 the U. S. Department of Defense charted a High-Order Language Working Group (HOLWG) as a joint service group with three tasks: (1) to identify computer language requirements for the 1980s and beyond (2) to evaluate existing languages, and (3) to recommend implementation and control of a minimum set. Some 23 languages were evaluated, but none were adequate. A series of requirements documents were refined into a final set for a new DoD-wide programming language. After a worldwide design competition the *Green language*, designed by an international team from Cii-Honeywell Bull, emerged the winner in April 1979. The language was standardized nationally [21] and internationally, even before the first compilers were in existence.

The language was named in honor of Ada Augusta Lovelace, the wife of the first Earl of Lovelace, and daughter of the poet Lord Byron. Lady Lovelace was well educated and had an unusually canny ability for mathematics. In her twenties, she was introduced to Charles Babbage's Differential Engine, and became the world's first computer programmer. She died of cancer in 1852, at the age of 36.

What Is Ada Like?

Ada is language with considerable expressive power, which includes facilities offered by several more classical languages as well as features found only in specialized languages, and in this sense it is a multidimensional language. It is sequential or block-structured like Pascal, hierarchical or module-structured like Modula-2, concurrent or process-structured like CSP, and low-level for machine-oriented programming. Pascal and LIS (a French language) were the main sources of inspiration for the language syntactical design, but Ada is much more complex than these languages. Following is an outline of the language main concepts.

Program Units.   In Ada, a software system architecture is organized as a hierarchical collection of program units. Each unit is defined, and provided, in two parts, namely a specification and a body. Entities declared in the specification are visible (i.e., exported) to other units, whereas entities local to the unit's body are invisible (i.e., nonexported) outside the unit. These import/export (I/E) aspects of units have an effect both at compile-time and at run-time. Compile-time I/E controls visibility, whereas at run-time it controls existence.

TABLE 6. Ada History

Jan	1975	HOLWG formed
Apr		Strawman
Aug		Woodenman
Jan	1976	Tinman
Apr		DoD Directive 5000.29
Nov		DoD Directive 5000.31
Jan	1977	Ironman
		Competition starts
Jun	1978	Steelman
	1979	Prel. Ada Ref. Man.
Jul	1980	Draft Standard Ada
Feb		Stoneman: Env. Reqs.
	1981	AJPO formed
		Ada® DoD Trademark
	1982	KIT/KITIA Formed
	1983	ACVC Operational
		MIL-STD-1815A
		First Validated Compiler
		Interim Ada Mandate
		(DeLaurer Memorandum)
	1985	Proposed MIL-STD-CAIS
	1986	ACVC Implementers Guide
	1987	General Ada Mandate
		(DoD Directive 3405.1)
		Weapon Sys. Mandate
		(DoD Directive 3405.2)
	1988	KIT/KITIA Dissolved
		Trademark dropped
	1989	DoD-STD-1838A (CAIS-A)
	1989	Ada 9x revision started
	1991	Congress passes law requiring Ada

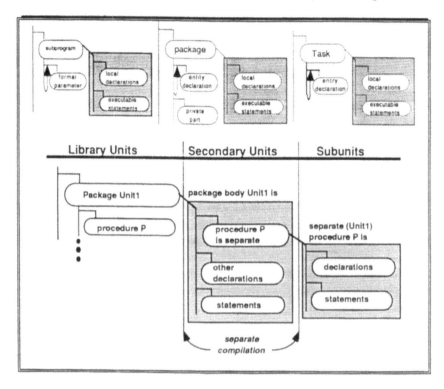

FIGURE 5.   Ada program units and compilation units.

The language defines three kinds of program units, namely packages, subprograms, and tasks, in order to allow the specification of distinct approaches to the dynamic behavior of the program (see Fig. 5).

Subprograms provide procedural abstractions, in the form of procedures and functions, which define operations applicable to objects, passed as parameters. Subprograms enforce traditional block-structured scope rules; a subprogram interface simply specifies the names, types passing modes and default values of parameters (if any). They can be overloaded (more than one subprogram with the same name in the same scope if their profile is sufficiently different in at least one argument), and can be used to specify programmer-defined operators.

Packages serve as organizational units providing a higher-level abstraction mechanism characterized by the exported entities (they can export objects, types, and even other units.) Packages, obviously a key concept in Ada, provide means for the separate control of visibility and existence. Unlike subprograms, packages do not really exist at run-time! They provide encapsulating environments affecting visibility (a compile-time phenomenon).

Tasks, are like specialized packages in that they encapsulate concurrent sequential processes (a "program" executing sequential statements activated implicitly) with an interface specifying a message-based communications protocol (entries); tasks provide a mixture of procedural and abstraction capabilities.

Compilation Units.   Incremental software development (top-down or bottom-up) is directly supported by separate compilation. A *library unit* is simply the stand-alone compilation of a subprogram or package specification. Their corresponding bodies, or *secondary units*, may also be provided in separate compilations. The body of a (local, i.e., nonlibrary) program unit may also be compiled separately as a *subunit*, in which case, a "body stub" is placed in the enclosing unit at the place where the actual body would normally occur (see Fig. 5). The separate compilation of unit bodies creates a tree-like hierarchy; whereas the hierarchy of library units specifies a linear dependency relationship among the units involved. Subunits allow compilation of program units that are too specialized to be suitable as library units.

Packages and subprograms, either local as program units or global as library units, can be made *generic*; this is to say, that they can be defined as translation-time, optionally parameterized, template units from which actual units can be *instantiated* (created). Again, the instantiation of a generic unit may result into a (global) library unit or (local) program unit. Notice that tasks cannot be made generic. Generics allow the specification of abstract units completely delaying the association of specific arguments until more specialized units are needed. Generic declarations can be parameterized with objects, types and subprograms.

Types.   Properties of types are assessed in order to group together related, i.e., functionally associated, types into type categories. A type category is a generalization of a type entity and specifies a family of types. Type categories are recognized and can thus be described in Ada programs, form a set of basic types. They serve to group common properties into related type families which from the *Ada type hierarchy*. This hierarchy serves as an organization mechanism for classifying new types. In Figure 6 we illustrate the Ada type hierarchy and the operations/attributes available for each category of types. The notion of type categories is also important for generics, which are generalizations of type entities, and in this sense, generic units are similar to object-oriented classes (discussed later).

The language provides facilities for introducing new types at the various levels in this hierarchy. Most types in a program are created and thus named by the programmer (*declared types*), others are named by the compiler and unknown to the programmer (*anonymous types*), and yet others are declared in the STANDARD environment (*predefined types*). We use the term *metatype* to refer to constructs which allow the creation of types. Instances of a metatype are (actual) types. There is a different metatype for each type category.

In the hierarchy shown in Figure 6, operations and attributes are defined for types, and passed down to subordinate types. The top of the hierarchy specifies properties "shared" by the rest of the subordinate types, and so on. This top is the type LIMITED PRIVATE, next, is the category LIMITED, for which the operations":=" (assignment) and "=" (equality) are defined and passed down, and so on. Anonymous types are implicitly derived from some existing type. Predefined type definitions are implementation dependent, are derived from anonymous "universal" primordial types. Compilers "derive" actual types used in a program from these predefined types. Derived types are important for AI programming. They will be discussed in more detail later.

Support for Software Design and Structure

Design is the process of translating software specifications into software structures. Good software structure is characterized by modular architectures, where each module has a well-defined *interface*, specifying both the needs from the outside and the abstractions provided, and a *body* hiding implementation details to prevent programmers from using the interface

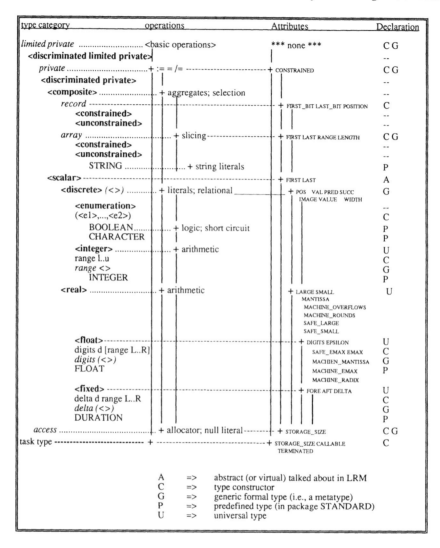

FIGURE 6.   Ada Type Hierarchy.

in unintended ways. The former considers the interface as the introduction of an abstract layer (global abstraction), whereas the latter introduces a number of subordinate modules (local abstractions) (see Fig. 7a). This produces a design architecture which depicts linear as well as tree-like hierarchical relations among the comprising modules [22]. This is illustrated in Figure 7b. Global abstractions are introduced in order to increase reliability and reusability; they interface provide new primitives, at a higher level, which can be used to form more primitives, at a lower level, and so on, creating a linear hierarchy of *levels of abstractions.* Local abstractions introduce a tree-like hierarchy of *levels of information hid-*

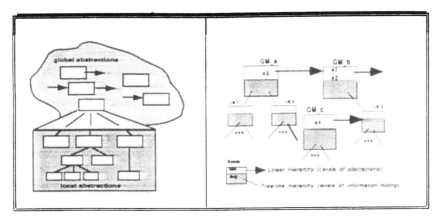

FIGURE 7. Structural hierarchies. (a) Kinds of abstraction. (b) Hierarchical intermodule relations.

ing; they tend to reduce the amounts of changes that may be necessary during evolutionary "maintenance."

A *design paradigm* provides the designer with encapsulating views for both the decomposition and composition of a specification's structure. These structural components are arranged into an overall architecture based on a framework as prescribed by the design school. Design decisions for devising these constituent parts are governed by a set of principles or axioms, firmly stated and ideally strongly enforced by a design paradigm. In other words, a design paradigm specifies the way in which the "right" software *static structure* can be determined. Several design paradigms have been proposed over the years. The best known design paradigms are listed in Table 7.

Modern languages provide good support in some areas and are more deficient in some other areas; in general, it is difficult to provide a language supporting all paradigms. The Ada language provides facilities supporting most of the design paradigms above, to a greater or lesser degree, as well as development approaches for programming-in-the-large in a multiuser program library environment. Language features supporting a design paradigm are those constructs related to program text control, visibility, and separate compilation.

Of paramount importance to programming AI applications is the provision of facilities dealing with object-oriented ideas. Ada supports this paradigm at the design level very well, although, at the programming level some of the object-oriented notions are not directly supported (but not forbidden either). We will discuss Ada support for object-oriented programming shortly, but first a few words about programming paradigms in general.

Support for Programming Paradigms

The mapping of design structures into programming language structures constitutes the next step in the software development process after design. A *programming paradigm* provides a set of principles for building program structures based on an execution model of the underlying computational engine. If specifies a way to devise the software *dynamic structure*. Program execution is a fundamental notion in computer programming, it defines the way to instruct the computer as to what to do next as reflected by the different control struc-

TABLE 7.   Software Paradigms

Design Paradigms	Programming Paradigms
• Function-oriented design [23]: functional blocks (modules) are devised by inspecting the flow of data.	• Procedural programming [27–29]: specify what the program does and how it does it. Modules contain control flow infrastructure.
• Data-oriented design [24]: software modules are obtained by mapping data structures into program structures. Structure clashes are solved by intermediate structures.	• Concurrent programming [30]: modules themselves control their own independent execution thread; control flow based on the occurrence of events.
• Entity-oriented design [25]: software components (modules) are identified by grouping entities, attributes and their relationships. Entities and attributes are usually data structures.	• Object-oriented programming [31]: non-procedural based on the idea of Modules representing objects' classes containing control infrastructure.
• Object-oriented design [26]: software components (modules) are formed by a tree-like hierarchy which allows properties to be inherited (i.e., "shared") down from parent to children components.	• Functional programming [32]: A style of programming in which no assignments or global properties are maintained (i.e., no side effects).
	• Logic programming [33]: Nonprocedural programs with axioms and a formula to be proved as input, and information about the proof as output.

tures. Control approaches have been the subject of programming methodology research for many years. Obviously, the first programming paradigms were defined in terms of the concrete model of how computers serially execute instructions. Programming paradigms can be classified according to where the decision control infrastructure resides into the categories listed in Table 7. More recently, abstract notions of execution control not necessarily directly supported by the physical hardware have been introduced. This requires additional system software, known as virtual machines, such as run-time kernels for "apparent" concurrent execution, inference engines for solving logic programming queries, interpreters supporting functional programming, and environments emulating objects and classes.

Procedural models, based on the idea that active subprograms operate on passive data objects sent as arguments, are widespread in conventional software development. The current state-of-the-art is characterized by data abstractions emphasizing modularity, information hiding and extensibility, where objects are said to be instances of a type. Supporting languages are general-purpose, which means that they are widely available (at least on traditional hardware/operating systems computing systems), able to coexist with other languages and to cope with every major application area.

Until recently languages were designed mainly to support a given programming paradigm. Ada supports procedural control very well by means of subprograms. It also has an excellent set of facilities for concurrent programming, including real-time control. The less traditional paradigms object-oriented, functional and logic programming are supported in a less elegant manner. This is discussed in the next section.

ARTIFICIAL INTELLIGENCE SOFTWARE DEVELOPMENT

In this section we look specifically at AI software technology. We discuss many of the most commonly used techniques and approaches for developing AI applications, together with corresponding Ada examples.

AI has a wealth of languages, techniques, and methods of its own. These techniques and methods, which evolved since the early 1960s, range from basic programming concepts such as dynamic and flexible data structures to unique and novel integrated environments with powerful databases and programming paradigms, with their own interpreters and programming shells. It is convenient, for our purposes, to group the various approaches commonly used by the AI community into three categories, namely basic methods and techniques, computational models and languages, and support environments. We will discuss each of these in turn.

Basic Methods and Techniques

Most commonly used techniques, intrinsic in a typical AI programming setup, include complex and flexible data structures (such as frames which treats data as objects and forms the basic for knowledge representation techniques), adaptive programming facilities (e.g., dynamic memory allocation, late binding, relaxed typing, etc.), and libraries of routines as for example to perform symbolic manipulations and pattern matching.

Flexible Data Structures

The idea of keeping together facts about a "concept" and linking these representations is of paramount importance for developing AI systems. The *frame*, first introduced by Minski [*34*], was defined for such purposes; it is a widely used data structure, and one of the most basic data representation techniques. Frames are used to represent knowledge in terms of semantic networks, to implement object-oriented programming by combining inheritance relations with message passing, and, together with rule-base systems and constraints, to build blackboard architectures and planning systems.

What is a Frame? A frame is a collection of information encapsulated in the form of a record structure each consisting of a set of slots containing values and associated processing functions. Frames can be organized hierarchically. Records at lower levels of this hierarchy can access attributes of frames at higher levels.

Although frames can be naturally expressed in such languages as LISP, several special frame-oriented systems have been introduced [*35*]. Frame structures have also been successfully implemented in Ada [*36*]. Ada provides specific language mechanisms, known as private types, which unify the representation and the operations of programmer-defined data types. The concept of private types is virtually the same as that of an abstract data type, it introduces a type name and the associated set of operations, but places the type's actual definition inside the private part of a package. The type definition is thus not exported.

TABLE 8.   An Ada LISP-like Lists Manipulation Package

```
generic
     type Data is private;
package LISP_Lists is

     type Exprs is (empty, atom, list);

     type S_Expr (Kind : Exprs := atom);

     type Link is access to S_Expr;

     type Elem (Kind : Exprs := atom) is record
               case kind is
                    when empty    => null;
                    when atom     => Value  : Data;
                    when list     => Next   : Link;
               end case;
          end record;

     type S_Expr (Kind : Exprs := atom) is record
               CAR      : Elem (kind);
               CDR      : Elem (list);
          end record;

- - construct a list from either an atom, other lists, or combinations thereof
     function cons (Left, Right    : S_Expr)          return S_Expr;
     function cons (Left, Right    : Data)            return S_Expr;
     function cons (Left      : Data; Right : S_Expr) return S_Expr;
     function cons (Left      : S_Expr; Right : Data) return S_Expr;

- - extract components of a list
     function car  (L   :     S_Expr)      return Elem;
     function cdr  (L   :     S_Expr)      return Elem;

- - append to a list      (Notice operators overloading for convenient
- -                                   use in infix notation)
     function "&" (Left,  Right : S_Expr)          return S_Expr;
     function "&" (Left : Data;  Right : S_Expr)   return S_Expr;
     function "&" (Left : S_Expr; Right : Data)    return S_Expr;

end LISP_Lists;
```

From an AI programmer point of view, each frame is fundamentally a list of lists; this allows program control of the dynamics of the frame system. The capability of dynamically creating/deleting data structures is, obviously, at the heart of any proposed linguistic solution. Dynamic data structuring in the form of *lists manipulation* is done in Ada basically as it is done in LISP. In LISP, all data is represented as S-expressions. An S-expression is either an "atom" or a list of S-expressions. An atom represents an actual *typed* value such as a numeric atom, in the form of an integer or a floating point number, a literal atom (e.g., names), or a character atom, array atom, etc. A list of S-expression is given in parentheses, each member separated by spaces; a list of two S-expressions (normally separated by a dot) is a special list known as "cons". A cons consists of an ordered pair of S-expressions. There is no question that Ada features more than suffice the basic requirements expressed here, namely defining and constructing data structures at run-time. Table 8 presents a prototypical generic Ada package providing a set of facilities for handling LISP-like lists.

In Ada, objects are *strongly typed*; thus, before an operation is performed, its operands are checked to ensure that they correspond to the appropriate type. This prevents nonsensical operations, but more importantly it allows overloading resolution. Two objects are only compatible if their types are compatible. But, what exactly does this mean for Ada? It means *name equivalence*, and requires that the two objects be given the same type name, and thus type checks are performed at compile time. (This is in contrast to traditional procedural languages where structural equivalence is used, requiring that the two objects have the same signature, e.g., Pascal.)

The strong typing philosophy of Ada seriously restricts the dynamic creation of heterogeneous data structures at the heart of AI programming. But, at the same time, it supports the idea of classes in which objects of the same class respond to the same set of messages! in other words, objects of a given type can only respond to operations defined for that type.

This problem can be alleviated by using generic units. We can say that Ada generics allow the creation of "type-less" algorithms since the generic specification is defined for no specific type, but a family of related types (generic formal types also known as type variables), delaying the actual association of specific types until the generic instantiation. Consider the list example in Table 8. Because of these strong typing rules, an instantiation of the LISP_Lists package is required for different type of values to be held in the cells of a list. If we need a list of INTEGERs, we simply need to instantiate the package for the predesigned type INTEGER as shown in Table 9. The package can be instantiated with any type at or below the family of PRIVATE types (see Fig. 6).

When using access types to define dynamic data structures such as lists, objects are continually taken off free memory. Many of these "cells" are temporary. If there is no way of reclaiming this space back into the application program, then it is likely that storage overflow will occur. The process of reclaiming unused cells back into the available memory is known as *garbage collection*. In Ada, automatic garbage collection is not required; however, the language reference manual does not preclude it either, and an implementation is free to provide it.

Recall that an Ada object of an access type provides access to dynamically allocated objects. Ada access types are strongly typed in the sense that the objects accessed by a given access type are all of a given specified type. More importantly, the use of Ada objects referred to by access types is much safer than similar concepts in other languages (e.g., Pointers in Pl/I and references in Algol 68). The problem with dangling references does not surface with Ada access types. Let us explain this further.

The main reason for the "predictable" behavior of access types, is that the accessed

TABLE 9.   Using the LISP_List Package

---

with LISP_Lists;

package Int_Lists is new LISP Lists (INTEGER); . . .

with Int_Lists; use Int_Lists; - - direct visibility of operators

X, Y, Z : S_Expr;   - - create three lists of integers

A, B : Elem; . . .

X   :=   cons   (1, 2);   - - the list (1 2)

Y   :=   cons   (1, null);   - - the list (1)

A   :=   car (X); - - produces the value 1.   Same effect with: A := X.car

B   :=   cdr (X); - - produces the value 2.   Same effect with: B := X.cdr

Z   :=   cons   (5, cons (cons   (6,   cons (1, 2)),   (8));
                                  - - the list   (5   ((6   (1 2))   8))

X   :=   (Z & (Y & (Z & cons (A, B))));

---

objects of a given type form a COLLECTION whose scope is that of the access type. On the one hand, the collection disappears when the scope is exited, and by then any corresponding access object would also disappear; so there would not be a possibility for an access object to point to or to reference a non-existing object. Ada programmers may directly control the size of the space use for each specific access collection (see Table 10 for an illustration).

On the other hand, when a dynamic Ada object is inaccessible (because no other objects refer to it either directly or indirectly) then the storage that it occupies may be reclaimed by an automatic garbage collector. Alternatively, implementers of packages

TABLE 10.   Storage Control in Ada

---

type List is access Cell;

for List'STORAGE_SIZE use

    500 * (cell'SIZE / SYSTEM.STORAGE_UNIT);
    - - this specifies actual size of List collection to be big enough to hold at
    - - most 500 Cells. Exception STORAGE_ERROR will automatically be
    - - raised if an attempt is made to create Cell 501th!

procedure Free is new UNCHECKED_DEALLOCATION (Cell, List);
    - - allows programmer controlled deallocation of Cells

PRAGMA CONTROLLED (list); - - informs the compiler that we are
    - - controlling the collection List so that any automatic garbage
    - - collection should not take place for this access type.

---

providing dynamic data structures, may explicitly deallocate no longer needed objects and keep track of the space made thus available. This is the preferred approach since it not only makes the software more implementation independent, but it also gives better timing control in a real-time situation. The Ada feature supporting programmer controlled storage allocation is the generic UNCHECKED_DEALLOCATION procedure. Table 10 illustrates the use of this procedure.

Returning to our discussion on the frame data structure, we can use the list package to create frames. Yen [37] has developed an Ada package that encapsulates a uniform model of dynamic objects together with an automatic garbage collection mechanism. The package allows for "type-less" programming, in the sense explained above, and thus to construct with less difficulty Lisp-like data structures in Ada. Table 11 shows an excerpt of a modified version of a frames package as proposed by Yen.

Frame's slots can be used not only to keep attribute values but also to connect frames in a number of ways. Such connections result in a representation of domain knowledge and taxonomy by the creation of (the illusion of) levels of abstraction. In this way, frames provide an organizational scheme for knowledge bases. Such a system of connected frames is known as a *semantic network* [38]. Semantic nets were originally designed to represent the meaning of words (semantics), and have their roots in in the notion that human knowledge is structured as an association of concepts linked together in a network. According to Tanimoto [39], "any system in which the modules of knowledge may be described as nodes in a labeled graph may be called a semantic net." An early example of using Ada to implement semantic nets is found in [40].

Adaptive Control Flow

Adaptive control flow is an important ingredient for programming an AI application. It refers to the capability of defining algorithms recursively in terms of themselves, and the dynamic association of executable code with procedural (or functional) abstractions.

Recursion. Ada provides very good *recursive programming* facilities. Both procedures and functions can be called recursively. Furthermore, because of the separation between a subprogram declaration and its body, mutually recursive subprograms are possible. Table 12 illustrates recursion in Ada.

Care must be taken with regards to the PRAGMA IN_LINE. The effect of this pragma is to expand inline the subprogram body at the place of each corresponding call. This has incidence on reducing execution time (by eliminating the actual call) at the expense of increasing space usage. Obviously, a recursive call to such a subprogram may cause storage overflow. The instantiation of generics inside a recursive program may also have a similar problem.

Demons. In a frame system, a slot may be provided with a default value and/or with information related to that slot. This attached information can take several forms. It may be a constraint that must be satisfied by the filled-in value for the slot, or it may be a "procedural attachment" (also known as *demons*) used to determine the value for the slot (commonly referred to as *if-needed* procedural attachments) or which are triggered after a value is filled in for the slot (this is called an *if-added* procedural attachment).

This attachment of information to slots provides great flexibility. Frames can thus be made to represent many more of the details of knowledge relevant to the problem, without loosing organizational effectiveness. In this way, programs are treated as data; and it opens the door to self-generative code.

Ada does not allow the dynamic association of names with executable statements.

TABLE 11.   A Frames Ada Package

```
with Dynamic_Memory, LISP_Lists;

package Frame_Data_Structure is

    package M renames Dynamic_Memory; - -          re-export package
    package L is new LISP_Lists (Data);
. . .

Not_Slot_Info      :   constant STRING   :=   "Argument is not a SLOT";
Not_Unit_Info      :   constant STRING   :=   "Argument is not a UNIT";
. . .

subtype Value             is M.AcsObj; - -   rename types for readability
subtype Values_List       is M.AcsObj; - -   all of the same type! to allow
subtype Facet             is M.AcsObj; - -   heterogeneous structures
subtype Slot              is M.AcsObj;
subtype Unit              is M.AcsObj;
subtype KB                is M.AcsObj;
subtype Unit_List         is M.AcsObj;
. . .

type Slot is record
        Name      :   Name_Str;
        Val       :   Values_List;
        Default   :   Values_List;
        Derived   :   Values_List;
        V_type    :   Value_Type;   - - local, default, inherited
        Facets    :   . . .
    end record;
- - constructor/accessor subprograms for Slots
    function Create_Slot          return Slot;
    function Slot_Name            return Name_Str;
    function Slot_Val             return Values_Lists,
    . . .
    procedure Slot_Name  (S  :   Slot;   Name   :   Name_Str);
    procedure Slot_Val   (S  :   Slot;   Val    :   Values_Lists)
    . . .

- - constructor/accessor subprograms for Units
    . . .
```

The same effect may be simulated by task types (which can be associated with variables and passed as arguments to subprograms) or by generic formal subprogram parameters. But in either case, the corresponding unit bodies must be available at link time at the latest. Ada tasks have a hybrid behavior in that they are both program units (with specification and body) and types (from which objects can be created). A task is a program unit that can itself encapsulate an object, by defining its interface through entries (messages), and specifying

TABLE 12.   Recursion in Ada

- - the following are two mutually recursive subprograms

procedure F (. . .); - - this is simply the declaration of F

procedure G (. . .) is - - this is the declaration of G and its body
begin
. . .
    F(. . .); - - call to F which in turns has a (recursive) call to G
. . .
end G;

procedure F (. . .) is - - this is the body of F
begin
. . .
    G(. . .); - - call to G which in turns has a (recursive) call to F
. . .
end G;

---

when and under what conditions messages are to be accepted (the task behavior which implements the methods).

Symbolic Manipulation and Pattern Matching

Reusability is one of Ada's strongest points, and library units (an intrinsic concept of the language) is *the* mechanism for the provision of reusable software. The LISP-like list manipulation package introduced above, is a good example of such reusable components. Facilities for LISP-like *pattern-directed computation* on list structures [41] have also been developed. The operation that drives a pattern-directed computation is that of finding a pattern in the data, and is generally identified with the processing of character strings. A pattern determines the structure of the string to which it is matched. Applicative pattern-directed computing requires the pattern matched to retain a value that can be acted upon by other functions. In this way, patterns are generalized into more powerful objects called *forms*. The value returned by a pattern is either false (no match) or a parse tree specifying the structure of the string that correspond to the portions of the pattern matched.

In the Ada implementation of pattern-directed computation found in Tanimoto [39], "patterns would consist of sequences of primitive matching functions, literal values, or other patterns. The matching would return a success/failure boolean, a tree of values representing the portions of the subject list that were matched by each pattern component, and a tree of pointers into the subject to allow Markov-style substitution or replacement of matched values." Table 13 shows the specification of an Ada package devised to sport this idea of pattern-directed computing.

To mimic LISP-like structures in Ada is beneficial. In fact, there have been several automatic translation systems from LISP into Ada; a good discussion of the topic is given by Baker [42]. Strong typing has been one of the major problems to be solved in such translations. The use of predefined library packages makes the translation more straightforward, and in fact, lessens any concerns about "loosing" the LISP environment as illustrated in the many examples shown in this section. Ada is also capable of coexisting with other lan-

TABLE 13.   Ada Package for Pattern-Matching

with LISP_Lists;

package Pattern_Matcher is

    package Str_Lists is new LISP_Lists (STRING); use Str_Lists;

    type Result is record
            Success   :   BOOLEAN   :=   False;
            Tree   :   S_Expr;
        end record;

function Match	(Pattern,	Subject	:	S_Expr;	
	L_Anchor,	R_Anchor	:	BOOLEAN)	return Result;
function Match	(Pattern,	Subject	:	STRING;	
	L_Anchor,	R_Anchor	:	BOOLEAN)	return Result;
function Match	(Pattern		:	S_Expr;	
	Subject		:	STRING;	
	L_Anchor,	R_Anchor	:	BOOLEAN)	return Result;
function Match	(Pattern		:	STRING;	
	Subject		:	S_Expr;	
	L_Anchor,	R_Anchor	:	BOOLEAN)	return Result;
function Parse	(Start_S,	Subject	:	S_Expr;	
	Label		:	BOOLEAN)	return Result;
function Parse	(Start_S,	Subject	:	STRING;	
	Label		:	BOOLEAN)	return Result;
function Parse	(Start_S		:	S_Expr;	
	Subject		:	STRING;	
	Label		:	BOOLEAN)	return Result;
function Parse	(Start_S		:	STRING;	
	Subject		:	S_Expr;	
	Label		:	BOOLEAN)	return Result;

- - selectors
    function "/"   (List   :   S_Expr;   Index   :   NATURAL) return S_Expr;
    function "*"   (Tree   :   S_Expr;   Index   :   NATURAL) return S_Expr;
    . . .

guages via the standard pragma INTERFACE (its availability though is implementation dependent).

Computational Models

AI computational models, such as lambda calculus and first-order predicate calculus, are radically different from the traditional stored program model of the Von Newmann machine. Under these paradigms we find various styles of AI programming, such as logic programming, functional programming, and object-oriented programming. Specialized languages, like LISP and PROLOG, have been devised to provide convenient notations in which to express these ideas. COMMON LISP is the de facto standard in the United States for developing AI applications. PROLOG seems to attract more attention in Europe, where there is a working group studying its standardization.

We discuss each of these paradigms in turn.

Logic Programming

Logic or predicate programming is based on primitives for defining facts and rules (declarative programs, similar to pattern-matching computing).

Probably one of the most widely used AI techniques are *"production systems."* A production system consists of a collection of condition-action pairs called production rules stored in a rule base, together with a database of known facts of the problem domain, state information of the current solution, and a procedure for "firing" the production rules called the inference mechanism. In this framework, a program is not a procedural sequence of instructions, but a set of declarative (i.e., nonprocedural) statements providing information about the problem.

These tools are based on the idea of "programming in logic." This form of logic programming is commonly done by using predicate calculus expressions called "Horn Clauses" in which at most one the literals of the expressions is unnegated. Basically, a production rule consists of an IF part (or left-hand side, antecedent, or conditional part) that when evaluated to TRUE produces the THEN part (or right-hand side, consequent, or action). Algorithms are not completely under the control of the programmer, but of the underlying control mechanism (or inference engine). Programmers must master this underlying process in order to specify a correct set of assertions (facts and goals to prove). Although rules are representable using a frame structure, special languages and environments have been developed, notably PROLOG. Interpreters for these languages are purely procedural programs and thus better written entirely in modern software engineering languages like Ada. Several Ada implementations of PROLOG (inference engines) have been developed [*43, 44*]. Two approaches can be observed as follows:

> Internal Approach: create Ada packages implementing inference systems. Sequential as well as concurrent approaches have been proposed. Table 14a presents an interesting generic approach to building an inference engine. Each rule in this inference engine is implemented as a separate task, which serves to demonstrate parallelism at the rule level. Table 14b shows an example of declaring rules using such a package.
>
> External Approach: provide an interface between Ada and the inference-oriented system.

Other "languages" and systems supporting logic programming have been designed and implemented in Ada. Notably ALLAN [*45*] and PROVER [*46*]. ALLAN is a language that, although based on PROLOG, uses an Ada-like syntax, adding explanation capabilities and confidence factors typically found in expert systems shells. Table 15 shows an excerpt of a Knowledge base described in ALLAN.

In PROVER, users supply facts and rules to prove a goal or possibly multiple goals; the systems uses a generalized first-order logic resolution algorithm to repeatedly deduce new facts or to generate new subgoals until all alternatives are exhausted or a special valid state has been reached. PROVER takes advantage of Ada strong typing and represents all

TABLE 14a.   An Inference Engine Ada Generic Package

---

generic

    with function Rule
        return BOOLEAN;

    with procedure ReCycle;

package Rule_Registration is

    procedure Cycle;

end Rule_Reg;

package body Rule_Reg is

    task Rule_processor is
        entry Cycle;
    end Rule_Processor;

    task body Rule_Processor is
    begin
    loop
        if Rule then ReCycle;
        end if;

        select accept Cycle;
        or terminate;
        end select;

    end loop;

    end Rule_Processor;

    procedure Cycle is

    begin
        Rule_Processor.Cycle;

    end Cycle ;

end Rule_Reg;

---

    generic

        with procedure Cycle_Rules
    package Monitor is
        procedure ReCycle;
    end Monitor ;

    package body Monitor is

    task Monitor is
        entry ReCycle;
    end Monitor ;

    task body Monitor is
    begin
        loop

        select
            accept ReCycle;
            Cycle_Rules;
            or terminate;
        end select;

        end loop;

    end Monitor;

    procedure ReCycle is
        begin
            Monitor.ReCycle;
        end ReCycle ;

    end Monitor;

Source: Ref. *47.*

TABLE 14b.   Using the Ada Inference Generic Package of 14a

---

procedure Cycle_Rules;

package T_Monitor is new Monitor   (Cycle_Rules);

function Rule_1   return BOOLEAN is
    begin   . . . end Rule_1;
package Rule_1_P is new Rule_Registration   (Rule_1,   T_Monitor.ReCycle);

function Rule_2   return BOOLEAN is
    begin   . . . end Rule_2;
package Rule_2_P is new Rule_Registration   (Rule_2,   T_Monitor.ReCycle);

. . .

procedure Cycle_Rules is
    begin
        Rule_1_P.Cycle;
        Rule_2_P.Cycle;
    end Cycle_Rules;

TABLE 15.   A KB Described Using ALLAN, An Ada Logic-Based Language

---

GLOBALS
    ?Girls_how_like_join   :=   0;   – – comments are similar to Ada's

SEMANTICS
    Likes (symbol, symbol);   female (symbol);

FACTS
    assert likes   (john, bill)   [1.0]; – –   []   confidence factor
    assert likes   (john, wine)   [0.0];
    assert likes   (mary, bill)   [0.5];
    assert likes   (sue, john)   [1.0];
    assert female   (sue);   assert female (mary);

RULES
    1:   start when likes (john, ?x);
    2:   likes (john, ?x)   when likes (?x, wine) [0.1]   "John . . . ";
    3:   likes (john, ?x)   when female (?x) and likes (?x, john) and
         ?Girls_how_like_john   :=   ?Girls_how_like_john + 1 [0.95]
         "John likes girls";

END;

TABLE 16.   Well-formed Formula Data Structures in PROVER

```
type wff_kind is    (if_then_wff, if_then_else_wff,
               and_wff, or_wff, not_wff,
                    existential_wff, universal_wff,
                    if_and_only_if_wff,
                    literal_wff, variable_wff, list_wff);

type wff_type       (kind    :    wff_kind); - - an incomplete type

type wff_ptr_type is access wff_type;

- - every wff has an associated polarity

type polarity is (positive, negative, both);

type wff_type       (kind    :    wff_kind) is record - - the actual type
     Polarity       :    polarity_kind;
     case kind is
     when if_then_wff
          =>  if_if_then_wff               :    wff_ptr_type;
              then_if_then_wff             :    wff_ptr_type;
     when if_then_else_wff
          =>  if_if_then_else_wff          :    wff_ptr_type;
              then_if_then_else_wff        :    wff_ptr_type;
     when and_wff
          =>  left_and_wff                 :    wff_ptr_type;
          =>  right_and_wff                :    wff_ptr_type;
     when or_wff
          =>  left_or_wff                  :    wff_ptr_type;
          =>  right_or_wff                 :    wff_ptr_type;
     when not_wff
          =>  not_wff                      :    wff_ptr_type;
     when existential_wff
          =>  existential_wff              :    wff_ptr_type;
     when universal_wff     ...
     when if_and_only_if_wff     ...
     when literal_wff    ...
     when variable_wff      ...
     when list_wff       ...
```

---

assertions as an abstract tree whose leaves are linked lists. Table 16 shows details of the data structure. Following is an example of assertions as presented to PROVER.

$$\forall x \forall y \; \forall z \; (if \; (x > y \; \wedge \; y > z) \; then \; x > z)$$

Expert Systems.   Many of the AI techniques discussed so far can be integrated to form a computer system (or program) that performs a series of activities commonly carried out by skilled or knowledgeable humans. These systems are known as *expert systems*. There

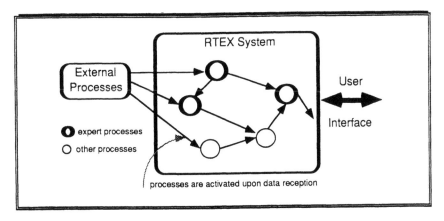

FIGURE 8.   RTEX architecture.

have been several Ada-based expert systems tools implemented [48, 49], some of which are commercially available such as ART-Ada [50], CHRONOS [51], and CLIPS/Ada [52].

The RTEX system [48] is an industry-oriented system for developing embedded real-time expert systems. The system integrates advance software engineering and real-time concepts through the use of Ada, with object-oriented (concurrent) programming, real-time inferencing, symbolic matching and signal understanding. Data in RTEX is kept in messages, initialized by a burst of messages and which can come from external sources. RTEX provides a concurrent object-oriented approach in which objects do not react on every incoming message (a discussion on object oriented programming is given below), but they known how to react on specific combinations of messages. Message protocol corresponds to the left-hand side of the production rules, whose associated action parts correspond to the methods. In this sense, RTEX is also a data driven language in which execution control is triggered by the arrival of input data. This accounts for the high degree of parallelism in the system. Figure 8 illustrates the relationships between RTEX expert processes (implemented as Ada tasks) and regular tasks.

The Helsinki Prolog System-HPS [53] provides advanced programming tools integrated into a programming environment to support modular Prolog systems development. HPS was implemented in Ada, with some parts using Prolog primitives (the system implements a superset of the Edinburgh Prolog Language). The user interface is provided out of a library of routines by using Ada PRAGMAS at the implementation environment. HPS consists of several components, including an interpreter-virtual machine to execute Prolog programs, a compiler to produce a more efficient execution of predicates by the virtual machine, an editor which ties together a syntax checker, a translator, and a library manager in order to allow the incremental execution of intermediate programs during the editing of source code. All these components are integrated in a seamless fashion. Table 17 shows an excerpt of the Ada task implementing HSP's shell. This implementation using tasks allows for concurrent queries to be handled graciously by the Ada run-time kernel. It also permits the association of timing constraints, and thus to control the use of resources spent in solving the queries in Prolog.

TABLE 17.   HPS Shell Implemented as an Ada Task

```
task HPS_Shell is

entry Solve - - -
        (Query                    :    in Prolog_Query; - - a string
        Time_Limit                :    DURATION  :=  DURATION'LAST);

entry Result
        (Success                  :    out Success_Kind; - - y/n/notyet
        Answer                    :    out Bindings;
        More_Answers              :    out BOOLEAN;
        Errors                    :    out BOOLEAN;
        Error                     :    Error_Kind);

entry More_Results
        (Continue                 :    in BOOLEAN'
        Time_Limit                :    DURATION  :=  DURATION'LAST);

end HPS-Shell;


HPS_Shell.Solve    (Time_Limit => 10,
                    Query => "father (X, Joe), mother (Y,X)",);
```

Functional Programming

Functional programming refers to a programming style in which elementary forms of dynamic function definition and self-modifying code, with very flexible control flow and dynamic scoping, are provided together with a mechanism to evaluate them. The idea is to use factor-forming operations combining primitive functions into more complex ones, and so on. This approach also eliminates the need for variables and conventional "procedural" descriptions.

Ada also allows function forming operations for defining mappings or applicative operators: a function that takes another function as input (e.g., apply-to-all mappings). This is a powerful form of control structure which determines how a function is to be applied to a data structure, and is achieved in Ada by using generic functions with other functions as parameters which can then be used to derive other functions and so on. Table 18 presents a modified example from [54] of such approach.

Functional programming is a pervasive style found in LISP, structured around applying functions (operators) to linked lists of arguments, which may themselves be functions. Dynamically definable functions is a topic closely related to *self-generative code*: techniques used in LISP and others interpretative languages in which a function or program segment is developed at run-time. This means that programs can be modified as data, and data structures can be constructed and directly executed as programs.

Ada does not offer this capability. In fact, it is only possible if and only if the language involved is the "native language" of the underlying computational engine (being it hardware or software). The LISP language permits this type of programming of representing program code and data identically by requiring an interpreter. Of course, if there is an Ada

TABLE 18.   Functional Programming in Ada

```
generic
     type Domain is private;
     type Codomain is private;
     with function F(X  :     Domain) return Codomain;
     with function G(X  :     Domain) return Domain;
function Composition (X     :     Domain) return Codomain is
begin
     return F(G(X));
end Composition;


generic
     type T is private;
     with function P     (X  :     T)   return BOOLEAN;
     with function F     (X  :     T)   return T;
     with function G     (X  :     T)   return T;
function Conditional (X) is
     begin
          if P (X)
               then return F (X);
               else return G (X);
          end if;
     end Conditional;


. . . . . . . . . . . . . . . . . . . . . . . . . . . . . . . . . . .

function Sub2 is new Composition
(F => Sub1, G => Sub1, Domain => FLOAT, Codomain => FLOAT);

function Sub3 is new Composition (SQRT, Sub2, FLOAT, FLOAT);

function ABS is new Conditional (FLOAT, GEZ, Id, NEG);
```

---

machine that directly executes Ada code (either virtually or physically) then dynamically definable functions are possible in Ada.

Nevertheless, Ada provides a different view of programs as data, in the form of constant task objects, which opens up new possibilities for "controlled" generative programs. Like other data objects in Ada, a task object belongs to a type, limited private and thus can be used anywhere a limited private type object can be used, i.e., as actual generic parameter, as subprogram actual parameter, or as a package private. Even though we know their structure, we cannot manipulate task types as literal values, and cannot be dynamically generated at run-time.

Self-modifying programs are mathematically undecided and may have unpredictable results! Therefore they should be avoided. "One can argue that this is a nonissue since one can certainly write an Ada program that interprets an array of virtual instructions!"

Object-Oriented Programming

We start by noting that the use of the term "object-oriented" is inconsistent among different audiences (especially among Ada and non-Ada cultures). In the Ada world, object-oriented basically means being able to encapsulate an object's properties inside a package. In general, the object-oriented paradigm attempts to model the problem domain based on a non-procedural and uniform use of objects in which objects apply operations (methods) on themselves. In the object-oriented paradigm, operations, in the form of messages, are sent to objects, in contrast with conventional programming in which objects are sent as arguments to subprograms.

The computational model for the object-oriented programming paradigm is based on the notions of objects as class instances, messages and methods. Semantically, an *object* represents an abstraction of both real-world entity and of the computer capabilities to store and manipulate information. An object implementation is encapsulated into modules called classes, and are viewed from the outside and from the inside. A fundamental notion is that classes can be organized and grouped hierarchically according to their degree of specialization depicting the structure of relative inheritance relations; thus, specialized (sub)classes are said to inherit information and behavior from more general (super)classes. Objects can only be accessed via *messages* defined in their associated class interface. This set of messages defines the objects external view also known as message protocol. The set of corresponding *methods* define the object's internal view. A method is the procedure invoked for responding to a message; it specifies what happens when an object receives the associated message.

The attractiveness of these ideas was recognized early, especially in the area of simulation. The programming language Sumula [55], developed in the mid-1960s, was the first to introduce the idea of classes and object instances. These ideas appeared nearly simultaneously in AI [56], and have achieved a high degree of sophistication in frame-based languages. Explicit awareness of the idea, including the use of the term object-oriented programming, came from Smalltalk, developed at the XEROX Palo Alto Research Center in the 1970s [57]. Object-oriented programming has prompted the development of newer languages such as Eiffel [58], CommonLoops [59], Flavors [60], Trellis/Owl [61], etc., and the adaptation of existing ones, for example, Objective-C [62] and C++ [63], Object-Pascal [64], Object-Logo [65], ObjectAda [66], etc. In fact, a wide variety of languages claim to support the object-oriented paradigm.

Bonafide object-oriented languages (e.g., Smalltalk) are not considered general-purpose languages. These languages still suffer a significant performance penalty when compared with procedural languages.

In what follows, we present a mapping into Ada of the fundamental notions of object-oriented programming. It is worth noticing that the design of the Ada language is more than a decade old based on requirements of some 16 years ago! However, the language quite remarkably satisfies many modern concerns.

Object Encapsulation: Packages.   Ada packages represent the chief mechanism for encapsulation and hiding. Its structure was illustrated in Figure 5 above. The essence of packages is their ability to define local entities, implemented in the package body, and the provision of entities exported through the package specification. They bind data and subprograms tightly together limiting data to a highly localized region of code. The binding of underlying data with associated collection of subprograms is called encapsulation. Inaccessibility to the internal structure is called hiding.

Ada packages are object oriented in the sense that they export definitional means for creating instances of objects and a set of subprograms that operate on those objects. Objects' state variables can be totally hidden in the package body.

A single object can be implemented in Ada as a package. We call such packages *single object packages*, or SOPs for short. The SOP specification exports the message protocol, while the package body hides the corresponding methods and data structures, the latter representing instance variables or the object's state. Object packages achieve the maximum degree of information hiding possible, since the object represented can only be accessed via the exported protocol (subprograms). Table 19(a) shows an example, modified from [67], of

TABLE 19. Ada Object Packages

(a)   single object package

- - - - - - - - - - here is the message protocol

```
package Directory_Object is
    procedure Insert
    (N:in Name; Num:in Number);
    procedure Look_Up
    (N:in Name; Num:out Number);
end Directory_Object;

packages body Directory_Object is
    type Dir_Node;
    type Dir_Ptr is access
        Dir_Node;
    type Dir_Node is record

- - declaration of instance variables

        Entry_name      :   Name
        Entry_number    :   Number;
        Left, Right         Dir Ptr;
    end record;
    Dir_Root         :   Dir_Ptr;

    - - this is the actual object

    - - methods provided as body stubs

procedure Insert . . . is separate;

procedure Look_Up . . . is separate;


begin . . . ; - - initialize directory object

end Directory_Object;
```

```
(b)    Multiple Object Package

generic
package Directories is
- -        . . . as in Directory_Object
end Directories;

package body Directories is
- -        . . . as in Directory_Object

- -   the following two instantiations
- - create two similar but distinct
- - objects, denoted by Home_Dir and
- - Work_Dir respectively.


package Home_Dir is new
Directories;
packages Work_Dir is new
Directories;
- - we can now access these objects in
- - the usual way:


Work_Dir.Insert    (Me, 764_6052);

Home_Dir.Insert    (Me, 250_5038);
. . . ;

Work_Dir.Look_Up

    ("Norris,G.", Number);
```

- - the object is accessed as follows:
Directory_Object.Insert (N => "George", Num => 250-5038);

an SOP. The capability to instantiate multiple objects can be obtained in a number of ways. The simplest approach would be to make the single-object package a generic package, we call this combination *Multiple Object Package*, or MOP. Each instantiation of this generic package creates a new SOP. This is illustrated in Table 19b.

Classes: Ada Types.   Conceptually, a type is a template that describes common Ada object's properties. Properties associate objects to a particular kind of data structure and, by implication, to the operations which may be performed on the objects of the type. An object declaration specifies an instance of a type, and constrains it to the type's signature (i.e., a set of values and operations). Methods are implemented in Ada as operators, subprograms, and built-in attributes. Both operators and subprograms can be overloaded. *Overloading* refers to the ability of a subprogram identifier (or operator) to denote several methods simultaneously (within the same lexical scope), each specifying distinct actual operations. This is a useful feature for supporting abstract polymorphism (see below).

A package exporting a type, and a set of *related subprograms* implements the idea of a class. We call this an *object-class package*, or OCP (Table 20). A related subprogram is one in which at least one of the parameters is of the exported type. Type is an object creation facility and thus serves as the "constructor." Object instances are created by Ada object declarations from the given type; these instances exist outside the package themselves.

Ada provides a rich selection of types, and thus, a decision must be made on how the instances of the type (viz the objects) are to be created, this affects the choice of type implementation and the degree of information hiding. This is to say, that the way a type is defined controls the degree of information hiding. The highest degree of information hiding is provided by the so called *opaque* types, which completely hide the structure of the exported type inside the package body. This is implemented in an OCP by exporting a *limited private type* defined as an access type to an incomplete type specified in the private part of the package and fully defined in the package body. An incomplete type simply introduces a type name and omits its definition until later. See Table 20b for an illustration.

At the other extreme of the spectrum we have a *open* OCPs; they export the *full type* declaration, making its structure totally known outside the package; open packages have the lowest degree of information hiding. A full type declaration introduces a new type name specifying a data structure as defined by the actual type definition.

In between these two extremes we have *private* and *limited private* OCPs which export a *private or limited private type*, respectively. Of course, private types are more open than limited private, since assignment and equality are available from them. A Private type introduces a type name and places the type definition inside the private part of the package. The definition is thus not exported outside the package. In Table 20a, the exported type is a task type; thus, each object declaration actually creates a new concurrently executing process; we say that these objects are active. A key issue is that the type exported here is a *limited private* type and restrict the access to the objects created only to the subprograms exported.

Polymorphism.   Procedural abstractions that operate uniformly and unambiguously on values of "different" types are said to be *polymorphic* abstractions. This is possible by defining these abstractions in terms of "type variables" or metatypes rather than specific types. A generalized form of metatypes, known as generic formal types in Ada, can be used for parameterizing program units not in terms of a specific type but a family of related types. In this way, the unit is said to be polymorphic and operates on arguments of the whole family of related types. Table 21 shows an example of a polymorphic function in Ada.

Subclasses and Hierarchies: Adaptability.   Factorization is a design principle associated with the need for *adaptation*. This form of class refinement is implemented by an

TABLE 20.   Ada Object-Class Packages

(a)   Active Objects
Package Directories is

    task type Directory
        entry Insert (N:in Name;Num:in Number);
        entry Look_Up (N:in Name;Num:out Number);
        end Directory;

end Directories;

package body Directories is
            type Dir_Node;
-- . . . as before, except that instance
--   variables are inside the task
            task body Directory is separate;

end Directories; . . .

-- the following declarations create two instances of type Directory

Home_Dir, Work_Dir   :Directory; . . .
-- messages sent by specifying the corresponding object's entry
Home_Dir.Insert(Me, 250_5038);
Word Dir.Look Up(your, Number);

    (b)   Multiple Object Package
package Directories is
    type Directory is limited private;

            procedure Insert (D:in out Directory;N:in Name; Num:in Number);
        procedure Look_Up (D:in out Directory;N:in Name;Num:out Number);

private
    type Dir_Node; – – incomplete type
    type Directory is access Dir_Node;
end Directories;

package body Directories is
    type Dir_Node is record
-- full declaration of incomplete type above
-- ... as before, but no local object is needed
end Directories; . . .

-- the create two instances of type Directory
Home_Dir, Work_Dir   :Directory; . . .
Insert (Home_Dir, Me, 250_5038);
-- notice that object is sent as an argument
Look Up (Word Dir, Your,Number);

TABLE 21.   An Ada Polymorphic Function

---

generic
   type T is range <>; -- family of all integer types
function Swap (x : T) return T; . . .
type My_Int is range -10 . . 25;
type Your_Int is new INTEGER range 100 . . 200;
-- Here we introduce three instances of this function
function T is new F (INTEGER); -- i.e., STANDARD.INTEGER
function T is new F (My_Int);
function T is new F (Your Int);

---

abstract class. An abstract class is created when subclasses share part of their protocol and yet neither one is a subclass of the other; furthermore, instance creation from the common superclass, i.e., the abstract class, is not logically desirable. A generic OCP allows the introduction of abstract classes in Ada.

In Ada, basic operations are defined only for base types and passed down to subordinate types in the Ada type hierarchy (see Fig. 6). Hierarchies are evidence of a form of abstraction at work. It defines tow complementary notions, namely that of Generalization and that of Specialization. *Generalization* suggests abstracting away detailed differences of several "class" descriptions, and presenting commonalties factored out as a more general superclass. *Specialization* is the refinement process inverse to generalization, allowing the introduction of details by "generating" subclasses from existing classes via the specification of additional characteristics. The result is a taxonomy of classes, organized in partial order and encompassing the software engineering principles of abstraction, decomposition, hiding, and encapsulation.

Specialization can be done by adaptation from parameterized components (e.g., Ada generics), or by inheritance from superclasses. In its simplest form, *inheritance* is available in Ada in the form of *subtypes* which inherit their properties from their base types. A subtype declaration does not create a new type, it merely allows the imposition of constraints on an existing (base) type. These restrictions refer to structural characteristics and not to the set of operations of the base type. Operations specified in terms of a subtype are defined for its base type and all other subtypes of this base type.

A more powerful form of inheritance in Ada is that provided by *derived types*, another form of defining a new type whose definition is inherited from that of an existing "parent" type. The new definition may add constraints to the properties inherited. The new (derived) type inherits data structure definitions including initial values (i. e., instance variable names), and the corresponding set of operations (i.e., messages and methods) from its parent type. The derived type can change base type attributes by applying representation clauses; it can also add operations to those inherited, or provide new methods for any of the inherited operations (by using overloading). Figure 9 illustrates the difference between subtypes and derived types.

In this way, similar classes of objects may be externally different manipulated by different operations, or internally different responding to same operations by executing different algorithms. This refers to the ability of a type to inherit, add, or inhibit existing base type properties (i.e., basic operations and, to some extend, data structures). The class refinement

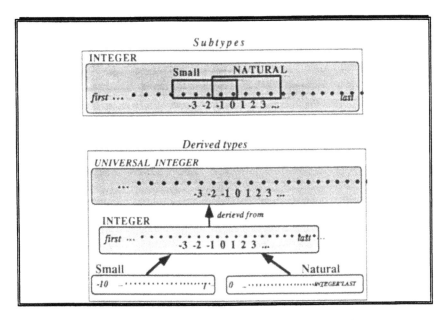

FIGURE 9.   Inheritance using Ada subtypes and derived types.

TABLE 22.   Subclassing Example in Ada

---

package Points is -- super class OCP

    type Point is record   --   inherits record ops.
           X, Y : INTEGER :=;
    end record;

    procedure Draw   (P :   Point);
    procedure Delta_X   (a :   INTEGER);
    procedure Delta_Y   (a :   INTEGER);

end Points;

package Circles is   -- subclass OCP
    type Circle is new Point;   -- inherits Draw, Delta_X, Delta_Y
    function Circle   (a,b,c   :   INTEGER) return Circle;
    procedure Draw (C :   Circle); -- redefines inherited procedure Draw
    private
        c :   point;   -- center
        r :   INTEGER   -- radio
end Circles;

---

model is directly supported by the inheritance mechanism of Ada's derived types and the Ada type class hierarchy. Table 22 illustrates subclassing in Ada.

If the generic package declaration is parameterized then more specific classes can be instantiated, each possessing different characteristics as specified by the actual generic parameters. See Table 23 for an example.

Support Environment

It is generally accepted that AI applications are considered on a different realm of software construction quite apart from traditional software systems. What makes AI software so unique and nonconventional? AI is essentially an experimental discipline, if a discipline at all, with no well-established uniformly applied theoretical frameworks against which to test models. *Validation is done by an actual implementation/experimentation cycle generally known as prototyping.*

The basic roadblock is that traditional software technology lack the powerful development environments in use for AI software practice. The idea of providing development environments for Ada which possess the same flexibility as those found in AI shops has been suggested and some environments have been developed.

Classic-Ada [68], is such an environment. This system borrows much of its interface from Smalltalk. It incorporates a language processor, to convert the class descriptions into vanilla Ada, an object-base with an object–base reporter, which is analogous to an Ada program library and associated library management tool, a builder which extracts information form the object-base in order to build data structures dynamically for binding and for inheritance, and a collection of packages, called the executive, generated by the builder and used at run-time to solve message references (runtime).

More recently [64] an integrated software engineering environment merging Ada technology with AI techniques, based upon LISP, has been successfully developed (see Figure 10). This environment includes "a compatible object-oriented extension of Ada, which includes all Ada mechanisms (types, packages, generics, tasking, etc.), object concepts (classes, methods, inheritance and dynamic binding) and memory managing functions." It also includes a natural language rule definition capability, an inference engine, and an interpretative environment with a user-friendly interface suitable for prototyping. Furthermore, the intermediate representations used allows Ada code to "coexists" with LISP. Rules are

TABLE 23.   Metaclass example in Ada

---

generic
    type x_Coordinates is (<>);
    type Y_Coordinates is (<>);
package Points is -- super class OCP
    type Point is record   -- inherits record ops.
        X   :   X_Coordinates;
        Y   :   Y_Coordinates; end record;
    procedure Draw (P   :   Point); . . .
end Points;

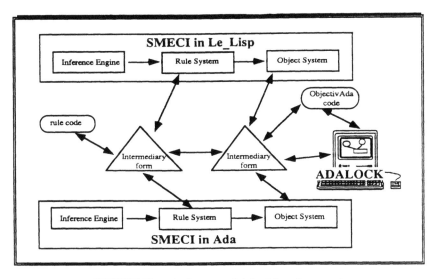

FIGURE 10.   An integrated Ada-AI environment.

translated to the intermediate form from where actual Ada or Le-Lisp code can be generated.

The interference engine was completely implemented in Ada. The graphical interface, called ADALOOK, as implemented in Le_Lisp with access to a graphical tool box. This interface facilitates visualization of an ObjectivAda software architecture with the corresponding dependencies between the various program units, and allows the browsing of entities (e.g., classes, packages, tasks, types, etc.) at the various levels of detail. A translator is provided to generate Le_Lisp code from ObjectivAda.

CONCLUSIONS

The issues discussed are summarized in Figure 11. We tried to answer the question of whether the Ada language and modern software engineering technology, are capable of supporting typical AI requirements. Another important question addresses embedded time-sensitive AI systems issues. All we can say on this is that a substantial amount of research is needed from which a sound scientific foundation for real-time AI computing could evolve. Much work has been done in some related areas, but little has been accomplished in their combined application. Efficiency considerations, for example, have never been a real concern of AI research which is not based on what is doable with current technology; and usually, non-cost-effective features at the time of their introduction become so due to advances in technology. Correctness is established through a trial-and-error process requiring a high degree of experimentation.

AI technology does not support real-time. There is no good model of behavior from a resource utilization point of view for searching, rule base, etc. For example, scanning potentially huge search spaces leads to serious performance limitations. Searching speed depends on quality of heuristics. Search heuristics without backtracking eliminates space requirements (and helps bounding time); clearly the search algorithm requires that the state vari-

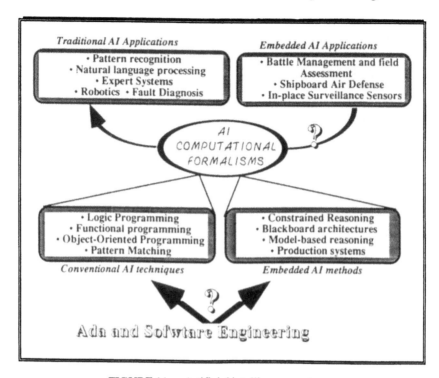

FIGURE 11.   Artificial intelligence systems.

ables for each stage during the search frontier be preserved, allowing the ability to backtrack and examine alternate paths. Adaptability and complexity preclude the use of static scheduling policies; automatic garbage collection exacerbates the predictability problem, and makes it virtually impossible to guarantee latency.

AI technology generally lacks facilities for integration with traditional computer software and systems, and for dealing with embedded real-time applications. For instance, CommonLisp, a language widely used in the United States only has two primitives that deal with time, one for reading a clock and the other for delaying (waiting) execution for a specified number of seconds. CommonLisp does not specify whether and how multiprocessing and multiprogramming is to be done, nor how concurrent processes should interact and communicate.

Most of today AI building tools are provided on dedicated special purpose computer systems or workstations supporting a collection of AI techniques like frames, pattern matching, production systems, demons, single and multiple inheritance, etc. However, AI applications are notoriously unportable due to their dependency on these specialized development environments. Lack of AI standard language constraints the range of possible solutions, for example, recommendations cannot be made for Ada (and its environment) to accommodate for a specific language or philosophy.

What about Ada and software engineering support for AI?   There are several factors other than data structures that characterize AI programming. These include symbolic manipulation and pattern-machine computation (rather than procedural control flow), interactive (i.e., interpretative) languages and environments, language sensitive editors (rather than text-oriented editors) and higher level (object-oriented) debugging facilities.

In summary, AI is supported by Ada technology at various levels:

AT THE LANGUAGE LEVEL
AT THE SUPPORT LEVEL (i.e., programming environment & run-time kernel)
AT THE LIBRARY LEVEL

The language has clear and modern control and data structuring mechanisms and powerful abstraction facilities with a comprehensive support for modularity. Furthermore, it has been shown that run-time performance is much better in Ada than in current interpreted typical AI languages. The notion of hierarchy of type categories is very beneficial; it serves as an organizational mechanism for classifying new types. Each new type is assigned a category, from where it is explicitly derived or instantiated.

Ada may be used as both native AI language or as implementation language. Tool Integration is important here: use FRAMES for knowledge-rep, then access Knowledge-base with PROLOG/LISP-like notation, and possibly switch to Ada for final system; interaction may take place via wide-spectrum user interface (graphics and natural language), coupled with translation between notations. Object-oriented programming, although not forced in Ada is not forbidden either, i.e., inheritance is explicit.

Ada specifies a multilayered, open-ended environment (APSE), with a standard tool interface (the Cais). An APSE typically include all facilities and tools which a software designer requires throughout the life cycle, such as methodology-specific tools, language-specific tools, applications-specific tools. Embedding inference capabilities into the environment provides a multi-paradigm programming approach with very high level of expressiveness (i.e., declarative programming) and real-time and embedded systems capabilities. This introduces an interesting mixture opening up newer possibilities for prototyping and engineering software.

Tools can be provided for automatically converting sentences written in a "functional notation" into Ada (generic) instantiations. The Ada RTK can provide LISP/PROLOG-like interpretative capabilities, "interface programs" (written in Ada) can be used to handle the necessary typing, subprogram calls, and error handling. The executable analysis becomes some sort of system prototype, which could be automatically converted into Ada programs. It is also possible to keep a common intermediate representation allowing the exchange of information between Ada and AI languages, notably LISP.

Packages, obviously a key concept in Ada, not only directly support encapsulation, but also promote separate compilation, supporting multiple-library and programming-in-the-large. The provision of Ada packages that mirror corresponding LISP-like structures makes programming an AI application in Ada in a manner highly isomorphic with more traditional AI techniques (as for example using LISP). Furthermore, it allows exploration of new concepts using LISP which are then immediately transferable into Ada. The translation from AI-specific notations into Ada makes it possible to convert AI systems into executable code which runs more efficiently on standard computers and is especially useful for embedded systems applications.

As fundamental approaches to knowledge-based systems grow more stable, so Ada becomes a suitable implementation language for such systems. In fact, Ada can be effective not just despite some of its limiting features (e.g., strong typing and static scoping), but because of them. The safety offered by these features reduces development time and increases reliability. Ada strong typing while feared to convey a loss of flexibility, have proven to be quite the contrary, providing a system that is much easier to customize than corresponding LISP prototypes.

Although Ada has desirable features for AI programming, it makes few concessions for "direct" AI development. In other words, software engineers may feel comfortable in using Ada for AI programming, whereas AI researchers would not find the language as natural for AI programming. Any inconveniences for supporting AI, for which the language was not specially designed, are secondary to the language final success but mainly related to using a new language to tackle old problems for which specially designed tools abound. But, the continued use of specialized AI languages may retard the expected widespread of Ada.

AI technology supports programming-in-the-small, experimental programming and prototyping, but not software engineering.

The application of software engineering techniques is key to limiting system complexity and for the successful production of reusable software components. Software engineering presents a coherent view of the software production process from a wealth of principles, techniques, and methods that promise to improve productivity and the quality of the products. All in all, the Ada programming language possess a wealth of constructs and environment tools (such as compiler-enforced configuration management) that provide direct support to modern software engineering technology.

"Hand-crafted demonstration systems" must give way to products showing standards that "exist" in conventional software systems. There are of course differences in specification, testing and development of AI software, but unless some thought is given to the software engineering aspect few programs will advance beyond the demonstration stage.

Although AI has provided many useful software techniques, their widespread use in industry has been slow. Simply rewriting them in Ada does not necessarily address the more fundamental issues of design and timing verification, and proper documentation.

The challenges ahead are centered on finding a suitable software engineering technology that is capable of satisfying a high degree of AI specific requirements.

We have studied the suitability of the Ada language for the development of AI applications and found that there are some impediments to a proper solution to the kinds of problems typically addressed in this domain. Only a few restrictions are more intrinsically related to the language design.

One AI technique for which Ada does not offer complete support is the capability of producing "self-generative" code in which there is a uniform view of programs and data. This is, however, only possible if and only if the language involved is the native language of the underlying machine (virtual or physical). Nonetheless, self-modifying programs are mathematically undecidable and may have unpredictable results. Such techniques should be avoided in embedded, military AI applications. Ada does, however, provide a view of programs as data (in the form of constant task objects) which in fact opens up newer possibilities for "controlled" generative software.

Ada support for AI is undoubtedly. Ada is here to stay, not only because of the key role being played by DoD, but mainly due to fact that the high-level concepts being put forward by the language form an excellent basis for system design.

As an international standard, the Ada language is currently under review, a process known in the community as Ada9X. Early in this decade, the X is likely to be 3, the MIL-STD-1815B will be official, and although the revision is rather conservatory, requiring only those changes in the language that produce the most benefits with the least detraction from

Ada83, it is envisioned that it will posses better support yet for the issues discussed in this paper, notably object-oriented technology.

ACKNOWLEDGMENTS

Parts of this manuscript benefited from comments made to an earlier draft by two colleagues, professors H. Hamburger and C. Stewart. Many thanks to them. I am also in debt to my wife Leigh for her encouragement, support, and patience during the writing of this article.

REFERENCES

1. *"The Reference Manual for the Ada Programming Language"* U.S. Department of Defense, ANSI/MIL-STD-1815A. Washington, DC, February 1983.
2. S. Tanimoto, *the Elements of Artificial Intelligence*, Computer Science Press, New York, 1990, p. 6.
3. P. Bonasso (Ed.), *Practical Artificial Intelligence: Techniques and Applications in Government Systems,* The MITRE Corp., Bedford, MA, 1990.
4. E. Charniak and D. McDemott, *Introduction to Artificial Intelligence* Addison-Wesley, Reading, MA, 1987.
5. C. V. Ramamorthy, S. Shekhar, and V. Garg, "Software Development Support for AI Programs," *IEEE Computer*, 30–40 (January 1987).
6. P. Zave, "A Compositional Approach to Multi-paradigm Programming," *IEEE Software,* 15–24 (September 1989).
7. J. Stankovic, "Misconceptions About Real-Time Computing: A Serious Problem for Next-Generation Systems," *IEEE Computer, 21*(1), 10–19 (October 1988).
8. R. Michalski and P. Winston, "Variable Precision Logic," *Artif. Intell., 29*(2), 121–146 (1986).
9. J. L. Díaz-Herrera, "The Ada-AI Interface," National Computer Conference, Chicago, June 1987.
10. Y. Mizuno, "Software Quality Improvement," *IEEE Computer, 15*(3), 66–72 (March 1983).
11. R. N. Charette, *Software Engineering Environments: Concepts and Technology,* McGraw-Hill, New York, 1986.
12. Electronic Industries Association,*The DoD Computing Activities and Programs: 1985 Specific Market Survey,* Washington, DC, 1985.
13. B. W. Boehm, "Software Engineering," *IEEE Transact. Computers, C-25,* 1226–1241 (December 1976).
14. MIL-STD-2167A *Software Development,* Washington DC (February 1983).
15. B. W. Boehm, "A Spiral Model of Software Development and Enhancement," *IEEE Computer, 21*(5), 61–72 (May 1988).
16. W. Agresti (Ed.), *New Paradigms for Software Development,* IEE Tutorial, Computer Society Press, Washington D.C., 1986.
17. "Use of Ada in Weapon Systems," U. S. Department of Defense Directive No. 3405.2, March 1987.
18. Department of Defense, "Common Ada Programming Support Environment (APSE) Interface Set (CAIS)," October 9, 1986.
19. MIL-STD-1638A "Common Ada Programming Support Environment (APSE) Interface Set (CAIS-A)" April 1990.

20. T. H. Probert, "Ada Validation Organization: Policies and Procedures," MITRE Corp, McLean, VA, MTR-82W00103, June 1982.

21. P. Fonash, "Ada—Program Overview," *Signal,* 27–31 (July 1983).

22. J. L. Diaz-Herrera, C. Gonzalez, and P. Wang, "The Development of a Flight Control System in Ada," WADAS'86, Washington, D.C., March 1986.

23. H. D. Mills, "Structured Programming: Retrospect and Prospect," *IEEE Software,* 58–66 (November 1986).

24. J. D. Warnier, *Logical Construction of Programs,* Von Nostrand Reinhold, New York, 1976.

25. M. Jackson, *System Development,* Prentice-Hall International, Englewood Cliffs, NJ, 1983.

26. G. Booch, "Object-Oriented Development," *IEEE Transact. Software Eng., SE-12*(2) 211–221 (February 1986).

27. O-J. Dahl, E. W. Dijkstra, and C. A. R. Hoare, *Structured Programming*, Academic Press, New York, 1972.

28. D. Parnas, "On the Criteria to be Used in Decomposing Systems into Modules," *Comm. ACM, 15*(21) 1053–1058 (1972).

29. B. Liskov and S. Zilles, "Programming with Abstract Data Types," *SIGPLAN nOTICES, 9*(4), 50–59 (1974).

30. A. Burns and G. Davies, "Pascal_FC: A Language for Teaching Concurrent Programming," School of Studies in Computing, University of Bradford, Bradford, England, 1981.

31. B. Shriver and P. Wegner, (Eds.), *Research Directions in Object-Oriented Programming*, MIT Press, Cambridge, MA, 1987.

32. P. Henderson, *Functional Programming: Application and Implementation*, (Prentice-Hall International, Englewood Cliffs, NJ, 1980.

33. R. Kowalski, *Logic for Problem Solving,* American Elsevier, New York, 1979.

34. M. Minsky, *A Framework for Representing Knowledge,* MIT AI Laboratory, AI Memo, Boston 1974.

35. J. M. Wright, M. S. Fox and D. Adam, *SRL/1.5 User's Manual,* Carnegie-Mellon University, Robotics Institute, 1984.

36. M. D. Walters and S. M. Martz, *Frame-Based Knowledge Representation in Ada*, Boeing Military Airplanes (March 1987).

37. M. Yen, "Using a Dynamic Memory Management Package to Facilitate Building Lisp-like Data Structures in Ada," in *Proceedings of AIDA '90,* pp 85..100, J. Baldo, J. L. Diaz-Herrera, and D. Littman, (Eds.) George Mason University, Fairfax, VA, 1990.

38. R. J. Brachman, "What IS-A Is and Isn't: An Analysis of Taxonomic Links in Semantic Networks," *IEEE Computer,* 16(10),30–36 (October 1983).

39. Ref. 2.

40. D. Scheidt, D. Preston, and M. Armstrong,"Implementing Semantic Networks in Ada," in *Proceedings of AIDA '86,* J. L. Díaz-Herrera and H. Hamburger,Eds., George Mason University, Fairfax, VA, 1986.

41. L. H. Reeker and K. Wauchope, "Pattern-Directed Processing in Ada," *Second International Conference on Ada Applications and Environment,* Miami, FL, April 1987.

42. H. G. Baker, "The Automatic Translation of LISP Applications into Ada," *Proceedings of the 8th Annual Conference on Ada Technology,* 1990, pp. 633–639.

43. L. Lander, et al., "The Use of Ada in Expert Systems," in *Proceedings of AIDA'86,* J.

L. Díaz-Herrera and H. Hamberger, Eds., George Mason University, Fairfax, VA, 1986.

44. P. O. Bobbie, "Ada-PROLOG: An Ada System for Parallel Interpretation of PROLOG Programs," in *Proceedings of AIDA '87*, J. L. Díaz-Herrera and H. Hamberger, Eds. George Mason University, Fairfax, VA, 1987.

45. F. Ice et al., "Raising ALLAN: Ada Logic-Based Language," in *Proceedings of AIDA '87*, J. L. Díaz-Herrera and H. Hamberger, Eds., George Mason University, Fairfax, VA, pp. 155–165.

46. R. Burback, "PROVER: A First-Order Logic System in Ada," in *Proceedings of AIDA '87*, J. L. Díaz-Herrera and H. Hamberger, Eds., George Mason University, Fairfax, VA, 1987, pp. 166–190.

47. M. M. Adkins, "Flexible Data and Control Structures in Ada," in *Proceedings of AIDA '86*, J. L. Díaz-Herrera and H. Hamberger, Eds., George Mason University, Fairfax, VA, 1986, pp. 9-1–9-17.

48. A. R. De Feyter, "RTEX: An Industrial Real-Time Expert System Shell," in *Proceedings of AIDA '88*, J. L. Díaz-Herrera and J. Moore, Eds., George Mason University, Fairfax, VA, 1988, pp. 6-1..6-22.

49. P. A. Wright, "Ada Real-Time Inference Engine-ARTIE," in *Proceedings of AIDA '88*, J. L. Díaz-Herrera and J.Zytokow, Eds., George Mason University, Fairfax, VA, 1989, pp. 83–93.

50. S. D. Lee, "Toward the Efficient Implementation of Expert Systems in Ada," in *Proceedings of the TRI-Ada Conference,* ACM/SIGAda, December 1990.

51. J. L. Martin, "A Development Tool for Real-Time Expert Systems," *Alsynews, 3,* 1 (March 1989).

52. Artificial Intelligence Section, NASA Johnson Space Center, *CLIPS Version 4.3 Reference Manual*, 1989.

53. P. Kilpeläinen, et al.; "Prolog in Ada: An Implementation and An Embedding," in *Proceedings of AIDA '89*, J. L. Díaz-Herrera and J. Zytkow, Eds., George Mason University, Fairfax, VA, 1989.

54. R. N. Meeson, "Function-Level Programming in Ada," *IEEE* Comp. Science Program on Ada Applications and Environment, pp. 128–132 (1984).

55. O-J. Dahl, K. Nygaard, and B. Myhrhaug, *The SIMULA67Common Base Language,* Pub. S-22 Norwegian Computing Center, Oslo, 1969.

56. M. R. Quillian, "Semantic Memory," in *Semantic Information Processing,* M. Minsky, Ed., MIT Press, Cambridge, MA, 1968, pp. 216–270.

57. A. Golberg and A. Kay (Eds.), "*Smalltalk-72 Instructional Manual,*" Xerox PARC technical report, March 1976.

58. B. Meyer, "EIFFEL: Programming for Reusability and Extendibility," *SIGPLAN Notices, 22*(2), 85–94 (February 1987).

59. D. G. Bobrow, et al., "CommonLoops: Merging Common Lisp and Object-Oriented Programming," *ACM OPSULA '86*, 17–29 (1986).

60. D. Moon, "Object-Oriented Programming with Flavors," *SIGPLAN Notices, 21*(11), 1–7 (November 1986).

61. C. Schaffert et al., "An Introduction to Trellis/Owl," *SIGPLAN Notices, 21*(11), 9–16 (1986).

62. B. J. Cox, *Object Oriented Programming: An Evolutionary Approach,* Addison-Wesley, Reading, MA, 1987.

63. B. Stroustrup, *The C++ Programming Language*, Addison-Wesley, Reading, MA, 1986.
64. L. Tesler, "Object Pascal Report," Apple Computer, 1985.
65. *"Object-Logo 1.5"* Coral Software Corporation, Cambridge, MA, 1985.
66. C. Fornarino and B. Neveu, "Ada and LeLisp: A Marriage of Convenience for AI," in *Proceedings of AIDA '89*, J. L. Díaz-Herrera and J. Zytkow, Eds., George Mason University, Fairfax, VA, 1989.
67. J. Welsh et. al., *The Ada Language and Methodology*, Prentice-Hall, Englewood Cliffs, NJ, 1987.
68. V. J. Kovarik and S. Nies, "Extending the Object-Oriented Paradigm within Ada," J. L. Díaz-Herrera and J. Moore, Eds., George Mason University, Fairfax, VA, November 1988.

JORGE L. DÍAZ-HERRERA

DATABASE MANAGEMENT SYSTEMS: AN INTRODUCTION

At the outset, it should be noted that many detailed and authoritative books and papers have been published which deal with this very complex subject area in a far more thorough form than does this brief article. The following material was, in fact, researched for presentation to the ASLIB Computer Group Conference on Software for Information Management, which was held at the Polytechnic of Central London on September 27, 1983.

ORIGINS AND BACKGROUND

Up until the 1950s, computer installations were concentrated in government defense establishments to tackle specialized military and scientific information-processing tasks which could justify the enormous expense. During the 1950s a number of commercial installations were established among the very largest firms, and these typically concentrated on batch processing of billing and other commercial applications. Virtually every application had to be written in assembler language with embedded instructions defining simple serial files unique to each application. The lack of any significant system analysis techniques also contributed to the "on-off" character of each application.

Obviously, a substantial number of problems surrounded this approach, not the least of which were lengthy development time and the near impossibility of performing ongoing maintenance with different staff. It was in the attempt to address some of these problems that the "first generation" of software was created by hardware suppliers in the form of input/output routines, very basic "operating systems," and some early systems analysis techniques.

During the mid-1960s management began to see the potential value of the computer for control purposes. The existing applications already contained a good deal of data concerning such items as sales transactions, customer addresses, and so on, which offered the promise of status and performance monitoring. At the time, these goals were described as "integrated management information systems" and required far more comprehensive data files, which tended to rely upon an excessive amount of data duplication. Two or more applications could be holding information such as inventory descriptions in their respective file structures, which led to inconsistency problems as updates occurred.

It was in the attempts to address these sorts of problems that the "second generation" of software was developed to offer more generalized file management facilities, data integration, and simple reporting facilities. Data analysis techniques also began to develop significantly. It is important to bear in mind from our present perspective as users of on-line terminal systems that all of these applications were operating in batch mode.

Integration became a key objective, which implied a need for far more sophisticated linking structures capable of representing complex relationships between data elements while minimizing duplication. It is also important to note that a good deal of development was being carried out to speed up data retrieval, and General Electric introduced a list-processing package around this time which provided indexing and retrieval techniques which are commonly used today.

The late 1960s were characterized by further growth in the number of large data processing installations, many of which were unable to respond to control and planning requirements without a more generalized and comprehensive data management environment. Several of these firms set out to develop the forerunners of today's "database management systems" (DBMS). They can be described more accurately as "database systems" and were aimed at providing better throughput, some data integrity control, access controls, and a medium for coordinating a growing list of data management functions. The fundamental design objective was to make systems more easily manageable.

Corporate database management systems gained wide acceptance in the 1970s and are sometimes referred to as the "third generation" of software. This far more mature DBMS provided facilities to cope with multiple on-line access control, the reorganization of relationships between data elements, data protection (privacy), recovery, and data independence.

FUNCTIONS OF A DBMS (DESIGN OBJECTIVES)

The main functions and benefits of true DBMS can be described as

1. Integration
2. Data independence
3. Data retrieval, analysis, modification, and storage
4. Privacy
5. Integrity controls and recovery methods
6. Compatibility
7. Concurrency support
8. Support of complex file structures and access paths

Integration

Integration is the ability to ensure that data items need not be duplicated when additional applications call for their use. The benefits could be seen to be in the reduction of physical storage requirements, but, as we shall see further on, this was not always the case. The real gains are to be found in the ability to update an item and have the change recognized throughout the system.

Data Independence

Independence is the ability to separate the database and associated management functions from application programs.

If a program is able to access and manipulate data through a suitably flexible and generalized interface, then changes in the application programs will not always require changes to be made to the database. Conversely, a radical restructuring of the database, as is sometimes necessary, will not necessarily affect the application programs.

Data Retrieval, Analysis, Modification, and Storage

These are the most frequently used operations of the DBMS and will be incorporated in the interface or command language provided for the application programs. A design objective here is to provide the functionality in such a way as to minimize the amount of coding in individual applications.

A great deal of coordinated work has gone into the specification of guidelines to be followed by DBMS products, and it is worth mentioning the role of the CODASYL Data Base Task Group (DBTG). CODASYL, the Conference of Data Systems Languages, was set up in 1959 to make contributions toward "the design and development of techniques and languages to assist in data systems analysis, design and implementation" and played a definitive role in the specification of COBOL, the Common Business Oriented Language, among other notable developments. In 1969 a special Data Base Task Group of CODASYL was formed to concentrate on principles specific to DBMS and produced a fairly detailed description of how such systems should be structured. As a result, we often hear the phrase "CODASYL compliant" attached to particular DBMS products which conform to the guidelines.

Privacy

The system must have facilities which restrict the retrieval and modification of data by unauthorized applications and individuals.

Privacy is usually provided through the provision of password systems, which allow passwords to be associated with types of data, whole files, or even individual records and some operations. Several systems even allow data to be "encrypted" to further ensure that even if retrieved the data will be difficult to interpret.

Integrity Controls and Recovery Methods

Integrity and recovery are assured by the enforcement of certain rules governing the data and the provision of some form of automatic "audit trail" as insurance against possible system failure.

Integrity rules can be fairly simple (i.e., the data item must be a 10-digit number with two decimal places) or highly complex (i.e., the data item must conform to an established range of values or must reside in a defined list, for example). Recovery systems typically allow an application or applications to be restarted after a system failure and will play back the transactions which occurred before the failure.

If we bear in mind that there may be many "users" of the database performing updates independently of each other, the design of such a facility appears quite complex.

Compatibility

This is the ability of the DBMS to function in concert with the desired machine environment, programming languages, and data as initially available.

To function efficiently the DBMS must integrate closely with the computer's hardware and software architecture, and as the environments vary considerably from one manufacturer to another the DBMS must be tailored appropriately. The programming languages interfaces must also be provided individually and are sometimes offered as separate chargeable extensions to the DBMS core system. External data usually have to be "loaded" into the DBMS and come fully under its control. Fortunately, ASCII and other less general standards make this less difficult than during the early days when data storage formats were designed to suit each new requirement.

Concurrency Support

The DBMS must have the ability to manage the kind of multiuser access problems which can arise when more than one task or user tries to write or read while another writes to a particular item of data at the same time.

Support of Complex File Structures and Access Paths

If we consider a bill of materials application for the production of large aircraft, we put this range of tasks in sharp relief. An aircraft is made up of many hundreds of subassemblies which, in turn, are made up of hundreds of components. There are hundreds of suppliers/manufacturers involved, and a number of them will be supplying what are really the same rivets, gaskets, and so on.

The spectrum of functions described in the preceding subsections should be supported by the DBMS with reasonable efficiency to achieve the cost and performance goals of the applications. It is worth noting that every DBMS implies an overhead. Recovery systems involve extra storage, and the processing of the audit trail in parallel with the applications' manipulation tasks and the DBMS itself will be a substantial processing "task" for the computer.

COMPONENTS OF A DBMS

Every DBMS will have a data definition language (DDL) and a data manipulation language (DML). Most now offer query and reporting systems (QRS) and it is often these facilities which attract customers to one system as opposed to another.

Data Definition Language

The DDL is the vehicle through which the database designer specifies the rules governing the data to be stored and retrieved. It will allow him/her to specify the types and formats of the "fields" and to sometimes attach validation criteria. The DDL will also allow the designer to describe how individual items relate to each other in the context of our previously mentioned bill of materials application. Access privileges and other characteristics are also assigned with the assistance of the DDL.

Having gone through the extremely exacting task of setting up the design of the database with the DDL, some provision should exist for the later restructuring and change of data base as requirements vary. Most DBMS software supports these tasks also through the DDL.

Data Manipulation Language

The DML will provide those operations required by application programs, which typically are

Creating records	Connecting records
Disconnecting records	Deleting records
Finding records	Retrieving data
Modifying data	Initializing recovery
Locking records	
(multiuser concurrency management)	

Query and Reporting Systems

Query languages are going through significant development as suppliers strive to provide more "friendly" and powerful user interfaces than their competitors. The QBE (query by example) approach and IBM's SQL are both examples of systems which try to get away from forcing query statements to follow rigid syntax or to imply knowledge of the data base structure. Such systems become important when the database is to be accessed on an ad hoc basis by individuals who cannot be expected to have any particular systems expertise.

Reporting facilities within most DBMS products are often simple listing routines not designed to meet highly complex reporting environments such as those associated with trading results, multisection invoices, and even statistical analysis reports. However, the presence or lack of such tools, even if from separate suppliers, can be key to a project's success as weeks can be spent coding a complex report in a traditional language such as COBOL or FORTRAN.

CLASSIFYING DBMS PRODUCTS

Virtually every recognized author on the subject of DBMS software has his/her own classification criteria and each tends to reflect a different perspective. Having said this, a relatively simple means of viewing the many different products available today is suggested by James Martin (*Principles of Data-Base Management*). Martin, who is prominent in this field, suggests that DBMS can be described by the way they represent data to the user.

Before carrying this idea further it is important to stress that the way in which data are represented to the user does not necessarily bear any resemblance to the way the data are actually physically stored; there are several examples of this divergence among products such as ADABAS, which can present a "relational" view of the data while actually storing it under DL/1, a "hierarchical" structure.

The Hierarchical, or Tree Structure

As can be seen in Figure 1, the tree structure is characterized by the separate subsets of field items being linked uniquely through pointers to nodes in the next higher level. Our diagram shows just two levels of a system which could have many, but all linked with the same principle. As already mentioned, DL/1 is a good and fairly well-established example of this type.

The advantages of this structure include the simplicity of the individual pointers and the relatively efficient access afforded to the individual elements. Maintenance and change of this type of structure, though tedious, is straightforward and could be carried out by someone other than the original data base designer. Unfortunately, many important structures, including our bill of materials system, cannot be represented without an excessive amount of data duplication.

The Plex, or Network Structure

A network-structured DBMS, such as IDMS, gets around this problem through its ability to support far more complex pointers which do not insist on this uniqueness between particular data elements and their nodes (see Fig. 2). Many of the most complex relationships can be directly represented with this type while minimizing physical storage requirements. It is this type which can sometimes be described as CODASYL compliant.

Defining a network-style of database requires considerable skill and planning, and changing such systems is difficult. If the original designer who is familiar with the relation-

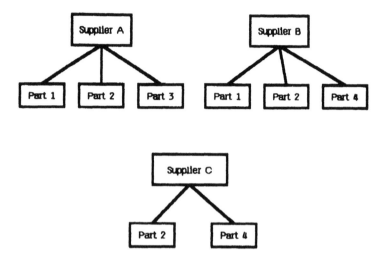

FIGURE 1.   The hierarchical, or tree structure.

ships is not available, then maintenance and change can consume undesirable numbers of man-months.

The Relational Structure

The relational model is a radically different approach to the problems in that it concentrates on simplifying the view of the database into one made up of "flat tables" without any explicit pointers and on supporting data management operations specified by a very precise form of mathematics. The model was developed largely in the IBM research laboratories in the early 1970s, and the most authoritative written works on the subject are those of E. F. Codd (e.g., "Relational Completeness of Data Base Sublanguages").

The process of designing the database as a series of "flat tables," or "relations," as they are described by the specialists, is called "normalization" and involves a series of logical steps to arrive at a design which optimizes clarity and minimizes data inconsistencies. This procedure is a valuable technique of database design generally and need not be taken as useful only in the context of relational databases.

Normalization and the relational calculus—a precise, nonprocedural mathematical language for defining the actual data management operations—are the basis for relational DBMS. The conceptual result of combining the two is a generalized data management environment, which is easily visualized and manipulated. As is suggested by our simple exam-

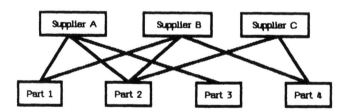

FIGURE 2.   The plex, or network structure.

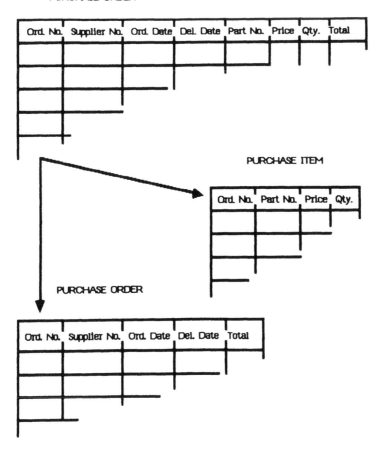

FIGURE 3.   The relational structure.

ple in Figure 3, even fairly complex data relationships are transformed into simple tables which the DBMS should be able to dynamically "join" together to form new tables with the desired attributes or domains (columns) included. Obviously, any two relations to be joined must possess a common attribute or domain and at least some equivalent elements within those attributes or domains.

Among the many benefits inherent in the relational model are the following:

1. Ease of visualization: Some fairly complex relationships in the tree or plex structures are easily represented, and it becomes much more feasible to present an inexperienced user with access to the database. This last characteristic is partly responsible for the tremendous growth in the use of relational systems since 1980 in spite of some of the problems.
2. Precision: While a network or plex representation can be quite confusing, relationships expressed as joined tables are precise in meaning and quickly reveal inconsistencies in the data base content or design which could otherwise take

some time to uncover. A consequence is improved maintenance, which was a preeminent design criterion in the first place.

3. Security: Sensitive data items can be isolated into separate relations and passworded for security in such a way as to prohibit their inclusion in a particular user's view. Encryption is also possible.

4. "Relatability": If the DBMS supports the operations defined in the calculus, then pointers and indices are not needed to define the relationships between data elements, and the applications will be able to use the DBMS to construct any logical view which is consistent with the data. This is a major departure from the systems previously discussed as they required the "view" to be implemented in specific access paths.

5. Ease of implementation: The physical storage of flat files can be less complex than the storage of tree and plex structures. Hardware and software devices to assist in rapid file searching are more feasible with files which avoid complex pointer linkages.

6. Data independence: There is a need for most data bases to grow by adding new fields and new files. The data will be used in new ways. If the data base is in a normalized form with data independence in the software, the data can be restructured and the data base can grow without, in most cases, forcing the rewriting of application programs.

7. Data manipulation language: With the data organized into flat structures, the manipulation sublanguage can be simple to use and extremely powerful in its range of operations.

On a less positive note, however, the relational model does imply either frequent searches to affect the desired joins or the underlying presence of highly complex pointers. This increase in input/output traffic between the central processing unit (CPU) and the mass storage units could probably be handled more efficiently by content-addressable storage technology such as ICL's CAFS systems, which does not require the CPU to "read" unwanted data.

Extended Network Structure (Post-CODASYL)

At least one DBMS implementation is currently available, MDBS III, which supports what its developers describe as "extended network structures." The original CODASYL DBTG recommendations did not include any requirement for the DBMS to be able to directly represent "many to many" relationships, which, unfortunately, occur frequently in the real world. If we consider the very simple illustration in Figure 4 of a relationship between employees and jobs, this becomes clear. There can be many employees assigned to a particular job and any of these employees can also be working on other jobs in parallel. MDBS III is said to support the ability to represent these relationships directly with the DDL.

The comments applied earlier to network or plex structures are also relevant here but with an added cautionary note that maintenance and change of this type of system could be even more difficult.

FIGURE 4.   Extended network structure (post-CODASYL).

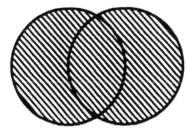

FIGURE 5.   Union (X ∪ Y).

Of all the representations discussed here, the relational model is the one which has captured the most recent interest, if not so much actual use in "production" environments, because of its inherent ease of use and maintainability. Because of this it may be useful to have some yardstick against which we can evaluate the strengths of the growing number of products promoted with the "relational" tag. The two fundamental ingredients, as already said, are the support of the "tabular" view of the data base and the compliance with relational calculus. The calculus describes a discrete number of operations which the DML should be capable of performing and which fall into categories of common set operations and specifically relational operations. These are briefly outlined as follows:

1. Union (Fig. 5): This is the ability to create a new table which contains all the tuples (these are rows or, sometimes, records) found in either X or Y or both. The new table should not contain any duplicate tuples.
2. Intersection (Fig. 6): Following this operation the new table should contain only those tuples which are common to both X and Y.
3. Difference (Fig. 7): The resulting table should contain those tuples which are unique to either X or Y but only those common to both.
4. Product ($X \times Y$): This operation is more difficult to display graphically as it is actually the Cartesian product of two sets. In it, each tuple of X is paired with all the tuples of Y. If X has n tuples and Y has m tuples, the resulting product will have $n \times m$ tuples, each with $n + m$ attributes (columns).
5. Join: This is the uniquely relational operator, which allows one to relate two sets by common attributes to produce a new set of tuples consisting of those which have identical values for the common attributes.
6. Selection (X where $A \leq n$ or $B \geq m$): This is the ability to produce a subset of tuples which conform to a logical selection criterion.

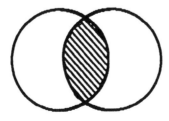

FIGURE 6.   Intersection (X ∩ Y).

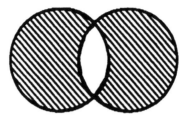

FIGURE 7.   Difference (X - Y).

7. Projection: Sometimes also referred to as "cut and paste," this operation allows a new table to be produced which contains only those attributes chosen from the given relations.

8. Division $(C \div X)$: If the DBMS supports the previous operations, then it can be assumed that this one is possible to achieve as it can be expressed in terms of the others in the calculus:

$$(C - [(C[X{\cdot}A, X{\cdot}B] \times X) - C])[X{\cdot}A, X{\cdot}B]$$

DATA MANAGEMENT: A BROADER VIEW

DBMS certainly are not always the most appropriate tools for achieving results. Virtually all such products require considerable development time and expertise, including those faithful to the relational model. This is an important point as many of the recent "shoppers" considering DBMS products are interested primarily in rapid application development and ease of use benefits, and in the end they generally procure other types of products which are often better suited to providing results when measured against these criteria.

No DBMS has yet been developed which can satisfy all data processing requirements, and in the early 1970s, parallel developments began to produce other specialized tools to deal with data retrieval, report generation, file management, and, of course, information retrieval. Today there are a large variety of such tools available, several of them on microcomputers.

Data retrieval packages typically assume the presence of either a certain DBMS product to which they are specifically adapted or the presence of the data in a host-standard file format. They usually offer a more flexible data inquiry language to programs, and sometimes to end users, than does the DBMS itself; and they may also support report-formatting facilities, which can dramatically speed up the creation of new report layouts. Teleprocessing monitors, such as CICS, are unique to large-scale mainframe computers and are designed to isolate the handling and monitoring of terminal-based transactions from the main application's program logic. File and data management systems, on the other hand, tend to address a much broader range of functions, from file creation and maintenance to screen and report formatting, and often compare quite favorably with DBMS DML facilities. They usually are far easier to use than a full-blown DBMS and are sometimes considerably cheaper to license. Having said this, they usually do not provide strengths in the areas of privacy, recovery, and multiuser locking. A good DBMS is also capable of providing quite rapid response times on large columns of data by virtue of the indexing techniques employed, while file and data management systems usually rely upon the hardware manufacturer's standard searching methods.

Application generators and/or fourth-generation languages go a step further in that they eliminate the need to use a traditional programming language in conjunction with the data management facilities. The user is presented with a comprehensive environment for file creation and change, data entry and update, and inquiry and reporting; and facilities for creating complete systems through putting the functions together under logical control. Some of these systems are even capable of generating compiled object code for run-time efficiency and are specifically designed to improve programmer productivity.

DBMS SELECTION CONCEPTS/QUESTIONS

The software tools so far discussed have all been specifically designed to assist with the management of data which have a fairly rigid structure, such as the information stored in the logical tables in Figure 3. Data which are in the form of "free text," on the other hand, are more typically the domain of specialized information retrieval systems such as HARWELL'S STATUS package, which imposes a less rigid structure on the data "records" and can provide inquiry access with fewer constraints.

So how, then, does one choose the best tool for a project?

The short answer to this is "with great difficulty" because selection criteria will usually vary from project to project. In the simplest case the user will already have access to and experience with a tool capable of doing the job, but as this is an unusual circumstance most users will have to weigh the importance of the following issues:

Is there any freedom in the choice in hardware?
How large is the data set to be "managed"?
How stable are the relationships between data elements?
How complex are the relationships?
Are very rapid response times a key issue?
How much time is available for development?
Is concurrency/recovery a major issue?
How much programming and systems analysis expertise is on hand?
Is free-text management/retrieval required?
In what form are the data presently held?
Who will take on the future responsibility for maintenance?

As a general rule of thumb, a full DBMS is best suited to projects involving large volumes of data with complex but stable relationships. A high level of systems expertise must also be available, together with a healthy budget. Projects which need to cope with changing data relationships but still involve high volumes may benefit from the features of the relational approach.

Small volumes of data are the province of some of the other tools mentioned, and there are many cases where even quite large columns (1,000,000 records or more) have been successfully tackled with fourth-generation languages.

There are a growing number of microbased products appearing, which are capable of tackling important jobs. In several cases the limitations are those of the machine and its operating system rather than design problems in the packages themselves. Examples of these are DBASE II, CONDOR 3, INFORMIX, and MDBS III.

DBASE II   From Ashton-Tate for around £400 on MS-DOS, CP/M, and CP/M 86, this package is a sound data management tool which can work with two files concurrently and has built-in facilities for application development.

CONDOR 3 From M.O.M. Systems for £95 to £195 on MS-DOS, PC-DOS, CP/M, CP/M 86, and MP/M, CONDOR is capable of representing far more complex relationships, is based upon the relational model, but requires the use of a traditional programming language such as PASCAL or BASIC to implement a complete menu-driven application.

INFORMIX From Relational Database Systems, Inc., for $1,600 under UNIX, PC-DOS, and MS-DOS, INFORMIX is also capable of dealing with quite complex relationships and performs most of the relational operations. Unlike CONDOR, INFORMIX supports transaction logging and automatic recovery.

MDBS III From Micro Database Systems for £2,085 under UNIX, CP/M, CP/M 86, MP/M, PC-DOS, and MS-DOS, MDBS III is a full extended network structure DBMS which appears to be complete in all respects. Not a "user friendly" tool, MDBS requires expertise and another programming language.

FUTURE DIRECTIONS

There can be no definitive conclusion to any discussion on data management and data base systems as the rate of technological change dictates that any approach will be outmoded rather quickly. A quick review of where we have come from makes this clear. Promising developments are under way on several fronts, which inevitably will affect the picture, and among these are LANs (local area networks), ICL's CAFS (content-addressable file store), IDBMs (intelligent database machines), and the "fifth" generation of software which could integrate data base management, information retrieval, word processing, business planning, graphics, application generation, and communications with some descendant of "mouse" technology. We live in exciting times.

BIBLIOGRAPHY

Brown, P. S., "Data Privacy and Integrity: An Overview," presented at the 1971 ACM SIG-FIDET Workshop on Data Description Access and Control, November 1971.

CODASYL, "Data Base Task Group. October 69 Report," AMC, 1969.

Codd, E. F., "Relational Completeness of Data Base Sublanguages," IBM Research Laboratory, San Jose, CA, March 1972.

Date, C. J., *Relational Data Base Systems: A Tutorial, Proceedings of 4th International Symposium on Computers and Information Science*, Plenum, New York, 1972.

Martin, J., *Principles of Data-Base Management*, Prentice-Hall, Englewood Cliffs, NJ, 1976.

Palmer, I., "DataBase Systems: A Practical Reference," CACI INC.-International, 1975.

Plyter, N. V., "INFO, a Relational Database Language," paper presented to the international INFO User Group Conference, February 1982.

LAWRENCE A. KURTZ

DISTRIBUTED ALGORITHMS

INTRODUCTION

Distributed computer systems and distributed information processing are steadily advancing and eventually will replace conventional computer designs built around a large central processor. Most computer systems today can already be regarded as distributed systems in certain respects.

Only in the present decade, the impetus from VLSI technology* (in the small) and local and wide area networks (in the large) has added greatly to the significance of distributed processing as a viable alternative to the physical limitations of even the largest single processor systems and the inordinate investments that they require. With hardware costs declining and commercially supported interconnection technologies now available, it certainly becomes more economical to achieve high performance by utilizing dedicated computing units running independently in parallel, rather than through the use of extremely complex (and hence subject to frequent and complete failures) high-speed single components.

In many ways though, *distribution and concurrency* actually create a great number of new challenging problems for the computer scientist.

WHAT IS DISTRIBUTED? HOW IS IT DISTRIBUTED?

Communicating Sequential Processes

User jobs and system routines generally are independent units (tasks) which could proceed in parallel if sufficiently many processors were available. In a distributed environment, any implementation of concurrency definitely requires mechanisms which enable concurrently executing units to exchange information (communication, cooperation) or to coordinate their action (synchronization).

Each of these independent units of execution (or task) in a system may be called a *process*. In the 1960s, E. W. Dijkstra and others promoted the view that *concurrent activity can best be modeled by a set of cooperating processes which alternate between independent activities and periods of communication.*

Breaking up tasks into processes is a start toward multiple processor systems. Each process is a natural unit to allocate to an available processor.

---

*VLSI stands for "very large-scale integration." With the advent of VLSI technology, it has become possible to embed ("integrate") circuits of tens of thousands of components in a surface of a single chip.

Distributed Computer Systems

A *distributed system* may be considered as a collection of n user *processes* (nodes) connected by e *direct communication links*, which constitutes the interconnection network of the distributed system.

Each process deals with only a *local* nonshared memory, *local* variables, and a *local* clock; each process can communicate only by sending messages to and receiving messages from its neighboring processes (nodes) in the network.

With respect to the communication behavior, distributed systems can be roughly classified as *asynchronous* or *synchronous* ones. In a fully asynchronous system, transmission and queuing delays experienced by a message along a communication link usually are assumed to be a *finite* (non-zero), but *unpredictable* amount of time. In a fully synchronous network, all clocks at all sites are assumed to tick simultaneously and any message sent at time t is received and processed at time $t + 1$.

THE NOTION OF A DISTRIBUTED ALGORITHM

The notion of *distributed algorithm* is basically founded on both notions of *distributed system* and *communicating sequential processes*. Distributed algorithms may thus be characterized by the following "identity":

Distributed algorithm = Processes + Messages

A distributed system consists of a collection of interconnected processes (nodes) which exchange data by use of messages. The orderly exchange of information requires that the nodes conform to some pre-established agreements or rules which constitutes a *protocol*. A protocol specifies both the format of the information packages transmitted and the actions to be taken for sending and receiving as well as the communication ("control") between the nodes to set up or maintain a connection. A protocol thus embodies all the necessary actions to let the network function.

In a packet-switching network, some strategy is required for directing packets via the communication subsystem. An optimal strategy should deliver the largest possible number of packets in the shortest possible time. Packets of a message are sent ("hopped") from node to node to reach their destination, but need *not* all follow the same path. Thus, sequence numbers are needed in the packet and the receiving host may have some difficulties in assembling the incoming message correctly. The *routing algorithm* of the network must *avoid congestion* of packets on the net and be protected *against failures of some part of the net*. All routing algorithms are based on maintaining routing tables either at a central node or distributed over all nodes. These routing tables contain information about connections, distances and delays to be expected along various links.

We may therefore draw a short (nonexhaustive) list of some control and protocol distributed algorithms:

Mutual exclusion and election distributed algorithms
Deadlock prevention and detection distributed algorithms
Termination of distributed algorithms
Distributed routing algorithms (e.g.,construction of a spanning tree of the network, etc.)
Distributed algorithms for the control of data transfers
Distributed algorithms for the control of duplicated data

In the sequel, examples of major distributed algorithms are given. First, we propose examples of distributed protocol algorithms, such as electing a leader processor, or *process*,* and constructing routing schemes in different configurations of distributed systems and interconnection networks.

Election and Spanning Tree Construction Distributed Algorithms

Two closely related basic computations in a distributed system are the *election*, and the *spanning tree construction* procedures. The solution of these two distributed problems are at the basis of most control and coordination mechanisms employed in distributed systems (e.g., mutual exclusion, synchronization, reset of a system after a possible failure, etc.); they are also closely related to other basic distributed computations (e.g., minimum finding, traversal, etc.). The election problem, and hence the spanning tree problem, can be solved deterministically only if each process has associated with a distinct identification value, its identity, from a (possibly infinite) index domain *I*: the election problem and the spanning tree construction problem cannot be (deterministically) solved but with one *unique* identity randomly chosen from *I* by each one process.

(a) The distributed election process consists in changing from an initial system configuration where every processor is in the same state (say *candidate*), to a final configuration where exactly one processor is in a predefined state (say, *elected*) and all other processors are in another predetermined state (say, *defeated*). In such a procedure, there is no a priori restriction on which processor should become elected (Fig.1).

Description of the Algorithm

The ring is of size n. Each processor P_i keeps the largest identity it has seen so far in a local variable MAX_i $(1 \leq i \leq n)$. Each processor goes through the following three stages.

Stage 1 (initialization)

    MAX_i: = id_i;
    SEND MESSAGE $<id_i>$ on the ring;
                         /* recall the ring is unidirectional */

Stage 2 (election)

    Repeat the following steps, UNTIL the end of the election is signaled by receipt of a message $<!>$:

    IF MESSAGE $< id_j >$ is received from a neighbour **THEN**

        IF $id_j > MAX_i$ **THEN** $MAX_i = id_j$;
                              PASS on MESSAGE $<id_j>$

        ELEIF $id_j = MAX_i$ **THEN**   /* P_i has won the election */
                                SEND MESSAGE $<!>$ on the ring

        FI;

---

*The notion of processor and process are similar in the applications which are addressed herein.

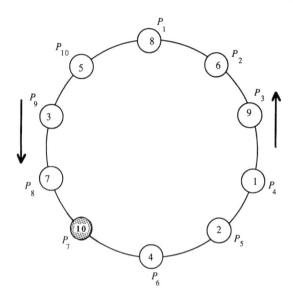

FIGURE 1.   An optimal distributed election algorithm on a unidirectional ring, the Algorithm of Chang and Roberts (1979).

Stage 3 (inauguration)

If a message <!> is received, the election is terminated and MAX_i holds the identity of the leader;

If this processor was elected in Stage 2, then the inauguration is over; otherwise, pass on message <!> and **stop**.

Notice that the elected leader P_i is the one and unique processor on the ring which eventually receives back (from its other port) its own message $<id_i>$; messages emitted from other processors are all killed at some point along the ring. Also note that the latter algorithm, as most distributed election algorithms, is an *extrema-finding* algorithm; the elected leader is the processor with the largest identity.

Message and Time Complexity of the Algorithm

The message complexity of the algorithm is the number of messages required by the algorithm. One may compute the *worst-case message complexity* of the algorithm, *viz.* the maximum number of messages used in any execution of the algorithm. Similarly, one may also compute the *average message complexity* of the algorithm, *viz.* the expected number of messages required in any execution of the algorithm. Along the same lines, the *worst-case* and the *average time complexity* of the algorithm are defined as the *maximum* and *expected* running time of the algorithm, respectively.

Assume there are k processors which start the algorithm. Clearly, the worst-case message complexity for k starting processors arises when the participating processors' identities are ordered in *decreasing* sequence. In such a case, a message initiated by any active processor must traverse all smaller processors and all passive processors. Therefore, the total number of messages required in the election stage (Stage 2) is *at most*

$$n + (n - 1) + (n - 2) + \cdots + (n - k + 1) = nk - \frac{k(k - 1)}{2},$$

and since (n-1) more messages<!> are needed for inauguration (Stage 3), the worst-case message complexity of the algorithm with k starting processors is thus

$$nk - \frac{k(k - 1)}{2} + (n - 1).$$

Now if *all* processors are starters ($k=n$), the worst-case message complexity of Chang-Roberts algorithm is clearly

$$\frac{n(n + 1)}{2} + (n - 1) = \frac{1}{2}n^2 + O(n).$$

Where O(n) ("big oh of n") stands for the order of magnitude of the remaining function of n when n is large enough, viz. $\frac{3}{2}n-1$.*

If the identities of processors are randomly ordered, a message initiated by the i-th highest active processor traverses $\frac{n}{i}$ links *on the average* before it is discarded by a higher processor. This yields the result that the expected message complexity of Chang-Roberts algorithm with k starting processors is

$$\sum_{i = 1}^{k} \frac{n}{i} + (n - 1) = nH_k + (n - 1).$$

Where H_k is the k-th harmonic number, $H_k = \sum_{i=1}^{k} \frac{1}{i}$, with asymptotic expansion $H_k = \ln k + \gamma + O(n^{-1}) = \ln k + O(1)$.

Hence, the expected number of messages required by the algorithm when *all* processors are starters ($k=n$) is, for n large,

$$nH_n + (n-1) = n\ln n + O(n).$$

Note that the above result implies that the election algorithm of Chang-Roberts is *average-case optimal*,† although its *worst-case* message complexity, $O(n^2)$, is far from being optimal (worst-case optimality also achieves $\Theta(n \lg n)$ in this class of algorithms).

---

*More precisely, "big oh," O, is an asymptotic notation defined as follows:
$a(n)=O(f(n))$ implies the existence of two (unspecified) integers M and N such that $a(n) \leq M f(n)$ for $n \geq N(a(n))>0$. Thus the statement $a(n)=O(f(n))$ may be taken as saying that $f(n)$ provides an upper bound, up to a multiplicative constant, on $a(n)$, when n is large.

Whenever $f(n)$ *also* provides a lower bound, up to a multiplicative constant factor, on $a(n)$ when n is large, $a(n)=\Theta(f(n))$ ("Theta of $f(n)$").

†In the case, *average-case optimality* means that, with respect to the *expected message complexity*, the latter algorithm achieves the best possible within its class, i.e. the class of distributed extrema-finding algorithms on undirectional rings. Its expected message complexity is thus $\Theta(n \lg n)$.

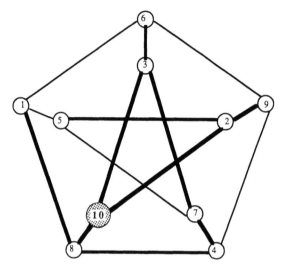

FIGURE 2.   Construction of a spanning tree of an arbitrary network.

From the above analyses, it is straightforward that the worst-case and average time complexity of Chang-Roberts algorithm are $O(n)$, and even $\Theta(n)$. Indeed, clearly, the number of comparison operations is optimally linear in n in both cases.

(b) The distributed spanning tree construction roughly operates as the construction of a certain *routing tree* within a given interconnection network by choosing links which can be easily determined during the election procedure. The elected node is thus the root of the constructed spanning tree of the underlying graph of the network (Fig. 2).

Let $G=(V,E)$ be the underlying graph of the distributed system, where V is the set of nodes/processes and E is the set of (undirected) edges/links in the graph/system: $|V|=n$ and $|E|=e$.

A spanning tree of the communication network is found here by a "depth first search" distributed algorithm (see Fig. 2) which selects the edges of G, one after the other, without building any cycle in the graph. Therefore, subtrees (of G) are maintained at each point in the algorithm, and a spanning tree of the network eventually is constructed.The elected leader is thus the root of the constructed spanning tree of G: the process with identification number **10** in the drawing.

Other Various Distributed Protocol Algorithms

Tasks Synchronization in a Distributed System

One of the main problems arising in distributed computing is the synchronization of the tasks performed by several computers within a network. In such a context, tasks are denoted by *processes*. Synchronizing tasks thus consist in pacing the processes' evolution, *viz.*, making new instructions complementary with respect to the previous ones. This makes it possible to obtain a (so called) *legal* sequence of these instructions.

In Figure 3 the system is composed of n cars (the processes) competing to park in a given parking area of m places (here, $m=3$).

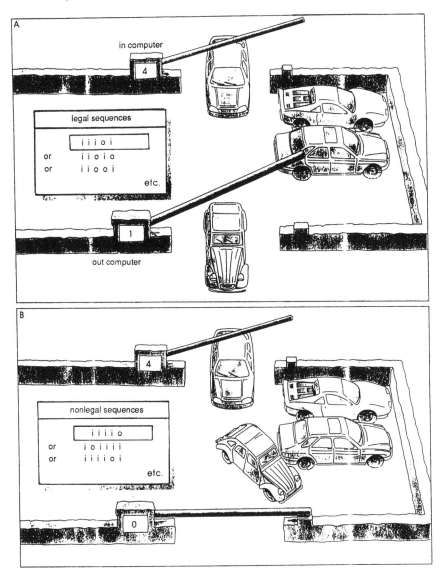

FIGURE 3.   The parking synchronization.

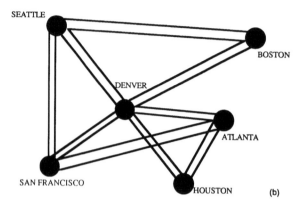

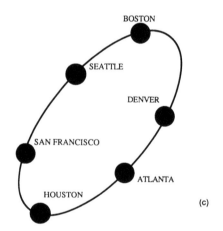

FIGURE 4.   Virtual ring network.

For each one car, instructions are:

- drive into the parking (*way in*)
- park the car
- drive out of the parking (*way out*)

    The two instructions for which synchronization is needed and, by all means, has to be ensured are "*drive in*" and "*drive out*". A *legal* sequence of these instructions may easily be defined as some sequence of i*n*(s) and o*ut*(s) such that the number of **i** does not exceed the number of **o** by more than 3. In other words, the difference of the number of cars admitted and the number of cars departing must not be larger than the number of available parking places!

The sequence **i i i o i** depicted in scheme (A) is a legal sequence of instructions. By contrast, the sequence **i i i o i** depicted in (B) is not a legal sequence of instructions, since the fourth car entering is registered before a parking place became free.

Such an example illustrates the question of "allocating resources" in a system (herein, the resources are the parking places). In computer science, this problem arises very frequently, for example, whenever several computers are linked to one printer.

Synchronization of Several Computers (Local Area Network), and Circular Configuration of a Network (Virtual Ring Topology)

In order to synchronize the execution of a given distributed program for several computers, a simple method consists in establishing a circular network configuration which connects them (Fig. 4).

Such a circular configuration of computers we call a *virtual ring* in order to emphasize the fact that the computers are not connected via *physical* links, but via *logical* links. Logical links may be materialized by means of any arbitrary communication channels.

Consider the network depicted in (B). Its advantages lie in the fact that each city is physically connected with any other via at least two (direct) links; such a property is most important in case of link failure. Indeed, it may be easily seen on scheme (B) that the physical link connecting Houston to San Francisco actually passes via Atlanta (or via Denver, in case of link failure). The ring drawn in (C) is thus a *virtual ring*. Such a framework is advantageous since it settles a natural order relation between computers in each site on the ring. It makes it possible to perform a very simple circulation of the control messages exchanged. It also brings *fairness* to the sites, namely virtual ring avoids a (possible) exclusion of some sites.

Distributed Protocol Algorithm for Solving the "Mutual Exclusion Problem" (E. W. Dijkstra, 1974).

A distributed system cannot work without sending and receiving messages. Here is an outline of the type of algorithms used to ensure a reliable circulation of communication messages from any site to any other on a virtual ring of computers (see Fig. 5). The following algorithm was proposed by E. W. Dijkstra in 1974. In order to describe and explain this algorithm, it might be easier to regard computers as Sioux indians: their piercing eyes represent here the communication channels connecting the computing machines on the ring.

Consider n Sioux indians with numbers $1, 2, 3, \ldots, n$ seated on the skirts of a wood, and arranged so that each Sioux (with number i) can see the Sioux with the preceding number in the sequence (i.e., Sioux with number i-1). This predecessor with number $(i$-1) we will call the *left neighbour* of Sioux with number i. Moreover, we are concerned with a *circular "chain"* of Sioux indians: the left neighbour of Sioux with number 1 is Sioux with number n.

While they are thus seated on watch, Sioux decide to enter meditation, this according to a very precise ritual. At any given time, one Sioux *at most* must meditate, and his meditation may last a finite but unpredictable delay time (occasionally no time at all if he is not in a good mood for meditation). In order to perform such a rite, Sioux indians light a fire and assume the following protocol:

RULE No. 1:

FOR each Sioux with number 2, 3, ... UNTIL n:

FIGURE 5.   Circular chain of Sioux Indians in meditation.

IF his left neighbour (Sioux with number i-1) has his fire on, while he himself
has his fire out, or conversely
THEN Sioux with number i may start entering meditation.

WHEN he decides to stop meditation, he either lights or puts out his fire (according to whether his fire was out or on).

RULE No. 2:
FOR Sioux with number 1:
IF Sioux with number n and he himself (number 1) both have their fires on or
both out
THEN Sioux with number 1 may start again entering meditation.
WHEN he (number 1) decides to stop meditation, he lights or puts out his fire
(according to whether his fire was out or on).

At the beginning, all fires are out and the meditation privilege is granted to the Sioux
with number 1 who may meditate if he wants to. When he gets tired, he lights his fire. Sioux

with number 2 may then see for himself that he is now allowed to enter meditation. Note that, according to this protocol, he is the only Sioux allowed to meditate.

When the second Sioux has been meditating as he pleases, he, in his turn, lights his fire (at step depicted in the drawing, Sioux with number 8 is thus allowed to enter meditation), and so on until all fires are eventually burning.

Thanks to this protocol, the ritual is obeyed. Besides, no Sioux is bound to continuously observe his left neighbor in order to see if his fire is on or out. By contrast, he needs only make some sporadic observations to compare his neighbour's state with his own, and take a decision. Moreover, the protocol has the advantage of being reliable. Indeed, if a Sioux retires from the Sioux assembly for a while, it is sufficient that his left and right neighbours should be aware of his retirement, so that they can see each other, and the protocol can go on as follows.

If a Sioux has a new left neighbor with lower number, he operates according to Rule No. 1. In the reverse case, he is at the end of the "chain" and thus operates according to Rule No. 2.

Within a distributed system, Sioux indians are computing machines, and their piercing eyes are communication networks. Thanks to the protocol described above, the circulation of messages is ensured for any computing machine, with periodic examinations of the state of the neighbouring machine.

Of course, both machines can exchange other types of information as well.

The Simple Termination Protocol Algorithm (E. W. Dijkstra 1983).

Among the questions arising with the advance of distributed systems, one of the major problems is the *termination problem* of a distributed computation.

Consider a set of processes distributed onto several computers, which cooperate to complete the same given job. *When* can we consider the program performed by these processes in the system *fully terminated*? The answer to this question is crucial in distributed computing. It may be easily seen how a "naive" method cannot at all solve the *distributive termination* problem, although it seems so trivial (Fig. 6).

Suppose n computers cooperate to perform a common job. Each computer is in either the *active* state, or in the *inactive* state. An active computer may ask another computer to perform a certain job. If the latter is inactive, it then becomes active. An active computer stops when its given job is finished: it then becomes inactive. When all computers are inactive, the global job is considered terminated.

However, how can these computers all agree in order to decide in concert that their jobs are all terminated? In general, one computer is charged with such a decision task.

All computers depicted in Figure 6 are distributed on a circular configuration of network, *viz.* a virtual ring.

Herein, inactive computers are *uncolored* ones (or computers colored *grey*), while active computers are colored *red*. Now suppose computer N_0 is charged with the termination detection of the program. Also consider that termination detection is executed by means of a circulating token from computer N_0 to computer N_6 on the ring, i.e., according to the natural order $0, 1, 2, \ldots, 6$ (the token is materialized with a particular message).

Thus, whenever the token leaves some active computer, it is colored *red*. In the reverse case, whenever the token leaves an inactive computer, it is colored *grey* (or not colored). On the drawing, the token has just left computer N_4, which is inactive since it is grey. The token is thus grey.

Whenever N_0 becomes inactive, it controls the state of other computers. So N_0 sends

FIGURE 6.   Have you finished soon?

the grey token to N_1. If N_1 is inactive it passes on the grey token to N_2. Otherwise, if N_1 is active, it passes on the red token to N_2.

Whenever a computer receives the red token it passes on the token unchanged to its next neighbour on the ring, whatever its own state may be. At the end of the round, N_0 will thus receive a red token and therefore it will learn that at least one computer along the ring is still active. By contrast, any computer which receives the grey token will change the color of the latter according to its own state; *viz.*, if it is inactive it passes on the grey token, and if its is active it passes on the red token, and so forth.

Therefore, one might think that if N_0 receives back the grey token after a whole round on the ring, it really proves that all computers are inactive indeed, and that jobs are finished.

This is *wrong*! This method is actually incorrect since the circulation of the token on the ring is *not instantaneous*.

To make this point clear, suppose, for example, that the grey token is received by computer N_4 (grey), whereas in the meantime when the token was passing from N_1 to N_4, this latter computer sent a message to N_1, thus reactivating it (see the arrow in the center of the drawing), and itself became inactive (grey). Then N_4 would have emitted the grey token which might certainly reach N_0 as grey, while in contrast N_1 would still remain active.

To solve the problem Dijkstra found, in 1983, a solution which requires the dissociation of the "color" of a computer from its state of activity: a given computer may now be in the inactive state, and at the same time be colored red. The following rules should then be carried out within the system:

RULE No. 1

Whatever the color of the received token, if an active computer receives the token it keeps it until it becomes inactive. If (or when) the computer is inactive, it passes on the token (the color of which is ruled according to Rule No. 3) to the next computer on the ring, in the order $0, 1, \ldots, n$.

RULE No. 2

A computer becomes or remains red when it orders some other computer for a job.*

RULE No. 3

The token becomes or remains red when it leaves a computer.

RULE No. 4

When the token leaves a computer, the latter becomes grey.

Thanks to the above four rules, one may now claim that a job is terminated whenever the token has visited *all* computers on the ring and *finishes grey upon receipt in* N_0. In the reverse case, the token becomes grey again and renews its visiting round on the ring with the first computer.

It may be seen how the above procedure eventually terminates correctly. Indeed, whenever all computers stop their job with no token, they are all grey. If N_0 is unable to conclude whether the whole job is terminated or not, the token must go another round along the ring until it returns grey.

On the other hand, a more complicated problem is set in proving that one does not *wrongly* decide that the termination is completed.

However, correct solutions to this problem have been proposed.

SELECTED BIBLIOGRAPHY

Apt., K., "Correctness Proofs of Distributed Termination Algorithms," *ACM Toplas, 8,* 3–8 (1986).

Chang, E. J. and R. Roberts, "An Improved Algorithm for Decentralized Extrema-finding in Circular Configurations of Processes," *Comm. ACM,* 22 (5), 281–283 (May 1979).

Comtet, L., *Analyse combinatoire,* Tomes I et II, Presses Universitaires de France, 1970.

Dijkstra, E. W. and C. S. Scholten, "Termination Detection for Diffusing Computations," *Inform. Proc. Letters, 11*(1), 217–219 August 1980.

Dijkstra, E. W., W. H. J. Feijen, and A. J. M. von Gasteren, "Derivation of a Termination Detection Algorithm for Distributed Computations," *Inform. Proc. Letters, 16* 217–219 (1983).

Feller, W., *An Introduction to Probability Theory and Its Applications,* Vol. 1, Wiley, New York, 1968.

Franklin, W. R., "On an Improved Algorithm for Decentralized Extrema-Finding in Circular Configuration of Processors," *Comm. ACM, 25*(5), 336–337 (May 1982).

Hoare, C. A. R., "Communicating Sequential Processes," *Comm. ACM, 21*(8), 666–677 (1978).

Knuth, D., *The Art of Computer Programming,* Vol 1 and 3, Addison Wesley, Reading, MA, 1968 and 1973.

---

*This very rule makes it possible for N_0 to detect if a computer has been activated by another computer which itself became inactive.

Lamport, L., Reading, MA, "Time, Clocks and the Ordering of Events in a Distributed System," *Comm. ACM, 21*(7), 558-565 (July 1978).

Lavault, C. "Exact Average Message Complexity Values for Distributed Electionon Bidirectional Rings of Processors," *Theor. Comput. Sci., 73,* 61-79 (1990).

LeLann, G., "Distributed Systems: Towards a Formal Approach, "*IFIP Congress, Toronto,* August 1977, pp. 155-160.

Pachl, J. E., Korach, and D. Rotem, "Lower Bounds for Distributed Maximum-Finding," *J. ACM,* 380-401 (October 1984).

Raynal, M. *Distributed Algorithms and Protocols*, Wiley, New York, 1988.

Raynal, M., *Networks and Distributed Computations: Concepts, Tools and Algorithms,* MIT Press and North Oxford Academic, Harvard, 1988.

Santoro, N., "On the Message Complexity of Distributed Problems," *Int. J. Computer Inform. Sci. 13,* 131-147 (1984).

Tel, G., *The Structure of Distributed Algorithms*, Ph. D. thesis, University of Utrecht, The Netherlands, 1989.

CHRISTIAN J. P. LAVAULT

EVALUATION OF SOFTWARE

OVERVIEW

Due to the rapid and significant decrease in the cost of computer hardware, along with the concurrent rise in the availability of software to perform a wide range of specialized functions, a large population of users are faced with the task of selecting and evaluating computer software. This article looks at the general nature of application software selection and evaluation. Topics include sources of software, need for software selection, locating software, the selection process, and the evaluation and comparison of software.

SOURCES OF SOFTWARE

Traditionally, application software, or computer programs that perform one or more user-specified tasks, was custom designed by experienced programmers in-house,. Today, application software is available in three additional forms: modular, "canned", and "turnkey." Modular software is a programming tool, such as VisiCalc or DB Master, that enables persons with limited programming skills to develop useful computer programs with a minimum of effort. Canned software is the prewritten, mass-marketed software available from a variety of vendors. A complete package, which includes all the hardware, applications programs, training, and maintenance, is known as a turnkey system. Generally, a turnkey system is bought or leased with ongoing charges for maintenance and software support. Canned and modular software require more participation on the part of the user for implementation.

A variety of commercial sources produce and distribute software. Only 15 to 20 years ago, manufacturers virtually gave software away. At that time, hardware cost exceeded software cost. In comparison, software was cheap, and hardware could not be marketed unless it did something useful. Because IBM unbundled software from computer systems in 1969, hardware manufacturers have become software vendors as well. Manufacturers are acquiring software houses and will contract to write custom–made programs or sell, as general-purpose programs, custom-written programs developed for other users. Even in the personal computer market, IBM has been selling software direct to its largest customers.

Many businesses have found that it is uneconomical to maintain in-house programming staffs. As a result, software houses have become a growth industry. There are more than 3,000 software houses at the present time. Some concentrate on contract or custom-designed software, but the trend is toward writing mass-produced, mass-marketed, general application software.

A third commercial source is the software broker who acts as intermediary between the developer and the buyer. The products and services that brokers offer vary greatly. There are some good packages by designers who lack marketing resources and some mediocre packages designed for one installation and patched for package sale. Some brokers are fully staffed to install, maintain, and support packages, whereas others point to the original developer for these services.

Initially, retail hardware/software stores supported the hobbyist but are now eyeing the lucrative small business market. One chain of office equipment/computer stores, in the west and southwest, and even bookstores, are now selling software. The advantage these stores have over other commercial sources is that they are local, and with the exception of bookstores, offer some level of support for the software they sell. In some cases, they can adapt or develop special application packages. Frequently, they offer a saving on a total hardware/software package. The disadvantages are that the software is usually limited to "best sellers" and rarely is under warranty. Also, salespersons often attempt to fit users' needs to the software that the store carries or the software with which they are familiar. This does not always guarantee the best match.

There are also a number of miscellaneous commercial sources. Some large corporations have created spinoff companies in an attempt to recoup investments, or make a profit, from programs developed in-house. However, many of these companies fold as fast as they open because they lack the time, talent, or money to market their product. Software can be bought, without support or warranty, through mail-order houses. Various databases that serve as software locators will vend software as well. A marketing tool developed by Ocean Data Systems, known as C-DOS, permits the downloading of demonstration programs from a database for preview before ordering. In the future, disks may be produced and sold on-site using a similar system.

The commercial software scene is currently undergoing rapid and significant changes. Many of the thousands of software companies will go out of business over the next few years. The cottage era of software production is coming to an end. The new entrants in the software market, such as CBS, McGraw-Hill, Dow Jones, and the international accounting firm of Arthur Young and Company, are large corporations that have established marketing and distribution systems.

It is predicted that the largest companies, such as IBM, will concentrate on the Fortune 1000 companies that now account for 24% to 33% of the market. The small companies that survive the market shake-up will either be writing application software for the big companies or catering to needs of specialized vertical markets. Vertical market suppliers are better able to target their audience and develop their distribution channels. Furthermore, specialization makes it easier to provide software training and support.

Competition in the marketplace has had a positive impact on application software. Commercial outlets have increased support to maintain and attract customers. Also, producers have become responsive to user criticism. In response to consumer demands, multiapplication software has been introduced to combine several applications into a single package. Currently, these packages combine word processing, electronic spreadsheets, and database management tools. In addition, designers are attempting to make software easier to use by eliminating the need for extensive control languages and keystroking by introducing innovations such as the mouse and windowed software.

Another new direction for the software industry is the crediting of software authors with the development of a specific package. In the past, software has been identified only by title or distributor. Author identification makes it easier for the consumer to identify not only specific software packages but quality products as well.

In addition to the commercial sources mentioned, there are a number of other ways to acquire software. User groups offer the free exchange of programs developed by their members. Some groups have an extensive bank of programs, as well as national connections. Although most of these center around hobbyists, there are a few that are work or profession oriented. Most hobbyists work for a living, so it is possible to find some application software even within their ranks. The quality of this software is highly variable and seldom screened. Although some will argue that these programs have undergone many revisions and enhancements, most are poorly documented and often difficult to support.

A function that user groups serve is to exert pressure on commercial producers to provide and service quality products. Professional user groups are especially effective in this respect. The banking and insurance industries have written software standards for their respective fields.

Programs can be found in books and periodicals. They do, however, require time to type the lines of code and to learn to operate. The majority of programs found in these sources are geared to the hobbyist or educator, although there are also some general application programs, particularly for small businesses.

Finally, there is the category of public domain software, available through a multitude of sources—educational agencies, hobbyists, software exchanges, information centers, electronic bulletin boards, and dial-up services. Public domain does not necessarily mean free; it simply means not copyrighted. A few software clearinghouses have been established to promote the sharing of ideas and programs. Materials often can be obtained for the cost of a disk. Softswap, operated by the San Mateo Office of Education and Computer Using Educators, and the Apple Avocation Alliance are but two examples of such clearinghouses. The quality and depth of their banks depend on whether they screen materials and the length of time they have been in operation. School districts, universities, and other local educational agencies are sources of public domain software, as many are recipients of federal grants to develop programs and support computing. Lists of projects sponsored by the National Science Foundation and the National Institute for Education can be obtained by writing to these agencies.

NEED FOR SOFTWARE SELECTION

Selection of proper program packages is what makes a computer system an efficient tool. According to Browstein and Lerner, 50% of data processing software is acquired with selection conducted by personnel with little or no selection experience [1]. Given the fact that there is no such thing as an exact fit of canned software and the complexity of software prevents total debugging, selection should be of concern. Many people buy microcomputers before they have determined their needs or the availability of useful programs to satisfy those needs. The result is a hardware system without the necessary software to get the job done. Either little software is available or the available software is not compatible with the target machine. A useful approach when selecting a system is to select the software first. There is evidence that this approach is being followed, as the current market in hardware is being software driven.

It is often more advantageous to buy rather than write software. Writing original software is a laborious, time-consuming process. There is a high demand for qualified programmers, particularly in any given application area. The best programmers are working for software houses or computer manufacturers and not for individual companies or low-paying institutions. Commercial software offers the advantage of being ready to use immediately, without the need of in-house programmers and with the cost and performance established. Generally, commercial software is better documented than in-house software, which makes support and maintenance easier. Of course, the possible disadvantages of inefficiency, inflexibility, expense, poor support, poor documentation, and lack of acceptance have to be weighed against the in-house production of tailor-made software, which gives the user full control.

Ten years ago there was no software industry. The microcomputer, more than any other factor, has changed that. Today, a $2,000 microcomputer provides the same capabilities that a $250,000 mainframe did 10 years ago. The dramatic drop in hardware price has made computing power available to individuals and institutions with limited resources who had never dreamed that computing would be within their reach. Although hardware has decreased in price, the same cannot be said for software, particularly in the newer application areas. Software accounts for 70% to 80% of the cost of a computer system.

With so much software available, selection is an important part of the acquisition process. A survey conducted by Sofsearch International, based on product listings for all types of computers in its database, showed a minimum of 32,241 packages available in 90,000 operating versions. Broken down, there were 25,509 application packages of which 19,122 were pertinent to business, a profession , or an institution [2]. As a means of comparison, 10,000 application packages were identified in 1982. This shows a growth in 2 years of roughly two and one-half times the number of products. In 1983, software sales reached $2.2 billion (approximately the size of the record industry) with predictions of $11.7 billion by 1988. And most software sales are packages under $10,000 [3].

THE PROBLEM OF LOCATING SOFTWARE

Due to the multitude of application packages available, some searching is required to determine whether there is a package that will meet one's needs. A preliminary report of a computer technology survey in nonprofit organizations shows that 77.8% of the respondents express moderate or great difficulty in finding or developing software [4]. Ten years ago, a similar lack of awareness of existing programs led to much duplication of efforts. Practically every installation was writing its own payroll package. This explains why so many payroll packages are available today.

Rather than there being a problem of not enough information, there is a problem of information scatter. Software advertisements are appearing not only in computer magazines but also in professional journals. In addition, these periodicals frequently review specific software and announce new software as well as products under development. A number of journals and magazines publish annual buyer's guides. Many software advertising brochures are sent, unsolicited, to schools, libraries, and businesses. Computer newsletters, electronic bulletin boards, and popular magazines are also sources of information.

However, only a finite portion of the commercially available software has been captured bibliographically. Bibliographic access can be gained, primarily, through one of three tools: indexes, directories, or evaluative reference/locator services available in both print and on-line format.

There is a great range and variety in the information these tools provide. Indexes generally lead to review articles appearing in the periodical literature. In many indexes, "review" or "evaluation" appears as a subheading under the heading "computer programs." However, finding a review for a particular piece of software is difficult. Only a small amount of software has actually been reviewed critically. Directories provide everything from a simple listing of software by name and/or vendor to comprehensive descriptions of the programs.

In the category of reference/locator services are those tools that evaluate or compare similar programs, which are frequently updated. On-line services are updated more often—usually monthly. In addition to descriptive data and review citations, on-line services may provide abstracts of reviews and permit software purchase, usually with discounts of 10% to 40%. On-line services also offer a greater number of entry points. They may be searched by application type, title, or computer brand or operating name, producer, producer's address, memory range, release data, price, or availability of warranty.

A derivative of the on-line locators are the personal software locators. These specially trained consultants search the electronic databases and provide printouts and applicable reviews for their customers. An annotated list of some locators and other tools used for identifying software is provided in the Appendix. This list is by no means comprehensive but is intended to demonstrate the type and scope of these tools.

In spite of the many print sources available, much of what is considered by users to be good application software is found serendipitously. Word of mouth is the most common way to learn of software. Most published software selection guides recommend speaking with other users in the field and attending conferences as a starting point for locating software.

Although bibliographic control of commercial software is still in its infancy, public domain software is virtually uncontrolled other than by the developers themselves. Tapping into this software source is done almost exclusively through direct contact. Professional organizations, user groups, electronic bulletin boards, and software exchanges are ways of initiating this contact. Because so little software has been reviewed, talking with users in the field is not only a good way to find out what is available but also a way to gather preliminary information for the selection process.

SOFTWARE SELECTION PROCESS

A review of the literature pertinent to software selection and evaluation seems to suggest two basic approaches to the selection of canned software. One could be labeled the marketplace or infusion method. This approach attempts to determine what software is available and how to fit it to an operation or how to make an operation fit the software. This was the approach taken, if not recommended, when relatively little software was available. Users were often relieved or amazed to see that something "worked" and did not question the quality. The result was the fostering of many poor products.

Partially in response to the many mediocre products, a more analytical approach is now recommended. Training for implementing this approach is now under way. Many guides and articles are being written for specific and general audiences on the selection of prewritten software. Perhaps, most significantly, these guides are directed to the user rather than to data processing personnel.

The first step in the process is to perform a needs assessment by taking a careful look at how things are being done, the flow of the work, and the objectives. While this information is being gathered, there is a question to keep in mind: Is automation appropriate? In about one quarter of the cases, the manual system is found to be efficient. Because of the aura surrounding technology, it is often assumed that automation is superior to other methods. As maturity and experience with software develops, some of the mystique that makes it appealing is dispelled. On some occasions, more relevance is achieved by other means. If automation is the answer, the self-analysis is still important for identifying and correcting errors before incorporating them into the automated process.

After the decision to automate and buy software has been made, it must be determined what the software is to do and how it is to do it. Consideration should be given to which functions are mandatory and which are"nice to have." At this stage, software requirements and specifications should be written. Because the software may be in use for a long time, thought should be given to future demands and functions. When establishing minimums for performance, a good rule of thumb is to use present minimums plus 25%.

Identifying potential packages and gathering preliminary information is the next step in the process. Sources for identifying and locating software have already been discussed. The type of information accumulated at this stage should include name, vendor, hardware, and system requirements, overview of functions and features, capacity, and price.

Packages that clearly fail to meet the objectives and specifications established earlier can be eliminated. It will be obvious if the hardware requirements are different from those available or are too costly to obtain. If objectives are not met, the package should be eliminated rather than altering the objectives to suit the package. With the amount of application software that is being produced and improved, there is little reason to settle for a package that offers less than is desired. Some waiting or additional searching may be required.

After the field has been narrowed by the selection process, a detailed evaluation and comparison of the remaining packages takes place. This is discussed in more detail in the next section.

The evaluation should lead to a decision and the negotiation and/or purchase of the appropriate software package. If an expensive package, one that requires modification, or custom software is being purchased, the vendor's responsibilities and software performance should be committed to a written contract. Typically, the vendor will try to assume minimum responsibilities. For this reason, standard contracts are discouraged. What is to be done, by whom, how, when, and at what cost is important, especially if the vendor is providing the majority of training, support, and maintenance.

EVALUATION AND COMPARISON OF SOFTWARE

In the past, software evaluation was generally considered to be the domain of the data processing department. However, many of today's potential software buyers are not affiliated with a data processing department. Furthermore, a programmer's opinion of what constitutes good application software is not necessarily the same as that of the end user. On the other hand, a novice may view even the slowest, most inflexible software as a remarkable improvement of a manual system.

If there is a unique problem that will require a considerable amount of special or expensive software and there is no time or personnel to conduct an analysis of present conditions, identification of software, and comparison of packages, an outside consultant should be employed. Such a consultant should have expertise in the application area and no vested interest in any products under consideration. It is therefore questionable to use a software or hardware salesperson as a consultant. The temptation exists to fit the application to the available product rather than match the software with the application. Knowing hardware and software is not enough for choosing application software. It is important that a consultant have a full appreciation of the intricacies of the application and the user's objectives.

For many, there is no decision to make concerning the hiring of an outside consultant. It is simply outside the budget, or the cost of the software itself does not warrant this type of expenditure. The end user, however, is not a bad choice for evaluator. Who other than the user has a better understanding of present conditions and desired objectives and requirements? Those who train users to evaluate software agree that by using subject expertise and knowledge, users can become effective evaluators. Confidence in the user's own expertise must be bolstered. Basically, this requires the demystification of software through knowledge and experience. The process of identifying software and gathering information itself can provide a great deal of background.

The person or persons selected to do software evaluation should possess three characteristics: (a) expertise in the application area, (b) general knowledge of any existing hardware system, and (c) no vested interest in the performance or nonperformance of a software package. If the end user is not directly involved with the evaluation, he/she should at least provide some liaison. This will be beneficial not only in choosing the most appropriate software but also in implementation later.The make and model, language, operating system, capacity, and peripherals constitute the required hardware knowledge. Fear of automation or an attitude known as the "not invented here syndrome" can interfere with objective evaluation. In simple terms, use the expertise at hand to best advantage when choosing evaluators.

In order to evaluate software, there is a need to establish some points of reference or criteria. Unlike other purchases, software does not stand alone. Criteria can be categorized as being application specific or nonapplication specific. The application-specific criteria are the features that meet the objectives and requirements identified during the selection process. The nonapplication-specific criteria fall into three broad areas: (a) technical and operational, which deal with the design concepts, ease of use, and hardware compatibility; (b) implementation and maintenance, which deal with documentation, training, modification, vendor support, and vendor reliability; and (c) price, which includes the direct purchase or lease costs, as well as the indirect costs such as training, modification, enhancement, conversion, and operation.

Much has been written concerning the need for establishing criteria, and numerous checklists can easily be located. This in itself creates difficulty. Rather than simplifying the process, elaborate evaluation forms run the risk of creating confusion. They have become so cumbersome that one can easily lose sight of the overall performance of a a software package. Another difficulty is that most checklists are general in nature and tend to foster a mechanical approach to viewing software.

Educators who, as application users, have had considerable practice in evaluating software during the last few years have begun to question what constitutes valid evaluation criteria. The idea that not all criteria are created equal is emerging. Recent forms attempt to assign weights or ranks to the criteria. However, numbers should not be relied on to convey important substantive matters. What is needed is a way to distinguish between deficiencies that may be easily remedied and those that cannot be remedied without overall reconceptualization. In the end, evaluation of software, as with most performance items, is subjective. Although a checklist is convenient for comparing similar programs, it should be used as an informative rather than authoritative tool.

The user must develop confidence in his/her own ability to evaluate software. This requires some knowledge of what is available and how it works. By keeping abreast of the current literature in one's own field, occasionally browsing through popular computer magazines, and talking with software vendors and users, one can develop an appreciation for what is available. Reading software reviews, as part of the identification and information-gathering step, helps the potential user to formulate the criteria that he/she will use to evaluate and compare software packages.

A skeletal checklist can provide the user with a format for identifying and prioritizing application-specific criteria without prejudicing viewpoint. In such a checklist, criteria can be divided into three parts: (a) application suitability; (b) controls and security, which should provide for backup or copy in addition to restricting access; and (c) operational performance. Once all criteria have been determined, they can be ranked by the user with the highest number assigned to the most important characteristic. As a particular package is evaluated, the evaluator can assign a number between 0 and 10 for each characteristic. By multiplying the characteristic's value by the assigned rating, the evaluator can produce a numerical score comparing similar software packages.

For personal, or "buy, don't buy"decisions, a four-section criteria list identifying application features, technical and operating requirements, implementation and maintenance requirements, and price range should be sufficient. It is possible to include both mandatory and "nice to have"features by marking mandatory items with an asterisk or other distinguishing marks. A sample of such a checklist is provided in Table 1.

Actual use of a software package on the user's own equipment, with real data and situations, is the best means for evaluating software against established criteria. The evaluator should also consider the ease or difficulty of interaction, whether data are checked for validity before processing, and whether the screen displays are appropriate. Some vendors, particularly in the educational field, will permit a 30-day preview period. If the vendor does not permit preview, one should attempt to arrange a bench-mark test on the vendor's equipment. Most local retail vendors have some type of demonstration facilities. If remoteness or need for a large file conversion makes a benchmark test impractical, the vendor should be asked to identify nearby installations where the package can be observed in operation under conditions as close as possible to those of the intended user. Arrange for a visit and prepare specific questions based on the criteria list. Be sure to inquire about any difficulties or unmet claims with either the package or the vendor.

If none of these previous methods is available, the vendor might conduct a partial demonstration of the software or provide a special demonstration version of the program. Caution should be exercised in these circumstances. Often, only the best and most impressive features are shown while faults are suppressed.

Reviews are better used in deciding whether to preview a piece of software rather than in place of preview. Reviews can become obsolete because software can be quickly and easily changed. Also, the version reviewed may be different from the one under consideration. Expertise and background of the reviewer is another question. Many reviews are unsigned and unsolicited. Some magazines do not publish negative reviews. Even if a review is favorable, the reviewer may have used different objectives, worked under different conditions, or looked only at the diskette and not at the entire system. Software should not be purchased sight unseen.

While previewing software, look at the accompanying documentation and vendor's service and reliability. Is the documentation provided written in clear, concise English? Is sufficient information provided for training and operation? Is technical information, needed for repair and maintenance, included in addition to tutorials and operating instructions? Will source codes be provided or obtainable should the dealer not be available for support? The vendor's stability, reliability, and expertise of personnel should be investigated, especially if the vendor is to provide training and maintenance or a custom project. Determine the provision, the time, and the cost of services.

With so many canned programs available, it is probably worth the time and effort to search for a software package rather than attempt to write application software in-house. Plenty of information and resources concerning software selection and evaluation exist, and the user, with some background, can become an effective evaluator. The most crucial step is to carefully identify the objectives and specifications that the software is to meet. It is doubtful that any one software package will meet all requirements exactly. The key questions are how much adaptation is required and is it acceptable? The final consideration is the availability and extent of support. The specific method applied to the selection and evaluation of software, as well as its thoroughness, will depend on the available resources—finances, personnel, and time.

REFERENCES

1. I. Brownstein and N. B. Lerner, *Guidelines for Evaluating and Selecting Software Packages*, Elsevier, New York, 1982, p.1.
2. "News and Notes," *Libr. Software Rev., 3*, 18 (March 1984).
3. A. Pollack, "Slugging It Out on the Software Front," *The New York Times*, October 16, 1983, Sec. 3, p.1.
4. "1983 Annual Survey of Computer Technology in Nonprofit Organizations." *Libr. Software Rev., 3*, 14 (March 1984).

APPENDIX: SOURCES FOR IDENTIFICATION OF SOFTWARE

Indexes

Computer Science Resources: A Guide to Professional Literature. Contains references to a number of resources that address the subject of software.

Computer Literature Index. Covers fairly technical magazines and journals in the fields of computers and data processing.

Consumer Index to Product Evaluation and Information Sources.

The Digest of Software Reviews: Education.

Microcomputer Index. Bimonthly coverage of articles and reviews from almost 50 microcomputer periodicals. Includes a subject index whose entries refer to abstracts appearing in the second section.

Small Computer Program Index. Bimonthly guide to listings in personal and small computer magazines and books in the United States and Great Britain (contains printed programs).

Directories

General

Apple II Blue Book. Where-to-find-it guide and descriptions of over 5,000 programs.

Data Sources. Quarterly guide to hardware, data communications, software, and services.

Freeloader 500 Software Library.

IBM PC Software Guide. Contains detailed information on over 3,000 PC and XT software programs from 1,100 suppliers.

ICP Directory. Multivolume annual guide with over 8,000 packages for types and size of computers (no evaluations).

International Directory of Software. Indexes products by category; includes description of software and suppliers profile.

International Software Directory. Available in two volumes: microcomputers and minicomputers. Based on the International Software Database.

On-Line Micro Software Guide and Directory. Directory of product descriptions.

Small Systems Software and Services Sourcebook.

The Software Catalog. Contains extensive data on 25,000 microcomputer packages.

The Software Directory. Includes brief descriptions of software.

Sourcebook. Directory of small systems software and services.

Skarbet Software Directory. For Apple computers.

Educational

Educational Software Directory. Lists titles of more than 500 programs for Apple, Pet, and TRS-80 (no evaluations).

The Educational Software Selector (TESS). Contains comprehensive and detailed information on the availability of educational software for microcomputers for nursery school through graduate school (citations to reviews).

Reference Manual for Instructional Use of Microcomputers. Cross-references over 1,000 educational software programs. Indexes journals and books and contains some evaluations.

School Microware: A Directory of Education Software. Description of software for classroom use with Apple, TRS-80, Pet, and Atari. Brief descriptions are organized by grade level, subject area, and hardware system (no evaluations).

Swift's Educational Software Directory. Directory of educational software.

Library-Specific

Directory of Information Management Software. Provides basic product information on commercially available packages for libraries and information and record centers.

Library and Information Sciences: A Directory of Computer Software Applications.

Reference/Locator Services

Print

Application Software Reports. Limited number of packages described.

Computer Software

Datapro Directory of Software. Over 2,000 packages, indexed by vendor and product; includes information on function, hardware, and peripherals required and price, maintenance, documentation, and training.

Datapro Directory of Microcomputer Software. Over 2,000 packages for microcomputers; includes vendor profiles, hard-to-locate supplies, features on software and basic product information; identifies best packages according to user ratings.

Micro-Courseware PRO/FILES. In-depth evaluation of educational courseware by EPIE/ Consumers Union.

MicroSIFT Courseware Reviews. Educators' guide to evaluated, field-tested software.

Micro Software Report: Library Edition. Focuses on software programs designed for the microcomputer; mainframes and minis included if interface with micro available.

Software Reports. Updated, loose-leaf reference guide to evaluated educational software. Stated criteria used to evaluate courseware in 20 subject areas.

On-Line

C-DOS (Ocean Data Systems). Permits search of database and demonstration of software at computer stores.

The Computer Database (DIALOG File 275).

DISC (BRS). Cover-to-cover indexing of journals in microcomputing with peripheral coverage of minis, EDP, and information science.

FileSoft (BRS/Search and BRS/After Dark). An expansion of On-line MicroSoftware Guide and Directory. Contains information on over 2,000 microcomputer packages exclusive of games and entertainment.

The International Microcomputer Software Database (DIALOG File 232). World's largest software database updated monthly.

MENU (The International Microcomputer Software Database). A personal software locator updated daily with printouts sent via Federal Express on the day of search. Included with printouts are any available reviews. Discount on purchase of software ranges from 10% to 25%.

Microcomputer Index (DIALOG 233). Indexes over 25 English language microcomputer periodicals cover to cover in addition to other publications.

ON-LINE SOFTWARE LIBRARY (Searchmart's Free Access Library). Menudriven searches. The database contains about 2,000 packages for mainframes, minicomputers, and microcomputers. Descriptive information may or may not include manufacturer's comments.

One Point Electronic Catalog (ITM). Menu driven with browse or search options. Brief printout includes subject and performance ratings from independent evaluators. Product description includes highlights of key functions, review abstracts, and user comments. Discount, 15% to 40%.

RICE (BRS). A database comprised of information on the state of the art in educational computer applications.

Sofsearch International, Inc. A personal software locator offering 15% to 40% discounts on over 40,000 software packages. Does not include product description or reviews.

The Software Catalog (DIALOG File 232). Contains information of 50,000 software products for minicomputers and microcomputers. Primarily used as a marketing tool.

GLOSSARY

Analyst. A person skilled in the definition and the development of techniques for solving problems, especially techniques for solutions on a computer.

Application Software. Programs designed and written to solve specific user-oriented problems.

Benchmark Problem. A problem used to evaluate the performance of computer and/or software, relative to each other.

Database. An organized grouping of data elements.

Debugging. The process of identifying and correcting errors in programs.

Documentation. All paperwork, manuals, and documents used to maintain a complete record of a system's design, user responsibilities, data entry, and operating instructions.

Evaluation. The process of studying the characteristics and performances of software packages to determine the relative merits of each.

Field. A set of one or more characters treated as a unit of data.

File. An organized collection or records directed toward some purpose; for example, a file of inventory records.

Maintenance. Maintaining software by making repairs, updates, and enhancements.

Modular. A programming tool that enables persons with limited programming skills to develop useful computer programs with a minimum of effort. Examples are VisiCalc and DB Master.

Object Language. Machine language.

Operating System. Collection of computer programs for accomplishing such housekeeping functions as input/output control, memory allocation, and program read-in.

Software Package. Data, programs, and assistance provided by a vendor, which may be partially modified for the configuration of the user's computer system.

Source Language. Language, other than machine language, in which a program is originally written.

System Software. Programs designed around the internal environment of the computer to directly or indirectly support processing.

Throughput. Total useful information processed or communicated.

Turnkey System. Computer, peripheral equipment, software, documentation, supplies, and installation supplied by the manufacturer to provide a total hardware/software system. Generally geared to a particular function or application.

Unbundling. Pricing strategy in which the services, programs, training, and so forth, are sold independently of the computer hardware by the computer hardware manufacturer.

User Group. An organization composed of users of software packages.

Utility Program. Standard program for performing frequently required system tasks, such as sorting, merging, selecting, editing, copying, or printing out the contents of a file.

Vertical Market Software. Specialized software designed for limited markets.

JUDY SPEEDY

EXPERT SYSTEMS FOR COMPUTER-INTEGRATED MANUFACTURING

EXPERT SYSTEMS: WHAT ARE THEY?

An expert system might be looked at as ". . . a computer program that knows what it knows, knows what it doesn't know, and knows what to ask for to solve the current problem and stores all added knowledge for future use" [1]. The essence is that the program has some intelligence and some expertise.

The concept of expert systems is to make use of a strong base of knowledge and an inference (reasoning) system that can reason with the knowledge base in such a way that it can solve meaningful problems. The human expert tends to have very extensive knowledge about a certain domain and perhaps does not use extremely strong reasoning processes. When this concept was realized by the artificial intelligence (AI) researchers, the field of expert systems was born.

Expertise can be put into systems in three fundamental ways: (a) by being told, (b) by induction from examples, and (c) observation and discovery [2]. These are quite comparable to the ways in which humans learn.

COMPUTER-INTEGRATED MANUFACTURING: WHAT IS CIM?

There are many definitions for CIM, a recent one defining CIM in terms of the intent: ". . . it is the logical organization of individual engineering, production, marketing, and financial functions within a computer-integrated environment" [3]. A philosophy of building expert systems was discussed at the Fifteenth International Programmable Controllers Conference and Exhibition [4].

An expert system for injection-molded plastic parts diagnoses and solves about 75%–85% of the problems and avoids holding up production [5]. McDonnell Douglas Research Laboratories have been developing AI techniques for the CIM area and expect AI to become ". . . indispensable in the factory of the future . . ."[6]. Carnegie-Mellon University is working on several expert systems that are being built for industrial use [7]. ". . . the wonder is thousands of other companies have not tried them . . . . The total risk can be as little as $10,000—but the reward can be 10 or 20 times as much" [8].

SOME EXPERT SYSTEM DEVELOPMENTS

Expert systems are not generally available for specific applications, but there are several expert system "shells" on the market. Each shell must then have a knowledge base before it can solve specific problems. Expert systems have been tried in several applications within the CIM domain.

Heuristic programming has been used to interpret drawings and to prepare CNC (Computer Numerical Control) instructions for a three-axis mill [9]. The drawing interpreter constructs three-dimensional data from two-dimensional drawings, which is no trivial problem. The CNC programming heuristic will give a diagnostic if the part cannot be machined. The CNC program has only been tested on plane surfaces and cylindrical faces in the principal directions.

GARI is a program for planning the sequence of machining cuts for mechanical parts using weighted pieces of advice from machining experts. GARI generates a machining plan from a model of the part. It knows the set of candidate cuts beforehand, and the system must decide how they are to be executed and in what order. GARI has a conflict resolution facility that allows it to reject some advice and accept other advice [10].

The factory of the future will use AI techniques in all aspects of planning and control, including design, processing, handling, assembly, and inspection. It is not yet clear as to the decision-making level responsibility. Some areas of manufacturing have not been attacked by the application of techniques that will result in major improvements in productivity [11]. It is essential that we develop a science of CIM before we can have an automation revolution. We rely too much on centuries of experience, human skills, and knowledge in the discrete parts of manufacturing business [12].

Hi-Mapp (Heirarchical and Intelligent Manufacturing Automated Process Planner) incorporated some AI techniques into process planning. A part is represented by its features, and the system also uses information about the available materials, tools, and machines. Hi-Mapp works toward a goal state that consists of a partial ordering of the operations that provides a proper sequence of actions [13].

Scheduling on the factory floor has come into considerable attention in recent years. The development of schedules is a major problem on the factory floor because optimal schedules generally turn out to be the solution of a combinatoric problem. Carngegie-Mellon University has been conducting investigations into this area for some time. A prototype of their ISIS (Intelligent Scheduling and Information System) has been demonstrated on the factory floor. Another system, OPIS (Opportunistic Intelligent Scheduler) is being developed to handle the full range of scheduling constraints found on the factory floor and to explore the benefits of a dynamic approach to problem decomposition [14]. Operations Advisor (OA) is a forward-looking system for scheduling in the factory environment. OA uses prompts and windows and consists of an allocation module, a goals or targeting module, an interpretation module, a sensitivity analysis module, and a report generation module [15]. One company uses a simulation to build a model of the factory so that the system can eventually build a production schedule directed toward either the floor supervisor or higher levels of management [16].

A rule-based system for FMS (flexible manufacturing system) has shown a dramatic increase in flexibility and maintainability because events and constraints can be taken into account modularly and incrementally. Some results are shown in Ref. *17*.

Considerable work has been done in the diagnosis/repair area. Some expert systems are essentially a decision tree approach and do not incorporate any probabilistic capabilities. Other systems try to solve diagnosis/repair problems by assigning "probabilities" to events and to have the system calculate probabilities as the diagnosis proceeds [18]. Researchers at an aerospace company are studying a flexible general-purpose expert system with an inference engine that is usable in many domains. LES (Lockheed Expert System) can hook into ADA, FORTRAN, Pascal, and other available languages [19]. DETECTIVE is an on-line diagnostics expert system for the reporting of process malfunctions, their location, time, and reason and then offers advice for repair. The program runs on proprietary hardware [20]. SEE WHY is a simulation-based, fill-in-blanks approach to building factory models. It comes with built-in expertise with default values that the user can override [*16*]. A number of factory design systems have been in use for some time; most did not incorporate AI techniques. A recently developed system does include AI methodology [*21*].

The Materials Laboratory at WPAB has let a contract for developing real-time integration of vision and force control [*22*]. CML (cell management language) was developed for factory cell management when the cell consists of several diverse machines [*23*].

An expert system has been developed with a focus on the effective use of a performance prediction model in the capacity planning process. The system uses a "blackboard" approach [*24*].

The "Lexan" Resin Troubleshooting System is designed to solve production problems in injection molding. It is estimated that the expert system can solve 75%—85% of the problems. The high success rate results in a reduction of lost production time [*25*]. An automated photolithograpy line for wafer fabrication is said to reduce the cycle times by 80%. The control system uses a 32-bit microprocessor. The control system has expert systems interfaces for process analysis, process control, and equipment maintenance. These expert systems allow the quality control scientists to spend their time on more critical problems and provide for continuity with turnover in personnel. In addition to reducing the cycle times, the system is expected to increase the field [*26*]. Another approach to the solution of product/production problems is the use of a "browser" that looks at the manufacturing data base in an attempt to find problems that an engineer or production specialist would have difficulty finding. The browser could look at the database overnight and present its findings to the production specialist on the following morning. The first domain for the browser is in wafer fabrication where there are many steps in the production process, and statistical analysis may not provide adequate information for trouble shooting. The browser establishes hypotheses, tests those hypotheses on the actual manufacturing data base, and arrives at conclusions that are transmitted to the production specialist. To avoid endless search, the browser must make decisions as to where to stop to make a detailed investigation [*27*].

One model of a knowledge-based simulation (KBS), simulating the distribution center for a large corporation, was used to determine the best location of manufacturing facilities and distribution centers and to determine the distribution of inventories. The objectives were to maintain a uniform level of production, minimize the transportation cost (only full truckloads can be shipped), minimize inventory costs at the various entities, ship products on time and in the quantity requested, and not to force the retailer to have excess inventories [*28*].

The choice of cutting tool can be a difficult one when there are many cutting tools, many tool holders and adapters, and many machines. An expert system was constructed based on DCLASS, a classification and coding system. The system generates four lists, each being a subset of the previous one. The last list presents the five "best" tools to the user, with this list being ordered with the best at the top [*29*].

Syllog is a shell that uses facts and rules about how to use those facts (syllogisms). The Syllog shell was used to develop an expert system that determines the number of testers to use, the location of the testers, and the time at which testers must come line. The expert system shows promise of real-world usefulness [*30*]. Several expert systems that are used in the investment casting process are to be controlled by a more global expert system. Although the current research is concerned only with the investment casting process, it is though that the system can be used elsewhere. Another project addresses the problem of monitoring and controlling a complex dynamic process. DIFF (domain-independent form filler) is an expert system for planning and scheduling. A program for very large-scale integration (VLSI) design considers a design built from the system level, the cell level, the circuit level, and the physical design level. Programs are also under way for facility layout, scheduling, machine setup, and quality control [31]. OPGEN (operation sheets generator) is used to assist engineers in developing the manufacturing specifications for printed circuit boards [32]. In a manufacturing facility, two major cycles may be addresses: the order/process cycle and the product life cycle. The order/process cycle is attacked with expert systems for requirements, specification, and design, for intelligent manufacturing, for order logistics, and for sourcing [33].

Callisito is a project management system that looks at (a) activity management (planning, scheduling, chronicling, and analysis), (b) product configuration management (product configuration management and change management), and (c) resource management (estimation and acquisition of resources, assignment of responsibilities, and handling of critical resources to avoid bottlenecks) [34].

AI and simulation seem to be a desirable combination for simulation of activities on the factory floor. Simulation requires large amounts of memory and long times and, therefore, has not proven to be useful in finding the solutions to routine problems. The combination of expert systems with simulations may make simulation more useful [35]. An aid to automatic factory decision making uses a graphic interface and has simulation capabilities. The system is being written in PROLOG [36].

AN EVALUATION OF THE STATE OF THE ART OF EXPERT SYSTEMS

Expert systems are a way of the future; they are not widely used today and tend to be rather narrow in the domains in which they function. As evidenced by the previous materials, there is considerable research in expert system, particularly in their applications. Most of the systems mentioned previously are really in the laboratory stage of development.

The manner in which a human solves a problem is not known. We can only surmise that certain things happen within the human "intelligence system" and try to model them. Expert system applications will, of necessity, be relatively limited until we learn more about human intelligence.

There will be considerable money and effort directed toward the development of larger, more powerful systems that can function in complex domains. There are those who are detractors and probably rightly so, as too many systems are being promoted that do not really solve meaningful problems. This is a technology that is in its infancy and has a long maturation process ahead. However, it is felt that they are a way of the future; therefore, we must continue to perfect them.

REFERENCES

1. J. E. Biegel, "The Future Role of Expert Systems in Manufacturing," *Proceedings of the Eighth Annual Conference on Computers and Industrial Engineering*, G. Whitehouse and H. Eldin (eds.), Pergamon Press, New York, 1986, pp. 473–475.
2. A. Walker, "Knowledge Systems: Principles and Practice," *IBM J. Res. Dev., 29*(4), 2–13 (July 1985).
3. L Mannis, "Extending the Reach Toward CIM," *Manuf. Syst., 4*(11), 32, 35–36 (November 1986).
4. C. Sykes, "Expert Systems to Augment Process Controls,"*Autom. News, 4*(7), 59 (April 21, 1986).

5. C. Sykes,"Expert Systems Suited for Factories," *CAE (Computer-Aided Engineering)*, 5(8), 16 (August 1986).

6. K. G. Kempf, "Manufacturing and Artificial Intelligence," *Robotics*, 1(1), 13–25 (May 1985).

7. K. G. Kempf, "Expert Systems—'Key' to Production Future," *Autom. News*, 10 (June 13, 1983).

8. K. G. Kempf, "Expert Systems: The Risk/Reward Ratios," *Manuf. Syst.*,4(8), 56, 59 (August 1986).

9. K. Preiss and E. Kaplansky, "Solving CAD/CAM Problems by Heuristic Programming," *Comput. Mech. Eng.*, 2(2): 56–60 (September 1983).

10. Y. Descotte and J-C. Latombe, "GARI: A Problem Solver That Plans How to Machine Mechanical Parts," *Proceedings of the Seventh International Joint Conference on Artificial Intelligence*, American Association for Artificial Intelligence, Menlo Park, CA, 1981, pp. 762–766.

11. D. C. Anderson, J. J. Solberg, and R. P. Paul, "Factories of the Future: How Will Automation Research Be Integrated,"? *Comput. Mech. Eng.*, 2(4), 30–36 (January 1984).

12. H. Voelker and A. Requicha, "Geometric Modelling of Mechanical Parts and Processes," *Computer*, 10(12), 48–57 (December 1977).

13. H. R. Berenji and B. Khoshnevis, "Use of Artificial Intelligence in Automated Process Planning," *Comput. Mech. Eng.*, 5(2), 47–55 (September 1986).

14. S. F. Smith, M. S. Fox, and P. S. Ow, "Constructing and Maintaining Detailed Production Plans: Investigations into the Development of Knowledge-Based Factory Scheduling Systems," *AI Mag.*, 7(4), 45–61 (Fall 1986).

15. M. Ball, "AI-based Software for Factory Control Debuts from Palladian," *Autom. News*, 4(20), 14, 14 (November 1986).

16. M. Ball, "Factory Experts," *Autom. News*, 4(12), 14 (July 7, 1986).

17. G. Bruno, A. Elia, and P. Laface, "A Rule-Based System to Schedule Production," *Computer*, 19(7), 32–39 (July 1986).

18. T. Jupille, "Expert Systems are New Textbooks," *Res. Dev.*, 28(12), 52–55 (December 1986).

19. I. Stambler, "Researcher Build Flexibility into Lockheed Expert System," *Res. Dev.*, 28(10), 44–45 (October 1986).

20. E. Hoefler, "Real-Time Controls a Prime Concern at Control Expo 86," *Autom. News*, 4(12), 5, 11 (May 19, 1986).

21. E. L. Fisher, "An AI-Based Methodology for Factory Design," *AI Mag.*, 7(4), 72–85 (Fall 1986).

22. M. Ryan, "USAF Earmarks $23 Million for Expert Systems," *Autom. News*, 4(20), 24, 42 (November 10, 1986).

23. D. A. Bourne, "CML: A Meta-Interpreter for Manufacturing," *AI Mag.*, 7(4), 86–96 (Fall 1986).

24. G. J. Stroebel, R. D. Baxter, and M. J. Denney, "A Capacity Planning Expert System for IBM System/38," *Computer*, 19(7), 42–50 (July 1986).

25. G. J. Stroebel, R. D. Baxter, and M. J. Denney, "Research Trend-letter," *Res. Dev.*, 28(8), 29 (August 1986).

26. M. L. Shopbell and W. F. Hastings, "Automation Removes Contaminents from Fabrication Line," *Res. Dev.*, 28(10), 112–114 (October 1986).

27. D. C. Brown and P. Posco, "Looking for Trouble: Expert Browsing in Manufacturing Data Bases," *Comput. Mech. Eng.*, 5(3), 19–23 (November 1986).

28. Y. V. Reddy, M. S. Fox, K. Doyle, and J. Arnold, "INET: A Knowledge-Based Simulation Model of a Corporate Distribution System," in *IEEE Proceedings, Trends, and Applications–1983, Automating Intelligent Behavior: Applications and Frontiers,* 1983, pp. 109–118.

29. T. Traugher, "An Expert System for Tool Selection," *TI Eng. J.*, 21–26 (September/October 1984).

30. C. Fellenstein, C. O. Green, L. M. Palmer, A. Walker, and D. J. Wyler, "A Prototype Manufacturing Knowledge Base in SYLLOG," *IBM J. Res. Dev.,* 29(4), 413–421 (July 1985).

31. Y-H. Pao, "The Center for Automation and Intelligent Systems Research, Case Western Reserve University," *AI Mag.,* 7(1), 69–73 (Spring 1986).

32. R. S. Freedman and R. P. Frail, "OPGEN: The Evolution of an Expert System for Process Planning," *AI Mag.,* 7(5), 58–70 (Winter 1986).

33. F. Lynch, C. Marshall, D. O'Connor, and M. Kiskiel, "AI in Manufacturing at Digital," *AI Mag.,* 7(5), 53–57 (Winter 1986).

34. S. Sathi, T. E. Morton, and S. F. Roth, "Callisto: An Intelligent Project Management System," *AI Mag.,* 7(5), 34–51 (Winter 1986).

35. T. Baer, "Simulating the Factory," *Mech. Eng.*, 38–43 (December 1986).

36. M. G. Dyer, "Artificial Intelligence Research at the University of California, Los Angeles: Current Research in Robotics and Intelligent Manufacturing," *AI Mag.,* 6(3), 217 (Fall 1985).

JOHN E. BIEGEL

MUSIC PRINTING

INTRODUCTION

Music Printing

Music printing is the process of creating and reproducing pages of music notation. In order to do this a music printing system, whether it is computer controlled or not, must have a method by which pages of music notation can be formed and a mechanism by which copies of the music score can be produced. The process of forming pages of music is generally referred to as engraving. This term has been retained from the days when music scores were reproduced from metal plates on which music symbols were etched. Today, a variety of methods can be used for music printing, with computer technology being utilized in ever-increasing amounts.

Music Notation

Music notation is a language which uses symbols and graphic images to produce a visual representation of sound events. This representation is initially prepared by a composer or music arranger, is printed, and ultimately, is read by an instrumental performer or conductor. The primary function of music notation is to capture the musical intentions of a composer and to communicate those ideas to a performer. Music notation as the intermediary stage between composer and performer must represent the musical materials of the composer in such a way that they can efficiently and accurately be interpreted by a performer. This involves laying out the score in accordance with standard engraving conventions and placing the necessary music symbols properly on the page. Notation that is inaccurate or that contains unnecessary ambiguities may cause errors during performance; such a score is considered to be poorly engraved.

The Scope of Music Notation

Generally speaking, music notation encompasses a wide range of visual representations from simple tablature to elaborate graphical scores. This enormous variety is largely due to the nature of music composition and performance. Notation can provide only a limited amount of musical information, the remainder must be interpreted by a performer. A score will have a very different appearance depending on which aspects of the music are notated and on the degree of specificity desired by the notator. In a sense, a score can be anything a composer wants it to be provided it communicates his/her musical ideas. Although all visual representations of sound can be considered to be music notations, the majority of automated notation systems focus on music which has been represented using common music notation (CMN). This term refers to the notation conventions which were developed during the sixteenth century and which have been used to notate virtually all of Western art music. These scores have been the focus of most notation systems because of the large quantity of music published and because of the relative consistency with which the notational conventions are used. Only automated notation systems with a strong graphics-orientation are capable of accommodating the entire domain of music notation (Fig. 1).

Common Music Notation

CMN is a two-dimensional representation of sound events with pitch placed on the vertical axis and duration on the horizontal. Musical notes contain pitch information by their vertical position relative to a five line staff and duration or rhythmic information by the type of the symbol used (Fig. 2).. Additional performance information (e.g., loudness, articulation, etc.) can also be indicated on the score with standard symbols

Other essential elements in a CMN score are the meter, which indicates the basic rhythmic divisions of the music, and barlines, which break the score into groups of beats. Notes which are played simultaneously are aligned vertically on a staff or group of staves, and the music is read from left to right. Although a CMN score contains the essential musical information, many other aspects of the music (i.e., fluctuation of tempo, articulation of individual notes) are determined by the performer; the CMN score contains enough information to permit a faithful rendition of the composer's intentions while still allowing the performer some flexibility (Fig. 3).

Iconic and Algorithmic Elements

When viewed from a graphical perspective, one observes that CMN (and virtually all other music notations) contains both iconic and algorithmic objects [4]. The iconic objects are fixed symbols such as clefs, rests, and accidentals—their shape and size is constant and they can be placed on the score as a icon of glyph. (An engraver uses a metal stamp for each icon, a laser printer uses a font.) The variable or algorithmic objects are images such as beams, slurs, and note stems which vary in shape, length, and angle according to the notational context. In both traditional and automated methods of music printing it is the algorithmic objects which are more problematic. Whereas iconic objects can be positioned at a single fixed location on the score (similar to the methods used to place text on a page), the length or shape of algorithmic objects must be calculated according to the particular situation. As a result, music engraving, unlike text setting, requires a combination of fixed symbols and variable graphics (Fig. 4).

Traditional Methods

Score Preparation

Traditionally, the production of a musical score involved the following stages:

1. Preparation of the original score by the composer or music copyist (in legible hand-copy)
2. Preparation of a master copy of the score by the publisher or editor
3. Proofreading and correction of the master copy
4. Duplication of the master score

In nonautomated printing systems, the entire process must be repeated to produce the individual instrumental parts for performance.

Printing Techniques

Music typesetting or engraving has been practiced since the early sixteenth century and is still widely used in the music publishing industry. The engraving process involves cutting

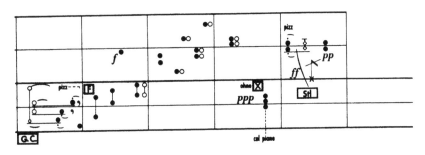

FIGURE 1   The domain of music notation: Example 2 reprinted with permission from Ref. 1; Example 4 reprinted with permission from Ref. 2; Example 5 reprinted with permission from Ref. 3.

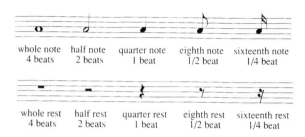

whole note   half note   quarter note   eighth note   sixteenth note
4 beats   2 beats   1 beat   1/2 beat   1/4 beat

whole rest   half rest   quarter rest   eighth rest   sixteenth rest
4 beats   2 beats   1 beat   1/2 beat   1/4 beat

FIGURE 2.   Standard music symbols.

each page of a score into a metal plate with the use of punches and cutting tools. The plate, when finished, is inked and the images on the plate are transferred to paper. Offset printing techniques are used to produce multiple copies of the master page. Before the actual engraving is done, the positions of all images must be calculated by the engraver and marked on the plate. If errors or omissions are discovered after the plate has been prepared, the faulty portion of the plate must be smoothed out and recut—a slow and awkward process. Although scores produced using plate engraving can be very elegant in appearance, the process requires highly skilled craftsmen and is extremely labor intensive.

Music autography is another common method of score preparation. Here, the score is prepared entirely by hand. Using a variety of calligraphic pens, the autographer draws the music with the aid of rulers, T-squares, and templates, and the finished page is printed using a photo-offset or lithographic process. In some instances the iconic elements (i.e., note heads, dynamic markings, etc.) are drawn with inked stamps to produce more consistency among images.

Music typewriters provide an alternative to engraving and autography. Although many models have been developed, the most commonly used is the Musicwriter, which was first introduced in 1955. A blank page is inserted into the Musicwriter and the music symbols (including staves) are typed onto the page by depressing the appropriate key on the keyboard. All typing is done with the right hand while the left hand moves the platen to the correct staff line or space. As one would expect, algorithmic images (i.e., slurs and beams) are not easily accommodated on these devices; often they are added by hand after the essential musical symbols have been placed on the page.

Scores may also by created using pressure lettering or acetates. These are sheets of music symbols which can be transferred onto the manuscript page by rubbing the adhesive

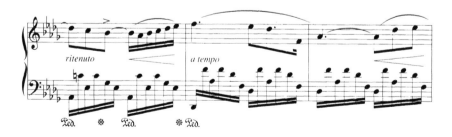

FIGURE 3.   Common music notation.

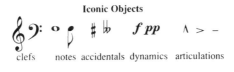

Iconic Objects

clefs   notes   accidentals   dynamics   articulations

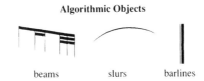

Algorithmic Objects

beams   slurs   barlines

FIGURE 4.   Iconic and algorithmic components.

backed character. The process is extremely slow and is more often used for corrections than for the production of complete scores.

The main problems with traditional engraving techniques are that:

1. They require that the page be carefully laid out and the positions of all images be calculated before the score can be created
2. The process is very slow
3. They require highly skilled craftsmen
4. Corrections are difficult and time consuming

Since all of the methods discussed above are manually intensive, the cost of printing music has risen along with the cost of skilled labor. In fact, virtually all professional engraving is presently done in countries such as Korea, where labor is relatively inexpensive. Also, the increased cost of production has led to a decrease in the quantity of scores published; many scores by composers of contemporary music exist only as photocopy reproductions of the composers' original manuscripts.

Reasons for Automating Music Printing

During the 1970s and 1980s, the prospect of computerized music printing became extremely attractive to music publishers; if much of the layout and image placement could be calculated by machine and if the images could be drawn neatly and accurately using laser printing technology, then the labor cost would be dramatically reduced. Another benefit of an automated system would be the elimination of many of the redundant tasks encountered in the traditional methods of engraving. Often many instruments in an orchestra are playing the same music and often entire sections of a score are repeated verbatim. Also, when an instrumental work is performed, the individual parts must be extracted from the full score; this requires that the entire work be recopied with the music for each instrument on separate pages. Making score transcriptions or transposing the work to another key (a frequent requirement in vocal music) necessitated a complete recreation of the score. All of these tasks would be easily handled by a computer. Finally, once the score had been entered into a computerized music notation system, proofing the score and subsequently correcting errors, making revisions or altering the pagination would be greatly simplified.

Despite the obvious benefits offered by computers, the music publishing industry has been slow to implement notation systems and to automate their production. The reasons that

FIGURE 5.   Various graphical representations of music data.

the computerization of music notation has been lagged behind advancements in other related areas (i.e., text editors, CAD systems) is due to the extreme complexity of musical
notation, the lack of research and development resources within the publishing industry,
and the unavailability of printing devices capable of producing "engraved-quality" output.
(In Leland Smith's MS system [5], scores were printed on a plotter at two or four times the
desired size and later photoreduced to increase the resolution.)

Unlike other languages, music notation does not have a clearly defined symbology
nor does it have a clearly specified syntax or set of rules which can be used to position the
symbols. Rather, scores have evolved historically in tandem with musical styles and notational conventions have been modified as needed. Since the primary objective of a musical
score is to communicate performance information, notational conventions must be flexible
in order to accommodate a range of musical styles. As a result, a comprehensive music editor must be able to take musical information that is well-defined and clearly organized, and
display it in a variety of ways depending on preferences of the individual involved, the musical context, and the style of the music. The translation from musical information to graphical representation is a complex process because there is no single correct notation for any
given musical datum. In the example above, all of the excerpts are different graphical representations of the same musical material (Fig. 5).

Another complicating factor in graphical representation of music is the increased
pitch and rhythmic complexity of twentieth century music which has forced composers to
invent new symbols and conventions. Although most of these symbols are extensions to
CMN, they are often not universally accepted nor are they used consistently by all composers and publishers. For example: in contemporary scores, there are at least six different ways
of indicating that a note is one quarter of a semitone sharp.

AUTOMATED MUSIC PRINTING

System Components

Hardware Requirements

Music printing systems require two hardware components: a computer for compiling, organizing, and displaying the musical data, and a printing device to produce the score. The
computers used in notation systems have, generally speaking, followed the evolutionary
trends of the computer industry. They have moved from mainframe computers to minicomputers to microcomputers, and have taken advantage of improvements in the quality of dis-

play monitors, in the development of interactive editing environments, and in increased microprocessor speed.

The printing devices used in notation systems initially produced comparatively poor quality printed output and this was one of the major factors in the slow acceptance of computer systems by professional music publishers. From the mid-1960s to the mid-1970s a variety of printing methods were used: dot matrix printers, computer-controlled typewriters [6], pen plotters [5], and photographic devices [8]. All of these printing methods produced resolution that was unacceptable to many publishers, although all were used to varying degrees for score production. With the advent of computer-controlled laser printers and phototypesetters in the late 1970s and 1980s, the printing component of notation systems became less of a limitation and the majority of new systems supported one or both of these methods. Currently, the standard resolution of a laser printer is 300–400 dots per inch (dpi), while phototypesetters can produce resolution up to 2500 dpi. Laser printer output is still considered to be below publishing industry standards and thus phototypesetters, although far more expensive, are preferred. One main advantage offered by laser printer technology is that all elements of a score (including slurs, beams, and text) can be drawn on the page. The iconic elements are usually drawn as a font (similar to the manner in which text characters are displayed), and the algorithmic elements are calculated mathematically and drawn with the correct shape, angle, and length (Fig. 6).

System Designs

Automated notation systems can be divided into two categories: publisher oriented and composer oriented [9] depending upon the purpose for which the system was designed.

Publisher-oriented systems generally run on minicomputers or high-speed microcomputers and output to laser printers, phototypesetters or pen-plotters. The emphasis in these systems is on high-quality output and precision of image placement; they attempt to produce "engraved-quality" scores. The hardware required by these systems is relatively expensive.

Composer-oriented systems tend to run on personal computers, are interactive in design, and often use synthesizers for score input and audio playback. These systems usually output to dot matrix or laser printers. Here, the emphasis is on efficiency of production rather than on printing quality. Composer-oriented systems are used to produce legible scores and to extract instrumental parts for performance. Since most systems of this type operate on microcomputers, the hardware required is relatively inexpensive.

FIGURE 6.   Output from laser printer (300 dpi) and phototypesetter (1200 dpi).

Software Designs

There has been a wide range of software designs in music printing systems. Fundamentally, two design approaches have been used. Most of the early designs (systems developed from the late 1960s through to the early 1980s) fall into the category of automated or batch systems. These programs take encoded scores, either from a standard music encoding language or from a proprietary representation, and convert the music data into a graphical score representation. In some cases the score is displayed on a computer screen for further editing, in others, the program outputs directly to the printer. Batch processing is a very efficient method of producing a score, but is limited in the complexity of music it can accommodate; since it is highly automated, it only generates music that adheres strictly to standard notational conventions.

The other category of software emphasizes user interaction. These programs usually utilize a high-resolution cathode ray tube (CRT) terminal and have a WYSIWYG (What You See Is What You Get) design. Such a system may convert a score automatically, but allows the user to modify the appearance of the score with interactive editing facilities. This design allows more flexibility than batch systems and can accommodate a wider range of graphical representations. However, because interactive systems are designed to allow the user to alter the images on the screen, they are often less efficient than automated systems. Most recent notation systems (i.e., systems developed since 1985) emphasize interactivity rather than automation. They are better able to replicate the appearance of engraved scores because they allow fine adjustment to the placement of images.

Music Printing Systems

There have been a variety of approaches to designing and developing music printing systems over the past two decades. In most of the early efforts, music notation was not the primary objective or focus of the development. Later, systems were designed specifically for editing and printing scores. A major limitation of the early music printing systems was that they did not allow modifications to be made to the layout of a score or to the position of individual music symbols. Since music notation is a highly complex language which permits variable representations, the automatic translation from encoded music data to graphical symbols sometimes produced aesthetically unsatisfying results. It became apparent that if a music printing system were to recreate the appearance of engraved music, the system had to allow the user to interact with the score before it was sent to the printing device. Thus, the model used by virtually all recently developed notation systems is:

1. The music data are entered into the system by typewriter keyboard, mouse or piano keyboard.
2. The positions of music symbols are calculated, and the score is displayed on a high resolution monitor.
3. Adjustments to the page layout and to the positions of the images are performed using the program's editing capabilities.
4. The finished score is printed.

Encoding Languages

Most music encoding languages were designed to be used in music applications such as musicological databases, thematic indices and music analysis research. In order to see printed output of the music data, notation programs were written to operate in conjunction with these encoding languages. These programs translate the encoded score data into a form

DARMS: !G !K- !M12:8 9E(10 9) 13Q 11E 9(8 9) R Q 9 / 10(9 10) 6Q 10E 11(10 9)

FIGURE 7.   DARMS code and corresponding printed score.

that can be used to drive a printing device. In most cases, the creation of a score is an auto-mated or batch process.

The most widely used music encoding language is DARMS (Digital Alternate Repre-sentation of Musical Scores) [*10*] which was initially developed by Stephan Bauer-Mengel-berg in 1964 and enhanced and extended over the years by Erikson, Wolff, Gomberg, Lincoln, McLean, and Dydo. DARMS was designed to be used both for musicological ap-plications and for automated music printing. Although it has been used most extensively in music databases, it was adopted as a frontend to notation systems by Hall (A-R editions printing system) and Dydo (The Note Processor) [*11*]. In DARMS, all score information is entered as ASCII code, which is then converted to a form readable by the specific applica-tion. Several dialects of DARMS have been developed over the years and there is some incompatibility between the dialects. Despite its ability to encode virtually any score re-gardless of complexity, DARMS has not been widely used for music printing because the task of encoding a score is error-prone and rather laborious. Figure 7 shows an example of one dialect of DARMS along with the score it represents.

Two other encoding languages which have been used for notation are MUSTRAN, developed by Jerome Weker at Indiana University in 1966, and Plaine and Easie, developed by Barry Brook and Murray Gould in the late 1960s [*12*]. The printing extension to MUSTRAN, called SMUT, was written by Donald Byrd in the late 1970s [*9*]. This program allows MUSTRAN-encoded score to be printed on pen plotters. The printing procedures used with Plaine and Easie were developed by Norbert Böker-Heil.

Perhaps the most important music encoding system is MS, which was developed by Leland Smith at Stanford University in the early 1970s [*5*]. Unlike most other encoding languages, MS was designed specifically for music printing. Originally written for the PDP-10 computer and Versatec plotter, a new version of the program, called SCORE™, was released in 1987 for the IBM™-PC and PostScript® laser printers. MS/SCORE is probably the most comprehensive notation system developed; it can accommodate virtually any style of music notation including early music and graphical scores and has sophisticated page formatting and part extraction capabilities. The score is entered as ASCII characters, the images are displayed on screen, and editing is done by altering the parameters associated with each music symbol. Recently, a conversion program has been added so that the music can be entered from a MIDI piano keyboard (Fig. 8).

Publisher-Oriented Systems

A number of publisher-oriented printing systems were developed in the 1970s and early 1980s for use in the music publishing industry. Although only a few publishers used com-puterized printing during this period and the quantity of scores that were produced by com-puter was relatively low, these systems demonstrated to the industry that music engraving and printing could be automated.

Most of the commercial music printing systems run on mainframe computers and output to phototypesetters. Most have relatively complex data entry methods requiring skilled operators. These factors make the systems inappropriate for small publishing houses and for individual composers or copyists. Some systems (i.e., Synclavier Music Engraving System by New England Digital Corporation) are commercially available, others (i.e., Amadeus Music Software by Kurt Maas) are available on a service bureau basis, while others (i.e., Dal Molin's Musicomp system , the A-R Music Engraving System and the Toppan Scan-Note System) are for in-house use only.

Development of Interactive Music Editors

Since one of the most crucial aspects of a music notation system is the ability to adjust the position of the images on the page, the introduction of interactive editing facilities proved to be an essential development for notation systems. The first program to emphasize interactive editing was Mockingbird [*13*] developed at Xerox PARC by John Maxwell and Severo Ornstein in 1983. This system was developed on the Dorado (Xerox 1132) computer as a research project in interactive editing and was never released commercially. A music composition could be played into the system on an electronic keyboard, displayed on the monitor and edited interactively with a mouse and pop-up menus. Although Mockingbird included sophisticated justification and transcription facilities, its most important feature was the ability to adjust the positions of the images and see the results immediately. The design advances made by Mockingbird led the way for a generation of composer-oriented notation systems with a similar interactive design.

Composer-Oriented Systems

With the increase in the performance and power of microcomputers during the mid-1980s, notation software was developed for small, inexpensive computers such as the Apple® Macintosh™. Previously, music software for microcomputers had focused on music pedagogy and simple sound synthesis. However, the graphical orientation and high-resolution monitors of these new microcomputers made them ideal for more advanced applications such as music notation. Most commercial programs were designed to be used by individual composers or music copyists and were loosely modeled on the Mockingbird design; they support interactive editing, usually by means of a mouse, and most permit piano keyboard input and audio playback through MIDI synthesizers.

The universal acceptance of MIDI (Musical Instrument Digital Interface) by the manufacturers of digital synthesizers during the 1980s had an important impact on the music software industry. MIDI is a protocol for communicating music performance information between computers and synthesizers. The availability of compatible synthesizers and MIDI interfaces to microcomputers simplified the task of entering musical data by means of

FIGURE 8.   Printed output from SCORE (IBM-PC and Apple LaserWriter).

a keyboard; any commercial MIDI synthesizer could be used as frontend to a notation program. In addition, it became possible to transfer MIDI data from other music applications such as sequencers directly to notation programs. Within the MIDI environment, it is possible to improvise a new composition on an MIDI synthesizer, record the performance on a sequencer program, then transfer the data to a notation program and print the finished score.

Among the first notation programs to utilize MIDI were Professional Composer™[14] by Mark of the Unicorn, which operated in conjunction with the Performer™ sequencer software and Personal Composer™ [15] by Jim Miller. The essential features of these programs were: MIDI keyboard input, display of the score for interactive editing (including score transposition and part extraction), playback through MIDI synthesizers, and output to dot matrix and laser printers. Although both of these programs had limitations in the complexity of scores they could accommodate and in the quality of their printed output, they represented a new direction for notation software—the vast majority of later composer-oriented systems followed the basic design of these programs.

The main enhancements found in subsequent programs were improved editing facilities, increased flexibility in the positioning of images, and adjustment of images and more sophisticated data conversion procedures. As laser printing technology improved and programs supported device-independent printing languages such as PostScript® [6] by Adobe Systems, Inc., the microcomputer-based systems were able to perform comparably to many publisher-oriented systems. NoetWriter™ [17] by Passport Designs and Finale™ by Coda Music Software are two examples of software packages which run on Macintosh computers and are capable of producing engraved-quality copy; Scores generated for the program can be printed on PostScript laser printers and phototypesetters and can be exported to a variety of desktop publishing applications (Fig. 9).

FUTURE PROSPECTS

Standardization

Despite the fact that MIDI has provided a communication protocol and standard file format, there still is no consensus on the internal representation of score data in computers, and thus no direct compatibility between notation programs. To overcome this problem, the American National Standards Institute (ANSI) established a subcommittee to develop a standard for machine interchange of musical information (MIPS-Musical Interchange Processing Standard). This standard, when introduced, will allow direct communication between all music applications, whether they are designed for music performance, notation, composition or analysis.

Optical Scanning

Although the use of a MIDI keyboard for score input has increased the efficiency of notation programs, the entry of music data remains the most time-consuming task in preparing a score. Although keyboard input is an efficient input method for relatively simple scores, it does not easily accommodate complex rhythmic materials or unusual notational conventions. Optical scanning of scores, however, has long been proposed as the most effective input method to a notation program. If an existing score, either printed or in rough draft, could be scanned and the music data captured, the score could be edited and altered, then printed. Initial research in optical scanning was done by Prerau [19] at MIT in the early 1970s. At that time, the technology was insufficient for the task and only very simple music could be accurately captured. Recently, research in the optical scanning of music has re-emerged and the prospects are much more promising. It is much more difficult to extract data from music scores than from text documents because of the high degree of variability in the position and graphical appearance of individual images. (For example, an eight note may have a flag above the note, below the note, or may be part of a beamed group of notes.) As research continues, several projects report high rates of accuracy with printed scores, although no system is yet capable of transcribing handdrawn music. The main centers of this research are Waseda University and Osaka University in Japan, McGill University and the University of Ottawa in Canada, and University of Surrey and University of Wales in Great Britain [11]. In addition, a number of commercial software companies are currently revising their programs to include optical scanning as a score input method. Although the early implementations of optical scanning in notation programs will have limitations, the dramatic increase in efficiency of this input method over all others makes it well worth pursuing.

Automatic Transcription

The direct conversion of sound into score has been an area of ongoing research at the Massachusetts Insitute of Technology [20], Stanford University[21], and Soviet Academy of Sciences [22]. At present, the transcription systems are limited to monophonic (i.e. single-voiced) or simple chordal music. With continued development, they may one day provide

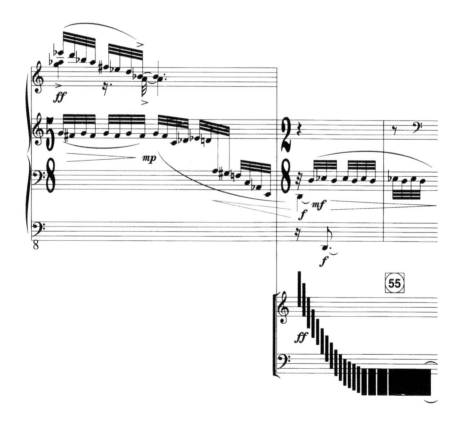

FIGURE 9.   Printed output from NoteWriter (Apple Macintosh and Linotronic™ photo-typesetting).

us with a totally automated music system—one that transcribes directly from live performance to printed score.

ACKNOWLEDGMENTS

Apple is a registered trademark of Apple Computers, Inc.
Macintosh and LaserWriter are trademarks for Apple Computers, Inc.
IBM is a trade mark of International Business Machines.
Linotronic is a trademark of Allied Corporation
PostScript is a registered trademark of Adobe Systems, Inc.
SCORE and NoteWriter are trademarks of Passport Designs Inc.
Professional Composer and Performer are trademarks of Mark of the Unicorn.
Personal Composer is a trademark of Jim Miller.
Finale is a trademark of Coda Music Software.

REFERENCES

1. J. Berlin, *Première Fantasie*, Editions du Centre National de la Recherche Scientifique, Cedex, France, 1976.
2. L. Berio, *Sequenza III*, Universal Edition, London, 1968.
3. M. Kagel, *Transición II für klavier, schlagzeug und zewi tonbänder*, Universal Edition, 1963.
4. K. Stickney, "Computer Tools for Engraved-Quality Music Notation," *Proc. AES 5th Int. Conf.: Music and Digital Technology*, Los Angeles, 1987.
5. L. Smith, "Editing and Printing Music by Computer," *J. Music Theory, 17*, 292–309 (1973).
6. L. Hiller, and R. Baker, "Automated Music Printing," *J. Music Theory, 9*, 129–152 (1965).
7. D. Byrd, "A System for Music Printing by Computer," *Computers Humanities, 8*, 161–172 (1974).
8. A. Dal Molin, "A Terminal for Music Manuscript Input," *Computers Humanities, 12*, 287–289 (1978).
9. D. Byrd, *Music Notation by Computer*, Ph.D. dissertation Department of Computer Science, Indiana University, University Microfilms, Ann Arbor, 1974.
10. R. Erikson, "The DARMS Project: A Status Report," *Computers Humanities, 9*, 291–298, (1975).
11. W. Hewlett, and E. Selfridge-Field (eds.), *Directory of Computer Assisted Research in Musicology 1988*, Center for Computer Assisted Research in the Humanities, Menlo Park, CA. 1988.
12. W. Hewlett, and E. Selfridge-Field (eds.), *Directory of Computer Assisted Research in Musicology 1987*, Center for Computer Assisted Research in the Humanities, Menlo Park, CA. 1987.
13. J. Maxwell, and S. Ornstein, *Mockingbird: A Composer's Amanuensis*, Xerox Palo Alto Research Center, Palo Alto, CA, 1983.
14. C. Yavelow, "Music Software for the Apple Macintosh," *Computer Music J., 9*(3), 52-67, (1985).
15. J. Miller, "Personal Composer," *Composer Music J., 9*(4), 74-75 (1985).

16. Adobe Systems Inc., *PostScript Language Reference Manual*, Addison-Wesley, Reading, MA, 1985.
17. K. Hamel, *NoteWriter II Reference Manual*, Passport Designs, Inc., Half Moon Bay, CA, 1989.
18. Coda Music Software, *Finale Reference Manual*, Coda Music Software, Bloomington, MN, 1988.
19. D. Prerau, "Computer Pattern Recognition of Printed Music," Proc. Fall Joint Computer Conf., 1971.
20. B. Vercoe, and D. Cumming, "Connect Machine Tracking of Polyphonic Audio," in *Proc. 1988 International Computer Conference*, Cologne, 1988, pp. 211–218.
21. J. Moorer, "On the Transcription of Music Sound by Computer," *Computer Music J.,* *1*(4), 32–38 (1977).
22. A. S. Tanguiane, "An Algorithm for Recognition of Chords," Proc. 1988 Int. Computer Conference, Cologne, 1988, pp. 199–210.

BIBLIOGRAPHY

Boretz, B. and E. Cone (eds.), *Perspectives on Notation and Performance*, W. W. Norton, New York, 1976.

Byrd, D., *Music Notation By Computer*, Ph.D. dissertation, Department of Computer Science, Indiana University, University Microfilms, Ann Arbor, 1974.

Hamel, K., "Issues in the Design of Music Notation Software," in *Proc. 1987 Int. Computer Music Conf.*, University of Illinois at Urbana-Champagne, 1987, pp. 325–332.

Hewlett, W. and E. Selfridge-Field (eds.), *Directory of Computer Assisted Research in Musicology 1987*, Center for Computer Assisted Research in the Humanities, Menlo Park, CA, 1987.

Hewlett, W. and E. Selfridge-Field (eds.), *Directory of Computer Assisted Research in Musicology 1988*, Center for Computer Assisted Research in the Humanities, Menlo Park, CA, 1988.

Rastall, R., *The Notation of Western Music*, J. M. Dent and Sons, London, 1983.

Read, G., *Music Notation*, 2nd ed., Allyn and Bacon, Boston, 1969.

Read, G., *Source Book of Proposed Notation Reforms*, Greenwood Press, New York, 1987.

Ross, T., *The Art of Music Engraving and Processing*, 2nd ed., Hanson Books, Miami, 1970.

Stone, K., *Music Notation in the Twentieth Century*, W. W. Norton, New York, 1980.

KEITH A. HAMEL

THE NUMERICAL SOLUTION OF MARKOV CHAINS

INTRODUCTION

It is possible often to represent the behavior of a physical system by describing all the different states that the system may occupy and by indicating how the system moves from one state to another in time. Under suitable conditions, the system may be represented by a Markov process. Examples of the application of Markov processes may be found extensively throughout the biological, physical, and social sciences as well as in business and engineering.

Each Markov process has associated with it a (possibly infinite) set of states. When the state space is discrete, the term Markov chain is used. The system being modeled by this process is assumed to occupy one and only one of these states at any given time. The evolution of this system is represented by transitions of the Markov process from one state to another. These transitions are assumed to occur instantaneously, in other words, the actual business of moving from one state to another consumes zero time. The fundamental property of a Markovian system, referred to as the Markov property, is that the future evolution of the system depends only on the current state of the system and not on its past history.

The information we would like to obtain from the model is a knowledge of the probabilities of being in a given state or set of states at a certain time after the system becomes operational. Most often this time is taken to be sufficiently long that all influence of the initial starting state has been erased. The probabilities thus obtained are called the *long-run* or *stationary* probabilities. Other measures of interest include the time taken until a certain state is reached for the first time, etc.

If we let q_{ij} denote the rate at which the system moves from state i to state j, then it may be shown that the stationary probability vector π, a row vector whose k-th element denotes the stationary probability of being in state k, can be obtained by solving the homogeneous system of equations $\pi Q = 0$. Alternatively, the problem may be formulated as an eigenvalue problem $\pi P = \pi$ where $P = Q\Delta t + I$ is the stochastic matrix of transition probabilities [Δt must be chosen sufficiently small so that the probability of two or more transitions occurring in time Δt is small, i.e., of order $o(t)$], Mathematically, the problem is therefore quite simple. Unfortunately, problems arise from the computational point of view because of the extremely large number of states which many systems may occupy. It is not uncommon for thousands of states to be generated even for simple applications.

In this article, most of our attention will be devoted to computational methods for stationary distributions of irreducible Markov chains. The final section, however, will treat the question of computational methods for transient solutions. We begin our discussions with an examination of the relative advantages and disadvantages of iterative and direct solution methods. We shall show that iterative methods are generally preferred, unless the infinitesimal generator has some special structure which makes a direct method more efficient. In subsequent sections we discuss direct methods and show how to implement them in a computationally efficient manner. Basic vector iteration methods are also considered, in particular, we examine the power method, forward and backward Gauss-Seidel, and SOR methods and preconditioned power iterations. Iterative methods that incorporate a subspace of vectors are treated. These go under the more generic name of *projection techniques*, and have been shown in comparison testing to be among the most effective for general Markov chain problems. We then turn to methods that are appropriate when the infinitesimal generator has a special block structure. We show that great care must be exercised when solving such systems using recursion, and provide conditions to indicate when recursive methods should and should not be used. We briefly introduce the *matrix-geometric* methods of Neuts. Again these may be applied when the infinitesimal generator is block Hessenberg and the individual blocks satisfy additional constraints. The final methods considered for the computation of stationary solutions are the decompositional methods. These are extremely valuable when the matrix is *nearly-completely-decomposable* (NCD), a situation which often arises in practice. Finally, as we mentioned above, methods for the transient solution are provided. Here most of our attentions will be given to the randomized method.

It is obviously impossible in a single article to cover the entire field of the numerical solution of Markov chains, a field that has been in constant evolution from the initial papers of Wallace and his colleagues [1-3]. To make up for this, we have provided an extensive bibliography at the end of this article. We hope that this will provide readers with all the further reading material they are likely to need. Some papers are of a general interest [4-7]. Although there currently are no texts devoted to the numerical solution of Markov chains, some that should provide valuable information are noted [8-14].

Finally, we would like to point out that most of the numerical methods discussed in this article have been incorporated into the software package, *MARCA: Markov Chain Analyzer* [15]. In addition to solution techniques, this package also provides a means for automatically generating infinitesimal generators from a general description of a Markov chain and of analyzing these generators for cyclic and near-complete-decomposable properties.

ITERATIVE AND DIRECT SOLUTION METHODS

Iterative methods of one type or another are by far the most commonly used methods for obtaining the stationary probability vector from either the stochastic transition probability matrix or from the infinitesimal generator. There are several important reasons for this choice. First, an examination of the iterative methods usually employed shows that the only operations in which the matrices are involved are multiplications with one or more vectors, or with preconditioners. These operations do not alter the form of the matrix. Thus compact storage schemes, which minimize the amount of memory required to store the matrix and which in addition are well suited to matrix multiplication, may be conveniently implemented. Since the matrices involved usually are large and very sparse, the savings made by such schemes can be considerable. With direct equations-solving methods, the elimination of one non-zero element of the matrix during the reduction phase often results in the creation of several non-zero elements in positions which previously contained zero. This is called fill-in and not only does it make the organization of a compact storage scheme more difficult, since provision must be made for the deletion and the insertion of elements, but in addition, the amount of fill-in can often be so extensive that available memory is quickly exhausted. A successful direct method must incorporate a means of overcoming these difficulties.

Iterative methods have other advantages. Use may be made of good initial approximations to the solution vector and this is especially beneficial when a series of related experiments is being conducted. In such circumstances the parameters of one experiment often differ only slightly from those of the previous; many will remain unchanged. Consequently, it is to expected that the solution to the new experiment will be close to that of the previous and it is advantageous to use the previous result as the new initial approximation. If indeed there is little change, we should expect to compute the new result in relatively few iterations.

An iterative process may be halted once a prespecified tolerance criterion has been satisfied, and this may be relatively lax. For example, it may be wasteful to compute the solution of a mathematical model correct to full machine precision when the model itself contains errors of the order of 5–10%. A direct method is obligated to continue until the final specified operation has been carried out.

Finally, with iterative methods, the matrix is never altered and hence the build-up of rounding error is, to all intents and purposes, nonexistent.

For these reasons, iterative methods have traditionally been preferred to direct methods. However, iterative methods have a major disadvantage in that often they require a very long time to converge to the desired solution. More advanced iterative techniques such as the method of Arnoldi, have helped to alleviate this problem but much research still remains to be done, particularly in estimating a priori, the number of iterations, and hence the time, required for convergence. Direct methods have the advantage that an upper bound on the time required to obtain the solution may be determined before the calculation is initiated. More important, for certain classes of problem, direct methods often result in a much more accurate answer being obtained in *less time*. Since iterative method will in general require less memory than direct methods, these latter can only be recommended if they obtain the solution in less time. Unfortunately, it is often difficult to predict when a direct solver will be more efficient than an iterative solver.

DIRECT SOLUTION METHODS

We are concerned with obtaining the stationary probability vector π from the equations:

$$\pi Q = 0, \pi \geq 0, \pi e = 1 \tag{1}$$

i.e., a homogeneous system of n linear equations in n unknowns. In this article the vector e is a column vector whose elements are all equal to 1. Also, we shall need to introduce the vector e_i, a column vector who's elements are all equal to zero except the i-th which is equal to 1. ·

The system of Eq. (1) has a solution other than the trivial solution ($\pi_i = 0$, for all i) if and only if the determinant of the coefficient matrix is zero, i.e., if and only if the coefficient matrix is singular. Since the determinant of a matrix is equal to the product of its eigenvalues and since Q possesses a zero eigenvalue, the singularity of Q and hence the *existence* of a nontrivial solution, follows. It is known that if the matrix Q is irreducible, there exists lower and upper triangular matrices L and U such that

$$Q^T = LU. \tag{2}$$

Once an *LU* decomposition has been determined, a forward substitution step followed by a backward substitution is usually sufficient to determine the solution of the system of equations.

For example, suppose we are required to solve $Ax = b$ with $det(A) \neq 0$ and $b \neq 0$ and suppose further than the decomposition $A = LU$ is available so that $LUx = b$. By setting $Ux = z$, the vector z may be obtained by forward substitution on $Lz = b$, since both L and b are known quantities. The solution x may subsequently be obtained from $Ux = z$ by backward substitution since by this time both U and z are known quantities. However, in the case of the numerical solution of Markov chains, the system of equations, $\pi Q = 0$, is homogeneous, i.e., $b = 0$, and the coefficient matrix is singular. In this case, the final row of U (assuming that the decomposition is such that the diagonal elements of L are set to unity) is equal to zero. Proceeding as indicated above for the nonhomogeneous case, we have

$$Q^T x = (LU)x = 0. \tag{3}$$

If we now set $Ux = z$ and attempt to solve $Lz = 0$ we find that, since L is nonsingular, we must have $z = 0$. Let us now proceed to the back substitution on $Ux = z = 0$ when $u_{nn} = 0$. It is evident that we may assign any non-zero value to x_n, say $x_n = \eta$, and then determine, by simple back-substitution, the remaining elements of the vector x in terms of η. We have $x_i = c_i \eta$ for some constants c_i, $i = 1, 2, \ldots, n$, and $c_n = 1$. Thus the solution obtained depends on the value of η. There still remains one equation that the elements of a probability vector must satisfy, namely that the sum of the probabilities must be one. Consequently, normalizing the solution obtained from solving $Ux = 0$ so that the conservation of probability condition holds, yields the desired unique stationary probability vector π corresponding to the infinitesimal generator Q.

An alternative approach to this use of the normalization equation is to replace the last equation of the original system with $\pi e = 1$. If the Markov chain is irreducible, this will ensure that the coefficient matrix is nonsingular. Furthermore, the system of equations will no longer be homogeneous (since the right-hand side is now e_n), and so the solution may be computed without problem.

Of course, it is not necessary to replace the last equation of the system by the normalization equation. Indeed, an equation could be replaced. However, this is generally undesirable, for it will entail more numerical computation. For example, if the first equation is replaced, the first row of the coefficient matrix will contain all ones and the right-hand side will be e_1. The first consequence of this is that during the forward substitution stage, the entire sequence of operations must be performed to obtain the vector z; whereas if the last equation is replaced, it is possible to read off the solution immediately, i.e., $z_1 = z_2 = \ldots z_{n-1} = 0$ and $z_n = 1$. The second and more damaging consequence is that substantial fill-in will occur since a multiple of the first row which contains all ones must be added to *all* remaining rows and a cascading effect will undoubtedly occur in all subsequent reduction steps.

Inverse Iteration

Inverse iteration is the method of choice for the direct solution of $\pi Q = 0$. Although this may sound rather like a contradiction in terms, inverse iteration, when applied to an infinitesimal generator matrix Q to obtain the stationary probability vector π, requires only a single iteration to determine π. It reduces to the standard LU decomposition method with special treatment of the zero pivot and the right-hand side vector.

Consider an iterative scheme based on the relation

$$x^{(k)} = (Q^T - \mu I)^{-1} x^{(k-1)}. \tag{4}$$

Let $x^{(0)}$ be an arbitrary column vector that can be written as a linear combination of the right-hand eigenvectors of Q^T; i.e.,

$$x^{(0)} = \sum_{i=1}^{n} \alpha_i v_i, \tag{5}$$

where the vectors v_i are the right eigenvectors of the matrix Q^T corresponding to the eigenvalues λ_i, i.e.,

$$Q^T v_i = \lambda_i v_i; \; i = 1, 2, ..., n. \tag{6}$$

Then

$$x^{(k)} = (Q^T - \mu I)^{-k} x^{(0)} = \sum_{i=1}^{n} \alpha_i (\lambda_i - \mu)^{-k} v_i \tag{7}$$

$$= (\lambda_r - \mu)^{-k} [\alpha_r v_r + \sum_{i \ne r} \alpha_i (\lambda_r - \mu)^k (\lambda_i - \mu)^{-k} v_i]. \tag{8}$$

Consequently, if for all $i \ne r$, $|\lambda_r - \mu| << |\lambda_i - \mu|$ convergence to the eigenvector v_r is rapid since $[(\lambda_r - \mu)/(\lambda_i - \mu)]^k$ will rapidly tend to zero. If $\mu = \lambda_r$, then the summation in Eq. (8) is zero and the eigenvector v_r will be obtained in a single iteration.

Note that when implementing inverse iteration, there is no need to explicitly form the inverse of the shifted matrix $(Q^T - \mu I)$. Instead, the approach generally adopted is to solve the set of linear equations

$$(Q^T - \mu I) x^{(k)} = x^{(k-1)}.$$

This obviously is identical to the original formulation in Eq. (4). If μ is not an eigenvalue of Q, then $(Q^T - \mu I)$ is nonsingular and for $x^{(k-1)} \ne 0$, an LU decomposition approach can be implemented without further ado.

If μ is an eigenvalue of Q (i.e., $\mu = \lambda_r$), then $(Q^T - \mu I)$ is singular. In this case the zero pivot which arises during the LU decomposition should be replaced by a small value ε. This should be chosen as the smallest representable number such that $1 + \varepsilon > 1$ on the particular computer being used. After one iteration, this approach results in a very accurate eigenvector.

In our particular case we are looking for the right eigenvector corresponding to the zero eigenvalue of Q^T. Therefore, letting $\mu = 0$ in the iteration formula, we get

$$(Q^T - 0I) x^{(k)} = Q^T x^{(k)} = x^{(k-1)} \tag{9}$$

and thus we are simply required to solve

$$Q^T x^{(1)} = x^{(0)} \tag{10}$$

Note that choosing $x^{(0)} = e_n$ reduces the amount of computation involved. The iteration simply reduces to the back substitution step

$$U x^{(1)} = \frac{1}{e_n}, \tag{11}$$

An appropriate normalization of $x^{(1)}$ will yield the stationary probability vector, i.e.,

$$\pi^T = \frac{1}{e^T x^{(1)}} x^{(1)}. \tag{12}$$

For more information on these and other direct methods, including sensitivity analyses, the reader should consult the relevant references [16–21].

Compact Storage Schemes for Direct Methods

Frequently the matrices generated from Markov models are too large to permit regular two-dimensional arrays to be used to store them in computer memory. Since these matrices are usually very sparse, it is economical, and indeed necessary, to use some sort of packing scheme whereby only the non-zero elements and their positions in the matrix are stored.

Assume, as is usually the case, that the coefficient matrix can be derived row by row. Then, immediately after the second row has been obtained, it is possible to eliminate the element in position (2,1) by adding a multiple of the first row to it. This process may be continued so that when the i-th row of the coefficient matrix is generated, rows 1 through $(i - 1)$ have been derived and are already reduced to upper triangular form. The first $(i - 1)$ rows may therefore be used to eliminate all non-zero elements in row i from column positions $(i, 1)$ through $(i, i - 1)$, thus putting it into the desired triangular form. Note that since this reduction is performed on Q^T, it is the columns of the infinitesimal generator that are required to be generated one at a time and not its rows.

This method has a distinct advantage in that once a row has been generated in this fashion, no more fill-in will occur into this row. It is suggested that a separate storage area be reserved to hold temporarily a single unreduced row. The reduction is performed in this storage area. Once completed, the reduced row may be compacted into any convenient form and appended to the rows which have already been reduced. In this way no storage space is wasted holding subdiagonal elements which, due to elimination, have become zero, nor in reserving space for the inclusion of additional elements. The storage scheme should be chosen bearing in mind the fact that these rows will be used in the reduction of further rows and also later in the algorithm during the back-substitution phase.

Since the form of the matrix will no longer be altered, the efficient storage schemes which are used with many iterative methods can be adopted. Note that this approach can not be used for solving general systems of linear equations because it inhibits a pivoting strategy from being implemented. It is valid when solving irreducible Markov chains since pivoting is not required in order that the LU decomposition of an infinitesimal generator matrix Q^T be performed in a stable manner.

SINGLE VECTOR ITERATIONS

The Power Method

The simplest iteration method for computing the dominant eigenvector of a matrix A is the single vector iteration

$$x^{(k+1)} = \frac{1}{\xi^{(k)}} A x^{(k)}$$

where $\xi^{(k)}$ is a normalizing factor, typically the component of the vector $Ax^{(k)}$ that has the largest modulus. For our situation the matrix of interest A is P^T. Since we know that the matrix has row sums equal to 1 and has 1 as the dominant eigenvalue, we can safely skip the normalizing factor and the above iteration takes the form

$$x^{(k+1)} = P^T x^{(k)} \tag{13}$$

$$= x^{(k)} - Q^T x^{(k)} \tag{14}$$

One problem with this simple scheme is that its rate of convergence can be very slow. The convergence factor for the eigenvector corresponding to the dominant eigenvalue λ_1 is given by λ_2/λ_1, where λ_2 is the subdominant eigenvalue. In situations where the eigenvalues cluster around λ_1, as is the case for nearly decomposable systems, the convergence can be unacceptably slow.

Gauss-Seidel Iteration and Successive Overrelaxation

Relaxation schemes are based on the decomposition

$$Q^T = D - E - F$$

where D is the diagonal of Q^T, $-E$ is the strict lower part of Q^T and $-F$ its strict upper part. The Gauss-Seidel iteration then takes the form

$$(D - E)x^{(k+1)} = Fx^{(k)}. \tag{15}$$

This corresponds to correcting the j-th component of the current approximate solution, for $j = 1, 2, \ldots n$, i.e., from top to bottom, by making the j-th component of the residual vector equal to zero. To denote specifically the direction of solution this is sometimes referred to as *forward* Gauss-Seidel. A *backward* Gauss-Seidel iteration takes the form

$$(D - F)x^{(k+1)} = Ex^{(k)} \tag{16}$$

and corresponds to correcting the components from bottom to top.

Note that convergence of the above (forward) iteration is governed by the spectral radius of $(D - E)^{-1} F$. Convergence may sometimes be improved by using the alternative splitting

$$\omega Q^T = (D - \omega E) - (\omega F + (1 - \omega)D)$$

which leads to the iteration, called successive overrelaxation, (SOR)

$$(D - \omega E)x^{(k+1)} = (\omega F + (1 - \omega D))x^{(k)}. \tag{17}$$

A backward SOR relaxation may also be written.

For many problems there exist some value of ω which provides the best possible convergence rate. The resulting optimal convergence rate can be a considerable improvement over Gauss-Seidel. The choice of an optimal, or even a reasonable, value for ω has been the subject of much study, especially for problems arising in the numerical solution of partial differential equations [22]. Some results have been obtained for certain classes of matrices. Unfortunately, very little is known at present for arbitrary nonsymmetric linear systems.

As a general rule, it is best to use a forward iterative method when the preponderance of the element mass is to be found below the diagonal for in this case, the iterative method essentially works with inverse of the lower triangular portion of the matrix and intuitively, the closer this is to the inverse of the entire matrix, the faster the convergence. On the other hand, the backward iterative schemes work with the inverse of the upper triangular portion and these methods work best when the non-zero mass lies above and on the diagonal. We point out that some specialized counter examples exist which make the above recommendations only rules of thumb [23].

Little information is available on the effect of the ordering of the state space on the convergence of these iterative methods. Examples are available in which Gauss-Seidel works extremely well for one ordering but not at all for an opposing ordering [24]. In these examples the magnitude of the non-zero elements appears to have little effect on the speed of convergence. It appears that an ordering that in some sense preserves the direction of probability flow works best.

For further information on convergence and convergence properties appropriate references are listed [8, 25, 26].

SSOR Iteration

The Symmetric Successive Overrelaxation method (SSOR) consists of following a relaxation sweep from top down by a relaxation sweep from bottom up. Thus, the case $\omega = 1$ corresponding to a SGS (Symmetric Gauss Seidel) scheme would be as follows:

$$(D - E)x^{(k+1/2)} = Fx^{(k)} \tag{18}$$

$$(D - F)x^{(k+1)} = Ex^{(k+1/2)} \tag{19}$$

while for arbitrary ω, it is:

$$(D - \omega E)x^{(k+1/2)} = (\omega F + 1(1 - \omega D))x^{(k)} \tag{20}$$

$$(D - \omega F)x^{(k+1)} = (\omega E + 1(1 - \omega D))x^{(k+1/2)} \tag{21}$$

The main attraction of SSOR schemes is that the iteration matrix is similar to a symmetric matrix when the original matrix Q^T is symmetric. This situation rarely occurs in Markov chain models. SSOR does however, help to reduce poor convergence behavior that results from a badly ordered state space.

Preconditioned Power Iterations

As was already mentioned the power method can be extremely slow to converge when the subdominant eigenvalue is very close to one. The relaxation schemes described above typically have a better convergence rate. This means that the iteration matrices corresponding to these schemes have an eigenvalue λ_2 farther away from 1 than the original matrix.

Preconditioning is a technique whereby the original system of equations is modified in such a way that the solution is unchanged but the distribution of the eigenvalues is better suited for iterative methods. In a general context, a preconditioning technique consists of replacing a system $Ax = b$ by a modified system such as $M^{-1}Ax = M^{-1}b$. Here M is a preconditioning matrix for which the solution of $Mx = y$ is inexpensive [27]. When the coefficient matrix is singular and the right hand side is zero, the method turns out to be equivalent to the power method applied to the matrix $(I - M^{-1} A)$.

We have seen that for the numerical solution of Markov chain problems, the power method may be written as

$$x^{(k+1)} = x^{(k)} - Q^T x^{(k)} \qquad (22)$$

$$= (I - Q^T) x^{(k)} \qquad (23)$$

Here preconditioning involves premultiplying the matrix Q^T with a matrix M^{-1}, generally chosen so that M approximates Q^T but is such that its LU decomposition can be efficiently determined. In this case, the iteration matrix $(I - M^{-1} Q^T)$ has one unit eigenvalue and the remaining eigenvalues are (hopefully) all close to zero, leading to a rapidly converging iterative procedure. We refer to such methods as *preconditioned power iterations, or fixed point iterations.*

Gauss-Seidel, SOR, and SSOR Preconditionings

A look at Eq. (15) reveals an interesting connection with the power method. We can rewrite Eq. (15) as

$$x^{(k+1)} = (D - E)^{-1} F x^{(k)}$$

$$(D - E)^{-1} \Big((D - E) - Q^T \Big) x^{(k)}$$

$$x^{(k)} - (D - E)^{-1} Q^T x^{(k)}$$

Comparing this with Eq. (14), we observe that the above iteration is simply the power method applied to the matrix

$$I - (D - E)^{-1} Q^T. \qquad (24)$$

Thus $(D - E)$ performs the role of the preconditioning matrix M. As a result we may view the Gauss-Seidel method as a preconditioned power iteration. It is an attempt to reduce λ_2, without changing the eigenvector.

The solution to the above system is identical with that of the original one. Its rate of convergence, on the other hand, may be substantially faster than that of the original problem. For this reason we will refer to the system (24) as the Gauss-Seidel preconditioned version of $Q^T x = 0$. Similarly one can define an SOR preconditioning and an SSOR preconditioning.

ILU Preconditioning

By far the most popular preconditioning techniques are the incomplete LU factorization techniques. These are sometimes also referred to as *combined direct-iterative* methods. Such methods are composed of two phases. First we start out by initiating an LU decomposition of Q^T. At various points in the computation, non-zero elements may be omitted according to various rules. Some possibilities are discussed in the following paragraphs. In all cases, instead of arriving at an exact LU decomposition, what we obtain is of the form

$$Q^T = LU - E$$

where E, called the remainder, is expected to be small in some sense. When this has been achieved, the *direct* phase of the computation is completed. In the second phase, this (incomplete) factorization is incorporated into an iterative procedure by writing

$$Q^T x = (LU - E)x = 0$$

and then using

$$LUx^{(k+1)} = Ex^{(k)}$$

or equivalently

$$x^{(k+1)} = x^{(k)} - (LU)^{-1} Q^T x^{(k)}$$

as the iteration scheme. Note that this is the same as solving the preconditioned (from the left) system of equations

$$U^{-1}L^{-1}Q^T x = 0$$

by the power method.

Here we describe three different incomplete factorizations. The first, which is called ILU(0), has been widely discussed and found to be successful especially when applied to systems of equations that arise in the solution of elliptic partial differential equations. Given the matrix Q^T, this ILU factorization consists of performing the usual Gaussian Elimination factorization and dropping any fill-in that occurs during the process. In other words,

$$Q^T = LU + E \tag{25}$$

where L is unit lower triangular, U is upper triangular, and $L + U$ has the same zero structure as the matrix Q^T.

The second incomplete factorization that we studied is a threshold based scheme. Here the decomposition proceeds in a manner similar to that described for the implementation of GE. However, after a row of the matrix has been reduced and before that row is recompacted and stored, each non-zero element is examined. If the absolute value of any element in the row is less than a prespecified threshold, then it is replaced by zero. Similarly, if any of the multipliers formed during the reduction are less than the threshold, they are also dropped from further consideration. The only exceptions to this drop threshold are the diagonal elements which are kept no matter how small they become. We refer to this incomplete factorization technique as ILUTH.

The final type of incomplete factorization we mention, is based on a realization that only a fixed amount of memory may be available to store the incomplete factors, L and U, so only a fixed number of non-zero elements are kept in each row. These are usually chosen to be the largest in magnitude. The algorithm proceeds in the same way as ILUTH. When a row has been reduced, a search is conducted to find the K largest elements in absolute value. This search is conducted over both the multipliers and the non-zero elements to the right of the diagonal element. As before, the diagonal elements are kept regardless of their magnitude. In our experiments, this incomplete factorization is referred to as ILUK.

Although the above three ILU factorizations are the only ones we considered, there are other possibilities [e.g., *28*]. However, we believe that ILU0, ILUTH, and ILUK will be the most effective for Markov chain problems.

PROJECTION TECHNIQUES

General Projection Processes

An idea that is basic to sparse linear systems and eigenvalue problems is that of projection processes [*29*]. Given a subspace K spanned by a system of m vectors $V \equiv [v_1, \ldots, v_m]$ a projection process onto $K \equiv span \{V\}$ finds an approximation to the original problem from the subspace K. For a linear system $Ax = b$, this is done by writing $x = Vy$ and requiring that the residual vector $b - AVy$ be orthogonal to some subspace L, not necessarily equal to K. If a basis for L is $W = span \{w_1, w_2, \ldots, w_m\}$ then this yields the condition:

$$W^T(b - AVy) = 0$$

or

$$\tilde{x} = V[W^TAV]^{-1}W^Tb \tag{26}$$

For an eigenvalue problem $Ax = \lambda x$, we seek an approximate eigenvalue $\tilde{\lambda} \in C$ and an approximate eigenvector $x \in K$ such that the residual vector $Ax - \lambda x$ is orthogonal to the subspace L. Writing again $x = Vy$ and translating this Petrov-Galerkin condition yields,

$$W^T(AVy - \tilde{\lambda}Vy) = 0$$

or

$$[W^TAVy] = \tilde{\lambda}W^TVy \tag{27}$$

which is a generalized eigenvalue problem of dimension m. The minimum assumptions that must be made in order for these projection processes to be feasible are that W^TAV be nonsingular for linear systems and that W^TV be nonsingular for eigenvalue problems. Clearly this will provide m approximate eigenpairs λ_i, x_i. In most algorithms, the matrix W^TV is the identity matrix, in which case the approximate eigenvalues of A are the eigenvalues of the $m \times m$ matrix $C = W^TAV$. The corresponding approximate eigenvectors are vectors Vy_i where y_i are the eigenvectors of C. Similarly the approximate Schur vectors are the vector columns of VU, where $U = [u_1, u_2, \ldots, u_m]$ are the Schur vectors of C, i.e., U^HCU is quasi-upper triangular. A common particular case is when $K = L$ and $V = W$ is an orthogonal basis of K. This is then referred to as an orthogonal projection process.

Subspace Iteration

One of the simplest methods for computing invariant subspaces is called subspace iteration. In its simplest form the subspace iteration can be described as follows [*30–33*].

Subspace Iteration

1. Choose an initial orthonormal system $V_0 \equiv [v_1, v_2, \ldots, v_m]$ and an integer k;
2. Compute $X = A^kV_0$ and orthonormalize X to get V.

3. Perform an orthogonal projection process onto *span* {V}.
4. Test for convergence. If satisfied then exit else continue.
5. Take $V_0 = VU$, the set of approximate Schur vectors (alternatively take $V_0 = VY$, the set of approximate eigenvectors), choose a new k and go to 2.

The above algorithm utilizes the matrix A only to compute successive matrix by vector products $w = Av$, so sparsity can be exploited. However, it is known to be a slow method, often much slower than some of the alternatives to be described next. In fact, a more satisfactory alternative is to use a Chebyshev-Subspace iteration: step 2 is replaced by $X = t_k(A)V_0$, where t_k is obtained from the Chebyshev polynomial of the first kind of degree k, by a linear change of variables. The three-term recurrence of Chebyshev polynomial allows to compute a vector $W = t_k(A)V$ at almost the same cost as A^kV. Performance can be dramatically improved. Details on implementation and some experiments are described by Saad [*34*].

Arnoldi's Method

A second technique used in the literature is Arnoldi's method [*35, 36*] which is an orthogonal projection process onto $K_m = span$ {$v_1, A^{v-1}, \ldots, A^{m-1} v_1$}. The algorithm starts with some non-zero vector v_1 and generates the sequence of vectors v_i from the following algorithm.

Algorithm: Arnoldi

1. *Initialize*: Choose an initial vector v_1 of norm unity.
2. *Iterate*: Do $j = 1, 2, \ldots, m$
   1. Compute $w := Av_j$
   2. Compute a set of j coefficients h_{ij} so that

$$w := w - \sum_{i=1}^{j} h_{ij}v_i \tag{28}$$

   is orthogonal to all previous v_i's.
   3. Compute $h_{j+1,j} = \|w\|_2$ and $v_{j+1} = w/h_{j+1,j}$.

By construction, the above algorithm produces an orthonormal basis of the Krylov subspace $K_m = span$ {$v_1, A^{v-1}, \ldots, A^{m-1} v_1$}. The $m \times m$ upper Hessenberg matrix H_m consisting of the coefficients h_{ij} computed by the algorithm represents the restriction of the linear transformation A to the subspace K_m, with respect to this basis, i.e., we have $H_m = V_m^T A V_m$, where $V_m = [v_1, v_2, \ldots, v_m]$. Approximations to some of the eigenvalues of A can be obtained from the eigenvalues of H_m. This is Arnoldi's method in its simplest form.

As m increases, the eigenvalues of H_m that are located in the outmost part of the spectrum start converging toward corresponding eigenvalues of A. In practice, however, one difficulty with the above algorithm is that as m increases cost and storage increase rapidly. One solution is to use the method iteratively: m is fixed and the initial vector v_1 is taken at each new iteration as a linear combination of some of the approximate eigenvectors. Moreover, there are several ways of accelerating convergence by preprocessing v_1 by a Chebyshev iteration before restarting, i.e., by taking $v_1 = t_k(A)z$ where z is again a linear combination of eigenvectors.

Preconditioned GMRES for Singular Systems

In this section we adopt the viewpoint that we are trying to solve the homogeneous system

$$Ax = 0 \tag{29}$$

The case of interest to us is when there is a nontrivial solution to (29), i.e., when A is singular. Then the solution is clearly nonunique and one may wonder whether or not this can cause the corresponding iterative schemes to fail. The answer usually is no and we will illustrate in this section how standard Krylov subspace methods can be used to solve (29) [37]. We start by describing the GMRES algorithm for solving the more common linear system

$$Ax = b. \tag{30}$$

in which A is nonsingular. GMRES is a least-squares procedure for solving (30) on the Krylov subspace K_m. More precisely, assume that we are given an initial guess x_0 to (30) with residual $r_0 = b - Ax_0$. Let us take $v_1 = r_0/\|r_0\|_2$ and perform m steps of Arnoldi's method as described earlier. We seek an approximation to (30) of the form $x_m = x_0 + \delta_m$ where δ_m belongs to K_m. Moreover, we need this approximation to minimize the residual norm over K_m. Writing $\delta_m = V_m y_m$ we see that y_m must minimize the following function of y,

$$
\begin{aligned}
J(y) &= \|b - A(x_0 + V_m y)\|_2 \\
&= \|r_0 - AV_m y\|_2 \\
&= \|\|r_0\|e_1 - AV_m y\|_2
\end{aligned}
\tag{31}
$$

Setting $\beta \equiv \|r_0\|_2$ and using the fact that $AV_m = V_{m+1}\overline{H}_m$ this becomes

$$J(y) = \|V_{m+1}[\beta e_1 - \overline{H}_m y]\|_2 = \|\beta e_1 - \overline{H}_m y\|_2 \tag{32}$$

from the orthogonality of V_{m+1}. As a result the vector y_m can be obtained inexpensively by solving a $(m + 1) \times m$ least-squares problem. We should point out that this procedure is also a projection process. More precisely, as is well-known, the minimization of $J(y)$ is equivalent to imposing the Gram condition that

$$r_0 - AV_m y \perp v \; \forall v \in \text{span } \{AV_m\}$$

which means that we are solving $A\delta = r_0$ with a projection process with

$$K = \text{span } \{r_0, Ar_0, \ldots, A^{m-1} r_0\}$$

and $L = AK$.

Details of this algorithm can be found in Saad and Schultz [38].

Preconditioned Arnoldi and GMRES Algorithms

Preconditioning techniques can also be used to improve the convergence rates of Arnoldi's method and GMRES. This typically amounts to replacing the original system (29) by, for example, the system,

$$M^{-1}Ax = 0 \tag{33}$$

where M is a matrix such that $M^{-1}w$ is inexpensive to compute for any vector w.

Thus in both the Arnoldi and the GMRES case, we only need to replace the original matrix A in the corresponding algorithm by the preconditioned matrix $M^{-1}A$. We may also precondition from the right, i.e., we may replace A by AM^{-1}. In this situation if $AM^{-1}z = 0$ we should note that the solution to the original problem is $M^{-1}z$, which requires one additional solve with M. If $M = LU$ then the preconditioning can also be split between left and right, by replacing the original matrix by the preconditioned matrix $L^{-1}AU^{-1}$.

BLOCK HESSENBERG MATRICES AND SOLUTIONS BY RECURSION

A matrix H is said to be upper Hessenberg if $h_{ij} = 0$ for $i > j + 1$. The following is an example of an upper Hessenberg matrix of order 6,

$$H = \begin{pmatrix} h_{00} & h_{01} & h_{12} & h_{13} & h_{04} & h_{05} \\ h_{10} & h_{11} & h_{12} & h_{13} & h_{14} & h_{15} \\ 0 & h_{21} & h_{22} & h_{23} & h_{24} & h_{25} \\ 0 & 0 & h_{32} & h_{33} & h_{34} & h_{35} \\ 0 & 0 & 0 & h_{43} & h_{44} & h_{45} \\ 0 & 0 & 0 & 0 & h_{54} & h_{55} \end{pmatrix} \tag{34}$$

H is said to be lower Hessenberg if $h_{ij} - 0$ for $i < j - 1$. A tridiagonal matrix is simultaneously both upper Hessenberg and lower Hessenberg. Irreducible Markov chains with infinitesimal generators that are upper Hessenberg are sometimes referred to as *skip-free-to-the-left*; the non-zero structure permits the process to move down (toward zero) by only one state at a time (and is therefore free of skips), but to move up by any number of states. Note that for a Markov chain with an upper Hessenberg transition matrix to be irreducible, all elements below the diagonal must be strictly greater than zero.

Infinitesimal generator matrices that are of Hessenberg form (either upper or lower) arise frequently in queueing models. The paradigm for the upper Hessenberg case is the M/G/1 queue; for the lower Hessenberg case, it is the GI/M/1. The M/M/1 queue has an infinitesimal generator that is tridiagonal.

The M/M/1 queue with service rate and arrival rate yields the following infinite infinitesimal generator

$$Q = \begin{pmatrix} -\lambda & \lambda & & & & \\ \mu & -(\lambda + \mu) & \lambda & & & \\ & \mu & -(\lambda + \mu) & \lambda & & \\ & & \mu & -(\lambda + \mu) & \lambda & \\ & & & \mu & -(\lambda + \mu) & \end{pmatrix} \tag{35}$$

From $\pi Q = 0$, it is obvious that $-\lambda \pi_0 + \mu \pi_1 = 0$, i.e., that $\pi_i = (\lambda/\mu)\pi_0$. In general, we have

$$\lambda \pi_{i-1} - (\lambda + \mu)\pi_i + \mu \pi_{i+1} = 0$$

from which we may derive

$$\pi_{i+1} = ((\lambda + \mu)/\mu)\pi_i - (\lambda/\mu)\pi_{i-1} = (\lambda/\mu)\pi_i.$$

Thus, once π_0 is known, the remaining values π_i may be determined recursively. For the $M/M/1$ queue it is easy to show that the probability that the queue is empty is given by $\pi_0 = (1 - \lambda/\mu)$.

This recursive approach may be extended to upper and lower Hessenberg matrices. When the transition probability matrix P of an irreducible Markov chain is upper Hessenberg, the global balance equations may be written as

$$\pi_j = \sum_{i=0}^{j+1} \pi_i\, p_{ij}, j = 0, 1, 2, \ldots$$

or equivalently

$$\pi_{j+1} = p_{j+1,j}^{-1}\left[\pi_j(1 - p_{jj}) - \sum_{i=0}^{j-1} \pi_i\, p_{ij}\right], j = 0, 1, 2, \cdots$$

This latter form exposes the recursive nature of these equations. If π_0 is known or may be determined, then all remaining π_i may be computed. If the matrix is finite then it is possible to assign π_0 an arbitrary value, 1 for example, to compute the remaining π_i and then renormalize the vector π s.t. $\|\pi\|_1 = 1$.

This may be viewed from a matrix approach by considering the corresponding homogeneous system of n equations in n unknowns:

$$\pi Q = 0$$

and partitioning it as follows

$$(\pi_0, \pi_*) \begin{pmatrix} a^T & \gamma \\ B & d \end{pmatrix} = 0, \tag{36}$$

in which a, d, and $\pi_* \in \mathcal{R}^{n-1}$, $B \in \mathcal{R}^{(n-1)\times(n-1)}$ and π_0 are scalars. We have

$$\pi_0 a^T + \pi_* B = 0 = \Rightarrow \pi_* B = -\pi_0 a^T.$$

If we assume that $\pi_0 = 1$ then the nonhomogeneous system of $(n-1)$ equations in $(n-1)$ unknowns (π_*) may be solved very efficiently for π_*, since the coefficient matrix B is triangular and has non-zero diagonal elements; it is simply a forward substitution procedure which is known to be stable.

Block upper (or lower) Hessenberg matrices are the obvious generalization of the upper (respectively lower) Hessenberg matrices just discussed. The figure below illustrates a finite block Hessenberg infinitesimal generator.

$$H = \begin{pmatrix} H_{00} & H_{01} & H_{12} & H_{13} & H_{04} & H_{05} \\ H_{10} & H_{11} & H_{12} & H_{13} & H_{14} & H_{15} \\ 0 & H_{21} & H_{22} & H_{23} & H_{24} & H_{25} \\ 0 & 0 & H_{32} & H_{33} & H_{34} & H_{35} \\ 0 & 0 & 0 & H_{43} & H_{44} & H_{45} \\ 0 & 0 & 0 & 0 & H_{54} & H_{55} \end{pmatrix} \tag{37}$$

The diagonal blocks are square matrices of order n_i, $i = 0, 1, \ldots, N$; the off-diagonal blocks H_{ij} $i \neq j$ have dimension$(n_i \times n_j)$. All of the elements of all of the blocks of Q are non-negative except the diagonal elements of the diagonal blocks which are all strictly negative. (As always the sum of elements across any row of Q is zero.)

Block Hessenberg matrices arise most commonly when the associated Markov process is two-dimensional, $\{X(t), Y(t)), t \geq 0\}$ on a state space $\{(\eta, k), 0 \leq \eta \leq N, 1 \leq k \leq K\}$ from which *single-step* transitions from state (i, k) to (j, l) are possible only if $i \leq j + 1$. The set of states $\{(\eta, k), 1 \leq k \leq K\}$ is sometimes referred to as level η. Thus the non-zero structure of a block upper Hessenberg infinitesimal generator permits the process to move down (toward level 0) by only one level at a time and to move up by several levels at a time. The process is said to be skip-free-to-the-left. A matrix that is both block upper Hessenberg and block lower Hessenberg is block tridiagonal and is sometimes referred to as a block Jacobi matrix.

As for their point counterparts, it sometimes is possible to develop recursive methods to solve block Hessenberg matrices for the stationary probability vector [see, e.g., *39–42*]. Unfortunately we can no longer guarantee the stability of these procedures. We illustrate this by considering a typical case.

In many two-dimensional Markov chains which represent queueing systems, the parameter η denotes the number of customers in the system and k denotes another aspect of the state of the queue. When the infinitesimal generator matrix is block tridiagonal the global balance equation may be written as:

$$(\pi_0, \pi_1, \ldots, \pi_N) \begin{pmatrix} A_0 & \Lambda & 0 & 0 & \ldots & \ldots & 0 \\ B_1 & A_1 & \Lambda & 0 & \ldots & \ldots & 0 \\ 0 & B_2 & A_2 & \Lambda & \ldots & \ldots & 0 \\ \vdots & \vdots & \vdots & \vdots & \vdots & \vdots & \vdots \\ 0 & 0 & 0 & 0 & B_{N-1} & A_{N-1} & A \\ 0 & 0 & 0 & 0 & \ldots & B_N & A_N \end{pmatrix} = 0, \qquad (38)$$

The matrices Λ are subblocks corresponding to customer arrivals. These blocks are often diagonal, for the arrival of an additional customer will not affect the state parameter k. The B_i subblocks correspond to transitions occasioned by a departure. Unlike arrivals, these may have an effect on the parameter k so that these blocks are seldom diagonal blocks. Diagonal blocks represent changes in the parameter k which do not alter the number of customers in the queue.

From the global balance equations, we have

$$\pi_{N-1}\Lambda + \pi_N A_N = 0 \qquad (39)$$

$$\pi_{N-1} = -\pi_N A_N \Lambda^{-1} \qquad (40)$$

If π_N is known, this gives π_{N-1}. In general, we find

$$\pi_i \Lambda + \pi_{i+1} A_{i+1} + \pi_{i+2} B_i + 2 = 0 \qquad (41)$$

$$\pi_i = -\pi_{i+1} A_{i+1} \Lambda^{-1} - \pi_{i+2} B_{i+2} \Lambda^{-1} \qquad (42)$$

and thus, if π_N is known we may easily compute all π_i.

If π_N is known in advance, it is then possible to compute all π_i in terms of π_N, using (39) and (41). The subvector π_N may then be obtained by solving a small system of equations and then substituted into the recursive relations to determine the remaining subvectors.

This procedure may be described in matrix terms by partitioning the infinitesimal generator matrix as:

$$Q = \begin{pmatrix} V & W \\ X & Y \end{pmatrix} \tag{43}$$

where the dimensions of V, W, X, and Y are, respectively, $NK \times (K + 1)$, $NK \times N(K + 1)$, $(K + 1) \times (K + 1)$ and $(K + 1) \times N(K + 1)$.

Note that the following relation is true for nonsingular W,

$$\begin{pmatrix} V & W \\ X & Y \end{pmatrix} \begin{pmatrix} I & 0 \\ -W^{-1}V & I \end{pmatrix} = \begin{pmatrix} 0 & W \\ X - YW^{-1} & Y \end{pmatrix} \tag{44}$$

so that solving

$$(\pi_*, \ \pi_N) \begin{pmatrix} V & W \\ X & Y \end{pmatrix} = 0 \tag{45}$$

is equivalent to solving

$$(\pi_*, \ \pi_N) \begin{pmatrix} 0 & W \\ X - YW^{-1}V & Y \end{pmatrix} = 0.$$

This allows us to obtain π_N by solving the small $N \times N$ system of equations

$$\pi_N(X - YW^{-1}V) = 0,$$

Now, given π_N, we can obtain π_* by solving the second set of equations (which defines the recurrence relationship)

$$\pi_* W = -\pi_N Y.$$

To solve $\pi_N(X - YW^{-1}V) = 0$, we first determine $YW^{-1}V$. This best achieved by setting $W^{-1}V = Z$ and then solving $WZ = V$ for Z. Once Z is found, we obtain the coefficient matrix by simply computing $(X - YZ)$. Since W is triangular, the system $WZ = V$ is easily solved for Z.

Note that the arrival rates, which are the components of Λ, are frequently small when compared to the service rates, the elements to be found in the blocks A_i and B_i. Thus $A_j\Lambda^{-1}$ and $B_{j+1}\Lambda^{-1}$ will be large. The matrices $A_j\Lambda^{-1}$ and $B_{j+1}\Lambda^{-1}$ will therefore have large norms and the substitution procedure will be unstable since small errors in π_{j+1} and π_j will be multiplied by large values in computing π_{j-1}.

From

$$\pi_{j-1} = -(\pi_j A_j \Lambda^{-1} + \pi_{j+1} B_{j+1} \Lambda^{-1}),$$

we may derive the following relationship among the errors induced during consecutive stages,

$$\epsilon_{j-1} = -(\epsilon_j A_j \Lambda^{-1} + \epsilon_{j+1} B_{j+1} \Lambda^{-1}).$$

This may be written as

$$(\epsilon_{j-1}, \epsilon_j) = (\epsilon_j, \epsilon_{j+1}) \begin{pmatrix} A_j \Lambda^{-1} & I \\ -B_{j+1}\Lambda^{-1} & 0 \end{pmatrix} = (\epsilon_j, \epsilon_{j+1}) E_j, \qquad (47)$$

and thus

$$(\epsilon_0, \epsilon_1) = (\epsilon_{N-1}, \epsilon_N) \prod_{j=1}^{N-1} E_j.$$

Hence, when the elements of $A_j \Lambda^{-1}$ and $B_j \Lambda^{-1}$ are large, we can only expect that

$$(\epsilon_0, \epsilon_1) \gg (\epsilon_{N-1}, \epsilon_N).$$

In other words, the recursive procedure is unstable.

In some cases it may be possible to reverse the procedure and to determine all subvectors $\pi_i = 1, 2, \ldots, N$ in terms of π_0, rather than in terms of π_N and if so, this reversed procedure can be very stable and efficient. Recall that the block Chapmann-Kolmogoroff equations have the form

$$\pi_{j-1}\Lambda + \pi_j A_j + \pi_{j+1} B_{j+1} = 0$$

and our recursive procedure was based on the relation

$$\pi_{j-1} = -(\pi_j A_j \Lambda^{-1} + \pi_{j+1} B_{j+1} \Lambda^{-1}).$$

The new recursive procedure is based on

$$\pi_{j+1} = -(\pi_j A_j B_{j+1}^{-1} + \pi_{j-1}\Lambda B_{j+1}^{-1}).$$

Unfortunately, in many cases the blocks B_i are singular and this approach cannot be used. Additionally, they seldom are as simple to invert as the Λ blocks since these latter are diagonal. In fact, it is the diagonal nature of the Λ blocks that makes the recursive techniques so tempting to use.

We wish to emphasize that great care must be taken when implementing recursive numerical procedures. In some instances they are very stable and efficient methods for determining the solution of Markov chains. However, in many and perhaps most cases they turn out to be unstable. The reader interested in using these techniques should carefully investigate the matrix norms of the diagonal, subdiagonal, and superdiagonal blocks of the transition rate matrix before proceeding.

MATRIX-GEOMETRIC SOLUTIONS

Much work has been carried out by Neuts and his colleagues [12, 43, 44] on infinite stochastic matrices whose stationary probability vector may be written in a *matrix-geometric* form.

Additionally, he has developed numerical techniques to compute these vectors. It is to these types of examples that we now turn.

Consider a two-dimensional irreducible Markov chain with state space $\{(\eta, k), \eta \geq 0, 1 \leq k \leq K\}$. Let the states be ordered so that the parameter k varies most rapidly. Assume further that the stochastic transition probability matrix has the structure

$$P = \begin{pmatrix} B_0 & B_1 & B_2 & B_3 & \ldots & B_j & \ldots \\ A_0 & A_1 & A_2 & A_3 & \ldots & A_j & \ldots \\ 0 & A_0 & A_1 & A_2 & \ldots & A_{j-1} & \ldots \\ 0 & 0 & A_0 & A_1 & \ldots & A_{j-2} & \ldots \\ 0 & 0 & 0 & A_0 & \ldots & A_{j-3} & \ldots \\ \vdots & \vdots & \vdots & \vdots & \vdots & \vdots & \vdots \end{pmatrix} \tag{48}$$

in which all submatrices, A_j, B_j, $j = 0, 1, 2, \ldots$ are square and of order K.

Since P is stochastic, $Pe = e$ and so $B_j e + \sum_{i=0}^{i} A_j e = e$ for all j. Note that the length of the vector e is determined from its context. For simplicity, we shall assume that the matrix A defined as $A = \sum_{i=0}^{\infty} A_i$ is stochastic and irreducible. This is certainly the case in most applications in which the matrix-geometric approach is used. The interested reader will find additional results in Neuts for situations in which these conditions do not hold.

Let the stationary probability vector π be partitioned conformally with P, i.e.,

$$\pi = (\pi_0, \pi_1, \pi_2, \ldots)$$

where

$$\pi_i = (\pi(i, 1), \pi(i, 2), \ldots \pi(i, K))$$

for $i = 0, 1, \ldots$ and $\pi(i, k)$ is the probability of finding the system in state (i, k) under steady-state conditions. From $\pi P = \pi$, we have

$$\pi_j = \sum_{i=0}^{\infty} \pi_{j+1-i} A_i \text{ for } j \geq 1, \tag{49}$$

$$\text{and } \pi_0 = \sum_{j=0}^{\infty} \pi_j B_j. \tag{50}$$

Additionally $\sum_{j=0}^{\infty} \pi_j e = e$, since $\pi e = e$.

Neuts defines a sequence of matrices $R(l)$ as follows:

$$R(0) = 0, \tag{51}$$

$$R(l + 1) = \sum_{j=0}^{\infty} [R(l)]^i A_i \text{ for } l \geq 0, \tag{52}$$

and under the conditions imposed above (specifically, the irreducibility of A) he shows that $R(l) \leq R(l + 1)$ for $l \geq 0$. Additionally, he proves that the sequence $R(l)$ converges to a matrix $R \geq 0$ for which the following theorems hold.

Theorem 1 (Neuts) If the Markov chain is positive recurrent, the matrices R^i, $i \geq 1$ are finite.

Theorem 2 (Neuts) If the Markov chain is positive recurrent, the matrix R satisfies the equation

$$R = \sum_{i=0}^{\infty} R^i A_i,$$

and is the minimal non-negative solution to the matrix equation

$$X = \sum_{i=0}^{\infty} X^i A_i.$$

Theorem 3 (Neuts) If the Markov chain is positive recurrent then

- for $i \geq 0$ we have $\pi_{i+1} = \pi_i R$
- the eigenvalues of R lie *inside* the unit disk
- the matrix $\Sigma_{i=0}^{\infty} R^i B_i$ is stochastic
- the vector π_0 is the positive left invariant eigenvector of $\Sigma_{i=0}^{\infty} R^i B_i$ normalized by $\pi_0 (I - R)^{-1} e = 1$.

Our interest is in Markov chains that are irreducible and possess a stationary probability vector. As such they are positive recurrent and satisfy the conditions of the above theorems. The stationary probability vector $\pi P = \pi$ is therefore given by

$$\pi = (\pi_0, \pi_0 R, \pi_0 R^2, \ldots),$$

and π_0 is found from theorem 3, part (iv).

We now turn our attention to the computation of the matrix R. In all cases considered by Neuts, this matrix can be determined by an iterative procedure which we describe below. Additionally, in certain instances, R can be obtained explicitly as a function of the elements of the infinitesimal generator.

To show how R may be obtained iteratively, consider the matrix equation

$$R = \sum_{i=0}^{\infty} R^i A_i.$$

From

$$R = A_0 + R A_1 + \sum_{i=2}^{\infty} R^i A_i,$$

we have

$$R = A_0 (I - A_1)^{-1} + \sum R_i A_i (I - A_1)^{-1},$$

and R may be computed by means of the iterative procedure

$$R_{l+1} = A_0 (I - A_1)^{-1} + \sum_{i=2}^{\infty} R_l^i A_i (I - A_1)^{-1},$$

using $R_0 = 0$ to initiate the procedure. As is shown by Neuts, the sequence R_e is monotone increasing and converges to R.

Notice that the inversion of $(I - A_1)$ and the matrix multiplications $A_i(I - A_i)^{-1}$ need be performed only once at the beginning of the procedure. Furthermore, in many applications $A_i = 0$ for $i \geq L$ where L is a small integer constant. In quasi birth-death processes, for example, $A_i = 0$ for $i \geq 3$ so that the iteration equation simplifies to

$$R_{l+1} = V + R_l^2 W$$

$W = A_2(I - A_1)^{-1}$. Note that, since A_1 is substochastic, $(I - A_1)$ is nonsingular.

It only remains to determine π_0. This vector may be computed from the first set of Chapmann-Kolmogorov equations with π_i written in terms of $\pi_0 R^i$. As in theorem 3 (iv) we get

$$\pi_0 = \pi_0(B_0 + RB_1 + R^2 B_2 + ...)$$

In many applications, $B_i = 0$ for all $i > L$, where again L is a small integer constant. The $(K \times K)$ matrix $(B_0 + RB_1 + R^2 B_2 + ...)$ is then easy to form and the vector π_0 may be subsequently determined by direct computation. In other applications, this will not be the case and the method of computing $(B_0 + RB_1 + R^2 B^2 + ...)$ will be dictated by the problem itself. Numerous examples have been provided by Neuts and his colleagues. The vector π_0, once computed should be normalized according to Theorem 3, $\pi_0(I - R)^{-1} e = 1$.

DECOMPOSITIONAL METHODS

A decomposition approach to solving Markov chains is intuitively very attractive because it appeals to the principle of divide and conquer: if the model is too large or complex to analyze in toto, it is divided into subsystems each of which is analyzed separately and a global solution then constructed from the partial solutions. Some of these methods have been applied to large economic models and most recently to the analysis of computer systems. Currently, a very large research effort is being devoted to these methods, by many different research groups. [See, e.g., *45–67*]. With the advent of parallel and distributed computing systems, their advantages are immediately obvious.

Ideally the problem is broken into subproblems that can be solved independently and the global solution obtained by "pasting" together the subproblem solutions. Although it is rare to find Markov chains that can be divided into independent subchains, it is not usual to have Markov chains in which this condition almost holds. An important class of problems that frequently arise in Markov modeling are those in which the state space may be partitioned into disjoint subsets with strong interactions among the states of a subset but with weak interactions among the subsets themselves. Such problems are sometimes referred to as *nearly-completely-decomposable (NCD), nearly uncoupled,* or *nearly separable.* It is apparent that the assumption that the subsystems are independent and can therefore be solved separately does not hold. Consequently an error arises. This error will be small if the assumption is approximately true.

The pioneering work on NCD systems was performed by Simon and Ando [68], in investigating the dynamic behavior of linear systems as they apply to economic models. The concept was later extended to Markov chains and the performance analysis of computer systems by Courtois [9]. The technique is founded on the idea that it is easy to analyze large systems in which all the states can be partitioned into groups in which:

Interactions among the states of a group may be studied as if the interactions among groups do not exist

Interactions among groups may be studied without reference to the interactions which take place within groups

Simon and Ando showed that in NCD systems (in which the above conditions are approximated), the dynamic behavior of the system may be divided into a *short-run* dynamics period, and a *long-run* dynamics period. Specifically, they proved the following results:

In the short-run dynamics, the strong interactions within each subsystem are dominant and quickly force each subsystem to a local equilibrium almost independently of what is happening in the other subsystems.

In the long-run dynamics, the strong interactions within each subsystem maintain approximately the relative equilibrium attained during the short-run dynamics but now the weak interactions among groups begin to become apparent and the whole system moves towards a global equilibrium in which the relative equilibrium values attained by the states at the end of the short run dynamic period are maintained.

Strong interactions among the states of a group and weak interactions among the groups themselves imply that the states of a nearly-completely-decomposable Markov chain can be ordered so that the stochastic matrix of transition probabilities has a block structure in which the non-zero elements of the off-diagonal blocks are small compared to those of the diagonal blocks. The irreducible, stochastic matrix P of order n, may be written as

$$P = \begin{bmatrix} P_{11} & P_{12} & \ldots & P_{1N} \\ P_{21} & P_{22} & \ldots & P_{2N} \\ \vdots & \vdots & \vdots & \vdots \\ P_{N1} & P_{N2} & \ldots & P_{NN} \end{bmatrix} \tag{53}$$

in which the subblocks P_{ii} are square, of order n_i, $i = 1, 2, \ldots, N$ with $n = \sum_{i=1}^{N} n_i$. We shall assume that

$$\|P_{ii}\| = 0(1), \quad i = 1, 2, \ldots N, \tag{54}$$

$$\|P_{ij}\| = 0(\varepsilon), \quad i \neq j, \tag{55}$$

where $\|.\|$ denotes the spectral norm of a matrix and ε is a sufficiently small positive number.

Let π be partitioned conformally with P, i.e., $\pi = (\pi_1, \pi_2, \ldots, \pi_N)$ and π_i is a (row) vector of length n_i.

Following the reasoning of Simon and Ando, an initial approach to determining the solution of $\pi P = \pi$ in the more general case when $P_{ij} \neq 0$ is to assume that the system is completely decomposable and to compute the stationary probability distribution for each component.

A first problem that arises with this approach is that the P_{ii} are not stochastic but rather strictly substochastic. A possible solution to this problem is to make them stochastic by adding the probability mass which is to be found on the off-diagonal blocks, $P_{ij}, j = 1, \ldots, N$ and $j \neq i$, into the diagonal block P_{ii} on a row by row basis. This off-diagonal probability mass can be accumulated into the diagonal block in a number of ways. For example, it can be simply added into the diagonal elements of the diagonal block (but this can lead to reducible blocks and numerical difficulties); it can be added into the reverse diagonal elements of the diagonal block to ensure that the diagonal block is irreducible; it can be distributed along the elements of a row of the block in a random fashion, etc. The way in which it is added to the diagonal block will have an effect on the accuracy of the results obtained. In particular, it may be noted that there exists a distribution of this probability mass that results in the exact answer π_i being obtained up to a multiplicative constant. Unfortunately it is not known how to determine this distribution without either a knowledge of the stationary probability vector π itself, or performing extensive calculations possibly in excess of that required to compute the exact solution. A simple solution to the problem of distributing the probability mass is to simply ignore it; i.e., to work directly with the substochastic matrices P_{ii} themselves. In other words, we may use the normalized eigenvector corresponding to the Perron root (the eigenvalue closest to 1) of block P_{ii} as the probability vector whose elements denote the probabilities of being in the states of this block, conditioned on the system occupying one of the states of the block.

A second problem is that once we have computed the stationary probability vector for each block, simply concatenating them together will not give a probability vector. The elements of each subvector sum to one. We still need to weigh each of the probability subvectors by a quantity that is the probability of being in that subblock of states. In other words, the probability distribution computed from the P_{ii} are conditional probabilities in the sense that they express the probability of being in a given state of the subset conditioned on the fact that the system is in one of the states of that subset. We need to remove that condition.

To determine the probability of being in a given block of states we need to construct a matrix whose element ij gives the probability of a transition from block i to block j. This must be an $(N \times N)$ stochastic matrix, and, in accordance with the Simon and Ando theory, should characterize the interactions among blocks.

To construct this matrix we need to shrink each block P_{ij} of P down to a single element. This is accomplished by first replacing each row of each block by the sum of the elements in that block row. The sum of the elements of row k of block i, j gives the probability of leaving state k of block i and entering into (one of the states of) block j. It no longer matters to us which particular state of block j is this destination state. Mathematically, the operation performed for each block is $P_{ij}e$.

To complete the operation, we need to reduce each column vector, $P_{ij}e$, to a scalar. As we have just noted, the k-th element of the vector in position ij is the probability of leaving state k of block i and entering into block j. To determine the total probability of leaving (any state of) block i to enter into (any state of) block j we need to sum the elements of this vector after each element has been weighed by the probability of being in that state (given that the system is in one of the states of that block). These weighing factors may be obtained from the elements of the stationary probability vector. They are the components of $\pi_i/\|\pi_i\|_1$. The ij^{th} element of the reduced $(N \times N)$ matrix is therefore given by

$$(A)_{ij} = \frac{\pi_1}{\|\pi_i\|_1} P_{ij}e, \tag{56}$$

where $\phi_i = \pi_i/\|\pi_i\|_1$. The matrix A is often referred to as the *aggregation matrix* or *coupling matrix*.

If P is an irreducible stochastic matrix, then A also is irreducible and stochastic. Let ξ

denote its left eigenvector, i.e., $\xi A = \xi$ and $\xi e = 1$. The i-th component of ξ is the stationary probability of being in (one of the states of) block i. It is easy to show that

$$\xi = (\| \pi_1 \|_1, \| \pi_2 \|_1 \ ..., \| \pi_N \|_1). \tag{57}$$

Of course, the vector π is not yet known, so that it is not possible to compute the weights $\|\pi_i\|_1$. However they may be approximated by using the probability vector computed from each of the individual P_{ii}. Consequently, the weights ξ_i can be estimated and an approximate solution to the stationary probability vector, π, obtained.

After this sequence of operations is performed, the result is an approximation

$$(\xi_1 u_1, \xi_2 u_2, ..., \xi_N u_N) \tag{58}$$

to π. The question now arises as to whether we can simply incorporate this approximation back into the decomposition algorithm to get an even better approximation. Note, however, that the u_i are used to compute the aggregation matrix and that using $\xi_i u_i$ in their place will have no effect on the probability vector which we compute from the aggregation matrix. It was found, however, that applying a power step to the approximation before plugging it back into the decomposition method had a very salutory effect. Later this power step was replaced by a Gauss-Seidel step and became known as a disaggregation step; forming and and solving the matrix A being the aggregation step. The complete procedure follows. The iteration number is indicated by a superscript in parenthesis on the appropriate variable names.

Algorithm: Iterative Aggregation/Disaggregation

- a. Let $\pi^{(0)} = (\pi_1^{(0)}, \pi_2^{(0)}, \ldots, \pi_N^{(0)})$ be a given initial approximation to the solution π, and set $m = 1$.
- b. Compute $\phi^{(m-1)}, = (\phi_1^{(m-1)}, \phi_2^{(m-1)}, \ldots, \phi_N^{(m-1)})$, where

$$\phi_i^{(m-1)} = \frac{\pi_i^{(m-1)}}{\| \pi_i^{(m-1)} \|_1;} i = 1, 2, ..., N. \tag{59}$$

- c. Construct the aggregation matrix $A^{(m-1)}$ whose elements are given by

$$(\mathbf{A}^{(m-1)})_{ij} = \phi_i^{(m-1)} P_{ij} e. \tag{60}$$

- d. Solve the eigenvector problem

$$\xi^{(m-1)} A^{(m-1)} = \xi^{(m-1)}, \quad \| \xi^{(m-1)} \|_1 = \sum_{i=1}^{N} \xi_i^{(m-1)} = 1 \tag{61}$$

- – e(i). Compute the row vector

$$z^{(m)} = (\xi_1^{(m-1)} \phi_1^{(m-1)}, \xi_2^{(m-1)} \phi_2^{(m-1)}, ..., \xi_N^{(m-1)} \phi_N^{(m-1)}). \tag{62}$$

– e (ii). Solve the following N systems of equations to find $\pi^{(m)}$:

$$\pi_k^{(m)} = \pi_k^{(m)} P_{kk} + \sum_{j > k} z_j^{(m)} P_{jk} + \sum_{j < k} \pi_j^{(m)} P_{jk}, \ k = 1, 2, ..., N. \tag{63}$$

- f. Conduct a test for convergence. If the estimated accuracy is sufficient, then stop and take $\pi^{(m)}$ to be the required solution vector. Otherwise set $m = m + 1$ and goto step b.

Let the matrix $(I - P)$ have the decomposition:

$$(I - P) = D - L - U, \tag{64}$$

where D, L, and U are, respectively, block-diagonal, strictly block-lower-triangular, and strictly block-upper-triangular matrices. In other words:

$$D = Diag\{I - P_{11}, I - P_{22}, ..., I - P_{NN}\}, \tag{65}$$

$$L_{ij} = P_{ij} \text{ if } i > j; \tag{66}$$
$$= 0 \ otherwise; \tag{67}$$

$$U_{ij} = P_{ij} \text{ if } i < j; \tag{68}$$
$$= 0 \ otherwise. \tag{69}$$

Let

$$J^{(m-1)} = Diag\left\{ \frac{\xi_1^{(m-1)}}{\| \pi_1^{(m-1)} \|_1} I, ..., \frac{\xi_N^{(m-1)}}{\| \pi_N^{(m-1)} \|_1} I \right\}. \tag{70}$$

Then

$$z^{(m)} = \pi^{(m-1)} J^{(m-1)}. \tag{71}$$

Furthermore, it is easy to show that the block Gauss-Seidel iteration method applied to step e(ii) can be written as

$$\pi^{(m)} = z^{(m)} L(D - U)^{-1} \tag{72}$$

Therefore, this aggregation/disaggregation method is equivalent to the iterative formula

$$\pi^{(m)} = \pi^{(m-1)} J^{(m-1)} L(D - U)^{-1} \tag{73}$$

It may be shown that π, the exact stationary probability vector, is a fixed point of Eq. (73).

We now turn our attention to some implementation details. The critical points are steps (c) through (e). In step (c), it is more efficient to compute $P_{ij}e$ only once for each block and to store it somewhere for use in all future iterations. This is only possible if sufficient memory is available; otherwise it is necessary to compute it each time it is needed.

To obtain the vector ξ from Eq. (61), the coupling system in step (d), any of the methods discussed in the previous section may be used, for the vector ξ is simply the stationary probability vector of an irreducible stochastic matrix A.

In step (e), each of the N systems of equations in (63) can be written as $Bx = r$ where B = $(I - P_{kk})^T$ and

$$r = \sum_{j > k} z_j P_{jk} + \sum_{j < k} \pi_j P_{jk}, k = 1, 2, ..., N.$$

In all cases, P_{kk} is a strictly substochastic matrix so that B is nonsingular. The vector r must have small norm if the system is NCD. If a direct method is used, the LU decomposition of $(I - P_{kk})$, $k = 1, 2, \ldots, N$ need only be performed once, since this remains unchanged from one iteration to the next. If an iterative method is used we have an iteration algorithm within an iteration algorithm. In this case it is advantageous to perform only a small number of iterations, (e.g., 30-40 of Gauss-Seidel) each time a solution of $(I - P_{kk})x = r$ is needed but to use the final approximation at one step as the initial approximation the next time the solution of that same system is needed.

In these methods, it is important to order the states so that the matrix has the block structure of Eqs. (54) and (55). Only after reordering the states, can we guarantee that the resulting transition matrix will have the property that directly reflects the structural characteristics of the NCD system. This may be accomplished by treating the Markov chain as a directed graph and utilizing some of the graph algorithms of Tarjan [69]. We have been successful in using a *depth-first search* (DFS) algorithm which searches in the forward (deeper) direction as long as possible. Details of the nonrecursive algorithm of DFS are given by Aho [70]. Coding details for DFS are given by Hopecraft and Tarjan [71]. The complexity of this algorithm is $O(|V| + |E|)$, where $|V|$ is the number of vertices and $|E|$ is the number of edges in the graph.

For more information on Iteration/Aggregation algorithms, including implementation details and the results of many test problems, the interested reader is referred to Stewart and Wu [72].

THE RANDOMIZATION METHOD FOR TRANSIENT SOLUTIONS

If $\pi_i(t)$ denotes the probability that a Markov chain with infinitesimal generator Q is in state i at time t, and $\pi(t)$ denotes the vector of all such probabilities, then it may be shown directly from the Chapmann-Kolmogorov differential equations that

$$\pi(t) = \pi(0)e^{Qt} \tag{74}$$

Here, e^{Qt} is the matrix exponential defined by

$$e^{Qt} = \sum_{k=0}^{\infty} \frac{(Qt)^k}{i!} \tag{75}$$

Moler and Van Loan [73] discuss 19 dubious ways to compute such a matrix exponential. For Markov chain problems, most methods for obtaining transient solutions are based on either readily available differential equation solvers such as the Adam-Bansforth/Moulton formulas or Gear's method [74], or on the method of randomization. Currently, there appears to be little to recommend a single method for all situations. Most methods experience difficulty when the infinitesimal generator contains both large numbers and small numbers (referred to as *stiff* in this context). Special methods have been devised for certain types of problems. For example, when the number of states is small, the problem stiff and the solution required at a large value of *t*, successive matrix multiplication (called *binary powering* [75] and *uniformed powering* [76] gives accurate results relatively efficiently. Since the available literature on ordinary differential equation solvers is widely available and well understood, we shall in this section concentrate our attention on the method of randomization. This method has attracted much attention, is extremely simple to program and often outperforms other methods, particularly when the solution at a single time point is needed. If the solution is required at many points, or if plots need to be drawn to show the evolution of certain performance measures, then a method based on one of the differential equation solvers may be preferable. There are several papers of general interest in this area [77–81].

The randomization technique [82–86] can be best understood by observing that it is simply a transformation of a continuous-time Markov chain

$$\{X(t), t \geq 0\} \tag{76}$$

into another continuous-time Markov chain

$$\{Y_{N(t)}, t \geq 0\}, \tag{77}$$

which becomes probabilistically equivalent to $\{X(t), t \geq 0\}$ when appropriate scaling factors are taken into account. The purpose of the transformations is to obtain a process from which the transient quantities of interest are more easily computed.

Consider any continuous-time Markov chain $\{X(t), t \geq 0\}$ on a countable state space S and assume it is defined by the pair: Q^x (the infinitesimal generator matrix) and $\pi(0)$ (initial state probability distribution vector). The randomization procedure may be applied to this process so long as the diagonal elements of Q^x are bounded; i.e., so long as there exist a Γ such that

$$q_{ii}^X \leq \Gamma \text{ for all } i \in S. \tag{78}$$

Now consider a different continuous-time Markov chain

$$\{Y_{N(t)}, t \geq 0\}, \tag{79}$$

defined also on the state space S and characterized by Q^Y and $\pi(0)$. In this process we insist that the mean sojourn time in a state be identical for all states. Specifically, we require that

$$|q_{ii}^Y| = \Gamma \text{ for all } i \in S. \tag{80}$$

An additional requirement is imposed in that every row of Q^Y must be a multiple of the corresponding row in Q^X. If we set

$$D = diag\{d_{00}, d_{11}, d_{22}, ...\} \tag{81}$$

where

$$d_{ii} = \frac{\max_j(|q_{jj}^X|)}{|q_{ii}^X|},$$ (82)

then it follows immediately that Q^Y obtained from

$$Q^Y = DQ^X$$ (83)

satisfies these conditions.

We may consider each row of Q^Y to be identical to the corresponding row in Q^X but expressed in different units. The unit conversion factors are given by the elements of the matrix D. It is in this sense that we say the processes $X(t)$ and $Y_{N(t)}$ are probabilistically equivalent. Both have the same initial state probability vector $\pi(0)$ and infinitesimal generator matrices related by $Q^Y = DQ^X$.

The time spent in any state by the process $X(t)$ is exponentially distributed with different mean sojourn time depending on the particular state. The time spent in each state by the process $Y_{N(t)}$ is also exponentially distributed but in this case the mean sojourn time is the same for all states. This common mean sojourn time is given by Γ^{-1}.

In the process $Y_{N(t)}$, it follows that the time between transitions from any state i to any state $j \neq i$ is exponentially distributed with parameter Γ and hence the transitions themselves may be viewed as being generated by a Poisson process with rate Γ. This is equivalent to taking the discrete-time Markov chain $\{Y_k, k = 0, 1, 2, \ldots\}$, in which transitions from i to $j \neq i$ occur at discrete points in time with probability p_{ij}, and randomizing these *points in time* by means of a Poisson process that generates them at rate Γ; hence the name *randomization*.

We introduced the elements of the matrix D in terms of unit conversion factors. From a probabilistic point of view, we may interpret d_{ii} as the probability that a transition occurs out of state i in the process $Y_{N(t)}$ at each of the randomized points in time at which it is observed. It then follows that the *effective* rates of transition for the process $Y_{N(t)}$ are given by $D^{-1}Q^Y = Q^X$ rather than by Q^Y. In other words, if we insist that at each of the randomized points in time at which the process $Y_{N(t)}$ is observed, transitions from state i occur with probability d_{ii} for all $i \in S$, then the process $Y_{N(t)}$ is probabilistically equivalent to the original process Q^X.

As an example, let $X(t)$ be defined on $S = \{0, 1, 2\}$ and suppose

$$Q^X = \begin{pmatrix} -2 & 1 & 1 \\ 3 & -8 & 5 \\ 1 & 2 & -3 \end{pmatrix}$$ (84)

We find

$$D = \begin{pmatrix} 4 & 0 & 0 \\ 0 & 1 & 0 \\ 0 & 0 & 8/3 \end{pmatrix} \text{ and thus } Q^Y = DQ^X = \begin{pmatrix} -8 & 4 & 4 \\ 3 & -8 & 5 \\ 8/3 & 16/3 & -8 \end{pmatrix}$$ (85)

Note that the stochastic transition probability matrix obtained by discretizing these continuous-time chains by means of the formula

$$P = Q\Delta t + I \tag{86}$$

where Δt, the discretization parameter is given by $\Delta t = \Gamma^{-1}$, is the same for both $X(t)$ and $Y_{N(t)}$. We have

$$P^X = P^Y = \begin{pmatrix} .750 & .125 & .125 \\ ..375 & .000 & .625 \\ .125 & .250 & .625 \end{pmatrix} \tag{87}$$

To summarize so far, we

1. Form the discrete-time Markov chain $\{Y_k, k = 1, 2, \ldots\}$ for which the one-step stochastic probability matrix is given by $I + Q^x/\Gamma$, where Γ is given by $\Gamma \geq max_i\{q_{ii}^X\}$.
2. Randomize the discrete points in time ($k = 0, 1, 2, \ldots$), (the points at which the discrete-time process Y_k is observed), by means of a Poisson process with parameter Γ to create the continuous-time Markov process $Y_{N(t)}$ which is, in turn a sense previously defined, probabilistically equivalent to $X(t)$).

We must now show how the transient solution of $\{X(t), t > 0\}$ may be obtained. It is given by the so-called *randomization formula* to which we now turn.

The Randomization Formula

The randomization equation states that:

$$p_{ij}^X(t) = \sum_{k=0}^{\infty} p_{ij}^Y(k)e^{-\Gamma t}(\Gamma t)^k/k! \tag{88}$$

where

$$p_{ij}^X(t) = Prob\{X(t) = j|X(0) = i\} \tag{89}$$

and $p_{ij}^Y(k)$ is the (i,j) element of $P^{(k)}$ ($= (P^X)^k = (P^Y)^k = P^k$), the k-step transition matrix of the discretized processes. This follows since

$$p_{ij}^X(t) = Prob\{X(t) = j|X(0) = i\} = Prob\{Y_{N(t)} = j|Y_{N(0)} = 1\} \tag{90}$$

$$= \sum_{k=0}^{\infty} Prob\{Y_{N9(t)} = j|N(t) = k, Y_{N(0)} = i\}Prob\{N(t) = k|Y_{N(0)} = 1\} \tag{91}$$

$$= \sum_{k=0}^{\infty} P_{ij}^Y(k)Prob\{N(t) = k\} = \sum_{k=0}^{\infty} P_{ij}^Y(k)e^{-\Gamma t}(\Gamma t)^k/k! \tag{92}$$

In establishing these equalities we use:

1. The definition of $p_{ij}^X(t)$ and the fact that $X(T)$ and $Y_{N(t)}$ are probabilistically equivalent,

2. The law of total probability, and

3. $Prob\{N(t) = k|Y_N(0) = i\} = Prob\{N(t) = k\}$ since $N(t)$ is independently of $Y_{N(0)}$.

We may also show the validity of the randomization Eq. (88) in a different fashion by showing that it is identical to the solution obtained for the transient state probabilities of the Kolmogorov forward differential equations. In matrix form, Eq. (88) may be written as:

$$P^X(t) = \sum_{k=0}^{\infty} p^k e^{-\Gamma t}(\Gamma t)^k/k! \tag{93}$$

We have

$$\pi(0)P^X(t) = \pi(t) \tag{94}$$

where $\pi(0) = (\pi_0(0), \pi_1(0), \dots)$ is the initial probability vector and $\pi(t)$ is the probability vector of the continuous-time process $X(t)$ at time t.

Multiplying both sides of (93) by $\pi(0)$, we get

$$\pi(t) = \sum_{k=0}^{\infty} \pi(0)P^k e^{-\Gamma t}(\Gamma t)^k/k! \tag{95}$$

The forward Kolmogorov differential equations may be written as:

$$dP^X(t)/dt = P^X(t)Q^X \tag{96}$$

For a given $\pi(0)$, this becomes

$$d[\pi(0)P^X(t)]/dt = \pi(0)P^X(t)Q^X \tag{97}$$

$$\pi(t) = \pi(t)Q^X \tag{98}$$

$$\pi(t) = \pi(0)e^{tQX} \tag{99}$$

In other words, solving the Kolmogorov forward equations for the transient state probabilities yields the state probability vector $\pi(t)$ of Eq. (99). But, from equation (95) we have

$$\pi(t) = \sum_{k=0}^{\infty} \pi(0)P^k e^{-\Gamma t}(\Gamma t)^k/k! \tag{100}$$

$$= \pi(0) \sum_{k=0}^{\infty} e^{-\Gamma t}(P\Gamma t)^k/K! = \pi(0)e^{(P\Gamma t - \Gamma t)} \tag{101}$$

$$= \pi(0)e^{\Gamma(P-I)t} = \pi(0)e^{tQ^X} \tag{102}$$

Thus the randomization equation (95) is precisely the transient solution of the Kolmogorov equations.

Implementation and Numerical Considerations

Among the numerical advantages of the randomization technique is the ease with which it can be translated into computer code and the control it gives over the truncation error. Let us first discuss the truncation error. In implementing the randomization method, we need to truncate the series in (95); i.e., we approximate $\pi(t)$ as:

$$\pi(t) \approx \sum_{k=0}^{T} \pi(0)P^k e^{-\Gamma t}(\Gamma t)^k/k! \tag{103}$$

Let

$$\pi^*(t) = \sum_{k=0}^{T} \pi(0)P^k e^{-\Gamma t}(\Gamma t)^k/k! \tag{104}$$

and let $\delta(t) = \pi(t) - \pi^*(t)$. For any consistent vector norm $\|.\|$, $\|\delta(t)\|$ is the truncation error. It is not difficult to numerically bound this error. If we choose T sufficiently large that

$$1 - \sum_{k=0}^{T} e^{-\Gamma t}(\Gamma t)^k/k! \le \epsilon, \tag{105}$$

then

$$\| \pi(t) - \pi^*(t)\|_\infty \le \epsilon. \tag{106}$$

This follows since

$$\| \pi(t) - \pi^*(t)\|_\infty = \tag{107}$$

$$\| \sum_{k=0}^{\infty} \pi(0)P^k e^{-\Gamma t}(\Gamma t)^k/k! - \sum_{k=0}^{T} \pi(0)P^K e^{-\Gamma t}(\Gamma t)^k/k!\|_\infty = \tag{108}$$

$$\| \sum_{k=T+1}^{\infty} \pi(0)P^k e^{-\Gamma t}(\Gamma t)^k/k!\|_\infty \le \sum_{k=T+1}^{\infty} e^{-\Gamma t}(\Gamma t)^k/k! = \tag{109}$$

$$\sum_{k=0}^{\infty} e^{-\Gamma t}(\Gamma t)^k/k! - \sum_{k=0}^{T} e^{-\Gamma t}(\Gamma t)^k/k! = \tag{110}$$

$$1 - \sum_{k=0}^{T} e^{-\Gamma t}(\Gamma t)^k/k! \le \epsilon \tag{111}$$

In implementing the randomization technique, we may code equation (95) exactly as it appears or we may partition it into steps $0 = t_0, t_1, t_2, \ldots, t_m = t$ and write code to implement

$$\pi(t_{i+1}) = \sum_{k=0}^{\infty} \pi(t_i)P^k \Gamma^k (t_{i+1} - t_i)^k/k! e^{-\Gamma(T_{i+1}-T_i)} \tag{112}$$

recursively for $i = 0, 1, \ldots, m - 1$. This second approach is the obvious way to perform the computation if the transient solution is *required* at various points $t_1, t_2, \ldots$ between the initial time t_0 and the final time t. It is computationally more expensive if the transient solution is required only at a single terminal point. However, even in this case it may become necessary to adopt the second approach when the numerical values of Γ and t are such that the computer underflows when computing $e^{-\Gamma t}$. Such instances can be detected a priori and appropriate action taken. For example, one may decide not to allow values of Γt to exceed 100. When such a situation is detected, the time t may be divided into $l = 1$ [$\Gamma t / 100$] equal intervals and the transient solution computed at times $t/l, 2t/l, 3t/l, \ldots, t$.

REFERENCES

1. V. L. Wallace and R. S. Rosenberg, "Markovian Models and Numerical Analysis of Computer System Behavior," *Proc. AFIPS Spring Joint Computer Conference, 28,* AFIPS Press, 1966.

2. V. L. Wallace and R. S. Rosenberg, "RQA-1, the Recursive Queue Analyzer," Technical Report No. 2, Systems Engineering Laboratory, University of Michigan, Ann Arbor, MI, 1966.

3. V. L. Wallace, "Towards an Algebraic Theory of Markovian Networks," in *Proc. Symp. Computer-Communication Networks and Teletraffic,* Polytechnic Press, New York, 1973.

4. V. A. Barker, "Numerical Solution of Sparse Singular Systems of Equations Arising from Ergodic Markov Chains," *Stochastic Models, 5,* 3 (1989).

5. C. C. Paige, P. H. Styan, and P. G. Wachter, "Computation of the Stationary Distribution of a Markov Chain,"*J. Statist. Comput. Simul., 4,*173-186 (1975).

6. B. Philippe, Y. Saad, and W. J. Stewart, "Numerical Methods in Markov Chain Modeling," Technical Report TR 89-21, North Carolina State University, Raleigh, NC 27695-8206, October 1989.

7. W. J. Stewart, "A Comparison of Numerical Techniques in Markov Modeling," *Comm. ACM, 21,* 144-151 (1978).

8. A. Berman and R. J. Plemmons, *Nonnegative Matrices in the Mathematical Sciences,* Academic Press, New York, 1979.

9. P. J. Courtois, *Decomposability; Queueing and Computer System Applications,* Academic Press, Orlando, FL, 1977.

10. I. S. Duff, A. M. Erisman, and J. K. Reid, *Direct Methods for Sparse Matrices,* Clarendon Press, Oxford, 1986.

11. A. L. Hageman and D. M. Young, *Applied Iterative Methods,* Academic Press, New York, 1981.

12. M. F. Neuts, *Structured Stochastic Matrices of M/G/1 Type and Their Applications,* Marcel Dekker, Inc., New York, 1989.

13. E. Seneta, *Non-Negative Matrices and Markov Chains,* Second ed., Springer-Verlag, New York, 1981.

14. J. H. Wilkinson, *The Algebraic Eigenvalue Problem,* Clarendon Press, Oxford, 1965.

15. W. J. Stewart, "MARCA: Markov Chain Analyzer. A Software Package for Markov Modeling." Technical Report 88-32, Department of Computer Science, North Carolina State University, Raleigh, NC, 27695-8206, 1988.

16. R. E. Funderlic and C. D. Meyer, "Sensitivity of the Stationary Distribution Vector for an Ergodic Markov Chain, *Linear Algebra Appl., 76,* 1-17 (1986).

17. R. E. Funderlic and r. J. Plemmons, "Updating LU Factorizations for Computing Stationary Distributions," *SIAM J. Alg. Disc. Meth.*, 7, 30-42 (1986).
18. G. H. Golub and C. D. Meyer, "Using the QR Factorization and Group Inversion to Compute, Differentiate and Estimate the Sensitivity of Stationary Distributions for Markov Chains," *SIAM J. Alg. Disc. Meth.*, 7, 273-281 (1986).
19. W. K. Grassmann, M. J. Taksar, and D. P. Heyman, "Regenerative Analysis and Steady State Distributions for Markov Chains," *Oper. Res.*, 33, 1107-1116 (1985).
20. W. J. Harrod and R. J. Plemmons, "Comparisons of Some Direct Methods for Computing Stationary Distributions of Markov Chains," *SIAM J. Sci. Comput.*, 5, 453-469 (1984).
21. D. P. Heyman, "Further Comparisons of Direct Methods for Computing Stationary Distributions of Markov Chains, *SIAM J. Alg. Disc. Meth.*, 8, 226-232 (1987).
22. D. M. Young, *Iterative Solution of Large Linear Systems,* Academic Press, New York, 1971.
23. L. Kaufman, "Matrix Methods for Queueing Problems," *SIAM J. Sci. Comput.*, 4, 525-552 (1983).
24. D. Mitra and P. Tsoucas, "Relaxations for the Numerical Solutions of Some Stochastic Problems," *Stochastic Models*, 4, 3 (1988).
25. G. P. Barker and R. J. Plemmons, "Convergent Iterations for Computing Stationary Distributions of Markov Chains," *SIAM J. Alg. Disc. Meth.*, 7, 390-398 (1986).
26. P. J. Courtois and P. Semal, "Block Iterative Algorithms for Stochastic Matrices," *Linear Algebra Appl.*, 76, 59-70 (1986).
27. O. Alexsson, "A Survey of Preconditioned Iterative Methods for Linear Systems of Algebraic Equations," *BIT,25*, 166-187 (1985).
28. R. E. Funderlic and R. J. Plemmons, "A Combined Direct-Iterative Method for Certain M-Matrix Linear Systems," *SIAM J. Alg. Disc. Meth.*, 5(1), 32-42 (1984).
29. Y. Saad, "Projection Methods for Solving Large Sparse Eigenvalue Problems," in *Matrix Pencils, Proc., Pitea Havsbad*, B. Kagstrom and A. Ruhe (eds.), Springer-Verlag, Berlin, 1982.
30. A. Jennings and W. J. Stewart, "Simultaneous Iteration for Partial Eigensolution of Real Matrices," *J. IMA*, 15, 351-361 (1975).
31. A. Jennings and W. J. Stewart, "A Simultaneous Iteration Algorithm for Real Matrices," *ACM Trans. Math. Software*, 7, 184-198 (1981).
32. G. W. Stewart, "Simultaneous Iteration for Computing Invariant Subspaces of Non-Hemitian Matrices," *Numer. Mat.*, 25, 123-136 (1976).
33. W. J. Stewart and A. Jennings, "A Simultaneous iteration Algorithm for Real Matrices," *ACM Trans. Math. Software*, 7, 184-198 (1981).
34. Y. Saad, "Chebyshev Acceleration Techniques for Solving Non-symmetric Eigenvalue Problems," *Math. Computation*, 42, 567-588 (1984).
35. W. E. Arnoldi, "The Principle of Minimized Iteration in the Solution of the Matrix Eigenvalue Problem," *Quart. Appl. Math.*, 9, 17-29 (1951).
36. Y. Saad, "Variations on Arnoldi's Method for Computing Eigenelements of Large Unsymmetric Matrices," *Lin. Alg. Appl.*, 34, 269-295 (1980).
37. Y. Saad, "Krylov Subspace Methods for Solving Large Unsymmetric Linear Systems," *Math. Comp.*, 37, 105-126 (1981).
38. Y. Saad and M. H. Schultz, "GMRES: A Generalized Minimal Residual Algorithm for Solving Non-symmetric Linear Systems," *SIAM J. Sci. Stat. Comput.*, 7, 856-869 (1986).

39. S. B. Gershwin and I. C. Schick, "Modeling and Analysis of Three-Stage Transfer Lines with Unreliable Machines and Finite Buffers," *Oper. Res., 31*(2), 354-380 (1983).

40. M. A. Jafari and J. G. Shanthikumar, "Finite State Spacially Non-homogeneous Quasi Birth-Death Processes," Working paper No. 85-009, Dept. of Industrial Engineering and Operations Research, Syracuse University, Syracuse, New York, 1985.

41. E. J. Muth and S. Yeralan, "Effect of Buffer Size on Productivity of Work Stations that are subject to Breakdowns," *Proc. 20 th IEEE Conf. on Decision and Control,* December 1981, pp. 643-648.

42. Wong, Giffin and Disney, "Two Finite M/M/1 Queues in Tandem: A Matrix Solution for the Steady State," *OPSEARCH, 14*(1), 1-18 (1977).

43. M. F. Neuts, *Matrix-Geometric Solutions in Stochastic Models: An Algorithmic Approach,* the Johns Hopkins University Press, Baltimore, 1981.

44. V. Ramaswami and D. Lucantoni, "Stationary Waiting Time Distributions in Queues with Phase Type Service and in Quasi Birth-Death Processes," *Stoch. Models, 1,* 125-136 (1985).

45. S. Balsamo and B. Pandolfi, "Bounded Aggregation in Markovian Networks," *Computer Performance and Reliability,* G. Iazeolla, P. J. Courtois, and O. J. Boxma (eds.), North Holland, Amsterdam 1988, pp. 73-92.

46. W. L. Cao and W. J. Stewart, "Iterative Aggregation/Disaggregation Techniques for Nearly Uncoupled Markov Chains," *J. Assoc. Comp. Mach., 32*(3), 702-719 (1985).

47. F. Chatelin, *Spectral Approximation of Linear Operators*, Academic Press, New York, 1984.

48. F. Chatelin, "Iterative Aggregation/Disaggregation Methods," in *Mathematical Computer Performance and Reliability,* G. Iazeolla, P. J. Courtois, and A. Hordijk (eds.), North Holland, Amsterdam, 1984, pp. 199-207.

49. F. Chateline nd W. L. Miranker, "Acceleration by Aggregation of Successive Approximation of Successive Approximation Methods," *Linear Algebra Appl., 43,* 17-47 (1982).

50. P. J. Courtois and P. Semal, "Bounds for the Positive Eigenvectors of Nonnegative Matrices and Their Approximation by Decomposition," *J. Assoc. Comp. Mach., 31,* 804-825 (1984).

51. B. N. Feinberg and S. S. Chiu, "A Method to Calculate Steady State Distributions of Large Markov Chains by Aggregating States," *Oper. Res., 35,* 282-290 (1987).

52. M. Haviv, "Aggregation/Disaggregation Methods for Computing the Stationary Distribution of a Markov Chain," *SIAM J. Numer. Anal., 24,* 952-966 (1987).

53. M. Haviv, "More on a Rayleigh-Ritz Refinement Technique for Nearly Uncoupled Stochastic Matrices," *SIAM J. Matrix Anal. Appl., 10,* 287-293 (1989).

54. D. S. Kim and R. L. Smith, "An Exact Aggregation Algorithm for Mandatory Set Decomposable Markov Chains," in *First International Workshop on the Numerical Solution of Markov Chains,* Marcel Dekker, Inc., New York, 1990.

55. R. Koury, D. F. McAllister, and W. J. Stewart, "Iterative Methods for Computing Stationary Distributions of Nearly Completely Decomposable Markov Chains," *SIAM J. Alg. Disc. Math., 5*(2), 164-186 (1984).

56. D. F. McAllister, G. W. Stewart, and W. J. Stewart, "On a Raleigh-Ritz Refinement Technique for Nearly Uncoupled Stochastic Matrices," *Linear Alg. Applications, 60,* 1-25 (1984).

57. C. D. Meyer, "Stochastic Complementation, Uncoupling Markov chains and the Theory of Nearly Reducible Systems," *SIAM Rev., 31*, 240–272 (1989).

58. P. J. Schweitzer, "Aggregation Methods for Large Markov Chains," *International Workshop on Applied Mathematics and Performance Reliability Models of Computer Communication Systems,* University of Pisa, Pisa, Italy, 1983, pp. 225–234.

59. P. J. Schweitzer, "Perturbation Series Expansions for Nearly Completely Decomposable Markov Chains," *Teletraffic Analysis and Computer Performance Evaluation,* O. J. Boxma, J. W. Cohen, and H. C. Tijms (eds.), Elsevier North-Holland, Amsterdam, 1986, pp. 319–328.

60. P. J. Schweitzer and K. W. Kindle, "An Iterative Aggregation-Disaggregation Algorithm for Solving Linear Systems," *Appl. Math. Comp., 18*, 313–353 (1986).

61. G. W. Stewart, "Computable Error Bounds for Aggregated Markov Chains," *J.Assoc. Comp. Mach.,, 30*, 271–285 (1983).

62. G. W. Stewart, W. J. Stewart, and D. F. McAllister, "A Two-Stage Iteration for Solving Nearly Uncoupled Markov Chains," Tech. Report TR 1384, Dept of Comp. Sci., University of Maryland, College Park, MD, 20742, April 1984.

63. G. W. Stewart, "On the Sensitivity of Nearly Uncoupled Markov Chains," in *Proc. first International Workshop on the Numerical Solution of Markov Chains,* Marcel Dekker, New York, 1990.

64. U. Sumita and M. Reiders, "A Comparison of the Replacement Process with Aggregation-Disaggregation," in *Proc. First International Workshop on the Numerical Solution of Markov Chains,* Marcel Dekker, New York, 1990.

65. Y. Takahashi, "A Lumping Method for Numerical Calculation of Stationary Distributions of Markov Chains," Research Report B-18, Department of Information Sciences, Tokoyo Institute of Technology, Tokyo, Japan, June 1975.

66. H. Vantilborgh, "Aggregation with an Error of $O(\varepsilon^2)$," *J. ACM, 32*, 161–190 (1985).

67. R. L. Zarling, "Numerical Solutions of Nearly Completely Decomposable Queueing Networks," Ph.D. dissertation, Department of Computer Science, University of North Carolina, 1976.

68. H. A. Simon and A. Ando, "Aggregation of Variables in Dynamic Systems," *Econometrica, 29*, 111–138 (1961).

69. R. J. Tarjan, "Depth First Search and Linear Graph Algorithms," *SIAM J. Comput., 1*(2), 146–160 (1972).

70. A. V. Aho, J. E. Hopcroft, and J. D. Ullman, *The Design and Analysis of Computer Algorithms,* Addison-Wesley, Reading, MA, 1974.

71. J. E. Hopcroft and R. J. Tarjan, "Efficient Algorithms for Graph Manipulation," *CACM, 16*(6), 372–378 (1973).

72. W. J. Stewart and W. Wu, "Iteration and Aggregation for the Numerical Solution of NCD Markov Chains," Copper Mountain Conference on Iterative Methods, Computational Math Group, University of Colorado at Denver, April 1990.

73. C. Molar and C. Van Loan, "Nineteen Dubious Ways to Compute the Exponential of a Matrix," *SIAM Rev., 20*(4), 801–836 (1978).

74. C. W. Gear, *Numerical Initial Value Problems in Ordinary Differential Equations,* Prentice-Hall, Englewood Cliffs, NJ, 1971.

75. A. L. Reibman, "A Splitting Technique for Markov Chain Transient Solution," in *Proc. First International Workshop on the Numerical Solution of Markov Chains,* Marcel Dekker, Inc., New York, 1990.

76. R. A. Marie, "Transient Numerical Solutions of Stiff Markov Chains," Proceedings:

20th International Symposium on Automative Technology and Technology. Florence, Italy, May 1989.

77. A. Bobbio and K. S. Trivedi, "An Aggregation Technique for the Transient Analysis of Stiff Markov Chains," *IEEE Transact. Computers, C-35*(9), 803–814 (1986).

78. R. A. Marie, A. L. Reibman, and K. S. Trivedi, "Transient Solutions of Acyclic Markov Chains," *Performance Evaluation, 7*(3), 175–194 (1987).

79. A. L. Reibman and K. S. Trivedi, "Numerical Transient Analysis of Markov Models," *Computers Oper. Res., 15*(1), 19–36 (1988).

80. A. L. Reibman, K. S. Trivedi, and R. Smith, "Markov and Markov Reward Model Transient Analysis: An Overview of Numerical Approaches," *Eur. J. Oper. Res., 40*(2), 257–267 (1989).

81. K. Trivedi, A. Reibman, and R. Smith, "Transient Analysis of Markov and Markov Reward Models," in *Computer Performance and Reliability*, G. Iazeolla, P. J. Courtois, and O. J. Boxma (eds.) North Holland, Amsterdam, 1988, pp. 535–545.

82. W. Grassmann, "Transient Solutions in Markovian Queueing Systems," *Computing Opns. Res., 4*, 47–66 (1977).

83. W. Grassmann, "Transient Solutions in Markovian Queues," *Eur. J. Opnl. Res., 1*, 396–402 (1977).

84. D. Gross and D. R. Miller, "The Randomization Technique as a Modelling Tool and Solution Procedure for Transient Markov Processes," *Oper. Res., 32*, 343–361 (1984).

85. A. Jensen, "Markoff Chains as an Aid in the Study of Markoff Processes," *Skandinavisk Aktuarietidskrift, 36*, 87–91 (1953).

86. B. Melamed and M. Yadin, "The Randomization Procedure in the Computation of Cumulative Time Distributions Over Discrete State Markov Processes," *Oper. Res., 32*, 929–943 (1984).

WILLIAM J. STEWART

OBJECT RECOGNITION AND VISUAL ROBOT TRACKING

INTRODUCTION

The major goal of artificial vision systems is to provide machines—be it robots, autonomous vehicles, or other automation equipment—with the flexibility they need in order to cope with variation in their environment. This contribution will primarily discuss the visual recognition of objects. The reader should not expect an exhaustive treatment of all possible algorithms which have been proposed over the past years. Yet, we hope he or she will gain a fair insight in the numerous subproblems involved and in the different directions taken by research. Special problems arise when vision systems and robots are expected to cooperate. As such systems will play an important role in the future, we devoted a considerable part to these developments.

In view of the remarkable performance of the human brain in dealing with visual input, the rather clumsy and often application-specific results obtained with modern machine vision systems make clear that there is still a long road of intriguing research in front of us. Nevertheless, where the environment can sufficiently be controlled, vision systems have entered the shop floor. Benefits include lower turnover times (especially in batch production), 100% instead of sampled inspection, automated gathering of fault statistics, reduction in labor cost, and elimination of special fixtures and pallets. Yet, although in many research areas the time before results are put into practice seems to be rapidly decreasing, in computer vision there is a growing mismatch between new algorithms' computational demands and available computer power. As a result, many industrial vision systems are still based on the type of features introduced in the early 1970s. For the future, much is to be expected from the integration of several new concepts. Hardware developments (further down-scaling, silicon on silicon, etc.), vision-CAD integration and new computational paradigms like interconnection-limited parallelism will boost vision potentials.

In general, recognition algorithms can be subdivided into three subsequent steps and is text is organized along this chronology: data acquisition is discussed first, followed by an overview of feature extraction. Actual recognition precedes a discussion on aspects of vision—robot integration. Finally, we sketch some possible evolutions toward more robust vision systems.

DATA ACQUISITION

In this section, we focus on the acquisition of image data. These can specify light intensity or distance to the visible points in the environment. Data are often noisy or sparse. Therefore, enhancement techniques are sometimes called for.

Gray-Level Images

Because a computer can deal only with finite sets of discrete numbers, intensity measurements will have to be stored with limited accuracy ('gray level quantization') for a limited

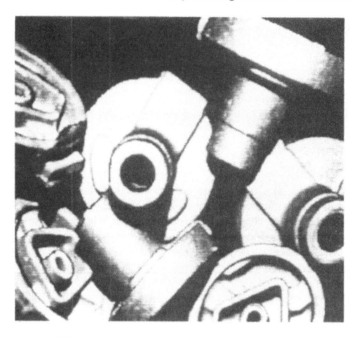

FIGURE 1.   512 × 512 intensity image of workpiece pile, with 256 possible gray levels (courtesy SRI).

number of locations placed along some grid ('sampling'). At each grid point, the intensity information is regarded as the mean value for a small area around the point. This area is a so-called pixel (also picture cell, pel). Intensity images usually have 8 bits or 1 out of 256 gray levels at each point. Figure 1 shows a gray level image of a pile of workpieces. Resolution is 512 × 512 and 256 possible intensity values. Vision algorithms sometimes use fewer bits, regularly as few as 1 bit ('binary vision'). The latter simplification is useful with high-contrast scenes where the distinction between pixels having intensity values above some selected threshold from pixels with below-threshold intensities successfully divides the image into objects and background. The sampling points will usually be arranged in a square grid. Alternative tessellations are rectangular (less attractive for meteorological applications but in consonance with video standards) or hexagonal. The latter scheme poses fewer ambiguities in defining connectedness (for the connectedness problem, see e.g., [1]) and exhibits a more regular and dense occupation of space, more similar to the human retina. Some sampling schemes are even more strongly based on such retina models. They apply decreasing spatial resolution when going from the image center to the outlines. Figure 2 shows a recently developed 'retina CCD' [2]. It should be noted, however, that square and rectangular gratings form the absolute majority in current vision applications, as they are directly linked with CCD element integration and traditional video standards.

The number of sampling points and quantization levels should be kept as low as possible. They have a direct impact on the data rate the vision computer has to process. Furthermore, a good choice of the sensor and the illumination can avoid many problems and simplify the algorithms to be used [3].

FIGURE 2.   Retina CCD with high resolution in the center and increasingly low resolution when going to the boundaries [2] (courtesy IMEC VZW).

FIGURE 3.   Range image for the same scene as in Fig. 1 (courtesy SRI).

Range Data

In 'range images' pixel values don't indicate light intensity, but distance from the sensor. Figure 3 is the range image for the scene depicted in Figure 1. Points lying far away are dark, points close to the camera are bright. In the following paragraphs we deal with the question of how to obtain such range images in practice [4]. Range acquisition methods requiring the projection of special illumination patterns are usually referred to as 'active,' the others are called 'passive.'

The most direct method is the 'time-of-flight' technique. With a laser and a coaxially placed photodetector it is possible to measure the time a light pulse signal (wave) travels from the sensor-source to the object and back. The signal traveling time is directly proportional to range. A similar principle is used with ultrasonic sensors, but resolution is rather low.

Most active methods instead make use of the triangulation principle, as is explained in Figure 4. The position of a laser spot on the object surface indicates depth at that position. Depth follows from the calculated intersection of the spot projection line and the viewing line connecting the projected spot and the camera lens center. Scanning the total scene with such a spot yields a complete range image. For each position of the spot a new image has to be taken. The spot can, without much difficulty, be extended to a line. Scanning has then only to be performed in the direction orthogonal to the line and the number of images can be reduced. Further extension to two-dimensional patterns is less straightforward as the points cannot be identified from a uniform illumination pattern. Encoding point positions within one pattern already has been proposed for 64 × 63 range images. Figure 5a shows this pattern projected on a face. It consists of 63 vertical 'lines,' each characterized by the black and white pattern of which. Figure 5b and c show the 3D reconstruction obtained by the triangulation for two different viewpoints. Other solutions use a limited set of masks which are projected subsequently and together build the position codes. Most of the patterns are binary for reasons of algorithm robustness.

Stereo employs at least two different intensity images of the same scene, usually taken simultaneously from different positions by different cameras. The underlying principle is also triangulation. Observing the position of a point through one camera, an infinite number of 3D positions on the line of sight through the point are possible. The second view will disambiguate the position to only one point in space, as this second line of sight will

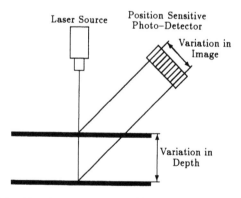

FIGURE 4.   Depth measurement with the triangulation principle.

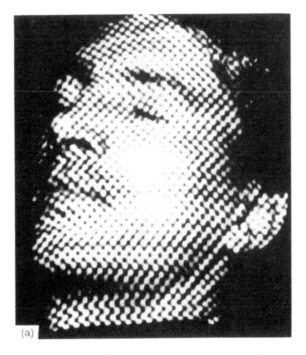

FIGURE 5. Illustration of a one-shot range finder. (a) The special pattern projected onto a face; (b, c) show the reconstructed surface viewed from different directions (courtesy ESAT).

intersect the first one. The fundamental problem is finding the 'correspondence points,' for each point in the first image the corresponding point in the second image has to be found. Once the configuration geometry is known, this search can be restricted to a line, referred to as the 'matching line' or 'epipolar line.' As far as the correspondence search is concerned, there are basically two strategies. The first approach searches for the corresponding points by use of a correlation measure. A neigbourhood around the point in the first image is optimally matched in the second image. This position is supposed to give the corresponding point. Besides the problem of high computational cost, this technique will be noise sensitive for small windows and it will have low resolution for large windows. As the images are taken from different positions the match will never be perfect. On the other hand, it makes few assumptions on the scene. Another approach has been developed, which does expect certain features to be present, but often poses fewer problems thereafter. By searching features like edges or corners in both images and matching these, topologically important feature groups are more easily matched [6, 7]. Whereas passive stereo uses normal day or indoor light, active stereo will create such features by projection of patterns. Finally, it should be noted that accuracy of the depth measurements can be increased by increasing the angle or the distance between the camera axes. But by doing so more and more points will be visible to only one camera and these occlusions will reduce the amount of points for which range can be obtained.

'Shape from shading' uses lighting with known direction and intensity. Gray levels of

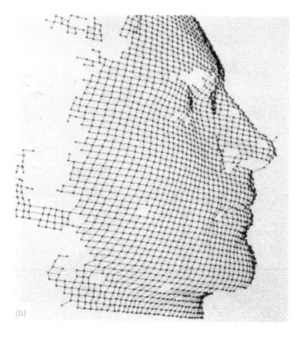

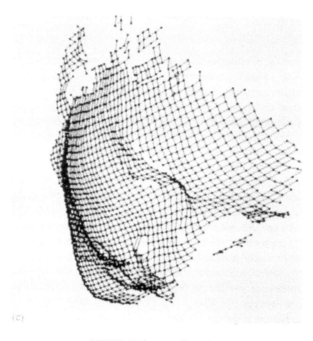

FIGURE 5.   continued.

object surface patches can then be brought into correspondence with their orientation. This process does not only require information on the sensor-illumination configuration, but also on the reflection characteristics of the surface. The complex relationship between gray levels and surface orientation can theoretically be calculated, but is usually derived from experiments and then stored in 'reflectance maps' for table-lookup. The orientation of an isolated patch cannot be derived uniquely. Local information for different patches is combined with extra assumptions on surface smoothness or with information obtained from other light source positions. A more elaborate account can be found in Ref. *1*.

Further passive methods include 'shape from texture' and 'shape from contour' [*8*]. Shape from texture [see, e.g., *9–13*] assumes a slanted and tilted surface to have a homogeneous texture. Homogeneity can have quite different meanings: constant number of texture elements ('texels') or constant edge length per unit area (edge extraction is explained in a later section), isotropy for texel edge orientation, or texels having a constant shape. Systematic inhomogeneity of the imaged texture is regarded as the product of projection. Surface orientations which allow the original texture to be maximally isotropic or homogeneous are selected. Sometimes active versions are used by projecting patterns onto the scene (e.g., circles). Shape from contour [e.g., *11, 14–16*] starts from a similar principle. From all possible deprojections of a given contour, the interpretation extremizing some performance index is chosen. As an example, for a closed contour area over perimeter squared gives an idea of contour compactness. Maximizing compactness for the possible deprojections of an ellipse yields a circle [*14*]. The ellipse is then interpreted as a slanted and tilted circle, in accordance with human perception. Several such indices have been proposed, most of them apply only for planar contours, however. The interpretation of twisted curves [*15, 16*] and the interaction between different contours in one scene [*17*] have not yet received much attention within the shape from contour context.

Only time-of-flight and passive or active triangulation approaches provide absolute distance, instead of relative depth cues or orientation. 'Shape-from-X' methods need to know the distance of at least one point or the object dimensions in order to obtain absolute range.

Regularization

The reconstruction of depth surfaces is typically an 'ill-posed problem.' A problem is ill-posed if no unique solution exists or if it does not continuously depend on the data (i.e., slight changes in the data cause drastic changes in the output). 'Regularization theory' has been put forward to render such problems well-posed [*18*]. Basically, the space of admissible solutions is restricted by imposing additional constraints and the solution to the original data is accepted to be nonexact. Rather than sticking solely to the data, a number of additional assumptions about the solution are made. Usually, these are some sort of smoothness assumptions. The solution then optimizes a functional which has several components, some of which measure the deviation from the data, while others penalize deviation from the assumptions. The solution is a compromise between these often competing forces and its exact form depends on the relative force weight. The 'regularization constant' specifying this relative importance is usually chosen heuristically, although some recent research is aimed at finding criteria for its automatic determination.

As an example, the range data obtained by one of the previous methods will be noisy. Therefore, one would like to smooth the results. Minimum energy solutions for membrane or plate models have been suggested. (An early but seminal contribution can be found elsewhere [*19*]. More recent research is discussed in Refs. *20–22*). The corresponding functionals to be extremized reflect the desire to both stay close to the measurements and yet have a smooth solution. The reconstructed surface corresponds to the equilibrium state of the membrane or plate. Membrane models assume smoothness of the range data, while plate models additionally impose smoothness on the surface normal. Let us illustrate this by the membrane analogue. At each of the measured range positions a spring is attached at one end. When the other ends of the springs are connected to a membrane, this will stretch and eventually reach an equilibrium state, corresponding to minimal energy. Springs are assumed to have zero potential energy at length 0, that is when the reconstructed surface contains the data point. If the membrane-connected (mobile) ends are considered as the new positions for the original data (fixed end of the spring), it is clear that in general the new position won't coincide with the original ones. The membrane has the effect of smoothing the original data. Problems occur at steep edges and discontinuities, which are also blurred. Recent developments propose modifications to the functional in order to leave the discontinuities intact. It should be noted, however, that these approaches require a lot of computation time, what so far keeps them out of the realm of real-time vision. We explained the principle on the basis of range data, because this best matches intuition when discussing membrane and plate surfaces. Of course, if image intensities are the input, completely analogous processing is possible for their enhancement. As an example, Figure 6a shows a noisy intensity image. Figure 6b shows intensities as a 3D plot. Height indicates intensity here. Figure 6c illustrates the effect of fitting a plate: noise is reduced but the steep edge is blurred also. Figure 6d shows the corresponding 3D plot. Figure 6e and f show the effect of including 'tears' in the plate. The discontinuity is preserved and in the neighbourhood of the tear tips edge propagation is facilitated. The final results for the intensity image and the 3D plot are shown in Figure 6g and h, respectively. Noise has been reduced, but edges have survived. Higher computational load and the theoretical problems of dealing with nonlinear energy functionals pose problems.

FEATURE EXTRACTION

Once the image is available, the amount of information has to be reduced. Processing will concentrate on ever fewer data of ever higher semantic content. One of the first steps usually is to 'segment' the image, i.e., to identify regions which somehow form separate entities. A further reduction can be realized by scrutinizing on a limited set of features extracted from the segmentation result. Some relevant aspects are discussed in subsequent paragraphs. These features should be carefully selected in order to make the recognition process efficient and reliable.

Segmentation

A scene usually will contain several objects, having several faces. Feature extraction usually starts with a division of the scene into its constituent components. Objects have to be distinguished from one another and from the background. Also, the different faces and subparts of one object have to be kept apart during further processing. This 'segmentation' problem is attacked by two strategies or a mixture of these. The first one is based on the detection of edges and boundaries. These are then assumed to separate the different entities. As an alternative, regions with homogeneous characteristics are gradually grown up to the point where they meet. These regions are then identified with the entities. Both strategies are now discussed somewhat further. Although we do in terms of gray level images, similar methods can be applied to range images.

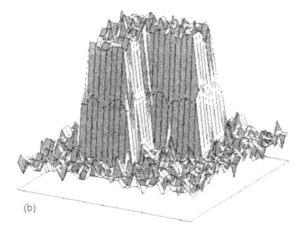

FIGURE 6. Regularization by a 'tearing plate' model: (a) the original noisy intensity image, (b) 3D plot of original intensity data, (c) fitting a plate blurs the image, (d) 3D plot of blurred intensity data, (e) initiation of a tear at high tension location, (f) propagation of the tear, which is facilitated because of increased tensions at the tear tip, (g) final result image, (h) final 3D plot, noise has been reduced without blurring the edges, which are made explicit by the system and are drawn in black [5] (courtesy ESAT).

The first approach starts with local edge detection. Most methods start from intensity gradients, obtained by convolution with bandpass filters. Several types of convolution masks have been proposed, depending on specific heuristics or theoretical optimizations. Especially locations with large gradient magnitudes are of interest. Most methods include some nonlinear operations, for example (adaptive) thresholding or nonmaximum suppression. The final goal is to arrive at clear, linked, and one-pixel thick edges. Figure 7b shows edges extracted from the gray level image in Figure 7a. The algorithm is being implemented on chip. Figure 7c shows the floorplan of the very large-scale integrated (VLSI) design. One clearly sees that edges are still not prefect. Without bringing in task-specific knowledge or

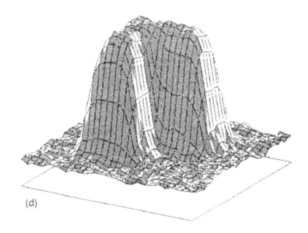

FIGURE 6.   continued.

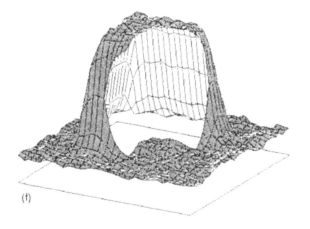

(f)

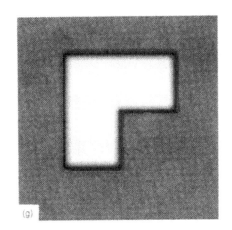

(g)

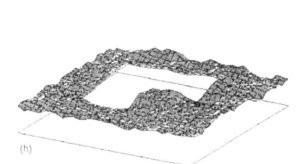

(h)

FIGURE 6. continued.

(a)

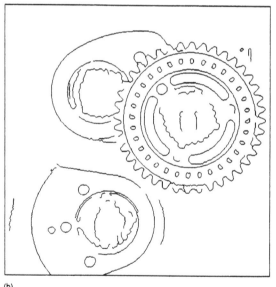

(b)

FIGURE 7.   From image (a) edges are extracted and shown in (b). (c) The schematic layout of a VLSI chip implementing the algorithm (courtesy ESAT-IMEC).

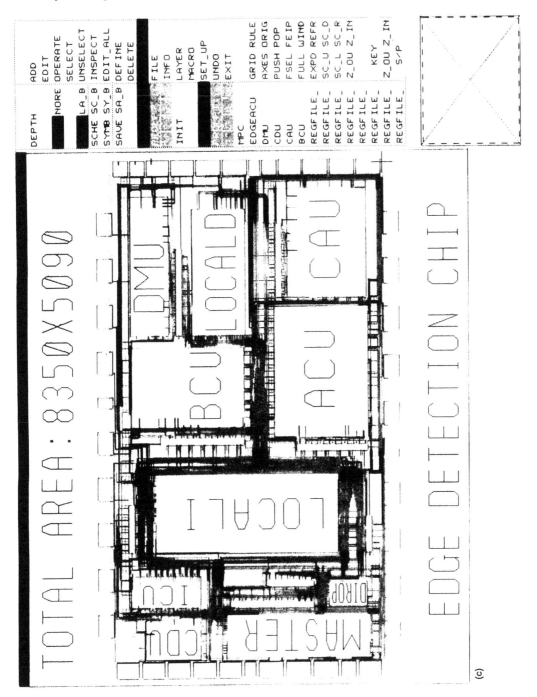

(c)

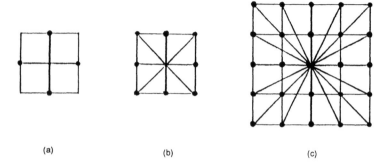

FIGURE 8.   Some chain codes: (a) 4-direction Freeman code, (b) 8-direction Freeman code, (c) generalized chain code [after *25*].

feedback from higher level scene interpretation, no method will be able to form the clean line drawings one would like to obtain. This particular implementation will yield video-rate edge extraction from gray level images. Sophisticated edge detectors can be found in Refs. *23* and *24*. After edge point linking, object boundaries are often described by 'chain codes.' The transition from one point of the contour to the next is given by a code number which uniquely corresponds with the step direction. On a discrete grid, the number of possible directions is limited. Figure 8a shows the 4-direction Freeman code, Figure 8b the 8-direction Freeman code, and Figure 8c the 'generalized chain codes' of 'length' 1 and 2. Advantages of the latter over the classic Freeman code are the more smooth and compact description [*25*]. Objects can be completely described as strings of such code numbers. Care should be taken as simple chain codes do not behave isotropically. Changes in part orientation will adversely affect measurements based on such codes (e.g., the number of code steps as an estimate for perimeter or length). Proposed remedies range from simple to quite sophisticated [*26–28*].

Region growing is an alternative segmentation technique. First small regions with very homogeneous characteristics are formed (e.g., intensity, curvature value or sign in the case of range images). These small regions are then further extended along their borders until they meet. In subsequent steps, neighbouring regions can be combined if their values don't differ too much; alternatively, after a while, regions can be split again, to form new regions with higher homogeneity. These techniques are referred at as 'split-and-merge' [*29*]. Regions can be more concisely described by the characteristic's mean value or by some parametric fit to the surface. Some basic surface types are discussed in a later section. The region and the edge description are more or less complementary. The boundaries of the regions yield edges, and the areas circumscribed by edges yield regions. Not all edge detection techniques output closed edges, however.

Global Versus Local Features

Initially, features were derived from the complete object area or contour. Such 'global features' have the advantage that they unambiguously follow from the shape. A simple, flat object has only one area, one perimeter, one number of holes, etc. An important class of such measures are the moments, here illustrated for the binary case. The $(p+q)$th order moment $M[p,q]$ for an object O with x and y being the coordinates of the pixels in the image, and I intensity is defined as

$$M[p,q] = \sum_{(x,y)inO} x^p y^q I(x,y) \tag{1}$$

If, e.g., after thresholding, $I(x,y) = 1$ if the pixel belongs to the object and 0 if it is part of the background $M[0,0]$ gives the area of the object, $M[1,0]/M[0,0]$ and $M[0,1]/M[0,0]$ the coordinates of the centroid. To determine the orientation of the object, additional information on the second order moments is needed. Sense is specified by third-order moments. When the coordinates refer to the world coordinate system, the moments are 'main moments.' 'Central moments' take the centroid as reference point. Problems are to be expected with highly symmetric objects. Another class are the 'Fourier descriptors,' which are based on the Fourier transforms of the object silhouette [30,31]. The boundary is treated as a periodic function, for example, a complex function with x and y as real and imaginary parts.

On the other hand, input image quality usually is not sufficient and scene complexity too high in order for these global features to be robustly retrieved. They are unreliable if, for instance, objects can overlap. As a consequence, vision system designers gradually shifted toward the inclusion of features which are extracted from partial data, 'local features.' Edges often are not nicely connected strings of edge points, but rather patches of jaggy strings separated by gaps. Global features like perimeter cannot be estimated from such incomplete data, whereas local features like vertices or curvature extrema might at least to some extent still be available. The disadvantage of these local features is that they do not necessarily uniquely correspond to one part of the object. As an example, a shape might have several vertices. Bringing the object model and image instance into correspondence then requires structural model descriptions and additional feature mapping. Local edge feature descriptions often take the form of a sequence of 'critical points' separated by optimally fitted edge segments ('primitives') having a simple parametric description. Both points and primitives require only limited information to be stored. If there is no limitation on the length of the code steps, generalized chain coding becomes a polygonal approximation of the contour (i.e., the primitives are straight lines). Several other polygonal approximation algorithms are available and video rate implementations have been realized [32]. Curvature extrema (vertices!) play a crucial part in polygonal approximation as line linkage knots (the critical points), as well as in human visual processes. Sometimes higher-order approximations are used as primitives. Circular arcs and B-splines are among the most popular and new developments like NURBS (nonuniform rational B-splines) can be expected to gain interest [33] as they can serve as a unifying description, embedding B-splines, straight lines, circular arcs, etc. Such primitives, however, require more computing time. One strategy is to start from a polygonal approximation and to derive the higher-order description from it. With curved primitives, critical points often include inflection points. These are invariant under similarities, affine transformations, and projective transformations. The primitive-critical point type of scheme sometimes is replaced by a brute-force variant. A set of overlapping contour segments of constant length is used. Data reduction can be realized by working with an optimal subset. Robust recognition has been demonstrated this way [34, 35]. In the case of range data, local features are used almost exclusively. As in the aforementioned case of edge primitives, the local feature extraction typically boils down to a segmentation of the surface into primitives separated by critical lines. The simplest boundary representation is the polyhedral approximation (e.g., via triangularization). Surface patches can also be described by higher-order descriptions, at the cost of an increasing number of coefficients and increasing fitting complexity. There are many different types of parametric surface representations like Coon's patches and tensor product composite surfaces, B-spline surfaces being probably the best known. In the computer vision literature, one seldom uses these descriptions, but rather often a limited set of surface shapes is supposed to occur. Typical examples include planes, cylinders, spheres, and cones. The gaussian sphere offers an instrument for their detection. Superquadrics [*36, 37*] and NURBS [*33*] are candidates for unified description. More information on superquadrics is given later. Recent research has also focused on surface curves and regions that enjoy some global property, without imposing precise parametric descriptions: lines of curvature, asymptotes, bounding contours, surface intersections as critical lines and umbilic regions, and regions characterized by the constant signs of Gaussian and/or mean curvature as the primitives [*38, 39*]. One can then combine surface regions to spheres, surfaces of revolution, and, in general, volumes thought of as being structured around spines and points. More about this follows.

Scale–Space

In the description of contours, another noteworthy development has retained a great deal of attention over the last years. 'Scale-space' approaches describe contours at different resolutions by subsequent smoothing operations [*40–42*]. The smoothing is carried out by convolution with a Gaussian filter. When obtained with Gaussian filtering, it can be proved that a signal's (e.g., curvature or its derivative with arc length) zero-crossing (e.g., inflection points or curvature extrema, respectively) find their origin in the original signal. The technique thus yields a list of features, which really stem from the original high-resolution shape and are not merely spurious artifacts. An interesting theoretical result is the possibility to reconstruct the original contour from the zero-crossing (e.g., inflection points) by making the smoothing process continuous (i.e., by widening the Gaussian filter continuously). Smoothing one-dimensional contour descriptions has been criticized because such an approach is 'blind' to the actual 2-D shape in the image, and thereby unfortunately may yield unnatural results. After smoothing, closed contours are not necessarily rendered closed [*43*], and the topology of the original contours often is not taken into account [*44*]. Nevertheless, the idea of coarse-to-fine analysis is an important one. Not only have some remedies against the aforementioned problems been presented [*43–45*], this idea of descriptions at multiple resolutions is applied to several other applications in vision.

Parameter Spaces

Sometimes feature extraction can be simplified by first applying some mapping to a different space in which the features take on a simpler form. We will discuss only a few examples: the Hough transform, arc length space, the Gaussian sphere, and the log-polar mapping.

The Hough transform offers an instrument for the robust detection of curves with simple parametric descriptions [*46*]. We will illustrate the basic principle with extraction of straight lines. Assume that edges have been extracted and that one would like to find all straight segments. One essential advantage of the Hough transform is that it requires only isolated edge points. Edges don't have to be linked and thinned. Assume we have N edge points with image coordinates (x_i, y_i), $i \in [1, N]$. If point (x_k, y_k) lies on a straight segment for which the corresponding line equation is given by

$$y = ax + b \tag{2}$$

then more particularly

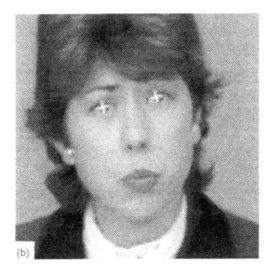

FIGURE 9.   Application of the generalized Hough transform: (a) the program extracts rectangular regions corresponding to car license plates and can easily be trained to recognize other shapes such as the circular pupils in (b) [45] (courtesy ESAT).

$$y_k = ax_k + b \qquad\qquad (3)$$

or

$$b = (-x_k)\, a + y_k \qquad\qquad (4)$$

If we reverse roles and interpret (a, b) as coordinates in the corresponding 2D parameter space, then the latter equation corresponds to a straight line having slope $-x_k$ and offset y_k. If we would construct such a line in parameter space for all points of the same straight segment in the image, all the parameter space lines would be seen to intersect in (a, b), yielding the unknown segment parameters. Of course, we cannot restrict this operation to collinear edge points. As one doesn't known which points form straight edge segments, one constructs the corresponding parameter straight line simply for each edge point in the original image. Each time a new line passes through a 'cell' of the parameter space, the cell's 'vote' is increased by one. Cells obtaining sufficient votes correspond to intersection points and most probably represent collinear edge points in the image. Similar strategies have been described for other simple parametric curves. If no parametric description of the target curve is available, then the generalized Hough transform can be used. Generalized Hough algorithms work with arbitrary, but a priori known shapes. Often it is supposed that the shape's location and orientation are known up to a translation parallel to the camera plane. Sometimes also rotation around an axis parallel to the camera axis is allowed, as well as scaling (e.g., as a consequence of changing distance from the camera). The more unknown parameters, the more computation time will be required. Figure 9a illustrates an application of a generalized Hough transform for the detection of car license plates [47]. The system was trained to find rectangular regions. Figure 9b shows output of the same program when trained on finding circular regions corresponding with pupils.

Whereas the Hough transform has been used widely for the detection of image features which are similar to models of apriori known shapes, arc length space has been introduced to facilitate the detection of similar edge segments within the image itself and of which shape does not have to be known [48, 49]. Possible applications are the detection of mirror symmetrical or parallel object outlines. Imagine two planar contours lying in parallel planes which are viewed from an orthogonal direction. Further imagine two points, one on each contour. Starting from fixed reference points on each contour, these two points are each characterized by their arc length, say s and s', respectively. If we interpret the pair (s, s') as coordinates in 2D space, then the original pair of points is mapped onto one point in this 'arc length space' (ALS). If a contour fragment F (containing point s_i) on the first contour is mapped onto a fragment F' on the second contour by a similarity transformations S, then the corresponding point $(s_i, S(s_i))$ lies on a straight line in ALS. Moreover, the sum or the difference of the tangential orientations for these point pairs should remain constant along these lines. The search for such lines can be made quite efficient by the following observation. Inflection points are mapped on inflection points under similarity transformations. This means that the point pair resulting from similarity mappings (the straight lines in ALS) should both correspond to inflection points or both correspond to noninflection points. Therefore ALS is divided into a special rectangular tessellation. The vertical and horizontal lines coincide with the positions of inflection points on the first and the second contour, respectively. The straight line mappings which really correspond to a similarity, should therefore cross a vertical and horizontal line simultaneously. Finding good candidates for similarity mappings is therefore largely reduced to searching sets of subsequent collinear tessel vertices. Only on such candidates should a more profound test be performed. Figure

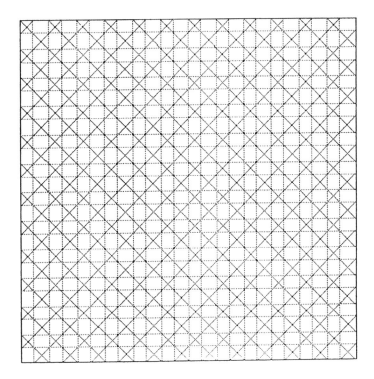

FIGURE 10. (a) Regular object contour, (b) its symmetries in arc length space [*48*] top left to bottom-right lines represent rotational symmetries; top right to bottom left lines are mirror symmetries. (courtesy ESAT).

10a shows a simple contour, having a dihedral symmetry group (mirror and rotational symmetries). Figure 10b shows the corresponding symmetries in arc length space, together with the aforementioned tessellation. Notice that the symmetry lines pass through the tessellation vertices. Generalization toward the use of ALS for nonorthogonal viewing directions have been proposed [48]. It is based on the use of affine instead of euclidean arc length.

The Gauss mapping maps a surface point to a point on the unit sphere with the same normal direction [cfr. *1* and *50*]. Simple surface types yield simple curves on this 'Gaussian sphere.' Cylinders will be reduced to two points for the two planar sides and a great (geodesic) circle for the curved envelope. Polyhedra become a set of points and cones a point and a nongeodesic circle. If information on the 3D normal vectors to the surface is available, then the Gaussian sphere offers an instrument for the segmentation of the surface into such simple surface primitives. Sometimes the Hough transform is used for the detection of the curves on the Gaussian sphere.

As a final example, the logarithmic-polar mapping is used to create feature descriptions which remain invariant under scaling and rotation [51,52]. Thus, regardless of the distance of the camera to the object and the relative orientation, exactly the same features can be used for recognition. The log-polar mapping is as follows:

$$(x, y) \rightarrow (\ln) r, \phi \tag{5}$$

where (r, ϕ) are the usual polar coordinates corresponding to the cartesian (x, y) coordinates of the original rectangular grid. If one can find a reference point on the object and keep it aligned with the camera center ($r = 0$), then it is clear that scaling and rotation will amount to a simple shift in log-polar coordinates. Figure 11b shows a log-polar sampling of Figure 11a. It is clearly seen that image detail is preserved at the center, while sampling is more coarse in the periphery. A compromise between data reduction and detail at the center of gaze is established. Figure 11c shows the final mapping, in which some important types of rotation and scaling show up as a simple translation. Figure 2 depicts a CCD chip which directly captures intensity values in such a coordinate frame.

RECOGNITION

Subproblems

Generally speaking, setting up a recognition system requires at least solving three subproblems. First, a system can only recognize parts it 'knows' in some way or another. An internal description of the different parts has to be generated, in the sequel referred to as object 'models.' Then the system should somehow be trained, in other words, it should be told which features to look for and in what order. More ideally, it could learn this autonomously, partly from comparisons between models and partly from experience. Finally, the actual recognition procedure has to be specified, involving data acquisition, feature extraction, and data-model matching. Older systems require human interaction for both modeling and training. In such systems, these two stages more or less coincide. Newer systems don't depend on human operators for the training. Features are selected automatically [e.g., *34*], recognition strategies are developed from experience [e.g., *35*], and recognition programs are generated automatically off-line [e.g., *53, 54*]. Training has become a more clearly separate entity from modeling. Attempts to allow systems to autonomously add new models to their database and to organize such databases to optimally assist in efficient recognition so far have not been successful.

FIGURE 11. (a) Original image, (b) Log-polar sampling, (c) Log-polar mapping [2] (courtesy DIST, University of Genova).

Besides the degree of occlusion (i.e., how strongly objects overlap), the difficulty of an image processing task is largely reflected by the degree to which three-dimensional information has to be inferred from two-dimensional data. If the object is completely flat, if it is looked upon from a perpendicular direction, and if no surface characteristics have to be judged, all information can be obtained from a binary silhouette image. If certain textures, elevations, or ridges on the surface are relevant, such surface characteristics as edges have to be extracted from a gray level image. If, moreover, the object is not resting in one of its stable positions or if it is viewed from arbitrary directions, three-dimensional geometric rea-

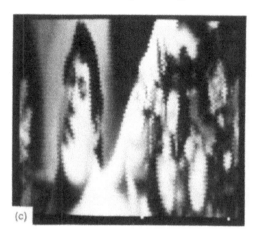

FIGURE 11.   continued.

soning is necessary. Then the correct model and the spatial transformation which most likely renders the two-dimensional data are searched for. This might be feasible if some 3D form elements like edges or vertices yield salient 2D features, but in the most general case with smooth surfaces this problem becomes untractable within reasonable time slots. Interpreting general two-dimensional intensity images still is beyond the ability of current computer vision systems. In principle inferring 3D descriptions from single 2D projections is impossible without making some additional assumptions about the scene and the objects it contains. Intensive research is going on in order to find such adequate additional assumptions. We described some earlier (shape-from-X). A noteworthy example is the SCERPO system [55]. SCERPO is largely based on a 'nonaccidentalness' assumption, stating that order in the image is most of the time genuine (e.g., straight lines in the image are projections of real straight edges, parallel image lines stem from really parallel structures, etc.). Instead of working with gray level information, one could in such cases of course directly extract range information using the specialized sensors discussed previously. Problems are then partially shifted from the interpretation stage to the acquisition stage.

As a conclusion, most industrial vision systems are basically 2D and intensity oriented. Yet, three-dimensional recognition has the potential of being viewpoint independent and generally applicable. But three-dimensional image processing faces different problems like generating high-resolution depth maps within very short time limits, the huge task of inferring form from two-dimensional intensity images, building precise object models appropriate for fast matching, or successfully segmenting surface data for the generation of primitives to be matched against. Additional information on 3D image processing can be found in the literature [50, 56] as well as in earlier sections. Moreover, industrial systems require interactive modeling and training. Recent research is aimed at eliminating this need. The coupling with CAD systems will play a crucial role in this respect.

Recognition Strategies

Three different types of recognition strategies will be outlined: template matching, feature vector classification, and structural methods.

Template matching consists of comparing, usually by correlation or subtraction techniques, a section of the image with a prestored pattern or 'template.' In order to find the same pattern in the image, the template is shifted over the image until both overlap precisely. In its general form, this approach is very time consuming, especially if the orientation (2D) or scale of the pattern are unknown. Then the process has to be repeated for several orientations or scales. Processing can be accelerated by first only comparing a subset of sparsely sampled points in the pattern mask and the image. Further processing is only envisaged when the subtemplate quality of match exceeds some threshold. The sensivitiy of template matching to minor mismatches increases with perimeter/area, which can be regarded as a measure of complexity. As a consequence, complex patterns which will often require more computations with other methods, simplify the determination of precise position and orientation with template matching. Template matching can also be applied to gray-scale imagery, but additional problems with lighting variations and surface changes due to stains and smears are to be expected. The generalized Hough transform, described by Ballard and Brown [57], is akin to this correlation type of processing.

The second strategy extracts a set of measures from a pattern and places the corresponding values and labels in a 'feature vector.' This feature vector is a one-dimensional array of fixed length. Typical features are simple characteristics like number of holes, perimeter, area, moments, and Fourier descriptors (i.e., the global features discussed in the preceding section. If there are N features and if they can be chosen appropriately, different object types will form different clusters in the N-dimensional feature space. This feature space is partitioned into several subspaces, corresponding to the different object types. Vectors of unknown objects have to be assigned to one of these subspaces. Minimum-average-loss Bayes classifiers and minimum distance classifiers are examples of popular assignment rules. With large numbers of features, the feature space quickly gets sparse and this type of decision making loses its efficiency. Recognition can also be organized in a sequential manner, where feature values are checked in a prescribed order, following a path in a decision tree. Care should be taken to make the measures in the vector invariant to translation, rotation, and possibly scaling or other transformations. Many global features already are invariant under some of these transformations. To this end, algebraic combinations of moments can be formed [58, 59] and normalized of Fourier descriptors has been proposed [60, 61]. Sometimes more local features are used by dividing the object in portions (e.g., angular or concentric sectors around its centroid). For each of the sectors several features are calculated, like the number of object pixels they contain or the number of changes between black and white. For each measure this yields a feature vector with the number of sectors as its dimension. These vectors are invariant under translation. Rotation results in a mere phase shift for the angular sectors. This approach is akin to log-polar mapping. Feature vector classification is a 'data-driven' method, in that first the different features are calculated solely from the image, irrespective of any considerations about the object models.

Structural methods, on the other hand, always contain some 'model-driven' aspects, in that the model is used to direct the feature extraction at some stage or to validate hypotheses. They use positional constraints (syntactic rules) imposed on the features (semantic primitives) with respect to each other. Although we didn't mention the underlying models so far, it is clear that these should support the type of strategy one is inclined to follow. This intertwining led us to their joint treatment in this section. Graphs are especially suitable for describing structure and classification in those cases is a question of graph matching (isomorphisms, maximal cliques . . .). Graph nodes correspond with features and the links represent the structural constraints. Linguistics have strongly influenced structural methods which are often formulated in terms of 'grammars' and 'sentence parsing' [62]. Structural

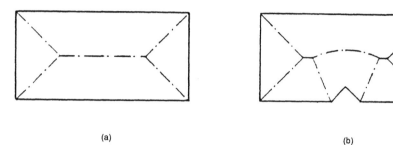

(a)   (b)

FIGURE 12.   (a) The symmetric axis transform (SAT) of a rectangle, (b) the SAT is drastically changed by minor changes to the pattern [*63*].

methods are the most powerful and robust. Most of the features used are local (i.e., they convey information about the shape of the primitives obtained from segmentation). The graph links usually refer to the positional relationships of the features, to the degrees of freedom in these relationships, and to the uncertainties on the corresponding values. Structural descriptions therefore allow to work with nonrigid objects composed of rigid subparts. The most direct matching would follow from explicitly listing the relations between every feature pair. With growing numbers of features in a model, this strategy clearly becomes unfeasible. Relations are often not independent and their number can therefore be reduced. Often only relations between neighbouring features are made explicit. Structural methods can only be full-fetched recognition processes if relations between any pair of features can be retrieved, especially for disconnected, distant features. A special type are the 'skeleton' descriptions, obtained from 'axis transforms.' The basic principle of axis transforms is to transform the silhouette of an object into a graph, which is called a 'skeleton.' Around each point of the SAT skeleton (symmetric axis transform) there exists a circle which is tangent to the boundary in at least two points [*63*]. The SAT consists of two parts: the structure of the skeleton and the radius of the corresponding circle at each of its points. The skeleton is used as a model fro structural recognition; that is, the object is described as interconnected components, each component corresponding to an axis of the skeleton. The computation of the skeleton is time consuming and the result is very sensitive to noise as can be seen from Figure 12. Alternative axis transforms like smoothed local symmetries (SLS) have been devised in order to overcome the SATs main difficulties [*64, 65*]. Some widespread 3D volumetric models are closely related to the skeleton idea. They are based on 'generalized cones' [see, e.g., *66*]. These descriptions start from a 3D space curve (the axis or spine) around which planar cross sections of the shape are specified. Usually, these cross sections are taken at right angles to the axis (generalized cylinders) and have some parametric form. 'Sweep functions' can then be used to describe the change of these parameters along the axis. Several spines form the skeleton of the object. A new result is the use of deformable cylinders which infer object shape under the guidance of limited image data (e.g., the bounding silhouette is used in combination with symmetry-maximizing 'forces') [*67*]. The advantage of this regularization-type approach is that the type of surface is no longer imposed on the model, but can dynamically be refined by incoming image information. Merely a tendency toward a certain type of regularity is imposed. Generalized cones are constructed around an axis. Similarly, many objects can be described around a point by

FIGURE 13. Example of 3DPO recognition strategy for the images 1 and 3 (a) detection of circular arc together with inferred circle, (b) structural information is used to guide a search for the smaller circle, which is successful, (c) proceeding like this, all degrees of freedom are removed and a unique object model remains, a hypothesis which is checked by projecting the model onto the scene and comparing the projection with the image measurements, (d) shows the structural CAD model which is known to the system [70].

specifying the radius from the point as a function of latitude and longitude angles (e.g., superquadrices) [36, 37]. The family of superquadrics includes such diverse shapes as cylinders, cubes, ellipsoids, and spheres. Less clearly specified sets of basic shapes can be based on the concepts of 'sticks, plates, and blobs' [68]. The relative dimensions of height, length, and so on determine the assignment of an object to a class. Geometrical and relational constraints are used for the interpretation of 2D views. From the basic shapes, more complex objects can be constructed by the logical operation of union, intersection, and difference. This 'constructive solid geometry' is popular in CAD, but lends itself less directly to object recognition, because only surface patches are visible but never whole solids. Moreover,

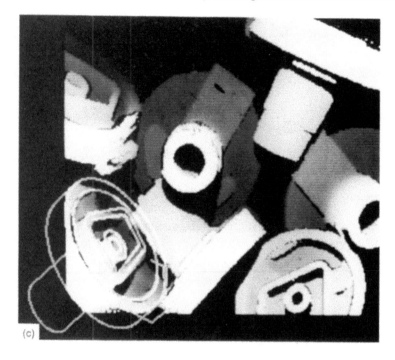

(c)

TWO-PART OBJECT MODELS

EXTENDED CAD MODEL   FEATURE CLASSIFICATIONS

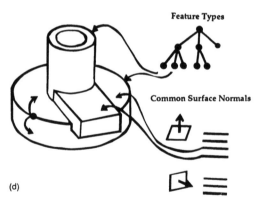

(d)

FIGURE 13.   continued.

these solids most of the time don't really correspond to a unique decomposition, but only reflect the designer's preference. A special interface between such models and the recognition's feature extraction has to be supplied. Generalized cylinders simplify this interface because the projection of the spine is also the spine of the projection. In the case of superquadrics, parameters rather easily follow from partial surface normals. Boundary representations ('B-reps') more directly relate to available features. Here the model consists of lists of surface representations (cfr. the description of primitives) together with their positional constraints and their domain of validity. The interested reader is referred to Besl et al. [69].

Let us illustrate the structural methods with an example: 3DPO, a program developed at Stanford Research Institute [70]. This program is an interesting example in several respects. It shows a nice integration of intensity and range processing, it uses models which can be derived from CAD systems, and it doesn't require interactive training. We will now start a description for the image of Figure 1. Based on the combined analysis of the intensity image in Figure 1 and the range image in Figure 3, a number of features are extracted. The system takes off by selecting a circle, based on a recognition strategy which was generated off-line. Starting from the circular arc illustrated in Figure 13a, a feature match is hypothesized, illustrated by the complete circle. The match is correct, the circular arc corresponds to the hypothesized circle in the model. As a next step, the position of a smaller circle is predicted, based on the position of the matched circle and the model (Fig. 13b). After the detection of such a sequence of features, at a certain point no ambiguity in object type or pose will remain. The recognition cycle for one object is then complete. Figure 13c shows the projection of the hypothesized object onto the scene. Recognition clearly has been successful. This stage is not only shown for illustrative purposes, however, but is part of the 'hypothesis generation—verification' paradigm. After a hypothesis has been generated, it will be checked by comparing the projected model and the actual scene.

Finally, we have to mention a straightforward, yet quite different approach. Rather than building one 3D model, one could as well store a set of 2D models of the object for different viewpoints. The number of possible viewpoints generally will be infinite, but such a large number of different models is fortunately not required. It is sufficient to store some 'aspects,' i.e., generic views which will only continuously change with changing viewpoint. For polyhedra, this means that no vertices or edges appear or disappear. The aspects are usually referred to as 'characteristic views' and are recognized by 2D structural methods [e.g., *53, 71, 72*].

VISION-ROBOT INTEGRATION

Active Vision

Problems in intepreting single 2D intensity images of 3D scenes can be alleviated by working with an image sequence instead. It is assumed that a relative motion between object and observer takes place. Not only can motion information between images be extracted from such a sequence ('optic flow'), which is often interesting in its own right, for example, for time-to-contact calculations [73-75]. The (sparse) optic flow field contains the image projections of the corresponding 3D velocities. Regularization is used to interpolate and enhance this field. In principle, from the optic flow field the real 3D velocity vectors and shape can be reconstructed under some simplifying assumptions. But in general, research has not come up with robust solutions to the 3D part of the problem. If the relative motion is known to the observer from other sources (e.g., knowing the robot motion and the object remaining at its position), then 3D information can be retrieved, often as the solution to well-posed problems. As an example, while moving around an object with a robot-held camera and tracking the object (i.e., keeping the object in the field of view), gradual refinements can be made to the description of the environment. Using image sequences rather than isolated frames can add robustness to an approach where it would otherwise fail. Several ill-posed problems can be rendered well-posed this way [8, 76]. Such 'active vision' has been demonstrated, for example, in stereo applications [e.g., 77] and dynamic shape-from-contour [78, 79]. The word 'active' as used here should not be confused with 'active' range finding. Certainly not all visual robot tracking is meant for active vision though, but certainly the ensuing years will show a clear tendency in that direction. Most often the processing of subsequent images is still done completely separately in robot vision applications, as if these images were unrelated snapshots. As vision becomes integral to robotic function, the more will robotic movement be designed to enhance the vision aspect of robotic motion. Let us now turn to robot aspects of visual tracking and some of the problems involved.

Robot control strategies are generally hierarchically organized and the main structure can be divided into two levels. The upper level is called path planning and the lower level is path tracking control. The path planning is concerned with the derivation of a scenario for the desired positions and velocities to be followed by the robot end-effector. The aim of path tracking control is to make the actual positions of the robot end-effector match those desired values. In dealing with a random environment, the position of the robot end-effector has to be monitored as it moves and errors must be corrected as soon as they are detected.

Broadly speaking, there have been three areas in which tracking techniques have been developed. The first involves sensorless tracking of an off-line planned path. Here it is assumed that the environment is deterministic, that the robot task is well-structured and that the positioning error of the robot is well within the permissible range prescribed by the robot task. Thus no on-line modification of the robot path will be necessary. The second situation involves a rather random environment but a well-structured robot task, like seam tracking in arc welding. In this case, the desired robot path is generally known in advance but could be subjected to significant variation in real-time. Therefore, on-line modification of the robot trajectory is necessary. The third area involves both a random environment and a variable robot task, such as mobile object handling. Here the object to be manipulated could be mixed with many other different objects and positioned randomly, for instance, on a conveyor belt with a random orientation. Moreover, the conveyor motion could be completely unknown except the form of motion (e.g., linear or circular). Thus the target motion has to be estimated using sensory data, deviations of the robot end-effector from the desired path should be compensated for as they are measured. The only solution to such a problem is then the utilization of dynamic tracking control techniques.

The second and third of these areas—both involving sensing—will now be examined. Discussion will be further restricted to vision-based robot guidance. Before going into any detail, however, some general aspects of vision-guided robot systems will first be discussed in the next section.

General Aspects of Vision-Based Robot Guidance

When integrated with a robot, computer vision can extend the feedback loop for robot positioning control to include relative end-effector position. As far as vision-based robot guidance is concerned, the system operations consist of a sequence of independent steps, known as the "look-and-move" structure as described below.

1. The vision system **"looks"** down at the scene of interest and infers the desired destination of the robot end-effector

2. Compute the difference between the current location of the robot end-effector and the desired one—the position corrections to be made by the robot end-effector
3. The robot end-effector **"moves"** to the desired position

If the visual servo control system is designed in such a way that the robot can accept new movement commands only after it has completed the previous one, then the "look-and-move" structure is said to be static. On the contrary, if position estimates can be updated as fast as they are measured and position corrections can be commanded while the robot is moving, the whole system can then be modeled as a dynamic closed-loop sampled-data system. Dynamic control has the potential to achieve fast response, but the role of computer vision as the feedback transducer will strongly affect the closed-loop dynamics of the overall system. At least two specific characteristics of the visual data must be taken into top account in control system design.

1. **Long time-delay**: Image processing algorithms are usually time consuming (additionally there always exists some execution time for the robot end-effector to arrive at a set point)
2. **Heavy noise corruption**: The uncertainty in visual data comes basically from three sources: (1) computer vision's lack or robustness against all kinds of image degradations; (2) the inevitable vibration of the camera when it is attached to the robot end-effector; (3) digitization and round-off effects during computations

As a result, direct use of the visual data for robot control purposes will obviously lead to a poor control accuracy and in the case of dynamic visual servoing this can even cause stability problems.

Vision-Guided Automatic Seam Tracking

As an example of the second type of tracking problems, we now discuss seam tracking. The idea of automatic seam tracking is not new and great effort has already been made to develop new sensor techniques for the large scale introduction of welding robots. Compared with other sensors, the noncontact visual sensor has appeared most promising.

The presence of the welding arc poses several problems for obtaining a meaningful image of the weld joints. The high-intensity light emitted by the arc adversely affects the contrast of the image; the streaks produced by the flying particles of luminescent spatter introduce noise into the image; the smoke emitted from the arc can obscure the scene, and so on. As a remedy, three special measures can be taken to overcome these problems: (1) Calibrate the camera in such a way that it views the seam a short distance, say 2 to 4 inches, ahead of the welding arc; (2) use a compact, high-intensity light source, say a laser projector together with a bandpass filter in front of the camera lense; and (3) shorten the exposure time to reduce spark streaks. The seam to be tracked is generally known and so can be programmed or taught to the robot in advance. But significant deformation in the welding line is expected in real-time due to the insufficiently accurate edge preparation of the weld joints, setting errors in both the weld joints and the rail on which the welding machine rides, and thermal distortion. Therefore, real-time measurement of the 3D seam geometry is necessary for accurate tracking of the welding line.

The most widely used technique for obtaining 3D information of the seam geometry is triangulation with structured illumination patterns. In real-time applications, both the laser projector and the image sensor are mounted on the robot end-effector and scan the surface of the weld joints in the direction perpendicular to the welding line. As the welding process is going on the actual trajectory of the welding line can then be detected step by step.

In this way automatic tracking is achieved and the welding torch can follow the actual welding line accurately in real-time.

It is obvious from the above discussion that the whole system is no more than a variant of the static look-and-move structure. But since the tolerance of arc welding itself is not so tight, the traveling speed of the torch is generally low, and the time delay has been automatically compensated for (scanning ahead of the torch), such a configuration is usually adequate.

Dynamic Tracking Techniques with Visual Feedback

Another important application area of robot vision is vision-based assembly. The main function of the robot in such applications is to pick up required objects and then put them to prescribed destinations. If the object remains stationary is space, the static "look-and-move" structure is generally sufficient since the look-and-move procedure can be repeated until a prescribed accuracy is achieved. Early vision-assisted robot systems were in fact dominated by this feature.

In order to handle a moving object, a critical constraint has to be imposed on the target motion. The camera will always be obscured, have too small a field of view, or be out of focus when the grasping robot tool has reached the vicinity of the object. This means that there will be a time period during which the vision system cannot provide any useful information and tracking has to be maintained. This time period may not be long but it could be long enough to cause unsuccessful grasping if the target moves in a random manner. Therefore, the target motion must be regular. No matter what kind of form it assumes, linear, circular, sinusoidal, or maybe a falling body parabola, it must be deterministic, that is, it can be measured or estimated with sufficient accuracy and the future position of the object can be predicted.

The robot motion can be decomposed into two submotions in mobile target handling; one for following the target motion and the other for eliminating both the positional and orientational displacement of the robot tool. Since the current displacement measured by the vision system is inherently the integration of the difference between the preceding target motion and the robot movement itself, the commanded movement of the robot tool at present will depend not only on the current displacement but also be correlated to some extent with the past. In view of the particularity of the visual data, the key is the accurate estimation of the target motion from the noisy visual data and the full compensation of the long time delay.

Control system design based on deterministic control strategies is appealing due to their maturity and the simplicity. But they are dependent on the explicit use of a stringent mathematical model of the system dynamics and the exact measurement of the true system state. In view of the complexity of robot control due to the coupled, time-varying, nonlinear dynamics of the robot and the particularity of the visual data, such a problem is best modeled as a stochastic optimal control problem. The optimal solution of it is well known and is given by the so-called separation theorem, that is, the optimal strategy is composed of two parts: a state estimator which generates the optimal estimates of the system state in terms of a suitably selected criterion, and a linear feedback controller which synthesizes the optimal control input on the basis of the state estimates. The long time delay can then be compensated for either by including it into the control law design or by the use of a predictive control strategy.

The Kalman filter is well known for being capable of generating minimum variance estimates of the state of a dynamic system from a sequence of noise-corrupted observations.

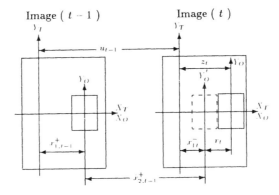

FIGURE 14.   State transition process of the Kalman filter.

Since its advent in the early 1960s, it has become a typical practice to utilize the Kalman filter in tracking control problems and so it is also an excellent candidate for robot tracking. Figure 14 shows schematically the state transition process of the Kalmar filter, where it is assumed that the target motion is linear with a constant speed, that the camera is mounted on the robot end-effector, that the visual data have already been transformed into the robot tool coordinates denoted by X_T and Y_T while X_O and Y_O are the object frame. The larger squares in the same figures are the field of view of the camera, the smaller rectangles stand for the target, $x^+_{1,\,t-1}$ and $x^+_{2,\,t-1}$ are the optimal estimates of the object position and the belt speed obtained at the preceding sampling instant, u_{t-1} denote the distance the robot end-effector is commanded to move during the previous sampling period. The best position prediction we can obtain at the same time instant is then x^-_{1t} as denoted by the dashed box. Let z_t denote the new observation of the target position, then the difference r_t between z_t and x^-_{1t} stands for the new information, called the innovation signal, brought in by z_t. By combining r_t with old state estimates and minimizing the estimation error covariance matrix, new state estimates can be obtained and new predictions of the target position can be computed in the same way.

Until now, it seems that the robot path could be easily planned by direct use of these state estimates. At most, we should use the position predictions rather than the current position estimate for the purpose of time-delay compensation. Generally, however, it is not the case, since the state estimates generated by the Kalman filter are optimal only in the sense that the estimation error covariances are minimum and by no means exact. Direct use of these estimates for robot control without taking into account the robot positioning error may still not satisfy the accuracy requirement for grasping.

In view of the dependence of the current displacement with the past, if we choose the path control data during each sampling period as the input signal $u(t)$ and the corresponding observations of the robot movement as the output signal $y(t)$, the positioning error of the robot will be automatically included in the output signal and $y(t)$ can be well described with the following ARIMAX (Auto-Regressive Integrated Moving Average eXogenous) model

$$y(t) = \sum_{i=1}^{n} a_i y(t-i) + \sum_{i=1}^{m} b_i u(t-i) + \xi_t / \Delta$$

where t is the index, Δ is the difference operator, i.e. $\Delta y(t) = y(t) - y(t - 1)$ and ξ_t is the discrete time white noise. For a systematic exposition of the model, the interested reader is referred elsewhere [80]. Starting with this formulation, the author proposed to use the generalized productive control (GPC) strategy for optimal control input synthesis. As a long-range predictive control strategy, the GPC is particularly suitable for controlling processes with long-time delay and so for visual servoing of robots [81, 82]. In the GPC, a set of free response predictions of the system output are first computed through the ARIMAX plant model by assuming a constant control input which is equal to that applied in the last sampling instant. Meanwhile, the expected movements of the robot tool for tracking are predicted in terms of the optimal state estimates. The differences between them should then be compensated for by increasing the control input. The optimal control input increments are then obtained by minimizing a quadratic form of these differences and the control input increments themselves. In this way, the influence of the uncertainties in both the visual data and the robot positioning system will all be reduced to their minimum and the time delay will be fully compensated for. As a result, perfect tracking of the moving object can be achieved.

Other examples of vision-guided robot tracking approaches include the learning control strategy proposed in Miller [83]. It is based on the cerebellar model arithmetic computer (CMAC) module. This approach uses a general learning algorithm to learn from on-line observations to reproduce, in a table lookup fashion, the relationship between available visual feedback parameters and system command variables. The significance of this approach lies in the fact that a priori knowledge about the system to be controlled is not a requisite. Therefore, it is easy to accommodate system changes.

A completely new structure, the image-based visual servo (IBVS) control approach, has been reported [84]. The key idea of this method is that image features are often continuous functions of the object position. Each optimally selected image feature can be used directly to control the motion of one robot joint. The issue of tracking moving objects has not really been addressed. More recently, extensions towards tracking of slowly moving objects have been reported [85].

A excellent example to conclude with is the ping-pong playing robot [86, 87]. Vision-control coupling is in between the very loose cooperation of static look-and-move and the strict link of IBVS. Special VLSI chips calculate the ball's moments. Camera pairs are used in a stereo set-up. Ball velocity is reported to reach 10 meters per second. Control is organized in a hierarchical structure, at the top of which is decided where the ball should go by the paddle return action. The dynamics of the collision is the lowest level in ball trajectory planning. Trajectories are kept in lookup tables. Not all goals are actually achievable and the system iterates between the numerical trajectory, posed calculations, feasibility tables, and an expert to modify system goals appropriately.

FUTURE DEVELOPMENTS AND CONCLUSIONS

Current vision systems are rather restricted in their applicability. Though state-of-the-art vision systems are still far from being able to assist in humanlike intelligent geometric reasoning, new developments, in software and hardware promote some idea about what to expect on the shop floor tomorrow. Their extra potentials will spur the increase of the input's dimensionality. The image resolution or the number of quantization levels could be increased. Multisensor information could be combined, as with multispectral (e.g., color) or range-intensity applications (data fusion). Sequences of images taken at different time slots, rather than single images could be interpreted. This would yield additional information on 3D motion parameters, surface shape, and time-to-contact ('optical flow' and active vision). Images could be stored and processed at multiple resolutions ('pyramid structures'), thereby not only increasing demands on memory and architecture parallelism but also algorithm efficiency. As the capabilities of next generation vision systems will not be sufficiently improved to envisage all these extensions, some choices will have to be made. Also the increasing task-specificity to be expected in robot design will encourage the diversification of vision systems, but the economic advantage of rather general-purpose systems which can be mass produced will have the opposite effect. Probably some forms of modularity and reconfigurable hardware will offer an attractive compromise.

Mixed architectures have received considerable research interest in the last few years. The architectures of future systems probably will combine processor arrays (SIMD) for low-level processing with multiprocessor architectures (MIMD) at higher levels. Higher levels will exercise more influence on lower level processing by the incorporation of feedback mechanisms.

Certainly, as the power of vision systems steadily increases, their role in industrial production will grow more prevalent and they will become an integral part of its environment with direct links to robot controllers and CAD/CAM databases.

ACKNOWLEDGMENT

The support of the Belgian Institute for Scientific Research in Industry and Agriculture (IWONL) is gratefully acknowledged. Also the authors are indebted to their colleagues who were so kind to supply them with the illustrations. Special thanks go to Radu Horaud, at Lifia, Grenoble, and to Giulio Sandini, at DIST, Genova.

REFERENCES

1. B. K. P. Horn, *Robot Vision,* MIT Press, McGraw-Hill, New York, 1986.
2. J. Van der Spiegel, G. Kreider, C. Claeys, I. Debusschere, G. Sandini, P. Dario, F. Fantini, P. Bellutti, and G. Soncini, "A Foveated Retina-like Sensor Using CCD Technology," in *Analog VLSI and Neural Network Implementations,* C. Mead and M. Ismail (eds.), DeKluwer, Boston 1989.
3. B. G. Batchelor, D. A. Hill, and D. C. Hodgson, *Automated Visual Inspections,* IFS (Publications) Ltd., Bedford, UK, 1985.
4. R. A. Jarvis, A "Perspective on Range Finding Techniques for Computer Vision," *IEEE PAMI, 5*(2), 122-139 (1983).
5. P. Vuylsteke and A. Oosterlinck, "Range Image Acquisition with a Single Binary-Encoded Light Patter," *IEEE Trans. Pattern Analysis Machine Intelligence, 5*(12), 148-164 (1990).
6. R. Horaud and T. Skordas, "Stereo Correspondence Through Feature Grouping and Maximal Cliques," *IEEE Trans. Pattern Analysis and Machine Intelligence, 11*(11), 1168-1180 (1989).
7. N. Ayache and B. Faverjon, "Efficient Registration of Stereo Images by Matching Graph Descriptions of Edge Segments," *Int. J. Computer Vision,* 107-131 (1987).
8. J. Aloimonos, "Visual Shape Computation," *Proc. IEEE, 76*(8), 899-916 (1988).
9. A. Witkin, "Recovering Surface Shape and Orientation from Texture," *Artif. Intell., 17,* 17-47 (1981).
10. J. Aloimonos, "Shape from Texture," *Biol. Cybernet., 58,* 345-360 (1988).

11. A. Blake and C. Marinos, "Shape from Texture: Estimation, Isotropy, and Moments," University of Oxford, Report No. OUEL 1774/89, 1989.
12. D. Blostein and N. Ahuja, "Shape from Texture: Integrating Texture-Element Extraction and Surface Estimation," *IEEE Trans. Pattern Analysis and Machine Intelligence, 11*(12), 1233-1250 (1989).
13. K. Kanatani and T. Chou, "Shape from Texture: General Principle," *Artificial Intelligence, 38*, 1-48 (1989).
14. M. Brady and A. Yuille, "An Extremum Principle for Shape from Contour," *IEEE Trans. Pattern Analysis and Machine Intelligence, 6*, 288-301 (1984).
15. S. Barnard and A. Pentland, "Three-Dimensional Shape from Line Drawings," *Proc. 8th Int. Joint Conference on Artificial Intelligence*, 1983, pp. 1062-1064.
16. H. Barrow and J. Tenenbaum, "Interpreting Line Drawings as Three-Dimensional Surfaces, *Artifi. Intell., 17*, 75-116.
17. R,. Horaud and M. Brady, "On the Geometric Interpretation of Image Contours," *Artif. Intell., 37*, 333-353.
18. M. Bertero, T. Poggio, and V. Torre, "Ill-Posed Problems in Early Vision," *Proc. IEEE, 76*(8), 869-889 (1988).
19   W. Grimson, "From Images to Surfaces: A Computational Study of the Human Early Visual System," MIT Press, Cambridge, MA, 1981.
20. D. Terzopoulos, "Multilevel Computational Processes for Visual Surface Reconstruction," *Computer Vision, Graphics, Image Proc. 24*, 52-96 (1983).
21. D. Terzopoulos, "Regularization of Inverse Visual Problems Involving Discontinuities," *IEEE Trans. Pattern Analysis and Machine Intelligence, 8*, 423-424 (1986).
22. A. Blake, and A. Zisserman, "Invariant Surface Reconstruction Using Weak Continuity Constraints," *Proc. IEEE Conf. Computer Vision and Pattern Recognition*, 1986, pp. 62-67.
23. J. Canny, "A Computational Approach to Edge Detection," *Proc. IEEE Trans. Pattern Analysis Machine Intelligence, PAMI-8*(6), 679-698 (1986).
24. F. Bergholm, "Edge Focusing," *IEEE Trans. on Pattern Analysis Machine Intelligence, 9*(6), 726-741 (1987).
25. J. Saghr and H. Freeman, "Analysis of the Precision of Generalize Chain Codes for the Representation of Planar curves," *IEEE Trans. Pattern Analysis and Machine Intelligence, PAMI-7*)6), 674-681 (1985).
26. F. Groen and P. Verbeek, "Freeman-Code Probabilities of Object Boundary Quantized Contours," *Computer Graphics and Image Proc., 7*, 391-402 (1978).
27. L. Van Gool, M. Goossens, and A. Oosterlinck, "Length Preserving Contour Coding with a Reduced Generalized Chain Code," *Proc. SPIE Intelligent Robots and Computer Vision, 579*, 64-71 (1985).
28. L. Dorst and A. Smeulders, "Length Estimators for Digitized Contours," *Computer Vision, Graphics, and Image Proc., 40*, 311-333 (1987).
29. S. Horowitz and T. Pavlidis, "Picture Segmentation by a Directed Split and Merge Procedure," *Proc. 2nd Int. Joint Conf. on Pattern Recognition*, 1974, pp. 424-433.
30. C. Zahn and R. Roskies, "Fourier Descriptors for Plane Closed Curves," *IEEE Trans. Computers, C-21*, 269-281 (1972).
31. E. Persoon and K. Fu, "Shape Discrimination Using Fourier Descriptors," *IEEE Trans. pattern Analysis and Machine Intelligence, PAMI-8*(3), 388-397 (1986).
32. R. Massen and E. Herre, "Real-Time Contour Vectorizer for Greylevel Images," *SPIE Proc. ECO2, Image Proc.*, III, 68-75 (1989).

33. P. Besl, "Geometric Modeling and Computer Vision," *Proc. IEEE, 76*(8), 936-958 (1988).
34. J. Turney, T. Mudge, and R. Volz, "Recognizing Partially Occluded Parts," *IEEE Trans. Pattern Analysis and Machine Intelligence, PAMI-7*(4), 410-421 (1985).
35. T. Knoll and R. Jain, "Learning to Recognize Objects Using Feature Indexed Hypotheses," *Proc. 1st Int. Conf. on Computer Vision,* 552-556 (1987).
36. A. Pentland, "Perceptual Organization and the Representation of Natural Form," *Artificial Intelligence, 28*(3), 293-331 (1986).
37. R. Bajcsy and F. Solina, "Three Dimensional Object Representation Revisited," *Proc. 1st Int. Conference on Computer Vision,* 321-340 (1987).
38. J. Koenderink and A. van Doorn, "The Shape of Smooth Objects and the Way Contours End," *Perception, 11,* 129-137 (1982).
39. M. Brady, J. Pone, A. Yille, and H. Asada, "Describing Surfaces," *Computer Vision, Graphics, and Image Processing, 32,* 1-28 (1985).
40. P. Burt and E. Adelson, "The Laplacian Pyramid as a Compact Image Code," *IEEE Trans. Comm., 31*(4), 532-540 (1983).
41. A. Witkin, "Scale-Space Filtering," in *Proc. 7th Int. Joint Conf. on Artificial Intelligence,* 1983 pp. 1019-1021.
42. F. Mokhtarian and A. Mackworth, "Scale-Based Description and Recognition of Planar Curves and Two-Dimensional Shapes," *IEEE Trans. Pattern Analysis and Machine Intelligence, PAMI-8*(1), (1986).
43. B. Horn and E. Weldon, "Filtering Closed Curves," *IEEE Trans. on Pattern Analysis and Machine Intelligence, PAMI-8*(5), 665-668 (1986).
44. J. Koenderink and A. van Doorn, "Dynamic Shape," *Biol. Cybernet., 53,* 383-396 (1986).
45. D. Lowe, Proc. 2nd International Conference on Computer Vision, Tampa, 1988.
46. J. Illingworth and J. Kittler, "A Survey of the Hough Transform," *Computer Vision, Graphics, and Image Proc., 44,* 87-116 (1988).
47. H. Mannaert and A. Oosterlinck, "A Recursive Self-Organizing Network for Object Recognition,"*Proc. Int. Joint Conf. on Neural Networks,* 1990, pp. 405-408.
48. L. Van Gool, J. Wagemans, and A. Oosterlinck, "Regularity Detection as a Strategy in Object Modeling and Recognition," *Proc. SPIE Applications of Artificial Intelligence, 1095,* 138-149 (1989).
49. L. Van Gool, J. Wagemans, and A. Oosterlinck, "Object Modeling and Redundancy Reduction: Algorithmic Information Theory Revisited," *SPIE Proc. ECO2, Image Processing III, 1135,* 82-89 (1989).
50. Y. Shirai, *Three-Dimensional Computer Vision,* Springer Verlag, New York, 1987.
51. G. Sandini and V. Tagliasco, "an Anthropomorphic Retina-Like Structure for Scene Analysis," *Computer Graphics and Image Proc., 14,* 365-372 (1980).
52. D. Braccini, G. Gambardella, and G. Sandini, "A Signal Theory Approach to the Space and Frequency Variant Filtering Performed by the Human Visual System," *Signal Proc., 3*(3), 231-240 (1981).
53. K. Ikeuchi and T. Kanade, "Modeling Sensors: Toward Automatic Generation of Object Recognition Program," *Computer Vision, Graphics, and Image Proc., 48,* 50-79 (1989).
54. C. Goad, "Special Purpose Automatic Programming for 3D Model-Based Vision," *Proc. DARPA Image Understanding Workshop,* 1983 pp. 94-104.
55. D. Lowe, "The Viewpoint Consistency Constraint," *Int. J. Computer Vision, 1, 57-72 (1987).*

56. P. Besl, *Surfaces in Range Image Understanding*, Springer Verlag, New York, 1988, pp. 936–958.

57. D. H. Ballard and C. M. Brown, *Computer Vision,* Prentice-Hall, Englewood Cliffs, NJ, 1982.

58. K. Park and E. Hall, "Form Recognition Using Moment Invariants for Three Dimensional Perspective Transformations," *Proc. SPIE Intelligent Robots and Computer Vision, 726*, 90–109 (1986).

59. C. Teh and R. Chin, "On Digital Approximation of Moment Invariants," *Computer Vision, Graphics, and Image Proc., 33*, 318–326.

60. T. Wallace and P. Wintz, "An Efficient Three-Dimensional Aircraft Recognition Algorithm Using Normalized Fourier Descriptors," *Computer Graphics and Image Proc. 13*, 99–126 (1980).

61. Kl. Arbter, "Affine-Invariant Fourier Descriptors," in *From Pixels to Features,* J. Simon (ed.), Elsevier, New York 1989, pp. 153–164.

62. K. Fu, "A Step Towards Unification of Syntactic and Statistical Pattern Recognition," *IEEE Trans. Pattern Analysis and Machine Intelligence, PAMI-8*(3), 398–404 (1986).

63. H. Blum and R. Nagel, "Shape Description Using Weighted Symmetric Axis Features," *Pattern Recognition, 10*, 167–180 (1978).

64. H. Asada and M. Brady, "The Curvature Primal Sketch," *IEEE Trans. Pattern Analysis and Machine Intelligence, PAMI-8*(1), 2–14 (1986).

65. J. Connell and M.Brady, "Generating and Generalizing Models of Visual Objects," *Artificial Intelligence, 31*(2), 159–184 (1987).

66. R. Nevatia, *Machine Perception,* Prentice-Hall, Englewood Cliffs, NJ, 1982.

67. D. Terzopoulos, "Symmetry-Seeking Models," *Proc. 1st Int. Conf. on Computer Vision,* 1987.

68. P. Mulgaonkar, L. Shapiro, and R. Haralick, "Matching 'Sticks, Plates, and Blobs' Objects Using Geometric and Relational Constraints," *Image and Vision Computing,* 2(2), 85–98 (1984).

69. P. J. Besl, and R. C. Jain, "Three Dimensional Object Recognition," *ACM Computing Surv., 17*(1), 75–145 (1985).

70. R. Bolles and P. Horaud, "3DPO: A Three-Dimensional Part Orientation System," in *Three-Dimensional Machine Vision,* T. Kanade (ed.), Kluwer, Boston, 1987, pp. 399–450.

71. I. Chakravarty and H. Freeman, "Characteristic Views as a Basis for Three-Dimensional Object Recognition, *Proc. SPIE Conf. on Robot Vision, 336,* 37–45 (1982).

72. Z. Gigus, J. Canny, and R. Seidel, "Efficiently Computing and Representing Aspect Graphs of Polyhedral Objects," *Proc. 2nd Int. Conf. on Computer Vision,* 1988; pp. 30–39.

73. B. Horn and B. Schunck, "Determining Optical Flow," *Artificial Intelligence, 17,* 185–203 (1981).

74. D. Heeger, "Optical Flow from Spatiotmeporal Filters," *Proc. 1st Int. Conf. on Computer Vision,* 1987, pp. 181–190.

75. H. Nagel, "On the Estimation of Optical Flow: Relations Between Different Approaches and Some New Results," *Artificial Intelligence, 33,* 299–324 (1987).

76. J. Aloimonos, I. Weiss, and A. Bandopadhyay, "Active Vision," *Int. J. Computer Vision, 2*(1) (1988).

77. O. Faugeras, F. Lustman, and G. Toscani, "Motion and Structure from Motion from Point and Line Matches," *Proc. 1st Int. Conf. on Computer Vision,* 1987, pp. 25–34.

78. A. Blake and R. Cipolla, "Robust Estimation of Surface Curvature from Deformation of Apparent Contours," University of Oxford, Report No. OUEL 1797/89, 1989.
79. E. Arbogast, "Reconstruction de surfaces a partir des contours critiques, dans un contexte multi-images," Technical Report LIFIA, Grenoble, RR784-I-IMAG 94, June 1989.
80. L. Ljung, *System Identification: Theory for the User,* Prentice-Hall, Englewood Cliffs, NJ, 1987.
81. D. Zhang, L. Van Gool, and A. Oosterlinck, "Generalized Predictive Control of a Vision-Based Robot Tracking System Using the Kalman Filtering Technique,"*Proc. IEEE Int. Conf. Control and Applications, 1989, RA-3-2.*
82. D. Zhang, L. Van Gool, and A. Oosterlinck, "Stochastic Predictive Control of Robot Tracking Systems with Dynamic Visual Feedback," *Proc. IEEE Conf. on Robotics and Automation* (1990).
83. W. Miller,"Sensor-Based Control of Robotic Manipulators Using a General Learning Algorithm," *IEEE J. Robotics and Automation, RA-3,* 157–165 (1987).
84. L. Weiss, A. Sanderson, and C. Neuman, "Dynamic Sensor-Based Control of Robots with Visual Feedback," *IEEE J. Robotics and Automation, RA-3,* 404–417 (1987).
85. J. Feddema and O. Mitchell, "Vision-Guided Servoing with Feature-Based Trajectory Generation," *IEEE Trans. on Robotics and Automation, RA-5*(5), 691–700.
86. R. Anderson, "Real-Time Intelligent Visual Control of a Robot," *IEEE Workshop on Intelligent Control,* 89–94 (1986).
87. R. Anderson, *The Design of a Ping-Pong Playing Robot,* MIT Press, Cambridge, 1988.

BIBLIOGRAPHY

Blake, A. and A Zisserman, *Visual Reconstruction,* MIT Press, Cambridge, 1987.
Brooks, R., *Model-Based Computer Vision,* UMI Research Press, Ann Arbor, 1984.
Castleman, K., *Digital Image Processing,* Prentice-Hall, Englewood Cliffs, NJ, 1979.
Coiffet, Ph., *Robot Technology*, Vol. 2, *Interaction with the Environment,* Kogan Page, London, 1983.
Duff, M., *Computing Structures for Image Understanding,* Academic Press, London, 1983.
Gonzalez, R. and P. Wintz, *Digital Image Processing,* 2nd ed., Addison-Wesley, Reading, MA 1987.
Hall, E., *Computer Image Processing and Recognition,* Academic Press, New York, 1979.
Huang, T. S. (ed.), *Image Sequence Processing and Dynamic Scene Analysis*, Springer-Verlag, New York, 1983.
Fischler, M., and O. Firschein, *Readings in Computer Vision: Issues, Problems, Principles, and Paradigms,* Morgan Kaufman Publishers, San Francisco, 1987.
Marr, D., *Vision,* W. Freeman, New York, 1982.
Pugh, A. (ed.), *Robot Vision,* IFS (Publications) Ltd., U.K., 1983.
Resnikoff, H., *The Illusion of Reality,* Springer Verlag, New York, 1989.

Rosenfeld, A. and A. C., Kak, *Digital Picture Processing,* Vols. 1 and 2, 2nd edition, Academic Press, New York, 1982.

Serra, J., *Mathematical Morphology and Image Analysis,* Academic Press, New York, 1982.

LUC J. VAN GOOL
DAO-BIN ZHANG
ANDRÉ OOSTERLINCK

OPTICAL AND OPTOELECTRONIC APPLIED SCIENCE AND ENGINEERING

INTRODUCTION

Roles of Optics

Optics is becoming significantly important in high technology industry. Its unique features can be exploited to enhance existing technologies. Optical systems are parallel in nature, photons (the carriers of optical information) do not interfere with one another, and they travel with the speed of light. Also, a majority of the physical quantities that are detected and processed are optical in nature. Therefore, it is obviously desirable to process these quantities by optical systems instead of converting them to other forms of energy. Examples are numerous, to name a few: pattern and character recognition, machine vision, quality control, and image processing.

Advantages of Optics

Optics introduces new features and flexibilities to the field of information processing and computing. Speed and parallelism are the main strengths of optics. Optical systems operate on the input data in parallel, as our visual system does when it sees an image. It does not operate on it a point at a time as the conventional sequential systems do. The information in the optical system propagates with the speed of light. Optics has the capability of performing global interconnections, with negligible interference or crosstalk. Broad communication bandwidth is the motivating factor behind the rapidly growing field of fiberoptics, which is capable of providing bandwidths in the terra hertz range. Also, optics is a three-dimensional technology, unlike electronics which is essentially two dimensional.

Hybrid Reality

Despite the advantages listed above , optics is not as well developed technologically as electronics. Electronics has mature materials, device and system technology, and it is highly flexible and integrable. Despite these advantages, electronics suffers from some inherent problems such as local interconnections, sensitivity to interference and crosstalk, planar technology, and narrow communication bandwidths. It is clear that some of the weaknesses of electronics are the strengths of optics and vice versa. Optics and electronics can complement each other to produce superior systems. Taking into account the advantages of both technologies, the hybrid systems seem to be the way to go at this time. Also there is an important reality of analog and digital systems. The majority of mature optical systems that exist today are analog. Analog systems are inaccurate and inflexible by their inherent nature, while on the other hand, digital electronics are very accurate and flexible. Therefore, in the foreseeable future, hybrid systems that combine analog optical and digital electronic systems, will be the optimum way to design and implement systems.

OPTICAL INTERCONNECTIONS

The miniaturization of electronic circuits is reaching some fundamental limits. As very large-scale integrated (VLSI) chips become smaller, denser, faster, and more complex, the interconnections between the different elements become the crucial design factor. As the VLSI chips get denser the interconnects become thinner and closer, which results in larger in larger stray capacitances. This limits the speed of the electric signals and causes crosstalk between the different signals. Connecting with light beams instead of electric signals might resolve these problems [1].

Optical interconnects have several advantages over their electrical counterparts. Optical signal propagation takes place at the speed of light in the medium and it is independent of the number of components receiving these signals. Also, photons (carriers of light) do not interact with one another. Two beams of light can pass through each other without any interaction. Therefore, optical interconnects are free from capacitive loading effects. The noninterfering property of photons makes optical interconnects immune to crosstalk. The effect of stray capacitances that exist between neighboring electrical paths increases with the bandwidth and causes cross-coupling of information. Optical interconnects do not engender such problems. Optical interconnects are free from planar or quasiplanar constraints. They have global interconnecting capabilities. Also the possibility of the interconnect reprogramming makes the optical interconnection an attractive technology.

Optical interconnects can be used at different levels of the hierarchy of computer systems. Optical interconnections within a chip, chip-to-chip, board-to-board, and between processors are all feasible.

Optical interconnects can be performed in different ways, namely free-space or guided-wave interconnects. Each of these configurations can be of different forms, and each has its own advantages and can differ from one application to another.

Free-Space Interconnects

An attractive means for exploiting optical beam noninteraction is to use free-space propagation with either focused or unfocused techniques. One application of the free-space interconnects is in intrachip clock distribution. The interconnects responsible for the clock distribution must convey signals to all parts of the chip at specific times. These requirements imply relatively long and dense electric paths with high capacitive loading, which results in propagation delays and slower operating speeds. Optical free-space interconnects can be utilized for the distribution of the clock signals to various parts of the chip [2]. Unfocused free-space interconnects can be used as shown in Figure 1. This interconnect is established by broadcasting the optical beam carrying the clock signal to the entire chip. A lens is used to collimate the light emitted by a modulated light source located at its focal point. The collimated beam illuminates the entire chip. The optical signal is received and converted to electric signal by photodetectors integrated in the chip. The signal reaches all the detectors at identical delay times from the light source. Hence in principle there is no clock skew. This system is inefficient due to the fact that only a small portion of the light beam falls on the photosensitive areas of the detectors and the rest of the beam is wasted. Focus free-space interconnects can be used for clock signal distribution as shown in Figure 2. This system uses a hologram to image the modulated optical source on the detectors. Obviously, this system is more efficient than the unfocused interconnect but it requires more precision in alignment. Clock distribution on the wafer level can follow the same techniques outlined above. On the board-to-board level, since the dimensions are larger, the signal can be sent to

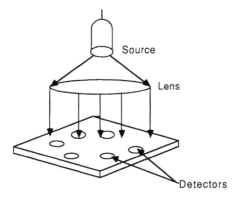

FIGURE 1.   Unfocused broadcast of the clock signal to the chip.

a part of the board using the focused method for the adjacent boards. While for nonadjacent boards, guided-wave interconnects are more suitable.

Free-space interconnects are also used in the more general case of data communications. In VLSI design the trend is to scale down feature size and increase chip size. This limits the operating speed of the chip by the delay time associated with the interconnections between different components of the circuit rather than the switching times of the components. Implementing the longer path interconnects optically can enhance the performance of the chip. An intrachip interconnect design proposed by Goodman et al. [2], which uses a holographic routing element is shown in Figure 3.

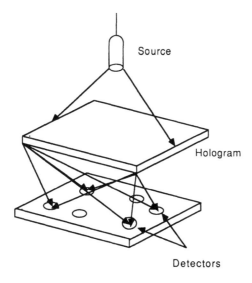

FIGURE 2.   Focused optical distribution of the clock signal using a hologram.

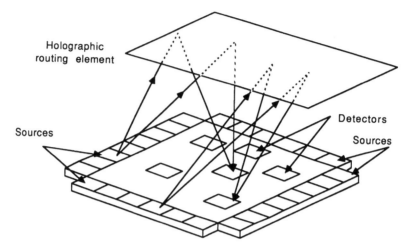

FIGURE 3.   An intrachip free space interconnection using a holographic routing element.

Free-space optical interconnects are also used in multiprocessor systems. Ishihara [3] reported the use of an optical interconnect system to replace the electric bus in multiprocessor systems. This high-speed optical communication bus consists of laser diodes, avalanche photodiodes (APD), and a cylindrical mirror as shown in Figure 4. This interconnect system allows greater flexibility and speed over the conventional bus design.

A comparison between electrical and optical interconnects is reported by Feldman et al. [4] based on power and speed considerations. They have shown that optical interconnects may be advantageous for intrachip communication in large area VLSI circuits or wafer scale integrated circuits, especially when high data rates and/or large fan-outs are required.

Guided-Wave Interconnects

In the guided-wave interconnects, light propagates through a medium which has a different index of refraction than its surroundings. This type of interconnection can be realized by optical fibers or integrated optical waveguides. The technology of optical fibers has been well developed during the past two decades, and today optical fibers with high efficiency and low dispersion are available. The integrated optical waveguides are usually made of $LiNbO_3$, but they can also be obtained by sputtering glass on a silicon wafer. The main advantage of integrated optical wave guides is that they are compatible with the VLSI technology. Integrated optical waveguides, however, suffer from relatively high loss especially in coupling light into and out of the waveguide channels.

Guided-wave interconnections can be used for communication between digital electronic computers or parts of a computer [2, 5]. The interconnections used for this application are at different levels. The highest level is the machine-to-machine interconnection which should be relatively long and have low loss. Optical fibers meet these requirements and they are already used for this purpose. Other levels are: processor-to-processor, board-to-board, chip-to-chip, and intrachip interconnects. Although optical fibers can be used at all these levels, they are more suitable for long distances. Bending problems make them unsuitable

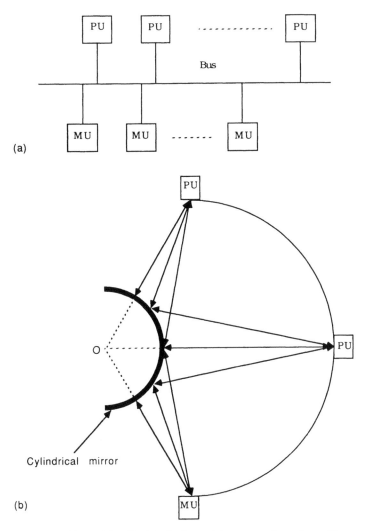

FIGURE 4.   Optical bus with cylindrical mirror: (a) common bus of a multiprocessor system, and (b) basic structure of a free space optical bus. In this figure, PU is a processing unit and MU is a memory unit, each has a laser diode and an avalanche photodiode to perform the communication between different modes of the system.

for lengths shorter than a few centimeters. For these cases, integrated optical waveguides or free-space interconnections are more suitable.

Another application of guided-wave interconnections is in optical data processing, where they are used to perform digital operations. Depending on the required operation, two types of systems are used for data processing: static (fixed) or dynamic (programmable) interconnections. In the first type, the same configuration is used to process any input data. In the second type, depending on the input data, the configuration is used to process any input data. In the second type, depending on the input data, the configuration is changed. Using fixed systems, operations such as discrete Fourier transformation and perfect shuffle

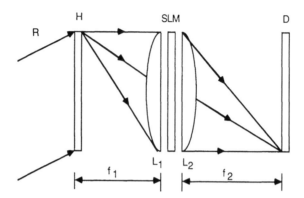

FIGURE 5.   Basic configuration for an N^4 interconnection network. H is a hologram array illuminated by reconstruction beam R, SLM is a spatial light modulator between two lenses L_1 and L_2 with their respective focal lengths f_1 and f_2, and D is a detector array or an array of nonlinear optical device.

can be realized [6]. Dynamic systems can be implemented by a combination of optical switches and integrated optical waveguides [7] or optical fibers [8]. Using this type of interconnection, more complex operations such as residue addition and multiplication [9], nonrecursive (FIR), and recursive (IIR) lattice filtering [8] can be performed.

Massive Holographic Interconnects

We want to connect an $N \times N$ input array of modulator elements (on a spatial light modulator, SLM) or of sources to an $N \times N$ output position array in such a way that each input is connected to each output with a selectable interconnection strength. This requires N^4 interconnections. For $N = 1000$, $N^4 = 10^{12}$. This large number of interconnections is almost certainly beyond current or future electronic capability.

The SLM input system can use reflective [2] or transmissive [10] SLMs. We show here the transmissive case (Fig. 5). It consists of a hologram array of linear dimensions H containing $N_h \times N_h$ holographic optical elements, an SLM of size S with $N_s \times N_s$ pixels sandwiched between two lenses with respective focal lengths f_1 and f_2, and a detector array D with $N_d \times N_d$ detector elements. The ij-th hologram in the array is imaged by the double-lens configuration onto the ij-th element of detector array. This hologram diffracts light from a reconstruction beam with an efficiency t_{ijkl} toward the kl-th pixel in the SLM. The same pixel receives a weighted fraction of the light diffracted also from all other holograms, but, assuming a linear interaction in the SLM, these are separated again on arrival at the detector array. Thus, ideally, each detector receives the sum of all the weighted beams just from a single hologram element. Mathematically, if the power transmittance of the kl-th pixel in the SLM is $a_{kl'}$ the total power received by the ij-th detector will be

$$b_{ij} = \sum_{k,l} t_{ijkl} a_{kl'} \tag{1}$$

where, for the time being, coherence effects have been ignored. This system in its ideal form may be viewed either as a matrix–matrix multiplier of a 4-D matrix by a 2-D matrix or as a vector–matrix multiplier with vectors of $N_s \times N_s$ dimensions,

$$B = \| \mathbf{T} \| A \tag{2}$$

The elements of the input vector (or matrix) are introduced by the transmittance of the SLM pixels with the hologram providing the fixed matrix $\| \mathbf{T} \|$. The output vector is read out from the detector array. Alternatively, we may consider this an interconnection network with N_s^2 channels that are interconnected by $N_s^2 \times N_h^2$ weighted interconnections that are hardwired for a given hologram array.

To implement the above architecture one must also devise a system for recording the required large hologram array. Within the present state of art, the practicality of computer-generated holography with electron beam writing appears to be out of the question for these large arrays. Thus one must resort to optical recording, preferably with computer assistance [11]. Several procedures may be envisioned for the implementation of the hologram recording process. The most obvious of these processes is based on the same optical system as the interconnection network itself (Fig. 5), where each element of the detector array is replaced one at a time by a point source. A useful realization of this point source may be the endface of a single-mode optical fiber that can be easily positioned and aligned with a computerized robotic arm. To record the *ij*-th hologram this source is positioned at the corresponding pixel on the detector array, oriented for optimal illumination of the SLM, and imaged onto the hologram by the two lenses. The SLM, sandwiched between the lenses, writes the desired interconnection pattern. This special lens configuration is useful to keep all incident ray angles on the SLM constant for a given hologram allowing for adjustments to take care of the angular variation of the SLM transmission characteristics. To attain small repeatable high-quality holograms, a random phase plane over the SLM may be useful [12].

In the above recording configuration it was assumed that an oblique reference beam, conjugate to the one indicated on the figure, is incident on the hologram. Alternatively, one may use a point source reference situated on the optical axis at the SLM plane. This will allow an axial reconstruction beam resulting in a reduced bandwidth requirement for the holograms and a simpler reconstruction configuration. The penalty for these benefits is removal of the central portion of the SLM and the introduction of aberrations induced by spherical-wave recording and reconstruction.

For the input array of sources we must go to a different geometry. This system is shown in Figure 6. We have drawn the system as though it consisted of a uniformly illuminated SLM rather than a source array because (a) that is one viable approach and (b) that allows a fully parallel explanation.

The system is operated here too by introducing the input vector a_{kl} in the SLM. Each element of the hologram array is illuminated by the reference beam through a corresponding pixel in the SLM, thus with a reference beam-intensity proportional to a_{kl}. The *kl*-th hologram diffracts light toward the *ij*-th detector in the array with an efficiency t_{klij}, this detector receives light from the *kl*-th hologram with a power proportional to $t_{klij}a_{kl}$. The overall power detected by this detector element is the sum of all the contributions (again ignoring coherence effects):

$$b_{ij} = \sum_{k,l} t_{klij}a_{kl} \tag{3}$$

This equation is of the same form as Eq. (1), which contains t_{ijkl} rather than t_{klij} and will be identical to it if the new $\| \mathbf{T} \|$ matrix is the transpose of the old one.

One possible procedure to record the hologram array is similar to the original architecture and uses the same system. This reinstalls some of the problems discussed earlier, but

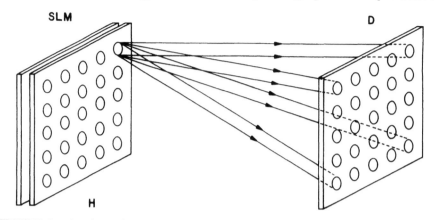

FIGURE 6.   An alternative method for arbitrary interconnect between N × N inputs and N × N outputs. SLM is the spatial light modulator, H is the hologram, and D is the detector.

can be dealt with more efficiently since for every hologram recording a single source is used.

The main initiative for this architecture was the reduction of the angular constraints on the SLM, and we already have seen that it also eliminates the need for the lenses. It turns out that there are also additional advantages: The polarization effects were also mainly related to the function of the SLM, and, therefore, they are absent here. Furthermore, there is no crosstalk on the SLM plane since it is practically in contact with the hologram. Thus in this architecture the only crosstalk (with an ideal SLM having infinite extinction ratio) is on the detector plane and is determined by the diffraction spot size of the hologram

$$S \approx \frac{\lambda f}{P_h} \qquad (4)$$

which should be smaller than p_d, where p_d, and p_h are the linear dimensions of the respective pixel sizes in the detector array and the hologram. Other problems can arise from coherence effects and aberrations.

The pixel size of the SLM is virtually unlimited for this architecture since each pixel serves only as the source of a reconstruction beam for a single hologram. Small SLMs available today my be used with a projection optical system to match its pixel size optically to that of the required hologram aperture.

The most obvious penalty for the benefits of this architecture is the reduced flexibility due to the requirement that there should be a one-to-one correspondence between the individual holograms and SLM pixels. Thus overlapping holograms are no longer allowed, and also the same number of SLM pixels as holograms must be used unless one allows the illumination of several holograms with a single SLM pixel or vice versa. This state of affairs is useful for many applications where the overall N^4 interconnections are not required.

Coherent superposition at the detector plane still takes place as with the original architecture, but here the superposition is from different holograms and not from different SLM pixels. To overcome this problem an improved version of this architecture will be possible eventually, with the development of large laser diode arrays that may be able to replace the SLM. The lasers in the array will be individually modulated to represent the input vector.

This modification lends an appreciable reduction in coherent noise, since each hologram is illuminated by a separate laser and each detector element receives a single signal from each hologram. Now the superposed beams on each detector element originate from different lasers and may be combined incoherently.

The diode array configuration will be superior to the various SLM configurations in speed, dynamic range, and signal to noise ratio. The only obvious problem is that such arrays are not yet available; however, ongoing research in this area [13] should provide the needed devices in the relatively near future.

OPTICAL COMPUTERS

Digital Optical Computers

Since the invention of the laser in 1960, there has been a growing interest in optical information processing. Analog optical processors, such as correlators and spatial filters, have been successfully developed. These processors can operate on two-dimensional arrays of data, hence they are capable of intensive computations. However, they suffer from two weaknesses: their accuracy is low (at best about 1%), and they are not flexible. To overcome these difficulties, research on digital optical computers has been pursued.

An important issue in digital computers is the number representation. Three number systems have been used for digital optical computers. These are: binary, residue, and signed digit. The binary number system has the advantage that the input and output data of the optical processor will be compatible with electronic computers. Among other advantages of this system are: high tolerance of noise and relatively easy implementation. However, since the digits in the binary system are dependent, it is not very suitable for parallel processing.

An alternative is the residue number system (RNS) in which the digits are independent of each other [14]. A residue number system is defined by choosing a set of numbers with no common factors $\{m_1, m_2, \ldots, m_n\}$ called moduli. Any integer number X within a dynamic range of $\prod_{i=1}^{n} m_i$ can then be presented by an n-tuple $(x_1, x_2, \ldots, x_n)$, where x_i is the remainder (residue) of X upon the division by m_i. The main advantage of the RNS is that the digits are independent, e.g., there is no carry in residue addition or multiplication. This makes the RNS suitable for parallel processing. Unfortunately, some operations, such as division and magnitude comparison, are difficult in residue arithmetic. This has limited the application of the RNS to the cases where the above operations are not largely used. When RNS is applicable it may be superior to power series methods because there is no roundoff error.

A third option is to use the signed digit number system introduced by Avizienis [15]. A special case of this system, known as modified signed digit (MSD), has been introduced to the optics community by Drake et al. [16]. This is a weighted number system of radix 2, in which three values (0, 1, and –1) are allowed for each digit. In the MSD system, each number has several representations. For example, decimal number 7 can be represented as 111 or $100\bar{1}$ or $1\bar{1}1\bar{1}$ or . . . , where $\bar{A}$ represents –1. Using this redundancy, carry propagation can be restricted to one digit to the left [16].

Several approaches have been proposed for the implementation of digital optical computers. Some of them are described below.

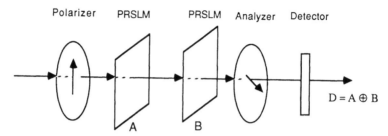

FIGURE 7.   Optical Implementation of (a) AND and (b) OR gates using controllable transparencies (CTs).

Optical Gates

One approach is to build the elements of a digital computer, such as gates and memories, with optical components. The advantage of this approach is that it can use the developed architectures of digital electronic computers and also benefit from the advantages of optics, such as massive interconnectivity, and two-dimensional input/output arrays.

Several techniques have been proposed for implementing optical gates. These techniques can be classified according to the characteristic of light that has been used for information coding. These characteristics are: amplitude, polarization, phase, and position. Amplitude coding is very suitable for binary data, where the two states of a bit are represented as the presence or absence of light. In the Soviet Union logic gates have been implemented by controlled transparencies [17]. In this method, depending on the value of the input data, these devices are made transparent or opaque. Figure 7 shows how logic operations AND and OR can be implemented.

Optical gates that work based on polarization of light have been developed for both binary and residue arithmetic [18, 19]. These devices are made of an electro-optic material, such as liquid crystal. By applying an appropriate voltage to a pixel (picture element) of a liquid crystal, the polarization of light will be rotated by a certain degree after it is reflected from or transmitted through that pixel. As an illustrative example, Figure 8 shows how the EXCLUSIVE OR operation can be implemented. The input light has a vertical polarization. The input signals A and B are applied to two cascade pixels. Each pixel, when activated rotates the polarization of light by 90°. The output analyzer allows only the light with horizontal polarization to be passed. As a result, an output signal will be detected if only one of the inputs is 1, i.e., $D = A \oplus B$.

Optical gates can also be realized by manipulating the phase of light. For example, Figure 9 shows an integrated optical inverted that works based on the phase change. A beam of light is entered from the left side and it is equally split between two channels. The lower channel has two electrodes. If the input signal A is 0, no voltage is applied to the electrodes. As a result, the two beams remain in phase and an output light will be detected, i.e., $D = 1$. If $A = 1$, a voltage is applied to the electrodes to change the index of refraction of the lower channel and to produce a 180° phase shift between the two beams. As a result, the two beams cancel each other in the output and no signal will be detected, i.e., $D = 0$. Therefore, the device acts as an inverted, i.e., $D = \overline{A}$. Other logic gates can also be implemented by integrated optical waveguides [20].

Optical gates based on positional coding have been proposed for implementation of residue arithmetic [21, 22]. In this technique, m_i positions are used for modulus m_i. De-

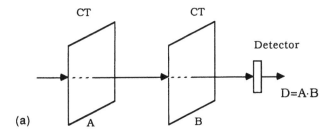

(a)

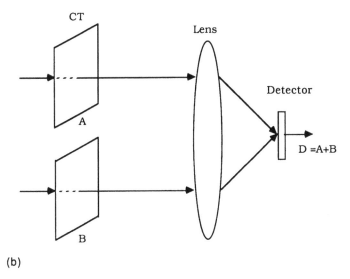

(b)

FIGURE 8. Optical implementation of EXCLUSIVE OR gate using polarization rotating spatial light modulators (PRSLMs).

pending on it value, the input number is coded as the presence of light in a particular position. The output is obtained by coupling the light from that channel to the appropriate output channel. For example, Figure 10 shows the implementation of residue addition modulo 4 using optical waveguides [23]. In this figure, one input number (N_1) is coded as the presence of a light beam in one of the input channels. Depending on the other number (N_2), some of the switching elements are activated to couple the light beam from the input channel to the appropriate output channel that corresponds to $N_1 + N_2$.

Although several optical gates have been demonstrated so far, they are not at a level to compete with the present integrated electronic gates. Today, research activities are mainly concentrated on other techniques that use unique characteristics of optics. Some of these techniques are described in the following sections.

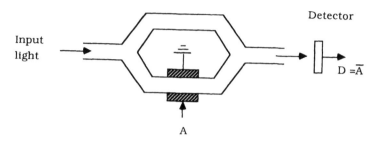

FIGURE 9.   An integrated optical implementation of NOT gate using electro-optical phase retardation.

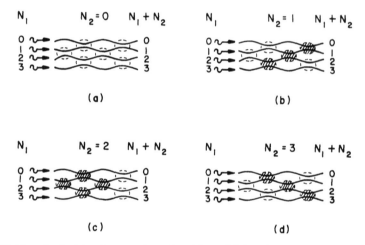

FIGURE 10.   Optical implementation of residue addition ($N_1 + N_2$) modulo four. The cases (a), (b), (c), and (d) correspond to $N_2 = 0, 1, 2,$ and 3, respectively. The activated switches are shown by hatched marks.

FIGURE 11.   Coding procedure for logic values of 0 and 1.

Table Look-Up

In the table look-up technique, the information about all possible cases of an operation is stored in a memory. The output for a particular case is then obtained by reading the result directly from the memory. This approach can provide the result faster than other techniques, since no calculation is performed during the process. However, for many operations of interest, the amount of information that needs to be stored is so large that the table look-up technique becomes impractical. For example, addition of two 16-bit numbers consist of $2^{16} \times 2^{16} \simeq 4.3 \times 10^9$ cases. One solution to this problem is to use the residue number system instead of the usual binary system. Since the digits in a residue number system are independent, several small tables instead of one large table are needed. For example, 16-bit addition can be realized using the set of moduli {3, 5, 7, 11, 13, 16}. Using this system, the total number of cases will reduce to only $3^2 + 5^2 + 7^2 + 11^2 + 13^2 + 16^2 = 629$.

Several optical implementations of the table look-up technique have been proposed by Huang et al. [21] for residue arithmetic. They used positional coding to represent the numbers and spatial maps to perform different operations. They proposed several architectures for implementing these maps using mirrors, prisms, gratings, and optical waveguides. Another method used by Guest and Gaylord [24] is to store the information as thick holograms in a photorefractive crystal, such as $LiNbO_3$. Goutzoulis et al. [25] have proposed the use of laser diodes and optical fibers, and have implemented a prototype look-up table for modulus 7.

Symbolic Substitution

Symbolic substitution for optical computing was first introduced by Huang [26]. In this technique, the input data are represented using a finite set of patterns. An operation is then performed by applying the corresponding substitution rules, where specific patterns are detected and replaced by the patterns that correspond to the result. The main advantage of this technique is that using the 2-D capability of optics, the same operation can be performed on several input data in parallel.

As an illustrative example, Figure 11 shows two patterns that can be used for coding there binary values 0 and 1. Each input number is represented by putting the patterns corresponding to its bits side by side. To perform an operation on a pair of numbers, the patterns of one number are placed on top of the patterns of the other numbers such that the corresponding bits are aligned. The operation is then performed by applying the substitution rules. For example, to perform binary addition, the substitution rules shown in Figure 12 are used. These rules, correspond to the four possible cases of 0 + 0, 0 + 1, 1 + 0, and 1 + 1. Because of the carry propagation, the addition of two n-bit numbers requires repeating these rules n times. One additional time is needed to ensure that the output carry is placed at the position of the most significant bit of the result. In the above example, positional coding was used for data representation. Another possibility is to use polarization coding, where the binary values 0 and 1 are coded by two orthogonal polarizations [27]. The advantage of this method is that the device area can be reduced.

An optical implementation of the symbolic substitution processor has been introduced by Brenner et al. [28]. This processor consists of four parts: pattern splitter, pattern recognizer, pattern substituters, and pattern combiner. The pattern splitter produces "sufficient" number of copies of the input pattern. This number is determined by the substitution rules for the desired operation. For example, four copies are needed to perform binary addition. Each pattern recognizer corresponds to one of the substitution rules and it can detect the locations at which the input pattern for that rule occurs. The pattern substituter replaces

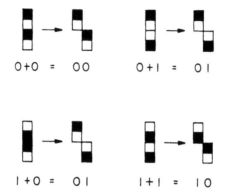

FIGURE 12.   Substitution rules for binary addition.

the detected pattern by the output pattern determined by the corresponding rule. Finally, the outputs of all the substituters are combined in one pattern. For most operations, such as addition, it is needed to repeat the substitution rules on the result pattern. This is obtained by a feedback from the output plane to the input plane.

New architectures have been proposed recently for optical implementation of symbolic substitution. These include the use of phase-only holograms [29], holographic matched filters [30], and diffraction gratings [31].

Symbolic substitution is a powerful technique and it is not limited to binary logic. Its application in performing addition and subtraction of modified signed digit numbers has been described by Bocker et al. [32]. Also, Goodman and Rhodes [33] have described the use of symbolic substitution in image processing.

Other Techniques

Other techniques have been pursued for the implementation of digital optical computers. Arrathoon and Hassoun [34] have studied the optical implementation of threshold logic gates. The advantage of this approach is that the number of gates required for implementation of a function can be significantly reduced. The problem is that, as the number of variables increases, threshold gates become more complex and sensitive to noise. Another approach is to develop special purpose computers using combinational logic, especially programmable logic arrays. Guilfoyle and Wiley [35] have proposed the application of acoustic-optic cells for this approach, while Murdocca et al. [36] have described the use of regular free space interconnections.

Although many digital optical computers have been proposed, so far only a few small-scale prototype processors have been developed, and it is not clear which architectures will succeed. To develop digital optical computers that can practically compete with the existing electronic computers, more progress should be made in the area of optical materials.

Algebraic Computers

The inherent parallelism and speed of optics make it very attractive for computing. For a long time optical processing was concentrated mainly on special purpose computation as in synthetic aperture radar, pattern recognition, correlators, spectrum analyzers, and the like. But it was realized that for optics to make it in computing, generic flexible architectures and algorithms to perform basic algebraic operations needed to be introduced. The basic algebraic problem, which about 70% to 80% of the scientific and engineering problems are reduced to, is solving a system of linear equations. Significant efforts were made for designing systems to perform linear algebraic operations, namely vector–matrix, matrix–matrix multiplications, vector inner and outer products, and solving systems of linear and nonlinear equations.

Cutrona [37] introduced an optical analog processor to perform vector-matrix multiplication. Multiplication of two matrices by coherent optical techniques was proposed by Heinz et al. [38], and was demonstrated experimentally by Jablonowski et al. [39] for a simple case of 2 × 2 matrices. Schneider and Fink [40] have introduced an incoherent optical matrix multiplication method. A very important method in multiplying a vector by a matrix was introduced by Bocker [41] and by Bromley [42] and an improved version was later described later by Monahan et al. [43] Stotts [44] suggested an integrated optical matrix multiplier. Higher accuracy matrix processors were introduced by Psaltis et al. [45], Collins et al. [46], Bocker [47], Athale et al. [48], and Psaltis and Athale [49].

Optical systolic processors were introduced by Caulfield et al. [50], Bocker et al. [51], and Casasent et al. [52]. Architectures and algorithms for solving systems of linear equations using optical processors were introduced by Caulfield et al. [53], Vijaya Kumar [54], Ghosh and Casasent [55], Cheng and Caulfield [56], Caulfield et al. [57], and Abushagur and Caulfield [58]. In the following subsections, we present some of the basic optical algebraic processors.

Scalar and Vector Multiplications

The basic representations of information in linear algebra are scalars, vectors, and matrices. In analog optics these representations can be achieved by the light intensity of a single element, a linear array, or a two-dimensional array of light sources, respectively, or by the transmittance value of either a single channel, a one-dimensional, or two-dimensional array of spatial light modulators. The basic arithmetic operations used are multiplication and addition and involve specific communication between the data elements. The multiplication operation in optics can be achieved by passing a light which represents a number through a transparency whose transmittance value represents another number. These can be combined spatially or temporally. The intensity of the light that emerges from the transparency represents the product of the two numbers. Addition can be achieved by combining two beams of light each representing a number. The resultant beam represents the sum of the two numbers. By using these two operations we can implement optically the basic linear algebraic operations as follows.

Scalar–Vector Multiplication. Consider the scalar quantity, a, which is to be multiplied by the vector **b**. The schematic diagram in Figure 13 depicts the optical system which performs the scalar–vector multiplication in parallel which has a time complexity of the first order, i.e., O(1). A light-emitting diode (LED) encodes the scalar a, one-dimensional transparency encodes the vector **b**, and a one-dimensional photodiode array produces the output vector **c**.

$$\mathbf{c} = a\mathbf{b}. \qquad (4)$$

The system is based on the waveguide design which is suitable for integrated optics. The light emitted by the LED encoding a is broadcast by the waveguide to all the elements of the transparency. The light transmitted by the transparency is then imaged on the detector array. The output of the photodiode array represents the vector **c**.

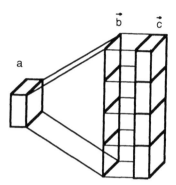

FIGURE 13.   An optical processor for a scalar-vector multiplication.

Vector–Vector Multiplication.   There are two operations which can be produced by the product of two vectors. The first is the inner product which is defined as

$$c = \mathbf{a}^T\mathbf{b}, \tag{5}$$

where the superscript T represents the transpose of the vector. Here we are assuming column vectors. The result of the inner product is a scalar quantity. Figure 14 shows the system which performs this inner product operation in parallel with O(1) time complexity. The second operation is the outer product which is defined as

$$\mathbf{A} = \mathbf{a}\mathbf{b}^T,$$

where $\mathbf{A}$ is an output matrix. If $\mathbf{a}$ is an $N \times 1$ and $\mathbf{b}$ is an $M \times 1$ vectors, then $\mathbf{A}$ will be an N × M matrix. For a sequential processor this requires an $(N \times \mathbf{M})$ multiplication and hence has a quadratic complexity of $O(N^2)$. Figure 15 shows an optical system which performs the outer product in parallel with time complexity of O(1). The system is two dimensional and in-

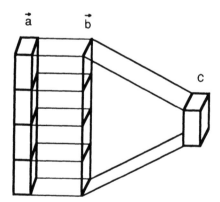

FIGURE 14.   An optical system for the inner product of two vectors.

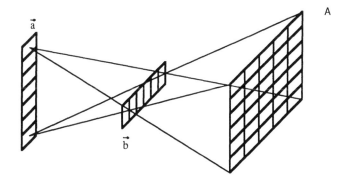

FIGURE 15.   An optical system for the outer product of two vectors.

volves two one-dimensional transparencies (or SLMs) to encode the vectors **a** and **b** and an output two-dimensional photodiode array. Each element of the vector **a** is broadcast to all the elements of **b**, while each element of **b** receives signals from each element **a**.

Vector–Matrix Multiplication.   This operation is one of the first which was implemented optically [59] and received a great deal of attention. It is defined as follows

$$b = Ax, \tag{6}$$

where **b** and **x** are $N \times 1$ and $M \times 1$ vectors, and **A** is an $N \times M$ matrix. This operation requires $(N \times M)$ multiplications and additions, and for a sequential processor it has a quadratic complexity with time complexity of $O(N^2)$. An optical system is shown in Figure 16 to perform this operation in parallel with time complexity of $O(1)$. The vector **x** is encoded by a one-dimensional array of light-emitting diodes (LEDs). The light emitted by each LED is expanded horizontally to illuminate a row of the mask which encodes the matrix **A**. The light emerging from each column of the mask is collected vertically to illuminate one element of the one-dimensional photodiode array.

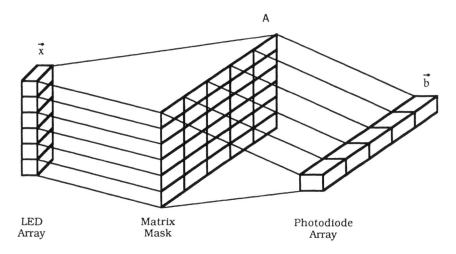

LED   Matrix   Photodiode
Array   Mask   Array

FIGURE 16.   An optical system for a vector-matrix multiplier.

Matrix–Matrix Multiplication.   The matrix–matrix multiplication operation is defined as

$$C = AB,$$

where A is an $N \times K$ matrix, B is a $K \times M$ matrix, and C is an $N \times M$ matrix. This operation requires $N \times K \times M$ multiplications and additions and for a sequential processor it has a time complexity of $O(N^3)$. This operation can be implemented optically in parallel using a vector–matrix multiplier processor.

Systems of Linear Equations Solvers

Solving a system of linear equations and determining the eigenvalues and the eigenvectors of a system are important problems. These arise in solving many physical problems, such as signal extrapolation, phased array radar, and image enhancement. In most practical cases, the matrices involved are very large ($\sim 1000 \times 1000$) and the required computations are very intensive. Although very powerful digital electronic computers have been developed, solving many practical problems is still very time consuming.

The Bimodal Optical Computer (BOC).   Analog optics is very fast, but results are inaccurate. On the other hand, digital electronics is very accurate but not as fast as analog optics. The advantages of both analog optics and digital electronics can be achieved in a compromised hybrid system that slows down the processor speed but in return increases the accuracy substantially. The bimodal optical computer (BOC) introduced by Caulfield et al. [57] is based on this idea. In the following discussion we will show how to solve a system of linear equations using the BOC.

Consider an $N \times N$ matrix A, and $N \times 1$ vectors x and b. A and b are given, and we want to solve the equation

$$A x = b \qquad (7)$$

to find the vector x. Equation (7) can be solved by analog optic techniques, such as the relaxation method [56]. Consider the hybrid system shown in Figure 17. First, an initial value for x is assumed and is written on the LEDs. Then the vector x is multiplied by the matrix A. The resultant vector y is compared with b using a difference amplifier, and the difference is feedback to correct x. This process of multiplying the new value of x with A and comparing y with b continues until the difference between y and b becomes negligible and the value of x converges to the solution of Eq. (7). This method of solving a system of linear equations is very fast. Its speed is limited only by the speed of the electro-optic devices and the feedback electronic system used and it can be in the nanosecond range.

Let us consider now the accuracy of the system. In writing the matrix A on the optical mask (which can be a photographic film or a spatial light modulator) and the vector x on the LED array, large errors are introduced because of the nature of these analog devices. Also reading the vector b from the photodiode array cannot be done accurately. Therefore, the system in Figure 17 does not solve Eq. (7) but instead it solves

$$A_0 x_0 = b_0, \qquad (8)$$

where the subscripts zeros indicate inaccuracies in the optics and electronics. The solution x_0 of Eq. (8) can be refined to get the vector x using the following algorithm.

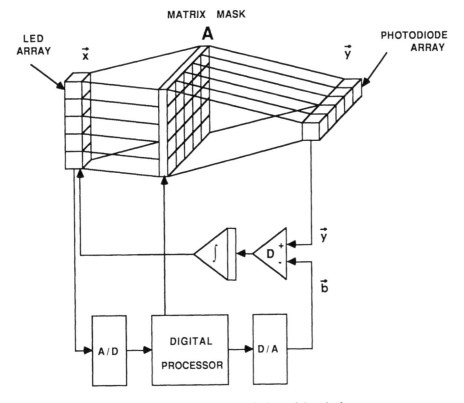

FIGURE 17.   Schematic diagram of a bimodal optical computer.

(a)   Solve the system in Eq. (8) for x_0 using the analog optical processor.

(b)   Store the solution x_0 with high accuracy in the digital processor. Use a dedicated digital processor to calculate the residue

$$r = b - A\,x_0 = A(x - x_0) = A\,\Delta x.$$

(c)   Use the optical analog processor to solve the new system of linear equations

$$A_0 y_0 = s\,r_0,$$

where $y = s\,\Delta x$ and s is a "radix," or scale factor which is chosen to use the dynamic range of the system efficiently.

(d)   Use other digital processor to refine the solution x_0 for x_1:

$$x_1 = x_0 + \Delta x$$

If the refined solution x_1 is accurate enough, terminate the iteration. Otherwise, return to (b) for a better solution.

The convergence and speed of the solution for the system of linear equations has been studied by Abushagur and Caulfield [58, 60], and Abushagur et al. [61]. The convergence of the iterative solution depends on two main factors. The first factor is the condition number of the matrix A_0 i.e., χ (A_0). This parameter is defined as

$$\chi(A_0) = \| A_0 \| \times \| A_0^{-1} \|,$$

where $\| A_0 \|$ is the norm of the matrix A_0. The smaller the condition number is, the faster the solution will converge. The second factor is the error involved in reading and writing A, x, and b using the electro-optic devices. The higher the accuracy of these parameters, the faster the convergence will occur.

A bimodal optical computer has been built and tested experimentally for solving a system of linear equations [63]. Although the accuracy of the analog processor was about 2 bits, a solution with 16-bit accuracy was obtained by the hybrid system after a few iterations. These experimental results show that a highly accurate hybrid system can be obtained from a low accurate analog processor.

Optical Systolic Processors. A systolic matrix–vector processing architecture was invented by Kung and Leiserson [63] and was implemented for optical systems by Caulfield et al. [50]. In this processor, the matrix-vector multiplication is achieved by point modulators (laser diodes or light-emitting diodes) images on an acoustooptic (AO) modulator as described by Casasent [64]. The matrix-vector multiplication processor is shown in Figure 18. In this system, M input modulators are imaged through M spatially separated regions of an AO cell. The Fourier transform of the light distribution leaving the AO cell is formed in

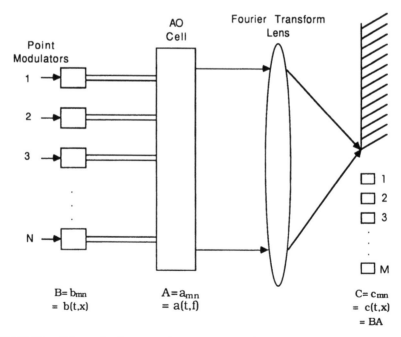

FIGURE 18. Schematic diagram of a frequency-multiplexed matrix acoustooptic systolic array processor.

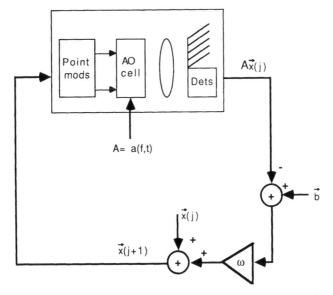

FIGURE 19.   Schematic diagram of an optical systolic array processor for a system of linear equation solver.

the back focal plane of the lens where it is detected by a linear photodiode array with parallel outputs. For the case of **M** vectors of length N, each vector is modulated on a separate temporal frequency, and all the vectors are present simultaneously in the AO cell. This is referred to as frequency multiplexing of the input data. When the N input point modulators are pulsed in parallel, the associated input vector multiplies all vectors in the AO cell. This produces the elements of **M** separate vector inner products. Each of these inner products leaves the AO cell at an angle proportional to its temporal frequency. The Fourier transform lens forms these **M** vector inner products on **M** separate photodetectors. The system performs a matrix-vector multiplication in parallel each T_B time.

This system can be used to solve a system of linear equations (7) using indirect iterative methods like the Richardson algorithm which is described by

$$x(j+1) = x(j) + \omega[\mathbf{b} - Ax(j)], \tag{11}$$

where ω is an acceleration or scaling parameter, and j is the iteration number. The architecture and data flow for this algorithm [65] is shown in Figure 19. This system works as follows: a vector **x**(0) is assumed as the initial solution and fed in parallel to the point modulators and the matrix A data are fed to the AO cell as $a(f,t)$. After the matrix data have been fed to the AO cell, the elements of the vector **x**(0) are applied to the point modulators. The matrix-vector product **Ax**(0) is produced in parallel on the detectors. The product **Ax**(0) is read and then operated on by **b** to produce the right-hand side of Eq. (11). The new solution **x**(1) is fed back into the point modulators for the second iteration. The same process of iteration will continue until a solution convergence is achieved when $\| \mathbf{x}(j+1) - \mathbf{x}(j) \|$ becomes small enough.

Expert Systems

An Expert System (ES) is generally understood as a computer system which emulates the reaction of human experts to input situations in some restricted field. We will use the example of medical diagnosis. The inputs are symptoms. The outputs are diseases. The discussion here is based on several prior papers [66–68] and is intended to be illustrative rather than exhaustive. The related area of reasoning with incomplete, uncertain, or even somewhat contradictory evidences can also be handled with optics [69].

We suppose there is an exhaustive list of possible symptoms $\{S_i\}$, $i = 1, \ldots, M$. There is also an exhaustive list of possible diseases $\{D_i\}$, $i = 1, \ldots, N$. The process of interaction with the optical ES might proceed as follows.

1. Insert information on that subset of $\{S_i\}$ already known.
2. Draw inferences on a subset of $\{D_i\}$ which are most likely in view of those symptoms.
3. For the most probable diseases, find the symptoms so-far unmeasured which most easily determine the presence of those diseases.
4. Insert the expanded set of symptoms and integrate until a "satisfactory" diagnosis is made.

The simplest assumption is that each symptom makes its own inference about every disease independently. Where S_k and S_s jointly determine results, the input should be the product $S_k S_s$.

We will represent each symptom with a range of values given by

$$S_i = \frac{S_i - \overline{S}_i}{\text{Max} \mid S_i \mid}.$$

Thus, in general, $-1 \le S_i \le 1$. We represent each diagnosis as a certainty

$$-1 \le d_i \le 1.$$

Here $d_i = 1$ means absolute certainty that this is the proper diagnosis; $d_i = -1$ means absolute certainty that this is not the proper diagnosis; and $d_i = 0$ means that no inference about this diagnosis can be made. For convenience, we write

$$S_i = S_i^+ - S_i^-,$$

where $S_i^+ \ge 0$ and $S_i^- \ge 0$. Likewise

$$d_i = d_i^+ - d_i^-$$

where $d_i^+ \ge 0$ and $d_i^- \ge 0$. For input, we use both in the reduced form (at least one of the two components is zero). The result will be in mixed form and should be reduced.

For both $\{S_i\}$ and $\{D_i\}$ we have line illuminators as inputs and line collectors as outputs. Consider the 2×2 case: $\{S_i\} = \{S_1, S_2\}$ and $\{D_i\} = \{D_1, D_2\}$. We initiate the inquiry by illuminating a 4×4 SLM with horizontal lines of light representing S_1 and S_2. We then collect along vertical paths to get d_1 and d_2. At the intersection between S_1^+ and d_2^-, for example, the SLM has a transmissivity (or reflectivity) of $e(S_1^+, d_2^-)$ which is two-way evidence. It is the evidence that disease D_2 is not present if symptom S, is positively present, and conversely. Thus we obtain outputs like

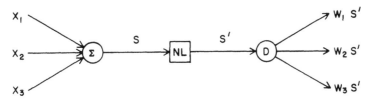

FIGURE 20.   Schematic diagram of an artificial neural network.

$$d_1^+ = e(S_1^+,d_1^+)S_1^+ + e(S_1^-,d_1^+)S_1^- + e(S_2^+,d_1^+)S_2^+ + e(S_2^-,d_1^+)S_2^-$$

for d_1^+, d_1^-, d_2^+, and d_2^-. From these we obtain normalized versions of d_1 and d_2.

The $d \rightarrow S$ direction works the same way. This time the ds are represented by line sources and we obtain outputs like

$$S_1^+ = e(S_1^+,d_1^+)d_1^+ + e(S_1^+,d_1^-)d_1^- + e(S_1^+,d_2^+)d_2^+ + e(S_1^+,d_2^-)d_2^-$$

These are used to guide future measurements.

If the spatial resolution of the SLM is insufficient to accommodate all of the Ss and Ds, we must, from time to time, rewrite it and rename the I/O channels. This is particularly easy to do with optically addressed SLMs. The various SLM patterns are stored as pages in a page-oriented holographic memory and recalled in parallel.

Neural Networks

Optical neural networks are the offspring of two parents: optical information processing and neural network theory. A brief overview of neural networks is presented to introduce the basic concepts to readers who may be unfamiliar with them.

It is now obvious that brains and digital computers function very differently. Digital computers are ideal for numerical solution of equations, numerical processing by iterative algorithms, sorting, formal logic, and probability calculation; in short algorithmically derived problems. Human brains tend to do those tasks slowly and poorly. Formal reasoning is hard but inspired guessing is easy. Biological brains are especially adept at very complex pattern recognition, generalization, abduction, intuition, problem finding, and language. These differences represent more than just a measure of the current limited state of computer development. It may also mean that brain-like architecture and function is much better adapted to these "characteristically biological" tasks than are digital computers. Neural networks, at present, are brain-inspired processors which utilize a very small number and only a very few of the types of structural components we find in brains, appropriately adapted for technological (electronic or optical) implementation. In contrast to conventional computers they are not necessarily algorithmically programmed with code but are adaptive, plastic, and may learn, although they can have "system algorithms" to make them function.

The basic component (cell) of a brain is a neuron. While biological neurons are very complicated, certainly more complicated than we now understand, artificial or technological neurons are very simple. Figure 20 shows such an artificial neuron symbolically. The components are

input signals, $\{x_i\}$
a summer, Σ
a nonlinear operator, NL $(\cdot)$
a distributor, D

The summer produces a signal

$$S = \sum x_i,$$

and the nonlinear operator produces a signal

$$S' = NL\ (s)$$

Usually $NL(\cdot)$ gives $S' = 0$ for low S, a fixed (saturated) S' for high enough S, and a monotonic transition region. The distributor sends signal W_jS' to neuron j, etc. Thus W_jS' becomes an input x to neuron j. Normally $1 > S' > 0$ and W_j can be either positive (excitatory to neuron j) or negative (inhibitory to neuron j).

Biological and technological neural networks are usually arranged in layers. A very simple feedforward, single layer neural network is shown in Figure 21. Such units can be connected in a forward direction from one layer to the next or backward or even laterally. The outputs of one layer become the inputs of another or, sometimes, the final outputs. Interconnect weights of zero are allowed. We can view the input set as a vector **x**. Each output neuron produces a sum

$$y_i = \sum_j a_{ij}x_j$$

We can view the y_i's as components of a vector **y** and a_{ij} as a component of a matrix **A**. Then we have

$$\mathbf{y} = \mathbf{Ax}.$$

The nonlinear operation works on each y_i, giving

$$y_i^1 = NL(y_i).$$

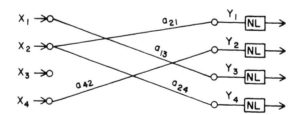

FIGURE 21.   A simplified model of a single layer biological (or technological) neural network.

In many neural networks, the system is far more complicated. Multiple layers, feed-back, and feed lateral operations occur. A bias may be added to effectively vary the threshold. Multiplicative as well as additive elements can occur. They also include "shunting" operations. In short, neurons need not be simple.

Neural networks carry out several types of operations. First, the network can learn (by themselves or with a teacher). Learning here means adjusting the strengths of the intercon-nections so that, to some degree, each input leads to the proper output. This operation is sometimes called long-term memory or simply LTM. Second, the network can apply what it has learned to new inputs by flowing them though the system to the output layers. In biol-ogy, short-term memory (STM) is a dynamic reverberatory pattern within the network which recalls previously stored patterns. In artificial neural systems, STM is sometimes used to mean use of the stored (LTM) patterns. In biology, these functions occur in the same system of hardware or "wetware." In technological neural networks, we can choose to use separate hardware of LTM and STM.

It is easy to show that digital computers and neural networks can each embody the other. From the beginning it was realized that Boolean operations could be performed by neurons. Likewise, since 1936, through Church's thesis [70], it has been widely believed that anything which can be calculated by any means (such as a neural network) can be calcu-lated digitally by a "Universal Turing Machine." In this sense, digital computers and neural networks are "formally equivalent." The neural network paradigm, however, often proves a useful one for associative memory, pattern classification, innovation, robustness, etc. It seems a natural fit for biology. We know of no biological Boolean operation. As we will see, it is also a "natural" application for optics.

Optical neural networks are made possible by adaptation of three other fields: "classi-cal" neural networks (the "connectionist model"), optical computing, and optical compo-nents. The needed adaptations of each are sketched in Figure 22 and elaborated somewhat below.

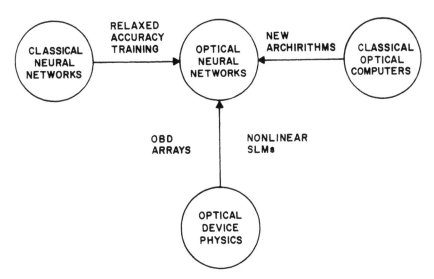

FIGURE 22.   Optical neural networks adapt components and concepts from three better developed fields to create some totally new potentialities. In this diagram, OBD represents optical bistable device.

A few general references can be recommended for readers who want to learn more about neural networks [*71–73*]. This is a vast and growing field. We will attempt a fair and balanced overview of the field but certainly not a complete literature survey. We have omitted many important papers because they were not necessary to the exposition.

There are sound reasons for using optics rather than electronics for implementing at least some neural networks. In this section, we want to make a few general observations.

The key ingredient of neural networks is the interconnection of neurons. There may be many neurons per layer with each neuron having high fan-in (number of input signals) and high fan-out (number of distributed signals). Very large fan-in/fan-out (10^3–10^6) is quite impractical for VLSI technology because it uses a unique discrete channel for each input or output. The space and power penalties in VLSI for these large fan-in/fan-out values are prohibitive. Most optical neural networks use unconfined or free space interconnections which avoid these problems by allowing freely crossing and overlapping interconnection paths. Thus large numbers of neurons and interconnections are the natural domains of optics. Figure 23 shows the region of advantage to optics clearly.

Power consumption is often a major advantage of optics. Most electronic digital computers use around 10^8 kT per fan-in and fan-out. Here k is the Boltzmann constant, T is the absolute temperature, and kT is the ambient thermal energy. Many optical processors operate at around 10^4 kT. Because coherent optics allows each proton to effectively perform the full fan-in of up to 10^6, the energy per fan-in can be much less than kT [*74*].

Of course, the general advantages and disadvantages of optics relative to electronics in computing apply here as well. These have to do with easy 3-D interconnection (with no soldering), natural parallelism, and insensitivity to electromagnetic inference.

As we will seek to show, optics is sometimes but not always preferable to electronics for implementing neural networks. It is *a* solution, not *the* solution to the problem of implementing neural networks.

The following optical interconnection methods comprise an essentially complete set of methods suggested to date:

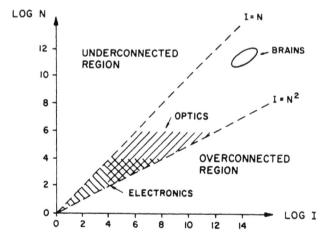

FIGURE 23.   Rough comparison of three implementation technologies for neural networks in terms of number of neurons *N* and number of interconnections *I*.

Fiberoptic fan-in/fan-out [75]
Holographic in-plane connection in integrated optics [4]
Optical parallel matrix-vector multipliers [76]
Lenslet array multiple imaging [77]
Thick holographic associative networks [78]
Fixed hologram arrays [79–82]

Of these methods, the last two offer the greatest number of parallel interconnections. We will concentrate our attention on them.

From the very early days of holography, the value of thick holograms as associative memories has been known [83]. Wavefronts representing paired two-dimensional (2-D) patterns are interfered in a three-dimensional (3-D) recording medium. If one wavefront is incident on the hologram, the other wavefront is reconstructed (approximately). Multiple pairs of wavefronts can be stored in this way. The various pairs must be recorded separately. If there are M pairs, each can use 1/M of the dynamic range of the recording medium. This leads to a 1/M signal-to-noise ratio decrease for each hologram relative to the M = 1 case [84]. What has changed recently is the use of photorefractive crystals as hologram recording materials [78, 85, 86]. These have several advantages over photographic media:

They can be millimeters rather than microns thick and thus offer very good selectivity and discrimination
These materials are reusable in "real time" and hence lead to continuous learning
Since only spatial differences in patterns cause refractive index changes, bias buildup is not a problem.

On the other hand, old recorded pairs fade as new ones are added. Furthermore even readout records the readout beam weakens the previously recorded memories. Thus, while there are many new promises and opportunities in photorefractive associate networks, additional research will be needed to optimize this approach.

Another holographic method which dates from the early days of holography is the page-oriented holographic memory (POHM) [87]. The basic idea of the POHM is to store many holograms side by side on the same substrate. The holograms are made in such a way that they have a common 2-D output plane. By deflecting a laser beam toward any hologram in the POHM, we cause the corresponding 2D "page" of data to appear in the output plane.

To use the POHM in neural networks only two major changes are required: address all of the holograms in parallel and (sometimes) place the "write plane" of an optically addressable Spatial Light Modulator (SLM) in the common output plane. Figure 24 shows one of many such configurations. Let the holograms be indexed by subscripts i and j. Since the output plane is an image of the hologram plane (through the transmissive SLM), it too is indexed by i and j. The input is a 2-D SLM whose picture elements or "pixels" are indexed by k and l. Let the amplitude of light from the i,j hologram toward the k,l pixel be called T_{ijkl}. If the transmission of that pixel is a_{kl}, then the light contributed to the i,j output from the k,l input is T_{ijkl}. Of course, all inputs contribute to that output which can be written

$$b_{ij} = \sum_{k,l} T_{ijkl} a_{kl}.$$

We can also write this in the form

$$\mathbf{b} = T\,\mathbf{a},$$

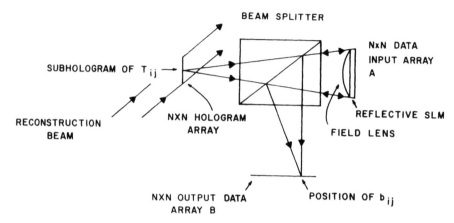

FIGURE 24.   An N^4 interconnection system.

where **a** is a 2-D input vector, **b** is a 2-D output vector, and T is a four-dimensional matrix or tensor. Since i, j, k, and l can all run from 1 to N, N^4 independent T_{ijkl}'s (interconnections) can be generated in parallel. Currently available components limit N to "only" 256 although $N = 1024$ (roughly 10^{12}) parallel interconnections appear feasible [88]. Of course, this is well beyond the capability of current or foreseeable electronics.

The "problem," which can be viewed as an advantage, of this approach is that the interconnect strengths are fixed. Once they are fixed, these neural networks cease to learn (or forget!). Fixed holographic memories are ideal for this situation because they can store vast numbers of interconnections and because they are readily and accurately copied (cloned).

PROJECTIONS

A critical point in the history of optical computing was passed in the late 1980s as workers more and more abandoned competition with electronics and began to emphasize activities which are

>   Important to the future of computing
>   Possible with optics
>   Impossible (or overwhelming impractical) electronically

The two activities now known are

>   Full parallel, weighted interconnect between a 1000 × 1000 input array and a 1000
>   × 1000 output array
>   Operations at energies less than kT per operation (on the average) using wave
>   particle duality.

Optics and electronics then become allies not rivals in the effort to make computers faster, smaller, power efficient, and less costly.

REFERENCES

1. L. D. Hutcheson, P. Haugen, and A. Husain, "Optical Interconnects Replace Hard-wire," *IEEE Spectrum, 24,* 30–35 (March 1987).
2. J. W. Goodman, F. I. Leonberger, S. Kung, and R. A. Athale, "Optical Interconnections for VLSI Systems," *Proc. IEEE, 72,* 850–865 (1984).
3. S. Ishihara, "Recent Advances in Optical Computing in Japan," *Proc. Photo-Opt. Instrum. Eng., 634,* 31–50 (1986).
4. M. R. Feldman, S. C. Esener, C. C. Guest, and S. H. Lee, "Comparison Between Optical and Electrical Interconnects Based on Power and Speed Considerations," *Appl. Opt., 27,* 1742–1751 (1988).
5. J. W. Goodman, "Optics as an Interconnect Technology," in *Optical Processing and Computing,* H. H. Arsenault, T. Szoplik, and B. Macukow (eds.), Academic Press, New York, pp. 1–32.
6. A. W. Lohmann, "What Classical Optics Can Do for the Digital Optical Computer," *Appl. Opt., 25,* 1543–1549 (1986).
7. J. Shamir and H. J. Caulfield, "High-Efficiency Rapidly Programmable Optical Interconnections," *Appl. Opt., 26,* 1032–1037 (1987).
8. B. Moslehi, J. W. Goodman, M. Tur, and H. J. Shaw, "Fiber-optic Lattice Signal Processing," *Proc. IEEE, 72,* 909–930 (1984).
9. M. M. Mirsalehi, J. Shamir, and H. J. Caulfield, "Three-Dimensional Optical Fredkin Gate Arrays Applied to Residue Arithmetic," *Appl. Opt., 28,* 2429–2438 (1989).
10. R. K. Kostuk, J. W. Goodman, and L. Hesselink, "Design Considerations for Holographic Optical Interconnects," *Appl. Opt., 26,* 3947–3953 (1987).
11. H. J. White and W. A. Wright, "Holographic Implementation of a Hopfield Model with Discrete Weightings," *Appl. Opt., 27,* 331–338 (1988).
12. Y. Tsunoda and Y. Takeda, "High Density Image-Storage Holograms by a Random Phase Sampling Method," *Appl. Opt., 13,* 2046–2051 (1974).
13. J. L. Jewell, Y. H. Lee, A. Schere, S. L. McCall, N. A. Olsson, J. P. Harbison, and L. T. Florez, "Surface-Emitting Microlasers for Photonic Switching and Interchip Connections," *Opt. Eng., 29,* 210–214 (1990).
14. N. S. Szabo, and R. I. Tanaka, "Residue Arithmetic and Its Applications to Computer Technology," McGraw-Hill, New York, 1967.
15. A. Avizienis, "Signed-Digit Number Representations for Fast Parallel Arithmetic," *IRE Trans. Electron. Comput., EC-10,* 389–400 (1961).
16. B. L. Drake, R. P. Bocker, M. E. Lasher, R. H. Patterson, and W. J. Miceli, "Photonic Computing Using the Modified Signed-Digit Number Representation," *Opt. Eng., 25,* 38–43 (1986).
17. E. A. Mnatsakanyan, V. N. Morozov, and Y. M. Popov, "Digital Data Processing in Optoelectronic Devices (Review)," *Sov. J. Quantum Electron., 9,* 665–667 (1979).
18. S. A. Collins, "Numerical Optical Data Processor," *Proc. Soc. Photo-Opt. Instrum. Eng., 128,* 313–319 (1977).
19. R. A. Athale and S. H. Lee, "Development of an Optical Parallel Logic Device and a Half-Adder Circuit for Digital Optical Processing," *Opt. Eng., 18,* 513–517 (1979)
20. H. F. Taylor, "Integrated Optical Logic Circuits," *Proc. Topical Meeting on Integrated and Wave Optics,* 1978, Tu C4-1 to Tu C4-4.
21. A. Huang, Y. Tsunoda, J. W. Goodman, and S. Ishihara, "Optical Computation Using Residue Arithmetic," *Appl. Opt, 18,* 149–162 (1979).
22. A. Tai, I. Cindrich, J. R. Fienup, and C. C. Aleksoff, "Optical Residue Arithmetic

Computer with Programmable Computation Modules," *Appl. Opt.,* 18, 2812–2823 (1979).

23. M. M. Mirsalehi, J. Shamir, and H. J. Caulfield, "Residue Arithmetic Processing Utilizing Optical Fredkin Gate Arrays," *Appl. Opt.,* 26, 3940–3946 (1987).
24. C. C. Guest and T. K. Gaylord, "Truth-Table Look-up Optical Processing Utilizing Binary and Residue Arithmetic," *Appl. Opt.,* 19, 1201–1207 (1989).
25. A. P. Goutzoulis, E. C. Malarkey, D. K. Davies, J. C. Bradley, and P. R. Beaudet, "Optical Processing with Residue LED/LD Lookup Tables," *Appl. Opt.,* 27, 1674–1681 (1988).
26. A. Huang, "Parallel Algorithms for Optical Digital Computers," *Tech. Digest, IEEE Tenth Int. Opt. Comput. Conf.,* 1983, pp. 13–17.
27. K. -H. Brenner, "New Implementation of Symbolic Substitution Logic," *Appl. Opt.,* 25, 3061–3064 (1986).
28. K. H. Brenner, A. Huang, and N. Streibl, "Digital Optical Computing with Symbolic Substitution," *Appl. Opt.,* 25, 3054–3060 (1986).
29. J. N. Mait and K. -H. Brenner, "Optical Symbolic Substitution: System Design Using Phase-Only Holograms," *Appl. Opt.,* 27, 1692–1700 (1988).
30. H. -I. Jeon, M. A. G. Abushagur, A. A. Sawchuk, and B. K. Jenkins, "Digital Optical Processor Based on Symbolic Substitution Using Holographic Matched Filtering," *Appl. Opt.,* 29, 2113–2125 (1990).
31. R. Thalmann, G. Pedrini, and K. J. Weible, "Optical Symbolic Substitution Using Diffraction Gratings," *Appl. Opt.,* 29, 2113–2125 (1990).
32. R. P. Bocker, B. L. Drake, M. E. Lasher, and T. B. Henderson, "Modified Signed-Digit Addition and Subtraction Using Optical Symbolic Substitution," *Appl. Opt.,* 15, 2456–2457 (1986).
33 .S. D. Goodman, and W. T. Rhodes, "Symbolic Substitution Applications to Image Processing," *Appl. Opt.,* 27, 1701–1714 (1988).
34. R. Arrathoon and M. H. Hassoun, "Optical Threshold Logic Elements for Digital Computation," *Opt. Lett.,* 9, 143–145 (1984).
35. P. S. Guilfoyle and W. J. Wiley, "Combinatorial Logic Based Digital Optical Computing Architectures," *Appl. Opt.,* 27, 1661–1673 (1988).
36. M. J. Murdocca, A. Huang, J. Jahns, and N. Streibl, "Optical Design of Programmable Logic Arrays," *Appl. Opt.,* 27, 1651–1660 (1988).
37. L. Cutrona, "Recent Developments in Coherent Optical Technology," *Optical and Electro-Optical Information Processing,* J. Tippet et al. (eds.), MIT Press, Cambridge, MA, 1965, Chap. 6.
38. R. A. Heinz, J. O. Artman, and S. H. Lee, "Matrix Multiplication by Optical Methods," *Appl. Opt.,* 9, 2161–2168 (1970).
39. D. P. Jablonowski, R. A. Heinz, and J. O. Artman, "Matrix Multiplication by Optical Methods: Experimental Verifications," *Appl. Opt.,* 11, 174–178 (1972).
40. W. Schneider and W. Fink, "Incoherent Optical Matrix Multiplication," *Opt. Acta,* 22, 879–889 (1975).
41. R. P. Bocker, "Matrix Multiplication Using Incoherent Optical Techniques," *Appl. Opt.,* 13, 1670–1676 (1974).
42. K. Bromley, "An Optical Coherent Correlator," *Optical Acta,* 21, 35–41 (1974).
43. M. A. Monahan, R. P. Bocker, K. Bromley, A. C. H. Louie, R. D. Martin, and R. G. Shepard, "The Use of Charge Coupled Devices in Electro-Optical Processing," *Proc. 1975 Intern. Conf. on the Applications of Charge-Coupled Devices,* 1975.

44. L. B. Stotts, "Integrated Optical Matrix Multiplier," *Appl. Opt., 15*, 2029-2031 (1976).
45. D. Psaltis, D. Casasent, D. Neft, and M. Carlotto, "Accurate Numerical Computation by Optical Convolution," *Proc. Soc. Photo-Opt. Instrum. Eng., 232*, 151-156 (1980).
46. W. C. Collins, R. A. Athale, and P. D. Stilwell, "Improved Accuracy for an Optical Iterative Processor," *Proc. Soc. Photo-Opt. Instrum. Eng., 352*, 50-56 (1982).
47. R. P. Bocker, "Optical Digital RUBIC (Rapid Unbiased Bipolar Incoherent Calculator) Cube Processor," *Opt. Eng., 23*, 26-33 (1984).
48. R. A. Athale, H. Q. Huang, and J. N. Lee, "High Accuracy Matrix Multiplication with a Magnetooptic Spatial Light Modulator," *Proc. Soc. Photo-Opt. Instrum. Eng., 431*, 187-193 (1983).
49. D. Psaltis and R. A. Athale, "High Accuracy Computation with Linear Analog Optical Processors: A Critical Study," *Appl. Opt., 25*, 3071-3077 (1986).
50. H. J. Caulfield, W. T. Rodes, M. J. Foster, and S. Horwitz, "Optical Implementation of Systolic Array Processing," *Opt. Comm., 40*, 86-90 (1981).
51. R. P. Bocker, H. J. Caulfield, and K. Bromley, "Rapid Unbiased Bipolar Incoherent Calculator Cube," *Appl. Opt., 22*, 804-807 (1983).
52. D. Casasent, J. Jackson, and C. Neuman, "Frequency-Multiplexed and Pipelined Iterative Optical Systolic Array Processors," *Appl. Opt., 22*, 115-124 (1983).
53. H. J. Caulfield, D. Dvore, J. W. Goodman, and W. T. Rhodes, "Eigenvector Determination by Noncoherent Optical Methods," *Appl. Opt., 20*, 2263-2265 (1981).
54. B. V. K. Vijaya Kumar, "Singular Value Decomposition Using Iterative Optical Processors," *Appl. Opt., 22*, 962-963 (1983).
55. A. Ghosh and D. Casasent, "Triangular System Solutions on an Optical Systolic Processor," *Appl. Opt., 22*, 1795-1796 (1983).
56. W. K. Cheng and H. J. Caulfield, "Fully-Parallel Relaxation Algebraic Operations for Optical Computers," *Opt. Comm., 43*, 251-254 (1982).
57. H. J. Caulfield, J. H. Gruninger, J. E. Ludman, K. Steiglitz, H. Rabitz, J. Gerfand, and E. Tsoni, "Bimodal Optical Computers," *Appl. Opt., 25*, 3128-3131 (1986).
58. M. A. G. Abushagur and H. J. Caulfield, "Highly Precise Optical-Hybrid Matrix Processor," *Proc. Soc. Photo-Opt. Instrum. Eng., 639*, 63-67 (1986).
59. J. W. Goodman, A. Dias, and L. M. Woody, "Fully Parallel High-Speed Incoherent Optical Method for Performing Discrete Fourier Transforms," *Opt. Lett., 2*, 1-3 (1978).
60. M. A. G. Abushagur and H. J. Caulfield, "Speed and Convergence of Bimodal Optical Computers," *Opt. Eng., 26*, 22-27 (1987).
61. M. A. G. Abushagur, H. J. Caulfield, P. M. Gibson, and M. Habli, "Superconvergence of Hybrid Optoelectronic Processors," *Appl. Opt., 26*, 4906-4907 (1987).
62. M. A. Habli, M. A. G. Abushagur, and H. J. Caulfield, "Solving System of Linear Equations Using the Bimodal Optical Computer (Experimental Results)," *Proc. Photo-Opt. Instrum. Eng., 936*, 315-320 (1988).
63. H. T. Kung and C. E. Leiserson, "Systolic Arrays (for VLSI)," *Sparse Matrix Proc. 1978*, Society for Industrial and Applied Mathematics, 1979, pp. 256-282.
64. D. Casasent, "Acoustooptic Linear Algebra Processors: Architectures, Algorithms, and Applications," *Proc. IEEE, 72*, 831-849 (1984).
65. D. Casasent, "Acousto-optic Transducers in Iterative Optical Vector-Matrix Processors," *Appl. Opt., 21*, 1859-1865 (1982).

66. G. Eichmann and H. J. Caulfield, "Optical Learning (Inference) Machines," *Appl. Opt., 24*, 2051–2054 (1985).

67. C. Warde and J. Kottas, "Hybrid Optical Inference Machines: Architectural Considerations," *Appl. Opt., 25*, 940–947 (1986).

68. H. H. Szu and H. J. Caulfield, "Optical Expert Systems," *Appl. Opt., 26*, 1943–1947 (1987).

69. H. J. Caulfield and I. Kadar, "Optical Parallel Dempster-Shafer Calculations," *Appl. Opt., 28*, 325–327 (1989).

70. A. Church, "An Unsolvable Problem in Elementary Number Theory," *Am. J. Math., 58*, 345–363 (1936).

71. D. E. Rumelhart, J. L. McClelland, and the PDP Research Group, *Parallel Distributed Processing: Explorations in the Microstructure of Cognition,* Vols. 1 & 2, MIT Press, Cambridge, MA, 1986.

72. R. P. Lippman, "An Introduction to Computing with Neural Nets," *IEEE ASSP Mag., 4*(2), 4–22 (1987).

73. S. Grossberg, "Nonlinear Neural Networks: Principles, Mechanisms and Architectures," *Neural Networks, 1*, 17–61 (1988).

74. H. J. Caulfield and J. Shamir, "Wave Particle Duality Considerations in Optical Computing," *Appl. Opt., 28*, 2184–2186 (1989).

75. R. Arrathoon, M. Rana, and T. Wang, "On the Limits of Fiber Optic Fan-in and Fan-out for Optoelectronic Logic," *Proc. Soc. Photo-Opt. Instrum. Eng., 936*, 327–332 (1988).

76. N. H. Farkat, D. Psaltis, A. Prata, and E. Park, "Optical Implementation of the Hopfield Model," *Appl. Opt., 24*, 1469–1475 (1985)

77. N. H. Farkat, S. Miyahara, and K. S. Lee, "Optical Analog of Two-Dimensional Neural Networks and Their Application in Recognition of Radar Targets," *Neural Networks for Computing,* American Institute of Physics, New York, 1986, pp. 146–152.

78. D. Psaltis, J. X. Yu, G. Gu, and H. Lee, "Optical Neural Nets Implemented with Volume Holograms," in *Technical Digest Topical Meeting on Optical Computing,* Optical Society of America, Washington, DC, 1987, p. 129.

79. H. J. Caulfield, "Parallel N^4 Weighted Optical Interconnections," *Appl. Opt., 26*, 4039–4040 (1987).

80. R. Clark, C. Hester, and P. Lindberg, "Mapping Sequential Processing Algorithms onto Parallel Distributed Processing Architectures," *Proc. Soc. Photo-Opt. Instrum. Eng., 880*, 20–28 (1988).

81. H. J. White, N. B. Aldridge, and I. Lindsay, "Digital and Analogue Holographic Associative Memories," *Opt. Eng., 27*, 30–37 (1988).

82. J. S. Jang, S. W. Jung, S. Y. Lee, and S. Y. Shin, "Optical Implementation of the Hopfield Model for Two-Dimensional Associative Memory," *Opt. Lett., 13*, 248–250 (1988).

83. R. J. Collier and K. S. Pennington, "Ghost Imaging in Holograms Formed in the Near Field," *Appl. Phys. Lett., 8*, 44–46 (1966).

84. H. J. Caulfield, L. Sun, and J. L. Harris, "Biasing for Single-Exposure and Multiple-Exposure Holography," *J. Opt. Soc. Am., 58*, 1003–1004 (1968).

85. Y. Owechko, B. H. Soffer, and G. J. Dunning, "Optoelectronic Neural Networks Based on Holographically Interconnected Image Processors," *Proc. Soc. Photo-Opt. Instrum. Eng., 882*, 143–153 (1988).

86. Y. Owechko, "Self-Pumped Optical Neural Networks," in *Technical Digest Topical*

Meeting on Optical Computing, Optical Society of America, Washington, DC, 1989, pp. 44–47.

87. F. M. Smits and L. E. Gallaher, "Design Considerations for a Semipermanent Optical Memory," *Bell Syst. Tech. J., 46,* 1267–1278 (1967).

88. J. Shamir, H. J. Caulfield, and R. B. Johnson, "Massive Holographic Interconnection Networks and Their Limitations," *Appl. Opt., 28,* 311–324 (1989).

MUSTAFA A. G. ABUSHAGUR
MIR MUJTABA MIRSALEHI
H. JOHN CAULFIELD

PACKET SWITCHING

INTRODUCTION: WHAT IS PACKET SWITCHING?

Packet switching is a statistical time division multiplexing method. Packet switching was invented to provide an efficient way to accommodate computer communication traffic that is *bursty** in nature.

Communication networks that existed prior to packet-switched networks were optimized mostly for voice communication (e.g., telephony). In such networks, it is assumed that the connection time (i.e., session) is relatively long, and that the bandwidth is (relatively) constantly utilized. These networks use what is commonly referred to as *circuit switching*. In circuit switching, the connection between any two users is preceded by a set-up stage, in which a communication channel is established between the two users. The set-up procedure involves reservation of communication hardware on the path connecting both sides. In particular, such a reservation involves dedication of a communication channel (e.g., bandwidth in FDM or time slot in TDM) for the whole time of the conversation. At the end of the conversation, the close procedure releases the channel that now can be dedicated to a new conversation. Circuit switching is based on the assumption that a conversation lasts for a period of time much longer than the set-up procedure, and that the channel utilization throughout the conversation time is relatively high. Thus, dedication of a line per connection makes sense.

When computer communication began to proliferate, measurements showed that computer-generated traffic is not suited to circuit-switched networks. In particular, computer traffic is more *bursty* in nature than voice traffic. Moreover, in some applications a conversation may be very short, on the order of set-up time. Thus dedication of a communication channel per computer connection results in very low utilization. Take, for example, a user editing a file. While typing, the user constantly sends characters over the connection line. However, while thinking there may be a long period of no activity. Dedicating a separate line per such a user results in low line utilization and high cost. Communication between machines† involves traffic that is also quite bursty, leading to an unacceptably low level of hardware utilization. Some sort of channel sharing was necessary and packet switching provides exactly this kind of sharing. In packet switching, a number of bursty traffic streams are (time) multiplexed onto a single channel. This statistical multiplexing is achieved by buffering (queueing) the incoming information at the channel entrance. In this way, the utilization of communication channels is increased.

In packet-switched network, when a large amount of data is to be conveyed, the data are fragmented into segments, each segment is assigned a header and a trailer that possibly

---

*Traffic *burstiness* is measured as the ratio of peak to average transmission bandwidth.
†For example, file transfer, distributed processing (remote procedure calls, distributed data bases), parallel processing.

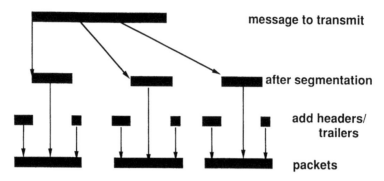

message to transmit

after segmentation

add headers/
trailers

packets

FIGURE 1.   The packet-switching principle.

contain addressing, control, and error-detecting information. The resulting structure is referred to as a packet (Fig. 1). The packets are then transmitted by the communication network (simultaneously with packets from many other users), travel independently through a network, and are received at the receiver site. At the receiver, the packets may be checked for any errors that occurred while in transit through the network. Occurrence of errors may require retransmissions of the erroneous packets by the transmitter. Correctly received packets are reassembled, and the information is passed to the destination machine. The process of communication of information over a communication network by means of dividing the information into segments that can independently travel through the network, is referred to as *packet switching*. Thus in packet switching, as opposed to circuit switching, communication hardware and software (links, switches, etc.) are shared by many users. Since statistical multiplexing of large number of users reduces the traffic fluctuations (i.e., burstiness), the transmission media is now better utilized. Moreover, for low-load operation, packet-switching features lower delay than circuit-switching because of the elimination of the set-up procedure in the packet-switched network. This is especially emphasized for transmission of data that is shorter than roundtrip delay between source and destination. Figure 2 demonstrates the lower delay of packet-switching as opposed to the circuit-switching delay.

The *message-switching* technique is similar to the packet-switching technique: messages are fed into a network without any set-up procedure and with no dedication of network resources. However, in message-switching, as opposed to packet-switching, there is no segmentation of messages into fixed size packets. Thus messages travel as units through the network. The message-switching technique has the advantage of simpler implementation, since no segmentation/reassembly process is required. On the other hand, the packet-switching technique, as opposed to the message-switching scheme, incurs lower retransmission penalty for a transmission error, lower delay due to the pipelining effect, and lower delay variations due to the law-of-large-numbers effect.

In order to operate properly, packet switching requires facilitation of such functions as addressing, routing, flow control, congestion control, error control, traffic priority classes, network management, billing, etc. Moreover, various traffic requirements (e.g., voice, video, and data integration), topology, cost, and other design parameters are imposed on the network. Consequently, a variety of different solutions were proposed to support these functions and to meet these requirements and parameters, which has led to the enormous diversity in, what is called today, packet-switched networks. In particular, the packet-

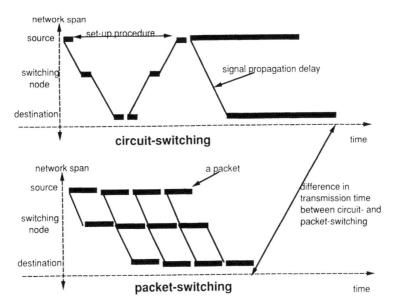

FIGURE 2.   Circuit- vs. packet-switching delay.

switching scheme is used in networks with different sizes; from local-area networks located in a single building (e.g., [*1*], FDDI), through metropolitan-area networks spanning an area of a city (e.g., 802.6), and up to wide-area networks with diameters of hundreds to thousands of miles (TYMNET, ARPANET, Telenet, Datapac, NSFNet).

The physical structure of a packet-switching network strongly depends on its span. In particular, a variety of solutions were proposed for the way a user interfaces with the network (referred to as *media-access control* or MAC). For example, in local area networks the MAC can be based on CSMA/CD* algorithm, as in Ethernet, or on token-passing algorithm, as in FDDI. Wide area packet-switching networks are usually composed of switching nodes interconnected by communication channels; i.e., links. In this arrangement, packets are passed from switching node to switching node until they arrive at the destination. This scheme is also referred to as *multihop*.

Standards play a central role in design and operation of communication networks. The purpose of standardization is to enable easy communication, interconnection, and integration of hardware and software created by different vendors. One of the best known standards is the *Open Systems Interconnection* (OSI) seven-layer architecture model [2] developed by International Standardization Organization (ISO) described below. Other standardization bodies are CCITT†, IEEE, EIA, ECMA, and others. Standards are concerned with nearly every aspect of communication networks; the physical media, the protocols, maintenance, administration, etc.

---

*Carrier Sense Multiple Access with Collision Detection.
†Comité Consultatif International des Téléphone et Télégraphique.

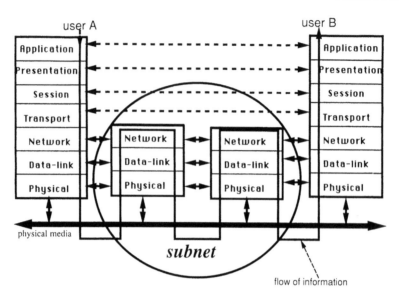

FIGURE 3   The ISO/OSI model.

PROTOCOLS IN PACKET-SWITCHING NETWORKS

A protocol is a set of agreements that control the way users access and transmit over communication networks. Protocols are needed to perform nearly every function and to facilitate interconnection of equipment manufactured by different vendors. Probably the most famous protocols architecture is the seven-layer model of ISO: the OSI model. The architecture, shown in Figure 3, divides the communication process into layers, each layer performs a specific set of functions. OSI model adopts the *envelope* approach, in which each layer after performing its function on the packet, appends its header and passes the packet to the layer above. At the receiving end the execution is reversed; each layer strips the packet from the layer's header, performs its functions and passes the packet to the layer above. For example, one of the functions of the *presentation* layer is encryption. At the transmitting site, the presentation layer receives a packet from the application, performs the encryption algorithm, appends its header, and passes the packet to the session layer. At the receiving site, the peer-presentation layer receives the packet from the session layer, strips its header, performs decryption, and passes the decrypted packet to the application.

OSI is a model for structuring communication protocols. It is not a protocol. There have been large numbers of protocols designed to be used in communication networks. Some of them are compatible with the ISO/OSI model, and some are designed according to other models (DEC-NET's DNA, IBM's SNA, etc). Among the more known network protocols is TCP/IP [3], used in ARPANET[5]. In all of the models, lower layers handle the actual transmission of the packet over the communication media and include function like media-access control, segmentation/reassembly, addressing and routing, etc. The higher layers are usually responsible for data formatting, sequencing, error handling, flow control, and connection management. Some of the techniques that are used to accomplish these functions are discussed below.

Connection Type

The packet switching technique can be used in the *connection-oriented* or in the *connectionless* mode. In the connection-oriented mode (virtual circuits, for example), there is a clear set-up procedure that precedes the actual exchange of data. This set-up stage usually involves reservation of buffer space and setting some information along the communication path, which will be used by all the packets that belong to the session. However, as opposed to circuit switching, connection-oriented packet switching allows sharing of the transmission media and possibly buffers among more than one session.

In the connectionless mode (e.g., datagram) packets are entered into the network as independent pieces; no set-up procedure is performed and packets that belong to the same session do not necessarily take the same route through the network.

Routing is done once in connection-oriented networks, during the set-up procedure, and per-packet in connectionless networks. Also, in connectionless networks, the header of each packet has to contain full destination address, while only a path identifier is required in connection-oriented networks. However, connectionless networks can more easily balance traffic, change configurations, and deliver short bursts of traffic with lower delay.

Addressing and Routing

Each packet carried by a packet-switching network contains an indication of the destination to which it is to be delivered. The actual addressing scheme depends mainly on the type of connection that the packet belongs to. For connection-oriented traffic, the initial set-up procedure sets up path from the source to the destination and associates an identifier with the chosen path. This identifier is used in each subsequent packet. For connectionless traffic, each packet carries the full destination address. The process of determining the route through the network is called *routing* and involves the distribution of the network status to individual nodes, if distributed routing algorithm is used, or to a central processing site, for centralized routing algorithm. This network status may include information on which links/nodes are operational or not, the delay through the switching nodes, etc.

Flow and Congestion Control

The statistical bursty nature of the traffic streams results in a queue building at times of higher activity. Buffers in the switching nodes are sized in such a way as to prevent their overflow. However, because of the statistical nature of the packet arrival there is a finite probability of buffer overflow. To avoid such condition, flow control procedures are introduced that allow a switching node to reduce or turn off incoming traffic. Flow control procedures are exercised at different levels in packet-switched networks. For example, when flow control is performed between two adjacent switching nodes, the sending node cannot have more than some preagreed number of outstanding packets, known as the *window size*. Each packet receive by the receiving node is acknowledged on a reverse channel and enables a new packet to be transmitted by the sending node. This scheme is known as *window flow control*, and can be used between different entities within the networks.* Other flow-control schemes (*rate-based* flow control, for example) are also common.

---

*Between adjacent switching nodes, as described, between network end points, between end users, etc.

When too much traffic is transmitted into a packet-switched network, the queues within the network build up, and the network delay increases sharply. This queue build-up phenomenon may result in packet loss due to buffer overflow, and may require retransmission of the loss packets. The increased delay may also trigger retransmission, since the user has no knowledge whether an awaited packet is lost or only excessively delayed. Such a state, in which some of the network bandwidth is lost due to overutilization of the network is called *network congestion*, and the scheme used to avoid or reduce network congestion are called *congestion-control* schemes. The congestion-control problem has been identified as one of the major problems in high-speed networks, mainly because of the increased storage capability of such networks. Accordingly, a wide spectrum of congestion-control techniques were proposed; bandwidth-reservation schemes, dynamic window flow-control, traffic shaping, etc.

Error Control

Errors occur in packet-switched networks because of two reasons: transmission errors (due to receiver thermal noise, for example) and packet loss (due to buffers overflow). Error control mechanisms are used in packet switching networks to detect and rectify errors created by each one of the two phenomena. In particular, CRC*[4] is used to detect transmission errors. CRC is done by appending a 16-bit long field to each packet. The value of the field is calculated for each packet by an arithmetic operation on the values of other packet fields. The receiver verifies whether a transmission error occurred by another arithmetic operation that includes packet fields and the value of the CRC. If an error occurred, the erroneous packet is dropped. Since packets are numbered by *sequence* numbers, the dropped packet will be detected and a request for retransmission will be issued to the transmitter. Sequence numbers are also used to detect lost packets and the same retransmission mechanism is used for recovery.

Different retransmission schemes are used to recover missing packets. The two best known are: *go-back-n* and *selective retransmission*. In the go-back-n scheme, all the information that follows a lost packet is retransmitted. In the selective retransmission scheme, only the lost packets are retransmitted, according to the request initiated by the destination. The go-back-n scheme has the advantage of simpler control, while the selective retransmission technique reduces the bandwidth penalty. It has been shown that go-back-n may have prohibitive cost in high-speed networks.

Additional Issues

The list of functions discussed above is by no means exhaustive. In addition to the functions associated with actual data exchange, there are issues that need to be carefully engineered for proper network operation; for example, OA&M (billing, architectural changes, traffic monitoring, etc.), traffic integration and priorities, security, etc.

SOME EXAMPLES OF PACKET-SWITCHING NETWORKS

Among the existing packet-switching networks, the X.25 is probably the best known. X.25 recommendation defined by CCITT deals with the lower three layers of the ISO/OSI model. In particular, the X.25 recommendation defines X.21 [5] as the physical layer and LAPB† as

---

*Cyclic Redundancy Check.
†Balanced Link Access Procedure.

the data-link layer. The third layer, referred to as packet layer, corresponds to the network layer and defines procedures for exchange of data and control information between DTE* and DCE† based on three types of services: virtual circuit, permanent virtual circuit, and fast select. X.25 defines procedure for call set-up, call clear, flow-control error-control, connection restart, etc. Additional recommendations (X.28, X.3, and X.29) were also defined to support terminal equipment (through PAD‡) that are not compatible with the X.25 standard.

The Ethernet is a well-known example of a local area network. Ethernet access scheme (which is very similar to the IEEE 802.3 Standard) is based on buss topology and on the CSMA/CD media access technique.

The new evolving standard of metropolitan-area network, the IEEE 802.6, is based on dual buss slotted architecture and special field in the packet format to allow slot reservations. The 802.6 packet format is quite similar to the ATM§ packet format defined as part of the B-ISDN‖ effort. In this context one should also mention SONET,☆ which defines the interface to the hierarchy of new generation of optical networks.

PERFORMANCE AND MODELING

With the proliferation of packet switched network, a lot of modeling, and performance analysis has been done (see e.g., [6,7]). Performance analysis of packet-switched network is mostly done using queueing theory and simulation. The main parameters of interest are; network throughput (number of packets per unit time), network delay (the time that elapses from the moment a packet enters the network till the time it emerges at the destination), error-rate (usually residual error-rate, since the network usually provides some error detection and correction mechanisms), jitter (the variation in network delay from packet to packet), and the availability (the duration of time the network is operational).

CONCLUSION AND FUTURE OF PACKET SWITCHING

The future looks promising for packet switching. Future networks are expected to be high-performance (high throughput, low delay) networks, based on the optical fiber media with transmission bandwidth of tens of Gbps [8]. Today's proposals for ATM Broadband ISDN, 802.6 MAN, and FDDI are based on packet switching in the hundred Mbps range.

In order to support high-performance communication, changes must be introduced in nearly every aspect of communication networks. For example, because of the high-rates involved, the amount of data in transit through the network increases by several orders of magnitude.❖ Thus, the penalty for retransmission of an erroneous packet significantly in-

---

*Data Terminal Equipment: a terminal equipment that is connected to the communication network (e.g., a user terminal or a computer).
†Data Circuit Terminating Equipment: equipment, which is part of the network, and to which a DTE is directly connected.
‡Packet Assemblers/Disassemblers.
§Asynchronous Transfer Mode
‖Broadband Integrated Service Digital Network
☆Synchronous Optical NETwork
❖For example, a 3000 mile T1 link can "store" about 4.7 Kbyte, but the same length of fiber link operating at 1.7 Gbps can contain as much as 5.3 Mbyte.

creases. Moreover, flow control and congestion control are much more difficult to implement. Furthermore, it is not clear whether the current structuring and implementation of communication protocols is adequate to provide future communication needs [9, 10]. Consequently, much of the current research on communication networks concentrate on proposing new schemes that are believed to be more powerful and that better match the future communication environment [10].

Also, much research is performed on optical networks (in particular, all-optical networks), in which the information is converted into light at the network entrance, propagates and is switched as light through the network, and is converted back to an electrical signal only at the network exit [11, 12]. Such approach, in principle, can provide enormous throughput with very low delay.

REFERENCES

1. *The Ethernet, A Local Area Network, Data Link Layer and Physical Layer Specifications*, Digital Equipment Corporation, Maynard, MA; Intel Corporation, Santa Clara, CA; Xerox Corporation, Stanford, CT; version 1.0, Sept. 30, 1980, and version 2.0, Nov. 1982.
2. M. Schwartz, *Telecommunication Networks; Protocols, Modeling and Analysis*, Addison-Wesley, Reading, MA, 1987.
3. D. E. Comer, *Internetworking with TCP/IP; Principles, Protocols, and Architecture,* Prentice Hall, Englewood Cliffs, NJ. 1988
4. A. S. Tanenbaum, *Computer Networks*, Prentice Hall, Englewood Cliffs, NJ, 2 ed., 1988.
5. P. Green (ed.), *Computer Network Architectures and Protocols*, Plenum Press, New York, 1982.
6. L. Kleinrock, *Queueing Systems*. Volume 1; *Theory*, John Wiley & Sons, New York, 1975.
7. L. Kleinrock, *Queueing Systems*. Volume 2; *Computer Applications*, John Wiley & Sons, New York, 1976.
8. Panel: Gigabit Network Applications, *IEEE Infocom'90*, San Francisco, CA, June 3-4, 1990.
9. S. Heatly and D. Stokesberry, "Analysis of Transport Measurements Over a Local Area Network," *IEEE Comm. Mag.* (June 1989).
10. Z. Haas, "A Protocol for High-Speed Communication over Broadbands ISDN," *IEEE Network Magazine*, January 1991.
11. P. R. Prucnal, "All-optical ultra-fast networks," *SPIE Fiber Telecommun. Comput. Networks, 715*, (1986).
12. Z. Haas and D. R. Cheriton, "Blazenet: A Packet-Switched Wide-Area Network with Photonic Data Path," *IEEE Transact. Comm.* (June 1990).

ZYGMUNT HAAS

PROFESSIONAL RESPONSIBILITIES IN A GLOBAL CONTEXT

Imbedded in the title of this entry, "Professional Responsibilities in a Global Context," are a number of complex concepts. The article begins with a discussion of the nature of professionalism and of who, exactly, constitute the professionals. It continues with an exploration of the dialectic of freedom and responsibility. Concentrating on the notion of obligation, it goes on to delineate responsibilities to one's self, to the profession, to one's country, and to the world. Indeed, one distinguishing attribute of the professional is his or her constant interaction with the enabling society or even larger, worldwide context. The article concludes with an understanding of how such professional responsibility might be realized—primarily through professional associations and their codes of ethical conduct.

THE NATURE OF PROFESSIONALISM

Professionalism, according to Smith [1, p. 50], is a word that "covers a multitude of sins. I always cringe when I hear *anyone* describe herself as 'professional,' because what usually follows is an excuse for inaction, an excuse for ethical irresponsibility." Before buying Smith's argument, however, consider the possible meanings for the word. "Professional" implies experience, expertise, learnedness, mastery, proficiency, authority, and specialization. All of these terms, considered synonymous with professionalism, bespeak a power that may—if unchecked—result in the abuses to which Smith alluded.

Perhaps most professionals can be characterized from both perspectives, as Merrill [2, p. 20] did of professional journalists: "They are both egoists and altruists." In his critical thesis on ethics and professionalism, Kultgen [3] went further. He explained that the professionalization of occupations can both harm and benefit society. In his view, the professions serve segments of society differentially—often disguising their self-interest behind a false ideology of expert service. He questioned whether professionalism's rules and ideals more typically mask self-interest or advance the physical and moral welfare of society.

Even a traditional definition of "professional" makes clear the fact that professionals have the *capacity* for great good and for genuinely moral purposes. Synthesizing the definitions found in most dictionaries results in a profile of the professional as one who engages in a particular pursuit, study, or science—typically one of the learned professions or any occupation requiring a high level of training and proficiency. Professionals are imbued with both authority and the practical experience in their area of knowledge to operate with an enviable degree of autonomy.

The literature of professionalism, of course, eclipses such dictionary meanings. Since the late 1930s, sociologists [e.g., Talcott Parsons, 4] have been studying the attributes of a professional in an effort to understand the increasingly important role professionalism plays. They began to examine the life patterns of individuals whose behavior, goals, and even personality were determined in large part by their professional functions.

By the late 1940s, the U.S. Census Bureau had developed a professional category in its occupational classification system. It went well beyond the three learned professions traditionally called "professions": law, medicine, and the clergy. The term "profession" has enjoyed its contemporary meaning at least since the seventeenth century and, in relation to medicine, at least since the time of the Hippocratic Oath—presumably in the fifth century BC. During the late nineteenth century, however, the three fields of medicine, law, and religion dominated public discussion of professionalism.

Since then, the boundary between professionals and nonprofessionals has become flexible and less distinct. Focusing too narrowly on the distinctiveness of the traditional professions would have sustained an elitism inconsistent with the increasingly egalitarian ethos of twentieth-century America. Thus the ranks of the professional, according to the U.S. Census Bureau, now include accountants, architects, artists, computer scientists, dentists, engineers, journalists, librarians, natural and social scientists, social workers, and teachers.

In the modern era, when professionalism moved beyond its historical origin in religion to encompass the humanities and the sciences, it also moved beyond morality and ethics to include the application of knowledge as well. For the first time, technological competence in a distinct intellectual discipline became a hallmark of a professional.

Of course, core criteria for the separation of a profession from an occupation vary widely. They depend in large part on who is doing the differentiating. Further, the voluminous literature on the characteristics of a professional suggests a continuum of professionalism rather than a dichotomy between profession and occupation [5]. Like Pavalko, Elliott [6] constructed such continua, with poles representing technical skill versus theoretical knowledge, routine versus nonroutine situations, programmed versus unprogrammed decisions, authority by institution versus authority derived from knowledge, limited versus extensive education, and so forth. Positions on the continua depend on the degree to which the occupation exhibits each characteristic [7].

Greenwood and his students [8] distilled much of the first three decades of the literature on professionalism. They concluded that the following five attributes characterize certain occupations as professions: systematic theory, authority, community sanction, ethical codes, and a culture. Greenwood cautioned, however, that these attributes are not exclusive to professions because nonprofessional occupations also possess them—albeit to a lesser degree.

Jackson [9] summed up the notion of professionalism in a single theme: "To qualify as a profession, rather than a vocation, a field of endeavor must be endemic to the human condition." He went on to explain that lawyers are professionals because of the need for government by law rather than by mob, that doctors are professionals because everyone needs mental and physical health, and that teachers are professionals because education is essential.

Systematic Theory

The first of Greenwood's [8] distinguishing characteristics of professionalism, *theory*, speaks to the element of superior technical skill—typically developed through lengthy training that is intellectual as well as practical. This type of theoretical knowledge often is called "esoteric," because it is not possessed by the population at large.

Authority

Professional *authority* is a related attribute. A professional, Greenwood [8] explained, has clients for whom he or she dictates what is best. Unlike customers, clients do not diagnose their own needs or criticize the quality of the service they receive. Why? Because they have surrendered these prerogatives to the professional authority whose judgment they value. Greenwood pointed out the risk inherent in any such superordinate-subordinate relationship: The subordinate member, such as the client, exchanges independence for a sense of security. In other words, the differential in level of power may lead to dependency.

The concept of "autonomy" is related to "authority." Professionals have the authority to employ their skills or esoteric knowledge autonomously. They are regulated primarily by their own norms and by their professional peers.

Traditionally, professionals such as doctors and lawyers worked independently; more recently, professionals such as computer scientists and engineers tend to work in organizations. In these contemporary cases, their autonomy may benefit society. Professionals working in organizations interact with other professionals outside the organization; that contact, in turn, introduces innovation into the organization and thus forces the organization to become more responsive to society.

Community Sanction

The third category of professional attributes, *community sanction*, represents one external way of limiting professional authority or the potential abuse of autonomy. Professionals receive their power and privileges either formally or informally from the communities in which they operate. Merrill [2] predicted that as society becomes more complex—as populations increase in size and in cultural diversity—the obligations of the professional will increase. Thus, recent sociological investigations have broadened to look at how professional associations operate in society and, most recently, in the global context.

Code of Ethics

Almost forty years ago, sociologists were describing a growing concern with Greenwood's [8] fourth attribute of professionalism: *a regulative code of ethics*. The reason? What Camenisch [10] considered the complexity of issues facing professionals and the variety and indeterminacy of "the professions." Without formal articulation of codes of ethics, Camenisch contended, professional ethics would be determined by whimsy or "the *ad hoc* proposals of individual authors" as a result of professionals' differing (and often unpredictable) modes of reasoning, relevant criteria, and grounds of obligation. (Durkheim [11], paraphrasing Aristotle, simply said that to some degree, morals vary according to the agents who practice them.) Thus Durkheim argued for a clearly focused and sustained effort to lay an ethical foundation for the professions irrespective of their particularity.

As early as 1915, Flexner [12] worried about the hazards inherent in the monopoly and authority most professionals enjoy. More specifically, Merton [13] echoed this concern by listing the abuses he recognized: charging unreasonably high prices for services, restricting entrance into the profession, diluting the caliber of performance without the clients' awareness, and frustrating efforts for change within the field.

Subscribing to a code of ethics may help overcome these hazards. Indeed, a moral dimension is inherent in professionalism—"the general expectation that professionals will be of good moral character" [14]. This ethical imperative encompasses the broad areas of fairness, justice, democratic values, and individual rights. Professionals who espouse this ethical philosophy reflect it in their behavior.

Professional Culture

Greenwood's [8] final attribute of a profession is its *culture*. He considered professional culture the single characteristic that most effectively differentiates professions from other occupations. In a consistent argument, Camenisch [10] actually defined professions as moral communities or subcommunities whose members bear a significant portion of any society's cultural traditions. Subcommunities, he said, also can be conceived of as groups of experts, fellowships of colleagues, and coalitions of similarly employed agents. (Others, he acknowledged, may see the professions as legally established monopolies whose lobbies represent substantial political power.)

Where Camenisch talked of subcommunities, Greenwood [8] described *subcultures* that each profession develops as its idiosyncratic variant of the professional culture. That culture consists of values, norms, and symbols. Together these three function as a basis of identification for the professional; the profession becomes a major reference group for its members, which helps control their behavior.

A professional group's social *values* represent its fundamental beliefs in the essential worth of the service it provides to the community. What Greenwood [8] called the "twin concepts" of professional authority and the monopoly most professions enjoy also represent group values. *Norms* guide action by presenting an appropriate range of behaviors for seeking and gaining admittance into the profession and for progressing within it. Norms suggest proper ways for soliciting clients and for dismissing them, for grooming proteges, for challenging outmoded theories or introducing new techniques, and so forth. *Symbols* include such meaning-laden items as insignias, emblems, history, folklore, distinctive dress, and stereotypes.

Other Attributes of the Professions

Other attributes not made explicit in Greenwood's [8] scheme include selectivity and exclusivity, minimum entrance requirements, an elite directorate that can expel irresponsible members, and a system of certification or licensing [15]. Camenisch [10] added centrality of the profession's activities to society's well-being in areas such as justice, health and long life, knowledge, and salvation. Ritzer [7] contributed the notions of recognition by the public and by the law that the occupation is a profession and community rather than self-interest, which is related to an emphasis on symbolic rather than monetary rewards. Gross [16] emphasized the professional's unstandardized product and Pavalko [5], a sense of commitment—long-term, if not life-long—that Camenisch [14] considered "atypical."

Camenisch [10, p. 4] also contended that the designation "professional" should not be extended to an occupational group "simply on the grounds that its members are educated, are competent at what they do, are generally trustworthy in their dealings with clients/customers, and desire the status of being a 'professional'." Instead, he argued for the imposition of the criteria described above—adding that any profession can be expected to exhibit a reasonable but not necessarily exhaustive number of these traits to qualify as such.

Finally, Caplow [17] envisioned professionalism as a lengthy sequence that begins with (a) the establishment of a professional association, continues with (b) a name change in an attempt to enhance "the image" to imply greater competence and (c) development of a code of ethics, and ends with (d) agitation for and attainment of legal restrictions on who may perform the services and establish the training facilities. Fenton [18] favored dissolving any disagreements over what constitutes a profession and focusing instead on how to educate for professionalism because she, like Caplow, believed that establishing a profession takes a long, long time.

PROFESSIONAL FREEDOM AND RESPONSIBILITY

"Professional freedom and responsibility" has become a phrase said almost as a single word. It bespeaks the Hegelian dialectic, or principle of contradiction inherent in thesis and antithesis. In other words, a thing is not only itself but something else as well. This dialectic, which represents the culmination of classical German philosophy, recognizes the need to reconcile conflicting concepts.

Within particular professions, freedom and responsibility take on special manifestations. For journalism educators, for example, professional freedom and responsibility encompasses free expression, ethics, media criticism and accountability, minority affairs, and public service.

Thus we see that with freedom, or the autonomy and authority professionals experience, comes a concomitant need for responsibility. According to Merrill [2], social responsibility or social ethics embodies the synthesis of that freedom and responsibility. As George Bernard Shaw put it so succinctly: "Liberty means responsibility. That is why most men dread it."

Freedom

Freedom, as a philosophical concept, is a correlate of responsibility. It is also culturally derived. For example, according to the Media Institute [19], the western concept of "freedom of information" does not exist in the lexicon of the New World Information Order (NWIO). Instead, freedom of information can be seen as one stage in a developing debate over global communication. As the MacBride Commission Report for UNESCO [20] made abundantly clear, the problems of professional communicators such as freedom of the press and the right to information are becoming more political, more economic, and more social in character as we enter the global era.

Traditionally, of course, freedom of expression has played a central role in the life of professionals because they are concerned with protecting and, indeed, encouraging the open circulation of ideas. As a group, professionals value the interaction that should lead to innovation and mutual understanding with other professionals in their field—whether those colleagues are associated with institutions of higher learning, governmental agencies, or community organizations around the world. With an appreciation for the diversity inherent in such global interaction, professionals should take care not to seek to impose any western view of freedom and responsibility.

Responsibility

To the extent that professionals continue to cultivate their own autonomy from the community's formal regulation, they must accept the responsibility for self-policing and for service to that community. A second, related source of obligation is the power of many professionals in contemporary society. Ryan and Martinson [21] have gone so far as to call professionals part of the ruling elite in American society.

Individuals accrue this power by virtue of their professional monopoly over crucial services, their membership in professional associations, and their above-average incomes. Taken together, these factors may explain the perception of a professional conspiracy against the public that has led to a serious erosion of the prestige and respect professionals once enjoyed [14]. These factors also provide a compelling rationale for the notion that any dominant people of power have the responsibility to be generous, compassionate, and stable in their dealings with others.

Society's investment in the professional is another important explanation for such obligation. As Camenisch [*14*, p. 55] put it, "The acceptance of a gift places one under an obligation to the donor and/or others designated by the donor." The "gift," in the case of professionals, includes the private and public monies spent on professional education (funding that goes well beyond any individual's tuition and scholarships or fellowships), financial support for research that helps create the body of esoteric knowledge, and funding for the institutions and structures in which professional activity occurs. Society provides this fiscal foundation for the benefit of its citizens who need professional services and not merely for the benefit of the professionals themselves.

The professional's promissory commitment in return must go well beyond the traditional and obvious moral obligations that include respecting clients' confidentiality, delivering adequate services, and refraining from taking sexual advantage of clients. This "larger moral reality" can be understood best by considering its constituent parts: responsibility to self, to the profession, to society, and—increasingly—to the world.

The nature of such responsibilities, in turn, can be determined by law or government, by the professional association, and by individual professionals. Alternatively, responsibility may be called "accountability," which suggests external, legal overtones, and "commitment," which suggests internal, intrinsic rewards. In other words, there are both legal and moral responsibilities. An example of the former, enacted in the global context, would be the MacBride Commission's [*20*] Recommendation #58. It suggested that governments pass laws requiring foreign news agencies to report what Third World governments tell them to report; penalties for failing to do so would include fines, jail, or expulsion. The remainder of this part of the entry, however, will deal primarily with the moral impetus for professional responsibility.

Individual Responsibility

Individual professionals typically accept the responsibility of dispensing the benefits of their special knowledge and expertise to those who need them. This notion is typified in the opening statement of the 1955 Declaration of Geneva of the World Health Organization: "I solemnly pledge myself to consecrate my life to the service of humanity." This ethical imperative seems to cut across all professions and thus characterizes individuals who bear the label "professional." Its manifestation in the behavior of individuals, of course, is problematic.

The actual conduct of a professional may or may not fit the relevant professional norm. Camenisch [*10*] contended, however, that in a pluralistic society such as the United States, a one-to-one correlation between normative statements about professions and about individual professionals would not be expected. His rationale lies in the motives behind the practitioner's professional decisions and behavior and the fact that professions espouse normative standards higher than most professionals currently attain.

Professionals who work solo and those who are employed in organizations have shown a somewhat different ethical stance in relation to responsibility to their clients. Wilensky [22] found that professionals in independent practice scored higher in orientation to clients than did salaried professionals, who seem less susceptible to such pressure. May [23] and Kornhauser [24] both found that professionals may in fact become overly responsive to their client's wishes and, in doing so, violate their own professional standards, compromise their professional judgement, or ignore the larger public interest.

We are left, then, with the understanding that in actuality a professional is what Parsons [*25*, p. 54] called "a type of independent artisan with particularly high social status."

This, in turn, helps explain the professional's ideology of service and predilection for association or guild-like—rather than bureaucratic—social structure among professionals.

Responsibility to the Profession

Every social group, including professional associations, is made up of individual members. Theories of economic decision making have shown that interests of the individual may not correspond with interests of the collective. At times, there may be more antagonism than agreement. However, the profession—typically through its association—attempts to reconcile the interests of its members. One major question involves the extent to which individuals members can be held accountable for policies of the professional group.

A second issue of responsibility to the profession concerns the particularistic nature of each profession. The professional obligations of a development program manager may differ dramatically from those of a computer scientist. In fact, there may be as many versions of professional responsibility as there are professions. In addition to distinctions among responsibilities of different professions, there may be opposing responsibilities. As Durkheim [11] pointed out in his treatise on "plurality of morals," doctors may be obligated to conceal the truth they know whereas other professionals—such as journalists—may experience a contrary duty.

Of major importance, however, is the understanding that since all professions enjoy a degree of autonomy, each must attempt to regulate its members' activities. In essence, this represents not only a plurality but a decentralization of ethics—one made increasingly complex in the global setting. This decentralized self-regulation makes sense in that the functions of a professional, which are not performed by the public at large, remain outside the common understanding. Thus the freedom of autonomy of the professional is relative; it is reduced somewhat by the professional association or, at least, by professional norms.

Within professional associations, some smaller body such as a committee typically oversees issues of professional responsibility. For example, this charge falls to the Committee on Professional Freedom and Responsibility within the Association for the Advancement of Policy, Research and Development in the Third World. The AAPRDTW's *Policies and Procedures* define the charge of the committee as follows:

> ... shall provide the overall policy guidelines on matters of professional ethics, scholarly responsibility and guidelines for involvement of Association members in events, actions or situations that may appear contrary to an acceptable practice or code of conduct. This committee shall also advise the Board on the question of the Association's relationship with other professional/scholarly bodies, institutions of higher learning, governmental and non-governmental organizations as well as community institutions.

Responsibility to Society

Earlier on, this entry established that to be a professional is to commit one's esoteric knowledge and skills to society's well being. Cheek [26, p. 11] went so far as to define a professional as "one who helps other members of society by employing his skills in their behalf, irrespective of his own interest."

Professionals take on their distinct role with an awareness of its technical and moral obligations. They enter into a reciprocal social contract or tacit agreement with society, an agreement typically based on trust. That is, society grants them financial support early on, followed by autonomy and monopoly, in exchange for professionals' extraordinary commitment and expertise. Camenisch [14] argued that even when this bargain is implicit, it is binding.

Global Responsibility

Despite encouraging progress in the wake of the international upheaval that characterizes the last decade of this century, oppression persists. The research and teaching of many professionals, in particular, should help their own students, their clients, their countries, and their world break through walls of repression, of silence, of ignorance, of poverty, and of isolation. Professional associations can and do take stands opposing the continued existence of anti-intellectualism, racism, extreme political ideologies, isolationism, sexism, chauvinism, and cultural elitism.

Associations often consider themselves responsible for opposing such oppression, in part by declining to engage in activities such as holding conferences with the parties responsible. The academic boycott of South Africa is but one recent example. At the same time, professional associations may encourage their members actively to support activities that enhance global responsibility, understanding, and respect. Through these means, they seek meaningful liaison with their counterpart scholarly, professional, governmental, and community organizations worldwide.

At the least, professional associations in developed countries tend to make their stances on relevant international concerns known. Their members may work toward change in developing countries through information sharing; setting uniform global standards; educational or training programs; boycotting or sanctioning what they consider irresponsible practices; sharing their professional expertise in program design, development, implementation, and evaluation; or encouraging legislative or other governmental action.

Questions about the extent to which professionals and their associations should avoid or seek out this kind of international involvement are intriguing to many western professionals. On the one hand, they do not avoid recognizing colleagues in countries such as Angola that are not recognized by the U.S. government. On the other hand, they cite the myriad complications inherent in a global commitment to professional responsibility.

Despite these challenges, globalizing the ethics of at least some professions has become a new priority. According to Merrill [2], for example, many journalists have perceived the need for the world's reporters and editors to professionalize and, concomitantly, to develop a universal concept of ethics. They consider the formulation of an international code both possible and appropriate, in spite of the difficulty of finding crosscultural commonalities.

International scholars of ethics, such as Merrill, view ethics not as culture bound, but, universal; they suggest the delineation of broad ethical principles rather than narrowly defined codes. Their ethical imperative includes such concerns as fairness, individual rights, and democratic values. One such scholar, Mowlana [27], posited four more specific principles that might be embraced by professionals in journalism world-wide: the prevention of war and promotion of peace; respect for culture, tradition, and values; promotion of human rights and dignity; and preservation of the home, human association, family, and community.

Mowlana did not suggest how journalists could institutionalize these principles. As a result, his work and that of others may be considered naive in the sense that it is idealistic and may underestimate the problematic nature of ethnocentrism, cultural relativism, and both political and cultural diversity. Numerous scholars [28, 29] have reminded us of the complication inherent in differences both within and between cultures.

A recent conference of the International Women's Media Foundation illustrates this complexity. There, the chasm between journalists from America and from other countries became clear; many reporters abroad work within oppressive regimes while still others are grappling with the problems intrinsic to new democracies. Participants came to understand that while U.S. journalists strive for objectivity, many of their international counterparts are forced into advocacy roles [30]. In fact, the New World Information Order has rejected the notion of a "free flow" of information because it is incompatible with the strict governmental control of media that characterizes many Second and Third World countries.

To illustrate further, Merrill [2, p. 232] quoted the opinion of Otto Schulmeister, publisher of *Die Presse* (one of the most established daily newspapers in Europe), that a journalist's morality stems from his or her background and value system; as a result, it is closely tied to one's national political and social context. Thus Merrill argued not for ethical "rules" but for basic attitudes or standards when nationalism merges with internationalism.

Another kind of integration becomes critical to any discussion of professional responsibility in a global context. As Amba-Rao [31] explained, technical and managerial professionals do not act in isolation. Despite the autonomy that characterizes any professionals and the locus of ethical responsibility that that engenders, they still must interact with the executive or top management of their multinational operation. Further, their organization or institution exists in a dynamic balance with a number of additional entities: the host country, the home country, any subsidiaries or parent companies, the industry, key external stakeholders, and the internal or employee public.

Amba-Rao [31] predicted ethical dilemmas that would arise out of the lack of moral consensus resulting from cultural, legal, and socioeconomic diversity. This problem is exacerbated when the norms of host and home country conflict or—according to Simpson [29]—when Third World countries fail to adequately regulate or enforce desired corporate action.

Professionals working in international enterprise often encounter such conflicts between their own or their professional norms and norms of the host country. As examples, Amba-Rao [31] alluded to levels of environmental pollution and consumer safety.

Donaldson [32] cited another typical example: bribery of elected officials. He explained that the practice of bribery undermines the public trust and violates one of his ten fundamental international rights, political participation. He contended that the right of political participation and other rights, such as subsistence, routinely are violated by professionals operating internationally. Acknowledging that cultural differences affect some standards, particularly political participation, he nonetheless considered this set of rights a universal and objective minimum. Thus Donaldson argued that regardless of the seemingly lower ethical standards of some host countries, professionals from First World countries are responsible for honoring certain minimal standards.

Consider more fully the oppositional concepts of ethical relativism and ethnocentrism. Brandt [33] held that indigenous norms should be respected even though they may contradict (and be "lower than") the norms of the home country. Amba-Rao [31, p. 8], however, questioned whether the behavior of professionals who follow the "higher" home-country norms implies "an ethnocentric superiority and disrespect for cultural diversity." Such extremes of ethnocentric behavior or cultural relativity are equally to be avoided, according to Donaldson [32]. From her exhaustive review of the literature of multinational corporate social responsibility, Amba-Rao [31] concluded that professionals in multinational organizations have the imperative of recognizing and balancing the mutual influences of host and home country and of helping develop convergence and consensus in moral judgments.

The next section of this entry discusses the role that codes of ethics can and do play in helping identify and enforce professional responsibilities throughout the world. First, though, one must identify what the problematic issues might include. Globalization supposes consideration of commerce, ecology, human rights, justice and fairness, health, democratic values, and communication.

More specifically, the literature frequently cites curbing hazardous technology, disposing of toxic waste, halting the export of dangerous products, sharing information and knowledge, supporting education and training, halting land degradation, increasing productivity, protecting the ozone layer, conserving forests and water, infusing stagnant economies, and enhancing global security. Certain professions, of course, logically would assume more responsibility in related areas. Engineers might be held accountable for ecological concerns while university professors might be responsible for higher education.

CODES OF PROFESSIONAL RESPONSIBILITY

The codes of rights and responsibility that characterize professions translate ethical philosophy into guidelines for behavior. As Kultgen [3] explained, professionals who wish to provide services with their enviable degree of autonomy must be held responsible for improving the institutions or societies that administer those services.

Perhaps the most effective codes are those that suggest what not to do to be responsible as well as propose what to do. They should reflect society's legitimate expectations of the profession. They also should reflect practice, rather than pretense.

At this point in the entry, then, we return to where we began: Are guidelines for professional responsibility developed to advance the welfare of the world served by professionals or are these rules and ideals merely camouflage for the self-serving professional with an entrepreneurial bent?

In his critical analysis of professional codes, Kultgen [2] also questioned what he considered a "harmful unconscious presupposition" of professionalism. He contended that professions are male domains because historically they have been populated by men; as a result, the language used in professional codes (equating the masculine with the generic) is, in his words, "freighted with disutility."

Other scholars have agreed that codes may not represent a panacea for encouraging and enforcing professional responsibility. Camenisch [14] cautioned that if codes are merely "public proclamations," they serve more as meaningless utterances than as mechanisms for holding professionals accountable to the commitments they ostensibly espouse as professionals. When this is the case, he suggested replacing self-government with licensing or making funding of professional training contingent on subsequent public service.

Laws, however, seem inadequate to the task of mandating professional, moral responsibility. They represent minimal and inflexible, rather than dynamic, standards. At best, "ethics" laws specify worst-case scenarios to be avoided rather than behaviors to be pursued.

Because professionals value the autonomy that characterizes them as professionals, they are willing to endorse codes of responsibility—a form of self-policing—more readily than regulation. Mtewa [34] pointed out, however, that the federal government's growing reliance on professionals who serve as consultants has accentuated the trend toward regulation there.

More often, professionals embrace a set of agreements that functions more as a compact than a contract with society. Their codes grow out of a consensus of senior members of professional associations. These leaders of the profession establish ethical standards from a loosely structured set of ad hoc rules, help develop a sense of responsibility among other members, arbitrate ethical disputes, and sanction members who violate the canon. As the product of a committee, the typical code reflects compromise and deliberately vague, rather than precise, wording. It may be politically or culturally biased as well.

Still, the development of a written statement of freedom and responsibility—whether detailed or perfunctory—represents the professional's search for an appropriate mechanism to foster accountability. Codes also engender a sense of community by promoting group identity. They help maintain the status of the professional as well. However, a code is effective only when it represents a central—rather than peripheral—concern of the professional complex.

No general agreement has been reached among professionals about the nature of such guideposts. However, as professionals grow in their moral sophistication one would expect a growing interest in codifying responsibility. Professions that are well developed and stable, operating in stable, developed countries, also tend to have codes of professional ethics that are stable and well developed. For example, the code of the American Medical Association can be traced to Hippocrates and the fifth century B.C.; a more contemporary code of ethics for physicians, developed by Thomas Percival in 1803, provided the basis for today's AMA code [35].

Such codes reflect the morality and the practices of the larger society. They may set forth the ethical priorities of the association as well as its role and mission. The Model Rules of Professional Conduct of the American Bar Association, for example, explicate the dual roles of adviser and advocate. More significantly, this code stands above most other, comparable codes in enunciating its profession's obligations to society.

Few codes, however, go beyond the context of the community or the nation. Associations of professionals who consider themselves "international" are the exception. For example, the statement on policies and procedures of the Association for the Advancement of Policy, Research and Development in the Third World describes its mission as concerned with the advancement of scholarly excellence, professional leadership, community service, and *international understanding*. The North American Public Relations Council, for a second example, represents thirteen organizations working together toward a uniform ethical code.

Mowlana [27] reminded us that developing any reasonable international ethic requires more than formulating and disseminating printed codes. Not only would any such code provoke controversy across cultural boundaries because of ethnocentrism but, typically, even among those of the same culture who belong to a single professional association.

The more typical situation of moral obligation extending only to the professional's indigenous society represents a central concern of this entry. Kultgen [3] is one of the few scholars of professional codes who has wrestled with appropriate boundaries of the moral community. He pointed out that few codes evince awareness of a community larger than one's own country.

One final, significant limitation of most existing codes is that they tend to reflect the sole point of view of the profession, rather than being multidisciplinary in character. An international perspective, however, seems to require the vital synergy of different professions from different cultures working together toward mutual understanding, development, and justice.

REFERENCES

1. B. Smith, "Racism and Women's Studies," in *But Some of Us Are Brave*, G. T. Hull, P. B. Scott, and B. Smith (eds.), The Feminist Press, New York, 1979, pp. 48-55.
2. J. C. Merrill, *Dialectic in Journalism: Toward a Responsible Use of Press Freedom*, Louisiana State University Press, Baton Rouge, 1989.
3. J. Kultgen, *Ethics and Professionalism*, University of Pennsylvania Press, Philadelphia, 1988.
4. T. Parsons, "The Professions and Social Structure," in *Essays in Sociological Theory Pure and Applied*, T. Parsons (ed.), The Free Press, New York, 1949, pp. 185-199.
5. R. M. Pavalko, *Sociology of Occupations and Professions*, Peacock Publishers, Itasca, IL, 1971.
6. P. Elliott, *The Sociology of the Professions*, Herder & Herder, New York, 1972.
7. G. Ritzer, *Man and His Work: Conflict and Change*, Appleton-Century-Crofts, New York, 1972.
8. E. Greenwood, "Attributes of a Profession," in *Moral Responsibility and the Professions*, B. Baumrim and B. Freedman (eds.), Haven Publications, New York, 1983, pp. 20-61.
9. P. Jackson, *Public Rel. J.*, 27-29, October 1988.
10. P. F. Camenisch, *Grounding Professional Ethics in a Pluralistic Society*, Haven Publications, New York, 1953.
11. E. Durkheim, "Professional Ethics and Civil Morals," in *Moral Responsibility and the Professions*, B. Baumrim and B. Freedman (eds.), Haven Publications, New York, 1983, pp. 33-41.
12. A. Flexner, "Is Social Work a Profession?," in *Proc. Natl. Conf. Charities and Corrections*, Chicago, pp. 576-590.
13. R. K. Merton, "Bureaucratic Structure and Personality," in *Studies in Leadership*, A. W. Gouldner (ed.), Harper, New York, 1950.
14. P. R. Camenisch, "On Being a Professional, Morally Speaking," in *Moral Responsibility and the Professions*, B. Baumrim and B. Freedman (eds.), Haven Publications, New York, 1983, pp. 42-61.
15. J. C. Merrill, "Three Theories of Press Responsibility and the Advantages of Pluralistic Individualism," in *Responsible Journalism*, D. Elliott (ed.), Sage Publications, New York, 1986, pp. 47-59.
16. E. Gross, *Work and Society*, Crowell, New York, 1958.
17. T. Caplow, *The Sociology of Work*, McGraw-Hill, New York, 1964.
18. M. Fenton, "More on Professionalism," *Public Rel. J.*, 28, 14-16 (August 1977).
19. T. G. Brown, *International Communications Glossary*, The Media Institute, Washington, DC, 1984.
20. *Many Voices, One World: Communication and Society, Today and Tomorrow: Towards a New, More Just and More Efficient World Information and Communication Order*. Report of the International Commission for the Study of Communication Problems, UNESCO, Kogan Page, New York, 1980.
21. M. Ryan and D. L. Martinson, "Social Science Research, Professionalism and Public Relations Practitioners," *Journalism Q.*, 67, 377-390 (1991).
22. H. L. Wilensky, "The Professionalization of Everyone?," *Am. J. Sociol.*, 70, 142-146 (1964).
23. J. V. May, *Professionals and Clients: A Constitutional Struggle*, Sage Publications, Beverly Hill, 1976.

24. W. Kornhauser, *Scientists in Industry: Conflict and Accommodation*, University of California Press, Berkeley, 1962.

25. T. Parsons, "Professions," in *International Encyclopedia of the Social Sciences*, Vol. II, L. Sills (ed.), Macmillan, New York, 1968, pp. 536–547.

26. N. H. Cheek Jr., in *The Professional in the Organization*, M. Abrahamson (ed.), Rand McNally, Chicago, 1967.

27. H. Mowlana, *Global Information and World Communication*, Longmen, New York, 1986.

28. D. J. Fritzsche and H. Becker, "Linking Management Behavior to Ethical Philosophy: An Empirical Investigation," *Acad. Mgmt. J.*, 27(1), 166–175 (1984).

29. J. R. Simpson, "Ethics and Multinational Corporation vis-a-vis Developing Nations," *J. Bus. Ethics*, 1, 227–237 (1982).

30. J. Flander, "Women Journalists' Global Village," *Washington Journalism Rev.*, 37–39, (January/February 1991).

31. S. C. Amba-Rao, "Multinational Corporate Social Responsibility, Ethics and the Third World Governments: Agenda for the 1990s," paper presented to the Association for the Advancement of Policy, Research and Development in the Third World, Mexico City, November 1990.

32. T. Donaldson, "Multinational Decision-Making: Reconciling International Norms," *J. Bus. Ethics*, 4, 357–366 (1985).

33. R. Brandt, *Ethical Theory*, Prentice-Hall, Englewood Cliffs, NJ, 1959.

34. M. Mtewa, *Consultant Connexion: Evaluation of the Federal Consulting Service*, University Press of America, Lanham, MD, 1980.

35. R. Gorlin (ed.), *Codes of Professional Responsibility*, Bureau of National Affairs, Washington, DC, 1986.

LARISSA A. GRUNIG
WILLIAM M. JOHNSON

PROJECT PLANNING AND CONTROL

Project planning and control are matched pairs in the management of a project. Planning involves thinking about the project's future and making explicit the project's objectives, goals, and those strategies necessary to bring the project through its life cycle to a successful conclusion on schedule, budget, and providing the required technical performance objective or "bundle of services" for the customer. Project control is the process of monitoring, evaluating, and comparing planned project results with actual results to determine the status of the project cost, schedule, and technical performance objectives. Control is also the constraining of resources through corrective action to conform to a project plan. First, a look at the conceptual framework of organizational planning and how project planning fits into this framework.

THE ORGANIZATIONAL CONTEXT

To plan a project is to make a rational determination of how to determine the resources required to support the project during its life cycle. Since projects are building blocks in the design and execution of organizational strategies, overall organizational planning is a prerequisite to effective project planning. Organizational planning consists of determining the probabilities and possibilities likely to impact an organization's future. A conceptual model of organizational planning includes:

A determination of the organization's *mission*—or "business" that the organization pursues in providing a "bundle of services" to its customers. The organizational mission is the most general and important strategic choice that must be made by the organization's leaders. An organizational mission is supported by *objectives*.

An organization's objectives are the ongoing purposes that must be achieved for maintaining competitiveness. Objectives serve as overall organizational performance criteria to be achieved and measured in the utilization of organizational resources. A computer company defines one of its objectives as "leap-frog the state-of-the-art in software technology every five years." Another company defines an objective as "providing technological leadership in our products and services." Organizational objectives are supported by *goals*.

Goals are milestones in the design and execution of organizational strategies, such as a performance goal of 15 percent on investment by a specific date. Goals are the basic components for measuring progress in attaining organizational objectives. One company stated a goal as: "We intend by the end of 1987 to complete the construction of a new flexible manufacturing systems facility to support organizational productivity program."

An organizational *strategy* is the design of the means through the use of resources, to accomplish the organizational goals, objectives, and mission. Strategies include action plans, policies, procedures, resource allocation schemes, programs, and *projects*. Since projects are building blocks in the design and execution of organizational strategies, they play an important role in preparing the organization for its future. To conceptualize a project and bring it through to a successful conclusion means that something that did not previously exist has been created which can be used to support a customer's future operational needs. Senior managers of an enterprise need to consider the "strategic fit" that a project is likely to have in supporting the strategies of an intended user or customer. Organizational planning provides the context in which project planning can be carried out.

THE ELEMENTS OF PROJECT PLANNING

In supporting organizational strategies project planning is carried out through the development of key supporting elements. These elements include:

A delineation of the project objectives—the desired future position of the project in terms of cost, schedule, and technical performance capabilities.

A determination of the project goals, or milestones which when successfully completed will lead to the adequate completion of the project. Project goals are defined in the context of the *work breakdown structure* leading to the "work packages" whose completion is essential to completing the project.

Project strategies are the plan of action required for the project along with accompanying policies, procedures, and schemas which provide general direction on how resources will be used to accomplish the project goals and objectives.

The organizational design of the project team and how that team interfaces with the parent organization and other organizations that provides products and services to support the project effort. Such an organizational design usually includes some variation of the "matrix-driven" organizational structure. The organizational design includes identification, negotiation, and resolution of individual and collective roles to support the project deliberations. The common denominator of this organizational design is reflected in the authority and responsibility patterns existing within the overlay of the project team on the existing *functional* elements of the organization.

The leadership style of the project manager, and how that style is reflected in the knowledge, skills, and attitudes of the project team in its organizational environment.

The information required to develop and support the project during its life cycle in the planning for, organization of, and control of the project resources.

The cultural ambience of the organization in which the project is being designed and executed. This ambience is a reflection of the beliefs, customs, knowledge, practices, and conventional behavior of the social groups in the project and its environment. The cultural ambience will have an influence on the character of the project and the efficiency and effectiveness with which the project is managed.

Finally, the techniques and methodologies used to gain insight into how the project resources should be allocated. These techniques and methodologies include scheduling, costing, modeling, and programming tools. All too often when the subject of project planning comes up only the use of the techniques and concepts such as PERT, CPM, or networking supported by appropriate software is envisioned. These techniques are valuable tools in the project planning process; project planning includes a much wider scope of activity which will be presented here.

Once a preliminary statement of the scope of the project is prepared, then action can be undertaken to do overall planning for the project. One of the most basic considerations in the planning for the project is the *work breakdown structure*.

THE WORK BREAKDOWN STRUCTURE (WBS)

The WBS is the basic cornerstone of the project. A WBS is a product-oriented family tree division of hardware, software, services, and other work elements which organizes, defines, and graphically displays the product or service to be created as well as the work to be accomplished, in order to achieve the specified purpose of the project. The logical subdivisions in a WBS are the specific *work packages*. A work package (WP) is a unit of work required to complete a specific job, such as a piece of hardware, a report, an element of software, which is the responsibility of one operating unit with the organization. The identification of a work package provides for the assignment of the work package to a unit of the organization for which responsibility and accountability can be charged. In the development of the WBS, a scheme is contrived for dividing the project into subelements: major groups are divided into tasks, tasks are subdivided into subtasks, and so on. The organization of the WBS should follow an orderly identification scheme: each WBS element is given a distinct identifier. With an aircraft, for example, the WBS might look like this:

- 1.0 Aircraft
- 1.1 Fuselage
- 1.2 Engines
- 1.3 Wings
- 1.4 Communications equipment
- 1.5 Ground support equipment
- 1.6 And so forth

A graphic representation of the WBS can facilitate its understanding. By using succeeding indented numerical listings, an understanding of the total project and its integral subsystems can be facilitated. For example:

1.0
  1.1
    1.11
      1.1.1.1
        1.1.1.1.1
          And so forth

Use of the WBS

When properly developed, the WBS can serve many key purposes in the planning and control of the project. These purposes provide the means for:

A model of all the products and services involved in the project to include support and other tasks.

A way to show the interrelationships of the work packages to each other, the overall project, and to other activities in the organization.

How to pinpoint authority-responsibility-accountability in the structure of the organizational "matrix" created by the overlay of the project team on the existing organizational functions. Each work package can be assigned to a specific individual on the project team.

A focus for estimating cost, schedules, and risk assessment on the project. Each work package can be assessed by an "expert" drawn from somewhere with the supporting organizational units as to the work packages cost, schedule, and risk considerations. By breaking down the project into the work packages, a unit of work is sufficiently defined so that the required organizational expertise can be brought to bear on the evaluation and planning of the project.

Establishes a basis for controlling the application of resources on the project.

Gives team members a reference point for getting committed to the project. Each member of the team, as well as other participating people, can identify with a specific work package for which they are expected to provide support in the development of that work package.

The WBS provides a common identifier and management thread by which the project can be developed, produced, and put in its operational environment environment. Estimating the project cost is an important task task of project planning.

PROJECT COSTS

The cost estimate of the project work packages should be done by the "experts" who are best qualified to determine the likely actual costs that will be incurred on the project. The development of the project costs are essential in controlling the application of resources on the project. Such costs can be used to produce timely reports on the actual project costs versus the estimated costs. The cost estimates can be used to produce a detailed monthly cost breakdown for each work package of the project. These cost breakdowns can be useful in providing a report which shows weekly actual cost with estimated cost as well as comparing actual manhours with target manhours in manufacturing or construction.

A *cost account* is considered the basic level at which project performance is measured and reported in the organizational cost accounting reports. This account represents a specific work package identified by the WBS, usually tracked by information on a daily or weekly time report which ties in with the organizational cost accounting system.

The cost accounting organization should provide a qualified person to serve as a member of the project team. This individual can provide valuable assistance in estimating costs on the project, and in designing and monitoring a cost tracking system to keep the project team appraised of the cost parameter of the project at all times. Costs are, of course, related to the schedule under which the project is being developed and produced.

PROJECT SCHEDULE

The project master schedule, along with supporting schedules, reflected in a graphic or logic network representation, is necessary in order to deal with the time element of managing the project. The schedule establishes the time parameters of the project and provides help to the team in determining the timeframe in which the manpower and equipment loading will be performed on the project. A schedule is an integral part of project control. An effective project schedule has these characteristics:

It is understood by the project team, and the team members have confidence in the credibility of the schedule.

The schedule provides the means for identifying and highlighting critical work packages and tasks on the project.

It is kept current, modified as required to reflect the changing project parameters, and has predictive value in the control of the project.

Sufficient detail is contained in the schedule so that it provides a basis for committing, monitoring, and evaluating the use of project resources.

Based on credible time estimates considering the availability of resources.

Consistent with other projects and organizational commitments that share the common resources in the enterprise.

The process of developing the project budget is clear. However, it should be remembered that the schedule is a reflection of the judgment of the team members who work together to develop the time elements of the project. As in estimating cost on the project work packages, it is advisable to go to the experts to garner their judgment on how long each work package should take to develop. The overall project objectives, goals, and strategies provide a convenient basing point from which to begin the scheduling process. After the WBS has been developed then the work packages and all supporting tasks can be put into their proper sequence and logic in the schedule. A realistic estimate of the work package and associated timing can be done at this point through the intereaction of the project team and supporting functional experts. During the scheduling process the synergy of the work package schedules with the overall project schedule should be determined. Inconsistencies and overlaps of timing elements should be resolved. During the scheduling process the consistency of the evolving schedule with the project costs and the "deliverables" expected to provide a baseline for the technical performance objectives of the project should be done. Finally, when the project schedule looks good it should be reviewed and approved by the senior and functional managers of the organization so that all concerned know of the commitments that are being made about the use and timing of resource utilization in the enterprise.

SCHEDULING TECHNIQUES

There are many types of scheduling techniques that can be used. Any good book on project management will explain the use and advantages, and disadvantages of the different types. Project software for schedule and cost planning are explained and are available in the contemporary project management literature. A word of caution in the use of project planning techniques: use the simplest system that will provide you with what is needed. Don't overkill. Manual techniques do quite well for projects that have less than one hundred work packages. For larger, more complex projects, software techniques are a must, and are sufficiently developed for a wide range of different types and sizes of projects. The best known scheduling techniques include:

Bar charts which consist of a scale divided into units of time (e.g., days, weeks, or months) across the top and a listing of the project work packages or tasks down the lefthand side of the chart. Bars or lines are used to indicate the schedule and status of each work package in relation to the time scale. Bar charts are easy to develop and to understand—they provide a simple picture of the timeframe of the project. A variation of the bar chart is the milestone chart which replaces the bar with lines and triangles to indicate project status. Bar charts are easy to prepare, but show limited information on work package interdependence and time-resource tradeoffs.

Network techniques such as PERT and CPM provide a measurement of time and work package relationships that neither the bar chart nor milestone chart show. The network diagram, which is basic to PERT/CPM provides a dynamic interrelated picture of events and activities and interrelationships relative to the project. The development of PERT/CPM schedules provides planning insight into the project as well as providing a standard for the tracking of time and cost considerations of the project during the implementation of the project resources.

Full desk scheduling techniques can be used when the number of work packages does not exceed 100. Full desk scheduling is done in the following manner. Write the work packages on 3 × 5 cards and use the top of a desk to put these work packages in their logical and time sequence. Have a few members of the project team together to put the cards in their proper place. During the placement of the cards the team members can discuss the logic and rationale for how the cards are arranged. After a general agreement is reached, use a polaroid camera and take a couple of pictures of the desktop. Wait a few days and get the team together again around the desk to verify, or change as needed, the layout of the cards. Take another picture. After this process has been done a few times, a good, simple project schedule can be obtained. Then the schedule can be put into a more permanent document.

A properly constructed schedule is an excellent way to depict the work sequence needed to carry the project through to a successful conclusion. Of course, any project requires the expenditure of funds to acquire and use the project resources.

FINANCIAL PLAN

Financial planning involves the development of action plans for obtaining and managing the funds to support the project through the use of a work authorization process. The project manager should be the one who controls the authorization of funds on the project. Most organizations have a document, typically called a *work authorization form*, which is an orderly and controlled way to delegate authority to expend money for resources for the project. Both in-house work and vendors should be authorized through the use of such a form. A work authorization document usually includes such essentials as: (1) the responsible individual/organization; (2) a work package designation; (3) a schedule; (4) cost estimate and funding citation; and (5) a statement of the scope of work to be done. Usually the work authorization form is a one-sheet format and should be considered a written contract between the project manager and the performing organization/person.

Many people are involved in the creation of a suitable project plan—the members of the project team and stakeholders from other supporting organizational elements such as the function units that provide specialized support to the project.

FUNCTIONAL PLANS

Each functional organization supporting the project should have a detailed operational plan that describes how the functional resources will be used to support the project. For example, the engineering design organization should have a plan on how the product hardware design will be carried out. After-sales service people should have a plan on how customer service is going to be provided to the customer after the project results have been delivered. Since people from different organizational elements are involved, organizational design planning is important.

ORGANIZATIONAL DESIGN PLANNING

Planning for the organizational design of the project team requires that the matter of authority and responsibility be dealt with in a forthright manner as soon as possible in the life cycle of the project. If the organization has used project management in the design and execution of strategies before, there are probably a few organizational design examples that can be used to develop the format for how to organize the project team. The biggest challenge in organizing for the management of the project centers around how the cross-functional teams characteristic of the "matrix" structure will be described and operated. In the matrix configuration, personnel are drawn from the organizational functional units to perform a specific task; the organization is temporary in nature, built around the purpose to be accomplished, rather than on the basis of functional similarity, process, product, or other traditional bases. When such a team is assembled and superimposed on the existing organizational structure, a *matrix organization* is formed. Figure 1 is a model of the matrix organization.

The matrix model is a network of interfaces between a project team and the functional

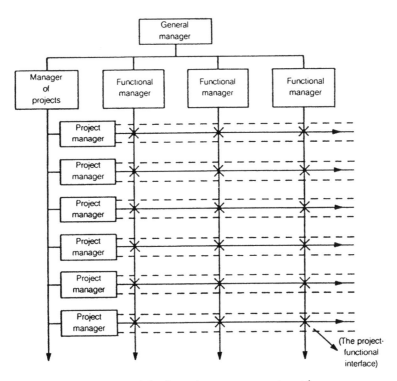

FIGURE 1.   A basic project management matrix.

TABLE 1.   The Project-Functional Interface

Project Manager	Functional Manager
• What is to be done?	• How will the task be done?
• When will the task be done?	• Where will the task be done?
• Why will the task be done?	• Who will do the task?
• How much money is available to do the task?	• How well has the functional input been integrated into the project?
• How well has the total project been done?	

Source: From Ref. *1*, p. 142.

elements of an organization. As additional project teams are laid across an organization's functional structure, more interfaces comes into existence. These interfaces, depicted in the lower right-hand corner of Figure 1, are where the focus of authority and responsibility come into play, largely determining who works with whom in the project affairs. A cursory review of Figure 1 would raise the suspicion that the individuals at the interface between the project and functional organizations would be working for two bosses, a apparent violation of the principle of "unity of command" which states that one should receive orders from only one individual in the chain of command. This apparent violation can be avoided by describing the basic dichotomy found in the matrix design around the syntax of the statements shown in Table 1. This basic dichotomy used to describe the organizational forces in the matrix organization should be used as a policy statement—a guide to the way people should think about their role in the matrix organization. The management of the organizational relationships in the matrix setting is multidimensional. Upward the project manager relates to the boss, horizontally to members of their project team, diagonally with the functional managers and to other representatives of organizations having a vested interest in the project to include customers, vendors, government agencies, local communities, and other stakeholders.

The literature in project management has given considerable attention to describing the matrix model of organization. All too many projects have been inefficiently and ineffectively managed because of a failure to understand and properly apply the matrix model of organization. In others, the nuances of the perceived violation of unity of command and the confusion resulting there from have caused difficulty. Today, thirty years after the first experiments with the matrix configuration began, there are still problems with its application and in its understanding. It is beyond the scope of this chapter to delve into the many reasons for its misunderstanding and misuse. The references at the end of the article can be used to pursue more details into the matrix.

An important part of project planning is to plan for the organizational arrangements that will be used in the management of the project team. A project team is like a football team. The individual and collective roles on the team have to be planned in advance so that all of the players know their own and the authority and responsibility of the other players. Project organization charting can serve a useful purpose here.

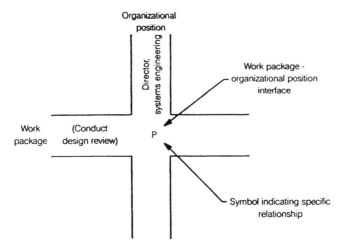

FIGURE 2.   Essential structure of a linear responsibility chart. From Ref. 1, p. 151.

PROJECT ORGANIZATION CHARTING

A *linear responsibility chart (LRC)* is a model of an organization that goes beyond the simple display of formal lines of communication, gradations of organizational level, departmentalization, and organizational territory portrayed in the traditional organizational chart found in most offices. The LRC reveals the work package-organizational position couplings in the organization. The chart shows who participates, and to what degree when a task on the project is to be carried out. It also helps to clarify the authority expectations when two or more organizational positions have overlapping involvement. It clarifies the authority relationships that arise when people share common work. Figure 2 shows the basic structure of an LRC in terms of organizational position and a work package, in this case "Conduct Design Review." The symbol P indicates that the director of systems engineering has the primary responsibility for conducting the system design review. Figure 3 shows an LRC for project-functional management relationships with a matrix organization. A different symbol is used in this sample. The development of such a chart, as part of the organizational planning activities of the project team, combined with the inevitable discussions that usually accompany such a development, can help greatly to facilitate an understanding of how the project team is organized, and how the day-to-day team roles will be carried out.

The project planning process is undertaken using a "work package" approach. A general guide to the major work packages that need to be undertaken in the project planning process are indicated below. If the project team has been able to develop all of these work packages, and put them into a reasonable plan format, then the key source elements required to support the project have been considered:

> Establish the strategic fit of the project.   Ensure that the project is truly a building block in the design and execution of organizational strategies and provides the project owner with an operational capability not currently existing or improves an existing capability. Identify strategic issues likely to impact the project.

Activity	General Manager	Manager of Projects	Project Manager	Functional Manager
Establish department policies & objectives	1	3	3	3
Integration of projects	2	1	3	3
Project direction	4	2	1	3
Project charter	6	2	1	5
Project planning	4	2	1	3
Project—functional conflict resolution	1	3	3	3
Functional planning	2	4	3	1
Functional direction	2	4	5	1
Project budget	4	6	1	3
Project WBS	4	6	1	3
Project control	4	2	1	3
Functional control	2	4	3	1
Overhead management	2	4	3	1
Strategic programs	6	3	4	1

Code

1: Actual responsibility
2: General supervision
3: Must be consulted
4: May be consulted
5: Must be notified
6. Approval authority

FIGURE 3.   Linear responsibility chart of project management relationships.

Develop the project technical performance objective.   Describe the project deliverable(s) that satisfies a customer's needs in terms of capability, capacity, quality, quantity, reliability, and efficiency, etc.

Describe the project through the development of the project WBS. Develop a product-oriented family tree division of hardware, software, services, and other tasks to organize, define, and graphically display the product to be produced, as well as the work to be accomplished to achieve the specified product.

Identify and make provisions for the assignment of the functional work packages. Decide which work packages will be done "in-house," obtain the commitment of the responsible functional work managers, and plan for the allocation of appropriate funds through the organizational work authorization system.

Identify project work packages that will be subcontracted. Develop procurement specifications and other desired contractual terms for the delivery of the goods and services to be provided by outside vendors.

Develop the master and work package schedules. Use the appropriate scheduling techniques to determine the time dimension of the project through a collaborative effort of the project team.

Develop the logic networks and relationships of the project work packages. Determine how the project parts can fit together in a logical relationship.

Identify the strategic issues that the project is likely to face. Develop a strategy for how to deal with these strategic issues.

Estimate the project costs. Determine what it will cost to design, develop, and manufacture (construct) the project, including an assessment of the probability of staying within the estimated costs.

Perform risk analysis. Establish the degree or probability of suffering a setback in the project's schedule, cost, or technical performance parameters.

Develop the project budgets, funding plans, and other resource plans. Establish how the project funds should be utilized and develop the necessary information to monitor and control the use of funds on the project.

Ensure the development of organizational cost accounting system interfaces. Since the project management information system is tied in closely with cost accounting, establish the appropriate interfaces with that function.

Select the organizational design. Provide the basis for getting the project team organized, including delineations of authority, responsibility, and accountability. At minimum, establish the legal authority of the organizational board of directors, senior management, project and functional managers, as well as the work package managers and project professionals. Use the LRC process to determine individual and collective roles on the project team.

Provide for the project management information system. An information system is essential to monitor, evaluate, and control the use of resources on the project. Accordingly, develop such a system as part of the project plan.

Assess the organizational cultural ambience. Project management works best where supportive culture exists. Project documentation, management style, training attitudes, all work together to make up the culture in which project management is found. Determine what project management training would be required. What cultural "fine tuning" is required?

Develop project control concepts, processes, and techniques. How will the project's status be judged through a review process? On what basis? How often? By whom? Ask and answer these questions prospectively during the planning phase.

Develop the project team. Establish a strategy for creating and maintaining effective project team operations.

Integrate contemporaneous state-of-the-art project management philosophies, concepts, and techniques. The art and science of project management continue to evolve. Take care to keep project management approaches up to date.

Design project administration policies, procedures, and methodologies. Administrative consideration often are overlooked. Take care of them during early project planning and do not leave them to chance.

Plan for the nature and timing of the project audits. Determine the type of audit best suited to get an independent evaluation of where the project stands at critical junctures.

Determine who the project stakeholders are and plan for the "management" of these stakeholders. Think through how these stakeholders might change through the life cycle of the project [1].

A SUMMARY OF PROJECT PLANNING

A project plan is like a map. It can guide the people on the general route required to get the project underway and see it through its life cycle. The effective action that is carried out around the project plan is what makes the project successful. Inactivity, or the wrong kind of action can create difficulties for the project, usually reflected in some compromise or failure of the project to accomplish its objective and goals. A project failure (or a project success)

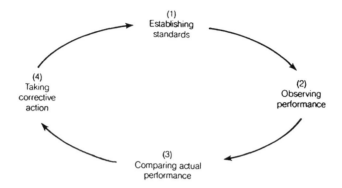

FIGURE 4.   The control system.

impacts the enterprise in which the project is a building block in the design and execution of organizational strategies.

Plans are specifications and simulations of the future of the project. Plans and control systems are interdependent forces in the management of a project.

PROJECT CONTROL

Project control follows project planning. Control is the process of monitoring, evaluating, and comparing planned results with actual results to determine the status of the project cost, schedule, and technical performance parameters. Control also involves the constraining of resources through corrective action to conform to the project plan. The managerial function of control may be visualized as having distinctive steps in a cycle as depicted in Figure 4. Effective control requires suitable information that gives insight into how well the project team is accomplishing the project results. By gleaning suitable information from all of the project activities that are underway explicit comparison can be made of the project plan and the results that have been accomplished to date. Control is done not so much to determine what has happened, although this is important information, but rather to become the basis for predicting what may happen in the future if the project's current thrust and trajectory are continued without any changes in the application of resources to the project. There are several distinct steps involved in the control process as reflected in Figure 4. As a starter it should be remembered that control can be carried out only if appropriate standards have been developed.

PROJECT STANDARDS

A standard is a touchstone—an acknowledged measure of comparison for determining value such as the value of the progress that has been made on a project. The expected value to be gained on a project is the degree to which the organizational resources has been used *efficiently* (doing things right) and *effectively* (doing the right thing). Standards to use in determining the efficiency and effectiveness with which the project is being managed are derivatives of the project plan. Some key standards commonly found in project plans and used in the control process include: scope of work, work breakdown structure (work packages), project specification, cost estimates and budgets, master and ancillary schedules, financial forecasts and spending plans, quality, customer satisfaction, project team satisfaction, senior management satisfaction, reliability, physical quantities of work, vandor plans, productivity, and strategic fit in the strategy of the owner's organization. It often is forgotten that effective control is preceded by effective planning. In the development of the project plans careful foresight should be exercised to see if the plans that are being developed contain the needed standards of performance against which monitoring, evaluation, and control can be carried out. Once the standards of performance have been developed and accepted by the project team, then oversight of the project activities have to be carried out.

PERFORMANCE OVERSIGHT

Oversight of the project's performance is watchful surveillance of what is happening in the use of resources that are impacting the cost, schedule, and technical performance parameters of the project. To maintain oversight means that sufficient information is available on the project to make an intelligent comparison of planned and actual performance on the project. Such information can come from both formal reports and project team meetings, and from letters, memoranda, and other documentation. Informal sources include casual conversation, observations, "management by walking around," and listening to everything that is being said about the project. Sometimes rumors and gossip can give insight into problems that are coming up in the project work.

Project review meetings are a useful place to garner information on how well things are going on the project. Review meetings should be held at the following levels to determine the indicated status of the project:

> The work package level (cost, schedule, and technical performance)
> The functional manager's level (quality and quantity of the technical resources brought to bear on the project)
> The project team level (total synergy of all the project's parameters)
> The general manager's level (adequacy of project and functional support)
> The customer's level (strategic fit)

Review at all of these levels is important. All of the effort underway on the project should come under focus at the project team level so that the cost, schedule, and technical performance considerations can be evaluated.

The basic purpose of carrying out a review of the project is to determine how well the project is doing, and if there are deviations from the performance standards, what caused these deviations.

COMPARING PLANNED AND ACTUAL PERFORMANCE

To compare is to examine in order to note the similarities or differences of planned and actual results. Two key questions need to be asked on a continuing basis: (1) How is the project doing? and (2) If there are deviations to the planned allocation of resources, what caused these deviations, and why were they caused?

Both the senior managers and the project team should maintain oversight of the project's activities. By analyzing the planned results vis-a-vis the actual results, a determination can be made as to what corrective action is required. Some potential deviations that are likely to occur, such as the original cost estimates may have been faulty. Perhaps there has been an unproductive use of the project resources. Projects which require a notable advancement of the technology where unknown forces operate always run the risk of overruns. A deviation such as a cost or schedule overrun is not the problem. In all likelihood such an overrun is a *symptom* of something else, and should be investigated accordingly.

Research in project management provides insight into why schedule overruns happen. In one research effort Ashok and Wilemon found several reasons for product development delays: poor definition of product requirements; technological uncertainties; lack of senior management support; lack of resources; and poor project management. Poor project management involved lack of monitoring of the project's progress, lack of control systems, poor team and cross-functional meeting management practices, complex matrix management structures, and undefined and conflicting roles. In a few cases the respondents in the research study expressed resistance to project controls. In the same research it was found that the major concerns during the new product development process were: management and organizational style; lack of attention to details; limited support for innovation; lack of strategic thinking; and poor manufacturing capabilities. The researchers believe that the reasons for product development delays are manageable. They suggest that the following major categories of management improvement can have positive influence: senior management support; early integration of functional expertise in new product development; availability of resources and their management; and an organizational environment that supports teamwork [2].

Corrective action is required when the oversight of the project indicates that reallocation of the resources needs to be done.

CORRECTIVE ACTION

Corrective action can consist of replanning, reprogramming, reallocation, or realignment of the resources. Perhaps the way in which the project is managed and organized is required. Since the corrective action on the project usually centers around one of the cost, schedule, or technical performance parameters, care should be taken to insure that the "ripple" effect of the action taken is considered. If the project is behind schedule and additional resources such as manpower are put on the project, the cost of parameters of the project will change. If the technical performance objectives are in jeopardy, putting more resources on the project will change the cost and schedule parameters. The resulting additional resources may impact other project development efforts underway in the enterprise. Under such conditions the senior managers need to evaluate carefully the strategic fit of the project—for if the project is behind schedule, it may well be that an important *goal* of the enterprise is in trouble. In highly competitive product development efforts such delay can put the enterprise out of the competitive game.

Corrective action is a people-based activity. Sometimes project and senior managers forget this and only provide for the development of sophisticated information systems buttressed by computer technology which provides impressive output documents on the status of the project. These can be valuable—if the managers recognize that the information in such documents is time dependent and may not reflect the true status of the project. The experiences of a project manager who managed a large national project is worth noting.

On this large project there were state-of-the-art information systems supported by computer capabilities to provide data on the status of the project. Weekly schedule-cost-technical performance reports crossed the desks of the key people on the project—project manager, functional managers, work package managers, team members, and senior managers of the enterprise. Unfortunately, these reports were running about three to four weeks behind what was happening on the project. The delay was caused because of the time required to collect the information, reporting the information to all of the organizational levels, and because of the inevitable "sanitizing" to weed out the "bad news" that might reflect unfavorably on a manager. By the time the information reached the managers who had the authority to modify the reallocation of resources on the project, events had overtaken the project. Forward control, the ability to perceive the likelihood of future events that could impact the project, could not be done. To correct the lack of timely intelligence on the status of the project, the following remedial actions were undertaken:

> Review meetings at all levels were increased.
>
> Each Monday morning the project manager spent a few hours on the telephone with each project work package manager and certain other key project "stakeholders" discussing the status of the project efforts. After these phone calls, the results were discussed with the team members during a review session. The project manager then presented the findings to his boss and to the customer.
>
> The project manager made special efforts to have lunch with as many of the team members as possible during the week. Select senior managers were invited to these informal luncheons to discuss and listen to what was really happening on the project.
>
> All members of the project team were encouraged to "listen to everything" as much as possible from other project participants. Informal talks over coffee, cocktails, or a few brief comments in the hallway during the day provided useful tidbits of information, which when pursued further, provide useful project control intelligence from time to time.

People control projects, not computers or information systems. Computer and information technology can provide powerful tools for the generation and comparison of information relative to the project. But people have to review that information and decide what decisions need to be made and implemented to realign, or leave alone, the current schemas to change the application of resources on the project.

Senior managers need to be particularly alert to how projects are being managed in the organization.

SENIOR MANAGEMENT PROJECT CONTROL

Senior managers gain valuable information on how well the enterprise is being prepared for its future by keeping eyes on how well the project development and implementation processes are being carried out in the enterprise. Projects, as mentioned earlier in this chapter, are building blocks in the design and execution of organizational strategies. Each project represents in some way an improved (at least a changed) product or organizational process for external and internal customers,. If there are no product or process development projects underway in the enterprise, then a strong argument can be made that the enterprise is doing little to prepare itself for the future. In today's competitive environment, *any* organization faces change from the changing competitive and environmental forces that the enterprise encounters. Although a desirable state, stability in the face of changing social, political, economic, legal, technological, and competitive forces is a wishful but not realistic state. Stability today comes from the ability to manage the enterprise so that specific product and process development efforts are underway at all times. By maintaining surveillance over the network of product and process development projects in the enterprise, senior managers have an excellent basis for determining how well the enterprise is being prepared for its likely unstable future.

As the forces in the environment change, the enterprise managers require intelligence on whether and the "stream of projects"underway in the organization needs modified, or if it should be left alone; even if it should be taken around the corner and be "shot between the eyes" when there is no compatible strategic fit within the organization's future direction. Senior managers need to ask a few key questions about the strategic fit of the stream of projects flowing through the organization:

> Will the project make money for the enterprise?
> Will the project results be available to fit the firm's timetable for improving future competitiveness?
> Is there a "customer" for the project results?
> Will the project results be available in the quantity and quality required to meet or exceed competitive needs?

Information and insight turned up as a result of asking and obtaining answers to these questions can provide guidance to senior managers as to when remedial action is required to "fine tune" the stream of projects underway in the organization. If sufficient information is not available on a particular project, perhaps an audit of that project is in order.

PROJECT AUDITS

An informal or formal audit of the project can be used as a useful project control technique. Such audits can provide an independent appraisal of where the project stands, and how well the management of the project is being carried out. By having an independent team do an audit on the project, additional insight can be provided to the key project decision makers. Such audits should be done in the spirit of a fact-finding enterprise and not as a fault-funding witchhunt. If the project teams accepts that the audit is being carried out to truly help the management of the project, and that it is not a subtle effort to find a scapegoat, then coopera-tion is likely to follow. On the other hand, if the project team suspects that the audit is a crafty form of witchhunt, their cooperation will be equally crafty, and probably they will keep hidden as much as possible any current or expected problems on the project. The audit report can serve as a focus around which to exchange ideas, information, problems, oppor-tunities, solutions, and remedial strategies to help out the project and the enterprise.

Some companies conduct audits on their key projects on a regular basis. Such audits are a way of life in the organization, to be expected and to be done in the spirit of better project performance. An audit team for any particular project is formed from the teams working on other projects. All teams members know that they likely will be called on to serve as an audit team member on other projects in the enterprise. Such service is an ac-cepted useful policy in the company, and an opportunity for the audit team members to gain knowledge and additional skill on how to manage projects in the enterprise. When an audit report is submitted on a project, a debriefing is held for all of the key managers in the com-pany on the results. In the process everyone learns something useful that can be applied on the other projects that are underway in the enterprise.

Project planning and control state-of-the-art techniques are to be found in the project management literature. In this chapter, the generic and basic approaches to managing pro-jects have been described. The theory and practice of additional information on project management can be found in the Project Management Institute (PMI), a professional organization that provides many benefits to its membership.

PROJECT MANAGEMENT INSTITUTE

In 1969 the *Project Management Institute* was formed whose objectives are to [3]:

> Foster professionalism in the management of projects
>
> Identify and promote the fundamentals of project management and advance the body of knowledge for managing projects successfully
>
> Provide a recognized forum for free exchange of ideas, applications and solutions to project management challenges
>
> Stimulate the application of project management to the benefit of industry and the public
>
> Provide an interface between users and suppliers of hardware and software project management systems
>
> Collaborate with universities and other educational institutions to encourage appropriate educational and career development at all levels in project management
>
> Encourage academic and industrial research in the field of project management
>
> Foster contacts internationally with other public and private organizations, which relate to project management, and cooperate in matters of common interest

SUMMARY

The summary treatment of key matters involved in the management of projects as described, if properly designed and executed, can help immensely in maintaining global competitiveness.

Planning and control of the project activities is a major responsibility of the project team. Senior managers, who see the project as a way to prepare the enterprise for an uncertain and competitive future, need to get involved in the planning and control of the project.

The closing bibliography provides further references on the details of project planning and control. Planning for and control of the project resources can be as complex as one wants, or as simple as needed to get the job done. The contemporary literature on project planning and control cited in the bibliography and in PMI publications can be useful, but the sophistication of the techniques that are used should not exceed the sophistication of the project. A firm philosophy of the usefulness of project planning and control processes, combined with good common sense of what to use in tracking the use of project resources will pay handsomely in producing effective, and efficient project results.

REFERENCES

1. D. I. Cleland, *Project Management: Strategic Design and Implementation*, Tab Professional and Reference Books, Blue Ridge Summit, PA, 1990.
2. A. K. Gupta and D. I. Wilemon, "Accelerating the Development of Technology-Based New Products," *Calif. Mgmt. Rev.*, 24–44 (Winter 1990).
3. Project Management Institute Brochure, P. O. Box 43, Drexel Hill, PA 19026.

BIBLIOGRAPHY

Awani, A. O., *Project Management Techniques*, Petrocelli Books, Inc., New York, 1988.

Badiru, A. B., *Project Management in Manufacturing and High Technology Operations*, John Wiley and Sons, Inc., New York, 1988.

Briner, W., M. Geddes, and C., Hastings *Project Leadership*, Gower Publishing Company, Brookfield, VT, 1990.

Cleland, D. I. and W. R. King (eds.) *Project Management Handbook*, 2nd Edition, Van Nostrand Reinhold, New York, 1988.

Dinsmore, P. C., *Human Factors in Project Management,* American Management Association, New York, 1990.

Gareis, R. (ed.), *Handbook of Management of Projects*, MANZsche Verlags, Vienna, Austria, 1990.

Levine, H. A., *Project Management—Using Microcomputers*, Osborne McGraw-Hill, Berkeley, CA, 1986.

Rosenau, M. D., Jr., *Project Management for Engineers*, Lifetime Learning Publications, Belmont, CA, 1984.

Rosenau, M. D., Jr. and M. D. Lewin, *Software Project Management,* Lifetime Learning Publications, Belmont, CA, 1984.

DAVID I. CLELAND

RASTER GRAPHICS

INTRODUCTION

The term *raster graphics* is most familiar to those who have studied the field of computer graphics. It refers to a subset of imaging technologies that has made a profound impact on our society. The term is hardly a household word, but one example of *raster imaging* is seen by many people daily—the television. Raster imaging currently is the most widely used form for manipulating images electronically, and in the broadest sense it refers to technology for image capture, manipulation, transmission, and display (i.e., photocopiers, video cameras, and facsimile machines). However, raster imaging is a far broader topic than raster graphics.

Raster graphics is used to describe how computers are used to synthesize still images and animation sequences. However, it does not describe all of computer graphics. Raster graphics specifically refers to the generation and display of images represented by a dot matrix. Raster displays are composed of discrete spots of light, often referred to as pixels or pels (i.e., picture elements). If one looks very closely at a video display screen the individual pixels can be seen. Conversely, there are some computer graphic techniques that operate solely in the continuous domain (i.e., pen plotters that can mechanically draw continuous lines, as well as vector display screens). In raster display systems the electronics and the software must control each individual pixel as a separate step in the display process. The discrete nature of a raster display can be readily understood by imaging a view through a screen door. When standing close to a screen door, the eye can still see many variations within the small square holes. Despite the fact that there are only a finite number of light-sensing structures in the eye, images are perceived as continuous variations in intensity and color. A raster image is like a view through a screen door, except that only one color is used to fill a square—usually accounting for the contribution of all the colors within the square (see Fig. 1).

Beginning in the late 1970s and continuing into the 1990s, there has been a rapid growth in the use of raster graphics. It is being used as a vehicle for many applications in business, manufacturing, scientific research, and medicine. In fact, computer workstations—because of their display screens—owe their existence to the raster graphics medium. Currently the most user-friendly human–computer interfaces are those that use raster graphics to implement the *desktop metaphor*. These user-friendly interfaces have helped expand the community of computer users, and again the linking of computers to raster displays has been instrumental in achieving this. Today, there are many professionals who work on perfecting raster graphics hardware, algorithms, and applications.

This article surveys the field of raster graphics, concentrating on the technology used for image generation and on the various applications for which it has been used. Initially a brief history is given, in order to explain how raster graphic techniques emerged. First, we present a brief outline of some of the devices that are specific to raster graphics. Next is a survey of those fields that make substantial use of raster graphics and raster images. We then

FIGURE 1.   Illustration of (a) a screen door and (b) a rasterized scene, right.

cover some of the methods that are used to represent raster images, and the geometric models that are used to synthesize them. We discuss a subset of the most common computer algorithms used to generate raster images, including the following procedures: rasterization, hidden surface removal, and shading. Finally we discuss *aliasing*, a problem that arises whenever discrete samples are taken from a continuous source.

THE EVOLUTION OF RASTER GRAPHICS

If one traces raster graphics back to its origins it might start with the invention of the cathode ray tube (CRT). The first extensive use of computer graphics occurred in the mid-1960s and was vector oriented due to the types of display devices that were available [*1*]. *Vector* or *calligraphic* displays were initially expensive, and could plot lines on a screen by moving the electron beam along arbitrary linear paths. This required a refresh buffer for storing plotting commands, and a fast processor for converting plot commands into control signals that directed the electron beam. In the late 1960s, direct view storage tubes provided more cost-effective plotting of high precision lines and text. By the mid-1970s technology was available for building affordable raster graphics hardware. From then on, vector graphics and raster graphics became two distinct categories of computer graphics.

For many years vector graphics and raster graphics serviced a different set of needs, dictated by various applications. Vector graphics usually were applied in fields where line drawings were needed (e.g., drafting, scientific plotting, cartography, etc.). In these fields the ability to display detailed pictures with a high degree of accuracy was important, and the resolution of the raster devices could not meet these requirements. Early raster graphics devices could only display images that were 640 lines high and 480 picture elements across. Despite this limitation, raster displays exhibited certain properties that were beyond calligraphic displays; the most significant was the ability to display grey-scale images. Raster graphics were applied initially in fields where two-dimensional grey-scale or color images were needed (e.g., computer vision, simulation, and graphic arts). By the late 1980s most of the applications that used vector graphics migrated toward raster graphics. This occurred due to several improvements in raster display technology (e.g., increased spatial/color resolution, faster display processing, and cheaper displays).

FIELDS THAT USE RASTER GRAPHICS

Business and Presentation Graphics

Raster graphics has been used throughout the business community to organize information in the form of pie charts, bar graphs, scatter plots, and many other forms. This application has grown steadily since the late 1970s. A variety of turnkey systems were developed that were specifically geared toward the creation of two-dimensional graphical presentations. By the mid-1980s presentation graphics had become more fully integrated into desktop publishing systems, allowing documents to easily include high-quality illustrations. Industry standards were developed such as *postscript*, which has further fueled growth in desktop publishing.

Graphics Workstations and Personal Computers

Many professionals and students have had some contact with workstations or personal computers. For a short time, a workstation was distinguished from a *graphics* workstation, but that time is already past. By the mid-1980s, many workstations provided a mouse-driven window system as the interface, and had replaced the standard alphanumeric display with a general purpose raster graphics display. This trend has also occurred in the evolution of personal computers.

Window System Interfaces

The first example of a workstation with a mouse-driven window system was developed at Xerox Palo Alto Research Center in 1978, and was called the Alto. The Alto set the standard around which most workstations are designed today. A self-sufficient computer with a bilevel raster display, that was connected to a network called "Ethernet." The system's graphics capabilities were exploited by creating a user interface that mimicked a real desktop—*desktop metaphor*. The Star interface, also developed at Xerox PARC, was another well-known implementation of a virtual desktop graphical interface [2]. The concept has since been adopted and refined by many vendors of computer software and workstations. Like a desktop, information could be on pages that were freely arranged—even overlapping. When this window-based paradigm was applied it resulted in a substantial improvement in productivity, because multiple windows offered what appeared like parallel access and execution. Information could be manipulated within a common framework, sometimes through menu selections. The interface became even more graphics oriented through the use of graphical icons and object-oriented paradigms. By using this paradigm, abstract entities became tangible things and could be directly manipulated using the mouse.

Computer-Aided Design

The field of computer-aided design continues to use a variety of computer graphics techniques, with some types of CAD more than others relying on raster graphics. There are CAD applications that are two-dimensional—typically in designing electronic circuits—as well as three-dimensional. In CAD systems for integrated circuit design, raster graphics often are used to display symbols that represent gates and paths. Color is often used to represent different materials and highlight junctions. Raster displays are preferred for viewing small regions, but for inspection of larger areas—where extremely high resolution is needed—the preferred output device is a large plotter.

Raster graphics also are used in three-dimensional CAD systems. When three-dimensional geometry is to be manipulated, raster techniques are used to display a variety of primitives: lines, arcs, splines, planes, curved surfaces, and solids. For many geometric modeling operations, vector graphics techniques are adequate, but for some operations there are some advantages that raster techniques offer. For most designs, a physical model is made to evaluate its look and feel; but, more and more, computer-generated images are being used to perform this type of evaluation. Raster images can show what a product will actually look like before it goes into production. Realistic images can reveal defects in functionality or can be used to evaluate aesthetics.

Raster graphics can also be used to visualize the results of analysis. Computer models are often subjected to tests by analysis software, in which they are tested for durability under stress, resistance to heat, and many other factors. The results of these tests are hard to evaluate by looking at the raw numbers, and raster graphics is often used for visualization of these results. In architectural design, scale models are constructed and used to evaluate lighting and aesthetics. Raster graphics has been slow in replacing these models because the lighting effects are difficult to model. New shading algorithms have been developed recently that can accurately simulate the effects of scattered light in real environments. The flow of photons as they bounce and scatter throughout the environment is modeled by a technique known as *radiosity* (discussed later).

Entertainment and the Arts

Animation

Raster graphics is used extensively by the entertainment industry. Anyone who watches even a little TV probably has seen examples of computer-generated animation. Computer-generated animation is far cheaper to produce than traditional forms of animation. These animations are used to produce children's cartoons, commercials, and lead-in footage.

Video Games

The video arcade of today is a strong example of our hunger for ever more sophisticated graphics displays. Today's video games have much higher quality graphics displays than those introduced 10 years ago. Some arcade games have realistic three-dimensional figures, and use techniques that were state of the art only a few years ago. One very old animation technique that is still heavily relied upon is called *iconographics*. In this technique, moving figures are stored as a set of small subimages (bitmaps). When a sequence of these bitmaps are displayed, figures can appear to move smoothly. Many figures can be mixed with a background image, creating a complex moving scene.

Fine Art

Raster images have been used as a new medium for artistic expression, in both still frames and computer-generated animations. Two-dimensional Paint programs were initially the most common tool for generating still art. This electronic medium may be more restrictive than traditional media, in that the limited repertoire of the programs can inhibit certain styles. However, computer-based media eliminates some of the restrictions inherent in traditional media. In electronic media it can be easier to reproduce work, make changes, and try different alternatives (see Digital Painting). These properties are also exhibited in systems that use three-dimensional image synthesis. The same animation tools used by commercial animation producers and research laboratories are also being used for creating fine works of art.

Medical Imaging

Medical imaging techniques, collectively known as tomography, includes such techniques as magnetic resonance imaging (MRI) and positron emission tomography (PET). Raster displays are used to view these images, and assist the physician in diagnosis and treatment planning. The data that result from these scanners is a three-dimensional array of samples, each representing various types of tissue. Projecting slices of the data onto the display is straightforward, but this can be a hit or miss proposition. Volume rendering is a process in which the viewer is allowed to see through many areas where the tissue is not too dense. In this way many features that exist in three-dimensional space can be seen in a single view (discussed later). In some cases, the surfaces of organs and bone are extracted in order to highlight important structures. There is clear evidence that these techniques are dramatically improving the planning of radiation therapy, as well as implant and reconstructive surgery.

Military

Simulators

The military has been using raster graphics for more than two decades. The most well-known example is in the flight simulators that are used to train military pilots. Early systems used cameras that were mechanically guided over physical models of terrain and projected these pictures into the cockpit canopy. Eventually advancements in image synthesis made it possible to use computer-generated animation to create visual feedback for the pilot. These systems are very expensive, because images must be generated at very high rates—60 times per second. However, the benefits have been well established; it is safer and cheaper to start pilot training with a simulator than it is to use real aircraft. Flight simulators are also used extensively in training commercial airline pilots. In the future, other forms of military and civilian training may also benefit from simulators (i.e., training for tanks, ships, trucks, cars, etc.).

Computer Vision

Another military application that uses raster images is computer vision. Computer vision is in some sense the opposite of image synthesis. In image synthesis one tries to derive a two-dimensional image that accurately represents a three-dimensional model, while in computer vision one tries to derive a three-dimensional model from a two-dimensional camera image. For military applications, the goal might be to automatically target or spot an enemy. In industry, computer vision can be used to control assembly robots, or to look for defective products—*inspection*.

Scientific Visualization

Visualization is a classic technique that has been used in many fields long before computers were around. When assisted by computers it allows large amounts of data to be presented in graphical form. These presentations are intended to impose a structure on the data that makes it easier to observe significant features. Below are a few examples of how visualization has been applied.

Finite-Element Analysis

Finite-element analysis is a numerical technique for simulating the effects of stress, heat, fluid dynamics, and other physical processes. The results of these types of algorithms are numbers, which in raw form are difficult to interpret. Raster images are an ideal medium for visualizing the results of finite-element analysis, often using pseudocolor to reveal areas of interest. Volume rendering, previously mentioned under medical imaging, can be used for visualizing data taken from solids and fluid systems.

Molecular Modeling

Another application where raster imaging is heavily used is in visualizing systems of molecules. Molecular modeling is being used to design new chemicals and medicines.

Weather Patterns

Finite-element analysis and volume rendering are also used for visualization of weather patterns. By observing how storm systems develop researchers are hoping to find better ways of predicting the movement of storms.

REPRESENTATIONS FOR IMAGE GENERATION

Image Representations

The most convenient structure for organizing images is a two-dimensional array of intensities. Color images containing three primaries—red, green, and blue—can be represented by three separate intensity arrays. Alternatively each primary can be coalesced into a single 24 bit or 32 bit word and stored in a single two-dimensional array. Frame-buffer hardware, which will be described later, must typically store images in this fashion. In general, this representation stores more information than is necessary, and a variety of compression schemes have been developed. However, in computer graphics applications, it is also important for representation to provide some means of efficient random access.

Quad Trees

A very well-known method, that both reduces storage and facilitates random access, is the quad tree [3]. Quad trees work best when applied to square images with dimensions that are a power of two. A quad tree is formed by recursively splitting an image into quadrants. Quadrants are stored in a quad tree as nodes of degree four: all nodes have exactly 4 or 0 children. A code can be used to indicate whether the area covered by a node is completely filled by the same intensity or has some variations. If there are any variations within that region, the tree node will have four children. Otherwise, it is a leaf node and uses a single intensity to represent the region. Figure 2a shows a bilevel image represented with a sparse quad tree.

   The algorithm for random access starts at the root of the tree, and searches down a single path until a leaf node is found. The worst case complexity for any single access is $O(\log_2 n)$, where n is the resolution in pixels along one side of a square image. For an image that is 256×256 pixels, a single random access traverses at most 8 nodes, and at most 9 nodes for an image that is 512×512. Other operations can be performed efficiently on quad trees, including set operations (i.e., union and intersection).

Octrees

The quad tree structure can be extended to represent spatial decompositions called *octrees* [4]. If a three-dimensional space is bounded by a cube, then the raster equivalent of the pixel is replaced by a square volume element or *voxel*. As in quad trees the decomposition works best when the resolution is restricted to powers of two. The space is split along three differ-

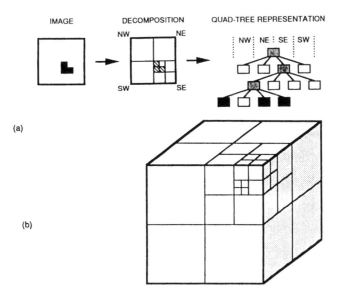

FIGURE 2. (a) Quad tree; (b) Octree.

ent axes, creating eight octants (Fig. 2b). Each node in the octree can have only 0 or 8 children, and leaf nodes can be labeled as either completely occupied or completely empty. Many of the properties of complexity that exist for quad trees also hold true for octrees. This form of spatial decomposition is used for medical imaging as well as solid modeling.

Surface Representations

A large variety of representation schemes exist for three-dimensional surfaces: polygons, parametric surface patches, superquadrics, binary partitioning trees, implicit surfaces, etc. Space permits only a brief description of the first two: polygons and parametric surface patches. Both of these representations are the most widely used in computer graphics.

Polygonal Approximations

Many surfaces can be adequately represented by a collection of polygonal faces. Models of terrain and architectural structures are most often modeled using polygonal faces. Some algorithms are general purpose enough to handle concave polygons while others can operate properly only on convex polygons. Usually all algorithms require that all polygons are planar. Figure 3a shows an object represented by polygons.

Polygons can be stored as either a list of vertices, or can be stored as part of a polygonal mesh. Meshed polygons require more storage, but a typical hidden surface algorithm requires only about half the amount of computation along the edges where adjacent polygons meet. Each vertex in the surface description is minimally defined by a three-dimensional coordinate. In some cases other values are stored, such as the following: normal vectors, texture map indices, color, coefficients for transparency, etc.

Polygonal approximations offer a few advantages over other representations. They are easily transformed and clipped, and they are the easiest primitive to render using hidden-line and hidden-surface algorithms. One major disadvantage, is the polygonal approxima-

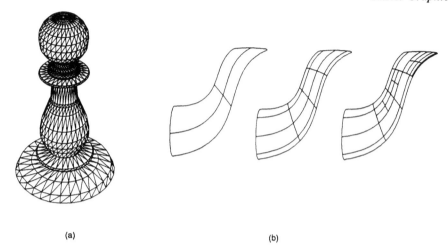

(a)   (b)

FIGURE 3.   (a) A polygonal surface. (b) Networks of bicubic patches.

tions are not always smooth enough. The inaccuracy of the approximation is most noticeable along the silhouette edges, and can produce visible shading discontinuities.

Curved Surface Representations

Curved surface representations are used when smoother approximations are needed, the most common form being the parametric surface patch. A parametric surface patch is described by Mortenson as the following: "A curve-bounded collection of points whose coordinates are given by continuous, two-parameter, single-valued mathematical functions" [5]. They are expressed in the following form

$$x = f_x(u,v) \qquad y = f_y(u,v) \qquad z = f_{z(u,v)}$$

where $u,v \in [0,1]$.

A variety of parametric functions can be used (i.e., equations of a plane, sphere, ellipse, etc.), but for free formed curved surfaces polynomial equations are used. A bicubic patch is commonly used for piecewise networks of patches, because the cubic polynomials allow continuity of the tangent vectors. As a result the illumination of the surface appears smooth across the boundaries of adjacent patches. Figure 3b shows half of a teapot spot represented by a piecewise network of bicubic patches. From left to right the figure shows how surface patches can be subdivided without altering the shape of the surface. The spout on the far right shows that subdivisions can be adaptively applied, a property that is used in some rendering algorithms [6].

COMPUTER HARDWARE FOR RASTER GRAPHICS

Any computer system that uses raster graphics needs to include a few standard components. The most basic requirement is a video display screen, a refresh buffer (also called a framebuffer), and circuitry that can generate a video signal from the contents of the refresh buffer. These components can be found in many variations, but they all function in a similar manner. Another category of hardware that is used in raster graphics systems include devices that are designed to speed up the process of image generation. The reader should be aware that this section is by no means an exhaustive survey of computer graphics hardware, It merely provides some background information on a few of the most well-known examples.

Display Screens

The most common form of raster display screen is the cathode ray tube (CRT). This includes most television sets, video display terminals, and personal computers. A black and white CRT is a large vacuum tube, with a thin phosphor coating painted on the inside surface where the image appears. When the phosphors are struck by an electron beam, they become fluorescent (emitters of light). In a standard CRT the phosphor spots loose fluorescence soon after the electron beam stops hitting them. For this reason, a picture must be refreshed 30–60 times per second. In a single refresh cycle the electron beam is swept along a series of horizontal scan lines until all picture elements have been struck. The intensity of the light at each pixel is controlled by varying the intensity of the electron beam. Color CRTs apply this same principle using phosphors that emit different colors. Each colored pixel consists of a triad of red, green, and blue phosphors. A different electron beam is used for each primary color; as an example, only the beam assigned to the color red can hit the red part of the triads.

There are other types of display that use completely different techniques to generate raster images. One that has become popular for calculators, lap-top computers, and small portable TVs is the liquid crystal display (LCD). LCDs can be made flatter than a CRT, and draw less power. There are two general types of LCD: front lit and back lit.

Frame-Buffers

An essential component for any raster graphics system is the frame-buffer. The frame-buffer serves as the memory for storing images along with the appropriate refresh circuitry for driving the CRT. Frame-buffer memory is dual-ported, providing two separate paths: one for the rendering computer to write/read intensity values and the other for reading values that refresh the display. There are at least as many memory locations in the frame-buffer as there are pixels on the display screen. Figure 4 shows a diagram of a typical frame-buffer, with 8 bits of memory per pixel. By using a color lookup table, the number of bits per pixel only limits how many colors can be viewed simultaneously, which can be smaller than the range of colors that can be represented. The value stored in pixel memory is used as an index into a color lookup table, and the value from the table is what encodes the color. In the diagram, an 8 bit pixel indexes a table with 256 values, and the table values are encoded as 12 bit color values—4 bits per primary. The three fields in the color map are used as inputs to three digital to analogue converters, and subsequently form part of the video signal that controls the CRT.

Acceleration Hardware

Frame-buffers store images and control the display, but there are also some examples where hardware is used for image generation (i.e., generating intensities from geometric primitives). In some cases a single dedicated processor is used for all image generation steps, while in other cases hardware targets specific parts of the process. Dedicated hardware is often necessary when general purpose computers are too slow.

The one part of image generation that varies the least is the transformation and clipping process. The fact that this part varies the least makes it the prime target for designing acceleration hardware. One well-known example was developed by Clark [7], called "The

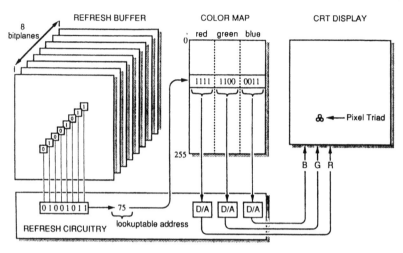

FIGURE 4.   Diagram of a frame-buffer with a color lookup table [based on a figure in Ref. *1*].

Geometry Engine." The geometry engine was a pipeline of special purpose hardware that used custom chips, for speeding up viewing transformations, clipping, and scaling to device-specific screen coordinates.

The processes that follow transformation and clipping are collectively referred to as the rendering stage, and here as well, special purpose hardware has been used to attain faster processes. One well-known example of this was developed by Fuchs [8], and is called pixel planes. Pixel planes used integrated circuits in which computational elements were part of the memory of the frame-buffer. In the first design, the computational elements could store linear equations, which could be evaluated to determine which pixels lie within a polygon. Edge equations would be broadcast to all computational elements, which would rasterize the polygon in parallel. This resulted in a fixed time to render a polygon, regardless of how many pixels it covered. The complexity grew linearly in proportion to the number of edges in a polygon. This was a major achievement, since the rendering stage often involves most of the computation in generating raster images. Since its first implementation pixel planes has evolved into an even more powerful architecture, and is no longer limited to solving linear equations.

ALGORITHMS FOR RASTER GRAPHICS

Computer Algorithms for Two-Dimensional Graphics

Digital Painting Tools

Paint programs are tools that allow artists and designers to interactively paint into a frame-buffer. These tools often incorporate concepts borrowed from traditional media (i.e., canvas/paper, a palette of colors, and brushes in various shapes and sizes). In a typical raster painting tool the brush is displayed as a cursor, and is positioned using a mouse or tablet. Pressing a mouse button or exerting pressure on a stylus causes intensities (pigment) to be transferred from the brush into the pixel memory. In some cases the color transfer uses a

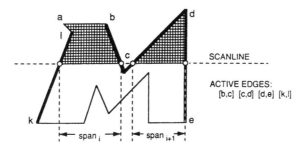

FIGURE 5.   Illustration of edge parity fill.

blending between the brush color and the color in the frame-buffer. Raster painting can be done in a freehand manner, or it can be more precisely controlled by geometric primitives.

Lines, Curves, and Polygons

Raster graphics often involves the use of geometric primitives to create pictures. Lines, circles, and circular arcs can be rasterized using simple and efficient algorithms. Brezenham's algorithm is probably the most well-known algorithm for rasterizing line segments and circles [1]. Free-form curves that are represented by polynomials can be rasterized efficiently by using a forward difference method to generate short-line segments [5].

The most common method of rasterizing a polygon (i.e., filling its interior), uses an x-sorted edge list and is called *edge parity fill* [9]. The algorithm works on the assumption that shaded segments along a scanline lie between odd-numbered and even-numbered edges in an x-sorted list of active edges. Given a y-sorted list of edges, the algorithm uses *insertion sort* to maintain an x-sorted list of edges that intersect the current scan-line—all perfectly horizontal edges are excluded. Scanlines are processed starting from the top of the display. When edges are first entered into the list of active edges an increment is computed which changes the x coordinate as it is cut by successive scanlines. Edges stay in the x-sorted list until the bottom end point is reached. Figure 5 shows an example of filling a polygon using edge parity.

Three-Dimensional Hidden Surface Algorithms

Hidden surface algorithms create raster images by projecting all visible three-dimensional surfaces onto a viewing plane. Prior to rendering three-dimensional models undergo perspective projection. Everything that lies outside of the viewing frustum is clipped away. For polygonal models a scan-conversion similar to the parity fill described above can be used. If no polygons intersect, and polygons are rendered starting from back to front (i.e., from farthest to nearest to viewer) there is no need to sort the pixels for hidden surface elimination. However, when polygons are rendered in random order or polygon intersections occur, visibility must be tested at each pixel. When visibility tests are required, depth values must be interpolated along all edges that bound the polygons. When successive pairs of edges are paired for parity fill, depth values must also be interpolated across each span.

Depth Buffering

In depth buffering, each pixel must provide for storage depth values, (also referred to as a z-buffer). For each pixel in a span between edge pairs, the algorithm tests the computed z-value with the one currently residing in the z-buffer. If the new value is closer to the

FIGURE 6.   Flat, Gouraud, and Phong shading.

viewer, both the z-buffer's z-value and the pixel's intensity are over written. Otherwise the old z-value and its corresponding intensity-value are left intact.

Rendering techniques compute intensities that simulate illumination of surfaces by a light source. The simplest techniques use surface normals and a point light source. The three most common forms of surface illumination are: flat shading, Gouraud Shading, and Phong shading. Figure 6 shows a chess pawn illuminated with these three illumination techniques. Notice that flat shading clearly shows the structure of the underlying polygonal model while Gouraud and Phong shading create smooth variations in intensity.

Gouraud Shading

In 1975 Gouraud presented an algorithm for smooth shading curved surfaces [10]. Gouraud used the angle between the normal vector and a vector pointing toward the light source to determine a diffuse intensity. These intensities were computed at each vertex of a polygonal approximation to the surface. During the rendering stage, a depth-buffering algorithm would linearly interpolate the intensities—just as depth is—along each polygon edge, and similarly the intensities would be linearly interpolated across every span. One noticeable artifact in this type of shading is the second-order discontinuities often referred to as *mach bands*. These subtle discontinuities in the rate of change of the intensities is noticeable along polygon edges when a coarse approximation is used. The algorithm is still widely used in many graphics systems.

Phong Shading

In 1975, Phong presented an algorithm that added the effects of highlights that appear on glossy surfaces [11]. In this algorithm the normal vectors are interpolated along edges and along spans instead of the intensities. The intensity is calculated for each pixel using the interpolated surface normals $\mathbf{N}$, the vector to the light source $\mathbf{L}$, and the vector to the eye $\mathbf{E}$. Phong's illumination model combined Gouraud's diffuse illumination term

$$I_{\text{diffuse}} = \frac{\mathbf{L} \cdot \mathbf{N}}{|\mathbf{L}||\mathbf{N}|}$$

with another term that models the contribution of reflected light to create specular high-lights.

$$I_{\text{specular}} = (\mathbf{N} \cdot \mathbf{H})^n$$

where

$$\mathbf{H} = \frac{\mathbf{E} + \mathbf{L}}{|\mathbf{E} + \mathbf{L}|}$$

While this improves the quality of the illumination model, it falls short of accurately model-ing how light interacts with surfaces in the real world. Subsequently, illumination models were developed that modeled the actual roughness of surfaces, creating more realistic light-ing effects [12–14]. The most noticeable difference between the Phong model and the Tor-rence Sparrow model is the Fresnel effect, where light that glances even roughened surfaces produces a peak in reflectance. This phenomena can be observed by holding a sheet of paper in front of a light and looking at it edge on.

Texturing

A variety of other clever techniques were developed to create more complexity without im-pacting the complexity of the rendering algorithms. *Texture mapping* was developed by Catmull [15], as a technique to add fine variations in intensity by indexing a lookup table. Texture indices u and v are interpolated along edges and spans just as intensities are in Gouraud shading. This technique was later extended by Blinn [13] to index values that per-turbed the surface normals at each pixel. This technique, called *bump mapping*, created the illusion of relief patterns on the surface. Bump maps create a more realistic impression of texture when objects move during animated sequences.

Shadowing

The illusion of realism in a computer-generated scene is greatly enhanced by adding shad-owing effects. Depth-buffering algorithms can generate scenes with cast shadows from a single light source by first generating a range image as seen from the light source [16]. Once the range image is computed, the rendering algorithm uses the inverse transformations to project pixel depths into object space, then into the screen space of the range data. A shadow is detected when the range data are closer then the projected depth value, and the intensity is appropriately diminished. In the case of multiple light sources, a different range image would be needed for each light source, and additional projections would also be necessary.

Ray Tracing

Ray tracing algorithms provide a more elegant solution to the hidden-surface problem, be-cause many visual effects (e.g., shadowing, interobject reflections, refraction, and depth-of-field effects) can be simulated without the special treatment that scanline algorithms require. Turner Whitted was the first to combine most of these effects into a single ray-trac-ing algorithm [17]. There currently are a large number of ray-tracing algorithms. The fol-lowing general description characterizes most implementations.

In order to efficiently model the effects of light on a scene, ray tracing focuses on only the visible portions of light by starting from the eye and following the light backwards through the scene. The algorithm proceeds as follows.

Step 1.   For each display pixel a primary ray is traced, which emanates from the eye and projects into object space. Those primary rays that hit nothing produce a background color, while all others result in processing Step 2.

Step 2.   Trace secondary rays; A ray to the light source (light-ray) can detect shadows if it intersects an object. In addition, depending on the properties of an object, some of the following secondary rays are traced:

  a. If the object is reflective, trace an additional ray (reflection-ray).
  b. If the object is not opaque trace an additional ray through the surface, with its direction determined by Snell's law (transmitted-ray). The equation for computing this ray uses the primary ray, the normal vector, and an index of refraction.

For all secondary rays intersection tests are made. If a reflection ray or a transmission ray intersects an object, Step 2 is recursively applied for each intersection, until no more reflection-rays or transmitted-rays are needed. In practice, a limit must be set on how many times Step 2 can be applied, since there are cases in which an infinite series of rays can be generated.

The result of this algorithm is a tree of rays rooted at each pixel. The intensity can then be computed by a traversal of the tree, and the use of the illumination model described by Whitted [17]. This algorithm is an ideal candidate for parallel processing, because the ray calculations for each pixel are independent of the surrounding pixels.

The most time-consuming portion of any ray-tracing algorithm is the code that computes the intersection of rays with objects. For each ray, all objects in the scene must be tested, usually sped by testing against a bounding volume first. For some objects (i.e., spheres and quadratic functions) the intersection calculations have closed form solutions. Polygon intersections require two steps: first an intersection with the plane of the polygon is computed, then the intersection point is tested to see if it lies within the polygon. Other types of surface representation (i.e., bicubic patches) require either a subdivision algorithm similar to [6] or an iterative root-finding algorithm. Often a bounded method for root-finding such as *regula falsi* is desired. Convergence is slower than Newton-Raphson iteration, however convergence is guaranteed.

Radiosity

Traditionally, the light scattered from a diffuse object was either disregarded or at best characterized as a constant. Radiosity is a technique that attempts a more comprehensive modeling of how light scatters and reflects in a complex 3D environment [18]. An enclosure is modeled by a series of perfectly diffuse surfaces. Each surface is subdivided into smaller surface elements, each of which is treated as a separate emitter/receiver of light. The radiosity measure b_j is the rate per unit area at which light energy leaves the surface element j and is determined by the following equation:

$$B_j = E_j + \varrho_j H_j$$

where,

E_j = rate of direct energy emission from element j
ϱ_j = reflectivity of surface j
H_j = incident radiant energy arriving at element j

The incident radian energy arriving at element j depends on three things: the radiosity of all other elements, the degree to which they can be "seen" from element j, and their proximity to element *j*. The degree of contribution is called the form factor. The equation for H_j then involves the radiosity of all elements and the form factors F_{ij} for each potential pairing.

$$H_j = \sum_{i=1}^{N} B_i F_{ij}$$

Combining the above equations yields a single equation for every surface element.

$$B_j = E_j + \varrho_j \sum_{i=1}^{N} B_i F_{ij} \quad \text{for } j = 1, N$$

The result is a set of N linear equations and N unknown values for b_j. Standard gaussian elimination techniques are then used to determine the intensity at each surface element. While this computation is quite expensive, it relies on geometry alone and is independent of the view point.

Volume Rendering

Volume rendering represents a special class of algorithms that attempt to render solid volumes as opposed to just the visible surfaces. Its usefulness for medical imaging was mentioned previously, but it is also useful for a variety of scientific visualization applications. Traditionally, computed tomography data was visualized with standard surface rendering techniques, combined with methods for extracting surface geometry from a series of slices. Volume rendering describes approaches that sample the volume data directly, and generates a pseudo x-ray image [19]. The following describes a general volume rendering technique known as *additive reprojection*.

Each volume element is assigned an opacity coefficient, which may correspond to the tissue density at that location. Starting from the eye, rays are traced through a pixel and projected into a three-dimensional voxel array. Starting at the voxel closest to the eye the algorithm traverses all voxels that intersect the ray. As each voxel is encountered, intensity values and opacity values are accumulated. When the accumulated opacity reaches a threshold, the algorithm stops traversing ray intersections, because the medium from this point to the eye can be considered opaque. At this point the accumulated intensities of all traversed samples are averaged, yielding an intensity for the corresponding pixel.

ALIASING: INHERENT PROBLEMS WITH DISCRETE SAMPLING

Whenever images are captured or synthesized, that process can be considered as one of sampling. The process usually starts with a continuous source (i.e., continuous surface primitives), and collects discrete samples. Sampling at the resolution of the display device assumes that the variations in the scene will be gradual enough for the samples to accurately represent it. In practice there are many cases where details are too small to be picked up by a raster scan process. A well-known theorem in signal processing literature, known as *the sampling theorem*, states that a band-limited signal can be precisely reconstructed given a sufficient number of equally spaced samples and an appropriate filtering process [20]. If the image that is being sampled contains high frequency components (i.e., there are many variations within a small area), then more samples will be needed to accurately represent the

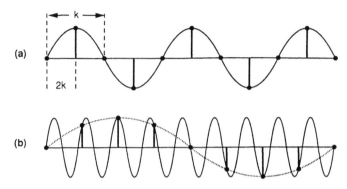

FIGURE 7.   Illustration of point samples (a) within Nyquist limit, and (b) below Nyquist limit. Note how the undersampled high frequency masquerades as a low frequency, hence the term alias.

original image. In practice more samples will be needed than there are pixels in the display, and the raster image will be reconstructed, by filtering the samples.

The sampling theorem states that the minimum sampling frequency, known as the Nyquist frequency, is twice the highest frequency that appears in the signal being sampled. When a signal is undersampled—below the Nyquist frequency—the samples cannot adequately reconstruct the original signal, and aliasing can occur. Aliasing is a term that describes false signals that are not in the original signal, but are introduced due to an inadequate rate of sampling. Figure 7 shows what happens when a one-dimensional signal at frequency k is sampled at and below the Nyquist frequency $2k$.

Aliasing is a recurrent problem in generating raster images, since it often involves the discrete sampling of a continuous source. In still frames aliasing most often occurs in the form of jagged or fragmented edges, and moiré patterns. A number of researchers have worked on developing rendering techniques that eliminate aliasing. Many systems that generate raster images today include some form of antialiasing.

Sampling Techniques for Antialiasing

Super Sampling

One straightforward technique for antialiasing is called supersampling. Given enough memory, an image can be oversampled, producing samples of at least twice the resolution of the display. A filtering process is then applied to the high resolution samples, to generate a raster image that matches the resolution of the display. Figure 8 illustrates the process of three times oversampling. Notice that all high resolution point samples—the small dots— that fall in between the actual pixels of the display—the large dots—contribute to the surrounding pixels. The degree to which a sample contributes to a pixel is determined by its distance from the center of a two-dimensional filter, which is centered at each pixel. The extent of the filter is illustrated by the large circles that overlap.

Stochastic Sampling

A major problem with brute force supersampling, is the additional cost of computing so many samples. In practice, aliasing can occur even when the sampling density is very high, and in fixed grid supersampling, N times oversampling requires N^2 samples per pixel. Fewer

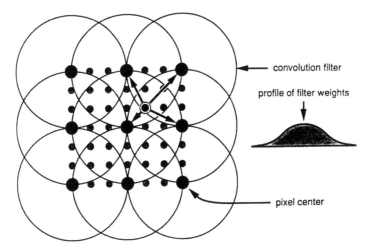

FIGURE 8.   Three times oversampling along a uniform grid.

are needed if a nonuniform sampling method is used. Stochastic sampling is a form of super sampling where the high-resolution samples are generated with random offsets. When stochastic sampling is used, the artifacts appear as noise in the image rather than aliases (false signals) [*21, 22*].

Area Sampling

Another approach to antialiasing is analogous to the screen door concept mentioned in the Introduction. Here each pixel is modeled as a rectangular area instead of a point sample. Graphical primitives are sampled by accumulating all fragments that partially cover a pixel, and calculating the area-averaged intensity of all visible parts of all fragments [*23*].

Texture Filtering

Texture maps are often plagued by aliasing, and most algorithms that use texture mapping rely on some form of filtering operation. Currently, the most efficient techniques for antialiasing texture, though not the most accurate, is through mip maps [*24*] or the slightly more accurate summed area tables [*25*]. The mip map technique performs all filtering in advance, storing multiple filtered texture maps at various resolutions. During rendering, the density of the texture is computed, then used to select intensities from the appropriate texture map. Since the resolution of the mip maps decrease by a factor of two in each step, intensities from intermediate resolutions are calculated by interpolation between adjacent texture maps. Summed area tables are a variation of the mip map technique, where a single table of sums is stored instead of prefiltered textures. The rectangular region that covers a pixel is computed and used to retrieve the sum of all intensities in that area from the table. The sum is then divided by the area of the rectangle, yielding the average intensity within the region.

Temporal Aliasing

Aliasing takes on some slightly different characteristics when generating computer animation.

When 2D raster images are generated for animation, the process starts with continuous motion and collects image samples at regular time intervals. When objects are moving too fast aliasing in the time domain can cause strobing, making objects appear to move in a jerking fashion. This effect shows up on old western movies where wagon wheels appear to roll in the opposite direction as they should. By extending the sampling techniques used in spacial sampling to the time domain, these artifacts can be suppressed. The sampling theorem holds true in this domain as well. The time interval between samples must shrink as objects speed up, otherwise some areas of the image will completely miss any fast moving objects. When interlaced video is used to display the images, one must also consider how even and odd fields are juxtaposed in time by the display.

REFERENCES

1. J. D. Foley and A. Van Dam, *Fundamentals of Interactive Computer Graphics*, Addison Wesley Publishers, Reading, MA, 1982.
2. D. C. Smith, et al., "Designing the Star User Interface," *Byte,* 7(4), 242–282 (1982).
3. G. M. Hunter, "Efficient Computation and Data Structures for Graphics," Ph.D. dissertation, Dept. of Elec. Engineering and Computer Science, Princeton University, Princeton (1978).
4. D. Meagher, "Octree Encoding: A New Technique for the Representation, the Manipulation, and Display of Arbitrary 3-D Objects by Computer," Technical Report IPL-TR-80-111, Image Processing Laboratory, Rensselaer Polytechnic Institute, Troy, NY (1980).
5. M. E. Mortenson, *Geometric Modeling*, John Wiley & Sons Publishers, New York, 1985.
6. E. E. Catmull, "A Subdivision Algorithm for Computer Display of Curved Surfaces," Ph.D. thesis, University of Utah UTEC-CSc-74-133 (1975).
7. J. H. Clark, "The Geometry Engine: A VLSI Geometry System for Graphics," *Comput. Graph.,* 16(3), 127–133 (1982).
8. H. Fuchs, "Distributing a Visible Surface Algorithm Over Multiple Processors," *Proc. ACM Annual Conf.,* Seattle, 1977.
9. T. Pavlidis, *Algorithms for Graphics and Image Processing*, Computer Science Press, Rockville, MD, 1982.
10. H. Gouraud, "Continuous Shading of Curved Surfaces," *IEEE Transact. Computers,* 20(6), 623–628 (June 1971).
11. B. T. Phong, "Illumination for Computer Graphics," *Comm. ACM,* 18(6), 311–317 (June 1975).
12. K. E. Torrence and E. M. Sparrow, "Polarization, Directional Distribution, and Off-Specular Peak Phenomena in Light Reflected from Roughened Surfaces, *J. Opt. Soc. Am.,* 56(7), 916–925 (July 1966).
13. J. F. Blinn, "Computer Display of Curved Surfaces," Ph.D. thesis, University of Utah (1978).
14. R. L. Cook and K. E. Torrence, "A Reflectance Model For Computer Graphics," *Comput. Graph.,* 15(3), 307–316 (1984).
15. E. E. Catmull, "Computer Display of Curved Surfaces," *Proc. IEEE Conf. on Computer Graphics, Pattern Recognition and Data Structures*, 1975.
16. L. Williams, "Casting Curved Shadows on Curved Surfaces," *Compute. Graph.,* 12(3), 270–274 (1978).
17. J. T. Whitted, "An Improved Illumination Model for Shaded Display," *Comm. ACM,* 23(6), 343–349 (1980).

18. C. M. Goral, "Modeling the Interaction of Light Between Diffuse Surfaces," *Comput. Graph. 18*(3), 213–222 (1984).
19. R. A. Drebin, L. Carpenter, and P. Hanrahan, "Volume Rendering," *Comput. Graph., 22*(4), 65–74 (1988).
20. R. N. Bracewell, *The Fourier Transform and Its Applications,* Second Edition, McGraw-Hill, New York, 1978.
21. M. A. Z. Dippe and H. W. Erling, "Antialiasing Through Stochastic Sampling," *Comput. Graph., 19*(3), 69–78 (1985).
22. R. L. Cook, "Stochastic Sampling in Computer Graphics," *ACM Trans. Graph., 5*(1), 51–72 (1986).
23. L. Carpenter, "The A-Buffer, an Antialiased Hidden Surface Method," *Comput. Graph., 18*(3), 103–108, 1984.
24. L. Williams, "Pyramidal Parametrics," *Comput. Graph., 17*(3), 1–11(1983).
25. F. C. Crow, "Summed-Area Tables for Texture Mapping," *Comput. Graph., 18*(3), 207–212 (1984).

DAVID M. WEIMER

REASONING ABOUT KNOWLEDGE:
A SURVEY CIRCA 1991

INTRODUCTION

Although *epistemology*, the study of knowledge, has a long and honorable tradition in philosophy, starting with the Greeks, the idea of a formal logical analysis of reasoning about knowledge is somewhat more recent, going back to at least von Wright [*1*]. The first book-length treatment of epistemic logic is Hintikka's seminal work, *Knowledge and Belief* [*2*]. The 1960s saw a flourishing of interest in this area in the philosophy community. Axioms for knowledge were suggested, attacked, and defended. Models for the various axiomatizations were proposed, mainly in terms of possible-world semantics, and then again attacked and defended [see, e.g., *3-5*].

More recently, reasoning about knowledge has found applications in such diverse fields as economics, linguistics, artificial intelligence, and computer science. While researchers in these areas have tended to look to philosophy for their initial inspiration, it has also been the case that their more pragmatic concerns which often centered around more computational issues such as the difficulty of computing knowledge, have not been treated in the philosophical literature. The commonality of concerns of researchers in all these areas has been quite remarkable, as has been attested by the recent series of interdisciplinary conferences on the subject [*6-8*].

This survey attempts to identify and describe some of the common threads that tie together research in reasoning about knowledge in all the areas mentioned above. Also briefly discussed is some of the more recent work, particularly in computer science, and some lines for future research are suggested. This should by no means be viewed as a comprehensive survey. The topics covered clearly reflect the biases of the author.

THE "CLASSICAL" MODEL

We'll begin by reviewing the "classical" model for knowledge and belief (now over 30 years old!), the so-called *possible-world* model. The intuitive idea here is that besides the true state of affairs, there are a number of other possible states of affairs, or possible worlds. Some of these possible worlds may be indistinguishable to an agent from the true world. An agent is then said to *know* a fact φ if φ is true in all the worlds he thinks possible. For example, an agent may think that states of the world are possible: in one it is sunny in London,

This is a greatly revised and updated version of an article entitled "Reasoning About Knowledge: An Overview" that appears in *Theoretical Aspects of Reasoning About Knowledge: Proceedings of the 1986 Conference*, J. Y. Halpern (ed.), Morgan Kaufmann, San Francisco, 1986.

while in the other it is raining in London. However, in both these states it is sunny in San Francisco. Thus, this agent knows that it is sunny in San Francisco, but does not know whether it is sunny in London.

The philosophical literature has tended to concentrate on the one-agent case, in order to emphasize the properties of knowledge. However, many applications of interest involve multiple agents. Then it becomes important to consider not only what an agent knows about "nature," but also what he knows about what the other agents know and don't know. It should be clear that this kind of reasoning is crucial in bargaining and economic decision making. As we shall see, it is also relevant in analyzing protocols in distributed computing systems (in this context, the "agents" are the processes in the system). Such reasoning can get very complicated. Most people quickly lose the thread of such nested sentences as "Dean doesn't know whether Nixon knows that Dean knows that Nixon knows that McCord burgled O'Brien's office at Watergate" [see Ref. *9* for a further investigation of similar sentences]. But this is precisely the type of reasoning that goes on in a number of applications involving man agents.

In order to formalize this type of reasoning, we first need a language. The language considered here is a propositional modal logic for n agents. Starting with primitive propositions $p, q, r, \ldots$, more complicated formulas are formed by closing off under negation, conjunction, and the modal operators $K_1, \ldots, K_n$. Thus, if φ and ψ are formulas, then so are $\neg\varphi, \varphi \wedge \psi$, and $K_i\varphi, i = 1, \ldots, n$. As usual, we take $\varphi \vee \psi$ to be abbreviation for $\neg(\neg\varphi \wedge \neg\psi)$ and $\varphi \Rightarrow \psi$ to be an abbreviation for $\neg\varphi \vee \psi$.

The formula $K_i\varphi$ is read "agent i knows φ." The K_is are called modal operators; hence the name modal logic. We could also consider a first-order modal logic that allows quantification, but the propositional case is somewhat simpler and has all the ingredients we need for our discussion.

We can express quite complicated statements in a straightforward way using this language. For example, the formula

$$K_1K_2p \wedge \neg K_2K_1K_2p$$

says that agent 1 knows that agent 2 knows p, but agent 2 doesn't know that agent 1 knows that agent 2 knows p. We view possibility as the dual of knowledge. Thus, agent 1 considers φ possible exactly if he doesn't know $\neg\varphi$. This situation can be described by the formula $\neg K_1\neg\varphi$. A statement like "Dean doesn't know whether φ" says that Dean considers both φ and $\neg\varphi$ possible. With these observations, we can deal with the sentence above, "Dean doesn't know whether Nixon knows that Dean knows that Nixon knows that McCord burgled O'Brien's office at Watergate." If we take Dean to be agent 1, Nixon to be agent 2, and p to the statement "McCord burgled O'Brien's office at Watergate," then this sentence can be captured as:

$$\neg K_1\neg(K_2K_1K_2p) \wedge \neg K_1\neg(\neg K_2K_1K_2p).$$

When reasoning about the knowledge of a group, it becomes useful to reason not just about an individual agent's state of knowledge, but also about the knowledge of the group. For example, we might want to make statements such as "everyone in group G knows φ." It turns out to be useful to be able to make even more complicated statements such as "everyone in G knows that everyone in G knows φ," and "φ is common knowledge among the agents in G," where *common knowledge* is, informally, the infinite conjunction of the statements "everyone knows, and everyone knows that everyone knows, and everyone knows that everyone knows that everyone knows, ..."

Common knowledge was first studied by David Lewis, in the context of conventions [10]. Lewis points out that in order for something to be a convention, it must be common knowledge among the members of the group.

Common knowledge also rises in discourse understanding. If Ann asks Bob "Have you ever seen the movie playing at the Roxy tonight?," then in order for this question to be interpreted appropriately, not only must Ann and Bob know what movie is playing tonight, but Ann must know that Ann knows that Bob knows, etc. (This is discussed in great detail by Clark and Marshall [9], although see Perreault and Cohen [11] for a slightly dissenting view).

Interest in common knowledge in the economics community was inspired by Aumann's seminal result [12]. Aumann showed that if two people have the same prior probability for an event and their posterior probability for the event (i.e., the probability they place on the event after getting some possibly different pieces of information) are common knowledge, then these posterior probabilities must be equal. This result says that people with the same prior probabilities *cannot agree to disagree*. Since then, common knowledge has received a great deal of attention in the economics literature, with issues being examined such as the number of rounds of communication information required before the posteriors for an event become knowledge [13, 14] and whether it is reasonable for rationality to be common knowledge [see 15 for a survey].

In order to express these notions, we augment the language with modal operators E_G ("everyone in the group G knows") and C_G ("it is common knowledge among the agents in G"), for every nonempty subset G of $\{1, \ldots, n\}$. Thus, we can make statements such as $E_G p \land \neg C_G p$: everyone in G knows p, but p is not common knowledge.

Kripke structures [16] provide a useful formal tool for giving semantics to this language. A Kripke structure M is a tuple $(S, \pi, \mathcal{K}_1, \ldots, \mathcal{K}_n)$, where S is a set of *states* or *possible worlds*, π associates with each state in S a truth assignment to the primitive propositions (i.e., $\pi(s)(p) \in \{\mathbf{true}, \mathbf{false}\}$ for each state $s \in S$ and each primitive proposition p), and $\mathcal{K}_i$ is an *equivalence relation* on S (recall that an equivalence relation is a binary relation which is reflexive, symmetric, and transitive). $\mathcal{K}_i$ is agent i's *possibility relation*. Intuitively, $(s, t) \in \mathcal{K}_i$ if agent i cannot ditinguish state s from state s from t (so that if s is the actual state of the world, agent i would consider t a possible state of the world). We take $\mathcal{K}_i$ to be an equivalence relation, since it corresponds to the situation where, in state s; agent i considers t possible if it has the same information in both s and t. This type of situation arises frequently in distributed systems and economics applications. However, it is also possible to consider possibility relations with other properties (e.g., reflexive and transitive, but not symmetric); most of the discussion goes through with very few changes if we change the nature of the possibility relation.

We now define a relation $\models$, where $(M, s) \models \varphi$ is read "φ is true, or *satisfied*, in state s of structure M."

$(M, s) \models p$ for a primitive proposition p if $\pi(s)(p) = \mathbf{true}$

$(M, s) \models \neg\varphi$ if $(M, s) \not\models \varphi$

$(M, s) \models \varphi \land \psi$ if $(M, s) \models \varphi$ and $(M, s) \models \psi$

$(M, s) \models K_i\varphi$ if $(M, t) \models \varphi$ for all t such that $(s, t) \in \mathcal{K}_i$

$(M, s) \models E_G\varphi$ if $(M, s) \models K_i\varphi$ for all $i \in G$

$(M, s) \models C_G\varphi$ if $(M, s) \models E_G^k\varphi$ for $k = 1, 2, \ldots$, where $E_G^1\varphi =_{\text{def}} E_G\varphi$ and $E_G^{k+1}\varphi =_{\text{def}} E_G E_G^k\varphi$.

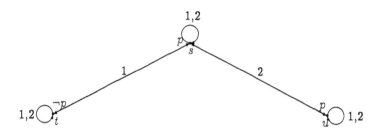

FIGURE 1.   A simple Kripke structure.

The first clause shows how we use the π to define the semantics of the primitive propositions. The next two clauses, which define the semantics of $\neg$ and $\wedge$, are the standard clauses
from propositional logic. The fourth class is designed to capture the intuition that agent i
knows φ exactly if φ is true in all the worlds that i thinks are possible. The fifth clause defines the semantics of $E_G\varphi$ in the most obvious way: $E_G\varphi$ holds if each agent G knows φ,
i.e., if $K_i\varphi$ holds for all $i \in G$. Finally, the last clause captures the intuitive definition of
common knowledge discussed above.

These ideas are perhaps best illustrated by an example. One of the advantages of a
Kripke structure is that it can be viewed as a labeled graph, that is, a set of labeled nodes
connected by directed, labeled edges. The nodes are the states of S; each node is labeled by
the primitive propositions true and false there, and there is an edge from s to t labeled i
exactly if $(s, t) \in \mathcal{K}_i$. For example, suppose $\Phi = \{p\}$ and $n = 2$, so that our language only has
one primitive proposition p and there are only two agents. Further suppose that $M = (S, \pi,$
$\mathcal{K}_1, \mathcal{K}_2)$, where $S = \{s, t, u\}$, p is true at states s and u, but false at t (so that $\pi(s)(p) = \pi(u)(p)$
$=$ **true** and $\pi(t)(p) = $ **false**), agent 1 cannot tell s and t apart (so that $\mathcal{K}_1 = \{(s, s), (s, t), (t, s),$
$(t, t), (u, u)\}$), and agent 2 cannot tell s and u apart (so that $\mathcal{K}_2 = \{(s, s), (s, u), (t, t), (u, s), (u,$
$u)\}$). This situation can be captured by the graph in Figure 1.

If we view p as standing for "it is sunny in San Francisco," then in state s it is sunny in
San Francisco but agent 1 doesn't know it (since he considers both s and t possible). On the
other hand, agent 2 does know that it is sunny in state s, since both worlds that agent 2 considers possible at s (namely, s and u), the formula p is true. Agent 2 also knows the true
situation at state t, namely, that it is not sunny. It follows that in state s agent 1 knows that
agent 2 knows whether or not it is sunny in San Francisco (since in both worlds agent 1
considers possible in state s, agent 2 knows what the weather in San Francisco is). Thus,
although agent 1 does not know the true situation at s, he does know that agent 2 knows the
true situation. (And so, assuming that agent 2 were reliable, agent 1 knows that he could find
out the true situation by asking agent 2.) By way of contrast, although in state s agent 2
knows that it is sunny in San Francisco, he doesn't know that agent 1 doesn't know this fact.
(In one world that agent 2 considers possible, namely u, agent 1 does know that it is sunny,
while in another world agent 2 considers possible, s, agent 1 does not know this fact.) All of
this relatively complicated English discussion can be summarized in one mathematical
statement:

$$(M, s) \models p \wedge \neg K_1 p \wedge K_2 p \wedge K_1(K_2 p \vee K_2 \neg p) \wedge K_2 \neg K_1 p.$$

What about common knowledge? It is not hard to check that the formula $\psi = K_2 p \vee K_2 \neg p$ is true at all three states s, t, and u in M. Taking $G = \{1, 2\}$, an easy induction on k now shows that in fact $E_G^k \psi$ is true at all three states, for all k. Thus, $(M, s) \models C_G \psi$.

Note that in both s and u, the primitive proposition p (the only primitive proposition in our language) gets the same truth value. One might think, therefore, that s and u are the same, and that perhaps one of them can be eliminated. This is not true! A state is not completely characterized by the truth values that the primitive propositions get there. The possibility relation is also crucial. For example, in world s, agent 1 considers t possible, while u he doesn't. As a consequence, agent 1 doesn't know p in s, while in u he does.

How reasonable is this notion of knowledge? What are its properties? One way of investigating this issue is to try to find a complete characterization of the *valid* formulas, that is, those formulas that are true in every state in every structure.

If we ignore the operators E_G and C_G for the moment, the valid formulas in the language with only K_i can be completely characterized by the following *sound* and *complete* axiom system, due to Hintikka [2]; i.e., all the axioms are valid and every valid formula can be proved from these axioms.

A1. All instances of propositional tautologies.
A2. $K_i \varphi \wedge K_i(\varphi \Rightarrow \psi) \Rightarrow K_i \psi$
A3. $K_i \varphi \Rightarrow \varphi$
A4. $K_i \varphi \Rightarrow K_i K_i \varphi$
A5. $\neg K_i \varphi \Rightarrow K_i \neg K_i \varphi$
R1. From φ and $\varphi \Rightarrow \psi$ infer ψ (modus ponens)
R2. R2. From φ infer $K_i \varphi$

A1 and R1, of course, are holdovers from propositional logic. A2 says that an agent's knowledge is closed under implication. A3 says that an agent only knows things that are true. This is the axiom that is usually taken to distinguish *knowledge* from *belief*. You cannot know a fact that is false, although you may believe it. A4 and A5 are axioms of introspection. Intuitively, they say that an agent is introspective: he can look at his knowledge base and will know what he knows and doesn't know. These are numerous papers in the philosophical literature discussing the appropriateness of these axioms [see *4* for an overview]. Philosophers have tended to reject both of the introspection axioms for various reasons.

The validity of A3, A4, and A5 is due to the fact that we have taken the $\mathcal{K}_i$s to be equivalence relations. In a precise sense, A3 follows from the fact that $\mathcal{K}_i$ is reflexive, A4 from the fact that it is transitive, and A5 from the fact that it is symmetric and transitive. By modifying the properties of the $\mathcal{K}_i$ relations, we can get notions of knowledge that satisfy different axioms. For example, by taking $\mathcal{K}_i$ to be reflexive and transitive, but not necessarily symmetric, we retain A3 and A4, but lose A5; similar modifications give us a notion that corresponds to belief, and does not satisfy A3. [See *17* for a survey of these issues, as well as a review of the standard techniques of modal logic which give completeness proofs in all these cases.)]

However, the possible-world approach seems to commit us to A2 and R2. This suggests a view of our agents as "ideal knowers," ones that know all valid formulas as well as all logical consequences of their knowledge. This certainly doesn't seem to be a realistic model for human agents (although it might perhaps be acceptable as a first approximation). Nor does it seem to even be an adequate model for a knowledge base which is bounded in terms of the computation time and space in memory that it can use. We discuss some approaches to this problem of *logical omniscience* below.

Once we include the operators E_G and C_G in the language, we get further properties. These are completely characterized by the following additional axioms:

C1. $E_G\varphi \leftrightarrow \wedge_{i \in G} K_i\varphi$
C2. $C_G\varphi \leftrightarrow E_G(\varphi \wedge C_G\varphi)$ (fixed point axiom)
RC1. From $\varphi \Rightarrow E_G(\varphi \wedge \psi)$ infer $\varphi \Rightarrow C_G\psi$ (induction rule)

The fixed point axiom says that common knowledge of φ holds exactly when the group G is in a particular situation where everyone in G knows that φ holds and that common knowledge of φ holds. It turns out that this is the key property of common knowledge that makes it a prerequisite for agreement and coordination. The induction rules gives us a technique to verify that common knowledge holds in a certain situation. The reason for its name is that once we know that $\varphi \Rightarrow E_G(\varphi \wedge \psi)$ is valid, then we can show by induction on k that $\varphi \Rightarrow E_G^k(\varphi \wedge \psi)$ is valid for all k, from which we can conclude that $\varphi \Rightarrow C_G\psi$ is valid.

How hard is it to tell if a given formula defines a valid property of knowledge? We can give an answer in terms of complexity theory. [See *18* for an introduction to complexity-theoretic notions mentioned below such as co-NP completeness.] It can be shown that if a formula ψ is valid if it is true at every state in every structure with at most 2^n states, where n is the length of ψ viewed as a string of symbols. From this result, it follows that the validity is decidable: there is an algorithm that, given a formula φ, can tell whether or not it is valid. However, deciding validity is not easy. If we consider systems with just one agent, then it is co-NP-complete, just as it is for propositional logic [*19*]. But once we consider systems with two or more agents, any algorithm that decides validity requires space polynomial in the size of the input formula, even if we do not include common knowledge in the language. Once we include common knowledge, the complexity goes up to exponential time [*17*]. We return to the implication of these complexity results in a later section.

A CONCRETE INTERPRETATION: DISTRIBUTED SYSTEMS

While it is not clear whether or not the model presented above is appropriate for human reasoning, it can capture quite well much of the reasoning that goes on in analyzing distributed systems. Indeed, the distributed systems point of view allows us to give quite a concrete interpretation to states in a Kripke structure.

A distributed system consists of a collection of processes, say $1, \ldots, n$, connected by a communication network. The processes communicate with each other over the links in the network. Each process is a state machine, which at all times is in some state. This state is a function of its initial state, the messages it has received, and possibly some internal events (such as the ticking of a clock). We can then view the whole system as being some *global state*, which is a tuple consisting of each process' local state, together with the state of the *environment*, where the environment consists of everything that is relevant to the system that is not contained in the state of the processes. Thus, if we are studying a message-passing system, consisting of communicating agents, the state of the communication line (whether it is up or down, or whether there are any messages in transit on the line) may be part of the environment state. Similarly, if we consider a system of sensors observing some terrain, the environment state may include features of the terrain not contained in the state of any of the sensors.

A system is not a static entity. To capture its dynamic aspects, we define a *run* to be a function from time to global states. Intuitively, a run is a complete description of what happens over time in one possible execution of the system. A *point* is a pair (r, m) consisting of a run r and a time m. At a point (r, m), the system is in some global state $r(m)$. We define a system $\mathcal{R}$ to consist of a set of runs; intuitively, these runs describe all the possible executions of the system. For example, in a poker game, the runs could describe all the possible deals and betting sequences.

We can associate a Kripke structure with a distributed system by taking the states in the structure to be all the points in the system. The $\mathcal{K}_i$ relations are defined by $((r, m), (r', m')) \in \mathcal{K}_i$ if process i has the same local state in global states $r(m)$ and $r'(m')$. Note that this definition makes $\mathcal{K}_i$ an equivalence relation. The primitive propositions in this setting would be statements like "the value of process i's local variable x is 0" or "process j's current state is σ."

This particular way of capturing knowledge in distributed systems is taken from Halpern and Fagin [20]. Slight variants of it have been used in most of the papers that attempt to define formal models for knowledge in distributed systems [21–24]. Interestingly, essentially the identical notion of knowledge was developed independently by Rosenschein and his co-workers [cf. 25, 26] and used for describing and analyzing situated automata in AI applications.

Note that in this model, knowledge is an "external" notion. We don't imagine a process scratching its head wondering whether or not it knows a certain fact φ. Rather, a programmer reasoning about a particular protocol would say, from the outside, that the process knows φ because in all global states consistent with its current state (intuitively, all the global states that the process could be in, for all it knows) φ is true. This notion of knowledge is information based, and does *not* take into account, for example, the difficulty involved in computing knowledge. Nor could a process necessarily answer questions based on its knowledge, with respect to this definition of knowledge. So on what basis can we even view this as knowledge?

There are two reasonable answers to this question. The first is that it corresponds to one common usage of the word. When trying to prove properties such as lower bounds on the number of rounds required to complete a given protocol, the kinds of arguments that one often hears have the form "We can't stop after only three rounds, because process 1 might not know that process 2 knows that process 3 is faulty." Now this informal use of the word "Know" is exactly captured by the definition above. Let φ say that process 2 knows that process 3 is faulty. Then process 1 doesn't know φ exactly if there is a global state of the system that process 1 cannot distinguish from the actual state where φ does not hold; i.e., where process 2 doesn't know that process 3 is faulty.

The second answer is that this notion gives us a useful formalization of our intuitions, one that gives us important insights into the design and verification of distributed protocols. A good illustration of this is the *coordinated attack problem*, from the distributed systems folklore [27]. The following presentation is taken from Ref. *23*.

Two divisions of an army are camped on two hilltops overlooking a common valley. In the valley awaits the enemy. It is clear that if both divisions attack the enemy simultaneously they will win the battle, whereas if only one division attacks it will be defeated. The generals do not initially have plans for launching an attack on the enemy, and the commanding general of the first division wishes to coordinate a simultaneous attack (at some time the next day). Neither general will decide to attack unless he is sure that the other will attack with him. The generals can only communicate by means of a messenger. Normally, it takes the messenger one hour to get from one encampment to the other. However, it is possible that he will get lost in the dark or, worse yet, be captured by the enemy. Fortunately, on this particular night, everything goes smoothly. How long will it take them to coordinate an attack?

Suppose the messenger sent by General A makes it to General B with a message saying "Let's attack at dawn." Will General B attack? Of course not, since General A does not know he got the message, and thus may not attack. So General B sends the messenger back with an acknowledgment. Suppose the messenger makes it. Will General A attack? No, because now General B does not know that General A got the message, so General B thinks General A sends the messenger back with an acknowledgment. But of course, this is not enough either.

In terms of knowledge, each time the messenger makes a transit, the *depth* of the generals' knowledge increases by one. Suppose we let the primitive proposition m stand for "A message saying 'Attack at dawn' was sent by General A." When General B gets the message, $K_B m$ holds. When A gets B's acknowledgment, $K_A K_B m$ holds. The next acknowledgment brings us to $K_B K_A K_B m$. Although more acknowledgments keep increasing the depth of knowledge, it is not hard to show that by following this protocol, the generals never attain common knowledge that the attack is to be held at dawn.

In that case, what about using a different protocol? This does not help either. As long as there is a possibility that the messenger may get captured or lost, then common knowledge is not attained, even if the messenger in fact does not deliver his messages. It would take us too far afield here to completely formalize these results [see *23* for details], but we can give a rough description. We say a *system* R *displays unbounded message delays* if, roughly speaking, whenever there is a run $r \in R$ such that process i receives a message at time m in r, then for all $m' > m$, there is another run r' that is identical to r up to time m except that process i receives no messages at time m, and no process receives a message between times m and m'.

Theorem 3.1 [23]

In any run of a system that displays unbounded message delays, it can never be common knowledge that a message has been delivered.

This says that no matter how many messages arrive, we cannot attain common knowledge of message delivery. But what does this have to do with coordinated attack? The fact that the generals have no initial plans for attack means that in the absence of message delivery, they will not attack. Since it can never become common knowledge that a message has been delivered, and message delivery is a perquisite for attack, it is not hard to show that it can never become common knowledge among the generals that they are attacking. More precisely, let *attack* be a primitive proposition that is true precisely at points where both generals attack.

Corollary 3.2

In any run of a system that displays unbounded message delays, it can never be common knowledge among the generals that they are attacking; i.e., if G consists of the two generals, then C_G (attack) never holds.

We still do not seem to have dealt with our original problem. What is the connection between common knowledge of an attack and coordinated attack? As the following theorem shows, it is quite deep. Common knowledge is a prerequisite for coordination:

Theorem 3.3 [23]

In any system for coordinated attack, when the generals attack, it is common knowledge that among the generals that they are attacking. Thus, if R is a system consisting of a set of runs of a protocol for coordinated attack, and G consists of the two generals, then at every point (r, m) of R, we have

$$(R, r, m) \models attack \Rightarrow C_G \ (attack).$$

Putting together Corollary 3.2 and Theorem 3.3, we get

Corollary 3.4

In any system for coordinated attack that displays unbounded message delays, the generals never attack.

This result shows not only that coordinated attack is impossible (a fact that was well known) [28], but shows *why* it is impossible. The problem is due to an unattainability of common knowledge in certain types of systems.

In fact, as results of Halpern and Moses [23] show, common knowledge is unattainable in a much wider variety of circumstances. Roughly speaking, common knowledge is not attainable whenever there is any uncertainty whatsoever about message delivery time. Common knowledge can be attained in "idealized" systems where we assume, for example, that events can be guaranteed to take place simultaneously. However, in the more common less-than-ideal systems, common knowledge is not attainable. Given that we also showed that common knowledge is a prerequisite for agreement, we seem to have something of a paradox here. After all, we often do reach agreement (or seem to!) Do we in fact get common knowledge, despite the results that say we cannot?

Two solutions to the paradox are suggested by Halpern and Moses [23]. The first involves a number of variants of common knowledge that are attainable under reasonable assumptions, and may suffice in practice. For example, we can consider a temporal variant called *ε-common knowledge*, which essentially says that "within ε time units everyone knows that within ε time units everyone knows that . . . ." Just as common knowledge corresponds to simultaneous coordination, ε common knowledge corresponds to coordinating to within ε time units. Further discussion of variants of common knowledge can be found elsewhere [22, 23, 29–33a,b].

This approach still does not explain the pervasive feeling that we do (occasionally) attain common knowledge. The second approach attempts to deal with this issue. It is based on the observation that, although common knowledge may not be attainable, an agent may reach a state that it cannot distinguish from common knowledge *from within the system*. Thus, an agent can essentially act as if he has common knowledge. [See *23, 34* for more details of this approach.]

The analysis of the coordinated attack problem shows the power of a knowledge-based approach to understanding distributed protocols. Numerous other papers have carried out knowledge-based analyses of protocols [e.g., *21, 29–33*a, b, *35–40*]; an overview of the earlier work can be found in Ref. *41*. These papers suggest that the knowledge-based approach can indeed give useful insights. In cases where simultaneous agreement is required, as in some variants of the well-studied *Byzantine agreement problem* [42, 43], common knowledge again turns out to play a key role [see 29, 31]. For other protocols, common knowledge is not required; depth two knowledge (*A* knows that *B* knows) or depth three knowledge (*A* knows that *B* knows that *A* knows) may suffice.

THE PROBLEM OF LOGICAL OMNISCIENCE

The model of knowledge described earlier gives rise to a notion of knowledge that seems to require that agents possess a great deal of reasoning power, since they know all the consequences of their knowledge and, in particular, they know all tautologies. Thus, the agents can be described as *logically omniscient*. While this notion of knowledge has been shown to be useful in a number of applications, it clearly is not always appropriate, particularly when we want to represent the knowledge of a resource-bounded agent. What is an appropriate notion of knowledge in this case? That may depend in part on the context and the application. In this section we consider a number of approaches to dealing with what has been called the logical omniscience problem.

One approach that has frequently been suggested is the syntactic approach: what an agent knows is simply represented by a set of formulas [44, 45]. Of course, this set need not be constrained to be closed under logical consequence or to contain all instances of a given axiom scheme. While this approach does allow us to define a notion of knowledge that does not suffer from the logical omniscience problem, by using it, we miss out on many of the merits of a knowledge-based analysis. If knowledge is represented by an arbitrary set of formulas, we have no structure or principles to guide us in our analysis. A somewhat more sophisticated approach is taken by Konolige [46], who considers starting with a set of base facts, and then closing off under a (possibly incomplete) set of deduction rules. But even here we lose the benefits of a good underlying semantics.

A semantic analogue to the syntactic approach can be obtained by using *Montague-Scott structures* [47]. The idea here is that a formula corresponds to a set of possible worlds (intuitively, the set of worlds where it is true). Rather than representing what an agent knows by a set of formulas (syntactic objects), we represent what an agent knows by a set of sets of possible worlds. Since each set of possible worlds corresponds to a formula, the two approaches are similar in spirit. Formally, we take a Montague-Scott structure to be tuple $M = (S, \pi, C_1, \ldots, C_n)$, where S is a set of possible worlds and π defines a truth assignment at each possible world, just as in the case of a Kripke structure, while $C_i(s)$ is a set of subsets of S for each $s \in S$. We can now define $\models$ for all formulas. All clauses are the same as for Kripke structures, except in the case of formulas of the form $K_i\varphi$. In this case we have

$$(M, s) \models K_i\varphi \text{ iff } \{t \mid (M, t) \models \varphi\} \in C_i(s).$$

Thus, agent i knows φ if the set of possible worlds where φ is true is one of the sets of worlds that he considers possible.

The Montague-Scott approach has a great deal of power; by putting appropriate conditions on the sets C_i we can capture many interesting properties of knowledge, without committing to others. For example, agent i's knowledge is closed under implication [i.e., $(K_i\varphi \wedge K_i(\varphi \Rightarrow \psi)) = K_i\varphi$ is valid] if $C_i(s)$ is closed under supersets for each $s \in S$ (i.e., $T \in C_i(s)$ and $T \subseteq T'$ implies $T' \in C_i(s)$). Similarly, agent i knows all tautologies if $S \in C_i(s)$ for all $s \in S$. (See 48 for more details on how the fine-tuning that is possible with the Montague-Scott approach.) Since we do not require that $C_i(s)$ be closed under supersets nor that it contain S, the Montague-Scott approach does not suffer from the major problems of logical omniscience. However, because it is a *semantic* approach, it cannot avoid having the following property: if φ and ψ are equivalent, then so are $K_i\varphi$ and $K_i\psi$. An agent cannot distinguish logically equivalent formulas (even if they have different syntactic structure). Thus, we have the following inference rule, which is sound for Montague-Scott structures:

$$\text{From } \varphi \equiv \psi \text{ infer } K_i\varphi \equiv K_i\psi.$$

Of course, whether this a problem depends on the particular application one has in mind.

While the Montague-Scott and the syntactic approach have a great deal of expressive power, one gains very little intuition about knowledge from these approaches. In these approaches knowledge is a primitive construct (much like the primitive propositions in a Kripke structure). Arguably, these approaches give us ways of *representing* knowledge, rather than *modeling* knowledge. We now investigate a few approaches that retain the flavor of the possible-world approach, yet still attempt to mitigate the logical omniscience problem.

One approach is to base an epistemic logic on a nonstandard logic, rather than on classical logic. There are a number of well-known nonstandard logics, including *intuitionistic logic* [49], *relevance logic* [50], and the four-valued logic of Belnap [51, 52] and Dunn [53]. Typically, these logics attempt to reformulate the notion of implication, to avoid some of the problems perceived with the notion of material implication. For example, in standard logic, from a contradiction one can deduce anything; the formula $(p \land \neg p) \Rightarrow q$ is valid. However, consider a knowledge base into which users enter data from time to time. As Belnap points out [52], it is almost certainly the case that in a large knowledge base, there will be some inconsistencies. One can imagine that at some point a user entered the fact that Bob's salary is $50,000, while at another point, perhaps a different user entered the fact that Bob's salary is $60,000.

Fagin et al. [54] define a logic of knowledge that is based on a nonstandard propositional logic called *NPL*, which is somewhat akin to relevance logic, and where, among other things, a formula such as $(p \land \neg p) \Rightarrow q$ is no longer valid. The possible worlds are now models of NPL. Agents are still logically omniscient, but now they only know NPL tautologies, rather than classical tautologies. This has some advantages. In particular, it can be shown that questions of the form "Does $K_i\varphi$ logically imply $K_i\psi$?," where φ and ψ are propositional formulas in conjunctive normal form, can be decided in polynomial time (which is not the case for standard logics of knowledge). This is an important subclass of formulas. If we view φ as representing the contents of a knowledge base and ψ as representing a query to the database, then it essentially amounts to asking whether a knowledge base that knows φ also knows ψ.* Thus, under this interpretation of knowledge, queries to a knowledge base of the form "Do you know φ?" can be decided quite efficiently (assuming φ is in conjunctive normal form).

Yet another approach has been called the *impossible-world approach*. The idea here is that the possible worlds, where all the customary rules of classical logic hold, are augmented by "impossible" worlds, where they do not [55a,b–58]. For example, in an impossible world, it may be the case that $p \land \neg p$ holds, while this cannot be the case in a possible

---

*We might also consider asking whether φ logically implies ψ rather than whether $K_i\varphi$ logically implies $K_i\psi$. It turns out that these two questions are equivalent in the context of NPL [54].

world. It is still the case that an agent knows φ if φ is true in all the worlds that he considers possible, but now an agent may consider impossible worlds possible. Thus, an agent may not know all tautologies of classical logic, since in some of the worlds he considers possible (i.e., the impossible worlds), these tautologies may not hold.

Although there are impossible worlds in a structure, when we consider what are the *valid* formulas in the impossible-world approach, we only consider the standard possible worlds. The intuition here is that although the agent may be confused and consider impossible worlds possible, we, the logicians looking at the situation from the outside, know better.

There are many variants of the impossible-world approach, depending on how one constructs the impossible worlds. One variant is considered by Levesque [59]. In Levesque's impossible worlds, a primitive proposition may be either true, false, both, or neither. This also makes Levesque's approach closely related to relevance logic and to the logic NPL discussed above. Indeed, it can be shown that Levesque's structures are essentially equivalent to NPL structures. The only significant difference between Levesque's approach and that of Fagin *et al.* [59] is that Levesque considers only possible worlds–those that obey the laws of classical logic–when it comes to validity, whereas Fagin et al. consider all worlds. Just as in the context of NPL, checking whether $K_i\varphi$ logically implies $K_i\psi$ for propositional formulas φ and ψ in conjunctive form can be decided in polynomial time.*

Levesque [59] restricts attention to *depth one* formulas, where there are no nested occurrences of Ks. He also restricts to the case of a single agent. Lakemeyer [60] has extended Levesque's approach to more deeply nested formulas; his approach can also be extended to deal with multiple agents. Patel-Schneider [61] and Lakemeyer [62] have also considered extensions to the first-order case which attempt to preserve decidability for a reasonable fragment of the logic.

Yet another approach to dealing with logical omniscience is to have truth in all possible worlds be a necessary but not sufficient condition for knowledge. Fagin and Halpern take this approach [63]. Their *logic of general awareness* is essentially a mixture of syntax and semantics. It starts with a standard Kripke structure, and adds to each state a set of formulas that the agent is "aware" of at that state. Now an agent (explicitly) knows a formula φ at state s exactly if j is true in all worlds the agent considers possible at s *and* φ is one of the formulas the agent is aware of at s. Thus, an agent may not know a tautology, even if it is true at all the worlds that he considers possible, simply because he is not aware of it. Similarly, an agent who knows φ and $\varphi \Rightarrow \psi$ may not know ψ because he is not aware of ψ.

There are a number of different interpretations we can give the notion of awareness. For example, we could say that an agent is aware of a formula if he is aware of all the concepts involved in that formula. Perhaps the most interesting interpretation is a computational one, where an agent is aware of a formula if he can figure out whether the formula is true (perhaps using some specific algorithm) within a prespecified time bound. Under this interpretation, the awareness set at state s would consist of those formulas whose truth the agent can figure out given the information it has acquired at state s.

This interpretation has been investigated in the context of the distributed systems model discussed in the previous section in work of Moses [64]. Moses presents a logic of resource-bounded knowledge, where he tries to make sense out of notions such as "an agent can compute φ in polynomial time." This does not mean that φ can be proved (in some appropriate axiom system) in polynomial time, but rather that the truth of φ at a particular

---

*Indeed, this result was first proved in Ref. *59* and then adapted to NPL in Ref. *54*.

state in a structure can be computed in polynomial time. Roughly speaking, this is true if there exists an algorithm A that gets i's local state as input, and computes in polynomial time whether φ is implied by the local state. The algorithm A must give the correct answer at all points in the system.

Typically, in AI applications, a situation has been characterized by a number of axioms and the question has been what else the agent knows, given that it knows these axioms. Since it is clear that agents do not always know the logical consequences of their knowledge, the standard approach has been to limit the deductive capabilities of agents by letting them carry out reasoning in a particular axiom system for a limited number of steps [*cf.*, the work of Konolige mentioned above; *45*]. The work of Moses is based on a quite different model-theoretic paradigm. Rather than describing a situation by a collection of axioms, the situation is described by a structure. (For example, the structure might be the system corresponding to a particular protocol.) Then, rather than counting the number of steps required to prove a fact, we consider the difficulty of checking that the fact is (known to be) true in the given structure. This turns the problem into an instance of *model checking*: computing whether a formula (in particular, one of the form $K_i\varphi$) is true at a given state in a structure. Techniques similar to those used in temporal logic [*65*] can be used to show that the complexity of model checking is polynomial in the size of the formula and the structure.

If an agent a considers only three worlds possible, it is quite easy for a to check, for any fact φ, whether or not he knows φ, simply by checking whether φ is true at the three worlds he considers possible. In particular, this is true if φ is a tautology. Notice that while it is easy for an agent to check that he knows any given tautology φ, he will not know that φ is a tautology. That would require checking other structures besides the one he finds himself in.

Of course, model checking can still be hard if there are a large number of possible worlds that need to be checked. Here we can imagine that, in practice, an agent carries out heuristics (such as checking the worlds that are most likely, in some sense). There is also the issue of how an agent goes about constructing the set of possible runs, this is typically relatively straightforward: the protocol defines the possible worlds, as we outlined earlier. In other contexts, the situation is not always so clear. In some cases, the best we can do is take the set of all worlds consistent with a certain collection of axioms. We briefly return to this issue in the next section. See Ref. 66 for further discussion of the model-checking paradigm in the context of epistemic logics.

KNOWLEDGE, COMMUNICATION, AND ACTION

Implicit in much of the previous discussion has been the strong relationship between knowledge, communication, and action. Indeed, much of the motivation for studying knowledge by researchers in all areas has been that of understanding the knowledge required to perform certain actions, and how that knowledge can be acquired through communication. This is a vast area; we briefly review some recent trends here.

Early work of McCarthy and Hayes [*67*] argued that a planning program needs to explicitly reason about its ability to perform an action. Moore [*68*] took this one step further by emphasizing the crucial relationship between knowledge and action. Knowledge is necessary to perform actions, and new knowledge is gained as a result of performing actions. Moore went on to construct a logic with possible-world semantics that allow explicit reasoning about knowledge and action, and then considered the problem of automatically generating deductions within the logic. This work has been extended by Morgenstern [*69*]; she views "know" as a syntactic predicate on formulas rather than a modal operator.

Another issue that has received a great deal of attention recently is the relationship between knowledge and communication. Levesque considered this from the point of view of a knowledge base that could interact with its domain via *TELL* and *ASK* operations [70]. He showed, somewhat surprisingly, that the result of *TELL*ing a knowledge base an arbitrary sentence in a first-order logic knowledge is always equivalent to the result of *TELL*ing it a purely first-order sentence (i.e., one without any occurrences of K). It is worth remarking here that it is crucial to Levesque's result that there is only one knowledge base (i.e., one agent) in the picture.

Characterizing the states of knowledge that result after communication is also surprisingly subtle. One might think, for example, that after telling someone a fact p he will know p (at least, if it is common knowledge that the teller is honest). But this is not true. For example, consider the sentence "p is true but you don't know it." When told to agent i, this would be represented as $p \wedge \neg K_ip$. Now this sentence might be perfectly true when it is said. But after i is told this fact, it is not the case that $K_i(p \wedge \neg K_ip)$ holds. In fact, this latter formula is provably inconsistent! It is the case, though, that i knows that $p \wedge \neg K_ip$ was true before, although it is no longer true now.

Even if we do not allow formulas that refer to knowledge, there are subtleties in characterizing the knowledge of an agent. Consider the following example from Fagin et al. [71]. Suppose that Alice has been told only one fact: the primitive proposition p. Intuitively, all she knows is p. Since we are assuming ideal agents, Alice also knows all the logical consequences of p. But is this all she knows? Suppose q is another primitive proposition. Surely Alice doesn't know q, i.e., $\neg K_Aq$ holds. But we assume Alice can do perfect introspection, so that she knows about her lack of knowledge of q. Thus $K_A \neg K_Aq$ holds. But this means if "all Alice knows is p," then she also knows $\neg K_Aq$, which is surely not a logical consequence of p! The situation can get even more complicated if we let Bob into the picture. For then Alice knows that Bob does not know that Alice knows q. (How can he, since in fact she doesn't know q, and Bob does not know false facts.) And knowing that Bob can also do perfect introspection, Alice knows that Bob knows this fact; i.e., $K_AK_B \neg K_BK_Aq$ holds! Thus, despite her limited knowledge, Alice knows a nontrivial fact about Bob's knowledge [see 71–76 for further discussion of these points]. Part of the difficulty here is due to *negative introspection*; that is, the fact that one has knowledge about one's own lack of knowledge. If we remove this feature from our model (i.e., discard axiom A5), things become much easier [cf., 77].

Part of the interest in understanding the issue above—roughly speaking, the problem of describing the set of worlds an agent a considers possible if "all a knows is φ"—is that it is closely related to the problem discussed earlier of how to construct the set of possible worlds. Consider an agent a in a system where the only way of acquiring information is by means of communication, and φ describes the conjunction of the facts that a has been told. In that case, then we can say that a is in one of the equivalence class of states in the essentially unique structure where "all agent a knows is φ."

KNOWLEDGE AND PROBABILITY

In many of the application areas for reasoning about knowledge, it is important to be able to reason about the probability of certain events as well as the knowledge of agents. This arises in distributed systems, since we want to analyze randomized or probabilistic programs. In game theory and economics, reseachers typically want to assume that agents have priors on certain events and make their decisions accordingly. Indeed, although researchers in economics and game theory did not use a logical language with operators for probability, probability has explicitly appeared in their framework all along, going back to the papers of Aumann [*12*] and Mertens and Zamir [*78*].

It seems straightforward to add probability into the framework that we have developed. As far as syntax goes, we can add statements such as $Pr_i(\varphi) = 1/2$ (according to agent i, the probability that φ holds is 1/2), and then close off under knowledge operators, to allow formulas such as $K_i K_j(Pr_i(\varphi) = 1/2)$ [this syntax is taken from *30*]. In order to be able to decide if a formula such as $Pr_i(\varphi) = 1/2$ is true at a state s, the obvious approach would be to put a probability on the set of worlds that agent i considers possible at s (where the exact probability used would depend on agent i's prior, or some information contained in the problem statement).

The difficulty comes in deciding what probability space agent i should use. This seems like it should be straightforward. A structure already tells us which worlds agent i considers possible at state s. All that remains is to make this uncertainty a little more quantitative (e.g., by assigning a probability to each of the worlds that agent i considers possible in such a way that the probabilities add up to 1.) To see that the situation is not quite so straightforward, consider the following example, taken from Ref. *30*.

Suppose we have two agents. Agent 2 has an input bit, either 0 or 1. He then tosses a fair coin, and performs an action a if the coin toss agrees with the input bit, i.e., if the coin toss lands heads and the input bit is 1, or if the coin lands tails and the input bit is 0. We assume that agent 1 never learns agent 2's input bit or the outcome of his coin toss. An easy argument shows that according to agent 2, who knows the input bit, the probability (before he tosses the coin) of performing action a is 1/2. There is also a reasonable argument to show that, even according to agent 1 (who does not know the input bit), the probability that the action will be performed is 1/2. Clearly, from agent 1's viewpoint, if agent 2's input bit is 0, then the probability that agent 2 performs action a is 1/2 (since the probability of the coin landing heads is 1/2); similarly; if agents 2's input bit is 1, then the probability of agent 2 performing action a is 1/2. Thus, no matter what agent 2's input bit, the probability according to agent 1 that agent 1 knows that the *a priori* probability of agent 2 will perform action a is 1/2. It seems reasonable to conclude that performing action a is 1/2. Note that we do not need to assume a probability distribution on the input bit for this argument to hold. Indeed, it holds independent of the probability distribution, and even if there is no probability distribution on the input bit.

Now suppose we want to capture this argument in our formal system. From agent 1's point of view, there are four possibilities: $(0, h)$, $(0, t)$, $(1, h)$, $(1, t)$ (the input bit was 0 and the coin landed heads, the input bit was 0 and the coin landed tails, etc.). We can view these as the possible worlds or states in a Kripke structure. Call them s_1, s_2, s_3, s_4, respectively; let S be the set consisting of all four states. Assume that we have primitive propositions A, H, T, B_0, and B_1 in the language, denoting the events that action a is performed, the coin landed heads, the coin landed tails, agent 2's input bit is 0, and agent 2's input bit is 1. Thus, H is true at states s_1 and s_3, A is true at states s_2 and s_3, and so on. Now suppose we try to put a probability space on S. It is clear that the event "heads," which corresponds to the set $\{s_1, s_3\}$, should get probability 1/2; similarly the set $\{s_2, s_4\}$ should get probability 1/2. On the other hand, there is no natural probability we can assign to the set $\{s_1, s_2\}$, since this set corresponds to the event "the input bit is 0," an event for which we do not have a probability.

In order to capture our informal argument, we can instead split up into two separate probability spaces, say S_0 and S_1, where S_0 consists of the points s_1 and s_2, while S_1 consists of the points s_3 and s_4. We can view S_i as the conditional space resulting from conditioning on the event "the input bit is i." We can view S_i as a probability space in the obvious way; for example, in S_0, we give each of the points s_1 and s_2 probability $1/2$. In each of S_0 and S_1, the probability of the event A is $1/2$. For example, in S_0, the event A holds at the point s_2, which has probability $1/2$. The fact that A has probability $1/2$ in each of S_0 and S_1 corresponds to our informal argument that, no matter what the input bit is (even if agent 1 does not know the input bit), the probability of A is $1/2$. Once we split up S into two subspaces in this way, the statement $Pr_1(A) = 1/2$ holds at all four points in S, thus $K_1(Pr_1(A) = 1/2)$ holds: agent 1 *knows* that the probability of A is $1/2$.

While dividing up S into two subspaces in this way captures our informal argument, it leads to an obvious question: What makes this the right way to divide S into subspaces? Suppose instead we had divided S into four subspaces $T_1, \ldots, T_4$, where T_i is the singleton $\{s_i\}$. When we view T_i as a probability space in the obvious way, the point s_2 must have probability 1. With this choice of subspaces, $Pr_1(A) = 1$ is true at the points s_2 and s_3, and $Pr(A) = 0$ is true at the points s_1 and s_4. Thus, all we can conclude is $K_1(Pr_1(A) = 0 \lor Pr(A) = 1)$. The agent knows that the probability of A is either 0 or 1.

Notice that there is a reasonable interpretation that we can give to the choice of $T_1, \ldots, T_4$. Before the coin is tossed, the agent can argue that the probability of A is $1/2$. What about after the coin has been tossed? There is one school of thought that would argue that after the coin has been tossed, A has been decided one way or another. Its probability is either 0 or 1, although agent 1 does not know which it is. From this point of view, dividing S into S_0 and S_1 captures the situation before the coin toss, while dividing it into $T_1, \ldots, T_4$ captures the situation after the coin toss. It is not a question of which is right or wrong; both choices are appropriate, but capture different situations.

This situation is studied in a more general setting in Ref. *79*. The argument there is that different partitions of the set of possible worlds into subspaces correspond to playing against different adversaries, with different knowledge. For example, the partition $T_1, \ldots, T_4$ corresponds in a precise sense to playing against an adversary that knows the outcome of the coin toss, while the partition S_0, S_1 corresponds to playing an adversary that does not know the outcome. The point of view allows us to clarify some important philosophical issues, as well as providing us with a means of analyzing randomized protocols.

OTHER WORK AND FURTHER DIRECTIONS

I have discussed what I see as many of the most important trends in research on reasoning about knowledge but, as I mentioned in the introduction, this is by no means a comprehensive survey. Let me briefly mention a few other topics that were neglected above due to lack of space and time:

- Using epistemic logics to better understand aspects of nonmonotonicity [see, e.g., *80-82* for further details].
- Connections between epistemic logics and *zero-knowledge proofs* [*83*]. In a zero-knowledge proof, a prover tries to convince a verifier of a certain fact (such that a particular number n is composite) without revealing any additional information (such as the factors of n). To make this precise, we need to invoke notions of computability and probability (since there is allowed to be a small probability of error). These notions can be formalized in epistemic logic by

combining the resource-bounded approach of Moses [*64*] with the logic of probability and knowledge of Fagin [*63*]; and see Halpern et al. [36] for details. Reasoning about knowledge and time, and how knowledge changes over time. In certain applications, we may want to say that our knowledge is stable over time unless we learn information to the contrary [see *80*]; this can be captured formally in structures where there is "no forgetting" [*84, 85*]. Unfortunately, assuming no forgetting implies makes formal reasoning about knowledge and time far more complex in a certain sense; Refs. *85-87* for more details.

- *Knowledge-based programming*: The analyses of several authors [*29-31, 37*] suggest that knowledge-based protocols (i.e., protocols that allow explicit tests for knowledge, so that an action of an agent can depend on its knowledge) provide a high-level way to describe the relationship between knowledge and action. Halpern and Fagin [*20*] provide a formal semantics for knowledge-based protocols. Ultimately, we might hope for a programming language that allows tests for knowledge, where the details of how the knowledge is computed are invisible to the programmer. While we are a long way from that point, the *agent-oriented programming* suggested by Shoham [*88*] can be viewed as a first step along these lines.

Research is currently proceeding in all these areas, as well as the ones mentioned earlier in this article. In earlier overview articles [*41, 89*], I concluded with suggestions for areas where further research needed to be done. The bibliography of this survey is testimony to the progress that has been made since these overviews were written. Nevertheless, there is much more that could be done. In particular, it seems to me that there are three areas where further research could lead to major progress:

- Analyzing more protocols using tools of knowledge. It would be particularly interesting to see if thinking in terms of adversaries can give us further insight into randomized protocols. Having a larger body of examples will enable us to further test and develop our intuitions.
- Getting more realistic models of knowledge, that incorporate resource-bounded reasoning, probability, and the possibility of errors.
- Getting a deeper understanding of the interplay between various modes of reasoning under uncertainty. In a system that needs to reason about and make decisions under uncertainty, it is important to do both qualitative and quantitative reasoning. Not surprisingly, there are many approaches to reasoning about uncertainty, including information theory, probability theory, variants of probability such as the Dempster-Shafer approach [*90*] or fuzzy logic [*91*], and many others. We should not expect that any one approach will be able to solve all of these problems. In any particular application, there will probably be some combination that is most appropriate. How do we decide?

I am optimistic that the next five years will bring us closer to a deeper understanding of all these issues.

ACKNOWLEDGMENTS

The presentation of the ideas in this article owes a great deal to discussions with Ron Fagin, Yoram Moses, and Moshe Vardi in the context of writing a book on reasoning about knowledge [*92*].

REFERENCES

1. G. H. von Wright, *An Essay in Modal Logic*, North-Holland, Amsterdam, 1951.
2. J. Hintikka, *Knowledge and Belief,* Cornell University Press, New York, 1962.
3. E. Gettier, "Is Justified True Belief Knowledge?," *Analysis, 23,* 121-123 (1963).
4. W. Lenzen, "Recent Work in Epistemic Logic, "*Acta Philosophic Fennica, 30,* 1-219 (1978).
5. J. Barwise and J. Perry, *Situations and Attitudes,* Bradford Books, 1983.
6. J. Y. Halpern (ed.), *Theoretical Aspects of Reasoning about Knowledge: Proc. 1986 Conf.* Morgan Kaufmann, San Mateo, 1986.
7. M. Y. Vardi (ed.), *Proc. Second Conf. Theoretical Aspects of Reasoning About Knowledge,* Morgan Kaufmann, San Mateo, 1988.
8. R. J. Parikh (ed.), *Proc. Third Conf. Theoretical Aspects of Reasoning About Knowledge,* Morgan Kaufmann, San Mateo, 1990.
9. H. H. Clark and C. R. Marshall, "Definite Reference and Mutual Knowledge," in *Elements of Discourse Understanding,* A. K. Joshi, B. L. Webber, and I. A. Sag (eds.), Cambridge University Press, New York, 1981.
10. D. Lewis, *Convention, A Philosophical Study,* Harvard University Press, Cambridge, 1969.
11. C. R. Perrault and P. R. Cohen, "It's for Your Own Good: A Note on Inaccurate Reference," in *Elements of Discourse Understanding,* A. K. Joshi, B. L. Webber, and I. A. Sag (eds.), Cambridge University Press, New York, 1981.
12. R. J. Aumann, "Agreeing to Disagree," *Ann. Statis., 4*(6); 1236-1239 (1976).
13. J. Geanaokoplos and H. Polemarchakis, "We Can't Disagree Forever," *J. Econ. Theory, 28*(1); 192-200 (1982).
14. R. Parikh and P. Krasucki, "Communication, Consensus, and Knowledge," *J. Econ. Theory, 52*(1); 178-189 (1990).
15. A. Brandenberger, "The Role of Common Knowledge Assumptions in Game Theory," in *The Economics of Information, Games, and Missing Markets,* F. Hahn (ed.), Oxford University Press, New York, 1989.
16. S. Kripke, "A Semantic Analysis of Modal Logic I: Normal Modal Propositional Calculi," *Zeitschrift für Mathematische Logik und Grundlagen der Mathematik, 9*; 67-96 (1963). Announced in *J. Symbolic Logic, 24,* 323 (1959).
17. J. Y. Halpern and Y. Moses, "A Guide to Completeness and Complexity for Modal Logics of Knowledge and Belief,"*Artif. Intell* (1992, to appear).
18. J. E. Hopcroft and J. D. Ullman, *Introduction to Automata Theory, Languages and Computation,* Addison-Wesley, Reading, MA, 1979.
19. R. Ladner, "The Computational Complexity of Provability in Systems of Modal Propositional Logic," *SIAM J. Computing, 6*(3), 467-480 (1977).
20. J. Y. Halpern and R. Fagin,"Modeling Knowledge and Action in Distributed Systems," *Distribut. Comput., 3*(4), 159-179 (1989).
21. K. M. Chandy and J. Misra,"How Processes Learn,"*Distrib. Comput. 1*(1), 40-52 (1986).
22. M. J. Fischer and N. Immerman, "Foundations of Knowledge for Distributed Systems," in *Theoretical Aspects of Reasoning About Knowledge: Proc. 1986 Conf.,* J. Y. Halpern (ed.), Morgan Kaufmann, San Mateo, pp. 171-186.
23. J. Y. Halpern and Y. Moses,"Knowledge and Common Knowledge in a Distributed Environment," *J. ACM, 37*(3), 549-587 (1990). An early version appeared in *Proc. 3rd ACM Symp. Principles of Distributed Computing,* 1984.

24. R. Parikh and R. Ramanujam,"Distributed Processing and the Logic of Knowledge," in R. Parikh (ed.), *Proc. Workshop on Logics of Programs,* 1985, 256–268.
25. S. J. Rosenschein and L. P. Kaelbling,"The Synthesis of Digital Machines with Provable Epistemic Properties," in *Theoretical Aspects of Reasoning About Knowledge: Proc. 1986 Conf.,* J. Y. Halpern (ed.), Morgan Kaufmann, San Mateo, 1986, pp. 83–97.
26. S. J. Rosenschein, "Formal Theories of AI in Knowledge and Robotics," *New Generation Computing, 3,* 345–357 (1985).
27. J. Gray, "Notes on Database Operating Systems," in *Operating Systems: An Advanced Course,* R. Bayer, R. M. Graham, and G. Seegmuller (eds.), Lecture Notes in Computer Science, Vol. 66, Springer-Verlag, New York, 1978. Also appears as IBM Research Report RJ 2188, 1978.
28. Y. Yemini and D. Cohen,"Some Issues in Distributed Processes Communication," in *Proc. of the 1st Int. Conf. on Distributed Computing Systems,* 1979, pp. 199–203.
29. C. Dwork and Y. Moses,"Knowledge and Common Knowledge in a Byzantine Environment: Crash Failures," *Inform. Computation, 88*(2), 156–186 (1990).
30. R. Fagin and J. Y. Halpern,"Reasoning About Knowledge and Probability: Preliminary Report," in *Proceedings of the Second Conference on Theoretical Aspects of Reasoning About Knowledge,* M. Y. Vardi (ed.), Morgan Kaufmann, San Mateo, 1988, pp. 277–293.
31. J. Y. Halpern, Y. Moses, and O. Waart,"A Characterization of Eventual Byzantine Agreement," in *Proc. 9th ACM Symp. on Principles of Distributed Computing,* 1990, pp. 333–346.
32. Y. Moses and M. R. Tuttle,"Programming Simultaneous Actions Using Common Knowledge," *Algorithmica, 3,* 121–169 (1988).
33a. B. Neiger and S. Touey, "Substituting for Real Time and Common Knowledge in Asynchronous Distributed Systems," in *Proc. 6th ACM Symp. on Principles of Distributed Computing,* 1987, p. 281–293; *J. ACM* (To appear).
33b. P. Panangaden and S. Taylor,"Concurrent Common Knowledge: A New Definition of Agreement for Asynchronous systems," in *Proc. 7th ACM Symp. on Principles of Distributed Computing,* 1988, pp. 197–209.
34. G. Neiger,"Knowledge Consistency: A Useful Suspension of Disbelief," in *Proc. Second Conf. Theoretical Aspects of Reasoning About Knowledge,* M. Y. Vardi (ed.), Morgan Kaufmann, San Mateo, 1988, pp. 295–308.
35. V. Hadzilacos, "A Knowledge-Theoretic Analysis of Atomic Commitment Protocols," in *Proc. 6th ACM Symp. on Principles of Database Systems,* 1987, pp. 129–34. A revised version has been submitted for publication.
36. J. Y. Halpern, Y. Moses, and M. R. Tuttle, "A Knowledge-Based Analysis of Zero Knowledge," in *Proc. 20th ACM Symp. on Theory of Computing,*1988, pp. 132–147.
37. J. Y. Halpern and L. D. Zuck,"A Little Knowledge Goes a Long Way: Simple Knowledge-Based Derivations and Correctness Proofs for a Family of Protocols," in *Proc. 6th ACM Symp. on Principles of Distributed Computing,* 1987, pp. 269–280. A revised and expanded version appears as IBM Research Report RJ 5857, 1987 and will appear in *J. ACM.*
38. M. S. Mazer, "A Knowledge Theoretic Account of Recovery in Distributed Systems: The Case of Negotiated Commitment," in M. Y. Vardi (ed.), *Proc. Second Conf. Theoretical Aspects of Reasoning About Knowledge,* Morgan Kaufmann, San Mateo, 1988, pp. 309–324.

39. M. S. Mazer, "A Link Between Knowledge and Communication in Faulty Distributed Systems," in *Proc. Third Conf. Theoretical Aspects of Reasoning about Knowledge*, R. Parikh (ed.), Morgan Kaufmann, San Mateo, 1990, pp. 289-304.

40. Y. Moses and G. Roth,"On Reliable Message Diffusion," in *Proc. 8th ACM Symp. on Principles of Distributed Computing*, 1989, pp. 119-125.

41. J. Y. Halpern, "Using Reasoning About Knowledge to Analyze Distributed Systems," in *Annual Review of Computer Science*, Vol. 2, J. Traub et al. (eds.), Annual Reviews Inc., 1987, Palo Alto, CA, pp. 37-68.

42. D. Dolev and H. R. Strong, "Requirements for Agreement in a Distributed System," in *Distributed Data Bases*, H. J. Schneider (ed.), North-Holland, Amsterdam, 1982, pp. 115-129.

43. M. Pease, R. Shostak, and L. Lamport, "Reaching Agreement in the Presence of Faults," *J. ACM, 27*(2), 228-234 (1980).

44. R. A. Eberle, "A Logic of Believing, Knowing and Inferring," *Synthese, 26*, 356-382 (1974).

45. R. C. Moore and G. Hendrix, "Computational Models of Beliefs and the Semantics of Belief Sentences, Technical Note 187, SRI International, 1979.

46. K. Konolige, *A Deduction Model of Belief*, Morgan Kaufmann, San Mateo, 1986.

47. R. Montague, "Logical Necessity, Physical Necessity, Ethics, and Quantifier," *Inquiry, 4*, 259-269 (1960).

48. M. Y. Vardi,"On the Complexity of Epistemic Reasoning," in *Proc. 4th IEEE Symp. on Logic in Computer Science*, 1989, pp. 243-252.

49. A. Heyting, *Intuitionism: An Introduction*, North-Holland, Amsterdam, 1956.

50. A. Anderson and N. D. Belnap, *Entailment: The Logic of Relevance and Neccessity*, Princeton University Press, Princeton, 1975.

51. N. D. Belnap,"How a Computer Should Think," in *Contemporary Aspects of Philosophy*, Oriel Press, New York, 1977, pp. 30-56.

52. N. D. Belnap,"A Useful Four-Valued Logic," in *Modern Uses of Multiple-Valued Logic*, G. Epstein and J. M. Dunn (eds.), Reidel, Dordrecht, 1977, pp. 5-37.

53. J. M. Dunn,"Relevance Logic and Entailment," in *Handbook of Philosophical Logic*, Vol. III, Reidel, Dordrecht, D. Gabbay and F. Guenthner (eds.), 1986, pp. 117-224.

54. R. Fagin, J. Y. Halpern, and M. Y. Vardi,"A Nonstandard Approach to the Logical Omniscience Problem," in *Proc. Third Conf. on Theoretical Aspects of Reasoning About Knowledge*, R. Parikh (ed.), Morgan Kaufman, San Mateo, 1990, pp. 42-55. To appear in *Artificial Intelligence*.

55a. M. J. Cresswell, *Logics and Languages*, Methuen and Co., London, 1973.

55b. J. Hintikka, "Impossible Possible Worlds Vindicated," *J. Philosoph. Logic, 4*, 475-484 (1975).

56. V. Rantala,"Impossible Worlds Semantics and Logical Omniscience," *Acta Philosophica Fennica, 35*, 18-25 (1982).

57. N. Rescher and R. Brandon, *The Logic of Inconsistency*, Rowman and Littlefield, New York, 1979.

58. H. Wansing,"A General Possible Worlds Framework for Reasoning About Knowledge and Belief, *Studia Logica, 49*(4), 523-539 (1990).

59. H. J. Levesque,"A Logic of Implicit and explicit Belief," in *Proc. Natl. Conf. Artificial Intelligence* (AAAI-84), 1984, pp. 198-202.

60. G. Lakemeyer,"Tractable Meta-Reasoning in Propositional Logics of Belief," in *Tenth Int. Joint Conf. Artificial Intelligence* (IJCAI-87), 1987, pp. 402-408.

61. P. F. Patel-Schneider,"A Decidable First-Order Logic for Knowledge Representation," in *Ninth Int. Joint Conf. Artificial Intelligence* (IJCAI-85), 1985, pp. 455–458.

62. G. Lakemeyer,"Steps Towards a First-Order Logic of Explicit and Implicit Belief," in *Theoretical Aspects of Reasoning About Knowledge: Proc. 1986 Conf.*, J. Y. Halpern (ed.), Morgan Kaufmann, San Mateo, 1986, pp. 325–340.

63. R. Fagin and J. Y. Halpern,"Belief, Awareness, and Limited Reasoning,"*Artificial Intelligence, 34*; 39–76 (1988).

64. Y. Moses,"Resource-Bounded Knowledge," in *Proc. Second Conf. Theoretical Aspects of Reasoning About Knowledge,* M. Y. Vardi (ed.), Morgan Kaufmann, San Mateo, 1988, pp. 261–276.

65. E. M. Clarke, E. A. Emerson, and A. P. Sistla,"Automatic Verification of Finite-State Concurrent Systems Using Temporal Logic Specifications," *ACM Trans. Programming Languages and Systems, 8*(2); 244–263 (1986). An early version appeared in *Proc. 10th ACM Symp. on Principles of Programming Languages,* 1983.

66. J. Y. Halpern and M. Y. Vardi, "Model Checking vs. Theorem Proving: A Manifesto," in *Principles of Knowledge Representation and Reasoning: Proc. Second Int. Conf.,* J. A. Allen, R. Fikes, and E. Sandewall (eds.), Morgan Kaufman, San Mateo, 1991, pp. 325–334.

67. J. M. McCarthy and P. J. Hayes,"Some Philosophical Problems from the Standpoint of Artificial Intelligence," in *Machine Intelligence 4*, American Elsevier, New York, 1969, pp. 463–502.

68. R. C. Moore,"A Formal Theory of Knowledge and Action," in *Formal Theories of the Commonsense World*, J. Hobbs and R. C. Moore (eds.), Ablex Publishing Corp., Norwood, NJ, 1985, pp. 319–358.

69. L. Morgenstern,"A First Order Theory of Planning, Knowledge, and Action," in *Theoretical Aspects of Reasoning About Knowledge: Proc. 1986 Conf.*, J. Y. Halpern (ed.), Morgan Kaufmann, San Mateo, 1986, pp. 99–114.

70. H. J. Levesque,"Foundations of a Functional Approach to Knowledge Representation," *Artificial Intelligence, 23*; 155–212 (1984).

71. R. Fagin, J. Y. Halpern, and M. Y. Vardi,"A Model-Theoretic Analysis of Knowledge: Preliminary Report," *J. ACM., 91*(2), 382–428 (1991).

72. J. Y. Halpern and Y. Moses,"Towards a Theory of Knowledge and Ignorance," in *Proc. AAAI Workshop on Non-monotonic Logic,* 1984, pp. 125–143. Reprinted in *Logics and Models of Concurrent Systems*, K. Apt (ed.), Springer-Verlag, New York, 1985, pp. 459–476.

73. H. J. Levesque, "All I Know: A Study in Autoepristemic Logic," *Artificial Intelligence, 92*(3), 263–309 (1990).

74. G. Lakemeyer and H. J. Levesque,"A Tractable Knowledge Representation Service with Full Introspection," in *Proc. Second Conf. Theoretical Aspects of Reasoning About Knowledge,* M. Y. Vardi (ed.), Morgan Kaufmann, San Mateo, 1988, pp. 145–159.

75. R. Parikh,"Logics of Knowledge, Games, and Dynamic Logic," in *FST-TCS*, Lecture Notes in Computer Science, Vol. 181, Springer-Verlag, New York, 1984, pp. 202–222.

76. W. R. Stark,"A Logic of Knowledge," *Zeitschrift für Mathematische Logik und Grundlagen der Mathematik, 27*, 371–374 (1981).

77. M. Y. Vardi,"A Model-Theoretic Analysis of Monotonic Knowledge," in *Ninth Int. Joint Conf. Artificial Intelligence* (IJCAI-85), 1985, pp. 509–512.

78. J. F. Mertens and S. Zamir,"Formulation of Bayesian Analysis for Games of Incomplete Information," *Int. J. Game Theory, 14*(1), 1–29 (1985).
78. J. F. Mertens and S. Zamir,"Formulation of Bayesian Analysis for Games of Incomplete Information," *Int. J. Game Theory, 14*(1), 1–29 (1985).
79. J. Y. Halpern and M. R. Tuttle,"Knowledge, Probability, and Adversaries," in *Proc. 8th ACM Symp. on Principles of Distributed Computing,* 1989, pp. 103–118.
80. Y. Shoham,"Chronological Ignorance: Experiments in Nonmonotonic Temporal Reasoning," *Artificial Intelligence, 36*, 271–331 (1988).
81. Y. Shoham and Y. Moses,"Belief as Defeasible Knowledge," in *Eleventh Int. Joint Conf. Artificial Intelligence* (IJCAI-89), 1989, pp. 1168–1173.
82. F. Lin and Y. Shoham,"Epistemic Semantics for Fixed-Point Nonmonotonic Logics," in *Proc. Third Conf. Theoretical Aspects of Reasoning About Knowledge,* Morgan Kaufmann, San Mateo, 1990, pp. 111–120.
83. S. Goldwassar, S. Micali, and C. Rackoff,"The Knowledge Complexity of Interactive Proof Systems," *SIAM J. Computing, 18*(1); 186–208 (February 1989).
84. R. Fagin, J. Y. Halpern, and M. Y. Varki,"What Can Machines Know? On the Epistemic Properties of Machines," in *Proc. National Conference on Artificial Intelligence* (AAAI-86), 1986, pp. 428–434. A revised and expanded version appears as IBM Research Report RJ 6250, 1988, under the title "What Can Machines Know? On the Properties of Knowledge in Distributed Systems," and will appear in *J. ACM.*
85. J. Y. Halpern and M. Y. Vardi,"The Complexity of Reasoning About Knowledge and Time, I: Lower Bounds," *J. Computer Sys. Sci., 38*(1), 195–237 (1989).
86. J. Y. Halpern and M. Y. Vardi, "The Complexity of Reasoning About Knowledge and Time in Asynchronous Systems," in *Proc. 20th ACM Symp. on Theory of Computing,* 1988, pp. 53–65.
87. E. Spaan,"Nexttime Is Not Necessary," in *Proc. Third Conf. Theoretical Aspects of Reasoning About Knowledge,* R. J. Parikh (ed.), Morgan Kaufmann, San Mateo, 1990, pp. 241–256.
88. Y. Shoham, "Agent-Oriented Programming," Technical Report STAN-CS-90-1335, Stanford, 1990.
89. J. Y. Halpern,"Reasoning About Knowledge: An Overview," in *Theoretical Aspect of Reasoning about Knowledge: Proc. 1986 Conf.,* J. Y. Halpern (ed.), Morgan Kaufmann, San Mateo, 1986, pp. 1–17. Reprinted in *Proc. Natl. Computer Conf.,* 1986, pp. 219–228.
90. G. Shafer, *A Mathematical Theory of Evidence,* Princeton University Press, Princeton, 1976.
91. L. A. Zadeh,"Fuzzy Sets as a Basis for a Theory of Possibility," *Fuzzy Sets and Systems, 1*, 3–28 (1978).
92. R. Fagin, J. Y. Halpern, Y. Moses, and M. Y. Vardi, *Reasoning About Knowledge,* 1991, To appear.

JOSEPH Y. HALPERN

REASONING IN UNCERTAIN DOMAINS:
A SURVEY AND COMMENTARY

THE TASK OF REASONING

When we attempt either to solve a problem or to make a decision an essential part of the effort can be called *reasoning*. Informally speaking, *reasoning* is the exercise of inferring information about some unobservable aspect of a situation based on the information about the observed aspects of the situation. For example, reasoning is performed to infer some information about a patient's internal subsystems based on the observable external symptoms; to infer an accused's role in a crime based on the available evidence; and to determine the possible intentions of an enemy force based on the available intelligence information. A number of formalisms for automated reasoning have been developed and these are based on a wide spectrum of theoretical frameworks, ranging from formal logics to theories of probability. We examine various types of objectives a reasoner may be trying to achieve and then examine the usefulness of various reasoning formalisms for attaining these objectives.

Types of Reasoning

As stated above, for a particular problem the reasoning exercise in a very general form can be viewed as follows:

> Given:
> - Information about the observed aspects of a particular problem
> - Knowledge about the domain to which the problem belongs
> Determine:
> - Information about some unobserved aspect of the problem situation

Depending upon the nature and type of the observed information and the objective of the reasoner, the reasoning task can be stated in a more precise manner. For example, when First-Order Predicate Calculus is used for representing knowledge then the reasoning task may be specified as follows:

> Given:
> - Observed aspects of the problem situation in terms of truth values of some predicates
> - Domain knowledge in the form of *wffs* of first-order predicate calculus
> Determine:
> - Truth value of some other *wff* of interest

Many decision-making tasks demand more than just an inference about an unobserved aspect of the situation. These tasks demand that the reasoning exercise should generate either *a hypothesis* or *an explanation* to justify the observed events. For example, given some symptoms, a reasoner may be asked to hypothesize a set of physiological processes to explain the symptoms. Based on the available information, a battlefield planner may be interested in hypothesizing an enemy's plan of attack. These hypothetizations can sometimes be more useful than knowing just the probability of the patient suffering from a particular disease, or the probability of being attacked by the enemy.

MODELS OF INQUIRY

Churchman in his book [1] presents a detailed discussion of various types of enquiring systems and their relevance to various reasoning situations. A summary of these models is also presented by Mitroff and Turoff [2]. When the above formulation of the reasoning exercise is viewed in the context of these models of inquiry, a better insight into the needs of a reasoning process is obtained. In this section we present a brief summary of Churchman's classification of inquiring systems.

The two primitives Churchman [1] uses are the concepts of *innate ideas*, and *inputs*. The innate ideas refers to some principles or theoretical truths about nature in which the reasoner believes. The inputs are the experimental observations made by the observer. A *fact-net* is an interconnection of inputs and innate ideas constructed by means of a given set of *relations* and *operators*. A fact-net is therefore a network of contingent truths.

Liebnizian Inquirer

A *Liebnizian Inquiring System* aims at constructing an optimal fact-net for a situation. Optimality becomes relevant because, for any given set of inputs, it may be possible to construct a number of different fact-nets. The Liebnizian Inquirer assumes that there is an optimal network and the process of building the network would converge to it because of the abilities inherent in the net building process. The Liebnizian inquirers represent a very general class of inquiring systems; some examples follow. The practice of Science can be viewed as a Liebnizian Inquirer. Every new scientific result is an "input" that can be linked into the network of older results, especially when the field is governed by a theory. The theory provides the *relations* and the *operators* for tying together the results in the form of a *fact-net* and corresponds to the *innate ideas* of the inquirer. A result or *input* that lies outside the largest net will often be ignored, whereas a result that enables the researchers to connect two hitherto unconnected nets will be acclaimed. These inquirers therefore do not discard the theories but look for networks containing all the inputs. Another example of such an inquirer is theorem proving and problem-solving machines where the primitives, axioms, and inference rules of the logic are the innate ideas and the various wff's are the inputs. The objective of the inquirer (theorem prover) is to make a network containing the wffs in order to determine if the desired wff is consistent with all the others.

A Liebnizian inquirer assumes the existence of an a priori model of the situation, (the innate ideas or the theory), and attempts to configure the inputs of the situation according to this model.

Kantian Inquirer

A *Kantian inquirer* does not presuppose the existence of one a priori model of the situation. The only a priori information assumed is for the basics such as a clock-event to enable the inquirer to observe the inputs. A Kantian inquirer initially contains a set of models. Each model is an independent set of innate ideas and may contain its primitives, axioms, and rules of inference, etc. An inquirer then selects a model from the set and builds a Liebnizian fact-net using the inputs and the innate ideas of this model. The inquirer then determines the extent to which this fact-net is "satisfactory" according to some criterion. The model that generates the most "satisfactory" fact-net is the solution for the inquiry. An example of such an inquirer is encountered in the social sciences where often the search is for a theoretical model in which all the observed data an be shown to fit properly.

Hegelian Inquirer

The *Hegelian model* of Inquiry seeks to develop the ability to see the same inputs from different points of view. The inquirer possesses a number of models, each of which is an independent set of innate ideas and may contain primitives, axioms, and rules of inference. Let us denote this set of models by W. Let I be a set of propositions which can possibly be true of the situation under consideration. Let D denote the set of inputs $d_1, d_2, \ldots, d_k$. Let X be an operator conjoining an element of D with an element of W, such that for every d_i in D and every W_i in W there corresponds one and only one element of the set I. That is, X maps elements of D for a given W onto the set I in a many-one correspondence. The set I is called the "information set" of a given set of models W and the operator X is called the interpretive operator. Thus for each element of W there corresponds an information subset, represented by $I(W_j)$.

Consider a set T of "theses," i.e., sentences stating something about the world, such that no element of T implies or is implied by any element of D, W, or I. C is a two-place function that transforms a T_i and a W_j into elements of the real number system. C represents the "degree of confidence" in T_i given the information in $I(W_j)$. This represents the credence of a thesis given that the world is accurately described by model W_j.

The inquirer selects a thesis A from the set T and undertakes to construct a "case" for supporting A, in effect, a defense of the thesis "A." This is achieved by selecting a W_{th} such that $W_{th} = max_j[C(A, I(W_j))]$. That is, the inquirer sets about showing that there is a way to look at reality, given by W_{th}, such that the inputs can be interpreted to support the thesis A.

The next thing a Hegelian inquirer does is to find a thesis B which is an antithesis of A, and also finds the model that supports B. B does not have to be a logical negation of A. For example, in the context of some battlefield intelligence information, if the thesis is that a "target will be destroyed," the anti-thesis may be "the attacking army will be destroyed" instead of "target will *not* be destroyed."

The next act of a Hegelian inquirer is to look at the two models of the world, the W_i's that support the thesis and the antithesis and examine the sources of conflict between them. It is hoped that the attempts to understand or resolve these conflicts would lead one toward the truth about the situation. The bigger model of the situation in the context of which the conflict can be understood is called the "synthesis" model of the situation.

Choosing a Model of Inquiry

The importance of the above stated categorization by Churchman is that it helps us see that different models of inquiry are more natural or useful in different problem domains. The choice depends on our knowledge and on our view of where the truth is likely to reside. If we think that "truth is in the model" and a good model (theory) is at hand, the Liebnizian model of inquiry, much used in the physical sciences, is most appropriate. This might also be called a top-down or model-directed approach. On the other hand, if in out view, "truth is partially in a model and partially in data" then one may pursue the Kantian model, which is the case in most social sciences. The Hegelian or dialectical model of inquiry is more appropriate to those domains where, in our view, the "truth" is likely to emerge from a clash between a thesis and an antithesis. Relatively ill-structured problem domains such as management, economics, law, politics, marketing, battlefield planning, and some poorly understood areas of medicine are examples where the Hegelian model of inquiry may be more appropriate.

The main point that one can conclude is that there are many approaches to inquiry, and depending on the problem domain, one approach may be more useful than the other. When we perform a reasoning exercise in some particular situation, it must be done in the context of the model of inquiry being pursued for the problem at hand.

In view of the above categorization, our earlier view of the reasoning can be refined to be presented as follows:

> Given:
> - Observed aspects of the problem situations in terms of the observed events (inputs)
> - Domain knowledge that provides basic facts for constructing models for various situations possible in the domain.
>
> Determine:
> - Some model that is in accordance with the observed events and satisfies some specified criterion of interestingness. This model may be obtained according to Liebnizian, or Kantian, or Hegelian models of Inquiry.
> - An inference about some unobserved aspect of the problem situation in the context of the above model.

APPROXIMATE REASONING

A problem faced in most reasoning situations is that all the information that may be relevant is not available and that which is available is confusing and not necessarily relevant.

Reasons for Approximation

Incompleteness of relevant knowledge is faced by reasoners in most reasoning situations. For example, the knowledge of only a few symptoms may not enable a reasoner to pinpoint a unique causal chain of physiological processes responsible for causing the observed symptoms. Similarly, the limited amount of available battlefield intelligence may fail to point toward a unique hypothesis about the enemy's plan. In situations of incomplete observed knowledge a number of hypotheses or explanations may be generated such that each of them is capable of explaining most if not all the observed symptoms. A reasoner now faces the problem of handling the multiplicity of hypotheses that explain a situation.

Another problem encountered by reasoners is of uncertainty of knowledge. In many situations we are often not in a position to insist that a statement about either an input or about an innate idea is absolutely true, but are willing to admit that it carries a degree of uncertainty. A number of attempts have been made to model this uncertainty either with or without using numbers.

Another problem encountered by reasoners is of imprecision of knowledge. The problem is encountered when the inputs and innate ideas may be imprecise in nature. For example, a Liebnizian inquirer may fail to include the input 'economy has an inflation rate of 3.87%' in a fact-net consisting of very precise inputs but may be able to connect the input "economy has a low inflation rate" in the same fact-net. The former input is very precise and the latter is less precise. In many situations of enquiry in our everyday life the factnets or models are constructed by choosing less precise predicates or propositions. That is, instead of discarding some input, we sometimes try to find a less precise version of the model in which the inputs can be included. This is one aspect which Churchman's discourse on models of inquiry has not addressed. The only calculus that has systematically addressed the issue of imprecision of statements is the theory of fuzzy sets.

Approximate Inquirers

If a reasoner working according to the Liebnizian model of inquiry is interested in determining the 'truth' value of some proposition by trying to form a fact-net containing it, then an approximate reasoner is interested in determining:

> Either the uncertainty associated with the proposition of interest, given the uncertainties associated with the inputs and innate ideas.
> Or an imprecise version of the proposition and the model such that the proposition can be proved to be 'True,' given the imprecisions associated with the inputs and the innate ideas.

An approximate reasoner working according to the Kantian model of inquiry is interested in determining an ordered list of a few models that best explain the inputs. The imprecision associated with some propositions included in a model may be a criterion for preferring it over another model.

An approximate reasoner working according the the Hegelian model of inquiry would be interested in determining pairs of models that support the thesis and the antithesis. Precision of the propositions in models may be a part of the criterion for preferring one model over the other.

In the preceding discussion we have used the idea of a model of a situation. We now look at the nature of models of a situation that may be used by various types of reasoners.

CAUSAL MODELS

In the preceding section we used the idea of models of a situation without going into the details of what a model may look like. That is, how the innate ideas about a situation, including its primitives, axioms, and rules of inference, etc. may be represented. For example, in the domain of medical diagnosis one knows the effects of various types of physiological processes and this knowledge should be included in any model of a patient's situation. What we need is some relationship operations between the physiological processes so that they may be interconnected to constitute a meaningful explanation of the observed symptoms.

The knowledge of causality relationships provides a basis for relating various events and thus providing a causal structure for a situation. Causal information appears to be the most convincing basis for relating various events. Tversky and Kahneman state [3]:

> It is a psychological commonplace that people strive to achieve a coherent interpretation of the events that surround them, and that the organization of events by schemas of cause-effect relations serves to achieve this goal.

The authors go on to show that in the context of human behavior, data that are given causal interpretation affect judgments, while data that do not fit into causal schemas are dominated by causally relevant data. A number of reasoning systems that seek to deal with the structures of situations have used causality information for interconnecting various events. In the domain of medical diagnosis the systems presented in Long et al. [4], Cooper [5], and

Kuipers [6] are some that use causal modeling of situations. The cause-effect structures for devices have also been used by Davis [7] for the Model-Based Approach to Reasoning. Methods for constructing causal models for devices have been presented [8, 9]. Philosophically there have been many problems with the idea of causality. Many have argued against our ever being able to establish the relationships of causality between various events. However, in this discussion, by causality we refer to the perceived notion of causality as experienced by humans. Such notions of perceived causality are the innate ideas from which our models of situations are constructed. And we use these innate ideas of perceived causality without questioning the validity of these perceived causality relationships.

In the following discussion we examine various systems for reasoning and their capabilities in various types of reasoning situations. We classify the systems in two categories—those based on formal logic and those based on numeric calculi.

FORMAL LOGIC

Most of the early reasoning frameworks developed in AI were based on formal logic and almost completely ignored the problems of approximate reasoning. Probability theory has been advanced as one framework most suited for handling uncertainty [10] but some non-numeric systems for handling uncertainty within the framework of formal logics have also been presented. Examples of such works include [11, 12]. Let us first look at some simple exercises of reasoning based on formal logic.

A formal theorem proving system is a Liebnizian inquirer [1]. The mechanism of theorem-proving activity is the same as the construction of a network of wffs to possibly derive the null clause—the activity similar to that of constructing a fact-net. The wffs and the axioms constitute a unique model of the situation and the attempt to prove a "theorem" is to determine whether the "theorem" can be deduced from the knowledge contained in the model.

Kantian and Hegelian models of inquiry require that more than one model of the situation be available to the inquirer. It is possible that the axioms corresponding to two different models of a situation may be inconsistent and therefore the framework of theorem proving does not belong to the Kantian and Hegelian models of inquiry.

Default Logics

Default logics present a framework which can possibly be used for implementing Kantian and Hegelian inquirers. In the frameworks of these logics, the reasoner possesses two types of knowledge: facts, and defaults. The facts are those pieces of information that are known to be always "true" in the world. The defaults are those pieces of information which may or may not be true in any particular situation. For example "Birds fly" is not always "true" in the world and is therefore not a fact. Since some birds fly and some don't, this piece of information may be assumed to be true in some descriptions of the world and not in others. This is thus a possible piece of *default* knowledge. An example demonstrating the use of such knowledge taken from [12] is as follows:

> **default1** $\neg$flies(X) $\leftarrow$ mammal(X)
> **default2** flies(X) $\leftarrow$ bat(X)
> **default3** $\neg$flies(X) $\leftarrow$ dead(X)
> **fact1** mammal(X) $\leftarrow$ bat(X)

fact2 bat(dracula)
fact3 dead(dracula)

Now let us say the input available to us is:

¬flies(dracula)

We can construct a theory that includes all the three facts and default1 and according to this theory we can explain the input. However, if the input available to us is:

flies(dracula)

then we can construct a theory with all the three facts and default2 to explain this input. The point is that logical inferences can be used within a theory, but when a number of theories may be possible the selection of an appropriate theory is of paramount concern. The exercise of reasoning concerns as much the task of inferencing as that of selecting a suitable theory. David Poole states [*12*]:

> Rather than expecting reasoning to be just deduction (in any logic) from our knowledge, we examine the consequences of viewing reasoning as a very simple case of theory formation.

The basic components used for constructing a theory are the facts and the defaults. In any theory, all the facts and some of the defaults are included in such a way that the theory remains consistent. In many situations it may be possible to construct a number of theories to explain some particular set of inputs. If the theory is to serve as a model of some situation and the reasoner is planning on taking some action based on this assumed model, then it may be required that only one of these models is selected. An alternative for handling such a situation is to determine all the theories that explain the evidence and then determine the utility of each possible action in the context of each theory. The framework of *Decision Theory* may then be used to select the optimal action. In this approach we would need to know the relative chances of each of the theories being the actual model of the situation. The other alternative is to order various possible theories according to some criterion specifying how interesting each is, and select the most interesting theory. Such an approach is suitable during a hypothesize-and-test cycle where we may want to determine the most interesting hypothesis and then verify it.

The inability of a reasoner to obtain all those inputs that may be needed to unravel the actual theory may have to be dealt with in one of the above two ways. The first option is closer to a Liebnizian inquirer and the second to a Kantian or Hegelian inquirer. In the first option numeric measures are used to indicate the uncertainty, and in the second the uncertainty is represented by accepting more than one model as the possible candidate.

Nonmonotonic Reasoning

In classical logic we can have only one theory, formed by a fixed set of wffs and axioms, to describe a particular situation. Any inferences that can be made within the context of this theory should still be possible when some new wff is added to the theory. That is, an inconsistent theory is not an acceptable description of a situation. It is so because we cannot have a model for an inconsistent theory. However, there are situations when in the absence of information we make certain assumptions and base our inferences on these assumptions. These inferences may be retracted when some new information is received. Such inferences have been referred to as the defeasible inferences. Logics that allow defeasible inferences have been called the nonmonotonic logics. The default logic discussed in the preceding section is also a nonmonotonic logic. Another system that provides a basis for defeasible reasoning is the nonmonotonic logic (NML) presented by McDermott and Doyle [13]. In this logic the language of first-order predicate logic is augmented with a modal operator M which can be read as "is consistent." For example, the formula

$$\forall x,y : \text{Brothers}(x,y) \land \text{MGetAlong}(x,y) \rightarrow \text{WillHelp}(x,y)$$

states that for all x and y, if it is known that they are brothers and it is consistent to assume that they get along with each other, then we can infer that they help each other. However, if at a later stage it becomes inferrable that they do not get along, then we would no longer be able to infer that they help each other. It is evident from the above example that an assertion is assumed to be *consistent* as long as no counter evidence becomes explicitly available. The set of possible semantic models for each syntactic theory may change drastically as new formulas are added to the syntactic theory. Each syntactic theory thus approximates the nature of the problem situation by making some assumptions. The set of assumptions made determines how our syntactic theory approximates the situation it is expected to represent. In default logic [14] these different theories take the form of different extensions. In NML we keep track of one line of reasoning during the process of determining inferences in a theory.

A basis for practical implementation of the nonmonotonic logics is provided by the Truth Maintenance System (TMS) [15]. This system keeps track of one line of reasoning by maintaining justifications for the assertions. Whenever a new inference results in a contradiction, the set of assumptions is revised so as to regain the consistency of the syntactic theory. The assumption-based TMS presented by Johan de Kleer [16] keeps track of all possible lines of reasoning in its structure and may be more useful than TMS [15] in many situations.

Some other mechanisms have also been developed for making assumptions to approximate the description of a situation in the absence of relevant knowledge. One such method is the *closed world assumption* made in the PROLOG environments. Several theories of *circumscription* [17–19] have also been proposed to deal with this problem. The circumscription works on individual predicates of a theory by forcing a model of the theory to be minimal in the sense that a predicate is true only for those cases for which it must be true to keep the theory consistent.

Modal Logics

The problem of representing uncertainty associated with a proposition, without having to use numeric measures, has been presented in many works. Much of this work has been done in the domain of modal logics. Segerberg [20] and Gardenfors [21] have presented modal logics which use formulas of the form $p \geq q$, and are interpreted as *p is more likely than q*. Halpern and Rabin have presented a modal logic LL [11] to reason about the Likelihood. In this logic the modal operator L captures the notion of being likely. That is, the formula lp represents the notion '*p is likely to be true.*' A model M for this logic can be viewed as a tree structure of states s. Each state s consists of a set of hypotheses that are taken to be "true for now." A state s_2 is a child of state s_1 if assuming s_1 to be true, an expert with his knowledge of the domain may call s_2 to be a likely state. Each state represents a set of consistent hypotheses. Also, a state does not represent a causal model of the situation being described, which in our view would be a desirable feature of any reasoner.

The problem of handling the level of imprecision has not been addressed within the framework of formal logics. It is possible to have two predicates for indicating "economy has low inflation" and "economy has an inflation rate between 2% and 3%," but there is no formalism that would automatically attempt to prove the former, a less precise statement, if the latter cannot be proved. That is, an attempt to form a fact-net with less precise statements would not be made automatically if the attempt with the more precise statements fails.

THE NUMERICAL APPROACHES

In many situations one seeks a causal structure underlying the observed symptoms. In cases of incomplete observable knowledge, it is difficult to uniquely identify an underlying causal model, and one may have to consider a number of causal models as possible candidates. If we are interested in the probability of some event, it may be determined by finding the fraction of possible causal models in which the event occurs.

Theories of Probability

A more useful probabilistic relationship from the point of view of reasoning is that of conditional probability. Let us consider two variables A and B with associated sets of discrete possible values $(a_1, a_2, \ldots a_k)$, and $(b_1, b_2, \ldots b_n)$. Let us say a reasoner knows the conditional probability values $P(a_i \mid b_j)$. Now whenever some event $B = b_l$ is observed, the probability values for the unobserved events $A = a_m$ can be computed by the reasoner.

In a reasoning situation where relationships among various aspects of a situation are known only in terms of conditional probabilities, the knowledge of observed events can in general be used to infer the probabilities of other unobserved events. The work done in the area of Bayesian Networks by Judea Pearl [22] has resulted in a framework for such reasoning. Some related work has also been presented [23, 24].

Bayesian Networks [22] are directed acyclic graphs (DAGs) in which the nodes correspond to propositional variables, the edges represent the conditional probability relationships between the linked propositions and the edges also signify causal relationships. In the network the causal relationships are quantified by the conditional probabilities of each variable given the state of its parent nodes. An example of a typical Bayesian network taken from Pearl [22] is shown in Figure 1. A Bayesian network is a graphical representation for the independence relationships embedded in the known joint probability distribution for the variables included in the network. This means that the joint probability distribution for variables $x_1, \ldots x_6$ of Figure 1 is such that it can be written as:

$$P(x_6 \mid x_5)P(x_5 \mid x_2, x_3)P(x_4 \mid x_1, x_2)P(x_3 \mid x_1)P(x_2 \mid x_1)P(x_1)$$

Each term in the above product can be associated with the set of edges incident at various nodes of the network. Such a network represents a reasoner's complete knowledge about the domain. In any particular instance of reasoning when some events (inputs) are observed, this network and the associated conditional probabilities can be used to determine the resultant probability values at all the other unobserved nodes of the network. An elegant and computationally tractable algorithm for updating the beliefs at the nodes of a singly connected network has been presented [22]. A singly connected network is one in which there is only one undirected path between any two nodes. The mechanism for updating the probability values at the unobserved nodes is based on local computations, wherein each node performs some computation and sends messages to its parent and child nodes. When

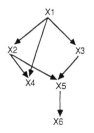

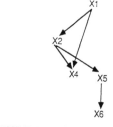

FIGURE 1.   A Bayesian network.

FIGURE 2.   The network of Figure 1 with node x3 excluded.

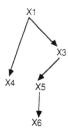

FIGURE 3.   An alternative model leading to a different inference about $x4$.

this process stabilizes we obtain the updated values at all the unobserved nodes. When the network is not singly connected, it has been shown by Cooper [25] that the problem of inference using belief networks is NP-Hard. If we work with the restriction of networks being singly connected only, then we would not be capturing the knowledge in problem domains in their entirety. Some work has been presented [26] to design special-case, average-case, and approximation algorithms for computations in Bayesian networks.

Let us look at probabilistic reasoning in Bayesian networks from the point of view of Churchman's classification. In the example of Figure 1 let us say that x_1 represents a disease, x_2 and x_3 represent possible physiological reactions initiated by the disease, x_5 represents the functioning level of some body organ, and x_4 and x_6 represent observable symptoms in a patient's body. Now let us say that in some case an x_6 event is observed and the reasoner is interested in knowing about some particular x_4 event. After performing the Bayesian computations, let us say we can find out the probability of the relevant x_4 event. But now let us consider the Bayesian network shown in Figure 2. It is the same as that in Figure 1 except that node x_3 is not included. A different probability value for the relevant x_4 event may be obtained when using the network of Figure 2. The network shown in Figure 3 is another alternative model of the world and may result in another inference about the x_4 event.

Let us consider the differences between the models of the situation represented by the three different networks. The network of Figure 2 considers x_2 to be the only possible cause of x_5; that of Figure 3 considers x_3 to be the only cause of x_5, and the network of Figure 1 includes both x_2 and x_3 as the possible causes of x_5. There may be still more possible causes of x_5 which are not included in any of these networks. In the context of network 2 we consider x_2 to be the only cause of x_5. That is, we are hypothesizing that all other causes are absent. In case of network 1 we do not know as to which of the two may have been the cause of x_5 and in the inference for x_4 we reflect the possibility of any of the two causes.

In any model of the situation it is sufficient to include only one cause for each such effect for which we need to know a cause. When two individual causes may be present we can view the effect as being caused by the interaction of the two individual causes, and then this interaction is the sole cause responsible for the effect. So we can say that a Bayesian network that includes all the known causes for each effect variable is a combination of all individual models that may be possible for the situation. An inference using such a network can be said to be based on the following: A number of models for the situation are known, and considering each of them to be possible, the inference reflects the effects of each possible model.

The Bayesian networks represent the knowledge of a causal relationship by means of conditional probabilities associated with the edges of the network. It has however been demonstrated [27] that conditional probabilities fail to capture the important information about the direction of causal influence and this information may be crucial in some instances of reasoning.

This type of reasoner is then closest to a Liebnizian inquirer. This inquirer, given a model of the situation, determines its logical consequences. The Bayesian network is then a model of the situation incorporating all known probabilistic relationships among the aspects of interest. The Bayesian networks cannot be used to construct a Kantian or a Hegelian type of inquirer where the reasoner needs to identify a suitable model from among all known models.

The use of probability theory for reasoning has also been explored by Lauritzen and Spiegelhalter [23]. Their techniques are also developed for a context in which a graphical structure represents the dependence relationship among propositions. Their method seeks to update probability information at all the other nodes when evidence is obtained at one of the nodes. Successive updates are performed when evidence at more than one node is available. About the model of the situation (the graph structure) the authors state:

> we assume a fixed model is currently being entertained and the numerical assessments are precisely specified, and our objective is to draw conclusions valid within this current structure, without any claim that the model is 'true'.

Therefore their techniques can also be used only by a Liebnizian inquirer, and Kantian and Hegelian inquirers, in their search for suitable models, would have to look for other techniques.

Theory of Evidence

Numeric calculi other than the traditional probability theories have also been developed and used in many reasoning systems. A popular calculus among these has been Shafer's theory of evidence [28].

If S is the universal set of events, then in probability theory the uncertainty information consists of a *probability density p* on the elements of S such that $p : S \rightarrow \{0,1\}$ and

$$\sum_{s \in S} p(s) = 1.$$

The theory of evidence defines a *mass function* which, it is postulated, is induced in us by the available evidence and assigns parts of finite amount of belief to subsets of S. Each assignment of a mass to a subset s of S represents that part of our belief which supports s without being able to allocate this belief among strict subsets of s. The *degree of belief* in a subset A of S, $bel(A)$ is defined as the sum of all masses that support either A or any of its strict subsets. That is,

$$bel(A) = \sum_{X \subset A, X \neq \phi} m(X).$$

The *degree of plausibility* of a subset A of S, $Pl(A)$ is defined as the sum of all those masses that can possibly support A. The possibility of a subset s supporting A means that the mass assigned to s can possibly gravitate to that strict subset of s which is also a subset of A. That is,

$$Pl(A) = \sum_{X \cap A \neq \phi} m(X).$$

When more than one mass function is available for a set S, they are combined using Dempster's rule which performs an orthogonal sum of the two mass functions. This method assumes the independence of the pieces of evidence, that is, an assumption which is made by a number of calculi but is difficult to enforce in most practical situations. The process of updating belief functions has been looked at from two different perspectives. There are some researchers who look at the belief and plausibility functions as the lower and upper envelopes of a family of probability distributions [29]. The techniques for updating with this perspective have been presented by Fagin [29]. In the view of some researchers the attempts to relate the theory of evidence to probability theory, as either a generalization or a speciali-zation, are not in the right direction and belief functions should be viewed in the light of their own framework. The ideas which view the updating process as only a transfer of belief in the light of new evidence are discussed in Smets [30].

Theory of Fuzzy Sets

The theory of fuzzy sets was originally developed by Lotfi Zadeh to capture and represent the notions that are imprecise, such as, "tall," "long," "young," etc. Systems for performing operations with these imprecise notions as operands, and to yield imprecise notions as re-sults have also been developed and examined [31–33]. From the point of view of a reasoner, this calculus provides a powerful formalism, and the only available one, for formally han-dling imprecise linguistic notions in any of the three types of inquirers. For a brief introduc-tion, let us consider the predicate *Low-Infl(x)*. Instead of evaluating to 'True' or 'False' for real-valued parameter x, the predicate acts as an elastic constraint on the acceptable values for x. For each x belonging to the set of real numbers, one can define $\mu_{\text{Low-Infl}}(x) \in [0, 1]$ as the extent of membership of the number x in the acceptable values for low inflation.

The grade of membership $\mu_{\text{Low-Infl}}(x)$ is also interpreted by Zadeh to be the possibil-ity, $\pi_{\text{Low-Infl}}(x)$, that the proposition is true with the value x. Necessity and possibility meas-ures have been defined for each proposition and can be easily computed.

This theory is very useful when one wants to make transitions between a very precise but uncertain proposition and a fuzzified and less precise but strictly true proposition. Magrez and Smets [34] present methods for computing the modalities (possibility and ne-cessity) of a more precise statement from the knowledge of a strictly true proposition. They also present a method for computing a strictly true proposition B from a proposition A qualified by necessity and possibility modalities.

A Liebnizian inquirer that fails to form a fact-net can attempt to construct another fact-net after making some of its propositions less precise. This is an aspect of reasoning we perform in our daily life but there is no formalism yet in artificial intelligence systems to simulate this capability. That is, our inability to precisely assess an enemy's strategy, based on incomplete and uncertain data, leads us to at least infer that an attack somewhere is imminent. The techniques presented by the theory of possibility for making transitions between related statements of varying precision are extremely useful for Liebnizian inquirers.

For example, if it is not possible to construct a model to infer that the inflation in the economy would be below 3%, we may try to find a less precise version of the proposition that can be supported by a model containing the available evidence. It may turn out that the available evidence within some model can let us infer the proposition "the inflation in the economy would be low" with complete certainty, that is with necessity equal to one. To determine the least imprecise version of a proposition that can be inferred with certainty is a type of reasoning that we perform very often. The framework of possibility theory helps us in designing such reasoners.

The same techniques can also be employed by the Kantian and Hegelian inquirers for constructing less precise or more precise models. This can be very useful in systems that perform adversarial arguments. In these situations one may want to advance a less precise proposition as argument instead of a proposition which can be countered as being not 'True' in at least some cases. To this end the theories of possibility and fuzzy sets provide a unique tool for the three types of inquirers.

FUSION APPROACHES

Formalisms for reasoning that are based on either formal logic alone or numerical approaches alone have addressed only limited and different aspects of an intelligent reasoning system. It is then natural that one would attempt to combine the representation and inferencing mechanisms of formal logic with those of the numeric approaches to build a more powerful reasoner. One such formalism is presented by Lee [35]. In this formalism fuzzy logic is used in conjunction with Robinson's Resolution Principle. In a first-order language L an n-ary predicate P represents a relation such that if U represents the universe then

$$P : U^n \rightarrow \{T,F\}.$$

In the fuzzy version M of the first-order language L the predicate P becomes a function from U^n into the $[0,1]$ interval. For example, if $P(x)$ represents "x is a large number" then $P(10^{10})$ may have a value 1, $P(10^{-10})$ may have a value 0, and $P(5370)$ may have a value of 0.3. It is assumed that the well-formed formulas are defined to be exactly the same as those in the two valued logic. Now if $T(S)$ denotes the truth value of a formula S of M, the evaluation procedure for a formula in M can be described as follows:

1. If S is the same as the ground atom A than $T(S) = T(A)$
2. If $S = -R$ then $T(S) = 1 - T(R)$
3. If $S = S_1 \wedge S_2$ then $T(S) = min[T(S1),T(S2)]$
4. If $S = S_1 \vee S_2$ then $T(S) = max[T(S1),T(S2)]$

With this formulation, it is proved in Lee [35] that if every clause in a set of ground clauses is something more than a "half truth" (i.e., $T(S) \geq 0.5$) and the most reliable ground clause has truth value *a* and the most unreliable clause has a truth value *b*, then we are guaranteed that all the logical consequences obtained by applying the resolution principle will have truth value between *a* and *b*. Unfortunately, the above result is restricted to ground clauses only. It is, therefore, not applicable to those situations in which a universal quantifier occurs in an axiom and the proofs involving this axiom require unification to be performed.

A number of formalisms in which numeric measures are associated with logical inferences have been examined by researchers engaged in designing expert systems. The Odds-ratio approach adopted in the PROSPECTOR system and Certainty Factors adopted in MYCIN are among the well known formalisms. Certainty Factors [36] work on the assumption that the knowledge represented by various rules is such that the independence assumption is not violated.

Rule-based expert systems are in spirit and principle based on the theoretical foundations provided by logic programming. A generalized framework for handling logic programs in which each literal is annotated by uncertainty knowledge has been presented by Kifer and Subrahmanian [37].

Let us consider a typical logic program. It contains clauses of the form

$$A \leftarrow B_1 \wedge B_2 \wedge \ldots B_k \tag{1}$$

An annotated clause, according to the formalism presented [37] has the following form:

$$A : \mu \leftarrow B_1 : \mu_1 \wedge B_2 : \mu_2 \ldots B_k : \mu_k. \tag{2}$$

Each annotated atom $B_k : \mu_k$ contains a usual atom B_k, and the annotation μ_k which may be either a constant, a variable or some other complex term and represents the uncertainty associated with B_k. Function *f*'s can be defined to compute the annotation of the atom in the head of the clause (*A*) when the annotations of all the (B_k) atoms are known.

An issue of interest is the following. Consider the case when two different ways of inferring the atom *A* exist. Since these are two different proofs of A, the final μ annotations for the atom *A* may be different in each proof. So, we obtain the two annotated atoms $A : \mu_1$ and $A : \mu_2$. According to Kifer [37], this is handled by the following type of inference rule

$$\frac{A : \mu_1, A : \mu_2}{A : F(\mu_1, \mu_2)} \tag{3}$$

where *F* is some function. When two different uncertainties are computed for some literal, the final uncertainty is defined as some function of the two different uncertainties. This is the same as is done in most numeric calculi for handling uncertainty and is useful in many applications. From the perspective of constructing causal models and arguments the reasoning needs to be done in a somewhat different manner. If *A* represents the variable *The-accused-is-Guilty* and two different proofs yield the atoms (*A* : 0.9) and (*A* : 0.05), then, to the opposing attorneys the function of two annotation values may not be of as much interest as the respective proofs by the opposing attorneys. Replacing the function *F* above by Max or Min, and keeping track of the various proofs may help us, but we would have to first search through all possible proofs before obtaining the desired argument (=proof). So, we see that the focus in these approaches is also toward a Liebnizian type of inquirer and not toward a Kantian of Hegelian type of inquirer.

THE MECHANICAL REASONER

A Liebnizian inquirer is suitable for well structured domains but one strongly feels the need for a Hegelian type of inquirer in most other situations. Let us examine a few examples. In problems of medical diagnosis the reasoner must proceed onward from an initial knowledge about the patient which consists of some observable symptoms and the medical history of the patient. The reasoner may then perform the following two steps:

1. Perform more tests etc. to determine a causal model of the physiological processes in the patient's body that explains the observed symptoms.
2. The above model being the diagnosis, determine a treatment that attenuates or removes the causes of undesirable effects.

The first task can be performed by a number of iterations of hypothesize-and-test steps. That is, given the knowledge about the symptoms, one hypothesizes one or more models and then performs tests to check the hypotheses. Information gained by performing the tests can be included in the next iteration to hypothesize new models. In the preceding section, Figure 2 and Figure 3 represent two possible models of the situation. Tests can be performed in the context of each model to verify the inferences for the unobserved nodes of the models.

The numeric approaches, in being consistent with their axioms and semantics, may not be applicable in many situations. For example, when dealing with the Iraqi threat to Saudi Arabia, President Bush declared that he has 'drawn a line in sand' and implied that Iraqi forces must not cross it. In this situation there is no sound probabilistic basis for quantifying the uncertainty associated with various events that may possibly be encountered if this 'line in sand' is crossed or not crossed. The logic *LL* of Halpern and Rabin [11] can determine the *likelihood* of a proposition p and we can find out if it is L^2p, L^3p, or L^kp, where L^2p stands for LLp meaning that it is likely that p is likely. According to the semantics of this logic L^kp holds if a state along a sequence of states representing "Likely successors of states" can be found in which L^kp is consistent. But the model for the logic represented by a tree of states must be made available before the reasoning can begin. For a new situation such as the one above, one needs a model in which all possible consistent states have already been included. The experts of the domain are expected to make this state-structure available to the reasoner who can then inquire if a proposition is likely or not, and if yes, in which state.

According to the semantics of *LL* [11] the knowledge of the expert that links various possible states of the world in the tree structure is her knowledge about various extralogical axioms, rules, and hunches embodying her past experience. Such an approach may be useful for domains where a manageable number of possible states of the situation is sufficient to handle most instances of the reasoning exercise. In a domain like medical diagnosis, or automobile fault diagnosis, it may be possible to construct the set of frequently occurring states. But it is not possible to maintain an enumerated set of all conceivable states that a situation may evolve into. For example, the situation created by the Iraqi invasion of Kuwait, and possible ways of dealing with it could not have been enumerated and kept ready for a reasoner.

The task of an intelligent reasoner is also to enumerate that subset of conceivable states of the world which may become very likely due to some observed developments. It is this capability to construct the hypothetical states that become relevant which we want the reasoner to possess. The enumeration of hypotheses can be done by constructing them from the very primitive innate ideas about the world. The primitives available for constructing possible states are the reasoner's knowledge of the axioms and rules governing the domain

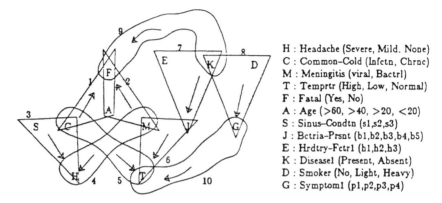

H : Headache (Severe, Mild, None)
C : Common-Cold (Infctn, Chrnc)
M : Meningitis (viral, Bactrl)
T : Temprtr (High, Low, Normal)
F : Fatal (Yes, No)
A : Age (>60, >40, >20, <20)
S : Sinus-Condtn (s1,s2,s3)
J : Bctria-Prsnt (b1,b2,b3,b4,b5)
E : Hrdtry-Fctr1 (h1,h2,h3)
K : Disease1 (Present, Absent)
D : Smoker (No, Light, Heavy)
G : Symptom1 (p1,p2,p3,p4)

FIGURE 4.   Example of domain knowledge hypergraph.

and his past knowledge. A Kantian or Hegelian inquirer is expected to select the optimal model when given some evidence, but if the number of possible models is so large that it is impossible to explicitly store each possible model then one must implicitly store these models by storing the basic components from which these models may be constructed.

The pieces of primitive knowledge that are useful for constructing causal models are the knowledge regarding individual causal relationships. Figure 4 shows an example where a hypergraph structure has been used to represent the knowledge of known causal relationships. A hypergraph structure is suitable because a hyperedge can easily capture the notion of some effect being caused by an interaction of two or more other aspects of the situation. A hyperedge can include more than two nodes of a graph in it and is represented in Figure 4 by either a closed curve or a polygon. For example, the hyperedge number 3 includes nodes S, C, and N and the arrow pointing to N signifies that an interaction between S and C causally affects N. Each subgraph of this hypergraph, such that only one cause is included for each effect, represents one possible causal model of some situation. The hypergraph consisting of hyperedges for all known causal relationships about a domain implicitly includes in it all possible models of various situations in that domain.

Consider the situation in which the presence of three types of bacteria, BA, BB, and BC is of interest. Also consider some organ C which can be found to be defective in one of the five different ways, say, d_1, d_2, etc. Now let us say the known causal links between the bacteria and the defects are the following:

> BA when present alone is highly likely to cause d_1 but may also sometimes cause d_2.
> BA and BB when present together, interact and this interaction is highly likely to cause d_3, and may also sometimes cause d_1.
> BA, BB, and BC when present together, interact and this interaction is highly likely to cause d_2 and may sometimes cause d_4.
> BB when present alone is highly likely to cause d_5 but may also sometimes cause d_2.

The hypergraph in Figure 5 includes a hyperedge for each of these possible causal relationships. Which defect is being caused is determined not by the presence of a particular bacteria, but by the presence of one or other causal relationship. A model of the situation should therefore hypothesize the set of causal relationships that are present and not that of

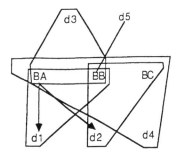

FIGURE 5.   Hypergraph model for possible causal links in bacteria example.

individual bacteria. That is, when one of the d_is is observed, the reasoner should hypothesize by selecting one of the hyperedges and not by selecting an individual bacteria.

When we use the joint probability distribution of all the bacteria and all the defects and use it to construct a Bayesian network as shown in Figure 6, we lose all the knowledge about individual causal relationships. Each edge between a bacteria and the defects represents a relationship summed up over all possible causal relationships according to which the bacteria could have affected the organ. Each edge therefore does not represent a single causal relationship, but a sum total of all those causal relationships of which the two connected nodes are a constituent, and is therefore not suitable when the objective of creating a model is to identify the active causal relationships.

A reasoner that constructs suitable causal models by finding appropriate subgraphs of the hypergraph has been presented [38]. Each hyperedge in this methodology also stores a joint probability distribution of all the nodes included in the hyperedge. This reasoner needs to know the criterion for preferring a model and the observed events. For example, the preference criterion could be "maximum probability for the event that the patient would die." The reasoner would then find that subgraph of the hypergraph which includes all the observed symptoms and is such that among all other possible models it satisfies the preference criterion. The algorithm is based on a heuristic search in the space of all possible subgraphs of the hypergraph. This reasoner can construct causal models and can work as a Hegelian or Kantian inquirer. This type of reasoner can be called a "constructive Reasoner" because the capability to determine the suitable model is like constructing an argument to support a suit-

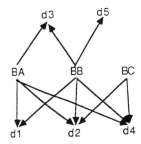

FIGURE 6.   A Bayesian network for bacteria example.

able thesis. This type of a reasoner can also be called a "hypothetical reasoner" because it can be used for hypothesizing suitable models of the world that may be of interest to the reasoner. For example, hypothetical models of the world in which an army may achieve victory may be needed to plan its offensive strategy and hypothetical models in which an army faces defeat may be used to plan its defensive strategy.

Any one of the various uncertainty calculi can be incorporated into such a mechanical reasoner. For example, if the preference criterion for hypotheses is in terms of the preciseness of inferred propositions then we can adopt the possibility calculus or the calculus of the fuzzy sets, whereas if uncertainty of one of the many options is of concern we may adopt a probability calculus.

CONCLUSION

We have examined various types of uncertainty calculi, reasoners and reasoning frameworks in the preceding sections. A mechanical reasoner in our view should be able to act like a Liebnizian, or a Kantian, or a Hegelian inquirer. Most existing formalisms are closer to Liebnizian reasoners and in our view a significant amount of work needs to be done to develop the latter two types of reasoners. These latter two types of reasoners capture many of the intelligent aspects of our day to day reasoning.

REFERENCES

1. C. W. Churchman, *The Design of Inquiring Systems: Basic Concepts of Systems and Organization*, Basic Books Inc., New York, 1971.
2. I. I. Mitroff and M. Turoff, "The Whys Behind the Hows," *IEEE Spectrum*, 62–71 (March 1973).
3. A. Tversky and D. Kahneman, *Judgement under Uncertainty: Heuristics and Biases*, Cambridge University Press, New York, 1982.
4. W. J. Long, S. Naimi, M. G. Criscitiello, and S. Kurzrok, "Reasoning About Therapy from a Physiological Model," in *MEDINFO 86*, R. Salamon, B. Blum, and M. Jorgensen (eds.), Elsevier Science Publishers B.V. (North Holland), Amsterdam, 1986, pp. 756–760.
5. G. F. Cooper, "NESTOR: A Computer-based Medical Diagnostic Aid that Integrates Causal and Probabilistic Knowledge," Ph.D. dissertation, Department of Computer Science, Stanford University, Stanford, CA, 1984.
6. B. Kuipers, "Causal Reasoning in Medicine: Analysis of a Protocol," *Cognitive Sci.*, 8, 363–385 (1984).
7. R. Davis and W. C. Hamscher, "Model-Based Reasoning: Troubleshooting," A.I. Memo No. 1059, MIT AI Laboratory, July 1988.
8. Y. Iwasaki and H. A. Simon, "Causality in Device Behaviour," *Artificial Intelligence*, 29, 3–32 (1986).
9. J. de Kleer and J. S. Brown, "Theories of Causal Ordering," *Artificial Intelligence, 29*, 33–61 (1986).
10. P. Chesseman, "In Defense of Probability," *Proc. IJCAI*, 1985, pp. 1002–1009.
11. J. Y. Halpern and M. O. Rabin, "A Logic to Reason About Likelihood," *Artificial Intelligence, 32*, 379–405 (1987).
12. D. Poole, "A Logical Framework for Default Reasoning," *Artificial Intelligence, 36*, 27–47 (1988).

13. D. McDermott and J. Doyle, "Non-Monotonic Logic I," *Artificial Intelligence, 13*(1) (1980).

14. R. Reiter, "A Logic for Default Reasoning," *Artificial Intelligence, 13*(1), 81–132 (1980).

15. J. Doyle, "A Truth Maintenance System," *Artificial Intelligence, 12*(3) (1979).

16. J. de Kleer, "An Assumption Based TMS," *Artificial Intelligence, 28*, 127–162 (1986).

17. J. McCarthy, "Circumscription—A Form of Non-Monotonic Reasoning," *Artificial Intelligence, 13*, 27–39 (1980).

18. J. McCarthy, "Applications of Circumscription to Formalizing Common-Sense Knowledge," *Artificial Intelligence, 28*(1), 89–116 (1986).

19. V. Lifschitz, "Closed World databases and Circumscription," *Artificial Intelligence, 27*(2), 229–235 (1985).

20. K. Segerberg, "Qualitative Probability in a Modal Setting," *Proc. 2nd Scandinavian Logic Symposium*, E. Fenstad (ed.), North-Holland, Amsterdam, 1971.

21. P. Gardenfors, "Qualitative Probability as Intensional Logic," *J. Philos. Logic, 4*, 171–185 (1975).

22. J. Pearl, "Fusion, Propagation and Structuring in Belief Networks," *Artificial Intelligence, 29*, 241–288 (1986).

23. S. L. Lauritzen and D. J. Spiegelhalter, "Local Computations with Probabilities on Graphical Structures and Their Application to Expert Systems," *J. R. Statist. Soc.*, series B, *50*(2), 157–224 (1988).

24. R. D. Shachter, "Intelligent Probabilistic Inference," *Uncertainty in Artificial Intelligence*, L. N. Kanal and J. F. Lemmer (eds.), North Holland, Amsterdam, 1986, pp. 371–382.

25. G. F. Cooper, "The Computational Complexity of Probabilistic Inference Using Bayesian Belief Networks," *Artificial Intelligence, 42*, 393–405 (1990).

26. K.-C. Chang and R. Fung, "Refinement and Coarsening of Bayesian Networks," in *Uncertainty in Artificial Intelligence 6*, North Holland, Amsterdam, 1991, pp. 435–445.

27. D. Hunter, "Causality and Maximum Entropy Updating," *Int. J. Approximate Reasoning, 3*, 87–114 (1989).

28. G. Shafer, *A Mathematical Theory of Evidence*, Princeton University Press, Princeton, 1976.

29. R. Fagin and J. Y. Halpern, "A New Approach to Updating Beliefs," in *Uncertainty in Artificial Intelligence 6*, North Holland, Amsterdam, 1991, pp. 347–374.

30. P. Smets, "The Transferable Belief Model and Other Interpretations of Dempster-Shafer's Model," in *Uncertainty in Artificial Intelligence 6*, North Holland, Amsterdam, 1991, pp. 375–383.

31. L. A. Zadeh, "Fuzzy Sets as a Basis for a Theory of Possibility," *Fuzzy Sets Systems, 1*(1), 3–28 (1978).

32. L. A. Zadeh, "PRUF A Meaning Representation Language for Natural Languages," in *Fuzzy Reasoning and Its Applications*, E. H. Mamdani and B. R. Gaines (eds.), Academic Press, New York, 1981, pp. 1–66.

33. P. Smets, "Elementary Semantic Operators," in *Fuzzy Set and Possibility Theory*, R. R. Yager (ed.), Pergamon Press, New York, 1982, pp. 247–256.

34. P. Magrez and P. Smets, "Epistemic Necessity, Possibility, and Truth. Tools for Deal-

ing with Imprecision and Uncertainty in Fuzzy Knowledge Based Systems," *Int. J. Approximate Reasoning,* 3(1), 35–57 (January 1989).

35.   R. C. T. Lee, "Fuzzy Logic and the Resolution Principle," *J. ACM, 19*(1), 109–119 (January 1972).

36.   B. G. Buchanan and E. H. Shortliffe, *Rule-Based Expert Systems: The MYCIN Experiments of the Stanford Heuristic Programming Project*, Addison-Wesley Publishers, Reading, MA, 1984.

37.   M. Kifer and V. S. Subrahmanian, "Theory of Generalized Annotated Logic Programming and Its Applications," to appear in the *J. Logic Programming.*

38.   R. Bhatnagar, "Construction of Preferred Causal Hypotheses for Reasoning with Uncertain Knowledge, Ph.D. dissertation, Computer Science Department, University of Maryland, College Park, MD, 1989.

RAJ K. BHATNAGAR

LAVEEN N. KANAL

SINGLE-AGENT AND GAME-TREE SEARCH

INTRODUCTION

Problem solving by exhaustive enumeration is a common computational technique that often relies on a decision tree framework to ensure that all combinations are considered. This approach is helped by a wealth of powerful tools for supporting tree searches. A related but slightly more general model is based on a state-space approach in which, from a given state of the system and a set of actions (i.e., given a description vector), the successor states are expanded until a specified goal is reached. Selecting an action transforms one state of a system into another, where perhaps a different set of actions is possible. A variety of general methods may be posed this way, for example, to find a sequence of actions that convert a system from an original to a final state with a prespecified set of properties (i.e., to seek a goal), or to find all such sets of actions (exhaustive enumeration), or to find the fewest actions needed to reach a goal (find a minimal cost solution), and so on.

Because these state transition problems can be described by graphs, which in turn are supported by a substantial mathematical theory, efficient methods for solving graph-based problems are constantly sought. However, many of the most direct classical methods for finding optimal solutions (e.g., dynamic programming) have a common fundamental failing: they cannot handle large problems (whose solution requires many transitions), because they must maintain an exponentially increasing number of partially expanded states (nodes) as the search front grows. Since storage space for intermediate results often is a more serious limitation than inadequate computing speed, heuristics and algorithms that trade space for time have practical advantages, rendering solutions that are otherwise unattainable.

To illustrate these points, and to provide insights into widely applicable and generally useful techniques that can be used to improve many optimization methods, we will consider the subdomains of single agent (one-person) and adversary (two-person) games. In both cases solutions can be found by traversing a decision tree that spans all the possible states in the "game." Since the order in which the decisions are made is not necessarily important, it is common for identical states to exist at different places in the decision tree. Under these circumstances such trees might be viewed as graphs. Because a tree is an intrinsically simpler structure, as well as being more regular than a graph, we will temporarily ignore such duplications, but later we will introduce methods that explicitly recognize and eliminate duplicates, and so reduce the effective size of the search space.

SINGLE-AGENT SEARCH

As an example of a single-agent search problem consider the popular N-puzzle game, which is typified by N distinct tiles on a rectangular grid plus a single "empty tile" space. The object of the game is to slide the tiles until all are in specified positions (a goal state). Humans can be adept at this problem, even when N is large, but solve it without regard to optimality (least tile movement). For computers a simple optimal algorithm exists, one which is general and can be applied to a wide variety of state-space search applications. Called A* [1], it is guaranteed to find an optimal solution, but because of its high memory requirements it can handle only small problems (N≤12). A more recent variation, Iterative Deepening A* (IDA*) [2] draws effectively on the notion of successive refinement and uses an interesting technique that can be generally incorporated in tree searches. As we show later the iterative deepening idea has been around for more than two decades in the computer chess community, where it is highly refined and enjoys great popularity. In IDA* the iterative technique controls elegantly the growth of memory needed in the expansion of a one-person game tree, but in such a way that an optimal solution is still guaranteed.

The essence of A* is the use of a heuristic evaluation function to guide the search by ordering successor states according to estimated cost of the path (set of transitions) from the start to the goal state. This is possible by using an evaluation function of the form:

$$f(n) = g(n) + h(n),$$

where $g(n)$ is the measured cost of the path from the start state (say node 0) to the current state, node n, and $h(n)$ is an estimate of the cost of the path from n to the goal state. If $h(n)$ never overestimates the remaining cost, A* is guaranteed to find an optimal (least cost) solution. The properties of $g(n)$ and $h(n)$ are easily seen from the simple N-puzzle example. Here $g(n)$ is exactly equal to the number of tile movements taken so far to convert the start state to the current state. Further, if $h(n)$ measures the sum of the Manhattan distances (i.e., the sum of the vertical and horizontal displacements of each tile from its current square to its goal state square), then it never overestimates the number of tile movements required. It is comforting to have an algorithm guaranteeing an optimal solution but, as with most state-space search methods, even an almost perfect evaluation function excessively produces partially expanded states. By analogy with a technique pioneered in computer chess programs to keep the time cost of search within reasonable bounds, Korf developed a simple mechanism to control a single agent search based on the A* evaluation function, and so find an optimal solution by ensuring that no solution of lesser cost exists. Korf's [2] iterative deepening version of A* eliminates the need to maintain open/closed lists of node state vectors, and has linear space complexity.

Iterative Deepening

Iterative Deepening A* is interesting and, as Korf shows, is more powerful than A*, in that it can find optimal solutions to some bigger problems, since its memory management costs are negligible, and space requirements are linear with depth. Even so IDA* is not universally successful, it can behave especially poorly on the traveling salesman problem. Again, illustrating with the N-puzzle, if node 0 represents the start state, a lower bound on the cost from the start position is:

$$d = f(0) = h(0),$$

since $g(0)$ is zero, so at least d tile movements are needed. Thus during the first iteration solutions of length d are sought. As soon as the condition

$$g(n) + h(n) > d$$

holds, the search from node n is discontinued. In problems of this type $g(n)$ increases monotonically, so that unless $h(n)$ decreases by an amount equal to g's increase the search stops quickly. Thus during each iteration a minimal expansion is done. If the goal state is not found, the depth of search is increased to the smallest value of $g(n) + h(n)$ attained in the previous iteration (always an increase of 2 for the N-puzzle), and the next iteration is started. The last iteration is usually the most expensive, especially if all the minimal cost solutions are sought. Even though more nodes may be expanded than for A*, the simplicity of the method makes IDA* the more useful algorithm in practice, because it eliminates costly mechanisms for maintaining the ordered list of states that remain to be expanded.

MIN-MAX SEARCH

So far we have considered how expansion of a game tree can be controlled by an evaluation function, and how the major shortcomings (excessive memory requirement) of a best-first state-space search can be overcome with a simple iterative depth-first search.

Iterative deepening is a powerful and general method whose effect can be further improved if used with some other refinements. These advantages can be seen better through the study of methods for searching two-person game trees, which represent a struggle between two opponents who move alternately. Because one side's gain (typically position or material in board games) usually reflects an equivalent loss for the opponent; these problems are often modeled by an exhaustive minimax search, so called because the first player is trying to maximize the gains while the second player (the hostile opponent) is minimizing them. In a few uninteresting cases the complete game tree is small enough that it can be traversed and every terminal (tip or leaf) node examined to determine precisely the value for the first player. The results from the leaf nodes are fed back to the root using the following back-up procedure. Given an evaluation function $f(n)$ which can measure the value of any leaf node from the first player's view: For a leaf node n

$$\text{MinMax}(n) = f(n) = \text{Evaluate}(n)$$

For any interior node, n, with successor nodes n_i

$$\text{MinMax}(n) = \underset{i}{\text{Max}}\ (-\text{MinMax}(n_i)).$$

Note that this formulation, referred to by Knuth and Moore [3] as *Negamax*, replaces the opponent's minimization function by an equivalent maximization of the negation of the successor values, thus achieving a more symmetric definition. Here Evaluate(n) is a function that computes the merit value of a leaf node, n, from the root node's viewpoint. For a true leaf (no successors) the merit value will be thought of as exact or accurate, and without error. Building exhaustive minimax enumeration trees for difficult games like chess and Go is impractical, since they would contain about 10^{40} or 10^{100} nodes, respectively. Evaluate(n) can also be used at pseudo-leaf (frontier or horizon) nodes, where it computes a value that estimates the merit of the best successor. Again the value will be designated as true or accurate, even though it is only an estimate (in some more sophisticated search methods an attempt is made to account for the uncertainty in the leaf values). Under the negamax backing up rule, the sequence of branches from the root to the best pseudo-leaf node is referred to as the *Principal Variation*, and the merit value of the leaf node at the end of the path is the one that is backed up to the root and becomes the value of the tree.

Fail-Soft Alpha-Beta

One early paper on computer chess [4] recognized that a full minimax search was not essential to determine the value of the tree. Some years later a little known work by Brudno [5]

```
function ABSearch (Position, Alpha, Beta, Height);
  if Height ≡ 0
    then return (Evaluate(Position[0]));            {frontier node}
  N = SelectNextNode (Position[0]);                 {get first move}
  if N ≡ null
    then return (Evaluate(Position[0]));     {leaf, no successors}
  Best = -∞;
  while N ≠ null do begin
    Merit = - ABSearch (Position[N], -Beta, -Max(Alpha,Best), Height-1);
    if Merit > Best then begin
      Best = Merit;                                 {improved value}
      if Best ≥ Beta then return (Best);              {cut-off}
    end;
    N = SelectNextNode (Position[N]);               {get next move}
  end while;
  return (Best);                           {return the subtree value}
end ABSearch;
```

FIGURE 1.   Fail-soft alpha-beta algorithm.

provided a theoretical basis for pruning in minimax search. From all these observations the alpha-beta pruning algorithm, was developed, and it remains today the mainstay for game-tree search. Of course many improvements and enhancements have been added over the years, and some of these will be explored here. An important point about the alpha-beta algorithm is that it is a simple branch and bound method, where the bound for all Max nodes (including the root) is named Alpha, and the bound for the Min nodes is named Beta. In effect, search can be viewed as taking place within a window or range of integer values Alpha to Beta with the underlying assumption that the integer value, V, of the tree lies in that range (that is, Alpha < V and V < Beta). Clearly if the initial values of Alpha and Beta are -∞ and +∞, respectively, the merit value of the tree will fall within that infinite range. In contrast, one popular enhancement to the alpha-beta algorithm, called *aspiration search*, artificially narrows these bounds, hoping to reduce the search space by cutting out more of the tree, and gambling that the true merit will still be found. To be most effective, aspiration search should include Fishburn's *fail-soft* idea [6]. The important theoretical point behind that idea is presented in Figure 1, which shows psuedo code for ABSearch (a basic version of the alpha-beta algorithm).

In Figure 1, the integer parameters Alpha and Beta represent lower and upper bounds, and Height is the remaining distance (in ply) to the search frontier. Also, Position [0] represents a pointer to the current node (state), and Position [N] is a pointer to the N-th successor of the current node. ABSearch returns the merit value of the subtree by using a recursive backing up process. One important feature of this skeleton is that the maximum depth of search is limited to Height from the root. Clearly this depth parameter can be manipulated to allow selective extensions of the search depth.

Aspiration Search

The essence of the fail-soft approach is the initialization of Best to -∞ instead of Alpha, as seems natural. Thus, even if the initial bounds (Alpha, Beta) are too narrow, after the search is complete we will know whether $V \leq$ Best $\leq$ Alpha, or whether Beta $\leq$ Best $\leq V$. That is, not only determine whether the search failed low or high, but also provide an upper/lower bound of the tree's true value. In the case of failure, the tree must be re-searched with correct bounds of either $-\infty$ to Best, or Best to $+\infty$, as appropriate. So far we have considered only a basic minimax pruning process incorporating a fail-soft mechanism, so that the best available merit value is returned when inappropriate Alpha-Beta bounds are chosen. Inclusion of this feature makes possible a useful variation, called aspiration search or narrow window search, which initially restricts the Alpha-Beta bounds to a narrow range around an expected value, V_0, for the tree. Thus at the root node an aspiration search might be invoked by setting Alpha = $V_0 - \varepsilon$ and Beta = $V_0 + \varepsilon$ and

$$\text{Best} = \text{ABSearch (Position, Alpha, Beta, Height)}$$

As a result, if the condition Alpha < Best < Beta is not met a re-search is necessary, as detailed in the following code:

```
if Best ≥ Beta then
    Best = ABSearch (Position, Best, +∞, Height);
if Best ≤ Alpha then
    Best = ABSearch (Position, -∞, Best, Height);
```

The advantages of working with narrow bounds can be significant, especially for games where it is easy to estimate V_0. However, early experimental evidence [7–9] shows that use of heuristics to estimate the search window in Aspiration Search still does not usually yield a performance comparable to the *Principal Variation Search* (PVS) algorithm [10]. The main disadvantage of Aspiration Search is that the estimate of V_0 is made strictly before the search begins, while for PVS the value of V_0 is continually refined during the search. Thus PVS benefits more from application-dependent knowledge that provides a good move ordering, and so almost guarantees that the value of the first leaf will be a good estimator of the tree's merit value. Nevertheless a problem remains: no matter how narrow the initial bounds, nor how good the move ordering, the size of the minimal game tree still grows exponentially with depth.

Approximating Game Trees

In practice, because game trees are so large, one must search a series of approximating subtrees of length Height, as the code in Figure 1 shows. Thus, instead of true leaf nodes, where the value of the node is known exactly, we have pseudo-leaf nodes or frontier nodes where the value of the unexplored subtree beyond this horizon is estimated by the evaluation function. In the simplest case the approximating tree has a prespecified fixed depth, so that all the frontier nodes are at the same distance from the root. This model is satisfactory for analytical and simulation studies of searching performance, but it does not reflect the current state of progress in application domains. For example, a typical chess program builds its approximating tree with three distinct phases. From the root all moves are considered up to some fixed depth, d (usually a constant), but if a node has only one or two legal successors (e.g., after a checking move in chess) it is not counted toward the depth, so the effective length of some paths could be $d + d/2$ (since in practice only one side at a time administers a series of checks). Once the nominal depth of the first phase is reached, a second phase extends the search by another constant amount (again force nodes are not counted in this extension), but at every new node only a selection of the available moves is considered. This heuristic is the dangerous and discredited practice of forward pruning. It works here because the exhaustive search layer finds short term losses that lead to long term gains (obvious sacrifices), while the next stage uses forward pruning to eliminate immediately losing moves and seemingly inferior short term continuations, thus reducing the demands on the third (quiescence search) phase. Although not ad hoc, this approach is ill-defined (although clearly some programmers have superior methods), but as we shall see it leads naturally to several good possibilities for a probabilistic way of controlling the width of the search.

The third (quiescent) phase of search is more dynamic. It is called a quiescence search, because its purpose is to improve the evaluation estimate of critical frontier nodes involving dynamic terms that cannot be measured accurately by the static evaluation function. In chess these terms include captures, checks, pins, and promotions. It is essential that these quiescence trees be severely restricted in width, only containing moves that deal with the nonquiescent elements. There have been several studies of desirable properties of quiescence search, but most noteworthy is the work of Kaindl [*11, 12*], the method of singular extensions by Anantharaman et al. [*13*], and the formalization of the null-move heuristic [14].

In summary, the three-layer search employs algorithmic backward pruning which is at first exhaustive, then uses limited forward pruning of seemingly obvious losing moves, and finally a highly directed selective search. Thus the use of heuristics increases with the depth of search, thereby introducing more uncertainty but extending the depth (frontier/horizon) along lines of greatest instability, thereby clarifying the outcome. This approach has many practical advantages and can be used equally effectively in many decision tree applications.

There is no theoretical model for these variable depth search processes. Analytical studies usually restrict themselves to the use of uniform trees (trees with exactly W successors at each node and fixed depth, D). The most commonly quoted result is the figure for the size of the minimal (optimal) game tree, which has

$$W^{\left\lceil \frac{D}{2} \right\rceil} + W^{\left\lfloor \frac{D}{2} \right\rfloor} - 1$$

leaf nodes. In Knuth and Moore's [*3*] terminology, the minimal game tree is made up of type 1, type 2 and type 3 nodes. Marsland and Popowich [*15*] call these PV, CUT and ALL nodes, respectively, to make it clearer where cut-offs may occur, as Figure 2 shows.

Principal Variation Search

An important reason for considering fail-soft alpha-beta is that it leads naturally to more efficient implementations, specifically Principal Variation Search (PVS), which in turn uses a *Null Window Search* (NWS). The fundamental idea here is that as soon as a better move (and bound) is found, an attempt is made to prove that the remaining alternatives are inferior. A null window is used so that no integer value can fall between these two adjacent bounds. Thus all remaining searches with that window will fail, hopefully low, proving the inferiority of the move. If the null window search fails high, then the move is superior to the previously best and the search will have to be repeated with the correct bounds, to find the proper path and value, as Figure 3 shows. Figure 4, on the other hand, illustrates exactly how the bounds are set and how the tree's merit value is backed up in a small example.

Thus the fundamental reason for the form of Figure 3 is now clear, it reflects the structure of a game tree in that at PV nodes an alpha-beta search (PVS) is used, while CUT and ALL nodes are initially visited by NWS.

Note that use of NWS is not essential, since in the PVS code of Figure 3 the line

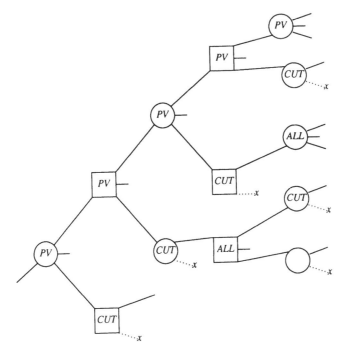

FIGURE 2.   Structure of a minimal game tree.

$$\text{Merit} = -\text{NWS (Position[N], -Alpha, Height - 1)}$$

can be replaced by

$$\text{Merit} = -\text{PVS (Position[N], -Alpha - 1, -Alpha, Height - 1)}$$

to produce a compact fully recursive alternative. This more compact implementation also illustrates better the notion of a null window. It encapsulates everything into one routine and is precisely the approach taken in an early description [7] and in NegaScout [16]. The use of NWS serves two purposes: first it makes possible a direct comparison with Scout [17] and also, as we shall see later, this separation helps the design of parallel game-tree search algorithms. Although Scout is a depth-first search it does not seem to be used in practice, perhaps, as Kaindl [9] points out, because it does not gain from the benefit that fail-soft alpha-beta provides.

Figure 3 explains how a "fail high" null-window search at ALL and CUT nodes is converted into a PVS re-search of a PV node. It also shows that the status of a node changes to PV whenever its value increases, so that it is re-searched by PVS. Reinefeld and Marsland [18] built on this model and developed some results for an *average* game tree, based on the

```
function PVS (Position, Alpha, Beta, Height);
    if Height ≡ 0 then return (Evaluate(Position[0]);
    N = SelectNextNode (Position[0]);
    if N ≡ null then return (Evaluate(Position[0]));
    Best = - PVS (Position[N], -Beta, -Alpha, Height-1);
    while SelectNextNode(Position[N]) ≠ null do
        if Best ≥ Beta then return (Best);                {CUT node}
        N = SelectNextNode (Position[N]);
        Alpha = Max(Alpha, Best);
        Merit = - NWS (Position[N], -Alpha, Height-1);
        if (Merit > Best) then
            if (Merit ≤ Alpha) or (Merit ≥ Beta)
                then Best = Merit
                else Best = - PVS (Position[N], -Beta, -Merit, Height-1);
    end;
    return (Best);                                        {PV node}
end PVS;


function NWS (Position, Beta, Height);
    if Height ≡ 0 then return (Evaluate(Position[0]);
    N = SelectNextNode (Position[0]);
    if N ≡ null then return (Evaluate(Position[0]));
    Best = -∞;
    while N ≠ null do
        Merit = - NWS (Position[N], -Beta+1, Height-1);
        if Merit > Best then Best = Merit;
        if Best ≥ Beta then return (Best);                {CUT node}
        N = SelectNextNode (Position[N]);
    end;
    return (Best);                                        {ALL node}
end NWS;
```

FIGURE 3.   Principal variation (null window) search.

notion of a research rate, and developed the theoretical conditions under which PVS is better than pure alpha-beta.

NegaScout and Scout

Fully recursive versions of PVS have been produced [7], but particularly interesting is Reinefeld's [16] NegaScout model, which Kaindl [9] shows to be a more efficient implementation of Scout [17]. NegaScout introduced an admissible (without error) pruning technique near the frontier in contrast to the more speculative *razoring* method of Birmingham and Kent [19], and the notion of a *futility cutoff*, best described by Schaeffer [20]. The essential idea behind razoring is that at the last move before the frontier the side to move will usually be able to improve the position, and hence the value of the node. In effect we assume that there is always at least one move that is better than simply passing, i.e., not moving. Therefore, if the current node merit value already exceeds the Beta bound, a cutoff is inevitable and the current node cannot be on the Principal Variation. This heuristic is widely applicable, but it is prone to serious failure. For example, in chess, where passing is not allowed, razoring will fail in zugzwang situations, since every move there causes the value for the moving player to deteriorate. More commonly, when the pieces are already on "optimal squares" most moves will appear to lead to inferior positions. This is especially true when the side to move has a piece newly under attack. The futility cutoff, on the other hand,

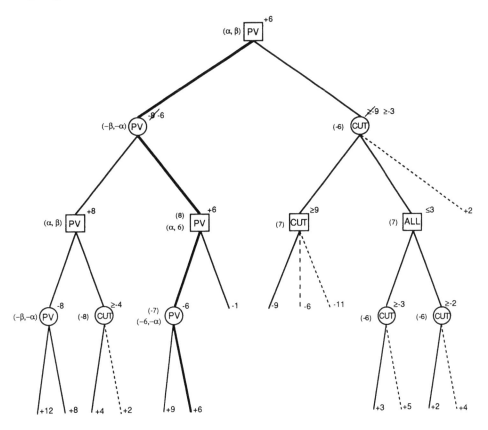

FIGURE 4.   Sample pruning of a minimax tree by PVS/NWS.

is a little safer. Again at the layer before the frontier, if the current node value is less than Alpha, only moves that have the potential to raise the node value above Alpha are of interest. This will include appropriate captures and all checking moves. It may be futile to consider the rest unless the current node value is close to Alpha. Abramson [21] provides an accessible review of razoring and other control strategies for two-player games.

Other Search Methods

As IDA* has shown, depth first searches have modest storage needs and can benefit from iterative deepening. For the two-person games there are several best-first searches, but they all suffer from the same excessive demands on memory and heavy overhead in maintenance of support data structures. Nevertheless, the state space searches are interesting on theoretical grounds and contain ideas that carry over into other domains. For example, Berliner's [22] best first B* algorithm returns a two-part evaluation range with pessimistic and opti-

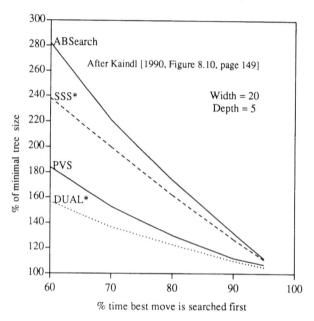

FIGURE 5.   Search of strongly ordered uniform trees.

mistic bounds. Since the real aim is often to find the best choice or move (with only secondary interest in the expected value), B* uses its bounds to identify that move. The best move
is the one whose pessimistic value is at least equal to the largest optimistic value of all the
alternatives. Note that it is not necessary to search intensely enough to reduce the range
intervals to a single point, just enough to find the best move, thus some search reduction is
theoretically possible. Later Palay [23] developed an algorithm called PB* to introduce
probability distributions into the evaluation function.

     SSS*, a best-first algorithm developed by Stockman [24], is also of special interest.
Closely related to A*, SSS* dominates the alpha-beta algorithm in the sense that it never
visits more leaf nodes. Also, with the change proposed by Campbell [25] to alter the order in
which the tree is traversed, SSS* expands a subset of the nodes visited by a normal alpha-
beta search, e.g., ABSearch (Fig. 1). But more efficient depth-first search algorithms, like
PVS, exist and they too dominate ABSearch. Statistically, most efficient of all is a variation
of SSS*, named DUAL* by Marsland et al. [26] which is formed by complementing the
actions at the min and max nodes. The duality has the effect of doing a directed (left to right)
search at the root node and SSS* below that. Thus DUAL* has lower memory requirement
(since it uses SSS* to search a 1-ply shallower tree), but otherwise shares the same burden-
some overheads. Although Reinefeld [27, Table 3.1, p. 102] has established the dominance
over an alpha-beta search on theoretical grounds, the statistical performance of these algorithms varies widely. In particular, SSS* does not do well on bushy trees (average width >
20) of odd depth, as Figure 5 illustrates for strongly ordered trees [10]. Such trees are intended to have properties similar to the game trees that arise during a typical application like
chess, yet permit a better comparison than is possible with random data. SSS* does not per-

form well here because the trees used were not random, rather the best move was searched first more than 60% of the time. DUAL* is best because of the directional search at the root. However, both SSS* and DUAL* share A*'s problem, namely that the CPU overhead to maintain the active states is more than five times that required for a depth-first search [26]. Thus, lower leaf nodes counts for SSS* and DUAL* do not normally translate into lower CPU utilization, quite the contrary. The idea for DUAL* came from a study of parallel SSS* algorithms [28] and opens a whole new world of game tree search studies.

Of the other new techniques, McAllister's [29] so called conspiracy number search is especially interesting. Although this method also makes heavy demands on computer memory, it is one of the class of probabilistic algorithms that attempt to measure the stability of search. A tree value is more secure (unlikely to change) if several nodes would have to "conspire" (all be in error) to change the root value. Application of this method is still in its infancy, although Schaeffer [30] has provided some working experiences and Allis et al. [31] make a comparison between SSS*, alpha-beta, and conspiracy number search for random trees. Since many game-tree applications require the search of bushy trees (e.g., chess and Go) some form of probabilistic basis for controlling the width of search would be of great importance.

Memory Functions for Iterative Deepening

The main problem with direct searches to prespecified minimal depth is that they provide inadequate control over the CPU needs. Since CPU control can be important in human–computer play, an iterative deepening method was introduced by Scott [32]. In its early form, rather than embark on a search to depth N-ply (and not knowing how long it might take), a succession of searches of length 1-ply, 2-ply, 3-ply etc. were used until the allotted time is reached. The best move found during one iteration is used as the first move for the start of the next and so on. Over the following years this idea was refined and elaborated, notably by Slate and Atkin [33] until by the late 1970s several memory functions were in use to improve the efficiency of successive iterations. It is this increased efficiency that allows an iterative deepening search to pay for itself and, with memory function help, to be faster than a direct D-ply search. The simplest enhancement is the use of a *refutation table*, as presented by Akl and Newborn [34]. Here, during each iteration, a skeletal set of paths from the root to the limiting frontier is maintained. One of those paths is the best found so far, and is called the Principal Variation (or Principal Continuation). The other paths simply show one way for the opponent to refute them, that is, to show they are inferior. As part of each iteration these paths are used to start the main alternatives, with the intention of again proving their inferiority. The overhead for the refutation table is best described in a new book by Levy and Newborn [35].

Transposition Table Management

More general than the refutation table is the *transposition table*, which in its simplest form is a large hash table for storing the results from searches of nodes visited so far. The results stored consist of: (a) the best available choice from the node, (b) the backed up value (merit) of the subtree from that node, (c) whether that value is a bound, and (d) the length of the subtree upon which the value is based. As with all hash tables, a key/lock entry is also required to confirm that the entry corresponds to the node being searched. The space needed for the key/lock field depends on the size of the hash table, but 48 bits is common. Problems with entry conflict error were initially dealt with by Zobrist [36] when he proposed a hashing method for Go. Much later, the application to computer chess was reviewed [37], with further insights by Nelson [*38*] and by Warnock and Wendroff [*39*]. The importance of the transposition table is twofold. Like a refutation table, it can be used to guide the next iteration, but being bigger it also contains information about the refutations (killer moves) in subtrees that are not part of the main continuation. Perhaps of greater importance is the benefit of information sharing during an iteration. Consider the case when an entry corresponding to the current subtree is found in the transposition table. If the depth field entry is not less than the remaining depth of search, it is possible to use the merit value stored in the entry as the value of the subtree from the node. This circumstance arises often, since transposition of moves is common in many two-person games. As a result, use of a transposition table reduces the effective size of the tree being searched; in extreme cases not only enabling a search of less than the minimal game tree, but also extending the search of some variations to almost double the frontier distance. More common, however, is use of the "move" from the transposition table. Typically that move was put there during a null window search, having caused a cut off, and is reused to guide the research down the refutation line.

Another memory function is the *history heuristic table*. This is a general method for identifying "killer moves," that is choices that have cut-off the search at other places in the tree [*40*]. The method is especially suited to cases where the choices (moves) at any node are drawn from a fixed set. For instance, without regard to the pieces, all moves on a chess board can be mapped into a 64 × 64 table (or even two tables, one for each player). Stored in that table would be a measure of how effective each move had been in causing cut-offs. Schaeffer found that simply using the frequency of prior pruning success is a more powerful means of ordering moves, than using application-dependent heuristic knowledge. Move ordering in turn dramatically improves the efficiency of directional searches like ABSearch and PVS.

Combined Enhancements

The relative efficiencies of these various alpha-beta enhancements are adequately captured in Figure 6, which presents data from a chess program Parabelle searching a suite of test positions. A direct N-ply alpha-beta search is taken as the 100% basis for comparison, based on frontier nodes visited. Figure 6 shows that under reasonable assumptions PVS is more efficient than Aspiration Search (although optimal aspiration windows will necessarily do better). Further, the memory function assists of transposition table (+trans), refutation table (+ref) and history table (+hist) for reordering the moves are additive and make a significant improvement in performance. The worsening result for the 6-ply search by PVS with transposition table (pvs+trans) may be attributed to overloading of the small (only 8K entries) transposition table. For comparison, a lower bound is provided by estimating the size of the minimal uniform game tree that approximates the average size of the trees that were generated during the search of the test suite (for Fig. 6, the average width of each node in the tree traversed was 34 branches). The oscillatory nature of these graphs can be attributed to the higher fraction of frontier nodes that must be evaluated in odd depth trees.

PARALLEL GAME-TREE SEARCH

In recent years the increased availability of small low-cost computers has led to an upsurge of interest in parallel methods for traversing trees and graphs. In the game-tree case, experience has been gained with a variety of practical implementations. Although many of the theoretical studies in parallelism focused on a dataflow model, by and large that model

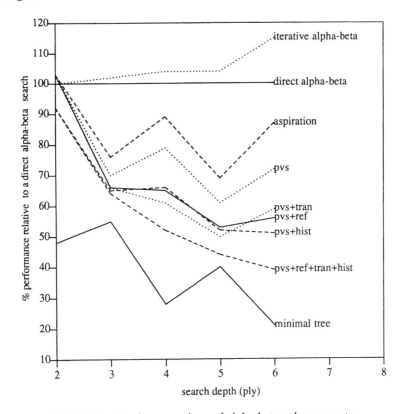

FIGURE 6.   Node comparison of alpha-beta enhancements.

could not account for pragmatic factors like communication and synchronization delays that inevitably plague physical systems.

The main problems faced by the designers of parallel tree-search systems are

a. How best to exploit the additional resources (e.g., memory and i/o capability) that may become available with the extra processors
b. How to distribute the work across the available processors
c. How to avoid excessive duplication of computation

Some simple combinatorial problems have no difficulty with point (c) and so, if work distribution is not a problem, ideal or even anomalously good speedup is possible [*41*].

In game-tree search the necessary information communicated is the improving estimates of the tree value. But, since uniprocessor solutions strive to minimize the size of the tree traversed by maximizing the pruning efficiency, parallel systems face the problem of unpredictable size of the subtrees searched (e.g., pruning may produce an unbalanced workload) leading to potentially heavy synchronization (waiting for more work) losses. The standard basis for comparison is speedup, defined by

$$\text{speedup} = \frac{\text{time taken (or nodes visited) by a uniprocessor}}{\text{time taken (or nodes visited) by an N - processor system}}$$

Although simple, this speedup measure can often be misleading, because it is dependent on the efficiency of the uniprocessor implementation. Also use of node counts does not help measure the communication and synchronization overheads. Thus good speedup may merely reflect a comparison with an inefficient uniprocessor design. On the other hand, poor speedup clearly identifies an ineffective parallel system.

Single-Agent Search

IDA* [2] has proved to be an effective depth-first method for single-agent games. Not surprisingly it has also been a popular algorithm to parallelize. Rao et al. [42] proposed PIDA*, an almost linear algorithm whose speedup is about 0.93N when N processors are used, even when solving the 15-puzzle with its trivial node expansion cost. It was thought to be even more efficient on the Traveling Salesman Problem, which entails a more expensive node generation process, but there the really efficient branch and bound algorithms are sequential (but not amenable to parallelization), so comparisons often overstate the success of the parallel methods. Powley and Korf [43] propose a parallel window search for IDA*, which "can be used to find a nearly optimal solution quickly, improve the solution until it is optimal, and then finally guarantee optimality, depending on the amount of time available." At the same time Huang and Davis [44] proposed a distributed heuristic search algorithm (PIA*) which they compare to A*. On a uniprocessor, PIA* expands the same nodes as A*. Although they claim that "this algorithm can achieve almost linear speedup on a large number of processors" [44], it has the disadvantage that its memory requirements are the same as for A*, and therefore is of doubtful practical value.

Adversary Games

In the area of two-person games, early simulation studies with a *Mandatory Work First* (MWF) scheme [45] and the PVSplit algorithm [10], showed that a high degree of parallelism was possible, despite the work imbalance introduced by pruning. Those papers recognized that in many applications, especially chess, the game trees tend to be well ordered because of the wealth of move ordering heuristics that have been developed [33, 46], thus the bulk of the computation occurs during the search of the first subtree. The MWF approach recognizes that there is a minimal tree that must be searched. Since that tree is well-defined and has regular properties, it is easy to generate and search. Also, nodes where all successors must be considered can be searched in parallel, albeit with reduced benefit from improving bounds. The balance of the tree can be generated algorithmically and searched quickly through simple tree splitting. Finkel and Fishburn [47] also favored this method and provided some analysis. The first subtree of the minimal game tree has the same properties as the whole tree, but its maximum height is one less. This so called principal variation can be recursively split into parts of about equal size for parallel exploration. PVSplit, an algorithm based on this observation, was proposed [25] and simulated [10]. Independently Monroe Newborn built the first parallel chess program, and later presented performance results [48, 49]. For practical reasons the tree was only split down to some pre-specified common depth from the root (typically 2), where the greatest benefits from parallelism can be achieved. This use of a common depth has been taken up by Hsu [50] in his proposal for large-scale parallelism. Limiting depths are also an important part of changing search modes and in managing transposition tables.

Advanced Tree-Splitting Methods

Results from fully recursive versions of PVSplit were presented for the Parabelle chess program [15]. These results confirmed the earlier simulation results and offered some insight into a major problem: In this N-processor system, N-1 processors were idle for an inordinate amount of time. This led to the development of variations that dynamically assign processors to the search of the principal variation. Notable are the works of Schaeffer [51] which uses a loosely coupled network of workstations, and Hyatt et al.'s [52] implementation for a shared-memory computer. That dynamic splitting work has attracted growing attention with a variety of approaches. For example, the results of Feldmann et al. [53] show a speedup of 11.8 with 16 processors (far exceeding the performance of earlier systems) and Felten and Otto [54] measured a 101 speedup on a 256 processor hypercube. This latter achievement is noteworthy because it shows an effective way to exploit the 256 times bigger memory that was not available to the uniprocessor. Use of the extra transposition table memory to hold results of search by other processors provides a significant benefit to the hypercube system, thus identifying clearly one advantage of systems with an extensible address space.

These results show a wide variation not only of methods but also of apparent performance. Part of the improvement is accounted for by the change from a static assignment of processors to the tree search (e.g., PVSplit), to the dynamic processor reallocation schemes of Hyatt et al. [52], and also Schaeffer [51]. These later systems tried to identify dynamically the ALL nodes of Figure 3 (where every successor must be searched) in the game tree, and search them in parallel, leaving the CUT nodes (where only a few successors might be examined) [15] for serial expansion. The MWF approach first recognized the importance of dividing work at ALL nodes and did this by a parallel search of the minimal game tree. In a similar vein Ferguson and Korf [55] proposed a "bound-and-branch" method that only assigned processors to the leftmost child of the tree-splitting nodes where no bound (subtree value) exists. Their method is equivalent to the static PVSplit algorithm, and yet realizes a speedup of 12 with 32 processors for Othello-based alpha-beta trees! More recently Steinberg and Solomon [56] also addressed this issue with their *ER* algorithm, and also considered the performance of different processor tree architectures. Their tenfold speedup with 16 processors was obtained through the search of 10-ply trees generated by an Othello program. They did not consider the effects of iterative deepening, nor exploit the benefits of transposition tables. As with similar studies, the fundamental flaw with speedup figures is their reliance on a comparison to a particular (but not necessarily best) uniprocessor solution. If that solution is inefficient the speedup figure will look good (e.g., by omitting the important node-ordering mechanisms). For that reason comparisons with a standard test suite from a widely accepted game is often done and should be encouraged. Most of the working experience with parallel methods for two-person games has centered on the alpha-beta algorithm. Parallel methods for more node-count efficient sequential methods, like SSS*, have not been successful [57], although the use of hashing methods to replace linked lists has not been fully exploited.

Recent Developments

Although there have been several successful implementations involving parallel computing systems [58], significantly better methods for NP-hard problems like game-tree search remain elusive. Theoretical studies often concentrate on showing that linear speedup is possible on worst order game trees. While not wrong, they make only the trivial point that where exhaustive search is necessary, and where pruning is impossible, then even simple work distribution methods yield excellent results. The true challenge, however, is to consider average game trees, or the strongly ordered model, where extensive pruning occurs, leading to unsymmetric trees and a significant work distribution problem.

For the game-tree case, many people consider the minimal or optimal tree model, in which the best successor is considered first at every node. Although idealistic, this model presumes the search of a highly structured tree, one which the iterative deepening searches approximate. Akl et al. [45] considered the search of minimal trees in their simulation of the Mandatory Work First method. Intuitively this is a nice idea, and yet it has not led to practical methods for the search of game trees. In practice average trees differ significantly from minimal trees, and so the underlying assumption behind MWF is undermined. Thus static processor allocation schemes like MWF and PVSplit cannot achieve high levels of parallelism, although PVSplit does very well with up to 4 processors. MWF in particular ignored the true shape of the minimal game tree under optimal pruning, and so was better with shallow game trees, where the pruning imbalance from the so called "deep cutoffs" has less effect.

Many people have recognized the intrinsic difficulty of searching game trees under pruning conditions, and one way or another try to recognize dynamically when the minimal game tree assumption is being violated, and hence to re-deploy the processors. Powley et al. [59] presented a distributed tree search scheme, which has been effective for Othello. Similarly Feldmann et al. [55] introduced the concept of making "young brothers wait" to reduce search overhead. Both of these systems have yielded impressive speedup results, but they may be overstated. The first system used a hypercube, so that the N-fold increase in processors was accompanied by an N-fold increase in memory not available to the uniprocessor. The second system used slow (8088) processors, so that the I/O time have been significant in the uniprocessor case.

Generalized depth-first searches [60] are fundamental to many AI problems, and Kumar and Rao [61] have fully explored a method that is well-suited to doing the early iterations of IDA*. The unexplored part of the trees are marked and are dynamically assigned to any idle processor. In principle this method could be used for deterministic game trees too. Finally we come to the issue of scalability and the application of massive parallelism. None of the work discussed so far for game tree search seems to be extensible to arbitrarily many processors. Nevertheless there have been claims for better methods and some insights into the extra hardware that may be necessary to do the job. Perhaps most complete is Hsu's recent thesis [50]. His project for the re-design of the Deep Thought chess program is to manufacture a new VLSI processor in large quantity. The original machine had 2 or 4 processors, but two new prototypes with 8 and 24 processors have been built as a testing vehicle for a 1000 processor system. That design was the major contribution of the thesis [50] and with it Hsu predicts, on the basis of some simulation studies, a 350-fold speedup. No doubt there will be many inefficiencies to correct before that comes to pass, but in time we will know if massive parallelism will solve our game-tree search problems.

REFERENCES

1. N. Nilsson, *Problem Solving in Artificial Intelligence*, McGraw-Hill, New York, 1971.
2. R. E. Korf, "Depth-First Iterative-Deepening: An Optimal Admissible Tree Search," *Artificial Intelligence, 27*(1), 97–109 (1985).
3. D. E. Knuth and R. W. Moore, "An Analysis of Alpha-Beta Pruning," *Artificial Intelligence, 6*(4), 293–326 (1975).
4. A. Newell, J. C. Shaw, and H. A. Simon, "Chess Playing Programs and the Problem of Complexity," *IBM J. Res. Dev., 4*(2), 320–335 (1958). Also in E. Feigenbaum and J. Feldman (eds.), *Computers and Thought*, 1963, 39–70.
5. A. L. Brudno, "Bounds and Valuations for Abridging the Search of Estimates," *Probl. Cybernet., 10*, 225–241 (1963). Translation of Russian original in *Problemy Kibernetiki, 10*, 141–150 (May 1963).
6. J. P. Fishburn, *Analysis of Speedup in Distributed Algorithms*, UMI Research Press, Ann Arbor, Michigan, 1984. See earlier Ph.D. thesis, May 1981 Comp. Sci. Technical Report 431, University of Wisconsin, Madison, 118 pp.
7. T. A. Marsland, "Relative Efficiency of Alpha-Beta Implementations," *Proc. 8th Int. Joint Conf. Artificial Intelligence*, Kaufmann, Los Altos, Karlsruhe, Germany, August 1983, pp. 763–766.
8. A. Musczycka and R. Shinghal, "An Empirical Study of Pruning Strategies in Game Trees," *IEEE Trans. Systems, Man Cybernetics, 15*(3), 389–399 (1985).
9. H. Kaindl, "Tree Searching Algorithms," in *Computers, Chess, and Cognition*, T. A. Marsland and J. Schaeffer (eds.), Springer-Verlag, New York, 1990, pp. 133–158.
10. T. A. Marsland and M. Campbell, "Parallel Search of Strongly Ordered Game Trees," *Computing Sur., 14*(4), 533–551 (1982).
11. H. Kaindl, "Searching to Variable Depth in Computer Chess," *Proc. 8th Int. Joint Conf. Art. Intell.*, Kaufmann, Los Altos, Karlsruhe, Germany, August 1983, pp. 760–762.
12. H. Kaindl, *Problemlösen durch Heuristische Suche in der Artificial Intelligence*, Springer-Verlag, Vienna, 1989.
13. T. Anantharaman, M. Campbell, and F. Hsu, "Singular Extensions: Adding Selectivity to Brute-Force Searching," *Int. Computer Chess Assoc. J., 11*(4), 135–143 (1988). Also in *Artificial Intelligence, 43*(1), 99–110 (1990).
14. D. Beal, "Experiments with the Null Move," in *Advances in Computer Chess 5*, D. Beal (ed.), Elsevier, New York, 1989, pp. 65–79. Revised as "A Generalized Quiescence Search Algorithm," in *Artificial Intelligence, 43*(1), 85–98 (1990).
15. T. A. Marsland and F. Popowich, "Parallel Game-Tree Search," *IEEE Trans. Pattern Analysis and Machine Intelligence, 7*(4), 442–452 (July 1985).
16. A. Reinefeld, "An Improvement of the Scout Tree-Search Algorithm," *Int. Computer Chess Assoc. J., 6*(4), 4–14 (1983).
17. J. Pearl, "Asymptotic Properties of Minimax Trees and Game Searching Procedures," *Artificial Intelligence, 14*(2), 113–138 (1980).
18. A. Reinefeld and T.. A. Marsland, "A Quantitative Analysis of Minimal Window Search," *Proc. 10th Int. Joint Conf. AI*, Kaufmann, Los Altos, Milan, Italy, August 1987, pp. 951–954.
19. J. A. Birmingham and P. Kent, "Tree-Searching and Tree-Pruning Techniques," in *Advances in Computer Chess 1*, M. Clarke (ed.), Edinburgh University Press, Edinburgh, 1977, pp. 89–107.

20. J. Schaeffer, "Experiments in Search and Knowledge," Ph.D. thesis, University of Waterloo, Waterloo, Canada, Spring 1986.

21 B. Abramson, "Control Strategies for Two-Player Games," *ACM Computing Sur., 21*(2), 137-162 (1989).

22. H. J. Berliner, "The B* Tree Search Algorithm: A Best First Proof Procedure," *Artificial Intelligence, 12*(1), 23-40 (1979).

23. A. J. Palay, *Searching with Probabilities*, Pitman, 1985. See earlier Ph.D. thesis (1983), Computer Science, Carnegie-Mellon University, Pittsburgh, 152 pp.

24. G. C. Stockman, "A Minimax Algorithm Better than Alpha-Beta," *Artif. Intell. 12*(2), 179-196 (1982).

25. M. S. Campbell, "Algorithms for the Parallel Search of Game Trees," Technical Report 81-9, Computing Science Dept., University of Alberta, Edmonton, Canada, August 1981.

26. T. A. Marsland, A. Reinefeld, and J. Schaeffer, "Low Overhead Alternatives to SSS*," *Artificial Intelligence, 31*(2), 185-199 (1987).

27. A. Reinefeld, *Apielbaum-Suchverfahren*, IFB 200, Springer-Verlag, Heidelberg, 1989.

28. V. Kumar and L. Kanal, "Parallel Branch and Bound Formulations for AND/OR Tree Search," *IEEE Trans. Pattern Analysis and Machine Intelligence, 6*(6), 768-778 (1984).

29. D. McAllister, "Conspiracy Numbers for Min-Max Search," *Artificial Intelligence, 35*(3), 287-310 (1988).

30. J. Schaeffer, "Conspiracy Numbers," *Artificial Intelligence, 43*(1), 67-84 (1990).

31. L. V. Allis, M. Meulen, and H. J. Van der Herik, "$\alpha\beta$ Conspiracy Number Search," in *Advances in Computer Chess 6*, D. F. Beal (ed.), Ellis Horwood, London, 1991, pp. 73-95.

32. J. J. Scott, "A Chess-Playing Program," in *Machine Intelligence 4*, B. Meltzer and D. Michie (eds.), Edinburgh University Press, Edinburgh, 1969, pp. 255-265.

33. D. J. Slate and L. R. Atkin, "CHESS 4.5-The Northwestern University Chess Program," in *Chess Skill in Man and Machine*, P. Frey (ed.), Springer-Verlag, New York, 1977, pp. 82-118.

34. S. G. Akl and M. M. Newborn, "The Principal Continuation and the Killer Heuristic," *Proc. 1977 ACM Ann. Conf.*, ACM, New York, 1977, pp. 466-473.

35. D. N. L. Levy and M. M. Newborn, *How Computers Play Chess*, W. H. Freeman & Co., New York, 1990.

36. A. L. Zobrist, "A New Hashing Method with Applications for Game Playing," Technical Report 88, Computer Sciences Dept., University of Wisconsin, Madison, April 1970. Also in *Int. Computer Chess Assoc. J., 13*(2), 169-173 (1990).

37. T. A. Marsland, "A Review of Game-Tree Pruning," *Int. Computer Chess Assoc. J., 9*(1), 3-19 (1986).

38. H. L. Nelson, "Hash Tables in Cray Blitz," *Int. Computer Chess Assoc. J., 8*(1), 3-13 (1985).

39. T. Warnock and B. Wendroff, "Search Tables in Computer Chess," *Int. Computer Chess Assoc. J., 11*(1), 10-13 (1988).

40. J. Schaeffer, "The History Heuristic," *Int. Computer Chess Assoc. J., 6*(3), 16-19 (1983).

41. T. Lai and S. Sahni, "Anomalies in Parallel Branch-and-Bound Algorithms," *Comm. ACM, 27*, 594-602 (1984).

42. V. N. Rao, V. Kumar, and K. Ramesh, "A Parallel Implementation of Iterative-Deepening A*," *Proc. 6th Nat. Conf. AI*, Seattle, July 1987, pp. 178–182.

43. C. Powley and R. E. Korf, "Single-Agent Parallel Window Search: A Summary of Results," *Proc. 11th Int. Joint Conf. AI*, vol. 1, Kaufmann, Los Altos, Detroit, 1989, pp. 36–41.

44. S. Huang and L. R. Davis, "Parallel Iterative A* Search: An Admissible Distributed Search Algorithm," *Proc. 11th Int. Joint Conf. AI*, vol. 1, Kaufmann, Los Altos, Detroit, 1989, pp. 23–29.

45. S. G. Akl, D. T. Barnard, and R. J. Doran, "Design, Analysis and Implementation of a Parallel Tree Search Machine," *IEEE Trans. Pattern Analysis and Machine Intelligence, 4*(2), 192–203 (1982).

46. J. J. Gillogly, "The Technology Chess Program," *Artificial Intelligence, 3*(1-4), 145–163 (1972). Also in D. Levy (ed.), *Computer Chess Compendium*, Springer-Verlag, New York, 1988, pp. 67–79.

47. R. A. Finkel and J. P. Fishburn, "Parallelism in Alpha-Beta Search," *Artif. Intell., 19*(1), 89–106 (1982).

48. M. M. Newborn, "A Parallel Search Chess Program," *Proc. ACM Ann. Conf.*, ACM, New York, October 1985, pp. 272–277. See also (March 1982) Tech. Rep. SOCS 82.3, Computer Science, McGill University, Montreal, Canada, 20 pp.

49. M. M. Newborn, "Unsynchronized Iteratively Deepening Parallel Alpha-Beta Search," *IEEE Trans. Pattern Analysis and Machine Intell., 10*(5), 687–694 (1988).

50. F. Hsu, "Large Scale Parallelization of Alpha-Beta Search: An Algorithmic and Architectural Study with Computer Chess," CMU-CS-90-108, Ph.D. thesis, Carnegie-Mellon University, Pittsburgh, February 1990.

51. J. Schaeffer, "Distributed Game-Tree Search," *J. Parallel Distrib. Computing 6*(2), 90–114 (1989).

52. R. M. Hyatt, B. W. Suter, and H. L. Nelson, "A Parallel Alpha/Beta Tree Searching Algorithm," *Parallel Computing, 10*(3), 299–308 (1989).

53. R. Feldmann, B. Monien, P. Mysliwietz, and O. Vornberger, "Distributed Game Tree Search," in *Parallel Algorithms for Machine Intelligence and Vision*, V. Kumar, P. S. Gopalakrishnan and L. Kanal (eds.), Springer-Verlag, New York, 1990, pp. 66–101.

54. E. W. Felten and S. W. Otto, "A Highly Parallel Chess Program," *Proc. Int. Conf. 5th Generation Computer Systems*, Tokyo, ICOT, November 1988, pp. 1001–1009.

55. C. Ferguson and R. E. Korf, "Distributed Tree Search and its Application to Alpha-Beta Pruning," *Proc. 7th Natl. Conf. Artificial Intelligence*, vol. 1, Kaufmann, Los Altos, Saint Paul, August 1988, pp. 128–132.

56. I. Steinberg and M. Solomon, "Searching Game Trees in Parallel," *Proc. Int. Conf. Parallel Processing*, vol. 3, University Park, PA, August 1990, pp. 9–17.

57. O. Vornberger and B. Monien, "Parallel Alpha-Beta versus Parallel SSS*," *Proc. IFIP Conf. Distributed Processing*, North Holland, Amsterdam, October 1987, pp. 613–625.

58. M. E. Guiliano, M. Kohli, J. Minker, and I. Durand, "PRISM: A Testbed for Parallel Control," in *Parallel Algorithms for Machine Intelligence and Vision*, V. Kumar, P. S. Gopalakrishnan and L. Kanal (eds.), Springer-Verlag, New York, 1990, pp. 182–231.

59. C. Powley, C. Ferguson, and R. E. Korf, "Parallel Heuristic Search: Two Approaches," in *Parallel Algorithms for Machine Intelligence and Vision*, V. Kumar, P. S. Gopalakrishnan and L. Kanal (eds.), Springer-Verlag, New York, 1990, pp. 42–65.

60. R. E. Korf, "Generalized Game Trees," *Proc. 11th Int. Joint Conf. on AI*, vol. 1, Kaufmann, Los Altos, Detroit, 1989, pp. 328–333.
61. V. Kumar and V. N. Rao, "Scalable Parallel Formulations of Depth-First Search," in *Parallel Algorithms for Machine Intelligence and Vision*, V. Kumar, P. S. Gopalakrishnan, and L. Kanal (eds.), Springer-Verlag, New York, 1990, pp. 1–41.

T. ANTHONY MARSLAND

STATISTICAL EXPERT SYSTEMS

INTRODUCTION

Statistical Expert Systems which merge statistical expertise as a knowledge domain with problem-specific inference rules of Artificial Intelligence have recently attracted a great deal of interest [1–3].

An expert system is a computer program that performs at the level of a human expert in a complex but narrow field. To qualify as an expert system, the program must operate in a domain in which expertise is an 'art,' based on experience and heuristic reasoning, rather than use algorithmic methods to solve problems. For example, fitting a curve through a cloud of data by nonparametric smoothing does not qualify as expert behavior—fitting is described by a well-defined algorithm. Choosing the most appropriate smoothing technique is expert behavior—it requires heuristic knowledge about what properties of the data are displayed by each technique, and which are important for the data set at hand. Recognizing that the smoothing comes from a given parametric family is also expert behavior. Although, in principle, this could be done by searching a set of possible curves, this set simply is too large to search exhaustively without some guiding heuristics.

Two types of expert systems which involve statistical reasoning are advice-giving programs and pattern-finding programs. Advice-giving systems have encoded within them rules for decision making in some domain, and have the goal of solving or pointing to solutions of a selected set of problems, for example, of diagnosing a disease, or determining an appropriate statistical analysis. Pattern-finding systems search through a database for interesting facts, for example, side effects of drug use, or rules for reaching certain conclusions.

Advice-giving expert systems involve statistical reasoning if they give statistical advice. (Many advice-giving programs also have devices to handle uncertainty in the data or vagueness in the rules, but I do not include this aspect in our definition of statistical reasoning.) Currently, advice-giving systems have been written in two modes. The consultant attempts to use its rules to solve the problem itself, and turns to a human expert only if it lacks either the data or the rules to continue. Because the program takes the lead in solving the problem, most consultant programs include explanation systems that allow the human expert to query the program's reasoning. Examples of consultant systems are MYCIN [4] which provides medical diagnosis and prescribes drugs for bacterial infections and REX [5] which does an expert job of least–squares linear regression.

Pattern-finding systems search a database to discover relationships. These systems use statistical techniques such as correlations and discriminants as well as knowledge about their domain. For example, the RX program [6], searches a medical database for possible

This article appeared previously in *Expert Systems* 5(3), Aug. 1988, 186–196. Reprinted with permission.

causal relationships, where causation is defined by lagged correlation. The program then uses medical knowledge to rule out common causes and clearly spurious correlations. Finally, both statistical and medical knowledge are used to test correlations, after controlling for other associated variables. The Odysseus system [7] attempts to create diagnostic variables by use of partitioning techniques in a medical database. No causality is assumed. The program attempts to find the symptoms associated with disease states, and thus to add rules to a diagnostic consultant. The program requires medical knowledge, statistical knowledge, and knowledge about the structure of plausible rules.

Typically, expert systems have more flexible language handling abilities. This means the user need not be annoyed so often by simple syntax and spelling errors.

More important, expert systems have heuristic knowledge which can guide the analysis and assist the interpretation of the results. For example, most linear regression packages note computational problems, such as singularity of the design matrix, since the numerical algorithms will fail, but few such packages note commonly occurring and readily detected problems such as integer-valued response variables or very small degrees of freedom for error, since these do not interfere with the numerical algorithms. An expert system may have encoded within it guidelines for the appropriate use of various statistical techniques. An expert regression package, for example, will draw the user's attention to violations of the normality assumptions and warn of problems like overfitting. At a higher level, an expert statistics package can advise a user who wants to know the 'relationship' between two variables, that a particular technique is suitable.

Many packages do provide diagnostics and other information automatically, but these often are buried within the output. The user with little statistical expertise may not understand the use of these statistics or may not know how to proceed if he does recognize a problem. (Some well-known packages produce statistics for the regression problem that most expert statisticians are familiar with.) An expert system examines the diagnostics and draws the user's attention to those with significant implications for the analysis, such as the existence of a highly influential point. The essential difference between a package and an expert system is in the phrase 'draw the user's attention.' The expert system computes, but does not print, all these relevant statistics. Like the human expert, the expert system interprets the results, and then advises the user on the appropriate course of action. Current packages rely on the user to recognize the important diagnostics, and to know how to proceed.

Of course, a statistical expert system need not have a numerical component. For example, an expert system knowledgeable about experimental design could assist a client in planning a study. The important points are that the expert system goes beyond a textbook by dealing with the problem presented by the user, not with the abstract case, and goes beyond the package by interpreting aspects of the analysis and bringing the important features to the attention of the user.

An expert system does not have the abilities of a human expert. In a narrow range of expertise, it may outperform a human expert due to the superior data retrieval and computational abilities of the computer. However, the human expert can perform in a far wider range of problems. He has 'world knowledge,' that is a broad range of knowledge that lies outside his field of expertise, and he learns readily both from experience and from other experts. To date, coding world knowledge into a program is not possible, and, although machine learning is an area of current research, programs still lack the understanding and insight of humans. The expert system has only domain knowledge, and has only a limited ability to extend that knowledge.

BUILDING AN EXPERT SYSTEM

The first expert systems were coded by programmers working in areas in which they had expertise, such as games. However, in fields of specialized knowledge, such as chemistry and medicine, the programming expertise and domain expertise are generally held by different individuals. Furthermore, expertise in these areas is often implicit, embodied in rules of thumb, and transferred, not only by textbook training, but also by 'hands-on' experience. Communication between the domain expert and the programming expert is a major problem.

One design strategy used to alleviate this problem was to separate the 'domain knowledge' of the system from its 'control knowledge' or 'inference engine.' The domain knowledge consists of the facts and heuristics known to the expert. For example, the knowledge that a t-test is a location is knowledge in the statistical domain. This knowledge usually is encoded as a series of rules. For example:

If the data are Gaussian, and the test is a test of location, use a t-test.

The 'control knowledge' is the problem-solving strategy used by the program. For example, in symbolic integration, many equivalent answers are possible, and only one is needed, but in medical diagnosis it is necessary to keep track of all possible diagnoses of the patient.

There have been two major consequences of this separation of domain knowledge and inference engine. First, the domain expert, with only a cursory knowledge of the inference engine, can add to and change the facts and heuristics in the knowledge base. The second is that the same inference engine can be used within different domains of expertise if the problem-solving strategies can be couched in similar terms. Only a new knowledge base must be constructed.

Knowledge acquisition systems such as TEREISIAS [4] and KAS [8] are programs designed to assist the domain expert in building a knowledge base. Inference engines and knowledge acquisition systems have been assembled into tools such as EMYCIN [9] and KAS which can, in principle, be used directly by the domain expert to build an expert system. The expert requires about the same level of programming skills required to use a statistical package. Whereas building an expert system from scratch can take years, systems can be built in a matter of months using these tools. For example Mycin, a medical diagnosis system, took four years to build, and SACON was built in about four months using the same tool [4]. Mycin has about 500 rules of domain knowledge, and Sacon has 170.

There are several types of inference engine now in use in various expert systems. EMycin assumes that all domain knowledge is encoded in production rules and that inference is done by backward chaining from the goal. A production rule is an 'if-then' statement, such as:

If the problem is to detect a difference in location, and if the data are paired, and if the differences are Gaussian, then the appropriate procedure is a paired t-test.

Backward chaining means that the inference engine starts from the goal, and seeks all information needed to attain that goal. In the example above, the goal is to determine the appropriate procedure to use. In order to determine this, it is necessary to determine the type of problem, if the data are paired, and if the differences are Gaussian; these become the new goals of the system. EMycin allows for multiple goals, and multiple conclusions.

A simple statistical expert system, XSAMPLE, as presented in Figure 3 for purposes of demonstration uses EMycin, the expert system building tool derived from Mycin.

Layout: TOP LEVEL

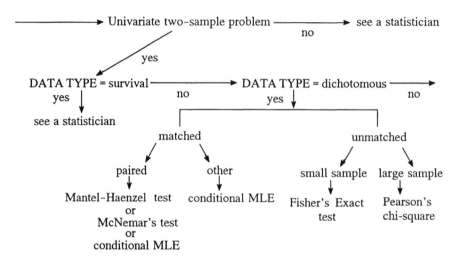

Layout: SECOND LEVEL

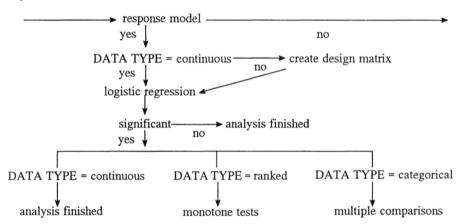

Layout: THIRD LEVEL

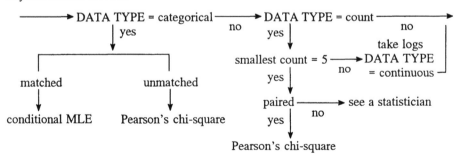

FIGURE 1.

Layout: FOURTH LEVEL

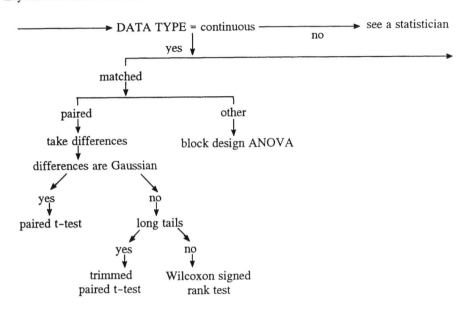

Layout: FIFTH LEVEL

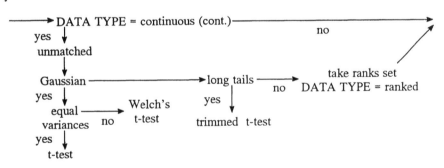

Layout: SIXTH LEVEL

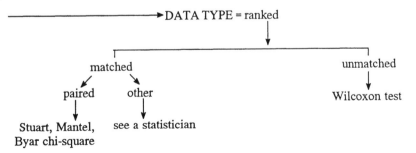

FIGURE 1. continued

Rule 007
This rule is tried in order to find out about the first thing you should do or the solution.

If: 1) The problem is prediction, and
           2) The type of data is unordered categories
Then: 1) It is definite (1.0) that the following is one of the first things you should do: create a design matrix,
           2) It is definite (1.0) that the following is one of the first things you should do: use logistic regression, and
           3) It is definite (1.0) that the following is the solution: use multiple comparison if the logistic regression is significant.

Premise: ($AND(PREDICTION = PREDICTION)
                (DATA-TYPE = CATEGORICAL)

Action: ($AND(SAME CNTXT PREDICTION PREDICTION)
                (SAME CNTXT DATA-TYPE CATEGORICAL)

PREMISE: ($AND(SAME CNTXT PREDICTION PREDICTION)
                (SAME CNTXT DATA-TYPE CATEGORICAL)

ACTION: (DO-ALL(CONCLUDETEXT CNTXT ADVICE(TEXT DESIGN)
                                TALLY 1000)
                        (CONCLUDETEXT CNTXT ADVICE(TEXT LOGISTIC)
                                TALLY 1000)
                        (CONCLUDETEXT CNTXT FINAL-ADVICE(TEXT
                                MULTIPLE) TALLY 1000))

Rule 038
This rule is tried in order to ascertain that the analysis is finished.

If: 1) This is not a two-sample one variable problem, or
           2) The solution is known
Then: 1) It is definite (1.0) that the analysis is finished,
           2) Display the first thing you should do, and
           3) Display the solution

Premise: ($AND($OR(INAPPROPRIATE)
                        (KNOWN CNTXT FINAL-ADVICE)))
Action: (DO-ALL(FINISHED)(PRINTCONCLUSIONS ADVICE)
                        (PRINTCONCLUSIONS FINAL-ADVICE)))

PREMISE: ($AND($OR(SAME CNTXT INAPPROPRIATE)
                        (KNOWN CNTXT FINAL-ADVICE))
ACTION: (DO-ALL(CONCLUDE CNTXT FINISHED YES TALLY 1000)
                        (PRINTCONCLUSIONS CNTXT ADVICE T)
                        (PRINTCONCLUSIONS CNTXT FINAL-ADVICE)))

FIGURE 2.

BUILDING XSAMPLE: A STATISTICAL EXPERT SYSTEM

XSample is a statistical assistant system, for advising on the appropriate analysis in the univariate two–sample location problem. The primary path of the decision tree is displayed in Figure 1 overleaf. A small set of rules, as they are interpreted by EMycin, is displayed in Figure 2. Part of a XSample run is displayed in Figure 3.

Which primary node of the tree is selected is determined by three variables, the data type, the design and the model. Five data types are considered; dichotomous, categorical, count, continuous and ranked. (If the study involves survival or lifetime data the client is advised to see a statistician. This was done to keep the problem small, since selecting an appropriate technique for survival analysis involved another large decision sub-tree.) Designs considered were matched and unmatched data. The two models depend on whether the grouping is the independent or dependent variable. If the grouping is the independent variable, the problem is to determine if there is a difference in distribution of the measured variable between the two groups. If the grouping is the dependent variable, the problem is to determine how group membership depends on the measured variable (that is, logistic regression or a related model).

The ordering of the primary nodes is not arbitrary. It is forced by the logic of EMycin. EMycin allows only backward chaining and conclusions reached by EMycin are irrevocable. For example, XSample asks questions about the differences between pairs, only if it has determined that a paired t-test may be an appropriate technique, that is, only under the node

CONTINUOUS = true
MODEL = difference-in-mean
N-MATCHED = 1

In statistics, attributes of the data may change as the analysis proceeds. For example, after taking logarithms, data that were originally counts may be treated as continuous, or data that were skewed may be considered Gaussian. Since EMycin does not allow re-evaluation of problem parameters, decision nodes must appear in an appropriate order, and dummy variables are occasionally needed.

Rules are entered using EMycin's knowledge acquisition routine. Rules may be entered in a simplified 'natural language,' more tersely in 'mathematical language,' or in Lisp. Examples of all three types of entry are displayed in Rule 007 in Figure 2. EMycin prompts for definitions of any parameters encountered, and translates the rules into all three modes, using simple templates. The templates for converting from mathematical language to Lisp are provided by EMycin. The templates for converting to natural language are provided by the human expert. For example, the template for the variable name 'ADVICE' is 'one of the first things you should do' and the template for its value 'DESIGN' is 'create a design matrix.' EMycin uses grammatical rules to create English-like sentences from the templates. Spelling correction is done automatically for known parameters, and other corrections may be done via a line editor. EMycin queries the user if rules give conflicting advice.

Rules fire when their premises are true. The first rule to be attempted is the goal rule. The action of the goal rule is to end the consulting session. The goal rule of XSample is Rule 038, displayed in Figure 2. Since the program attempts to resolve the truth of the premises of the rule, it will first attempt to determine if the problem is a univariate two-sample problem, and if it is, to find the appropriate analysis. The attempt to resolve the premises of the goal rule controls the firing of the other rules.

The consulting session is recorded in Figure 3. Notice that EMycin provides spelling

PROBLEM 1

1)   Are the data dichotomous, categorical, ordered, ranks, counts, or continuous?
        **RANKS
2)   Do you want to determine if there is a significant difference in the distribution
        in the groups (difference-in-mean) or predict group membership?
        **DIFF
= DIFFERENCE-IN-MEAN
3)   Are the data in the first group matched in any way to the data in the second
        group?
        **YES

The solution is as follows:
See a statistician.

FIGURE 3a.

PROBLEM 2

1)   Are the data dichotomous, categorical, ordered, ranks, counts, or continuous?
        **COUNTS
2)   Do you want to determine if there is a significant difference in the distribution
        in the two groups (difference-in-mean) or predict group membership?
        **DIFFERENCE-IN-MEAN
3)   What is the smallest count in the data?
        **WHY (i.e. WHY is it important to determine the smallest count?)

        (1.0) This will aid in determining whether the data are continuous.
              It has already been established that:
              (1.1) the type of data is the data are counts
              Therefore, if
              (1.2) the smallest count is greater than or equal to 5
              then
                    it is definite (1.0) that the data are continuous
              (ALSO:
                    it is definite (1.0) that the data have been tested to determine if they are
                    Gaussian
                    it is definite (1.0) that the data are Gaussien
                    Take the logarithm of the data)
              (RULE 013)
   (back to question3)
   **7
   Take the logarithm of the data.
4)   Are the data in the first group matched in any way to data in the second group?
        **Y
5)   How many experimental units in group two are matched to a single unit in
        group one?
        **1

Take the differences between pairs. From this point onward we refer only to the differences.

The solution is as follows:
Do a one-sample t-test on the differences.

FIGURE 3b.

correction and an explanation facility (the 'WHY' command). Due to an EMycin bug, the program has not attempted to resolve the first premise of the goal command, that is, has not first checked to ensure that this is a univariate two-sample problem. The program can give two levels of advice. The 'solution' is a single piece of advice, that signals the goal rule to finish the session. If the solution needs to be modified, for example, by reminding the user to create a design matrix, another variable, 'initial advice' is also printed. This problem displays a common piece of advice 'See a statistician.' This advice is basically a place-holder, indicating problems that do not have standard solutions, or nodes in the decision tree such as 'DATA-TYPE = survival' which are not currently handled by the program, but which could be added later.

My goal was to design a system that handled a consulting session with a user who was somewhat conversant with statistical language, but not knowledgeable in the full range of tools available to handle the two-sample problem. The proliferation of rules was limited by referring the client to a human statistician if the problem had no standard solution, or more properly belonged to the realm of survival analysis. As a result, although the problem domain was small, 38 rules were needed.

XSample does not access statistical packages. That is, it gives advice about which technique to use, but does not do any analysis for the client. This makes XSample very different from programs like Rex in which the consultant carries out the entire analysis. XSample does not have much knowledge about the data and must always query the client. In this mode, XSample is simply a summary of its decision tree.

Even this small system could be quite useful, however, if attached to a statistical package. This could be done without major revision to the current knowledge base, although new rules would have to be added to interpret the output of the package. Passing the information back and forth from the packages to the system would be a tedious programming task. Current systems which access statistical packages, such as RX [6] and Rex [5], handle this by allowing some rules to create calls to the associated package and then scanning the output for relevant values.

Although XSample does an adequate job of the actual data analysis task, it does not model a consulting session. A statistical consultant asks general questions of the type; 'where does this data come from?' 'how did you collect it?' and so on. XSample has no general world knowledge, nor does it understand natural language well. XSample enters the consulting session after the human consultant, through dialogue with the client, has narrowed the problem to selecting within a small set of possible models (techniques).

THE CONSULTANT VERSUS THE ASSISTANT

Since the idea of building a statistical consultant expert system was suggested by J. Chambers at the 1981 Interface of Computer Science and Statistics Interface [10], there has been considerable debate in the statistical community about the role of the program as a consultant. While some statisticians feel that a consultant system would assist users who currently use statistical packages without consulting a statistical expert, others worry about putting a yet more powerful tool in the hands of the untrained user.

The argument against the consultant program is that it lacks real world knowledge and natural language recognition, and therefore cannot pursue vague questions of the type 'where did this data come from?' or 'what are you trying to find out?' These are the questions that are often the crux of a session with a human consultant. That is, the task of the consultant is not just to suggest and carry out a statistical analysis of the client's data, but to clarify the premises, actions, and goals of the client.

It is useful, in thinking about this question to note that experts in other fields are also uncomfortable about using consulting systems. Comments like 'the computer cannot understand how sick the patient really is' (how complex this data set really is) or 'every patient (data set) is unique' were made by assessors of Mycin [4]. Yet in blind assessments Mycin compared well with human experts. Of course, these assessments are done only using cases for which the use of the program is already indicated.

There are two major differences between consultation systems for statistics and for those in other fields. In the first place, in a field such as chemistry or medicine, the computer consultant has knowledge about the problem domain. The statistical consultant, on the other hand, has knowledge about the statistics domain, not about the problem domain. Second, medical consulting systems are designed to be used by doctors, not by patients. The consulting system provides expert advice, when used by a general practitioner who has already recognized a class of possible disease states. However, given the current use of statistics packages by clients with only cursory knowledge of statistics, the builders of statistical consultation systems must realistically expect that these systems will be used by clients with little statistical expertise.

Figure 4 is a simple model of a statistical consulting session. The initial stages of the session consist of dialogue between the consultant and the client. The purposes of the dialogue are to reach a common vocabulary for discussion of the problem, to determine the characteristics of the available data, to determine the goals of the client, and finally, to determine a class of models (techniques) which may be appropriate. The second stage of the session is the analysis loop. At this stage, the data are examined in detail. Summaries such as

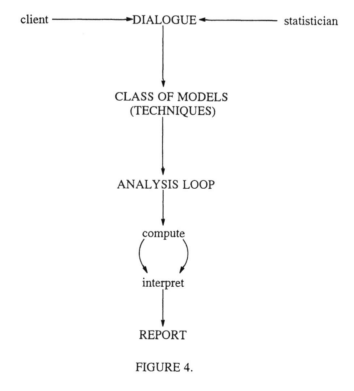

FIGURE 4.

graphic displays, tables and approximating equations may be used. Interesting features of the data are noted. Statistical tests are performed. The analysis stage is iterative. A careful analysis usually requires several cycles through the analysis loop. In each cycle, the data analyst, who may be the statistician or the client, examines interesting features, such as outliers, and associations between variables, and adjust the model. There may also be periodic returns to the dialogue step. The final step is writing the report on the statistical aspects of the problem.

Statistical consulting systems which can handle the dialogue stage of the consulting session could be built for very limited problem domains. For example, a system which could design and analyze clinical trials in a small medical domain may be possible, since a few hundred rules could probably handle most of the knowledge. However, the same system would not be able to handle similar statistical techniques in another domain, because the vocabulary of the problem and the accompanying domain knowledge would differ. It is at present feasible to build statistical consulting systems which can handle the dialogue stage of the consulting session for a general consultant.

It is more realistic to suppose that the statistical consulting system will enter the consulting session at the second stage, during the analysis loop. With access to a statistical package, the system can handle the iterations of the analysis loop, once a class of models has been identified. The system can also keep track of what it has done, and write a report.

In this sense, statistical consulting systems have the same limitations as medical consulting systems. Medical systems do not model the role of the general practitioner. Such a system would require too much world knowledge. Medical computer consultants work well in a very limited domain. The patient is already known to have a disease in a given (small) class (for example, meningitis) and the remaining task is simply to narrow the diagnosis further in order to prescribe appropriate treatment [11]. Similarly, the computer statistical consultant can do an expert job of the analysis once a class of techniques has been selected by the human consultant.

Many of the arguments between opponents and proponents of the use of the expert systems for statistics turn on this distinction. The opponents have focused on the dialogue stage of the consulting session. At present expert consulting systems do not handle this well. The proponents of expert systems have focused on providing expert analysis once the human expert has formulated a class of models. Programs such as Rex [5] demonstrate that this is a feasible task.

Statistical consultation systems can be useful for the applied statistician. Even a trained statistician cannot have expertise in all techniques he knows. It is far easier to identify a class of models which suit the problem, than to do an expert job of finding a specific model to fit a particular data set. Applied statisticians must often provide consulting support over a wide range of problem areas. Expert systems could provide them with much needed support, especially for new techniques.

Expert systems will be useful pedagogically. Just as the development of statistical packages has freed us from teaching students the details of the numerical alogorithms, the development of expert systems will free us from teaching nontechnical students the technical details of a good analysis. What must be taught are the uses and interpretation of statistical techniques.

For the time being, at least, statistical consulting programs, like statistical packages are an asset for a statistician, but carry the potential for abuse by the nonstatistician. Statistical packages reduced programming errors but did not prevent users from running an inappropriate analysis. Statistical expert systems, too, cannot prevent users from doing an inappropriate analysis, but they do ensure that the selected analysis is done well. Of course, if an inappropriate analysis is selected, the quality of the analysis is irrelevant. However, this is a problem which already exists. At least for that level of client with some statistical knowledge, the consulting systems can provide guidance, and can reduce some of the manual labor of performing the analysis loop.

STATISTICAL EXPERTISE AND EXPERT STATISTICIANS: CONCLUSIONS

Building an expert consulting system is like writing a textbook or a manual for a statistical package. It codifies and explicates existing statistical techniques and strategies. New techniques arise only minimally, when numerical summaries are required for visual displays, or gaps are discovered in current practice.

The development of tools like EMycin may, however, change the manner in which statistical software is developed. Commercial packages will undoubtedly begin to distribute expert systems with their routines, and such systems may even replace manuals. (The use of the term 'expert system' in this context is unfortunate, since it seems to imply more than such systems will actually deliver.) When expert system building tools like EMycin interface more readily with computational programs, it will be practical and attractive for new methods to be released by statistical investigators as expert systems, rather than as statistical algorithms.

Pattern-finding expert systems, such as RX and Odysseus, that try to find new knowledge in a data set have been somewhat neglected by statisticians interested in expert systems. These systems require both domain knowledge and statistical knowledge. They provide interesting laboratories for testing our ideas of the meaning of statistical ideas like causation. Besides, the data sets used in these systems are usually rich, and require new analysis techniques.

Whatever our feeling as statisticians about the role of expert systems, we cannot afford to ignore them (see the articles of Hand, Tukey, and Huber [2]). Expert systems involving statistical expertise will be built because of the utility to the builders, if not to the potential client. With the explosion of personal computing, writing statistical software has become a lucrative business. Statistical software wrapped in an expert system is that much more marketable. For example, both EMycin and BMDP [12] are now marketed for use on (different) personal computers, and a system which consults on any given BMDP routine could easily be written in a few days. Pattern-finding systems are still at a more primitive stage—they must be built from scratch—but are attractive research topics for students in Artificial Intelligence as well as being of obvious interest for institutions handling large databases. The same computer that collects patient records for a medical project could, in its 'spare time,' search for interesting relationships in the data and generate new hypotheses for research.

ACKNOWLEDGMENTS

I am indebted to C.C. White and D.J. White, University of Virginia, for their helpful comments. All errors are mine.

REFERENCES

1. H.W. Gottinger, *Elements of Statistical Analysis*, De Gruyter, Amsterdam, 1980.

2. W.A. Gale (ed.), *Artificial Intelligence and Statistics*, Addison Wesley, Reading, MA, 1986.

3. G.J. Hahn, "More Intelligent Statistical Software and Statistical Expert Systems: Future Directions," *Am. Statistician*, 39 (1985).

4. B.G. Buchanan and E.H. Shortliffe, *Rule-Based Expert Systems: The MYCIN Experiments of the Stanford Heuristic Programming Project*, Addison Wesley, Reading, MA, 1984.

5. D. Pregibon and W.A. Gale, "REX: an Expert System for Regression Analysis in Computer Science and Statistics," *Proc. 14th Symp. Interface*, K.W. Heiner (ed.), Springer-Verlag, New York, 1982.

6. R.L. Blum, "Discovery, Confirmation and Incorporation of Causal Relationships from a Large Time-Oriented and Clinical Data Base: The RX Project," *Computers Biomed. Res.*, 15 (1982).

7. D.C. Wilkins, W.J. Clancey, and B.G. Buchanan, "Learning by Watching: Transfer of Expertise for Classification," *Expert Systems Ninth International Joint Conference on Artificial Intelligence*, 1985.

8. F. Hayes-Roth, D.A. Waterman, and D.B. Lenant, *Building Expert Systems*, Addison Wesley, Reading, MA, 1983.

9. W. Van Melle, A.C. Scott, J.S. Bennett, and M. Peairs, *The EMYCIN Manual*, Heuristic Programming Project of Stanford University Technical Report HPP-81-16, 1984.

10. J.M. Chambers, "Some Thoughts on Expert Software in Computer Science and Statistics," *Proc. 13th Symp. Interface*, K.W. Heiner (ed.), Springer-Verlag, New York, 1981.

11. H.W. Gottinger, "Computers in Medical Care: A Review," *Methods Inform. Med.*, 2 (1984).

12. *BMDP Statistical Software*, University of California Press, Berkeley, 1983.

HANS W. GOTTINGER

STATISTICAL MEASURES OF LANGUAGES:
ENTROPY AND REDUNDANCY OF THE ENGLISH DICTIONARY

INTRODUCTION

The study of language statistics has a variety of real and potential applications and it can play a principal role in the design of suitable methods for intelligent human–machine interaction. The analysis of the English dictionary itself can give an insight into the origin, constituent parts, and human preferences in the use of specific sounds and thematic structures.

A well-established approach to the analysis of language involves n-gram (n consecutive and naturally occurring letters) statistics and their potential as units of identifiable information. A number of researchers have utilized the statistical results obtained, and various methods have been implemented for automatic correction of misspellings, speech recognition, translation, information retrieval, text compression, and others.

We present the inherent statistical characteristics, including the economy, entropy, and redundancy of the English dictionary, based on the *Shorter Oxford English Dictionary*. Our sample (stored on an ASCII file) contains 93,681 unique words in alphabetical order, separated by spaces within multiword records each 80 characters maximum. Nonalphabetic characters and a small number of words which are obsolete are excluded.

Experimental results show how the distribution of n-grams in the dictionary varies from the ideal as n increases from 2 to 5, that is, from bigrams to pentagrams; it is shown that the corresponding redundancy also increases from 0.1067 to 0.3409. The results presented are of interest because: (a) the dictionary provides a finite list for deterministic analyses, (b) each entry (word) appears only once, and (c) all entries, even rarely occurring ones, have equal weight.

Preliminary analyses established that the longest word is ANTHROPOMOR-PHOLOGICALLY with 23 letters, and the most frequent word lengths are: 9 characters with 13,171 occurrences, 8 characters with 13,041, 10 characters with 11,848, and 7 characters with 11,319 occurrences. These and other findings which are not in line with the statistics of free running text demonstrate very clearly the peculiar nature of the English dictionary which does require special consideration.

A BRIEF HISTORY OF SYMBOL SETS

The use of language exemplifies the principle of economy of words applied ever since humans were able to communicate, and it is apparent in the sense that very frequent words tend to be very short. There have been many attempts to utilize this principle.

In 1605 Bacon anticipated the binary notation for numbers and also the five-unit code: A=00000, B=00001, C=00010, etc. In 1617 Napier provided the first use of the binary system for calculation. In 1832 Morse designed a code in which the most frequent letters were given short codes (e.g., E=$'.'$, T=$'\_'$ A=$'.\_'$) and the least frequent letters were given the longest codes (e.g., Q=$'\_ \_.\_.'$). The length of each code was designed to be inversely related to its frequency of occurrence. This was not intended to be a compression technique but an attempt to minimize the length of the message transmitted. A year later, in 1833, Weber and Gauss invented the international teleprinter five-unit alphabet where the most frequent letters were the easiest to represent.

R. C. Eldridge produced a catalogue of 6,000 common English words. As he stated in 1911, the ultimate aim of the work was the introduction of a limited vocabulary for universal use. The various word lists contained in this catalogue were made from random columns of random pages of the *Buffalo Sunday News* in 1909. In 1943, Dr. Irving Lorge and Edward L. Thorndike produced the *Teacher's Word Book* of 30,000 most frequently occurring English words.

In 1948 Zipf [*1*] presented his ideas on the principle of "least-effort" and applied this in order to study the economy of words. However, one of the most important contributions to the application of this principle for the transmission of information and the development of communications in general, was the mathematical theory of communication by Shannon [*2*] in 1948 and a method for estimating the entropy and the redundancy of a language [*3*].

The relative entropy, symbolized by H-relative, is a statistical parameter which measures how much information is produced, on average, for each letter of a text in a language [*4*]. Also, sets of variable length keys with high relative entropy provide a high degree of discrimination among words and therefore facilitate the process of on-line searching.

Recent research in the new information technology which includes cable technology, mobile radio and satellite communications, together with increasing use of very large databases, have highlighted the need for a very effective method of storing and transmitting information. The analysis of the English dictionary itself can give an insight into the origin, constituent parts, and human preferences in the use of specific n-grams, sounds, and thematic structures.

More recently there has been an increasing interest in n-gram statistics and their potential as units of identifiable information. A number of researchers have utilized the statistical results obtained and various methods have been implemented for automatic correction of misspellings, speech recognition, translation, information retrieval, text compression, and others. Also, n-grams generated from some source data have been used to calculate the redundancy associated with that data. Note that the source data used in all studies so far were based on free-running text rather than on a finite list of well-defined entries such as the words in our dictionary.

N-GRAMS AND THEIR USAGE

An n-gram can be formed by extracting n consecutive letters from a piece of text which contains words formed by some alphabet. For example, 'BIBL' is a tetragram that can be extracted from the words BIBLE, BIBLIOGRAPHY, BIBLIOGRAPHER, etc.

Knowledge of the inherent characteristics of the written language, including n-gram statistics, is particularly important for the design of intelligent natural language processors, parsers, etc. A number of techniques [*5*] make use of such statistics for efficient information processing, in a limited sense, due to the lack of global statistics. Note that the use of n-grams has certain advantages over the use of dictionaries which require substantial secondary storage as well as unacceptably long processing times. Unfortunately, most of the statistical lists available include only the 50 most frequently occurring n-grams, although the sources used varied in size from 10,000 words to the very impressive size of 1 million words [*5*].

In his attempt to apply his new method of calculating the entropy of a set of symbols, words, etc., Shannon [3] stressed the importance of n-grams and the need for accurate lists, particularly with n-grams where n>3. The latter were not available at that time.

Today, the problem is not so much the actual calculation of n-gram statistics (although this is a very demanding task in terms of disk storage utilization and processing time) but the sample under analysis. The question is "To what extent the sample is representative of the corresponding universe of discourse?" It is interesting to note here that Yannakoudakis et al. [6] proved that it is possible to get reasonable compression ratios with a set of n-grams derived from specialized sources (e.g., bibliographic) even when these are applied to general material (e.g., computer programs and newspaper articles).

In theory, using the whole range of bigrams with spaces, 50% compression can be achieved, but then there will be 601 (maximum rank of bigrams) additional symbols and the need for a very large look-up table will incur overheads in the efficiency of the compression algorithm. Similarly, large tables will be required when the whole range of trigrams, tetragrams, etc. is used. The majority of n-gram compression techniques employ 128 most frequently occurring n-grams but this depends on the algorithm and quite frequently key-sets of 256 symbols are generated. This approach works satisfactorily.

N-grams where n>5 are not particularly useful because they are not frequent enough to justify their use as symbols in their own right. Lynch et al. [7] attempted to include heptagrams, octagrams, etc., but discovered that the INSPEC database contained only 142 octagrams (for a key-set limit of 30) and only 9 octagrams for a key-set limit of 100.

THE N-GRAMS OF THE ENGLISH DICTIONARY

There are two basic methods for generating sets of n-grams

Method A

This method involves the following steps:

1. Calculate unigram frequencies
2. Calculate the most frequently occurring bigrams and adopt an arbitrary lower limit
3. Calculate the most frequently occurring trigrams on the basis of bigram frequencies above the lower limit
4. Continue for tetragrams using trigram limits, for pentagrams using tetragram limits, etc. as in step (3) above

Method B

Here, a 'window' of fixed length n (n being the length of the n-gram) is moved across each word, all possible n-grams are extracted, sorted, and analyzed. This method was used by Yannakoudakis et al. [6], who generated lists of n-grams for n=1, . . ., 8.

Under method A it becomes very difficult to establish a reasonable lower frequency limit for each set of n-grams while there is always a possibility to miss certain n-grams, particularly where n>2. Under method B, all possible n-grams can be generated and analyzed. However, the problem with the latter method is the vast secondary storage space that is required to hold the lists of n-grams.

The implementation of each of these methods is discussed in the following sections.

During the creation of the various lists of n-grams it was assumed that each word started with a letter and terminated with a space. Therefore, the n-grams produced are of the form N_ and not _N.

Bigrams

The theoretical maximum number of distinct bigrams that can be found is $26 \times 26 = 676$ (without spaces) and $27 \times 27 = 729$ (with spaces) less 26 bigrams beginning with space, less 1 bigram of the form (space, space) which gives a total of 702. Clearly, these theoretical maxima can never be reached in practice because certain bigrams, such as JX, QQ, etc., simply do not exist in the English dictionary.

The number of distinct bigrams in the dictionary without spaces is 575, whereas the number of distinct bigrams with spaces is 601. Table 1 contains the top 100 bigrams of the dictionary.

Trigrams

The maximum possible number of distinct trigrams is $26 \times 26 \times 26 = 17,576$ (without spaces) and $26 \times 26 \times 27 = 18,252$ (with spaces). Appropriate storage arrays were used to hold the trigrams in each case. The 100 most frequently occurring trigrams are listed in Table 1.

The results established that the number of distinct trigrams without spaces is 6,551 and the number of distinct trigrams with spaces is 6,898. The total number of nondistinct trigrams is 648,046 without spaces and 741,701 with spaces. The number 741,701 was expected since it is obvious that

BIGRAMS (without spaces)=TRIGRAMS (with spaces).

Tetragrams

The identification and analysis of tetragrams presented completely different problems because it proved impossible to create a memory table of $26 \times 26 \times 26 \times 26$ giving a total of 456,976 entries, while at the same time reserving 6 numeric digits as a counter for each entry. This required a main memory with $456,976 \times 6 = 2,741,856$ entries. In the case of tetragrams with spaces the situation is even worse because we have 531,440 possible distinct tetragrams and therefore the requirement for a table of 3.2 Mb.

We decided to produce a very large subset of the tetragrams by applying method A, as discussed later. Subsequently, the list of the most frequently occurring trigrams which we had available became the basis for calculating as many tetragrams as possible.

It is clear that any number of n consecutive letters can form an n-gram, if and only if they can form an (n-1)-gram first [8]. In theory, each trigram, say XXX, can produce the following $26+26=52$ tetragrams:

AXXX	XXXA
BXXX	XXXB
CXXX	XXXC
DXXX	XXXD
⋮	⋮
⋮	⋮
⋮	⋮
YXXX	XXXY
ZXXX	XXXZ

It is obvious that the following combinations of letters must be trigrams at the same time:

AXX	XXA
BXX	XXB
CXX	XXC
DXX	XXD
:	:
:	:
:	:
YXX	XXY
ZXX	XXZ

We can thus conclude that the 200 top trigrams can produce up to $52 \times 200 = 10,400$ tetragrams without spaces and 10,800 tetragrams with spaces.

On the basis of these considerations, we decided that the only way to overcome the problem of defining large files was to create two tables: TOTAL-TETRAGRAMS-TABLE-A (200,26) and TOTAL-TETRAGRAMS-TABLE-B (26,200) with 5,200 entries of 6 digits each. It was then easy to keep counters of tetragrams of the form XXXA and BXXX., respectively ('XXX' being a trigram 'A' any letter after 'XXX', and 'B' any letter before 'XXX'). So, whenever a trigram XXX was found, either the tetragram BXXX or the tetragram XXXA was also assumed to exist. It then became necessary to search through the table of the 200 top trigrams using the binary-chop technique to locate any trigram with an average of $(\log_2 200) + 1 = 8$ accesses, the only extra requirement being the use of indexed tables.

The theoretical maximum number of distinct tetragrams that could exist in the dictionary is $26 \times 200 + 26 \times 200 = 10,400$ without spaces and $27 \times 200 + 27_2 \times 200 = 10,800$ with spaces. When the dictionary was analyzed, we found that the number of distinct tetragrams was 6,026 without spaces and 5,821 with spaces. This was not expected because, normally, the number of tetragrams with spaces is greater than the number of tetragrams without spaces. One explanation for this is the fact that although the number of tetragrams with spaces is very large compared with the number of tetragrams without spaces, there are many tetragrams which belong to the first category but they are terminating parts of many words. Therefore, they are repeated without being distinct at the same time. This obviously depends on the 200 top trigrams that are actually used in each case.

Using a simple formula (introduced later) we found that the theoretical total number of tetragrams is 554,486 without spaces and 648,046 with spaces. The actual total number of tetragrams we processed was 284,887 without spaces and 338,814 with spaces. Therefore, the results were produced by analyzing approximately half the tetragrams which actually exist.

The lists of the most frequently occurring tetragrams which were produced using method A are more than adequate for applications like key-set generation and compression techniques on the dictionary. However, for certain other applications, like misspelling correctors, they may not be adequate because the more n-grams are known the more effective the corresponding methods become. So, we decided to implement method B although the storage requirements here were 10 times larger than had been the case previously.

Method B produced 554,486 tetragrams without spaces and 648,046 tetragrams with spaces. The distinct number of tetragrams were: 35,921 without spaces and 38,651 with spaces. In the first case (without spaces) the lists of the 100 most frequently occurring tetragrams which were produced by both methods A and B were identical, whereas in the

TABLE 1   The Most Frequent n-Grams of the English Language

Rank	Bigrams		Trigrams		Tetragrams		Pentagrams	
1	E_	18149	LY_	6389	ESS_	4775	NESS_	3709
2	ER	15470	ESS	5616	NESS	3726	TION_	2645
3	Y_	14243	ER_	5297	TION	3288	ATION	2278
4	IN	14016	SS_	4912	ION_	3096	ABLE_	1602
5	TI	12592	ED_	4318	OUS_	2838	ALLY_	1310
6	TE	11618	AL_	4249	ING_	2316	ICAL_	1196
7	AT	11276	ATI	4148	ATIO	2302	ENESS	1044
8	AL	10834	ION	4140	ATE_	2209	LITY_	816
9	EN	10789	IC_	4062	ICAL	2087	CALLY	783
10	ON	10526	OUS	3981	BLE_	2029	TIVE_	780
11	AN	10117	NES	3966	ABLE	1983	MENT_	773
12	IC	10023	TE_	3865	LLY_	1596	ICALL	766
13	LE	9712	ON_	3808	ITY_	1554	NGLY_	766
14	S_	9171	ING	3773	ENT_	1520	INGLY	763
15	IS	9103	ENT	3558	IST_	1503	LESS_	755
16	NE	9066	TIO	3507	ISM_	1499	TICAL	715
17	ES	8931	LE_	3478	TIC_	1498	GRAPH	695
18	RE	8501	ATE	3449	ALLY	1324	ROUS_	648
19	RA	8486	TER	3332	CAL_	1286	ATIVE	630
20	ST	8447	US_	3050	TIVE	1232	SNESS	599
21	RI	8186	ICA	2884	TER_	1171	OGRAP	597
22	N_	8181	TIC	2870	ITE_	1153	INESS	563
23	NT	8025	BLE	2735	TED_	1151	ILITY	546
24	LI	7639	IST	2722	ENES	1134	OLOGI	545
25	AR	7636	CAL	2649	IAN_	1117	ATED_	543
26	OR	7472	NG_	2463	MENT	1096	INTER	515
27	R_	7271	ABL	2429	IVE_	1061	USLY_	514
28	SS	7078	NT_	2352	LESS	1051	OUSLY	513
29	LY	7040	INE	2309	OLOG	994	BILIT	505
30	T_	7030	AN_	2220	IZE_	970	LENES	489
31	IT	6825	ALL	2144	INE_	959	BLENE	453
32	RO	6707	RY_	2061	ATOR	884	USNES	444
33	D_	6698	ANT	2028	CALL	851	OUSNE	442
34	UN	6527	ST_	2004	ROUS	844	ATOR_	440
35	ED	6372	CON	1942	INGL	837	TORY_	434
36	CO	6259	IVE	1938	LITY	816	EROUS	433
37	L_	6148	TY_	1926	IOUS	815	SHIP_	430
38	CA	6145	ENE	1833	ELY_	809	IOUS_	428
39	IO	6019	TOR	1723	TICA	790	LING_	427
40	LA	5913	PER	1661	STIC	787	ENCE_	414
41	OU	5849	ISM	1653	GLY_	780	TIONA	413
42	US	5748	NE_	1651	NCE_	776	ISTIC	408
43	DE	5643	STI	1629	NGLY	770	ABLY_	404
44	DI	5280	LLY	1627	NTER	762	STIC_	403
45	NI	5216	RAT	1596	IAL_	729	LOGY_	401
46	NG	5143	DIS	1589	RAPH	725	LATE_	398
47	TA	4983	ITY	1579	GRAP	709	IONAL	394
48	EL	4907	SM_	1550	INTE	699	DNESS	388
49	TO	4877	ITE	1543	TOR_	691	VELY_	383
50	LL	4869	LIT	1523	OGRA	659	OLOGY	378
51	TR	4845	ALI	1519	SLY_	657	IVELY	377
52	ME	4818	IAN	1489	LOGI	655	EOUS_	376
53	LO	4688	LAT	1454	LATE	654	RATE_	375
54	ET	4609	MEN	1445	ATIV	650	TING_	371
55	IA	4549	TRI	1433	RATI	641	LOGIC	367
56	NA	4494	TRA	1423	ILIT	625	CTION	365
57	VE	4492	ERI	1418	TING	618	TABLE	363
58	CH	4462	LIN	1400	ANT_	614	FORM_	361
59	MA	4427	TIV	1368	LING	603	ABILI	354
60	OL	4358	TED	1365	SNES	602	ABLEN	354
61	HE	4337	NTE	1350	INES	595	IFORM	351
62	C_	4208	ATO	1338	IONA	591	NISM_	347
63	SE	4133	GRA	1322	ARY_	580	EDLY_	346
64	IL	4086	VE_	1320	ATED	573	LNESS	343

65	PE	4067	TIN	1318	ISH_	570	EMENT	342
66	OM	4011	LOG	1292	BILI	569	NATE_	336
67	SI	4005	LES	1277	RATE	565	TATIO	323
68	AB	4003	OLO	1273	STER	551	ANCE_	322
69	AC	3985	ONI	1262	ISTI	541	ATORY	322
70	BL	3981	VER	1260	BLY_	534	RATIO	320
71	TH	3976	RES	1245	LENE	533	GICAL	315
72	CE	3963	HER	1235	TATI	531	NOUS_	308
73	NC	3902	NTI	1231	ETER	529	NTLY_	308
74	UL	3783	INT	1225	ENTI	525	NIST_	303
75	MI	3753	IZE	1221	FORM	522	IBLE_	302
76	PH	3720	THE	1214	ORY_	522	RIAN_	296
77	HI	3658	RAN	1213	OUSL	519	ONAL_	295
78	UR	3594	DER	1195	ULAT	519	OGICA	293
79	ND	3537	IAL	1179	NAL_	517	CATIO	291
80	AS	3389	STE	1174	ICAT	514	ETER_	291
81	EA	3277	NCE	1172	USLY	514	LOUS_	287
82	HO	3233	RIC	1171	ENTA	513	ULATE	282
83	GE	3148	STR	1167	TRIC	512	ZATIO	282
84	MO	3098	NAT	1161	NDER	509	IZATI	280
85	OP	3064	ERA	1147	NIC_	505	RAPHI	278
86	PA	3059	PRO	1140	ATIC	500	TIVEL	277
87	HA	3024	ISH	1135	DLY_	500	EDNES	276
88	NO	3019	MAN	1135	RING	497	ICATI	271
89	OG	3010	AST	1131	MATI	495	METER	268
90	M_	2981	ILI	1126	ENCE	490	ULAR_	268
91	EC	2962	NDE	1125	ONAL	487	VENES	268
92	OS	2931	ARI	1124	THER	480	SION_	267
93	ID	2910	RIN	1119	BLEN	479	ATIC_	266
94	PO	2907	INA	1116	AGE_	473	LISM_	263
95	CI	2884	MAT	1102	INAT	472	IVENE	262
96	SH	2789	ITI	1100	NATE	468	RING_	262
97	EM	2717	CE_	1082	EOUS	467	ELESS	259
98	AM	2703	ECT	1070	RESS	467	ALITY	257
99	G_	2669	ROU	1066	TLY_	467	MATIC	257
100	NS	2649	LEN	1058	SHIP	465	LATIO	255

second case (with spaces) method B also produced the tetragrams 'USLY' and 'SHIP' with ranks 81 and 100, respectively.

The 100 most frequently occurring tetragrams produced by method B are listed in Table 1.

Pentagrams

In order to store a theoretical maximum number of pentagrams we require a large table of $27 \times 27 \times 27 \times 27 \times 27 = 14,348,907$ distinct entries. We used method A and the list of 200 most frequently occurring tetragrams in order to generate 4,012 distinct pentagrams without spaces and 3,906 distinct pentagrams with spaces. Only 109,495 and 148,181 pentagrams were processed in each case.

With method B we processed 461,789 pentagrams without spaces and 554,486 with spaces and found 89,114 distinct pentagrams without spaces and 99,590 distinct pentagrams with spaces. The number of 99,590 pentagrams implies that, on average, there is more than one unique combination of 5 letters (pentagrams) in each of the 93,681 unique words of the English dictionary we have used.

It is worth pointing out here some of the peculiar pentagrams of the English language. The pentagrams 'ZZETT,' 'ZZART,' and 'ZZOUL' with frequency 1 are associated with the words 'MOZZETTA,' 'IZZART,' and 'POZZOULANA,' respectively.

The lists of the 100 most frequently occurring pentagrams produced by methods A and B were quite different. The list produced by method B contained some newcomers, as for example 'ACEOU,' 'FULLY,' 'OSCOP' (in the list without spaces), and 'SHIP_,' 'IZATI' (in the list with spaces).

The 100 most frequently occurring pentagrams produced by method B are presented in Table 1. We discovered a maximum rank of 55,000 because the rest of the pentagrams have all frequency 1.

Calculation of Expected Number of n-Grams

There are many instances where it is very useful to be able to calculate, theoretically, the number of n-grams that exist in a given text or dictionary. This can, for example, enable the selection of an appropriate compression technique, or even predict how many n-grams will be necessary for its effective implementation.

We found it necessary to calculate, theoretically, the number of n-grams in the dictionary in order to verify the empirical results already obtained by the various programs. It is easy to establish that the total number of n-grams in a given text or dictionary can be given by the formula:

$$N(n) = \sum_{w=n}^{m} (w - n + c) f(w)$$

where:

$N(n)$ = Number of n-grams in the text (n=1,2,3, . . .)

m = The maximum word length (23 characters for the dictionary)

$f(w)$ = Frequency of words with length w

c = 1 (without spaces), 2 (with spaces).

TABLE 2.   The Distribution of Words According to Their Length

Word-length	Frequency
1	26
2	95
3	863
4	3207
5	5534
6	8949
7	11319
8	13041
9	13171
10	11848
11	9231
12	6710
13	4454
14	2632
15	1412
16	675
17	335
18	113
19	44
20	15
21	6
22	0
23	1

The word length distribution for the dictionary is given in Table 2 from which we were able to calculate the number of n-grams in each case. We found that the empirical results were identical with the results obtained theoretically (the number of n-grams processed is presented in Table 3).   As can be seen in the word length distribution (Table 2), the most frequently occurring word length in the dictionary is 9 characters (i.e., 14% of the words).

TABLE 3.   Number of n-Grams Processed

	Without spaces		With spaces	
	Total	Distinct	Total	Distinct
Unigrams	835,382	26	929,063	27
Bigrams	741,701	575	835,382	601
Trigrams	648,046	6,551	741,701	6,898
Tetragrams	554,486	35,921	648,046	38,651
Pentagrams	461,789	89,114	554,486	99,590

TABLE 4.   Percent Distribution of Certain Bigrams in Two Lists

Bigram	Words from the English dictionary	Words from list used by Suen [5]
ER	2.085	1.568
IN	1.889	1.835
TI	1.697	0.855
TE	1.566	0.846
AT	1.520	1.122
AL	1.460	0.766
EN	1.454	1.084
ON	1.419	1.276
AN	1.364	1.605
IC	1.351	0.480
LE	1.309	0.611
IS	1.227	0.893
NE	1.222	0.554
ES	1.204	0.891
RE	1.146	1.436

Suen [5] produced n-gram statistics as well as positional distributions from a list of carefully selected samples of natural language texts such as reports, editorials, texts on hobbies, humor, etc. printed in America in 1961. The most frequent word length was three characters constituting 23% of the total words processed.

As expected, the results obtained from the analysis of the dictionary varied a great deal from those of Suen [5]. Table 4 contains the percent distribution of bigrams in both our dictionary and the list used by Suen. It is clear that some of the most frequently occurring bigrams in the dictionary occur rarely in Suen's list, with the exceptions of the bigrams 'IN,' 'AN,' and 'RE.'

CALCULATION OF ENTROPY AND REDUNDANCY

The n-gram statistics can now form the basis for the interpretation and application of Shannon's mathematical theory of communication [2] upon the English dictionary. The interpretation can be based on the definition of completely new symbol-sets which contain quasi-equifrequent groups [8]. Because the n-grams here are complete, the ultimate quasi-equifrequent arrangement can be formed deterministically rather than by approximation as has been the case so far.

When Shannon [2] first published his mathematical theory of communication (often called information theory), he provided some generalizations about the efficiency in transmitting messages in noiseless channels, and also the possible savings due to the statistical structure of the original text/message under transmission. Although certain researchers still believe that Shannon's theory is restrictive and unhelpful, it is generally accepted that it has had a profound influence on the development of information technology during the past three decades.

Two concepts play the principal role in the mathematical theory of communication:

the 'entropy' and the 'redundancy' of a set of symbols or a language. These concepts are reinterpreted and applied here using the exhaustive n-gram lists we have generated.

The entropy is a statistical parameter which measures how much information is produced on average for each letter of a text in a language. If text is translated into the binary digits 0 and 1 in the most efficient way, the entropy measures the average number of binary digits required per letter of the original language.

Shannon was led to the definition of the entropy by the requirements of a quantity to measure how much information is produced by a coding process, or better, at what rate information is produced. It was found that the only quantity, say H, satisfying certain assumptions that were made, is of the form

$$H = -k \sum_{i=1}^{n} p_i \log_2 p_i$$

where k is a positive constant referring to the units selected. The mathematical definition of the entropy H can then be considered under:

(a) The entropy of a discrete set of probabilities $(p_1, p_2, \ldots, p_n)$ which is defined as

$$H = -\sum_{i=1}^{n} p_i \log_2 p_i$$

where n is better understood as the number of symbols in the encoding alphabet and p the probability of symbol i.

(b) The entropy of a continuous distribution with density function p(x) which is defined as

$$H = -\int_{-}^{+} p(x) \log_2 p(x) dx$$

The relative entropy or the relative uncertainty is given by the formula:

$$H - relative = \frac{H - actual}{H - maximum}$$

According to the properties of H, H-maximum is reached when the probabilities of occurrence of the symbols of a particular sequence are equal, i.e., when $p_1 = p_2 = \ldots = p_n = 1/n$ and therefore

$$H - maximum = -n(1/n) \log_2(1/n) = \log_2 n$$

The redundancy measures the amount of constraint imposed on a text in the language due to its syntactical rules where for every syntactic rule there is a constraint that must introduce some redundancy. The statistical structure of the language itself introduces a certain amount of redundancy. In English, for example, there is a strong tendency for R to follow E, for N to follow I, and for I to follow T (see Table 1).

The redundancy can be defined as the difference between H-maximum and H-actual expressed as a fraction of H-maximum:

$$Redundancy = \frac{H\text{--}maximum\text{--}H\text{--}actual}{H\text{--}maximum}$$

or

$$Redundancy = 1 - H\text{--}relative$$

Generally, it is desirable to maximize the relative entropy of a set of symbols and therefore minimize the redundancy associated with that set.

Shannon's statement about the equifrequency of symbols, and therefore, about rectangular distributions stands as the ideal. In such states we have no redundancy at all because H-relative=1, since H-actual=H-maximum. It is, however, obvious that equifrequency is very rarely encountered within information structures.

TABLE 5.   Information Content of Letters in the Dictionary

Letter	Frequency	Rank	p$_i$	-p$_i$ log$_2$ (p$_i$)
A	69,281	3	0.0829	0.2978
B	15,443	18	0.0185	0.1064
C	39,193	10	0.0469	0.2070
D	26,580	12	0.0318	0.1581
E	91,262	1	0.1092	0.3488
F	10,191	19	0.0122	0.0775
G	18,844	17	0.0226	0.1235
H	21,653	15	0.0259	0.1365
I	75,561	2	0.0905	0.3136
J	1,239	26	0.0015	0.0140
K	4,727	22	0.0057	0.0424
L	51,606	9	0.0618	0.2482
M	25,371	14	0.0304	0.1532
N	59,930	4	0.0717	0.2725
O	56,696	7	0.0679	0.2634
P	25,607	13	0.0207	0.1542
Q	1,546	25	0.0018	0.0164
R	58,037	6	0.0695	0.2673
S	52,812	8	0.0632	0.2517
T	58,187	5	0.0697	0.2678
U	31,702	11	0.0379	0.1789
V	8,298	20	0.0099	0.0659
W	4,932	21	0.0059	0.0436
X	2,618	24	0.0031	0.0258
Y	21,045	16	0.0252	0.1338
Z	3,021	23	0.0036	0.0292

Total=835,382; H-actual=4.1987

Table 5 contains the frequency of occurrence of the letters in the dictionary. The sum of the values in the last column of this table is equal to 4.19876 and is interpreted as the entropy (or uncertainty) of the ensemble. Therefore, H-actual=4.19876. H-maximum refers to the theoretical maximum entropy, this being achieved only when the letters of the alphabet are all equiprobable [9]. Consequently,

$$H-maximum = \log_2 26 = 4.70042$$

In practical terms the above number means that if letters of the English alphabet are selected randomly for inclusion in some unit of the dictionary, then on average 4.70042 attempts are required to identify any of the letters if they are all equiprobable. Thus,

$$H-relative = \frac{H-actual}{H-maximum} = \frac{4.19876}{4.70042} = 0.89327$$

$$Redundancy = 1 - 0.89327 = 0.10673$$

Therefore, the relative entropy in this ensemble is 89.3% and the redundancy is 10.7%. It is interesting that these results are similar to those obtained by Yannakoudakis [4] from a file of bibliographic records where it was found that the relative entropy is 89.9% and the redundancy is 10.1%. Another recent comparative study between Greek and English texts [10] proved that the relative entropy is 89.1% and 88.4%, respectively. The minimum redundancy in Greek appears in heptagrams (1.22%) while the minimum redundancy in English appears in the octagrams (5.35%). The overall redundancy of Greek words is 22.7% [10].

The relative entropy and the redundancy for bigrams, trigrams, tetragrams, and pentagrams in the dictionary are presented on Table 6. Note that,

TABLE 6.   Entropy and Redundancy of n-Grams

n-gram	Max-Rank	H-max	H-actual	H-relative	Redundancy
Unigrams					
no spaces	26	4.7004	4.1987	0.8932	0.1067
spaces	27	4.7548	4.2470	0.8931	0.1069
Bigrams					
no spaces	575	9.1674	7.6416	0.8335	0.1665
spaces	601	9.2312	7.6922	0.8332	0.1668
Trigrams					
no spaces	6,551	12.6774	10.4717	0.8260	0.1740
spaces	6,898	12.7519	10.3780	0.8138	0.1862
Tetragrams					
no spaces	35,921	15.1325	11.5577	0.7637	0.2363
spaces	38,651	15.2382	11.4715	0.7528	0.2472
Pentagrams					
no spaces	89,114	16.4433	10.8387	0.6591	0.3409
spaces	99,590	16.6037	10.1215	0.6095	0.3905

$$H-maximum = -log_2(MAX - RANK)$$

because the maximum rank is the number of distinct n-grams that exist in the dictionary.

An unexpected finding was the relatively low H-actual in the pentagrams. The reason for this is that even if the number of n-grams was large, most of these would occur once or twice and therefore their probability of occurrence would be very low. We found that of the 99,590 pentagrams that exist, 42,075 occur once, 16,665 occur twice, and 9,475 occur three times.

Since it is practically impossible to achieve absolute equifrequency among the symbols, we expected the distribution of n-grams to be far from the ideal rectangular distribution. However, given a relative entropy of 83.35% for bigrams, the rank-frequency distribution was perfectly acceptable and very close to a rectangular distribution [8]. The deviation from the ideal was worse in the trigram rank-frequency distribution, but still acceptable. The largest deviation from the ideal rectangular distribution was observed in the pentagrams (with spaces) where the relative entropy was 60.95% and the redundancy was 39.05% [8].

Zero Redundancy State and Prediction

According to information theory, the entropy H is calculated by a series of approximations using a function F which takes successively into account more and more statistics of the language; the entropy H becomes the limit of F as n tends toward infinity. F_n is given by the formula:

$$F_n = -\sum_{i,j} p(b_i, j) \log_2 p_{bi}(i) =$$

$$= -\sum_{i,j} p(b_i, j) \log_2 p(b_i, j) + \sum_i p(b_i) \log_2(b_i)$$

where:

b_i = (n–1)-gram
j = any letter following b_i
$p(b_i, j)$ = probability of the n-gram b_{ij}
$p_{bi}(j)$ = conditional probability of
letter j after the (n–1)-gram b_i
Thus, $p_{bi}(j) = p(b_i, j)/p(b_i)$

Therefore $H = \lim F_n$. F_n is taken equal to H-maximum of the letters that form the generalized alphabet for a particular sample.

Shannon applied the above formula for n=3 because there was lack of tetragram and pentagram statistics. The problem in calculating the entropy here is that we cannot be absolutely sure that F_n will always be positive.

An interesting (but not reliable) method of calculating the entropy of a given text is by applying Zipf's law $r*f=c$ [1]. If we were to apply this on the dictionary we would be faced with the following hypothetical and theoretical situation: Since all the words in the dictionary are unique, the probability of each occurring is 1/93,681 and with an average word length of 8.9 letters, the entropy becomes:

$$H = - \sum_{1}^{93681} (1/93,681) \log_2(1/93,681) = 16.51 \text{ } bits \text{ } per \text{ } word \text{ } or 16.51/8.9 = 1.85 \text{ } bits \text{ } per \text{ } letter$$

Here, of course, we assume equiprobability and therefore the quantity H refers to H-maximum.

In his book *Human Behaviour and the Principle of Least Effort* [1, pp. 20,21], Zipf gives some examples of extreme situations of economy, or what we call 'zero-redundancy state.' He states that from the viewpoint of the speaker (speakers' economy), the maximum economy or zero redundancy state will be achieved if the vocabulary consists of a single word (one character) with m different meanings. Now, from the viewpoint of the auditor (auditor's economy), maximum economy means *m* different words with one meaning each and with the minimum number of characters. We must point out here that some of Shannon's experiments produced English expressions which were pronounceable but at the same time not meaningful.

Although Zipf simply provided some theoretical cases of economy without any intention of applying them (this was impossible anyway), Shannon applied the formula H=lim F_n in his attempt to find out to what extent English is predictable. He gave some examples where a person tries to predict a letter in a text by simply knowing the previous three. The interpretation of such a methodology requires the use of multiple Markov chains.

A given text forms a multiple Markov chain of order *r*, if for any blocks of strings each consisting of *r* consecutive letters, the probability of the next block to be of a specific kind is the same as the probability of the next block to be of a specific kind given only the last block of the string.

Finally, if a language is a Markov process of order -1, it will be in the zero-redundancy-state. This implies that it will have no syntax, but only semantics, because every syntactic rule is a constraint which introduces redundancy.

REFERENCES

1. G. K. Zipf, "*Human Behavior and the Principle of Least Effort*, Addison-Wesley, Cambridge, MA, 1949.
2. C. E. Shannon, "A Mathematical Theory of Communication," *Bell Sys. Tech. J., 27,* 623-656 (October 1948).
3. C. E. Shannon, "Prediction and Entropy of Printed English," *Bell Sys. Tech. J., 30,* 50-64 (1951).
4. E. J. Yannakoudakis, "Towards a Universal Record Identification and Retrieval Scheme," *J. Informatics, 3*(1), 7-11 (1979).
5. C. Y. Suen, "N-Gram statistics for natural language understanding and text processing," *IEEE Transact Pattern Analysis Machine Intell.PAMI-1,* 2, 164-172 (April 1979).
6. E. J. Yannakoudakis and P. Goyal, "The Generation and Use of Text Fragments for Data Compression," *Inform. Proc. Mgmt., 18*(1), 15-21 (1982).
7. F. M. Lynch, J. H. Petrie, and J. M. Snell, "Analysis of the Microstructure of Titles in the INSPEC Data Base," *Inform. Storage Retrieval, 9* 331-337 (1973).
8. E. J. Yannakoudakis and G. Angelidakis, "An Insight into the Entropy and Redundancy of the English Dictionary," *IEEE Pattern Analysis Machine Intell.* (PAMI), *10*(6), 960-970, (1988).

9.   E. J. Yannakoudakis and A. K. P. Wu, "Quasi-Equifrequent Group Generation and Evaluation," *Computer J. 25*(2) 183–187 (1982).
10. E. J. Yannakoudakis, J. Tsomokos, and P. J. Hutton, "n-Grams and their implication to natural language understanding," *Int. J. Pattern Recog, 23*(5), 509–528 (1990).

EMMANUEL J. YANNAKOUDAKIS

SYMBOLIC COMPUTATION SYSTEMS

Not every scientist needs a symbolic manipulator, and not every scientist who needs one knows that he needs it [*1*].

INTRODUCTION

Symbolic computation systems are computer programs to perform symbolic mathematical computations, as described by Yun *et al.* [*2*]. They are based on data structures representing mathematical expressions and on algorithms for algebraic and analytical transformations. The availability of such software systems, together with the systems for numerical computation, enormously enhances the computing capabilities for scientific problem solving.

This article reviews the major advances in the design and implementation of symbolic computation systems of the last decade and the main capabilities of the currently available systems.

The pioneering work on differentiation by Kahrimanian [*3*] and by Nolan [*4*] in 1953 is often considered the first effort in the development of software for formal mathematical computation.

In 1960, the introduction of LISP stimulated and facilitated a wide programming activity in the area of symbolic and algebraic computation. Indeed a program for formal differentiation is the second most commonly written LISP program (the first obviously being the factorial function). In the successive years, J. Slagle studied how to invert the process of differentiation. His work [*5*] represents a first example of a special purpose symbolic computation system dedicated to the problem of indefinite integration.

The design and development of general purpose symbolic computation systems started in the 1960s. The first generation of such systems, including ALPAK, FORMAC, MATHLAB, and PM, provided a large number of different computing methods (e.g., polynomial and rational function algebra, polynomial factorization, Laplace transformation). MATHLAB also included facilities for interactive use and bidimensional output.

The successive period of the 1970s presented the development of a second generation of very significant and efficient systems, such as ALTRAN, CAMAL, MACSYMA, muMATH, REDUCE, SAC-1, and SCRATCHPAD I. Many of these systems, which allow for an interactive use, are still in use today.

A wide description of these two generations of systems can be found elsewhere [*2,6*].

In the 1980s, remarkable advances were made in system design and implementation, mainly due to methodological and technological achievements in symbolic computation and to the contributions of hardware and software industries and of commercial companies active in the field.

The development of symbolic computation systems in this decade has mainly followed two directions: the enlargement and enrichment of systems already available, as MACSYMA and REDUCE, an the design of new systems, as MAPLE and MATHE-

MATICA, especially designed to also be run on powerful workstations with graphic facilities.

In this same period, the SCRATCHPAD II project started at IBM Research Center in Yorktown Heights. This project represents now the most innovative achievement in symbolic computation system design and it has brought to a system of new generation, particularly suitable to treat applications with a strong algebraic characterization.

It must be noted that the development of symbolic computation systems has been the result of an international effort, as the systems often incorporate, at software level, most of the theoretical and algorithmic results obtained by the international research community and as they have often been developed with the contribution of several researchers and programmers visiting the development center from other research institutions. REDUCE and MACSYMA are very significant examples of this approach of incremental implementation.

The capabilities of symbolic computation systems are strongly influenced by the research achievements on algorithm design and implementation, as well as by the theoretical results on complexity. At the same time, theoretical advances in commutative algebra and logical theories have also given a strong background for the design of symbolic computation systems. Furthermore, the studies of the design and implementation aspects of graphic user interfaces and of numerical computation capabilities, to be integrated into a symbolic computation system, have deeply characterized the development of new systems.

The reader wishing to explore the topics further may refer to the recommended list of basic readings appended to this article.

RESEARCH BACKGROUND AND BASIC FEATURES

The record of accomplishments in symbolic computation which are relevant to system design and implementation is significantly large [7]. In particular, it includes basic results on the definition of practically fast algorithms, and the application of software engineering methods and techniques, mainly obtained in the last decade. Furthermore, it also includes other basic results of a theoretical or mathematical nature that have not yet been transferred into effectively usable algorithms or computing systems.

One basic problem in system design and implementation is the development of efficient data structures and algorithms to deal with arbitrary precision integers and rationals and with indefinite precision floating-point numbers.

Another important problem is the availability of fast algorithms for polynomial and rational function arithmetics and for solving algebraic equations and systems of algebraic equations.

The problems of computing polynomial gcds and of polynomial factorization have been deeply studied and significant improvements to their algorithmic solutions have been proposed over the years [8,9].

Several approaches were followed to define algorithms for the computation of gcd, mainly based on the extension of the euclidean algorithm and on the computation by homomorphic images. Probabilistic algorithms have also been proposed for sparse multivariate polynomials [10]. Many of these algorithms are available in the major symbolic computation systems and they can be selected by setting appropriate switches.

The effective and practical solution of the problem of polynomial factorization is based on the use of the algorithm for polynomial factorization over finite fields and, again, on the method of computing by homomorphic images [9]. Important theoretical results on this problem have also been obtained quite recently. Indeed the definition of algorithms for univariate and multivariate polynomial factorization in polynomial time is one of the most relevant accomplishments in the entire field of symbolic computation [*11,12*].

Closed form and approximate solutions of equations is a central issue in applications. In particular, computing the numerical approximation of the roots of a univariate polynomial can be done by effective algorithms based on the methods of root isolation and of interval refinement [*13*]. The definition of algorithms for the exact solution of a system of polynomial equations is based on the results obtained in the framework of the polynomial ideal theory. These algorithms construct the canonical basis, called the Groebner basis, of the ideal generated by the set of polynomials that defines the system of equations to be solved. The solution of the given system is then obtained from the canonical basis, by successive reductions [*14*].

Algorithmic solutions recently proposed for other important problems in symbolic computation have also characterized this decade. The solution to the problem of integration in finite terms given by Risch in 1970 [*15*] has been studied [*16,17*] and implementations of his algorithm are included in many of the currently available systems.

Analogous work has also been performed on the problem of summation in finite terms [*18*] and an implementation of related algorithms is available in MACSYMA.

Several practically usable results were obtained also for the problem of finding algorithms for solving differential equations and systems of differential equations in closed form [*19,20*]. Algorithms have been defined for the ordinary, linear and nonlinear, cases. They are available in many systems and have allowed users to solve significant problems in real applications [*21*].

The use of graphic workstations with high-resolution bitmapped displays has widely characterized the system development in this decade. Such workstations allow for the design of very sophisticated user interfaces, with multiple windowing facilities and pointing devices. These modern interfaces improved the input of expressions and the formatting and display of the output. They also offer the capabilities of manipulating expressions by specializing editing commands and mathematical operations using the mouse. Furthermore, the basic graphic capabilities incorporated into the interface offer powerful facilities for graphics and plots of mathematical expressions. This represents one of the best achievements in symbolic computation system design in the decade. The MATHEMATICA system remarkably exploited all these technological advances. New user interfaces have also been proposed for systems of past generation, such as MACSYMA. See Young and Wang [22] for a comprehensive presentation of the subject.

Another important aspect is related to the communication of a symbolic computation system with other computing environments, namely with programming languages dedicated to numerical computation, as FORTRAN, and with publishing languages, as TeX. Current systems offer facilities, at various levels, to produce outputs of symbolic computations in a format suitable for further processing. In particular, this possibility is very relevant to allow for the effective treatment of real applicative problems that generally require a combination of symbolic and numerical techniques for their solutions.

MAJOR SYMBOLIC COMPUTATION SYSTEMS

The number of symbolic computation systems designed and implemented can be certainly counted by the dozens. Most of them have been developed for special research and application purposes and they have been made available only to restricted groups of interested persons. Only a few consist of general purpose symbolic computing tools and they are widely distributed. These systems are in general very well maintained and documented, and they have been used extensively over the years.

In this section, five of these major general purpose systems are reviewed: DERIVE, MACSYMA, MAPLE, MATHEMATICA, and REDUCE. They are quite different in structure and in destination, and their presentation may give a good shape of the state of the art in the field.

DERIVE

DERIVE, designed by A. Rich and D. Stoutemyer, is the successor of the system muMATH. The system muMATH, implemented in the LISP-like language muSIMP, has been devised for architectures based on 8–16 bit microprocessors and maintained and distributed from 1976 to 1983. The evolution of personal computers (e.g., better performance, larger memory, graphics facilities) has brought to the design of DERIVE, which exploits the entire experience of the algorithm design and implementation of its ancestor muMATH and offers a much more friendly interface.

DERIVE is a LISP-based system designed for personal computers based on new microprocessors (e.g., INTEL 80286 and 80386), with graphics facilities, and running under MS-DOS. The system can be interactively accessed through a modern interface, based on windows (both overlaid and split-screen) and menus and it includes capabilities for 2D and 3D graphic output.

The system, described as "a mathematical assistant for your personal computer," offers a wide range of symbolic computation commands, including those previously offered by muMATH. DERIVE can be used easily as a pocket calculator. A general symbolic formula can be entered using standard mathematical operators and functions. The system displays the formula in a format which is very easy to read, by also raising exponents, and performs the requested operation. Formulas can be simplified, plotted, expanded, approximated, factored, placed over a common denominator, differentiated, and integrated. Equations and inequalities can also be solved, both analytically or approximately. Matrices can be operated by the usual linear algebra operations.

In particular DERIVE incorporates facilities for: exact arithmetics, polynomial and rational function algebra; simplification (controlled by a variety of appropriate flags); elementary function operations; differentiation; indefinite and definite integration; limits; linear algebra; algebraic and transcendental equations; differential equations; sums and products; power series; combinatorics and statistics; bidimensional and tridimensional graphics.

The possibility for the user to add new computational methods for specific purposes is also provided.

Even though DERIVE is a system conceived for machines with limited resources, it is sufficiently complete in terms of symbolic computation capabilities. However, the power and the flexibility for solving real applicative problems is necessarily quite limited and the size of data to be possibly manipulated by the available commands is also limited. Actually, the main interest in using DERIVE is for educational purposes. Indeed, in this direction it has gained a large recognition, due to the wide availability and the low cost, as well as to the very nice integration of the graphic facilities into the symbolic computation package.

The system is available for PCs running compatible MS-DOS or PC-DOS, or running the PS/2 system. The minimum requirement is 512 bytes of memory and one double-sided (360 k) 5.25 inch or one (720 k) 3.5 inch diskette drive. The system supports also different monitors. A version for NEC PC-9801 compatible personal computers is also available.

For further details on DERIVE and muMATH the reader is referred to read elsewhere [*23, 24*]. The system is distributed by: The Soft Warehouse Inc., 365 Harding Avenue, Suite 505, Honolulu, HI 96816.

MACSYMA

MACSYMA is an interactive LISP-based system designed and developed by the MATH-LAB Group at M.I.T., under the direction of J. Moses, since late 1960s.

The main goal of the MACSYMA project has been the design of a system incorporating as much mathematical knowledge as possible, in order to satisfy the scientific computing needs in science and engineering applications. MACSYMA is the result of a giant effort in software development and maintenance, which is sizeable in more than 100 man-years. It is a very large system with thousands of LISP functions allowing for the treatment of a variety of mathematical expressions, including indefinite precision floating-point numbers, partial fractions, special functions, power series, and tensors.

MACSYMA represents a powerful tool for an automated approach to mathematical problem solving in real applications. It combines symbolic and numerical capabilities and enlarges the possibilities of interaction among exact symbolic methods and approximation methods. The links to FORTRAN programming environments guarantees the applications of basic numerical analysis capabilities into the symbolic computation framework.

The system yields enormous increases in productivity by allowing one to obtain symbolic solutions very fast; then, the subsequent numerical calculations are carried out at reduced cost. It also guarantees a high degree of accuracy by using ultra-high-precision arithmetic and by producing symbolic solutions in place of numerical approximations. At the same time, when closed form solutions are not computable, algebraic approximation methods can be applied to obtain the desired precision without rounding errors.

The MACSYMA user can concentrate himself on the intellectual content of a problem, leaving all the computational details to the system. Actually, MACSYMA offers significant facilities to support a decision on the techniques to be used in many situations, and allows the user to easily define them.

Some of the most relevant capabilities of MACSYMA allow one to perform: simplification; polynomial and rational function algebra; polynomial factorization; linear algebra; differentiation and indefinite integration; limits and definite integration; differential equations; equations and systems of equations; power series expansion; indefinite summation; poisson series; linear transformations (e.g., Laplace transform); tensor manipulation; FORTRAN and TeX code generation.

The system is designed to assist mathematical problem-solving activities in sciences and engineering. In particular, heavy use of MACSYMA has been reported at several laboratories such as Jet Propulsion, Naval Research, Los Alamos National, Draper, MIT Lincoln, NASA Langley. Major application areas, where very relevant results have been obtained, include: acoustics, algebraic geometry; computer-aided design; control theory; decision analysis; economics; fluid mechanics; number theory; numerical analysis; plasma physics; structural mechanics; and solid-state physics.

MACSYMA was first developed for DEC and Honeywell computers. Then, the agreement reached between MIT and Symbolics Inc., for marketing the system, brought its implementation on Symbolics 3600 workstations. Presently, also versions for Apollos, Dec-Vax, IBM (PC/386), and Sun, are supported and distributed.

For further details on MACSYMA the reader may refer to Refs. *25–32*. The system is distributed by: The Computer Aided Mathematics Group, Symbolic Inc., 8 New England Executive Park, East Burlington, MA 01803, USA.

MAPLE

MAPLE is an interactive C-based system designed and developed by the Symbolic Computation Group of the University of Waterloo, Canada, since 1980.

The most significant characteristic of MAPLE is its compactness, which allows the system to be run on machines with relatively small memory, requiring only a few hundred kilobytes per user. In fact, the main motivation for the design and development of the MAPLE system has been to provide effective and efficient symbolic computation tools for a large number of users, such as students or novices. In particular, the need has been considered to guarantee the simultaneous access to a symbolic computation system to run on microprocessor-based workstations or on time-sharing computing environments, for educational applications as well as for general scientific and engineering applications. This goal generated two more specific objectives for the MAPLE system: portability and efficiency.

In order to reach such objectives, the MAPLE system has been designed to be a very compact system, and it has been developed by a specially designed macroprocessor. A small kernel of the system, implemented in C, includes some basic components, such as the number and polynomial arithmetic package, the memory management system, the input-output functions, the MAPLE programming language interpreter. The other parts are coded in the MAPLE programming language and are organized in a library of more than 1500 functions which is accessed on demand.

An important consequence of these designing characteristics of the MAPLE system is the possibility for the user to extend the capabilities of the system by defining its own functions, which assume the same status of the library system functions and therefore are processed equally fast.

The main computing capabilities of the MAPLE system provide facilities for: arbitrary precision integer and real arithmetic; simplification; polynomial and rational function algebra; integer and polynomial factorization, linear algebra; differentiation and indefinite integration; limits and definite integration; differential equations; equations and systems of equations; power series expansion; indefinite summation.

These facilities have been improved over the years both from the extension of the data domains on which they apply and from the efficiency points of view. The user easily accesses the system by a syntax based on typical mathematical notations. The current version of MAPLE also offers two-dimensional graphics, complete on-line help system with examples of the main commands, while a new graphic interface is under development.

The MAPLE system requires only one megabyte of memory for most of its applications. The structure of the system, with a small kernel of basic capabilities and a library of functions, has allowed MAPLE to be implemented on a broad range of computer architectures including Apollo, Apple Macintosh SE and II, Dec-Vax, IBM PC/386 under UNIX, Sun, and Cray and IBM mainframes.

For further details on MAPLE, readers are referred to the literature [*33–37*]. The system is distributed by: The Symbolic Computation Group, Department of Computer Science, University of Waterloo, Waterloo, Ontario, Canada N2L 3G1.

MATHEMATICA

MATHEMATICA is a general purpose system of new generation for doing mathematics by computer. It was designed by S. Wolfram in the last decade: the first version of MATHE-MATICA was released in 1988.

The main feature of MATHEMATICA is represented by its high-quality graphic interface and by its highly sophisticated graphic output capabilities. Actually, the system offers most of the basic symbolic and numerical methods strongly integrated via appropriate interfaces and enriched by the graphic tools.

The system is implemented in C and is structured with a kernel and an interface front-end module. The kernel consists of about 150 thousand lines of code and is implemented as a machine-independent module and allows one to perform basic symbolic and numerical operations. The front-end consists of about 50 thousand lines of code, represents the interface, and is designed to exploit the characteristics of specific machines.

The system can be used in many different ways. As a calculator MATHEMATICA allows computation with numbers, in particular with exact (arbitrary length) integers and rationals, arbitrary precision floating point, and complex numbers. It can also compute symbolically on polynomials and on rational functions by basic operations, such as arithmetic operations, expansion, factorization, decomposition, gcd, common denominator, and partial fractions.

As a numerical computing system MATHEMATICA allows one to handle many different mathematical functions, such as elementary trascendental, orthogonal polynomials, and special functions. All functions can be evaluated to arbitrary precision. Numerical matrix operation are allowed, as well as data analysis by generalized least-squares fit and Fourier transform, and numerical integration, summation, product, root finding, and minimization.

As a symbolic computing system MATHEMATICA allows for (partial) differentiation, integration, by the Risch method plus pattern matching, power series expansion, limits computation, and linear algebra. Furthermore, symbolic methods for analytical solution of algebraic (linear and polynomial) equations and systems of algebraic equations, by Groebner basis method, are also offered.

As a new generation system MATHEMATICA is amazing for its external interface and for its powerful graphics facilities. The user interface, enriched with both windows and menu-handling features, allows for input files, programs, or keyboard and produced output suitable for further processing by C, FORTRAN, and TeX. It also permits communication with external environments.

The system can be effectively used for two- and three-dimensional graphics, both in black and white and in color. The graphics produced are very impressive. They include functions for plotting single, multiple, and parametric curves, by adaptive evaluation point algorithm, default scaling to find regions of interest, options for curve color and style, and axes. Three-dimensional graphics include resolution-independent procedure, full hidden surface removal, and surface rendering by wire frames or shading.

The system also offers a very powerful programming language that allows users to augment the basic capabilities by building their own libraries for numerical and symbolic calculations and for specific graphic facilities. The new libraries are then accessed as speedily as the system library.

MATHEMATICA initially was developed for Apple Macintoshes. The standard version of the system runs on Macintosh Plus, SE, and II. The Macintosh II version runs on Macintosh II only. It requires 2.5 MB RAM, while 4 MB is recommended. Many new versions have been released, including versions for Apollo, Cray, Dec-Vax and Dec stations, Hewlett-Packard, and Sun. A version for MS-DOS 386-based machines is also distributed.

For further details on MATHEMATICA readers are referred to appropriate literature [*38–41*]. The system is distributed by Wolfram Research Inc., P.O. Box 6059, 201 W. Springfield, Suite 500, Champaign, IL 61821.

REDUCE

The system REDUCE was originally designed by A. C. Hearn in 1963 to solve problems in theoretical physics, and has grown to a general purpose symbolic computation system of wide use by thousands of scientists and engineers in several application areas.

REDUCE is an interactive system implemented in LISP by applying the classical technique of bootstrapping and macros. For this reason it has been made available for a very large number of different machines, ranging from small PCs to supercomputers. Indeed portability is the main feature of REDUCE.

After the original system REDUCE, a new version appeared in 1970: REDUCE 2. This version was characterized by the use of a new ALGOL-like implementation language, called RLISP, to facilitate the software development. REDUCE 2 was distributed to a large community of users worldwide.

The successive version REDUCE 3, distributed since 1983, was developed by A. C. Hearn with substantial contributions of others in implementing several new packages (e.g., packages for integration, multivariate factorization, equation solving). The user community itself continuously contributes in different ways to the enhancement of REDUCE, by adding new packages and by reporting problems and suggesting improvements. This process of development maintains REDUCE up to date with the current results in symbolic computation.

The basic system includes some fundamental functions to perform the most frequent and common symbolic operations. The present version includes facilities for: exact integer arithmetic; arbitrary precision real arithmetic; evaluation, substitution, and simplification of general algebraic expression; polynomial and rational function algebra; polynomial factorization; linear algebra; and differentiation and indefinite integration.

The simplification as well as the output processes can be controlled directly by the user by a number of programmable switches. A general purpose pattern-matching facility is also available, at user level, in order to allow for the definition of specific simplification rules and of computational methods not available in the standard version of the system. It is worth noting that the source code of REDUCE is distributed with the system. The user then can easily access the basic functions and extend the system with new capabilities of his or her particular interest. The REDUCE language, with an ALGOL-like syntax, supports this programming activity.

User-contributed packages offer facilities for several operations seen as very important from an application point of view. The package for indefinite integration of square roots, an extension of the basic package for analytical integration, allows one to integrate a wide range of expressions involving square roots of algebraic functions. A package for computing with algebraic numbers is also available. It allows for operations on polynomials with algebraic number coefficients. The differential geometry package is provided to support the study of differential problems and to compute in general relativity. The computation of Groebner bases, using the Buchberger algorithm, is offered by a specific package. It allows for operations on a variety of domains and for different term orderings.

A particular mention is for the GENTRAN package designed to output expressions in formats suitable for successive processing in FORTRAN, RATFOR, and C. This package furnishes a natural and effective tool to integrate symbolic and numerical computations into a single computing environment, as necessary in many applications where symbolic computation steps are often followed by numerical evaluations.

REDUCE has been applied to a variety of problems in the sciences and engineering, including theoretical physics, plasma physics, celestial mechanics, electrical network analysis, general relativity, numerical analysis, and turbine and ship hull design.

Reduce, in its present version 3.3, is distributed for at least twelve different architectures, ranging from PC compatible to CRAY X/MP, including Apollo, Apple, CDC, Dec-Vax, Hewlett Packard, and Sun.

For further details on REDUCE the readers are referred elsewhere [42– 44]. The system is distributed by Anthony C. Hearn, The Rand Corporation, 1700 Main Street, P.O. Box 2138, Santa Monica, CA 90406-2138.

DEVELOPMENT OF NEW PROJECTS

In addition to the systems presented in the previous section, other general purpose systems have received significant attention from the research and the user communities. Among these systems, particular mention is due to SCRATCHPAD II, mainly for the innovative principles of its design. So far, this system has been made available only to a restricted number of research centers, under joint study agreements with IBM. Therefore it cannot be considered a system available for real applications, as the other major systems described above. However, IBM plans to market SCRATCHPAD II commercially in the near future.

There are many other systems designed especially to treat problems in very specific application areas. In particular, a relevant production of special purpose systems occurred in areas such as celestial mechanics, general relativity, and quantum electro dynamics. The class of special purpose systems includes systems dedicated to solve problems in pure and applied mathematics. In this direction, the system CoCoA for solving problems in commutative algebra deserves explicit consideration.

The two sections following are devoted to a short presentation of SCRATCHPAD II and CoCoA. For a description of other systems the reader may refer to the list of basic readings.

SCRATCHPAD II

SCRATCHPAD II is a language for the implementation of a new general purpose computer algebra system, developed at the IBM Research Center in Yorktown Heights since the late 1970s. This very modern language is based on some general programming features (such as data abstraction and inheritance, taken from the object-oriented programming paradigm), which are so very important when developing sophisticated software as that for symbolic mathematics.

The formal specification of the data structures and of the algorithmic methods embedded in a symbolic computation system requires the implementation language to offer powerful mechanisms to express the rich set of relationships among the mathematical objects. Then, the language should allow one to code symbolic mathematics in a completely structured way, as in formal algebra. This is not the way other known systems have been developed, where, for instance, similar algorithms for different mathematical structures belonging to the same algebraic structure are designed independently without any consideration of the obvious similarities.

The SCRATCHPAD II system bases its implementation of abstract data types on categories. They provide a convenient and powerful method to model the mathematical structures and their relationships through multiple inheritance. A category designates a class of abstract mathematical structures, called domains, and specifies the admissible operations, together with the related properties to be satisfied. A large set of built-in categories is available, such as OrderedSet, Ring, Integral Domain, and FiniteField.

A domain is a category, as a set of attributes, plus a set of functions which actually implements the operations specified in the category, so as to satisfy their properties. All domains are created by special constructors and they represent the abstract data type of the language. There are basic domains, such as Integer and RationalNumber, and related subdomains, such as PositiveInteger. There also are parameterized domains, such as IntegerMod, Matrix, Polynomial, and Rational Function, which depend on given fixed parameters, such as a prime number or a coefficient domain.

SCRATCHPAD II can be used both as a desk calculator and as a programming language. The user can simply define objects and apply operations from built-in domains, he enters expressions and gets the computation done with powerful type checking assuring high degree of correctness. At the same time, the SCRATCHPAD II language allows one to create new domains or subdomains, by defining new algorithms and computational methods, and by also applying the inheritance mechanism available.

SCRATCHPAD II is certainly not specific to applications. It has been conceived as a tool for the implementation and the experimentation of mathematical algorithms and methods. It is a very large software package, including the library of facilities for the manipulation of various mathematical structures, the compiler and the user interface interpreter. The system has been initially developed for IBM mainframes. More recently, a version for IBM workstations, such as PC-RT, has been designed and implemented in order to verify the prospective of a wide distribution as a commercial product.

For further details on SCRATCHPAD II, see Refs. *45-47*. For information on the system one may contact Richard D. Jenks, IBM Thomas J. Watson Research Center, P.O. Box 218, Yorktown Heights, NY 10598.

CoCoA

CoCoA is a small interactive special purpose system for doing computations and supporting research activity in commutative algebra. The system has been designed and developed mainly in response to requests by mathematicians for a very simple and small system, to be easily accessible with a limited expertise on computers, and to be mainly used to check algorithms and theoretical ideas.

The first implementation of CoCoA started in 1987 and included basic capabilities for handling multivariate polynomial rings. The current version, implemented in standard Pascal, offers a quite large number of functionalities based on the most recent algebraic techniques, as the construction of Groebner basis of ideals. This version actually runs on any computer of the Macintosh family, and then is characterized by a very attractive user interface, consistently integrated into the classical Macintosh environment.

CoCoA gives the user greater freedom in organizing the computation by writing commands and expressions in a very simple and intuitive way. However, in order to keep the system small it has been decided, at the present stage of development, to make it nonprogrammable, and to omit facilities for arbitrary precision integer arithmetic. For the same reason the system is quite fast and immediately applicable to a wide range of typical computations in commutative algebra.

Further details on CoCoA are described by Giovini et al. [*49*]. For information on the system one may contact: Lorenzo Robbiano, Department of Mathematics, University of Genova, Via L. B. Alberti 4, 16132 Genova, Italy.

CURRENT TRENDS IN SYSTEM DESIGN AND IMPLEMENTATION

The characteristics and the power of the software systems currently available, as described in the previous sections, still are not adequate to answer the quantitative and qualitative needs of mathematical problem solving in different application areas.

Research and development in symbolic computation system design and implementation have been very intensive in the last few years, with significant contributions from industrial environments. However, the relevant achievements still are based on the traditional approach to software specification and design, with the only valuable exception of SCRATCHPAD II.

It seems necessary to further exploit the recent research results and to attack the problem from a completely new point of view. New structural characteristics of the desired systems must be defined, in order to allow the user to work in a different way. In particular, the role of a computer should be enhanced further from a pure computing instrument to a tool for supporting the creative and qualitative activity in mathematical problem solving. Two main goals have to be pursued, namely the effective and complete integration of the different computing paradigms (numerical, algebraic, and analytical) and the correctness of all the computations. In fact, the possibility for a qualitative analysis of the results must also be offered by allowing for the formal verification of the mathematical properties of the objects to be dealt with.

Presently, the research activity in the design and implementation of symbolic computation systems mainly considers the following topics:

> Abstract specification of mathematical objects
> Axiomatic definitions of the mathematical objects, with the consequent use of automated deduction mechanisms, as a new fundamental computing tool for qualitative analysis
> Algebraic and heuristic methods for applied mathematics, at a very high level of abstraction with respect to the domains where the problems are defined
> Object-oriented programming methodologies
> Numerical–symbolic interface
> High-quality graphics for the user interface

At the same time, particular attention is also devoted to computational aspects of parallel algorithms as well as to parallel symbolic computation system design.

These topics, with their theoretical and practical aspects, have been the subject of recent conferences on the design and implementation of symbolic computation systems [*50*] and on parallelism [*51*]. New interesting proposals of experimental systems have been presented. They confirm the trend toward the development of a new generation of symbolic computation systems where the broad features offered to the user is accompanied with a clean and smooth system design which guarantees correct processing and computing.

REFERENCES

1. W. S. Brown, SIGSAM Interview, *ACM SIGSAM Bull.*, 27, 7–16 (1973).

2. D. Y. Y. Yun and R. D. Stoutemyer, "Symbolic Mathematical Computation," in *Encyclopedia of Computer Science and Technology*, Vol. 15, J. Belzer, A. G. Holzman, and A. Kent (eds.), Marcel Dekker, New York, 1980, pp. 235-310.

3. H. G. Kahrimanian, "Analytic Differentiation by a Digital Computer," M.A. Thesis, Temple University, Philadelphia, 1953.

4. J. Nolan, "Analytic Differentiation on a Digital Computer," M.A. Thesis, M. I. T., Math Department, Cambridge, 1953.

5. J. R. Slagle, "A Heuristic Program that Solves Symbolic Integration Problems in Freshman Calculus," *J. ACM*, *10*, 507- 520 (1963).

6. J. A. Van Hulzen and J. Calmet, "Computer Algebra Systems," in *Computer Algebra—Symbolic and Algebraic Computation*, B. Buchberger, G. E. Collins, and R. G. K. Loos (eds.), 2nd ed., Springer-Verlag, New York, 1983, pp. 221-243.

7. B. F. Caviness, "Computer Algebra: Past and Future," *J. Symb. Comp.*, *2*, 217-236 (1986).

8. W. S. Brown, "On Euclid's Algorithm and the Computation of Polynomial Greatest Common Divisors," *J. ACM*, *18*; 478-504 (1971).

9. E. L. Kaltofen, "Factorisation of Polynomials," in *Computer Algebra—Symbolic and Algebraic Computation*, B. Buchberger, G. E. Collins, and R. G. K. Loos (eds.), 2nd ed., Springer-Verlag, New York, 1983, pp. 95-113.

10. R. E. Zippel, "Probabilistic Algorithms for Sparse Polynomials," Proc. EUROSAM '79, *Lecture Notes on Computer Science Series*, *72*, 216-226 (1979).

11. A. K. Lenstra, H. W. Lenstra, and L. Lovasz, "Factoring Polynomials with Rational Coefficients," *Math. Ann.*, *261*, 515-534 (1982).

12. E. L. Kaltofen, "Polynomial-Time Reduction from Multivariate to Bi- and Univariate Polynomial Factorisation," *SIAM J. Comput.*, *14*, 469-489 (1985).

13. G. E. Collins and R. Loos. "Real Zeros of Polynomials. Symbolic and Algebraic," in *Computer Algebra—Symbolic and Algebraic Computation*, B. Buchberger, G. E. Collins, and R. G. K. Loos (eds.), 2nd ed., Springer-Verlag, New York, 1983, pp. 83-94.

14. B. Buchberger, "Groebner Bases: An Algorithmic Method in Polynomial Ideal Theory," in *Multidimensional Systems Theory*, N. K. Bose (ed.), Riedel, Dordrecht, The Netherlands, 1985, pp. 184-232.

15. R. H. Risch, "The Problem of Integration in Finite Terms," *Trans. A.M.S.*, *139*; 167-189 (1969).

16. J. H. Davenport, "On the Integration of Algebraic Functions, " *Lecture Notes on Computer Science Series*, *102* (1981).

17. M. F. Singer, B. D. Saunders, and B. F. Caviness, "An Extension of Liouville's Theorem on Integration in Finite Terms," in *Proc. ACM Symposium on Symbolic and Algebraic Computation*, 1981, pp. 23-24.

18. R. W. Gosper, "Decision Procedure for Indefinite Hypergeometric Summation," *Proc. Natl. Acad. Sci.*, *75*, 1:40- 42 (1978).

19. M. F. Singer, "Formal Solution of Differential Equations," *J. Symb. Comp.*, *10*, 59-94 (1990).

20. E. Tournier (ed.), *Computer Algebra and Differential Equations*, Academic Press, New York, 1990.

21. R. Pavelle (ed.), *Applications of Computer Algebra*, Kluwer Academic Publ., Boston, 1985.

22. D. A. Young and P. S. Wang, "GI/S: A Graphic User Interface for Symbolic Computation Systems," *J. Symb. Comp.*, *4*; 365– 380 (1987).
23. C. Wooff and D. Hodgkinson, *muMATH: A Microcomputer Algebra System*, Academic Press, New York, 1987.
24. D. Stoutemyer, J. Rich, and A. Rich, *Derive User Manual*, The Soft Warehouse Inc., Honolulu, 1989.
25. P. S. Wang and R. Pavelle, "MACSYMA from F to G," *J. Symb. Comp.*, *1*, 69–100 (1985).
26. MACSYMA *Reference Manual, Version 13*, Symbolics Inc., East Burlington, MA, 1988.
27. *MACSYMA User's Guide*, Symbolics Inc., East Burlington, MA, 1988.
28. R. D. Drinkard, "MACSYMA: A Program for Computer Algebraic Manipulation," Naval Underwater Systems Center, NUSC Tech. Doc. 6401, 1981.
29. R. H. Rand, *Computer Algebra in Applied Mathematics: An Introduction to MACSYMA*, Pitman Publishing Inc., Marshfield, MA, 1984.
30. R. J. Fateman (ed.), *Proc. MACSYMA User's Conference*, NASA CP-2012, Washington, D.C., 1977.
31. V. e. Lewis (ed.), *Proc. MACSYMA User's Conference*, MIT, Lab. Comp. Sc., Cambridge, MA, 1979.
32. V. E. Golden (ed.), *Proc. MACSYMA User's Conference*, General Electric Co., Res. and Dev., Schenectady, NY, 1984.
33. B. W. Char, K. O. Geddes, M. W. Gentleman, and G. H. Gonnet, "The Design of Maple: A Compact, Portable and Powerful Computer Algebra System," *Lecture Notes and Computer Science Series*, *162*, 101–115 (1983).
34. B. W. Char, G. J. Fee, K. O. Geddes, G. H. Gonnet, M. B. Monagan, and S. M. Watt, "A Tutorial Introduction to Maple," *J. Symb. Comp.*, *2*; 179–200 (1986).
35. B. W. Char, K. O. Geddes, G. H. Gonnet, M. B. Monagan, and S. M. Watt, *Maple Reference Manual*, Fifth Edition, WATCOM Publications Ltd., Waterloo, Ontario, 1988.
36. B. W. Char, K. O. Geddes, G. H. Gonnet, M. B. Monagan, and S. M. Watt, *First Leaves: A Tutorial Introduction to Maple*, 2nd edition, WATCOM Publications Ltd., Waterloo, Ontario, 1988.
37. B. W. Char, K. O. Geddes, G. H. Gonnet, B. L. Leong, M. B. Monagan, and S. M. Watt, *First Leaves for the Macintosh: A Tutorial Introduction to Maple*, Books/Cole Publishing Company, 1989.
38. S. Wolfram, *MATHEMATICA: A System for Doing Mathematics by Computer*, Addison-Wesley, Reading, MA, 1988.
39. *MATHEMATICA for the Macintosh: User Manual*, Wolfram Research Inc., Champaign, IL, 1988.
40. R. Maeder, *Programming for Mathematica*, Addison-Wesley, Reading, MA, 1989.
41. A. Crandall, *Scientific Application of Mathematica*, Addison-Wesley, Reading, MA, 1989.
42. J. Fitch, "Solving Algebraic Problems with REDUCE," *J. Symb. Comp.*, *1*; 211–227 (1985).
43. A. C. Hearn, *REDUCE User's Manual*, The RAND Corp., RAND Publ. CP, Santa Monica, 1987, p. 78.
44. G. Rayna, *REDUCE: Software for Algebraic Computations*, Springer Verlag, New York, 1987.

45. J. H. Davenport, R. D. Jenks, MODLISP, *Proc. of the 1980 LISP Conference*, Redwood Estates, CA, 1980, pp. 65–74.

46. R. D. Jenks, "The SCRATCHPAD Language, Proc. of Symposium on Very High Level Languages, *ACM SIGPLAN Notices, 9*; 4 (1974).

47. R. D. Jenks and C. J. Sundaresan, "The 11 Keys to Scratchpad II: A Primer, Proc. EUROSAM '84," *Lecture Notes and Computer Science Series, 174*, 123–147 (1984).

48. S. M. Watt, R. D. Jenks, R. S. Sutor, and B. M. Trager, "The Scratchpad II Type System Domains and Subdomains," in *Computing Tools for Scientific Problem Solving*, A. Miola (ed.), Academic Press, New York, 1990, pp. 63–82.

49. A. Giovini and G. Niesi, "CoCoA: A User-Friendly System for Commutative Algebra," in *Design and Implementation of Symbolic Computation Systems*, A. Miola (ed.), Springer-Verlag, New York, 1990, pp. 20–29.

50. A. Miola (ed.), *Design and Implementation of Symbolic Computation Systems, Lecture Notes and Computer Science Series*, 429 (1990)..

51. J. Della Dora and J. Fitch (eds.), *Computer Algebra and Parallelism*, Academic Press, New York, 1990.

BIBLIOGRAPHY

Buchberger, B., G. E. Collins and R. G. K. Loos (eds.). *Computer Algebra—Symbolic and Algebraic Computation*, 2nd ed., Springer-Verlag, New York, 1983.

J. H. Davenport, Y. Siret, and E. Tournier, *Computer Algebra—Systems and Algorithms for Algebraic Computation*, Academic Press, New York, 1988.

A. Miola (ed.), *Computing Tools for Scientific Problem Solving*, Academic Press, New York, 1990.

D. Y. Y. Yun and R. D. Stoutmeyer, "Symbolic Mathematical Computation," in *Encyclopedia of Computer Science and Technology*, Vol. 15, J. Belzer, A. G. Holzman, and A. Kent (eds.), Marcel Dekker, New York, 1980, pp. 235–310.

ALFONSO M. MIOLA

SYSTEMS INTEGRATION: CONCEPTS, METHODS, AND TOOLS

INTRODUCTION

Computer and information science and technology have managed problems in widely different applications, providing the services for users in diverse areas of research, development, and industry. In the quest for correct and comprehensive solutions, new concepts, methodologies, and technologies have been invented, tested, and applied in order to meet the demand for well-designed systems. However, "well-designed" often has a very restricted frame of reference, addressing only the needs and attributes of a single application. System design concepts, methods, and tools usually focus on improving the process of development and maintenance, without paying much attention to the system's possibility of subsequent integration in a larger system context. This produces a situation where the resulting product functions according to a specification, targeted to define a project with predefined boundaries. The underlying technologies, system architectures, and semantic concepts are chosen to fit these restricted goals.

The result is that one ends up with a set of applications which is designed to perform individual component tasks without even acknowledging the presence of other applications. However, sooner or later, strategic planning and organizational requirements lead to the need to use data and services among different systems, and, consequently, to coordinate and integrate these systems. Coping with this objective usually makes it clear that a system is more than the simple sum of its parts. An integrated system, even if it is composed of existing applications, has its own characteristics and therefore its design and implementation have to be planned and conducted carefully.

Systems integration can be achieved either by gluing the already existing parts together or, preferably, by applying an integrated top-down approach, thus coordinating all integration and development activities in a common framework. To be able to handle the different possible forms of systems integration, it is necessary to identify the different active and passive components of the systems, their dependencies, and their uses. The "passive" components provide the infrastructure of the system (e.g., transport of data) which is used by the "active" components which comprise the functionality of the system by implementing a given application. The management of integrative processes can be discussed on the basis of such a framework of classified system parts.

Our discussion focuses on that part of systems integration related to computer science and information systems. From this viewpoint integration refers to integration of hardware/software systems, concepts, and technologies rather than modelling industrial production methods and their implementation. Thus, we shall assume that all parts of the system will be viewed on the level of their representations as a hardware/software system with defined interface to other computer applications, or will not be investigated under such a level.

This report on systems integration is organized as follows: First we identify the basic building blocks of a conceptual systems integration framework, based on a layered model which starts with basic technologies and goes on to the problems of concepts integration over multiple system parts. We proceed to discuss the basic attributes of the integration process and present two actual models for integration. The discussion concludes with a summary.

A FRAMEWORK FOR INTEGRATION

The following model of a layered approach, identifying the components in the systems integration task, is based on a framework originally presented by Nilsson et al. [1]. Basically, three different classes of technologies, methods, concepts, and/or tools are identified:

-Enabling technologies
-Integration architectures
-Global integration

Enabling technologies are the prerequisites for systems integration, providing us with the building blocks necessary to get started. Integration architectures describe the use of these building blocks in forming a system which is internally integrated and allows for further expansion. Global integration addresses the coordination and tuning of the system at its interface and addresses the semantic level.

Enabling Technologies

Enabling technologies address mechanisms, systems, and tools which can be used as a basis for systems integration. These components of the integration process make the possibility of systems integration easier. However, their existence alone does not guarantee that an integration process is taking place.

A typical starting point for any kind of integration effort is the use of clearly defined software and system engineering concepts and tools [2,3]; the application of database technology in user application [4] and as a design support tool [5]; and the coordinated introduction of networking. These three technologies must be at a mature level of development to serve as a basis for systems integration. This means that their application is standardized, predefined and supported by a coordinating system group.

Networking technology and the success of high-end PCs and workstations have a significant influence on the state of the art of systems integration. These factors and the emerging ability to integrate hardware and operating systems from a mainframe level to the PC level allow us to strive for integration solutions which would have been impossible before. On the other hand, it is networking and the concept of distributed computing that challenges both the software engineer and the database specialist to adapt within their domain of expertise and to create new and improved solutions which are facilitated by the new dimension of computing offered by reliable networks.

Nilsson, Nordhagen, , and Oftedal [1] identify the transfer of data between systems and the initiation of actions in other systems as the primary factors within the enabling technologies, calling them integration technologies. They specify the levels of integration technology as:

basic data transfer
transport services
file transfer protocols
remote procedure calls

The main attributes used to evaluate these levels of communication are reliability and effectiveness. The two basic strategies used to achieve the necessary level of integration quality are referred to as: (1) manual data transfer versus automatic data transfer; and (2) common database versus process to process communication.

In general, fully automatic data transfer (data transfer between applications without user intervention) is preferable. However, this presupposes a higher level of standardization and integration on the networking level. This is a good example of a system integration which starts by integrating the system parts themselves. The question of a common database versus process-to-process communication is not so much a question of the enabling technology, but rather leads directly to the level of integration architectures.

Besides the aforementioned basic enabling technologies, other techniques like artificial intelligence and new concepts like object-orientedness [7] and software reuse [8] should be mentioned here. On one hand, these new concepts can be used to support systems integration attempts and, on the other hand, they presuppose systems integration as a prerequisite for their own applicability. In any event, all these domains lack a standardized model of application and are, for the time being, difficult to integrate with other technologies. This prevents them from being of real use for systems integration, though it opens a wide area for research and future application [9].

Integration Architectures

The concept of integration architectures refers to idea that an integrated system should have a strategically chosen open architecture which is implemented on the basis of identified enabling technologies. Different architectures favor different forms of communication and integration and are objects of research in their own right. Standards help to reach agreement upon tested and approved system layouts and provide the means of achieving the level of industrial mass production.

There is no common theory or figure of merit which would indicate whether a given system architecture is able to handle integration. However, the simple fact that well-designed systems are in general easier to handle than comparable systems of lower quality holds also for systems integration. Widely used quality metrics like cohesion and coupling [10] force a system to be constructed in a modular manner from well-defined blocks and support the task of integration by achieving flexibility and adaptability. Furthermore, integrated systems should provide for easy expansion with regard to functionality and data.

Concurrent systems with message passing between processes and systems linked by a common data repository [1] are typical implementations of integrated architectures. On an abstract level, several forms of system architecture can be identified as follows:

Generic systems
Object-oriented systems
Channel-based systems

With integration as a major factor for systems, there will be a change from the prepacked, ready to use system, which is fixed in all its details to the generic system which can be adapted to its environment. This kind of system will be "parameterized" and able to be instantiated to different instances. Instances are adapted to run as slightly different versions of the generic system in different application environments. These application environments are similar to each other with regard to needed system functionality and layout, but still are different enough to trigger the need for adapted versions. Consistency rules will be necessary to ensure integrity during the instantiation process. Examples for research in this area can be found elsewhere [11,12].

Systems which follow a message-passing paradigm and have a high degree of reusability usually require attributes like flexibility, adaptability, and expansibility and tend to meet the need to be generic enough to be adapted to a given environment. Therefore, message-passing systems have a better chance of being used successfully as components or as a backbone for a targeted system in the integration process. Object-oriented systems [7], with their loosely coupled architecture based on message passing and with their hierarchy of classes, seem to be a possible prototype for these architectures. However, the matching of object-oriented systems to distributed systems and the integration of more traditional system architectures into the object-oriented paradigm, to form a common system architecture, are open questions.

A similar alternative is the class of system architectures often referred to as "channel-based approaches." The channel-based approach typically separates the passive components which provide the common infrastructure—the channel which transports data and files on the system level—from the "active" components of a system which constitute the functionality and data storage capacity of the system [13]. As in hardware architectures, active components, like hardware system components, use the given bus or channel architecture to communicate with each other in a standardized way, thus allowing one to modify functionality and data capacity on the basis of an open architecture of passive, message-passing components. Examples include the UNIX™ pipe mechanism [14], the co-tool concept [13], and, at least from its basic conception, the European Software Factory [15]. This architecture, like its hardware implementation, provides high modularity, easy extension, and good adaptability.

To apply these generic architectures successfully, it will be necessary to follow the approach of an "open" system. Specifications, design, and eventually implementation details should not be handled as proprietary information, but should be available for every interested user or vendor; the Bellcore OSCA™ architecture [16] is an example. As the current market situation shows, this open system approach seems to be feasible not only with regard to its technical dimension, but also to user satisfaction and earned profits.

An open system would have to define at least the following system parts [1] and, ideally, give some freedom to modify them:

    Basic architecture
    User interface
    Data storage and representation
    System functions
    Data transfer
    Used enabling technologies

Global Integration

Global integration focuses on the integrated system as a whole and not on the parts of the system. The major concern is to fine-tune the system architecture, to deal with interface problems, and to abstract implemented solutions and necessary improvements to provide standards.

In a system which has been planned and implemented with systems integration in mind, the activity of global integration may be reduced to a kind of final check on performance numbers, competent interface layout and functionality, and compliance with standards. However, if we consider very large systems which evolve over time or if we take into account systems which need a post-facto integration, global integration will exceed these kinds of system check mechanisms. In this case, global integration is a process of its own [17].

The activity of system tuning includes fine tuning of interfaces, data stores, and functions and data transfer according to operational needs, such as performance. System re-engineering is a major part of global integration activities in post facto integration of systems which are composed out of old system parts. In this context, re-engineering is a process that transforms the system into an approved system, without changing its externally visible functionality. Re-engineering and reusability are closely related. Results in transformation technology as applied to reuse and system development are presented By Cheatham [18] and Boyle and Muralidharan [19].

Re-engineering may entail reverse engineering, a method of going backward from code to design or from design to specification, to provide the engineer with a model of the system (-part) at the next higher level of abstraction. Starting from this recreated system description, changes are made and implemented.

Interface development [1] includes the task of providing a uniform user interface for the end user, even though he or she might work on different applications which constitute the integrated system. A uniform user interface acts like a filter between the actual system and the user. It translates the system output into the "language" of the end user and allows him to stay with the well-known structure and functionality of "his" interface.

In a highly integrated system, which encapsulates many different system parts, it will be necessary to work on an integration scheme to ensure a consistent use of concepts on a system-wide basis, not only on the level of syntax, but also on the level of associated semantics. Furthermore, it will be necessary to adapt the system structure as it is presented to the user according to the user's expectations and needs, similar to the concept of user views in database applications.

System standardization is a key method to achieve the very demanding and diverse tasks of global integration, to enable architectural integration, and to support development of enabling technologies. It would go beyond the scope of this discussion to describe the variety of standards under development or in use. Kuhn [20] gives a summary of the most important standards and relates the system integration process and some integrated architectures to the use of standards.

The basic idea of this approach is to build a layered system, in which the application uses system services only via the interface of organization (and national) standards, such as a "channel," thus ensuring consistent integration and change. Such a layered system consists of four layers, namely:

Layer-1: application
Layer-2: organization standard services
Layer-3: system Services: software standards, proprietary services
Layer-4: the operating system kernel

INTEGRATION MANAGEMENT

After having identified the fundamental concepts and components involved in systems integration on the level of computer applications and systems, the logical next step is to identify the basic concepts and alternatives for managing the task of applying, combining, controlling, and implementing these key elements.

With respect to approved software engineering methodology, the first step is to develop and to define the following terms:

A generic model for the process of integration itself
Methods to handle this process
Tools to support the different phases and tasks
Metrics, measurements, and control structures to guide it

Furthermore, we must take into account the special necessities and critical steps of effective systems integration, as seen from the point of view of practitioners who have to live and cope with a highly dynamic market; according to Seifert [21], effective systems integration includes the following four steps:

1. Process characterization
2. Re-engineering and process simplification
3. Convergence on a common architecture and data language
4. Automation of the process and systems

This model not only provides for the integration of new systems, but demands the characterization and improvement of existing solutions. It acknowledges and stresses the fact that "systems integration is more complex than linking together information systems and islands of automation." Systems integration is based on architectures and standards, as discussed earlier, and has as its ultimate goal to be automated to a large extent.

Following Lehman [22] and considering the immature nature of the field, the first task of a process engineer is to design a process and its supporting elements before tool support and distinct applications are considered. As soon as a process is defined and implemented within a supporting (tool-) environment, the product engineer can handle the development of applications in an integrated manner.

However, so far there is no agreed-upon or standardized process model or reference process architecture for systems integration which could be seen as a basic (and maybe generic) model in this field. Due to this fact, what we have seen so far are only the first attempts to standardize and to coordinate on either a company or national level.

An example for such an approach on company level to guide the integration process is the OSCA™ approach by Bellcore [16]. OSCA specifies a "strategic architecture to be used by Bellcore Client Companies to provide software interoperability." Interoperability is defined as the ability of software products to communicate with each other and the ability of users to communicate with any software product, irrespective of the internal implementations and the environments on which software products reside. However, even though there are some remarks on the process of system development and integration itself, the OSCA approach is targeted much more to define the framework for integration rather than the process itself.

On a national level, standards are in discussion in a variety of groups and organizations [23], including work for an abstract common reference model for software environments [24]. Such a reference model could be used as a metamodel for describing and integrating different specialized approaches and as a common framework for process definition. Once again, the approach of a common reference model is still mainly concerned with the definition of interfaces and integration architectures rather than being a model for a process. Nevertheless, it seems that it might be able to lay the basis for a common vocabulary and understanding, regarding methods and tools involved with such a systems integration process.

An integration process guided by metamodels and targeted at a predefined reference architecture must take into account at least the following dimensions of systems integration:

Services of the integrated system
Involved technologies, architectures, and mechanisms
Process management

Services describe what the user wants from an integrated system and how the system provides this in terms of functionality, data storage, and networking capabilities on a conceptual level. This step is not so much different from conventional systems analysis. However, it has to deal with a wide variety of ill-structured problems and a tendency to involve large systems as parts of an even larger integrated system. It asks for an extremely broad knowledge of the state-of-the-art and even possible future solutions. Furthermore, it is likely that an integrated system will tend to go beyond the scope of a single application domain. This leads to a demand for special education and a distinct methodology in order to be able to handle this situation of work on a "meta-level."

Work on this level includes identification, evaluation, and adaptation of a framework for the integrated system, including the use of basic technologies, integration system architectures, and global integration mechanisms. This work requires consulting with experts of the different domains of knowledge involved. These experts have to be coordinated and their efforts must be integrated according to a predefined process model.

As mentioned above, there is so far no standardized conceptual framework for defining the necessary process models. Nevertheless, two basic approaches involving models and methods are (1) the post-facto or bottom-up approach [17] and (2) the phased top-down approach [25]. These two models will be discussed in more depth.

The Post-Facto Approach

A post-facto approach, as opposed to pre-facto approaches, focuses on mechanisms used for interconnecting parts. It thus acknowledges that we lack a purely top-down approach for developing projects, but rather have to rely on a mixture of approaches, including bottom-up development strategies. Even if top-down development is the basic goal, software/hardware reuse, combined with a lack of adequate transformation mechanisms, may make a bottom-up scheme necessary to resolve incompatibilities and to integrate the existing (so far incompatible) components.

Furthermore, even though the top-down approach can handle many projects using a relatively well-structured plan based on the typical specification, design, and implementation cycle, integration of large systems will necessarily include the post-facto integration of systems (not only components) based on different technologies and developed at different points in time and with different goals in mind. Therefore, post-facto integration should not be characterized as a "black-art" used by engineers who have not been able to handle their systems adequately, but it should be considered as a research area of its own, leading to new methods and tools [17].

An overview of post-facto integration is given by Power [17]. According to his work, pure *pre-facto* design, with systematic development, has the following characteristics:

System design precedes parts design
Uniform parts
Monolingual environment
Tight coupling

Fine grained structure
Standardized reuse

On the other hand, pure *post-facto* systems, with "opportunistic development," have the following attributes:

Parts design precedes system design
Heterogeneous system
Multilingual environment
Loose coupling
Typically medium to large-size parts
Nonstandardized reuse

Evidently, post-facto integration faces the need to "glue" together nonstandardized and not directly compatible components. This software glue, which is a piece of coupling software between two given subcomponents, has the following functions:

Call assist mechanisms
Type conversions
Protocol matching
Interlanguage and interprocess communications

These pieces of coupling software are used to form a targeted system, in which each component is seen as an independent process. The indigenous interface of each component is transformed according to the given demands (stream-oriented interfaces are proposed by Power [17] by encapsulating the components with layers of software. Data objects which are shared between components are represented as external copies with synchronization mechanisms. Additional functionality and data structures are allowed, but should be handled outside the original components in the encapsulating software.

Post-facto integration allows us to see practice as it is and offers reuse on a level which can be used without major investments and requiring a long time to reach the break-even point. Thus, it seems that post-facto integration serves very well to develop a relatively loosely coupled system out of predefined and commercially available smaller systems. However, it inherits all the well-known drawbacks of bottom-up methodologies and loose coupling. Some of these consequences might not have the same importance on a level which couples systems and not mere system parts; however, maintenance and the quality of the system structure itself will suffer in particular.

Post-facto integration is much more concerned with integrating systems on the interface level and less concerned with the process of managing systems integration from a more management oriented point of view. Therefore, post-facto integration can be combined with more comprehensive integration approaches and used to allow the inclusion of alien subcomponents in an otherwise well-structured and specified system framework.

The Phased Top-Down Approach

Top-down approaches follow a traditional waterfall model of systems integration, by starting with a conceptual system and then deriving the system by incrementally refining the abstract concepts. These approaches provide a basis not only for technical integration, but also for the management of organizational and budgetary aspects. Even though the reuse and integration of existing (commercially available) solutions are supported, they focus on the uniformity and the degree of integration of the resulting system.

Eisner [25] proposes a top-down-oriented, two-phased process for large-scale systems integration. This approach is based on the identification of three main problem areas for systems integration:

Dealing with large and complex systems
Requirements difficulties
An overloaded procurement and acquisition process

Large and complex systems tend to make development and integration of systems a highly complicated process and require flexible but firm management of the development and integration process from the beginning, taking potential future changes in requirements and technology into consideration at the same time. Requirements of large and complex systems are inherently incomplete and have a tendency to change [22]. Thus, requirements can only be seen as a starting point for combined user–developer evaluation and are subject to changes, with mutual approval from the user and developer, which makes systems integration even more complex. Typical acquisition processes ask for quick on-the-spot decisions, influencing the future integration structure in unpredictable ways, and may lead to hard to correct system design errors. To overcome these difficulties, system development and integration is divided into the phases of (1) archetyping and (2) actual system building [25].

The second step, actual system building, is a relatively conventional step, based on the principles of systems engineering. Besides the technical part, it includes monitoring of progress, user training, and verification of assumptions (e.g., on system performance) made in the archetyping phase. This phase always follows the archetyping phase and can be performed either by in-house development of the integrated system or by an external contractor. In both cases, developers have to work according to the results of the preceding archetyping phase.

The first step, the archetyping phase, is independent from the subsequent building phase and constitutes the major improvements of the phased top-down approach as described here. It is again split up in two steps: architecting and prototyping.

Architecting uses a top-level design approach to construct a generic architecture of the system. Such a generic architecture allows one to integrate already existing components and provides a framework for interface definitions, performance and cost evaluations, etc. However, this architecture should be generic and robust enough to provide flexibility and adaptivity for changes in requirements and technologies. To achieve highly reliable results, sensitivity analysis and the use of simulation models are suggested for this stage.

The prototyping step is used to construct an "architected" and tested demonstration prototype of the system. This prototype is then used to verify the architecture and to check the assumptions made in the architecting step.

From our point of view, a comprehensive archetyping-oriented integration process, as proposed by Eisner [25] includes the three dimensions of integrated services, integration architecture, and process management. In its architecting step, it defines an integration architecture and addresses global integration issues without binding the system too early to existing solutions and technologies. This makes the architecting phase a critical step which has to be supported properly by methods, reference architectures, standards, and tools.

SUMMARY

In discussing the various issues related to the notion of systems integration, we have identified a framework for components of the integration process in terms of enabling technologies, integration architectures, and global integration activities.

Trying to map this framework to an integration process, we presented three basic elements of integration: services of the integrated system; involved technologies, architectures, and integration mechanisms; process management. These elements can be handled through the use of post-facto or phased top-down integration approaches.

In the relatively young area of structured systems integration, concepts and methods that can be used in the process of integrating systems need to be further investigated and standardized for use. This leads to a situation where methodological support and tools are still lacking or imported from other areas, such as software and requirements engineering. However, the areas of research which have to be investigated can be identified and related to possible solutions that may have significant impact on the state-of-the-art of systems integration in the near future.

ACKNOWLEDGMENT

We thank all the people who contributed to the success of the First International Conference on Systems Integration ICSI'90 by presenting their work and discussing their opinions. Our special thanks go to Professor Howard Eisner for his permission to use his not yet officially published paper for the discussion on phased top-down approaches and to Professor James McHugh for his valuable comments.

REFERENCES

1. E. G. Nilsson, E. K. Nordhagen, and G. Oftedal, "Aspects of Systems Integration," in *Proceedings of the First International Conference on Systems Integration*, Morristown, NJ, IEEE Computer Society Press, Washington, D.C., 1990, pp. 434–443.
2. P. A. Ng and R. T. Yeh (eds.), *Modern Software Engineering—Foundations and Current Perspectives*, Van Nostrand Reinhold, New York, 1990.
3. J. Garbajosa, J. R. Larre, J. Sanchez, N. Alfaro, and J. J. Galan, "Implementing Cooperation and Coordination in Software Engineering Environments," in *Proceedings of CASE '90, 4th International Workshop on Computer-Aided Software Engineering*, Irvine CA, IEEE Computer Society Press, Washington, D.C., pp. 163–167.
4. P. C. Lockemann and J. W. Schmidt (eds.), *Datenbank Handbuch*, Informatik Handbuecher, Springer Verlag, Berlin, 1987.
5. B. Strong, "Requirements for Database Support in Computer-Aided Software Engineering," in *Modern Software Engineering—Foundations and Current Perspectives*, P. A. Ng and R. T. Yeh (eds.), Van Nostrand Reinhold, New York, 1990, pp. 274–317.
6. S. B. Weinstein, "Telecommunications in the Coming Decades," *IEEE Spectrum*, 24(11), 62–68 (November 1987).
7. W. Kim and F. H. Lochovsky, *Object Oriented Concepts, Databases, and Applications*, ACM Press, Frontier Series, New York, 1989.
8. T. J. Biggerstaff and A. J. Perlis, *Software Reusability*, Vols. I and II, ACM Press, Frontier Series, New York, 1989.
9. *Proceedings of CASE'90, 4th International Workshop on Computer-Aided Software Engineering*, Irvine CA, IEEE Computer Society Press, Washington, D.C., 1990.

10. W. P. Stevens, G. J. Meyers, and L. L. Constantine, "Structured Design," *IBM Sys. J.*, *13*(2), 115–139 (1974).
11. J. Gougen, "Parameterized Programming," *IEEE Trans. Software Eng.*, *SE-10*(5), 528–543 (September 1984).
12. R. M. Mittermeir and M. Oppitz, "Software Bases for the Flexible Composition of Application Systems," *IEEE Trans. Software Eng.*, *SE-13*(4), 440–460 (April 1987).
13. V. Venugopal, "Integrated Tool Support in Object-Based Environments," in *Proceedings of the First International Conference on Systems Integration*, Morristown, NJ, IEEE Computer Society Press, Washington, D.C., 1990, pp. 171–176.
14. S. R. Bourne, *The Unix V Environment*, Addison Wesley, Reading, MA, 1987.
15. W. Schaeffer and H. Weber, "European Software Factory Plan—The ESF Profile," in *Modern Software Engineering—Foundations and Current Perspectives*, P. A. Ng and R. T. Yeh (eds.), Van Nostrand Reinhold, New York, 1990, pp. 613–637.
16. Bellcore—Bell Communications Research, "The Bellcore OSCA™ Architecture," Technical Advisory, TA-STS-000915, Issue 2, RFC #90-41, July 1990.
17. L. R. Power, "Post-Facto Integration Technology: New Discipline for an Old Practice," in *Proceedings of the First International Conference on Systems Integration*, Morristown, NJ, IEEE Computer Society Press, Washington, D.C., 1990, pp. 4–13.
18. T. E. Cheatham Jr., "Reusability Through Program Transformations," *IEEE Trans. Software Eng.*, *SE-10*(5), 589–594 (September 1984).
19. J. M. Boyle and M. N. Muralidharan, "Program Reusability Through Program Transformation," *IEEE Trans. Software Eng.*, *SE-10*(5), 574–588 (September 1984).
20. D. R. Kuhn, "On the Effective Use of Software Standards in Systems Integration," in *Proceedings of the First International Conference on Systems Integration*, Morristown, NJ, IEEE Computer Society Press, Washington, D.C., 1990, pp. 455–461.
21. L. C. Seifert, "Conference Chairman's Message," in *Proceedings of the First International Conference on Systems Integration*, Morristown, NJ, IEEE Computer Society Press, Washington, D.C., 1990, P. IX.
22. M. Lehman, "Software Engineering—The Role of CASE," Keynote Address at CASE'90, 4th Int. Workshop on Computer-Aided Software Engineering, Irvine, CA, December 1990.
23. CASE Standards Coordination Meeting '90, hosted by the 4th Int. Workshop on Computer-Aided Software Engineering, Irvine, CA, December 1990.
24. 4th Workshop on Integrated Software Engineering Environments (ISEE), sponsored by the National Institute of Standards (NIST) and IBM, Summary by W. Wong, NIST/NCL, Gaithersburg, MD, October 1990.
25. H. Eisner, "The New Process of Archetyping for Large-Scale Systems Integration," *J. Sys. Integration* (submitted).

WILHELM ROSSAK
PETER A. NG

Milton Keynes UK
Ingram Content Group UK Ltd.
UKHW020825141024
449569UK00008B/553